"Harl has written a terrific, fast-pasted history of the nomadic peoples of the Eurasian steppes. It is full of color and crackles with vitality—one almost feels the thundering of horses' hooves. One thing is certain, Harl leaves little doubt that civilization is not just built from brick walls and marble edifices, but from canvas tents and felt saddlecloths too."

—**Professor Lloyd Llewellyn-Jones, Cardiff University, author of** *Persians: The Age of the Great Kings*

KENNETH W. HARL

EMPIRES
OF THE
STEPPES

A HISTORY OF THE NOMADIC TRIBES
WHO SHAPED CIVILIZATION

HANOVER
SQUARE
PRESS

HANOVER
SQUARE
PRESS™

Recycling programs
for this product may
not exist in your area.

ISBN-13: 978-1-335-14682-3

Empires of the Steppes

First published in 2023. This edition published in 2024.

Hanover Square Press
22 Adelaide St. West, 41st Floor
Toronto, Ontario M5H 4E3, Canada
HanoverSqPress.com

Printed in U.S.A.

To my wife, Sema, ever patient and ever loving.
Canim, seni seviyorum sonsuz çünkü evet dedin.

Also by Kenneth W. Harl

Civic Coins and Civic Politics in the Roman East, A.D. 180–275

Coinage in the Roman Economy, 300 B.C. to A.D. 700

EMPIRES
OF THE
STEPPES

Table of Contents

Foreword

Ten years ago, I agreed to record a course with the Great Courses (formerly known as the Teaching Company) on the nomadic peoples of the Eurasian steppes. I created this course in response to requests by many customers for a course on the Silk Road. The course on DVD and streaming formats has since proved most popular. But I owe a debt of thanks to literary agent Adam Gauntlett, who approached me about writing a grand narrative of the nomadic peoples of the Eurasian steppes and how they contributed so much to the world in which we live.

Adam's timing was perfect because my wife and I, given our age and medical condition, were compelled to isolate during the COVID-19 pandemic in 2020–2021. I had to cancel my plans of a sabbatical leave overseas working in coin cabinets and numismatic institutes. Those who are familiar with my scholarship know that I publish on the coinages and economic history of the Roman world. Instead, I turned to writing a sweeping narrative covering forty-five centuries from the first steppe nomads who domesticated the horse and learned how to exploit the endless grasslands of Eurasia to Tamerlane (1370–1405), the Prince of Destruction, the last conqueror who based his empire on the invincible horse archers. I chose to close this book with Tamerlane's death. In less than two generations after his death, the handheld firearms of a military revolution ended the supremacy of the horse archer forever. At the same time, the European voyages of discovery turned the oceans into the highways of a new global economy that replaced the caravan routes of the Silk Road across the Eurasian steppes. The steppe nomads steadily lost their decisive role in history over the next two centuries.

I recognize that I have ventured far beyond the limits of my professional training as a Classical historian, devoted to the great books of Greece and Rome. Yet the story of these peoples on the Eurasian steppes has always fascinated me from a young age when I first read about the spectacular exploits of Attila and the Hun and Genghis Khan. As I was completing this book, I was excited to read initial reports that archaeologists might have uncovered the burial of Genghis Khan. If so, this discovery will be hailed the greatest archaeological find of the twenty-first century. This report is also a sobering reminder of how future breakthroughs in comparative linguistics, archaeology, and DNA analysis may modify some of what I have written. Yet I hope that I have presented an exciting, and plausible, narrative of these remarkable peoples that will stand the test of time.

In turning lecture notes into a book, I had to master over a decade of new scholarship. I also had to rethink the presentation and emphasis of this story. Hence, I wrote new chapters on the little-known Kushans, Rouran, Northern Wei, Hephthalites, and Karakhitans. I have treated at length the legend of Prester John that captured the imagination of Medieval Europeans and so led them to misunderstand the Mongols. In another chapter, I took up the story of the travelers Giovanni da Pian del Carpine, William of Rubruck, and Marco Polo, who returned from the Mongol court with new insights and information that forever shattered popular misconceptions of the Eurasian nomads, and so ultimately launched the European voyages of discovery to reach the Cathay of Kublai Khan. Above all, I gained a new appreciation for the genius of Kublai Khan, the most consequential ruler of the thirteenth century, who united rather than just conquered China. In each chapter, I have aimed to explain the impact of each of these nomadic peoples on their world and what their legacy means to us today.

I acknowledge my debt to the many scholars trained in the languages and literatures of Arabic, Persian, Sanskrit, Chinese, and Russian whose works I have consulted. My book rests on their collective research and insights. I am at home in the Classical, Byzantine, and Western Medieval worlds, and here, at a number of points, I have offered my own interpretation of events. I also gained, later in life, a knowledge of Turkish from working on archaeological excavations in Turkey for twenty-five years in the era before the pandemic. Even more important, I married my wife, Sema, a citizen of Turkey, and in eight years of marriage, I have learned more about Turkey and Turkish society than the previous twenty-five as an academic visitor studying in research institutes, museums, and dig houses.

I owe a debt of thanks to many people who have assisted and encouraged me to pursue this ambitious project. Foremost is my wife, Sema, whose patience, love, and encouragement enabled me to complete this book. Again I acknowledge my inestimable debt to Adam Gauntlett. My editor, Peter Joseph, and the entire staff of Hanover Square Press have been splendid in their work to turn a manuscript into a printed book. They all have my thanks for their patience and hard work. Among my friends and colleagues, I single out Jason David Sanchez, who is conversant in both Classical and modern Chinese, and is an independent scholar with expertise on the Silk Road and the reception of Buddhism in China. Jason read over the chapters dealing with China, and offered corrections, bibliography, and insights. Jason and my alumnus and friend Stefanos Roulakis have also been indefatigable companions on my travels across Anatolia in search of battlefields, sites, and roads of the Roman and Byzantine periods. I also thank my friend and colleague Professor Thomas R. Martin at the College of Holy Cross, a fellow Classicist who admires Chinese civilization. Tom reviewed not only the chapters on the Classical world, but also those of the Qin and Han Empires. I also must thank my colleagues Professors Samuel Ramer and Brian DeMare for their assistance in Russian and Chinese history, respectively. I especially appreciate my dear friend and colleague Professor Michael Kuczynski, who read over the text for its style. Finally, I must thank my alumnus and friend Patrick Vizard, who has been indispensable in assisting me in learning how to exploit the scholarly resources on the internet. They all contributed significantly to this book, and any errors are mine alone.

Prologue

Attila on the Road to Rome

In 452, Attila the Hun, the Scourge of God and most deadly enemy of Rome since Hannibal, descended upon Italy to avenge the ferocious, but indecisive, battle fought in Roman Gaul on the Catalaunian Plains in the previous year. This time he was determined to capture Rome, the eternal city, seat of the Roman Empire and Christianity. Even then, Rome still retained her luster and her look as the capital of the Mediterranean world, even though the cravenly Emperor Valentinian III resided at Ravenna, a modest, sleepy town protected by malarial swamps and with direct access to the sea.[1] Valentinian's colleague Marcian too acknowledged the seniority of Rome to his own capital Constantinople, New Rome, seat of imperial power in the East. For Attila, Rome was the ultimate prize. Her capture would make Attila master of the Roman Western Empire. But more important was that Rome would confer legitimacy on the nomadic, barbarian conqueror. Attila would avenge the insult of two years previously when his marriage to the empress Honoria was rejected by her brother Valentinian III and his court.[2] Attila would secure his bride and so ultimately rule as guardian (*parens Augusti*) for their children. Such a marriage might well have revived Roman power in the hands of a nomadic conqueror who could not possibly have ruled the empire from horse-back but instead through the imperial officials of Rome.

The rejection of the marriage proposal had denied Attila the expected recognition by Rome of his status as indispensable ally and lord, or to use the later language of the steppes kaghan, of the barbarian world from the Danube to the Volga River. His ancestors, either vassals or scions of the Xiongnu (pronounced Hunna in ancient Chinese), had engaged in centuries of diplomatic exchanges with both their nomadic overlord, the celestial kaghan, and the Chinese emperor who ruled by the Mandate of Heaven.[3] Whenever a charismatic conqueror of the Eurasian steppes achieved primacy, the emperor of the Han peoples acknowledged the newest conqueror of the warlike tribes of horse archers. The kaghans expected Chinese envoys who brought costly gifts, silk, imperial titles, and Chinese princesses as brides. To the Chinese court, these missions conveyed the "five baits," subsidies intended to turn the kaghan from a foe into an ally.[4] To the kaghan, the envoys rendered tribute to glorify his court, and to provide fancy gifts that he then distributed among the lesser khans of the tribes to secure their loyalty. Every great kaghan ruled a confederation comprising "Inner" and "Outer" tribes bound to serve in his army. Far lesser kaghans than Attila had even seized northern Chinese lands and ruled as Chinese-style emperors in their own right and sponsored Buddhism to uphold their legitimacy in the eyes of their Han subjects.[5] In 450, when the empress Honoria had sent a signet ring and message for assistance to Attila, he could only have interpreted it as a marriage offer from the imperial court of Rome.[6] But Roman princesses, unlike their Chinese counterparts, did not marry barbarian, pagan rulers. Hence, Attila waged war on the Western Roman Empire not only for loot and slaves, but also to assert his legitimate claim to be the greatest ruler of Europe and guardian of the Roman Empire.

In the spring of 452, Attila opened his second campaign against the Western Roman Empire by crossing the Julian Alps with a vast horde of allies summoned from the Germanic tribes of Central Europe and the nomadic tribes dwelling on the Pontic-Caspian (south Russian) steppes. Roman authors exaggerated the size of this army, numbered by them in the hundreds of thousands.[7] It was the largest barbarian host yet to invade Italy. The horse archers of Huns were dreaded as invincible warriors, who, with many remounts, could cover great distances swiftly and endure the harshest of conditions. Their sturdy horses were just as formidable, and they could even forge under snow during winter campaigns. Yet the Huns were but a fraction of his army, for they had dwelled on the grasslands of eastern Hungary and Transylvania (the former Roman provinces of Pannonia and Dacia) for nearly two generations. Attila also summoned his vassals among kindred nomadic tribes to the east on the south Russian steppes, and from among the East Germanic peoples of Central Europe: Ostrogoths, Gepidae, and Herulians. Among his Germanic subjects, poets already celebrated him as the greatest warrior of all time, so that under various renditions of his name, such as Norse Atli or Middle High German Etzel, Attila lived on as a hero of the northern peoples of Germany, England, and Scandinavia.[8] Finally, Attila recruited Roman deserters, captives, and renegades who served as his engineering corps so that Attila could capture walled cities. Attila, just like every other nomadic conqueror, appreciated the skills of the clever craftsmen and engineers of rival sedentary, bureaucratic empires.

In the spring and early summer of 452, Attila marched across northeastern Italy, encountering little resistance. The citizens of Aquileia, the strategic gateway of Italy, manned their walls and long defied Attila. The proud Latin colony had never been captured, and one imperial contender, Maximinus Thrax (235–238), had lost his throne and his head by his failure to capture Aquileia.[9] Yet Attila, inspired by an omen of white storks fleeing their nests on the rooftops of the doomed city, stirred his men to storm and sack the city.[10] The other cities of Venetia fell in quick succession: Concordia, Altinum, Patavium, Vicetia, Verona, Brixia, Bergamum (modern Bergamo), Ticinum, and Mediolanum (Milan). Most cities were ruthlessly sacked. Ticinum and Mediolanum were spared for unknown reasons. Survivors and refugees fled to the lagoons on the shores of the Adriatic Sea, where their descendants would found the city of Venice. At the former imperial capital of Mediolanum, Attila ordered the palace's mural of the emperor Theodosius I receiving submissive barbarians to be repainted featuring Attila, receiving two suppliant Roman emperors, Valentinian III and Marcian, offering tribute.[11] The anecdote, most likely reported by suave diplomat and historian Priscus, reveals much about Attila's aims and conception of himself. He sought universal rule in the fashion of nomadic conquerors who had preceded and who would follow him. For Romans, Attila was the first of such conquerors, but Chinese emperors had fought, courted, and intrigued against such conquerors for nearly seven centuries. With Attila, successive conquerors commanding invincible horse archers poured out of the Eurasian steppes to threaten Christian Medieval Europe for the next seven centuries. Attila, like all these conquerors, once he had welded the nomadic tribes into a confederation, strove to control the sources of wealth generated by the neighboring literate civilizations with cities, trade, and agriculture. For no pastoral nomads on the Eurasian steppes could prosper without trade with the agriculturalists and urban dwellers of the great civilizations of China, India, the Middle East, or Europe.

In the summer of 452, Attila appeared to be on the road to such a success. His army had penetrated to the Minucius River, a tributary of the Po, near Mantua, eighty miles southeast of Mediolanum, from whence he could cross the Po, secure the passes of the Apennines, and follow the Roman highway, Via Flaminia, down the Tiber to Rome, the Eternal City. His courtiers and advisers warned him that the far lesser Gothic King Alaric, a generation earlier, had looted the city and carried off captives only to die soon afterward—an evil portent for those risking the wrath of the Christian God. Yet Attila's host could surely have taken the city. Attila intended to rule over the Roman world with a Roman empress, whereas Alaric acted out of frustration to pressure the reluctant Emperor Honorius to grant him a command and his people land. In the summer of 452, the road to Rome lay open.

Flavius Aetius, the generalissimo (*magister militum*) of the Roman field army who dominated the court at Ravenna, had been taken by surprise by Attila's sudden invasion of Italy. The hostile monk Prosper of Aquitaine alleged that Aetius initially panicked and urged the imperial court to flee Italy.[12] Valentinian III stayed in his capital, Ravenna, protected by its malarial lagoons, and kept the ten thousand soldiers sent by his eastern colleague Marcian as reinforcements for the Western field army.[13] For three decades, Aetius had maintained Roman power in the West by his alliance with Attila, whose horse archers terrorized into dutiful loyalty the Germanic federates (*foederati*) settled on imperial lands in Gaul—Visigoths, Burgundians, Alans, and Franks. In 452, Aetius lacked sufficient soldiers to defend Italy because these vital German federates, who had fought the Huns to defend their new homelands in Gaul in the previous year, had no interest in opposing Attila in Italy. They remained north of the Alps, while Aetius was powerless to stop Attila's march on Rome.

Aetius had no choice but to treat for whatever terms Attila might grant. In the late summer of 452, a delegation headed by the three most distinguished Roman patricians arrived at Attila's camp on the banks of the Minucius River.[14] They were Trygetus, former Prefect of Rome and the envoy who had signed away Roman Africa to the Vandals, Gennadius Aviennus, consul of 450, who was long on lineage and short on ability, and the most impressive member, Pope Leo I, the Great, the impeccable defender of orthodoxy who defined the theology of the Western church. No contemporary report of the meeting has survived, but legend almost immediately supplied the answer. The imposing pontiff had conveyed through interpreters his admonishment that Attila risked his soul by an attack on the holy city of Saints Peter and Paul. Raphael, commissioned by Pope Leo X, captured the moment in a magnificent fresco of the legendary meeting in an apartment of St. Peter's in 1512–1514. Raphael dutifully painted the portrait of his Pope Leo for that of Leo the Great. Legend and painting epitomized the meeting of churchman and conqueror as the symbolic triumph of civilization over barbarism.

The historical reality was more mundane, and pressing. When the envoys arrived at his camp, Attila was facing shortages of fodder and food for his army, for Italy was facing a second year of famine. With the threat of starvation came the first signs of pestilence.[15] The Hun army had ravaged and stripped northeastern Italy, and Attila had lost valuable time in his siege of Aquilea. An advance on Rome would have arrived in the autumn. Attila would have gained the city but put his army at risk to the privations and disease of a siege. Furthermore, Attila had learned of the arrival of reinforcements from the eastern army, and reports of an attack on his borders on the Danube by the eastern army under another Aetius, general of the emperor Marcian.[16] Withdrawal was prudent. The terms discussed at the fateful meeting were never reported, but negotiations were sure to follow. Attila had proved that he could strike at will in Italy, and he could always return to claim his bride, the empress Honoria, should negotiations fail. Thereupon, the Hun army departed as suddenly as it had invaded. Once at his capital near Aquincum (modern Budapest) on the Upper Danube, Attila planned fresh campaigns for the next year, foremost against the defiant Eastern Roman emperor who refused to render the promised tribute. But Attila was never to set out again on the road to Rome or New Rome. In the winter of 452–453, he overindulged in a wedding celebration to his newest wife, a stunningly beautiful woman named Ildico.[17] He collapsed in a stupor into the marriage bed, burst a blood vessel, and drowned in his own blood. With his ignominious death, the Hun Empire fragmented soon after as his sons battled over the succession and vassal tribes rebelled. On the banks of the Nedao River, in 454, the Herulians and Gepidae, with the gold of the emperor Marcian, crushed the Hun army and shattered the empire of Attila.[18]

The career of Attila the Hun, memorialized in Medieval epic poetry, modern novels, and classic film, is perhaps more widely known than that of any other barbarian conqueror of the Eurasian steppes except for that of Genghis Khan. Parallels have often been drawn between Attila and Genghis Khan, his grandsons Batu, Hulagu, and Kublai Khan, and his emulator, Tamerlane, Prince of Destruction. Yet seven centuries earlier, a barbarian conqueror of the Eurasian steppes, Modu Chanyu (209–174 BC), had likewise posed an existential threat to imperial China.[19] Historians are now debating the role of each of these barbarian conquerors in shaping the history of Eurasia. Attila himself has been subject to interpretations, from an annoying wayward ally of Rome who exploited opportune times to attack, to a conqueror with a grand strategy and vision of empire. The scope of this work is to present the story of barbarian nomadic peoples, and their empires, from earliest times down to Tamerlane (1370–1405). For all of them had an impact on the great civilizations of China, India, the Middle East, and Europe. Seldom do they speak to us in their own words. So often we depend on the descriptions of their foes and victims. The Greek historian Herodotus (ca. 495–425 BC) gives us our first vivid description of Scythians, nomads dwelling on the south Russian steppes.[20] The Roman historian Ammianus Marcellinus, a pagan writing under Christian emperors, paints a similar description of the Huns when they first entered Europe.[21] Both authors have been criticized for resorting to stereotypes with a mix of fear and contempt for these nomadic barbarians. Likewise, Chinese or Muslim authors often show the same curiosity and disdain. The Han envoy Zhang Qian deplored the customs of the Xiongnu north of the Great Wall in 129–119 BC, and the Arab geographer Ahmad ibn Fadlan was shocked by the customs of the Turkish Bulgars on the lower Volga River in 921/2 AD, even though they had converted to Islam.[22] Despite their prejudices, these authors were eyewitnesses, or they based their reports on firsthand testimony. Therefore, their words must judiciously be weighed against other evidence furnished by archaeologists, philologists, biologists of historical genetics, or anthropologists. On a number of occasions, the barbarians speak for themselves, such as on the inscription from the Orkhon valley (today in Mongolia). Bilǧe (717–734), Kaghan of the Gök Turks, warns his tribesmen not to be seduced by the pleasures of Chinese civilization.[23] Genghis Khan is best known from his faithful portrait commissioned by Kublai Khan and the so-called *Secret History of the Mongols*, a Chinese redaction of the Mongolian original composed in the reign of Genghis Khan's son Ögedei.[24] From such sources, my aim is to tell the story of these barbarian conquerors and the empires they founded from their perspective, and so re-create them and their world, and how they changed it.

1

The Peopling of the Eurasian Steppes

S ir Aurel Stein, the indefatigable British linguist, archaeologist, and explorer, led four expeditions into Central Asia between 1900 and 1930.[1] There, in the buried caravan cities and caves of the Tarim Basin, Stein found troves of Buddhist and Manichaean documents between the fourth and eighth centuries AD, as well as mummies remarkably well-preserved due to the dry climate. The documents have illuminated the spiritual and commercial world of the Silk Road. They were written in a number of languages, and were recorded on different media and in different scripts. Among the languages were Sanskrit, Prakrit, Saka (an eastern Iranian dialect), Sogdian (another eastern Iranian dialect that was the lingua franca of the Silk Road), Tibetan, Tangut, Chinese, and a previously unknown language family that scholars have since dubbed Tocharian. The so-called Tarim Mummies, dating between 2000 and 300 BC, have shattered previous notions about the history of Central Asia. Subjected to DNA analysis, the mummies have now revealed, to the dismay of both Uyghur and Chinese nationalists, that the first inhabitants of the cities of the Tarim Basin were neither Turks nor Chinese.[2] Instead, testing since 2008 confirms that the first inhabitants shared DNA with today's European populations, while later immigrants from the Middle East and northern India arrived and intermarried with this indigenous population. Mummies of individuals with Mongolian features only date from the end of the first millennium BC. These scientific findings offer little comfort to Chinese or Uyghur nationalists today seeking historical justifications to claim Xinjiang or Uyghurstan as their homeland.[3] Instead, they confirm that Stein's discoveries of the manuscripts and mummies forever altered our understanding of the origins of the Indo-European languages, and the origins of the steppe nomads of Eurasia.

Sir Aurel Stein was the epitome of a Victorian scholar, gentleman, and confirmed bachelor who was always accompanied by a pet dog, invariably named Dash.[4] He was, however, born in Budapest to an accomplished Jewish family in 1862, although he and his brother were baptized as Lutherans and received a Classical training in the gymnasium, mastering Latin, Greek, French, and English. Aurel then obtained his doctorate in Sanskrit and Persian at Tübingen in 1883. He departed for further study in England the next year. Three years later, Stein was convinced by the Indologist Rudolf Hoernlé, whom he had met at a conference in Vienna, to travel to India. Between 1888 and 1899, Stein served as the Principal of Oriental College in Lahore. Throughout his life, Stein passionately read and translated Sanskrit and Persian texts, meticulously recorded his travels, penned a voluminous correspondence with colleagues and family, and published extensively on the antiquities of Central Asia. In 1900, he was inspired to undertake his own expedition upon reading the account of the Swedish explorer Sven Hedin's travels in Central Asia, which was published in 1898.[5] For his outstanding contributions, Sir Aurel was showered with honors, obtained British citizenship, and was knighted. But Sir Aurel Stein was not the first to excavate the lost cities of the Tarim Basin, for he owed a debt not only to Sven Hedin, who mapped Central Asia, but also to Hedin's mentor, the German archaeologist Ferdinand von Richthofen, who coined the name the Silk Road (*Seidenstraße*) and happened to be the uncle of the flying ace Manfred von Richthofen, the "Red Baron."[6] Sir Aurel was, however, the most celebrated, because he captured the imagination of the reading public of Great Britain, Europe, and North America by revealing the lost world of the Silk Road.

In 1907, during his second expedition, Aurel Stein excavated the Buddhist sanctuary the Mogao Caves, a complex of five hundred temples southwest of the Chinese garrison town of Dunhuang. Dunhuang stands at the eastern end of the narrow verdant Gansu corridor, flanked by the Gobi Desert to the north and the Tibetan highlands to the south. All caravans going to and from China passed through the city. Thankful merchants donated these temples between the fourth and fourteenth centuries. Within the complex, a great storeroom housed a trove of documents on palm paper, wooden tables, and Chinese paper. In return for offering a subvention to restore the temples, Stein convinced the Buddhist caretaker Wang Yuanlu to permit him to remove forty thousand documents, which are today the jewel of the Central Asian collection in the British Museum.[7] Stein intimated to Wang Yuanlu that he was devoted to Buddhist Saint Xuanzang, and perhaps that he might even be a reincarnation of the Chinese pilgrim who had recorded his travels along the Silk Road to India during the seventh century AD. In fact, Stein pinpointed lost caravan cities by consulting Xuanzang's itinerary. French, Japanese, Russian, and Chinese scholars followed with their own expeditions. Among the documents obtained by Stein were fragments in a hitherto unknown language written in a script adapted from Brahmi (the main syllabary used in Northern India). This new language, first deciphered by the German philologists Emil Sieg and Wilhelm Siegling in 1908, has been identified as Tocharian.[8]

Since the surviving Tocharian texts are primarily translations of Buddhist scriptures composed in Sanskrit, Prakrit, or Saka, philologists quickly identified two languages, Tocharian A and B, which were Indo-European in origin and descended from a mother language centuries earlier.[9] In their core vocabulary and grammar, these two Tocharian languages exhibit many conservative features that had not survived in other Indo-European languages. The texts, dating between the fifth and eighth centuries AD, have been found in the caravan cities among the northern rim of the Taklamakan Desert, stretching east from the city of Aksu to Turpan. At the time of the composition of the texts, Tocharian A was already a liturgical language that speakers of Tocharian B could scarcely understand. A third dialect, Tocharian C, was spoken along the southern rim of the Tarim Basin between the cities of Niya and Krorän (Chinese Loulan). Excavations have so far failed to yield fragments of any texts in Tocharian C, but the language can be surmised from the numerous Tocharian loan words detected in Saka and Prakrit commercial documents.

The decipherment of Tocharian as an Indo-European language astonished scholars at the beginning of the twentieth century, who had based their theories on the birth and dispersal of Indo-European languages on a proposal by Sir William Jones.[10] In an address on February 2, 1786, Jones proposed to the Asiatic Society (which he and Governor General Warren Hastings had founded two years earlier) that Latin, Greek, and Sanskrit shared so many similarities that they must have descended from a mother tongue in the distant past.[11] His address was published in 1788, and Jones went on to suggest that the Celtic, Germanic, and Iranian languages were likely members of this same family of languages, which has since been designated Indo-European. Sir William, who was appointed as one of three jurists to the Supreme Court of the Calcutta Presidency, had set sail for India in 1783. A precious linguist, he had, at a young age, mastered Greek, Latin, Hebrew, Arabic, and Persian, as well as understood the Celtic language because he had spoken Welsh as a boy. Once in India, Jones sought instruction in Sanskrit at Nadiya Hindu University, where he became enthralled with the beauty of the Sanskrit of the Vedas. In the nineteenth century, philologists, expanding upon Jones's proposal, had classified the Indo-European languages into two discrete families, one named the Centum branch in Europe (comprising Greek and the Celtic, Germanic, Romance, Illyro-Thracian, and perhaps Armenian languages) and the other, the Satem branch, comprising the Baltic, Slavic, Iranian, and Indian languages. The discovery of Tocharian shattered this neat division. Less than a decade later, the philologists were again surprised when the Czech scholar Bedřich Hrozný identified Hittite as yet another ancient Indo-European language, which had been spoken in central Anatolia (today Turkey) in the Bronze Age.[12] Hittite, along with its cousins Palaic and Luvian, was recorded on cuneiform clay tablets from the royal capital Hattusas (today Boğazköy), and these tablets dated between the sixteenth and thirteenth centuries BC.[13]

During his expedition to Krorän in 1907, Sir Aurel also discovered the burials of mummies whom he reported as people who appeared to be of Iranian or northern Indian origin. But he lacked the means of transporting the mummies safely to London, and so he reinterred them, erected over the site stone markers, and looked forward to a day when he or other explorers might return and recover the mummies for posterity.[14] That day came twenty years later when the Swedish archaeologist Folke Bergman excavated the earliest mummies from the Tarim Basin in the prehistoric cemetery at Qäwrighul, which had once stood on the shores of Lop Nur, a vast lake fed by the Tarim River.[15] Qäwrighul and its sister city Krorän now are ruins in the desert basin that was once the lake because of the river's change of course and centuries of human destruction of the poplar forests for fuel and building material. The mummies, dating from the Middle and Late Bronze Ages (ca. 1800–1000 BC), exhibited Caucasian features, and the burial goods, use of ocher paints to adorn the deceased's body, and clothing pointed to an origin far to the west. The so-called Cherchen Man, often dubbed Ur David, had reddish hair, blue eyes, an aquiline nose, and a fair complexion. He had died in his early fifties in ca. 1000 BC, and was interred along with his wife and infant son. He was clad in a red twill tunic and his body was painted with ocher pigments with sun patterns.[16] The contemporary Princess of Xiaohe was unearthed by Chinese archaeologists from a cemetery just west of Krorän (Loulan) in 2003. She had flaxen hair, long eyelashes, and a fair complexion.[17] She was wrapped in a white wool cloak with tassels and wore a felt hat, string skirt, and fur-lined leather boots—the garb suitable for life on the Eurasian steppes. The most controversial has been the Beauty of Krorän, discovered in 1980, who had died in her early forties, probably from lung failure after a lifetime of inhaling desert air mixed with sand and charcoal, in ca. 1800 BC. This lady, with lice-infested auburn hair and clad in modest clothing, lived a hard life as a member of a merchant community. Uyghur nationalists have hailed her the "Mother of the Nation," but in speech, culture, and ancestry, she was neither Turkish nor Chinese.

In 1996, Professor Victor Mair of the University of Pennsylvania headed an international team of geneticists, archaeologists, and linguists who studied the mummies in the museums of Xinjiang. Their findings have been confirmed by subsequent genetic studies.[18] Based on DNA analyses, the earliest inhabitants of the Tarim Basin were of European origin, although matrilineal descent for some individuals such as the Beauty of Kroran included Siberian ancestors. The burial goods, ceramics, and textiles pointed to a connection with the people of the Afanasievo culture, who had settled on the grasslands stretching from Lake Baikal to the Altai Mountains in ca. 3000 BC. The ancestors of the people of the Afanasievo culture, in turn, had migrated over one thousand two hundred miles across the central Eurasian steppes from the western or Pontic-Caspian (southern Russian) steppes, home to the Yamnaya culture (ca. 3500–2600 BC), where the mother tongue Proto-Indo-European (PIE) had evolved perhaps five centuries earlier.[19] No writing of the Bronze Age has survived from sites of the Lopur Basin, but the only plausible explanation can be that these individuals whose remains were mummified spoke an archaic Indo-European language that evolved into the Tocharian speech represented in the Buddhist texts of the fifth through eighth centuries AD. Chinese chroniclers of the Han and Tang dynasties report tall, fiery-haired, and light-eyed barbarians with full beards and in felt caps and leather leggings in the Western Regions (today Xinjiang), who traded in jade and horses.[20] Wall frescoes of the rock-cut Kizil Cave monasteries dating to the fourth through sixth centuries depict some native rulers, merchants, or Buddhist monks with red hair and fair-skinned features. The complex, often known as the Caves of the Thousand Buddhas, is seventy-five miles west of Kucha, a major oasis city on the northern side of the Tarim Basin. Kucha has yielded many documents in Tocharian B. The murals, dating between the third and sixth centuries AD, depict scenes from the life of the Buddha, and share close stylistic similarities to the contemporary art of Gandhara.[21]

The ancestors of the Tocharians, who dwelled in the cities of the Tarim Basin for nearly three millennia, had arrived from the Eurasian steppes in ca. 2000 BC. Yet these Proto-Tocharian speakers were not the first of the Indo-European speakers to depart from the original homeland on the Pontic-Caspian steppes in ca. 3300 to 3000 BC. The ancestors of the so-called Anatolian languages had migrated from the southwestern terminus of these same steppes into the Balkans perhaps five centuries earlier, in ca. 4000 BC.[22] At this time, PIE speakers practiced a mixed economy of hunting, herding, and cultivating barley. Both Tocharians and Anatolians were genetically and culturally related to the people of the Yamnaya culture (ca. 3600–2500 BC), who devised the nomadic way of life on the Pontic-Caspian steppes between the lower Dniester and middle Ural Rivers.[23] They already spoke dialects of a common language, dubbed PIE, the mother tongue of many of the languages of Europe, Iran, and India today. The immediate ancestors of the Yamnaya people had domesticated the horse as a source of winter meat, and later for riding.[24] The Yamnaya nomad applied the large disc wheel to great carts (*gers* in Mongolian) conveying mobile felt tent homes. Soon they learned to travel rapidly over great distances across the six thousand miles of Eurasian steppes, and so they could exploit the endless grasslands for their ever-growing herds and flocks.[25]

PIE, spoken over a wide area of over one hundred thousand square miles, is best seen as a continuum of dialects of a koine, or common tongue, which itself must have undergone significant changes over the centuries. As families, clans, and tribes frequently moved in search of pastures and water, they encountered and exchanged words, ideas, and goods with each other. Over time, as speakers of this koine PIE migrated away from the steppes, they evolved their own distinct language as they encountered new peoples. Philologists have reconstructed a lexicon of one thousand five hundred root words of the Yamnaya people's language, which is dubbed PIE based on comparison of cognates in ancient or conservative daughter languages (notably Greek, Sanskrit, Hittite, Tocharian, Early Germanic languages, Old Irish, and Old Lithuanian).[26] Philologists have even reconstructed the principles of grammar, morphology (in the conjugation of verbs and declension of nouns, pronouns, and adjectives), syntax, and the rules of euphony for vowels and consonants that determined sound shifts of PIE words in the daughter languages. The relationship among the daughter languages is easily demonstrated from common words of kinship. Hence, the PIE root word for father, *pH2tér, gave rise to *pater* in Greek, *pater* in Latin, *pitŕ* in Sanskrit, and *fædar* in Old English.[27] All Indo-European languages, both ancient and modern, share many such cognates for numerals, pronouns, common adjectives and verbs, and nouns denoting parts of the body, flora, fauna, geographic features, and direction. Even certain names of gods known in historical times descend from a common religious vocabulary. Most significant are the common words relating to the horse, wheel, and chariot. Six core words—two distinct words for wheel, axle, wagon, horse, and riding—shared by the daughter languages can be derived from the same PIE root word.[28] Such words associated with the pastoral way of life can only date from ca. 3600 BC, when the Yamnaya people adopted a mobile way of life. At the same time, archaeological excavations since the late nineteenth century reveal a significant decline of settlements on the steppes stretching from the Dniester to the Ural Rivers. Furthermore, this region was then home to the vast majority of the horses in the world (perhaps 85 percent).[29]

Archaeologists have illuminated the material world of the Yamnaya people of the Pontic-Caspian steppes. They were likely descended from earlier foragers, who had sustained themselves primarily by hunting, fishing, and gathering wild grains, nuts, fruits, and vegetables in ca. 6500–5000 BC. These foragers traded with the Neolithic agriculturalists of the Çris culture (between the Dniester and Lower Danube) and Celshanka culture (between the Lower Volga and Ural Rivers), who had learned farming from immigrants arriving in considerable numbers from the Neolithic settlements of Anatolia.[30] The inhabitants on the southern Russian steppes evolved a number of distinct local cultures with their own ceramics, material goods, and burial customs during the Eneolithic (or Chalcolithic Age), in ca. 4200–3800 BC. They had gained metallurgical skills in working gold, silver, and copper from the Neolithic villagers dwelling between the Bug and Danube Rivers, whose agrarian culture has been designated "Old Europe." They also traded with peoples of the Russian forests (likely ancestors of the Finno-Ugric speakers). When in 3600–3400 BC the Yamnaya culture emerged, it marked a dramatic widespread shift to a pastoral way of life across the steppes between the Dniester and the Volga, although farming was still practiced in the river valleys. The Yamnaya proved skilled craftsmen, learning the bronze technology from southeastern Europe or the Near East. They built thousands of shaft graves, covered by tumuli known as kurgans, across the steppes. These graves reflected the emergence of a powerful warrior aristocracy who could afford to bury precious objects.[31] The majority of the graves (80 percent) were of adult males, and the rest were likely those of ladies of high rank, so these kurgans were comparable to the later royal Scythian tombs of the sixth to fourth centuries BC.

To the southwest, the nomads of the Yamnaya culture likely raided the settlements of agriculturalists in the Balkans, because archaeology has revealed that many villages of the Tripolye culture in the lower basin of the Dniester and Danube Rivers were fortified.[32] To the south of the Yamnaya culture was the contemporary Maykop culture (named after its principal site) on the Kuban steppes, which stretched to the Caucasus and beyond into northeastern Anatolia.[33] The people of the Maykop culture were of mixed origin, and while their linguistic identity is a matter of scholarly controversy, they most likely spoke a non-Indo-European Caucasian language (which is today represented by Georgian). They too raised kurgans, produced fabulous "animal-style jewelry," and shared in the material culture of their nomadic neighbors to the north. They also had trade links across Transcaucasia to the earliest cities of Sumer (ca. 3600–3100 BC), so they too might have transmitted the smelting of bronze to their neighbors, the Yamnaya people.

By adopting their very way of life, the nomads of the Yamnaya peoples possessed in their ox-drawn mobile homes and horses the means to trek across great distances. Just as important, they traveled and traded widely so that they gained a far greater understanding of geography than any of their contemporaries. These two advantages have proved vital for the success of all later Eurasian nomads down to the Mongols. In response to drought, overpopulation, or invasion, nomads could quickly set out in search of new homes.

Speakers of the Proto-Anatolian languages (Hittite, Luvian, and Palaic) were the first to migrate from the Indo-European heartland. The Dniester River had long been the frontier between the steppe peoples and the agriculturalists of Old Europe (today south-eastern Europe). Fortification of settlements of the Late Tripolye culture and a shift in material culture likely mark the arrival of the ancestors of the Anatolian languages in the Balkans in ca. 4000–3800 BC. Gradually the Anatolian speakers moved south, and in ca. 2300 BC, they crossed the Bosporus and entered Asia Minor. They might have sacked the royal citadels of Troy II and Alaca Hüyük.[34] The Hittites, who called themselves Neshites, settled on the Anatolian plateau, while their kinsmen the Luvians settled in western and southern Asia Minor, and the Palaic speakers in north-western Asia Minor.

In the fashion of the later Seljuk conquerors, the Hittites imposed themselves as a ruling class over a far larger indigenous population called Hattians. They introduced wheeled vehicles and the horse, and at some point learned chariot warfare from their distant kins-men on the central Eurasian steppes. Also, just like the later Seljuk Turks, Hittites found the Anatolian grasslands on the central pla-teau similar to those of the Eurasian steppes and so ideal for herd-ing their livestock and for breeding horses. By 1900 BC, a dozen Hittite kingdoms had emerged in central Anatolia. At each royal center, Assyrian merchants, in search of silver, horses, mules, wool-ens, and leather, established a commercial colony (karum).[35] The Assyrians who had settled at Nesha (Kanesh in Assyrian records, and today Kültepe) maintained a regular correspondence with the home office in Ashur. From the Assyrian merchants, Hittite dy-nasts learned cuneiform writing and the arts of Mesopotamian civ-ilization. Abruptly, in ca. 1750 BC, the Assyrians abandoned their colonies, because Hittite monarchs incessantly warred against each other and disrupted trade. The most successful, Labarnas (1680–1650 BC), was remembered as the progenitor of the Hittite impe-rial family, and united central Anatolia. His successor and namesake lifted his father's curse on the citadel of Hattusas and built a new capital there. He assumed a new royal name, Hattusalis, "the man of Hattusas."[36] The Hittite rulers, styling themselves as the Great Kings of Hatti, forged the first imperial state in Asia Minor based on the power of their chariots.

The Hittites adapted the cuneiform script to their Indo-European language. Thousands of clay tablets recovered from the royal library at Hattusas are the oldest written records in an Indo-European language. The language of the texts reveals that the ancestors of the Hittites had departed at a time when PIE was still spoken as the koine across the Pontic-Caspian steppes. Hittite was not affected by shifts in pronunciation that gave rise to the division of PIE into Centum and Satem language families in ca. 2500 BC. Hittite, along with Luvian and Palaic, exhibits many archaic features that were common in early PIE.[37] Hittite grammar lacks the dual. It recognizes only two genders for nouns and pronouns (animate and inanimate rather than the three of masculine, feminine, and neuter in other Indo-European languages), and two tenses (as opposed to four to six in later Indo-European languages). Most remarkably, laryngeals, long posited by philologists as a class of consonantal sounds in early PIE, are found in Hittite, whereas they were abandoned in other Indo-European languages. Furthermore, written Hittite vocabulary, syntax, and perhaps accent were significantly modified by the indigenous languages of Asia Minor.

In ca. 3300–3000 BC, the ancestors of the Tocharians migrated next. They departed from the upper Ural basin, crossed 1,200 arid miles of Kazakhstan's steppes, and reached the grasslands between Lake Baikal and the western foothills of the Altai Mountains. There, in their new homeland, they created their own distinct Afanasievo culture.[38] The immigrants would have found the steppes between the Volga and Lake Baikal thinly settled, so they were soon isolated from their kinsmen of the Yamnaya culture. Hence, Tocharian, just like Hittite, never experienced many of the later modifications common to other Indo-European languages. The conservative, even archaic, character of the Tocharian languages was still evident in the Buddhist texts over thirty-five centuries later.[39] Furthermore, contrary to popular perceptions since the Middle Ages, the earliest nomads migrated not from east to west, but the reverse, from west to east. The Tocharians, who headed east from the original homeland, were later followed by the ancestors of the Indo-Iranian languages. Hence, Indo-European-speaking nomads brought the horse, the wheel, and the nomadic way of life to the central and eastern Eurasian steppes.

Meanwhile, on the Pontic-Caspian steppes, the PIE speakers of the Yamnaya culture proved ever more successful given the advances of their pastoral way of life. Success bred periodic surges in population; seasonal conditions produced spring flooding or summer droughts. In a search for water and pastures, families, clans, and tribes continually migrated beyond the horizons of the Yamnaya world, to the southwest, west, and east. By 2500 BC, the koine of spoken PIE had diverged into two daughter branches known as Centum and Satem.[40] Each family of languages, in turn, represented a broad spectrum of dialects that evolved further into the main Indo-European languages known today. This proliferation of mutually unintelligible languages resulted from the great distances traversed by descendants of the Yamnaya culture. The wide-flung communities of immigrants lost touch with each other. But from the very beginning, given the absence of writing, there never was a standard version of either a spoken Centum or Satem language. Instead, speakers in each region modified consonants and vowels according to ease of pronunciation, innovated on grammar and syntax for more precision, and adopted loan words from speakers of other languages to express new ideas or objects. In daily conversations, speakers of any language continually alter pronunciation. For example, in modern English, the conservative rules of spelling retain the hard guttural sound *k* before the nasal consonant *n* in such words as *know* or *knight*, even though speakers have ceased to pronounce the initial *k* sound since Chaucer's day. During the last three generations, many English speakers have swallowed the aspirate sound *h* of the relative pronoun *which* so that the spoken word is indistinguishable from the noun *witch*. Context rather than sound now determines the meaning of two words that have become homonyms. In the preliterate world of the Yamnaya culture, such changes occurred frequently, and each community agreed to its own rules of pronunciation. A broad range of such changes in the second half of the third millennium BC is represented by one such major shift of the PIE initial guttural consonant *kw* to a simple *k/[h]* sound in Centum languages (either a simple *k* or, in Germanic languages, a hard *h*) and in Satem languages into the initial *s/sh* sound. Among speakers of Indo-European languages in Central and Southeastern Europe, the initial *kw* sound was modified to a simple guttural sound *k*, made at the back of the tongue, when it preceded an open vowel such as *a*, *e*, or *i*, which is formed at the tip of the tongue. Hence, the word *centrum* resulted in Latin for the numeral one hundred—a change shared by the Italic, Celtic, and Germanic languages, as well as Greek.[41] Many centuries later, perhaps in ca. 750–500 BC, speakers of Proto-Germanic then altered this hard *c/k* sound into an aspirate; hence, *centrum* became *hundred* in modern English, *hundert* in modern German.[42] Among the speakers of what became the Balto-Slavic and Indo-Iranian languages, the initial hard *k* gave way to a softer sibilant *s* or *sh*, which was spoken at the tip of tongue just like the following vowel; hence, Sanskrit *satem* for the numeral. Speakers of Proto-Sanskrit also swallowed the medial nasal *n* in an original *santem* before dental consonants (*d*, *t*, *dh*, and *th*) so that the earlier *santem* was pronounced *satem* when the language was first put down in writing.[43]

The linguistic changes resulted from the far-ranging migrations of Yamnaya descendants out of the Pontic-Caspian steppes. The migrations are reflected in the archaeological record and recent DNA analysis of large samples of human remains recovered from graves. The distinct material culture of the Yamnaya culture gave way to a far more widely dispersed material culture designated Corded Ware, extending from Central Europe and southern Scandinavia across eastern Europe to the forests and steppes as far as the Volga River. The culture is named after its signature pottery with corded rings of lateral decoration—today a favorite image on Danish stamps and European bank notes.[44] These changes in material culture resulted from migrations by Indo-European speakers of nomadic ancestry. DNA evidence presented by Nicolas Patterson has now confirmed that the steppe peoples of the Yamnaya culture migrated in large numbers into central and northern Europe from 2600 BC on.[45] DNA analyses of skeletal remains indicate that well over half of the DNA among individuals possessed the same genes, on both the patrilineal and matrilineal sides, as those of the Yamnaya people. Such a dramatic change in demography resulted when Indo-European speakers moved first into the basin of the upper and middle Danube, and then into the rest of Central Europe and Scandinavia in the second half of the third millennium BC. The newcomers displaced or assimilated the indigenous population, who were themselves a mix of early hunter-gatherers of the Neolithic Age and agriculturalists from the Middle East who had crossed the Bosporus, and gradually migrated along the Danube into Central and Western Europe. From them sprang the language families of Celtic, Italic, and Germanic.[46] This major migration of steppe nomads, recovered by over a century of the exacting labors of philologists, archaeologists, and geneticists, added the third and most significant genetic and linguistic component in the making of the European populations of today.

Simultaneously, the ancestors of the Greek, Thraco-Illyrian, Macedonian, Phrygian, and Armenian languages, dwelling on the steppes between the Dniester and lower Don Rivers, either crossed the Carpathians and settled on the Transylvanian grasslands or pressed south across the lower Danube into the Balkans.[47] These newcomers' spoken languages, while classified within the Centum branch, also shared certain features with the Satem languages. By 1900 BC, Greek speakers entered the Hellenic peninsula, where they adapted the aesthetics, mores, and syllabary of the Minoans of Crete. The lords of Mycenaean Greece employed chariots, built citadels, and left the earliest records of the Greek language on clay tablets in the syllabary known as Linear B.[48] Thracians, Illyrians (who were likely the ancestors of the modern Albanians), and Macedonians remained in the Balkans. The Phrygians, whom Herodotus called neighbors of the Macedonians in the distant past, crossed from the Balkans into Asia Minor in the wake of the collapse of the Hittite Empire shortly after 1200 BC.[49] The Phrygians spread their language across Asia Minor. In the Roman Age, funerary monuments reveal that Phrygian was still spoken as late as the third century AD. The Armenians, likely kinsmen to the Phrygians, migrated farther east to their final homeland in the seventh and sixth centuries BC.

The speakers of the Satem languages migrated in two different directions. The ancestors of the Slavic speakers moved off the steppes into the forests of Russia, while the Proto-Baltic speakers (today represented by Lithuanian and Latvian) pressed northwest, settling along the shores of the Baltic Sea. In these dense forests, both groups encountered Finno-Ugric speakers (ancestors of modern Finns, Estonians, and Hungarians), who taught the newcomers the skills of hunting, trapping, and fishing in the northern climes.[50] By ca. 2000 BC, Proto-Indo-Iranian speakers, who might have migrated east from regions of the Corded Ware culture of Central Europe, already dwelled on the steppes straddling the lower Volga valley. There they had acquired spoke-wheeled light chariots and superior domesticated horses bred for endurance and a docile nature from local inhabitants whose material culture is dubbed the Sintashta culture (ca. 2050–1900 BC).[51] A royal kurgan at Sintashta dating to ca. 2050 BC has yielded the earliest intact chariot, destined to become the primary weapon of warfare in the Middle and Late Bronze Ages from the Near East to China. Over the next three centuries, Indo-Iranian-speaking nomads of the so-called Andronovo culture (ca. 2000–1450 BC) settled the central Eurasian steppes of Kazakhstan, the future heartland of the Scythians, nomads of the Iron Age who spoke eastern Iranian dialects.

The Indo-Iranians pressing east soon reached the western borders of the Tocharian-speaking peoples of the Afanasievo culture. The arrival of the Indo-Iranians might well have triggered the migration of the ancestors of the Tocharians to quit the steppes and seek new homes in the oases of the Tarim Basin, where they learned to cultivate the river valleys, and traded in jade and horses with the Han Chinese of the Shang Dynasty.[52] Other Indo-Iranian tribes, reaching the northern shores of the Aral Sea, pressed southeast and soon arrived at the banks of the Jaxartes River (Amu Darya). Once across the Jaxartes River, they grazed their horses, cattle, sheep, and goats on the grasslands of Ferghana, Sogdiana, and Bactria between the Jaxartes (Syr Darya) and Oxus (Amu Darya). There they encountered sedentary agriculturalists who were members of a culture known as the Bactria-Margiana Archaeological Complex (BMAC).[53]

The fortified towns and villages in the oases and middle and lower Oxus and Zeravshan valleys had long prospered as the nexus of trade routes extending to the central Eurasian steppes to the north, and west along the future Silk Road to the cities of Sumer and Akkad, and southeast across the Hindu Kush to the cities of the Indus Valley civilization called Meluhha in contemporary cuneiform texts, and Mleccha in the *Rig-Vedas*.[54] Transoxiana provided the literate cities of Iraq and India with a number of exotic products, notably lapis lazuli, tin, copper, spices, timber, slaves, and horses, prized by Sumerians and Akkadians for breeding mules. They had originally obtained horses in limited numbers from the people of the Sintashta culture on the lower Volga. The newcomers from the steppes entered into an economic symbiosis with the indigenous inhabitants that was to be repeated many times in the history of Transoxiana.[55] The Indo-Iranian nomads provided superior horses in far greater numbers to merchants engaged in the international trade to Mesopotamia and India. They traded leather, woolens, salted meat, and dairy products for grain, bread, fruits, and vegetables, and the finished goods of craftsmen. The newcomers gained from their hosts the domesticated Bactrian camel. In the Avestan and Vedic texts, the speakers of Iranian and Sanskrit used the same loan word for camel, *ushtra*, which is unrelated to the word for camel in other Indo-European languages.[56] In Transoxiana, the ancestors of the Indo-Iranians prospered and perfected their use of chariots, perhaps shifting from javelins to the composite bow as the favored missile weapon. They also learned the trade routes to the west and southeast.

The ancestors of the Iranians and Indo-Aryans long dwelled together as neighbors in Transoxiana. They shared a common speech and many cultural and religious practices. In historic times, they still worshipped the same gods known from the later *Rig-Vedas* and *Avesta*. They both practiced horse sacrifices, imbibed the same fermented beverage (*soma*), and were organized by occupations in a social hierarchy that crystallized in the caste of Hinduism. The *Rig-Vedas*, hymns to the early Indo-Aryan gods, and the *Garthas*, the oldest verses in *Avesta* (the scriptures of Zoroastrianism), represent the earliest forms of the Sanskrit and Iranian languages, which are very close in vocabulary, grammar, and syntax. These verses perhaps were first composed in the Late Bronze Age (1500–1200 BC).

The Vedic hymns were long recited orally until they were written much later, perhaps in the sixth century BC. But the hymns must have been repeatedly edited and redacted.[57] The earliest surviving Sanskrit documents are later still: the edicts of the Mauryan emperor Ashoka (269–232 BC), written in Brahmi script, which was based on the Aramaic alphabet of the sixth century BC.[58] The earliest surviving document of any Iranian language is the Persian text, written in cuneiform script, on the trilingual inscription at Behistun.[59] The Great King Darius I (521–486 BC), the victor in a civil war, commissioned the awesome monument in Akkadian, Elamite, and Persian, to proclaim his legitimacy.

In ca. 1500 BC, Indo-Aryan speakers departed from Transoxiana and traversed northern Iran, and settled on the grasslands of the al-Jazirah, a new homeland congenial to nomads arriving from the Eurasian steppes. When they arrived soon after 1500 BC, they found the Near East divided into warring states in the aftermath of the collapse of the Babylonian Empire. They imposed themselves as a warrior elite known as the *mariyanna* ("young warriors"), the equivalent of the Vedic Kshatriya caste.[60] These Indo-Aryans ruled over a far larger Hurrian- and Semitic-speaking population. They adopted cuneiform writing and Mesopotamian bureaucratic institutions to forge an imperial state in northern Syria and Mesopotamia called the Mitanni. These Indo-Aryan kings of the Mitanni corresponded on terms of equality with the Pharaoh of the New Kingdom, the Great King of Hatti, and the Kassite King of Babylon. In a treaty between the Mitannian King Kurtiwaza and Hittite Emperor Suppiluliumas (1344–1322 BC), the Mitannian gods invoked were Mitrasil, Arunasil, Indar, and Nasattyana. They are, respectively, the Vedic divinities Mitra, Varuna, Indra, and the Nasatya twins.[61] An Indo-Aryan master horse trainer, Kikkuli, in the service of the Hittite emperor, composed in his native language and Hittite a manual for training warhorses. The text, dating to the early fourteenth century BC, is the oldest record of the Indo-Aryan language.[62] The Hittite king Suppiluliumas invaded and overthrew the kingdom of Mitanni, and sacked its capital Washukanni (today an unidentified tell, or an artificial hill, in the vicinity of Tell Halaf in northern Syria). The Indo-Aryans of the Middle East abruptly disappeared from history.

Meanwhile, other Indo-Aryans migrated southeast, crossed the Hindu Kush, and entered the Punjab and Gandhara as immigrants, mercenaries, and invaders. Over the course of perhaps five centuries (ca. 1500–1000 BC), they settled in the lands of Meluhha. Scholars are still divided over whether these newcomers arrived as invaders or as successors to an urban civilization long in decline.[63] To be sure, the cities of Meluhha were already in decline; hence, many scholars posit ecological or environmental causes for the urban collapse. As yet, the limited number of ideograms stamped on Meluhhan glyphs are too few and too brief to be deciphered.[64] Records and historical accounts were likely written on palm leaf paper that disintegrated long ago. But if we had such historical texts, they would have revealed a concert of powers, rather than a single state, that had long warred among themselves in the fashion of the contemporary Near Eastern empires. Furthermore, the *Rig-Vedas* celebrate how the Aryans warred against the Dasas, the Dravidian-speaking people of Mleccha, who were subjected as the Sudra caste. Therefore, it is best to compare the Indo-Aryan migrations to those of the Germanic tribes who entered into the Roman Empire by invitation and invasion between the third and sixth centuries AD. In their new homeland, the Indo-Aryans recorded their ancestral rites of sacrifices and deeds of their gods in the verses of the *Vedas*, composed in an archaic Sanskrit and recited orally, only to be put down in writing centuries later. The newcomers from the Eurasian steppes also brought the horse, the spoked wheel, and the chariot, and they defined the linguistic and cultural future of India.[65]

In the early Iron Age (ca. 1000–750 BC), the Iranian-speaking nomads, collectively known as the Scythians, dominated the central Eurasian steppes and Transoxiana.[66] They replaced the light chariot with the mounted archer, equipped with the composite bow and astride a superior high saddle with leather toe loops as stirrups. This major shift in warfare enabled a new wave of migrations by Iranian-speaking nomads into the Near East, Iran, and the Tarim Basin from the ninth century BC on. The Scythians represented a confederation of diverse tribes, and later classical sources report among the many tribes the Dahae, Massagetae, and Saka. The Scythians had gained many benefits from their trade with the sedentary populations of Transoxiana and the forest peoples of Siberia. Foremost, they possessed a deep knowledge of geography and trade routes.

Eastern Iranians pitched their tents on the grasslands of Ferghana, which offered ideal grazing for their horses and livestock, and then crossed the Pamirs and settled in the western oases of the Tarim Basin, notably in the later caravan cities of Kashgar and Khotan. They brought their nomadic way of war and their distinct language, Saka.[67] A group of mummies from the Tarim Basin dating from the Iron Age (700–1 BC), tested for DNA, has confirmed this migration. The individuals were members of a population who shared ancestry with peoples of northern India and the Middle East. Murals of the Kizil Cave Monasteries of the fifth and sixth centuries AD depict many men and women with dark hair and slender figures typical of Iranians.[68] Men are shaven save for a handlebar mustache. Chinese and Persian literary sources report how Turkish kaghans, Persian shahs, and Chinese emperors prized Saka musicians, dancers, and courtesans. Some Saka-speaking tribes migrated even farther east into the Ordos triangle of the Upper Yellow River, where they came into contact with the warring states of Zhou China.[69] These Iranian nomads likely taught the steppe way of life, and way of war, to Altaic-speaking peoples of Mongolia, whose common tongue evolved into the later Turkic and Mongolian languages. The nomads dwelling on the Mongolian steppes proved adept pupils, for they would forge the confederation of the Xiongnu that would challenge imperial China.

Simultaneously, other Scythian tribes, perhaps under pressure from the Massagetae, migrated west, back to the ancestral homeland of the Pontic-Caspian steppes, in the eighth and seventh centuries BC.[70] They expelled a nomadic people who also spoke an Iranian dialect and were called in Greek sources Cimmerians. The Cimmerians fled across the grasslands of the Kuban, crossed the Caucasus by the Dariel Pass, and invaded the Near East in ca. 720 BC. The Cimmerians, the first nomadic horse archers to burst into the Near East from north of the Caucasus, quickly overran the Armenian plateau. In 714 BC, they defeated King Rusa I of Urartu, who ruled over the Hurrian-speaking kingdom centered around Lake Van that was the political heir of the Hittite Empire. Rusa had suffered a decisive defeat at the hands of the Assyrian king Sargon II the year before; in despair, he committed suicide.[71] The Cimmerians thereupon crossed the Upper Euphrates and entered Asia Minor, ravaging the northwestern provinces of the Assyrian Empire. In 705 BC, King Sargon II fell fighting in a great battle on the Cappadocian plateau against the rebel Hittite vassals of Tabal, supported by Cimmerian horsemen.[72] The rebels and their Cimmerian allies, however, had suffered heavily and failed to exploit their victory. In 696 BC, the Cimmerians, in alliance with King Rusa II of Urartu, invaded the Phrygian kingdom. The Phrygians, speaking an Indo-European language remotely related to Greek and Macedonian, were newcomers from the Balkans. In the Early Iron Age (ca. 950–750 BC), a succession of Phrygian kings, ruling under the dynastic name Midas (called Mita in Assyrian sources), united western and central Anatolia. Their massively fortified capital at Gordion, today seventy-five miles west of Ankara, succeeded to the role of Hittite Hattusas. Phrygian kings consulted Greek oracles and promoted trade with the Greek colonies on the Euxine and Aegean shores of Asia Minor. The last Midas, who was buried in the great tumulus of Gordion, suffered a catastrophic defeat at the hands of the Cimmerians, and he too committed suicide, reportedly by drinking bull's blood.[73] For the next fifty years, the Cimmerians rampaged across Asia Minor, raiding as far west as the Greek colonies on the Aegean littoral. In response, the Lydian king Gyges (ca. 680–644 BC), ruling from Sardes, made common cause with the Assyrian kings Esarhaddon and Ashurbanipal II against the invaders.[74] By 656 BC, the Cimmerians were driven back into Cappadocia and northeastern Asia Minor, where they settled and imposed their Iranian language and mores of the steppe way of life on the indigenous populations.

Finally, the most successful Iranian speakers migrated out of Transoxiana west across northern Iran and settled in the Media and Persia east of the Zagros mountains in the tenth and ninth centuries BC.[75] These Iranian-speaking nomads too excelled in horsemanship and archery. The Medes clashed with the Neo-Assyrian kings, and so they were compelled to organize an effective state centered on their capital, Ecbatana (today the massive mound Tappe-ye Hagmatān outside of Hamadan and still to be excavated). In 612 BC, King Cyaxares of the Medes allied with Nabopolassar, the Chaldean King of Babylon, against the Assyrians. The two monarchs captured and sacked the Assyrian capital, Nineveh, and so ended the Assyrian Empire.[76] In the fashion of the first Mesopotamian conqueror, Sargon of Akkad, Nabopolassar went on to unite the Fertile Crescent for the last time.[77] Cyaxares, commanding the invincible Median cavalry, expelled the Scythian invaders from northwestern Iran and forged a new imperial order comprising the lands of Iran, Transoxiana, and Afghanistan. Yet in the next generation, Cyrus the Great (559–530 BC), the vassal king of Persia, overthrew his overlord the Median King Astyages.[78] The Persians, kinsmen of the Medes, had settled in southwestern Iran, Persis (today Fars). They succeeded to the urban, bureaucratic state of Elam and its capital Susa, because the Assyrian monarch Ashurbanipal II had shattered Elamite power in 639 BC. In less than a generation, between 550 and 515 BC, Cyrus and his two immediate successors, Cambyses and Darius I, built the greatest empire of the ancient Near East, spanning three thousand miles from the shores of the Aegean to the Indus valley, and embracing perhaps forty million residents.[79] The Achaemenid kings of Persia ruled over an imperial order that rested on the bureaucratic institutions of Babylon and the horse archers of the Eurasian steppes. The Persians had proved to be the most successful of all the Iranian nomads who had migrated across and then off the Eurasian steppes in search of new homes.

In 500 BC, over the course of thirty-five centuries, Indo-European nomads had spread their languages from Europe to India. Those who peopled the central and eastern Eurasian steppes propagated a pastoral way of life based on the horse and the wheel. They transformed the steppes into a great land corridor, which would be traversed by future generations of merchants and missionaries, immigrants and conquerors. Those nomads such as the Anatolians, Tocharians, Indo-Aryans, and Persians who eventually settled new lands outside of the steppes exchanged their nomadic way of life for a settled one, based on agriculture and cities. They altered the linguistic and cultural map of Europe, the Middle East, and India. In so doing, they enriched, and even defined, the classic civilizations of Greece, the Middle East, and India.

2

Surviving on the Eurasian Steppes

In 1246, the Franciscan friar Giovanni da Pian del Carpine, envoy of Pope Innocent IV, was amazed by the size and numbers of ox-drawn carts with gigantic solid disc wheels (*gers*) conveying the mobile homes of the Mongols as he crossed three thousand miles of Eurasian steppes from Saray, on the Volga, to the Great Khan's capital at Karakorum in the heart of Mongolia.[1] The Greek historian Herodotus (490–425 BC) describes similar lumbering trains of carts conveying felt tents of the Scythians, the nomads of his day.[2] The wives drove great carts, while the men rode ahead marking the way and finding water and pastures for their herds and flocks. The wagon train conveyed round felt tents and their supporting poles that could be quickly assembled and dismantled.[3] Construction varied over the centuries, and from tribe to tribe, but a wagon and felt tent remained the center of a nomadic family, the *yurt* in Turkish. With such vehicles, nomads could move across the steppes swiftly in search of food, water, and pastures in a daily struggle for survival.

These grasslands extend over six thousand miles and cover over three million square miles, stretching from the lower Danube in the west across Russia and Siberia to the upper Amur River and the

Greater Khingan Mountains, which mark the western boundary of Manchuria. The climate and terrain are harsh, and nomads could afford no mistakes. On the open steppes, nomads are compelled to lay in stores and settle into shelters during frigid Arctic winters. Ahmad ibn Fadlan, ambassador of the Abbasid Caliph, set out across the central steppes for the lower Volga valley in the bitter winter of 921/2.[4] He later recollected how his survival depended on Turkic families, huddled in their *gers*, who received his party. Within the winter tent, privacy was impossible as each family member saw to his or her daily bodily needs. Yet his hosts graciously shared the warmth of their fire, and precious food and drink. Ibn Fadlan appreciated both the hospitality and probity of his hosts. His guides negotiated with each host the customary terms to borrow fresh horses vital for a winter crossing. Likewise, the missionary William of Rubruck reports how his guide insisted that the friar and his company don the warm clothing of the steppes—woolen kaftan, trousers, felt cap, and fur-lined coat and boots—before attempting a crossing in January 1246.[5] Should the Christians lag behind, the guide sternly warned, they would be on their own, because any attempt to rescue stragglers might endanger the group. Under the scorching summer sun, nomads were forever on the move, seeking water and pastures. Often the only shade from the unrelenting summer sun was found beneath the parked *gers* during brief breaks to take meals. Only the hardiest of humans and animals can survive these conditions.

At any time in Antiquity or in the Middle Ages, a nomadic *yurt* or tightly knit extended family wishing to cross the entire steppes would have been awed by the great distances, varied landscapes, and endless horizons as they migrated from west to east. These nomads would have trekked along a great land corridor with inland seas, lakes, and deserts to the south, and the dense coniferous forests of the taiga to the north. At the western end, they would have started their journey on the western edge of the South Russian or Pontic-Caspian steppes that stretch from the Carpathian Mountains and mouth of the Danube River, east to the lower Volga, and southeast to the northern slopes of the Caucasus.[6] They could have chosen to go in one of four directions. West, they had to cross the Carpath-

ian Mountains into Central Europe; to the south, they had to cross
the Danube's delta into the Balkans; to the southeast, they faced the
even more formidable Caucasus with only two passes: the Dariel
or Derbent that led them into the Middle East. In all cases, they
would leave the steppes for alien lands. Trekking directly east of
the Volga River, they would find the familiar pastures of the Central Eurasian steppes to the Altai Mountains. Today these steppes
constitute Kazakhstan, home to descendants of Turkish-speaking
nomads and in an area equivalent in size to Europe. To the south,
between the Caspian and Aral Seas, they would avoid venturing
into the forbidding Karakum (Black Desert). Traveling east from
the Volga, they would arrive at Lake Balkhash and its tributary the
Ili River that waters rich pastures. From here, they could travel
south across the Jaxartes River (Syr Darya) into Transoxiana or, in
Arabic, Mawarannahr (today the Republic of Uzbekistan). They
would have found this region between the Jaxartes (Syr Darya)
and Oxus River (Amu Darya) both familiar and unfamiliar. Between the lower (northern) courses of the two rivers that empty
in the Aral Sea stretches the forbidding Kizil Kum (Red Desert).
The Aral Sea, once a life-giving inland sea teeming with fish and
fowl, has today been drained dry in an ill-conceived and ecologi-
cally destructive Soviet project to irrigate cotton fields.[7]

Where once cattle and sheep grazed on the grasslands of the
Jaxartes's delta, the ancient land of the Khwarazm is now a vast
poisoned salt depression. Along the middle and lower courses of
the Oxus River and its tributary the Zeravshan, the land offered
ample pastures and water for their animals, but it also sustained irrigated fields and the caravan cities of the Silk Road. Invariably,
any nomads arriving in this region would need to come to terms
with the indigenous population. Once across the Jaxartes, our nomads could turn east into Ferghana (today Tajikistan), with ideal
grazing lands, and then cross over the Pamirs into the Tarim Basin
(today Xinjiang), an arid plateau and desert between the Tien Shan
to the north and Tibetan highlands to the south. If they settled in
the Tarim Basin, they would have given up their ancestral ways
for a sedentary life. The Tarim River and its tributaries cut fertile
valleys through the Taklamakan Desert that sustained agriculture

and the caravan cities of the Silk Road. They would have found two narrow corridors, skirting the desert to the north and south, and each with successive oasis cities that led east through the narrow grasslands of Gansu to the Yumen Pass, the fabled Jade Gate, and so the entrance into China. If, instead, our nomads chose to press east rather than south from Lake Balkhash, they would cross another formidable mountain range, the Altai, and so arrive on the Eastern Steppes of Outer Mongolia. To the south was the inhospitable Gobi of Inner Mongolia, and beyond the Huang He (Yellow River), and China. No nomads ever recorded in writing their experiences of traversing the steppes. Yet every nomadic family covered at least a significant stretch of these steppes during their lifetimes. The earliest nomads, speakers of Indo-European languages, would have made such journeys from west to east, but in the Middle Ages, first the Xiongnu and then Turkish tribes traversed these distances from east to west.

If our nomad families did not venture upon a trek in search of a new home, they still frequently traveled over a wide area to graze and water their horses and livestock. The wealth of any *yurt* was counted in horses, cattle, and sheep.[8] Frequently, unrelated families, clans, or tribes shared the same steppes according to customary arrangements. Nomads evolved rules of hospitality so vital for the survival of all. Hosts granted permission to neighbors or newcomers the right of passage over ancestral grasslands. They sealed these deals with feasts, exchanges of gifts, and marriages. All nomads negotiated such small-scale deals in which both hosts and guests profited. The arrangements often endured from generation to generation. It was impossible to draw maps designating specific areas as owned by any particular group, because land was merely a means to sustain horses and livestock rather than a capital asset of any group or private property. Each tribe ranged over a wide swath of the steppes that they had to share with others. In the early Middle Ages, between the fourth and sixth centuries AD, Iranian-speaking nomads who had dwelled on the central and western steppes for centuries forged many such small-scale arrangements with newcomers from farther east who spoke agglutinative, Altaic languages. Hence, many Iranian-speaking tribes might have easily accepted as their overlord Kaghan Bumin of the Gök Turks, because they had long contact with Turkish-speaking tribes over grazing rights.[9] Large-scale military operations, however, violently disrupted centuries-old patterns of seasonal herding and put the survival of all at risk. Mongol conquerors ordered vast stretches of the steppes cleared of all humans and livestock so that their warriors, and their strings of mounts, had ample water and pastures, and thus they could traverse great distances quickly. So ordered Genghis Khan when he marched against Khwarazm, or Batu, when he waged his western campaign, or Tamerlane, when he invaded the Golden Horde.[10] Empire building on the steppes always came at a high price, bringing famine and death to many, and sending others fleeing.

Therefore, survival on the steppes always depended on movement. Nomads, even when traversing familiar grasslands, surveyed the land and remained alert. They had to possess keen eyesight and hearing and an acute sense of smell if they were to forecast sudden changes in weather, to hunt game, or to espy foes on cattle raids.[11] Even today, many nomads size up strangers as friend or foe by their sense of smell. Men and women both had to calculate precisely the *yurt*'s daily needs of meat and dairy foods. Meats were often dried, salted, or boiled for preservation. The Huns, according to the Roman historian Ammianus Marcellinus, packed dried or salted meat under their saddles so that they could eat while mounted and ride into the night before halting to take a light supper.[12] Turks and Mongols fermented mare's milk into the strong alcoholic beverage called *qumis* (or *kumis* in Western Turkish languages). The Mongol khan Batu, according to the missionary William of Rubruck, described the process of fermenting the heady beverage. He also notes that Mongol Khan Batu reportedly kept a herd of three thousand white mares, milked daily, so that he could ply his warriors and foreign envoys with ample quantities of *qumis* for toasts at the banquets held in his tent.[13] Yet the staples of meat and dairy products alone were insufficient to sustain a healthy life. Those nomads bordering on the forests of Siberia supplemented their food supply by fishing, hunting, and gathering berries, acorns, and nettles. Friar Giovanni da Pian del Carpine was astonished, and disgusted, by the variety of rodents and fowl eaten by Mongol tribes in the thirteenth century.[14] Temujin, the future Genghis Khan, barely sustained himself and his family on such a meager diet when they lived as exiles in the forests.[15] All nomadic peoples had to trade with sedentary peoples for grains, fruits, vegetables, and manufactured goods. Even on the steppes, some inhabitants lived in villages and cultivated the land. Early inhabitants of the river valleys of the Pontic-Caspian steppes cultivated barley, vegetables, and fruits that they bartered with the nomads of the Yamnaya culture. On these same steppes centuries later, the Greek historian Herodotus reports how the high king of the Scythian nomads exacted tribute in grain from those of his subjects engaged in farming. Yet most nomadic peoples acquired much-needed foodstuffs, finely crafted goods, and luxuries in the market towns of literate urban civilizations along the rim of their world. The Scythians of Herodotus's day frequented Greek colonies of the Tauric Chersonesus (Crimea), where they traded salted meat, dairy goods, woolens, and horses for wine, olive oil, dried fruits and vegetables, and finely crafted goods.[16] Along the Great Wall, Turkish or Mongol nomads traded for necessities and luxuries in the markets regulated and protected by the emperor of China. Bilĝe, Kaghan of the Gök Turks (717–734), boasted on his monumental inscription in the Orkhon valley how he had courted and protected Chinese merchants who arrived bringing millet, rice, silk, and precious objects to the prosperity of his subjects.[17] When they were unable to trade, nomads would then raid. Hence, they were forever condemned in the writings of historians of the urban literate civilizations as rapacious barbarians, ignorant of agriculture and prone to violence. The stereotype has persisted to this day, but often nomads had little choice but to raid if they were to survive.

The chances of survival, and even prosperity, for the peoples of the Eurasian steppes increased significantly when merchants of imperial China and Rome regularly conducted long-distance trade across the Eurasian continent.[18] The commerce of the so-called Silk Road altered the lives of so many nomadic peoples from the third century BC on. In the first century AD, the four empires of Rome, Parthia, the Kushans, and Han China imposed a general peace that made such trade in luxuries predictable and profitable.[19] The commerce continued long after all four of these empires had

collapsed and were replaced by new imperial regimes, the Caliphate and Tang China, just as eager to promote the lucrative trade.

In the first century AD, a caravan sponsored by a consortium
of Aramaic-speaking merchants of Palmyra would have traversed
a well-known route from this oasis city in the Syrian desert on
Rome's eastern frontier.[20] The caravan would have skirted the Arabian desert to reach the middle course of the Euphrates River,
then turned southeast, following the river to the twin capitals of
the Parthian Empire, Seleucia ad Tigrim and Ctesiphon.[21] There
the Palmyrene merchants conducted their first major transactions,
with the assistance of resident kinsmen who acted as sureties before
Parthian market wardens. From Ctesiphon, the caravan crossed the
Zagros Mountains, and traveled east across northern Iran from Ecbatana (today Hamadan) to Margiane (Merv), and thence northeast, where it would have crossed the middle Oxus River, and then
made for the oasis cities most famous under their Medieval names
of Bukhara and Samarkand. At each major city, the Palmyrenes
were greeted by fellow countrymen, who were respected residents
of the city and so could represent their guests before local authorities. New camels could be purchased; supplies secured; guides and
escorts hired. Every stop included haggling in the market, and sam-
pling of the local delights and vices. At Samarkand (called Maracanda in Classical sources), the Palmyrenes had reached their final
destination. There they purchased Chinese silks from native Sogdian merchants, who, in turn, bought the luxury goods the Palmyrenes had conveyed from the Roman world or acquired along
the way. Sogdian merchants controlled the eastern extension of
the Silk Road.[22] From Samarkand, their caravans, loaded with the
goods of the Mediterranean world and Transoxiana, ascended the
Pamirs to reach Kashgar, at the western end of the Tarim Basin. A
Sogdian caravan could choose to follow the route along the northern edge of the Taklamakan Desert, or the southern route via Khotan. Both routes took the caravan to the celebrated Jade Gate, and
beyond into China. As they passed from city to city, the Sogdian
merchants on this caravan too operated with the assistance of resident kinsmen. They acquired en route jade, textiles, and slaves for
the Chinese markets. Their ultimate goal was either Luoyang or

Chang'an, capitals of the Han emperor, where they acquired the silk that sustained the entire trade.[23] Already in the first century AD, merchants operated along extensions of this prime route. Caravans from Margiane (Merv) followed the lower Oxus River to Bactra (Balkh), then crossed the Hindu Kush, and so reached Taxila (Takshashila in Sanskrit) in Gandhara.[24] From Taxila, the caravan might continue east to the sacred cities of the Ganges valley or press south, making for the port Barbaricum (near Karachi today), where merchants arriving by sea either from Charax on the Persian Gulf or Alexandria exchanged goods from the Roman world for Chinese silks.[25] From Bukhara, other caravans trekked down the Oxus River, skirted the southern and western shores of the Aral Sea, and then traversed the central Eurasian steppes to the Greek ports on the northern shores of the Black Sea. The routes persisted, and expanded, as new peoples succeeded to the commerce. Arab merchants of the Caliphate replaced the Aramaeans of the Roman age, and they vastly expanded the scale of the trade in Turkish slaves.[26] Baghdad and Damascus replaced, respectively, Ctesiphon and Palmyra as the international markets for silks, spices, and slaves. Sogdian merchants, however, maintained their monopoly over the eastern routes, despite the rise and fall of successive Chinese dynasties and Turkic kaghanates. Only in the eleventh century did Sogdian give way to Turkish as the language of commerce.

For the nomadic peoples, caravans of the Silk Road provided opportunities for enrichment, and survival. Nomads sold to caravans camels and horses in great numbers. The camel, either the Arabian dromedary or two-humped Bactrian one, was the preferred beast of burden over the mule. In the tenth century AD, the Oghuz Turks bred for the caravan trade a superior hybrid camel with greater endurance in the colder climate of the steppes that quickly replaced the Bactrian one.[27] A camel can convey a load 50 percent heavier than a mule. Camels conserve water, live four times longer than mules, and are far more resilient, capable of attaining twenty-five miles per day. Horses, especially the prized steeds of Ferghana, were also needed in great numbers for armed escorts and scouts. Local leaders of nomadic tribes negotiated lucrative deals with the merchant princes of caravans, providing supplies, fodder, rights of

passage over grasslands, and use of water sources. They also hired
out their warriors as guards and guides. Merchants stocked up on
many ordinary wares, dubbed tag items by economic historians,
which they could barter, sell, or hand out to nomads along the route.
Every Turkic or Mongol kaghan appreciated caravans for providing
life-giving goods and foodstuffs for his people, and the fancy prestige items that he could bestow on his faithful warriors. Starting
with Modu Chanyu, the indomitable ruler of the Xiongnu in the
second century BC, every conqueror who forged a tribal confederacy on the Eurasian steppes aimed to control at least part of the
Silk Road. They learned from the merchants the power of writing for record keeping, and so nomadic rulers, starting with Modu
Chanyu (209–174 BC), employed literate scribes who could adapt
existing scripts or devise new ones to keep records in the speech
of the nomadic peoples.[28]

Given a lifetime of movement and trade, nomads had to adapt and
learn different languages if they were to communicate effectively
with fellow nomads, caravan merchants, or vendors in the urban
markets of sedentary civilizations. Migration across the steppes inevitably resulted in linguistic change. But linguistic change was far
more complex than the displacement of one race by another—the
model followed by so many nationalistic historians or ideologues
since the late nineteenth century. Invariably nomadic peoples on
the move intermixed and assimilated with others en route to their
new homes or in seasonal herding of their livestock. Hence, any
identity of a people on the steppes was more a matter of common
language, culture, and shared historical experiences rather than racial descent. Anthropologists have theorized how speakers of one
language, who might have constituted a minority, could assimi-
late a larger body of speakers of another language. Steppe nomadic
peoples on the move in search of water and pastures adopted what
is called a "distributed" strategy for survival.[29] They were inclined
to modify, simplify, and adapt their own language as well as learn
other languages as part of a strategy of survival. Hence, every steppe
language was replete with loan words and phrases, expressing unfamiliar objects and concepts learned from other peoples. Often,
tribes or smaller communities on the Eurasian steppes were inclined

to adopt new languages to facilitate trade or to gain status. In the sixth and seventh centuries, many speakers of eastern Iranian dialects adopted Turkish to improve their standing in the eyes of their overlord, the kaghan of the Gök Turks. Yet nomads often resisted renouncing their ancestral tongue for that of the settled, prosperous populations with whom they regularly traded. As a matter of practicality, nomads learned a dominant language such as Chinese, Tocharian, Sogdian, or Arabic. They often employed as translators bilingual captives, political exiles, or craftsmen resident among them. Yet nomads, when they were not trading and raiding, spent most of the year among themselves, herding their animals, searching for pastures and water, or settling vendettas with ancestral foes. These small groups spoke their language among themselves, and perfected vocabulary, grammar, and syntax. Without writing, they prized recitation and memory. The two earliest written documents of the Turkish and Mongol languages, the Orkhon inscriptions of the eighth century and *The Secret History of the Mongols* of the thirteenth century, reveal that each language has changed little over the centuries, and each is still intelligible to modern speakers. During the long nights of winter months, bards entertained their hosts huddled in their winter tents by reciting formulaic lists of ancestors back many generations. Among Turks and Mongols, descent from the superior clans of white bones took precedence over those of the black bones.[30] In reciting such genealogies, poets inserted and expanded on the great deeds of ancestors. Among the Turks and Mongols, fabulous progenitors included the wolf and doe, sacred animals of Tengri, the lord of the eternal blue sky.[31] Genghis Khan could recite in verse his ancestors back five generations. Yelü Dashi, the founder of the Karakhitan Confederation, could count back nine generations.[32] By means of oral poetry, nomads not only preserved the memory of ancestors but also perfected the language, so vital to their identity. Therefore, for all their contact with envoys, merchants, and holy ones from the urban civilizations, nomads retained their language and so their identity. For every language is more than a means of communication; it is also an interpretation of the world, as anyone who is in a bilingual marriage quickly learns.

  In their daily struggle for survival, all steppe nomads also shared

similar outlooks on the divine forces of nature that governed their
lives. For all their differences in ritual and myths, Indo-European,
Turkic, and Mongol nomads agreed on religious fundamentals born
in response to their environment. They believed in the efficacy of
sacrificing domesticated animals, especially horses and cattle, in be-
seeching the gods.[33] As early as 5000 BC, inhabitants of the Pontic-
Caspian steppes already practiced animal sacrifice.[34] Among speakers
of both language families, Indo-European and Altaic, sacred and
legal languages were derived from the same root words, because
prayer, whether individual or communal, took the legal form expressed in Latin, *do ut des*, i.e., "I, the worshipper, give in order
that you, the divinity, may give in return." Above, they looked to
the endless blue sky that dominated their lives as the supreme lord
of the universe, invoked by the PIE speakers as Dyēws, and Tengri
by the later Turks and Mongols.

Due to the accidents of survival, scholars can reconstruct in
broad outline several of the principal deities of the earliest Indo-
European nomads based on cognates of the names of certain gods
among the daughter languages. They also have compared common
elements of myths shared by Indo-European speakers in historic
times (notably Vedic, Hittite, Greek, Roman, and Norse myths).
In contrast, far less can be surmised about divinities and myths of
Turkic- and Mongol-speaking nomads because they modified their
ancestral beliefs soon after they came into contact with missionaries and merchants of the Buddhist, Manichaean, or Muslim faiths.

The first nomads on the Pontic-Caspian steppes held in awe the
two principal features of their physical world: the eternal blue sky
above, and the grasslands rolling endlessly to the distant horizon.
Hence, an all-powerful, all-seeing lord of the heavens ruled above,
and his consort was the fertile earth. The PIE root words for the
two divinities have been reconstructed as Dyēws pH$_2$tér, "Sky Father," and Dhéghōm, "the broad one."[35] In historic times, this sky
god was represented by Zeus among the Greeks, Jupiter among the
Romans, and Tiwaz or Tyr in the Germanic and Norse pantheons. The divine name did not survive in the earliest religious texts
of Indo-Iranians. Zoroaster, prophet and reformer in the seventh
or sixth century BC, instituted a monotheistic creed, demoting

many of the ancestral gods to demons.[36] In India, thunder-wielding Indra reigned instead as king of the gods in the *Rig-Vedas*. The Hindu poets repeatedly invoked Indra and fire-breathing Agni, while they only mentioned in several hymns Father Sky, Dyáus Pitā, who had been demoted to a distant ancestor.[37] Dyēws impregnated Mother Earth, likely called Dhéghōm, with life-giving rains. From them sprang younger gods. Among them were divine twin brothers, later remembered as the equestrian Dioscuri (Castor and Polydeuctus) among the Greeks, and chariot-driving Asvins in Vedic hymns.[38] The Dawn, PIE Hausōs, was either an ageless maiden or one of an endless succession of maidens who were born and died with each rising and setting of the sun. The sun was also conceived as a maiden, whereas the moon was a divine youth. The stars were merely ornaments in the firmament that brightened the night rather than divinities. Nomads much later invested spiritual powers in the stars after they encountered the astrologers of China or the Near East. Tamerlane, last of the conquerors from the Eurasian steppes, was reared as a devout Muslim, so he consulted astrologers rather than shamans. Tamerlane, however, never let the forecasts of his astrologers dictate his military operations. After his spectacular victory at Delhi in 1397, Tamerlane excoriated his astrologers who warned him against joining battle. The astrologers got the message. Their lord wanted confirmation, not predictions, and so they foretold a glorious victory before the Battle of Angora six years later.[39]

The Yamnaya people were ever pragmatic in appeasing the fickle gods who governed their harsh environment, so they readily accepted new divinities who demonstrated their power by answering supplications. Hence, the membership in the Indo-European pantheon steadily increased over time, and new gods learned from neighbors were duly enrolled. The personalities and rites to the gods too changed as material life changed. The divine brothers in later myths were mounted on powerful steeds, or rode chariots across the sky. These attributes dated after the domestication of the horse and the invention of the light chariot. Goddesses of fate, best remembered as the Greek Moirai or Norse Norns, spun the fates of mortals as weaving became a vital female task within the *yurt*.

Hence, mortals constantly innovated on the attributes and powers of divinities as their own physical world changed. To be sure, poets versed in the stories of the gods and priests knowledgeable in sacrificial rituals inspired or led a conservative communal worship, but they lacked canon, creed, and even sanctuaries staffed by hereditary priests who could impose a conformity of worship. Yet the believers did agree on general points about the cosmos. Sky and earth formed a single flat reality, encircled by a great ocean. Humans sprang from primordial ancestors, invariably hermaphrodites, in a distant past. Distant lands in the far west were deemed abodes for the blessed few, while the dead crossed dark waters to enter a dismal netherworld guarded by a gigantic multiheaded hound, Cerberus in the Hellenic tradition or Sharvara, the spotted hound of the god Yama, in the Vedic.

For centuries, bards recited in alliterative verse myths about their gods and the mortal heroes who enjoyed divine favor. Virtually all of these myths were forgotten long ago as Indo-Europeans departed from their original home on the Pontic-Caspian steppes.[40] One myth did persist, a primeval combat between the lord of the eternal blue sky and an enormous serpent, sprouting many ferocious heads and spewing venom.[41] The poet Hesiod first records how Zeus slew the serpent monster Typhon, who led the Titans in an assault on Olympus when the giants piled Mount Pelion atop Mount Ossa so that they could scale the heavens.[42] In the many later retellings of the myth about how to slay a dragon, the lord of winds and rains usurped the role of father sky. In the *Rig-Vedas*, Indra, mounted in his chariot, wields his lightning weapon varja against Vritra, an evil serpent who has brought drought to the earth by penting up the waters.[43] Once Vritra is slain, the waters are released, and fertility returns to the world. In the Hittite epic, the storm god, under his Hurrian name Teshub, slays a similar many-headed serpent, Illuyanka.[44] A relief from the palace of Mild (modern Malatya, Turkey) dating from the eleventh century BC depicts Teshub and his son Sharruma attacking Illuyanka. Displayed in Ankara's Museum of Anatolian Civilizations, the relief is our earliest depiction of the cosmic combat between god and serpent. In the "Völuspá," the first poem of the Poetic Edda, a prophetess or völva recites the origins and end of the world in the earliest Norse alliterative verse. At Ragnarök, in his final combat, fiery-haired Thor, lord of thunder, hurls his magical hammer, Mjölnir, to slay his arch enemy, the Midgard Serpent, who has arisen from the ocean. But Thor staggers backward to his death, suffocated by the venom spewed over him by the mortally wounded serpent.[45] This myth of a cosmic battle between sky god and serpent endured because it symbolized the violent struggle at the dawn of creation.

Poets, operating in a world without writing, had many aids to recite myths of the gods and legends of heroes in alliterative verse. Drawing on phrases and epithets, well-documented in Homeric and Germanic epic verse, a poet, accompanying himself on a lyre, could improvise line after line of verse. Each recitation was thus an independent performance to thrill the listeners who knew well the stories.[46] Hymns to the gods, however, permitted far less creativity. They were memorized and transmitted in archaic language, because they were sung at ritual sacrifices. Today Brahmans still recite faithfully Vedic hymns in an archaic Sanskrit unintelligible to most Indians. The hymns were perhaps first recorded on palm leaf paper in the seventh or sixth century BC when scribes adapted the Aramaic alphabet to Sanskrit. The Brahmans, who monopolized the rites and prayers to the gods in historic India, were the spiritual heirs to the poetic prophets who had sung the earliest hymns to the Indo-European gods. The hymns meticulously record the butchering of sacrificial victims and the distributing of the meat, and the positioning of the altar according to the points of the compass. Indra, lord of rains and thunder, and the fire god Agni received most of the veneration in the hymns, whereas Vishnu and Shiva, the lords of later Hinduism, are not mentioned. The hymns are set in a timeless past, composed after the Indo-Aryans had entered the Punjab, the "land of the seven rivers" in the Vedic verse.[47] When the Brahmans composed the hymns, the Indo-Aryans had not yet settled in the Doab and valley of the Ganga, the later sacred land of Aryavarta. Nor do the poets of the *Rig-Vedas* betray any memory of the ancestral homeland on the Eurasian steppes, or even the trek of the Indo-Aryans across the Hindu Kush. Even so, the hymns of the *Rig-Vedas*, in purpose and form, descended from the first hymns offered in sacrifice to the ancestral gods common to all Indo-Europeans twenty-five centuries earlier. Likewise, the thirty-three Homeric hymns shared a similar descent. These hymns were written down, or perhaps dictated, in the seventh and sixth centuries BC.[48] The anonymous poets composed these hymns about the myths and rituals of the Olympians in the archaic language of the Homeric epics rather than any of the vernacular dialects of Greece. The sacred language of Greek and Sanskrit hymns sprang from a conservative, even fearful, spiritual outlook of the Yamnaya nomads. Prayers offered to the gods, along with proper sacrifices, must never be altered lest the gods take offense of errors or changes in wording, and so visit retribution upon the community.

The Xiongnu, who welded the first confederation of Altaic-speaking nomads on the eastern Eurasian steppes, and later, Turks and Mongols, also venerated the lord of the eternal blue sky, Tengri. As early as the fourth century BC, the god's name was rendered in Chinese ideograms as Chengli, the supreme god of the barbarian Xiongnu.[49] In the Orkhon inscription in the eighth century AD, Bilğe Kaghan of the Gök Turks stresses how he ruled by favor of Tengri, and so Bilğe Kaghan claims a Mandate of Heaven in a fashion akin to that of the Tang emperors of China. In the same inscription, he also praises his judicious mother, who is like the earth goddess Umay.[50] Turks and Mongols, just like earlier Indo-European nomads, revered the divine powers of earth and sky. They too often offered prayer individually to the gods, for no priestly caste ever emerged among Turkish and Mongol nomads. In the *Secret History of the Mongols*, Genghis Khan often gazes to the sacred Mount Burkhan Khaldun when he utters his prayers to Tengri or invokes the protective spirit of the mountain.[51] In return, he received dreams and portents from Tengri as warnings or assurances of victory.

Turks and Mongols revered shamans who could read from the charred shoulder bones of sheep the will of Tengri. In drug-induced trances and astride a sacred horse, shamans ascended a world tree to the highest, fifth, level of the heavens, where they would supplicate spirits to intercede on their behalf before the supreme celestial lord of the universe.[52] They inherited from their ancestors, who had once dwelled in the Siberian taiga, visions of a world tree and a reverence for the forest animals, wolves and bears, as guardians and progenitors. Kipchak Turkish villagers of Central Anatolia, whose families had been expelled from their homeland on the South Russian Steppes by the Tsarist regime in the nineteenth century, recount in their folklore what is likely an ancestral myth.[53] Tengri, in the guise of a white goose, flies over a boundless ocean. Beneath the waters, the white mother goddess, Ak Ana, implores him to create and fill the lonely universe with life. But in his act of creation, Tengri engenders Er Kishi, who turns to evil and misleads mortals into darkness. Hence, Tengri sends down to earth sacred animals as moral guides. The myth, which shares a dualist outlook with Manichaean and Zoroastrian concepts of the eternal clash between good and evil, could easily be interpreted as a moral allegory of the tenets of monotheistic creeds.

Propitiating the gods dwelling in the skies above was just as much an act of survival as piety, because nomadic peoples would consider a new divinity if their shamans or holy ones could demonstrate their power. Between the second century BC and the seventh century AD, missionaries carried new faiths to the caravan cities along the Silk Road, and to the steppe nomads dwelling along and beyond the frontiers of imperial China and Iran. Iranian- and Turkic-speaking nomads proved receptive to teachings of Buddhism, Manichaeism, Zoroastrianism, Nestorian Christianity, and Judaism, but they adapted rather than embraced the new faiths outright. When nomads visited the urban markets, they could only conclude that wealthy merchant princes enjoyed the favor of powerful divine protectors. Furthermore, merchant families poured their wealth into religious monuments as thank-offerings for prosperity. Many nomads embraced new faiths to secure the same divine favor, and they gained an additional advantage when they negotiated with merchants who were coreligionists.

The monks of Mahayana Buddhism scored spectacular success in converting Iranian- and Tocharian-speaking nomads, because they stressed the message rather than the sacred language of scriptures.[54] Monks translated Buddhist texts from Sanskrit or Prakrit into the widely spoken vernaculars Saka, Sogdian, Tocharian, and Chinese. Hence, monks could preach to nomadic peoples in their own language. Enlightenment did not depend on the Vedic hierarchy of caste, but rather on each individual following his or her own dharma. Pious acts netted karma, and so the hope of a superior reincarnation on the road to nirvana and the end of the cycle of births. Nomads easily reconciled the myths about their ancestral gods as previous incarnations of the Buddha. Buddhist merchants proved even more convincing missionaries. They were prosperous, literate, and conversant in several languages. They built palatial residences in caravan cities frequented by nomads. Many such lavishly decorated and furnished homes have been excavated at the Sogdian settlement at Panjikent (today in Tajikistan).[55] Panjikent, on the banks of the Zeravshan River, was the base for any caravan ascending or descending the routes across Pamirs to the Tarim Basin. Likewise, the frescoes of the Mogao Caves celebrating the life of the Buddha must have awed nomadic pilgrims, who would have visited after concluding their business at the Chinese outpost of Dunhuang. Furthermore, Buddhist merchants and monks traveled under the protection of great rulers, notably the Mauryan, Indo-Greek or Kushan emperors, all of whom were venerated as Dharmikasa or a follower of dharma.[56]

Few nomads dwelling on the Eurasian steppes embraced Zoroastrianism, a monotheistic creed reformed by the prophet Kartir, who doubled as spiritual adviser to the first two Sassanid Shahs.[57] The dualist doctrine of a cosmic struggle between Ahura-Mazda, the lord of light, and his evil adversary, Ahirman, should have appealed to many nomads. But the faith, while universal in appeal, was culturally and linguistically Iranian, and so closely linked with the Sassanid court.[58] Instead, another monotheistic faith, Manichaeism, which had arisen in the western borderlands of the Sassanid Empire, won many converts among Turkish nomads. Its prophet, Mani (215–273), too preached a dualism, but his doctrines transcended political and cultural barriers.[59] His scheme of cosmic redemption might well have been influenced by Buddhism. The Manichees, just like Buddhists, comprised a community of the enlightened, the "Elect," and the ordinary believers, "Hearers." The Elect perceived the falsehood of the material world, and sought reunion with the celestial particles of light, whereas the Hearers dutifully performed their allotted tasks in this lifetime with the hopes of attaining enlightenment in the next. Manichaean missionaries adapted myths of many peoples, preached in vernacular tongues, and used picture books and visual props to awe converts. In 762, Bögü Khan, who ruled over the third of the Turkish kaghanates on the Mongolian steppes, embraced Manichaeism.[60] His people, the Uyghurs, followed suit. Many Turkish- and Mongolian-speaking tribes of the eastern steppes still practiced Manichaeism in the time of Genghis Khan.

Nestorian Christians, condemned as heretics at the Third Ecumenical Council in 431, departed the Roman world for the caravan cities of Transoxiana and the Tarim Basin.[61] Nestorian missionaries originally preached in Syriac, a dialect of Aramaic, which was widely spoken along the western half of the Silk Road, but they soon translated their scriptures into Sogdian, Turkish, and Chinese. They even devised a script for Turkish. Nestorian Christians assumed the mores and dress of Central Asia, including the practice of multiple wives. Christian holy men had a reputation for healing and performing miracles. In the sixth century AD, Turkish mothers tattooed crosses on the foreheads of their children as a protection against plague.[62] Nestorian priests, who accompanied the exiled Sassanid Shah Kavad, who sought refuge among the Hephthalites in 496–498, converted a Turkish kaghan and his tribe when the priests ended a drought by summoning rains upon making the sign of the cross.[63] In the late eighth century AD, the court and nobility of the Khazar kaghanate converted to Judaism.[64] They too were impressed by wealthy and sophisticated Jewish merchants who had settled in the Khazars' settlement Atil at the mouth of the Volga River. Furthermore, the Khazar kaghans preferred a monotheistic creed that was favored by neither of his two principal rivals, the Orthodox emperor Constantinople and the caliph of Baghdad. Ultimately, the future on the western and central steppes rested with Islam. In the tenth century, numerous Turkish nomads converted to Islam, which they viewed as a religion of both victory and prosperity. The caliphs of Baghdad reigned over a mighty empire that defeated the armies of Tang China.[65] Under the caliphs' protection, Muslim merchants and mystics long traded and preached among the Turkish tribes. To this day, the national identities of the Turkish peoples are defined by Islam. Yet even the Turkish nomads of the tenth and eleventh centuries, when they converted to Islam, did so on their own terms. Theirs was a folk Islam adapted to their ancestral ways and beliefs. Shamans and Sufi mystics were both revered as mentors or *hocalar*. The Turks, like all other nomadic peoples, were ever pragmatic about their religion. They embraced the new without discarding the old, and so assured divine favor from both that was so vital for surviving on the Eurasian steppes.

Finally, the Eurasian steppes bred the hardiest of hunters and warriors, who engaged in incessant blood feuds, cattle rustling, and abducting of wives as marks of bravery and honor.[66] The horse was central to the lives of the nomads. The world's vast majority of horses in 5000 BC roamed across the Pontic-Caspian steppes. The species had long disappeared in its original homeland in the New World, and few horses survived across most of Eurasia.[67] The earliest Sumerian and Akkadian texts speak of horses as rare, wild ongars of Kur, impossible to tame or domesticate.[68] The first nomads on the Pontic-Caspian steppes domesticated the horse as a source of winter meat and hides perhaps as early as 4500 BC, but later nomads only ate horseflesh as a last resort. Several centuries later, ancestors of the Yamnaya people were experimenting with riding horses bareback and guided by copper or bronze bits and bridles. A rider could herd far many more cattle or sheep than a pedestrian drover. Riders could scout the paths of the *yurt* on the move, and ran down prey on the grasslands. Horses never pulled the heavy mobile homes (*gers*) of nomads or, until the tenth century in Europe, the heavy plows of peasants. Over the course of centuries, nomads bred horses for endurance and a more docile nature. It was only by 2020 BC that the warrior nomads of the Sintashta culture on the lower Volga produced the modern horse, capable of pulling a light chariot with spoked wheels or carrying a rider atop a saddle and guiding his mount with bit and bridle. Recent DNA analysis indicates the new breed of horse displaced other species across the expanse of the Corded Ware culture.[69] The Indo-Iranians soon after introduced the horse to the central and eastern steppes, Transoxiana, India, and the Near East. Nomads revered the animal, offering it in sacrifice to the gods and the honored dead. Herodotus first records such a sacrifice to the deceased high king of the Scythians. His kurgan, a burial chamber covered by an earthen mound, was flanked by horses, slaughtered, stuffed, and raised on poles.[70] Riders too were sacrificed, stuffed, and attached by stakes to the beasts. The Mongols similarly honored their revered dead. This ancient steppe ritual of the horse sacrifices survived in many locales in historic times. Each year, the Rhodians in Classical times sacrificed to Helios a chariot drawn by four white horses and driven off the island's cliffs into the Aegean Sea.[71] In the fourth and fifth centuries AD, Gupta emperors of India revived the Vedic version of the ritual (*ashvamedha*) to announce their rule over Aryavarta, the sacred heartland of India.[72] The designated horse was permitted to wander for a year, thereby staking out the emperor's realm, before it was offered in sacrifice.

Foremost, steppe nomads turned the horse into a vehicle of war, and so initiated two military revolutions. By ca. 2000 BC, Indo-Iranian speakers had bred superior warhorses that, when harnessed in teams of four, were capable of pulling a light chariot with spoked wheels. Chariots offered platforms from which warriors armed with either javelins or composite bows could rain deadly fire upon enemy infantry.[73] During the next four centuries, this military innovation had spread across Eurasia from Britain to China. The pharaohs of the Egyptian New Kingdom, the Great Kings of Hatti, and even the Mycenaean lords of Greece fielded armies of chariots in the Middle and Late Bronze Age. Chinese imperial armies depended on chariots rather than cavalry far longer because they lacked access to the sturdy horses of the Eurasian steppes. Then, at the dawn of the Iron Age, in ca. 1000 to 900 BC, the Scythians on the central Eurasian steppes abandoned chariots in favor of mounted horsemen armed with composite bows.[74] Successive improvements gave nomadic horsemen superior saddles and, by the sixth century AD, metal stirrups. Henceforth, nomadic horse archers excelled in the tactics of skirmishing and ambush, and in strategic movement and speed. Riding, archery, and fighting were the skills of every freeman of a tribe. In the Orkhon valley, Bilgĕ Kaghan of the Eastern Turks spent a month in the year 732 carving into a monolith Turkish runes celebrating his deeds. He reports how he won honor and enriched his tribe with spoils taken in thirty-eight campaigns. He also reports the names and colors of his warhorses, and praises those that fell in battle.[75] Kings, princes, and nobles across Eurasia learned to prize the warhorse from their nomadic foes. The Tang emperor Taizong, who preferred to be a warrior rather than a Confucian emperor, immortalized his six warhorses slain in battle with a monumental relief sculpture, accurate to the last detail, including the wounds each sustained in battle.[76]

Nomadic warriors, to the horror of their civilized neighbors, waged war violently. They were reared in the brutal conditions of the Eurasian steppes, and in tribal warfare, there were no prisoners. Ritual torturing of prisoners and head taking were lessons to the victors not to be defeated. Women often rode into battle with their men. Kurgans, burial monuments in Ukraine, include many Scythian warrior princesses, and Herodotus located the Amazons in the land of the Scythians.[77] Khutulun, a Mongol warrior princess, could outride and outshoot men, and also offered wise counsel to her father, Khan Kaidu, an implacable enemy of Kublai Khan.[78] Victory alone counted, and defeat meant death for all because victors could ill afford to feed large numbers of captives. Therefore, whenever nomadic armies burst into the civilized lands, they massacred on a colossal scale any populations that dared to resist. In part, they hoped to terrorize other foes into surrender, but they also were practicing the harsh rules of warfare on the steppes. Yet these warriors, when organized and inspired by a commander of genius, could win empires and decide the fate of civilizations.

3

Scythians and the Great King of Persia

On the southern steppes of Ukraine today, near the Don River, Darius, Great King of Persia at the head of the mightiest army yet assembled, pondered the meaning of a curious message sent to him by the Scythian king Idanthyrsus. The envoy delivered a bird, mouse, frog, and five arrows, and then departed without explanation. Darius immediately interpreted the message as submission by the Scythians. But Gobryas, Darius's senior adviser and brother-in-law, discerned the meaning. "Unless you Persians turn into birds and fly up in the air or into mice and burrow in the ground or into frogs and leap into lakes, you will never get home again but stay here in this country, only to be shot by Scythian arrows."[1] The exchange captures the strategic limitations of waging war against the elusive nomadic horse archers on the Eurasian steppes. Darius failed to bring the Scythian nomads to decisive battle, and so, in the autumn of 512 BC, he declared victory and withdrew.[2] Six months earlier, Darius had marched an army of seven hundred thousand from Asia into Europe, crossing the Bosporus on a bridge of ships. He then crossed the Danube and invaded the steppes. The Scythians rallied against the invader. They laid waste to the land, poisoned the wells, and harassed the Persians at a distance. Darius could not overcome famine and thirst even though his fleet conveyed supplies from the Mediterranean world.

Yet King Darius was not the first Persian king to wage war against the Scythians. Darius strove to emulate and avenge his illustrious predecessor Cyrus the Great, the architect of the Persian Empire, and lauded by Greek writers as the greatest conqueror until Alexander the Great. Fifteen years earlier, Cyrus attacked nomads in their homeland, the Massagetae, who were a Scythian tribe dwelling on the central Eurasian steppes just north of the Jaxartes River (Syr Darya), which was the northeastern frontier of the Persian Empire.[3]

This is the first report of a preemptive strike against nomads in their own homeland. It is also our first report of a nomadic warrior princess, Queen Tomyris, who led her people to victory over an invader. She thwarted the strategy of King Cyrus, who intended to break the power of the Scythians because Cyrus feared that the Scythians, if left unchecked, would raid and settle in the Upper Satrapies of Sogdiana and Bactria (Transoxiana). Initially, King Cyrus sought a diplomatic solution, proposing a marriage alliance to Queen Tomyris of the Massagetae. But she spurned Cyrus's offer of marriage whereby she would join the royal harem and her people would grace royal reliefs of Cyrus's palace as submissive subjects rendering tribute. Instead, she sternly warned off Cyrus, but should he attack, she proudly offered battle either on the Persian or Scythian side of the Jaxartes River. Cyrus must have been enraged by the defiant barbarian queen, for in Cyrus's world, the Persians had adopted the Near Eastern practice of secluding royal women in the harem. Cyrus arrogantly chose war. Yet Cyrus erred in perceiving the Scythians as inconsequential barbarians. The Persians shared with these nomads a common origin going back to the Indo-Iranian speakers who had first settled on the Central Eurasian steppes. Persians and Scythians alike valued the same martial virtues, and the same way of war. The Persians (and their predecessors and kinsmen the Medes) had built the first Near Eastern empire based on the power of cavalry.[4] Herodotus reports that every Persian boy was taught to ride, shoot the bow, and always tell the truth, and he adds, would that the Greeks be as good. These were the virtues of the

Persians' nomadic ancestors, and so Cyrus should have known better and avoided fighting his Scythian foes on the Eurasian steppes. Then again, Cyrus failed to realize that the Massagetae also knew well their Persian foe.

Cyrus lured his foe into a clever stratagem worthy of Genghis Khan. He abandoned his camp, laden with supplies and luxuries, and guarded by a small detachment. Then Cyrus feigned a withdrawal and concealed his main force in ambush. The Massagetae quickly overran the camp, plundered the stores, and drank themselves into a stupor. Cyrus thereupon burst upon the Massagetae and slaughtered them while still asleep. Cyrus defeated only an advance detachment of the Massagetae, but he captured the queen's son and heir Spargapises. Spargapises duped Cyrus into granting him liberty of the king's tent, and promptly committed suicide. Without a royal hostage, Cyrus was compelled to cross the Jaxartes and seek battle. Herodotus, who likely spoke to Persian eyewitnesses, marveled at the length and savagery of the fighting.[5] Persian and Massagetae horsemen harassed each other from afar by successive barrages of arrows. When both sides exhausted their arrows, they finally closed in a deadly melee. The Massagetae outmaneuvered and outfought the Persians. The slaughter was dreadful, and Cyrus fell in battle. Tomyris ordered Cyrus's body beheaded, and fulfilled her vow of avenging her son by plunging the head into a skin sack of blood and contemptuously telling the tyrant to drink his bloody fill. Later Greek historians invented more dignified deaths for Cyrus, but they could not cover up the defeat and humiliation.

Cyrus's defeat at the hands of the Scythians fixed the northeastern Persian frontier on the Jaxartes River; Darius's defeat put the empire at risk. His Greek subjects, the Ionians living on the shores of Western Asia Minor, could only read Darius's withdrawal as a sign of weakness. They furnished the squadrons that guarded the bridge of ships over the Bosporus and the lifeline of Darius's army on the Russian steppes. While Darius chased the Scythians across the steppes of southern Russia, Scythian envoys appeared at the camp of the Ionian Greeks, whose fleet was guarding the bridge of ships across the Bosporus.[6] They urged the Greek commanders to destroy the bridge and sail home. Darius and his army would have been trapped on the steppes to face a Russian winter. Miltiades, a leading Athenian noble and tyrant of the Greek cities of the Thracian Chersonesus (today Gallipoli), urged accepting the advice. The Ionians could rid themselves of the Persian despot and regain their freedom and autonomy—the cherished political notions of every city-state.[7] But the wily Histiaeus, tyrant of Miletus, convinced his fellow tyrants to remain steadfast to Darius, whose favor assured their personal rule over their resentful citizens. Freedom and autonomy of their citizens were not what Greek tyrants wanted. Miltiades was proved correct, and he later led the Athenians to victory over the Persians at Marathon. Histiaeus proved too clever for Darius, who suspected the ambitious Milesian tyrant might plot rebellion and carried Histiaeus off to gilded captivity at Persepolis.[8] Histiaeus, however, obtained his revenge, and release, by fomenting the great rebellion of the Ionian cities in 499 BC.[9] By a clever ruse, Histiaeus sent his slave from Susa to his son-in-law Aristogoras, the reigning tyrant in Miletus, with instructions to incite rebellion among the Ionians. The message had been tattooed on the head of the slave to avoid detection by Persian guards along the Royal Road. The Ionians rose in rebellion, launching fleets that they had ironically constructed on Darius's orders for his Scythian expedition. Failure on the steppes delivered to Darius a dangerous revolt among his Greek subjects. During the rebellion, the Scythians sought to exploit Darius's difficulty, for in ca. 495 BC, they crossed the Danube in force, ravaged the lands to the shores of the Sea of Marmara, and contacted the Spartans to join in an alliance to invade Persian Asia Minor.[10] It took six years for Darius's generals to put down the rebellion. This Ionian rebellion led to an even more disastrous war to punish the Greek city-states that supported the Ionian rebels. This Greco-Persian War climaxed in the failed invasion by his son Xerxes to conquer Greece in 480 BC. Thereafter, the Great King of Persia, struggling to control his western satrapies, never again challenged the Scythians.

Herodotus, the Father of History, recognized the pivotal geopolitical role of the Scythian nomads in his day, because he devoted one of the nine books in his history to just the Scythians. For Herodotus, the Scythians achieved the unimaginable, defeating, twice, the Great King of Persia who ruled the mightiest Near Eastern empire to date. The Great King ruled from his ritual capital of Persepolis over forty million subjects residing in the lands between the lower Danube and Indus Rivers.[11] In the course of two centuries, Persian kings repeatedly mobilized military expeditions numbering between two hundred fifty thousand and seven hundred fifty thousand combatants. The cavalry forces alone ranged between thirty-five thousand and fifty thousand. Royal officers imposed harsh discipline upon the diverse subject peoples called up for military service. Persian logistics and engineering were of the highest order.[12] No state in the Western tradition ever again mobilized such large field armies until Napoleon's invasion of Russia. In comparison, Royal Scythians, dwelling between the lower Danube and Volga Rivers, dominated a nomadic confederacy comprising diverse subject tribes pursuing both pastoral and agricultural ways of life. At most, the population on the western steppes might have numbered between five hundred thousand to one million souls. Farther east, from the northern shores of the Caspian Sea to the western slopes of the Altai Mountains, dwelled their kinsmen the Sauromatae, Dahae, Massagetae, and Sacae, who at most only nominally recognized the high king of the Royal Scythians. Given the disparity in numbers and wealth between the two combatants, Herodotus was correct to praise the Scythian victory over King Darius.

The Scythians, the first nomads known to us by name, spoke related Eastern Iranian dialects. Soviet, Russian, and Ukrainian scientists have tested the DNA of the human remains recovered from kurgans, the monumental Scythian tombs.[13] Members of the ruling class, at least among the leading tribes in southern Russia and the Kuban, were European in features, quite tall (often six feet or slightly taller), and with fair complexions, gray eyes, and reddish hair. The physician Galen of Pergamum and the historian Ammianus Marcellinus, writing in the imperial Roman age, similarly described the features of the Sarmatians, who were the latter-day Scythians in all but name.[14] In appearance, the Scythians and their successors, the Sarmatians, differed little from the Tocharians represented by the Tarim Mummies of the Bronze Age and later de-

pictions in paintings of Tang China. Both nomadic peoples likely
shared a common ancestry from the Indo-European speakers of
the Yamnaya culture. Yet Scythian kings ruled over subjects of diverse genetic origins and appearance. The cluster of Scythian burials near the western foothills of the Altai Mountains reveals mixed
Europid and Mongolid populations who had long intermarried
with each other. Language, religious practices, customs, and the
nomadic way defined the Scythians' ethnic sense of themselves far
more than genetic similarities.

The Scythians perfected the saddles and composite bow that revolutionized warfare on the Eurasian steppes. Scythian bowmen, clad
in leather trousers and felt caps, were a favorite subject for Greek
sculptors and vase painters. The Athenian tyrant Peisistratus hired
Scythian bowmen when he invaded Attica and seized the city for
the third time in 526 BC. He and his sons retained Scythian bowmen as their bodyguards. The Athenians, once they overthrew the
tyrants, retained the Scythians as the police force of the democracy
because the formidable, loyal foreigners could keep the unruly vot-
ers in order during boisterous meetings of the assembly. The finest
archers and horsemen of their day, the Scythians gained the respect
of Greeks and Persians alike.

The monarchs of the Royal Scythians prospered off the trade
with the Greek colonies on the eastern and northern shores of the
Black Sea and clustered along the southern littoral of the Crimea,
known as the Tauric Chersonesus in Classical sources. They also
exacted tribute in grain from the subject agriculturalists cultivating
the rich arable lands of the southern Ukraine. Greek merchants eagerly sought out grain, salted meats, leather, flax, honey, and slaves
to sustain the growing cities of the Aegean world. In turn, Greek
merchants brought wine, scented oils, dried fruits, textiles, finely
wrought cauldrons and rhytons, and drinking vessels in the shape
of a ram that functioned as an ornate funnel used in ceremonial
drinking bouts. All these goods proved vital to any nomad's survival on the steppes. The Scythians also protected and promoted the
transit trade between the lands of the Baltic, the source of amber
so prized in the Classical world, across the rivers of Russia, to the
Greek ports on the Euxine shores. From trade and tribute, Scyth-

ian kings amassed fancy gifts that they distributed to buy the loyalty of their vassal rulers.

We know so much about the habits and beliefs of the Scythians thanks to Herodotus, who perceptively described Scythian customs, thereby providing a model for subsequent Classical accounts of nomads. Herodotus's observations were based on eyewitness reports from Greeks who traded and intermarried with the Scythians.[15] The Scythians themselves have left us no writing, but the stunning gold objects, jewelry, and weapons from their monumental tombs, kurgans, attest to the sophisticated tastes of Scythian elites between the seventh and third centuries BC.[16] They also confirm Herodotus's view that the Scythian kings were worthy foes of the Great King, because they could expend their wealth in grand displays of their power by erecting and stocking with costly objects their kurgans.

Herodotus reports the ceremony of honoring a deceased Scythian high king who would have been called a kaghan by later Turks and Mongols. The body was embalmed with aromatics, laid out on a magnificent funeral bier, and then conveyed in an ornately decorated cart or *gers* throughout the realm. One such *gers* has been reconstructed because, afterward, it was broken up and deposited in a burial at Pazirik near the foothills of the Altai Mountains. Mourners of every rank offered up cut locks of their hair or their blood from self-inflicted wounds. The ceremonial procession lasted for months, and climaxed with the interment of the deceased king in a monumental subterranean grave or kurgan and celebrated with feasting and heavy drinking of wine and *qumis*, fermented mare's milk. Only after the ritual meal was the tumulus raised over the burial. But a final ceremonial farewell at the king's kurgan came even later:

> At the end of the year another ceremony takes place: they take fifty of the best of the king's remaining servants, strangle and gut them, stuff their bodies with chaff, and sew them up again—these servants are native Scythians, for the king has bought no slaves, but chooses people to serve him from amongst his subjects. Fifty of the finest horses are then subjected to the same treatment. The next step is to cut a number

of wheels in half and to fix them in pairs, rim downwards, to stakes driven into the ground; two stakes to each half-wheel; then stout poles are driven lengthwise through the horses from tail to neck, and by means of these the horses are mounted on the wheels, in such a way that the front pairs support the shoulders and the rear pairs the belly between the thighs. All four legs are left dangling clear of the ground. Each horse is bitted and bridled, the bridle being led forward and pegged down. The bodies of the men are dealt with in a similar way: straight poles are driven up through the neck, parallel with the spine, and the lower protruding ends fitted into sockets in the stakes which run through the horses; thus each horse is provided with one of the young servants to ride him. When horses and riders are all in place around the tomb, they are left there, and the mourners go away.[17]

The details of the tomb's construction and funerary rites described by Herodotus are borne out by Soviet, Ukrainian, and Russian archaeologists who have excavated numerous kurgans in the lower Dnieper valley, Kuban, and the steppes immediately west of the Altai Mountains. Across the Eurasian steppes, the Scythians set the standard for burial practices for all later nomads.[18] The Scythians sank a deep and wide burial chamber into the virgin soil of the steppes. Above the burial chamber, they then constructed a dwelling (replicating the felt tent) with massive wooden pillars to support a gabled roof. Upon interment, they covered the entire complex with a massive tumulus. The tumulus over the kurgan at Tsarzky measures fifty-five feet (seventeen meters) high with a circumference of 820 feet (260 meters).[19] Within the burial chamber, the deceased, either male or female, was provided with rich goods, including costly gold objects obtained from the Greek world or Near East. In the kurgan at Chertomlyk, dating from the fourth century BC, the tableware, ceramics, and weapons were carefully selected to provide the ruler with appropriately matched objects in his next life.[20] The walls of the burial chamber were fitted with hooks so that an entire wardrobe could be hung. Servants and wives (in the case of male burials) were either poisoned or strangled, and then neatly positioned around the deceased. Above the burial chamber, at ground level, horses caparisoned in their finest harnesses and saddles were dispatched by a single blow to the head. They too were arranged in neat pairs or groups. In 1897, renowned Russian archaeologist Nikolai Ivanovich Veselovsky excavated one of the best-preserved graves on the Kuban steppes, at Kostromskaya, dating from the seventh century BC.[21] The deceased was accompanied by thirteen servants and twenty-two horses, fit and magnificent beasts, although poorer warriors were sometimes accorded older or injured horses. The number of horses sacrificed varies from ten to four hundred. Royal burials were spectacular theater involving the slaying of many expensive horses, servants, and wives to accompany their master into the other world. Such ceremonies exalted not only the deceased but also the prestige and power of his dynasty. Even more telling, nearly one-third of excavated kurgans in the Kuban were of females, equipped with weapons. Hence, Herodotus placed the land of the legendary Amazons in Scythia, beyond the Caucasus Mountains.[22]

Today, Scythian objects take pride of place in Russian and Ukrainian art museums, while traveling exhibitions have dazzled millions who marvel at the intricate workmanship of Scythian jewelry, weapons, and rhytons. All visitors leave deeply impressed, in the words of King Pyrrhus, that these objects are not of the manner of barbarians.[23] For Scythians, the great burials were the single greatest communal undertaking after war. Construction of kurgans and rites involved thousands over many months. The kurgans, once completed, dominated the steppes, and acted as a focal point for memorial rites. The tumuli thus represented the most visible sacred space of the ancestors on the steppes. All nomads revered their ancestors, whose presence was never far from the living. Divination by shamans invariably involved their questioning of the ancestors. Sacrifices and rites to the deceased were performed each year under the eternal blue sky, whether conceived as the Indo-European god Dyeus (the progenitor of Classical Zeus and Jupiter) or Tengri of the Turks and Mongols. Kurgans and burial practices, while personal in purpose, were communal in impact.

The many expensive imported objects interred in kurgans attest to the uneasy symbiosis between nomadic Scythians and their Greek and Persian neighbors. Scythian rulers depended upon gifts obtained in trading or raiding to cement their power over a confederacy of tribes. Greek craftsmen responded to the demands of Scythian customers. For example, they exported from their shops rhytons and cauldrons decorated to native tastes for use in ritual drinking.[24] The material comforts of Hellenic civilization were alluring to some Scythians, who quit their traditional life for that of the Greek cities. In the third century BC, a Hellenized family of Scythian dynasts, the Spartocids, imposed their rule over the Greek colonies of the Crimea and the Taman peninsula.[25] The later Scythian dynasts of the Bosporus (today the Straits of Kerch) ruled over these Greek cities into the fourth century AD. As friends of Rome, they minted superb gold coins bearing the portraits of a Scythian monarch in the guise of a Cossack hetman, while the reverse carried the portrait of the Roman emperor.[26]

Yet many more Scythians adapted useful technology and products from the Greeks, but adhered to their ancestral ways. Over the next two millennia, successive nomadic peoples confronted the same dilemma of coming to terms with the far more numerous neighbors of the urban civilizations. Herodotus preserves two anecdotes that reflect the same concerns of Bilğe Kaghan of the Eastern Turks a thousand years later when he warned against too much contact with the Chinese. Anacharsis, who was later enrolled among the sages of Greece, ran afoul of his tribesmen by practicing the rites of Dionysus, which he had learned during his sojourn at Cyzicus, a Greek city on the southern shores of the Sea of Marmara.[27] He was slain for neglecting the ancestral gods in favor of a foreign deity. The Greeks hailed Anacharsis a philosopher, and credited him with writing treatises and laws. He reputedly warned the Athenian lawgiver Solon that his constitution was like a spider's web that ensnared the weak, but was easily ripped up by the rich.[28] To the Greeks, Anacharsis was a forerunner of the Cynics, but to the Scythians, he was an impious traitor. It was acceptable to respect the gods of other peoples, and their holy ones, but it was not acceptable to embrace them in preference to ancestral gods. The Scythian king Scylas faced rebellion among his subjects led by his own brother, because he came to favor Greek customs and rites.[29] He had long led a dual life, donning Greek clothing and speaking Greek whenever he visited one of the cities, while back on the steppes, he comported himself as a Scythian lord. Eventually, his addiction to Greek goods, wine, and poetry grew too much for his subjects. He fled to King Sitalces of the Thracians, but his host was intimidated to turn over Scylas to his brother Octamasades. Scylas was beheaded, and his skull, suitably bejeweled and gilded, joined the royal tableware. It was passed around at ceremonial toasts as a warning for future Scythian warriors to remain true to their code of valor.

The Royal Scythians, after defeating King Darius, dominated the western and central Eurasian steppes for the next two hundred fifty years. For the later Persian kings, the Scythians remained a constant threat along the northern frontier. During the fourth century BC, Ateas was respected by Greeks and Persians alike as the greatest high king of the Scythians.[30] His Scythians habitually raided across the Caucasus Mountains into the Persian satrapy of Armenia. To the east, other Scythians crossed the Jaxartes River and ravaged the hinterlands of the cities of the Upper Satrapies of Sogdiana and Bactria (Transoxiana). Along these northern frontiers of the Persian Empire, later Great Kings preferred diplomacy and rich gifts rather than warfare to cope with recalcitrant Scythians on the borders. Persian kings sought to direct trade between their subjects and nomads to border towns, and to regulate, rather than block, the movement of nomads across the frontiers. Many Scythians were permitted to settle within the domains of the Great King so that intermarriage and cultural exchange between newcomers and indigenous inhabitants nurtured a distinct frontier society.

For uncertain reasons, in the closing decades of the fourth century BC, the Scythian confederacy of Herodotus's day began to fragment. Vassal tribes on the Kuban and the steppes to the north and east of the Caspian Sea asserted themselves. By the opening of the third century BC, many of these tribes had migrated westward in search of new homes.[31] These latter-day Scythians were collectively dubbed Sarmatians, and they have sometimes been credited with first perfecting mounted, heavily armed lancers (*cataphracti*). If

so, they might have initially gained a tactical advantage over Scythian tribes still depending solely on light cavalry, but innovations
in war were the most fleeting of secrets on the steppes.[32] In speech
and way of life, the Sarmatians differed little from their former
Scythian masters. Yet no charismatic ruler arose to weld the Sarmatians into a new confederation. In part, each aspiring high king
faced too many competitors. None of them ever gained a monopoly over trade and amassed the wealth to buy the loyalty of vassal
tribes or to construct the magnificent kurgans to awe subjects and
vassals. In the second and first centuries BC, Sarmatian and Scythian princes both furnished mercenary cavalry and bowmen to the
Hellenistic kings who fought Rome. The celebrated poison king,
Mithridates VI Eupator (121–63 BC), king of Pontus in northeastern Asia Minor, hired Scythian horsemen for his three wars against
Rome. The Romans respected Mithridates as their deadliest foe
since Hannibal, and the greatest king after Alexander the Great.[33]
When the redoubtable king was driven from his realm in 63 BC, he
fled to the Greek cities of the Crimea. There he urged the Scythians to join him in a grand invasion against Rome. The Scythians
demurred; his Greek subjects rebelled.[34] The king committed suicide to avoid an ignominious fate of gracing a Roman triumph. A
faithful Gallic officer dispatched Mithridates by the sword, after
several futile attempts by the king to poison himself. For Mithridates
had acquired immunity by taking antidotes all his life.

It was also significant that Scythian imperial power had passed
when the Roman Republic was uniting the Mediterranean world.
Imperial Rome was expert in sowing dissension among barbarian
tribes beyond her frontiers. In the words of the Roman historian
Tacitus, "Long, I pray, may foreign nations persist, if not in loving
us, at least in hating one another; for destiny is driving our empire
upon its appointed path, and fortune can bestow on us no better
gift than discord among our foes."[35] Scythian and Sarmatian tribes
needed little encouragement from Rome to war among themselves.
Hence, imperial Rome long faced no existential threat from the
nomads of the Eurasian steppes.

In the early first century AD, two Sarmatian tribes, the Jazyges
and the Roxolani, quit their homes on the south Russian steppes

and, with Roman permission, settled as allies on the grasslands of Transylvania and Wallachia, respectively.[36] As a matter of policy, members of these tribes were allowed to settle on Roman territory, but Roman governors took the precaution of scattering the barbarian colonists in small settlements lest they settle a well-armed, and potentially hostile, tribe on imperial soil. As dutiful allies of Rome, the Sarmatians were paid to patrol the steppes opposite the Roman frontier along the middle and lower Danube. On three occasions in the late first and second century, these Sarmatians deserted their Roman alliance and joined Rome's enemies, Dacians or the Germanic Marcomanni and Quadi.[37] Imperial Rome quickly reimposed treaties on these Sarmatians, and recruited their cavalry into the imperial army. The Sarmatian recruits replenished the ranks of the imperial army and assured the loyalty of their tribes. In 175, the emperor Marcus Aurelius drafted into the imperial army 7,200 Sarmatian horsemen who likely represented half the warriors of the Jazyges. Six thousand of these were sent to Britain, where they patrolled the Scottish Lowlands immediately north of Hadrian's Wall.[38] The Sarmatians, who fought for Rome under their inflated leather dragons learned from the Chinese, introduced the fabulous dragon to their Roman officers. Classical authors, however, turned the benign, protective dragon of China into the fire-breathing monster of Western literature. Roman success in dealing with the Sarmatian tribes of Eastern Europe would leave Rome ill-prepared to meet a truly deadly nomadic foe, the Huns.

The Alans, kinsmen of the Roxolani and Jazyges, dwelled to the east, on the Kuban steppes north of the Caucasus. Their modern descendants, the Ossetians, still dwell there and preserve their distinct Iranian language and traditions. The Alans frequently raided across the Caucasus into Roman Asia Minor or Parthian Mesopotamia and Iran. Flavius Josephus, the perceptive Jewish historian, described one such horrifying raid by these newest "Scythians" in 72 AD.[39] Veteran Roman governors perfected tactics to counter such raiders. The Roman senator Arrian (Lucius Flavius Arrianus), governor of the Roman province of Cappadocia in Asia Minor, penned a manual on tactics based on his experience of fighting Alan cavalry in 135 AD.[40] He advises how a commander should draw up his battle line of legionaries, archers, and cavalry, backed up by field artillery, to counter nomadic horse archers. Arrian drew on both his own experience and lessons he had learned from reading the exploits of Alexander the Great. For Arrian wrote the definitive military history of the Macedonian conqueror who was the first commander ever to best nomads on the steppes.

4

Alexander the Great: Walling off Gog and Magog

I n the summer of 329 BC, Alexander, son of Philip, King of
Macedon, and commander of the Hellenic League, stood on
the banks of the Jaxartes (Syr Darya).[1] In his mind, he had
nearly reached the limits of the world, for, as Aristotle had taught
him, this river with its banks lined by fir trees must flow into the
Tanis (Don) and so empty into the Black Sea. To the north, beyond the river, lay steppes and then frozen wastes washed by the
Great Ocean encircling the earth. To his southeast lay the eastern
Caucasus (today the Hindu Kush) and then the great river valley of
the Indus at the extreme eastern limit of the world. For beyond this
river valley, India, was again the Great Ocean.[2] The Indus, flowing south and filled with crocodiles, must join the Nile. Alexander was apparently unaware that King Darius had known better,
for the Great King had sent the Carian explorer Scylax to navigate
the river in 515 BC.[3]

On the Jaxartes, Alexander confronted the task of defeating the
Scythians and securing the northeastern frontier of his world empire. In less than six years, Alexander had achieved the unimaginable: the overthrow of the Persian Empire, stretching from the
Aegean world to the Hindu Kush. He had fought under every con-

ceivable condition without a single defeat. He now commanded a grand army of seventy-five thousand comprising loyal Macedonians, Greek mercenaries, and new Persian subjects. As heir of Darius III, the last Achaemenid King of Persia, Alexander had to secure the rich Upper Satrapies of Bactria and Sogdiana between the Oxus (Amu Darya) and Jaxartes, today Transoxiana.[4] Hence, he, just like his Persian predecessors, had to reckon with the Scythians on the northern steppes, who would encourage and even ally with rebel Persian nobles of Bactria and Sogdiana. Wisely, the young conqueror planned no conquest of the steppes, but rather he aimed to chastise the nomads, and then fortify the frontier whereby he could regulate the nomads' movements across the Jaxartes.[5] After crossing the Jaxartes River, he lured the Dahae, the leading Scythian tribe, into a tactical trap.[6] Alexander sent forward as skirmishers his light cavalry, who quickly retired, drawing the Dahae into attacking the Macedonian phalanx backed up by archers. Meanwhile, the Dahae were caught by surprise as the heavy Macedonian cavalry encircled and attacked the Dahae in the flanks and rear. Over a thousand Scythian horsemen were trapped and slain with minimal loss to the Macedonians. The survivors sued for peace. Alexander granted them clemency, extended their trading rights, and recruited Dahae horse archers into his own army for the invasion of India.

Alexander the Great is still hailed the greatest military genius ever—a rank acknowledged by his emulators from Hannibal to Napoleon. He is also today the most recognized secular historical figure best documented by polls taken in the arbiter of American taste, the mall.[7] Yet it is easy to overlook his victory over the Scythians, for Alexander was the first to wage battle against nomads on the steppes and win decisively. Informed by superb reconnaissance, he devised a tactical deployment based on deception, surprise, and shock rather than amassing overwhelming numbers as Persian kings had done. Alexander thus ambushed nomadic horse archers who were themselves the masters of ambush. Alexander, however, had already studied his nomadic foe. Six years earlier, Alexander, then age twenty-one, waged a campaign to pacify the tribes of Thrace and Illyria. These Balkan tribes dwelling south of the lower Danube would provide a shield to guard Macedon against Scythian attacks from the north while Alexander was on campaign in Persia.[8] In early summer 335 BC, Alexander reached the southern banks of the lower Danube, the Ister, which Aristotle had taught him marked the northern limit of inhabitable Europe. Across the river, he confronted mounted horse archers of Getae, numbering 14,000, who had adopted the nomadic way of war from their Scythian masters. The Getae not only opposed Alexander's crossing but also, from the opposite bank, taunted him with threats that they would soon cross themselves once Alexander had withdrawn. Alexander reasoned that he could not secure his northern frontier unless he punished the nomads and imposed a treaty on them. At night, he led a daring crossing of one thousand five hundred cavalry and four thousand infantry, who swam across the river assisted by their leather knapsacks stuffed with straw. The Macedonians concealed themselves in a wheat field. At dawn, when the Getae descended from their camp to the northern banks of the Danube, the main Macedonian army on the river's opposite bank greeted them with a barrage of missiles from their artillery. The Macedonians then began to cross the river in force. The Getae, with their attention fixed on the obvious threat, were thrown into confusion when Alexander and his detachment suddenly arose from among the wheat stalks and charged the Getae in the flank and rear. Audacity and surprise delivered to Alexander his first victory over nomads. The Getae submitted, and, for a generation, dared not cross the Danube.

The Roman senator and historian Arrian, in his account of Alexander's military exploits, stressed both these victories over the nomads. In his own tactical manual, Arrian recommended an improved version of Alexander's battle line, stressing the importance of cavalry guarding the infantry's flanks and rear, large numbers of bowmen, slingers, and crossbow men, and, whenever possible, supporting field artillery.[9] A commander must keep strict discipline over his men lest they break ranks in pursuit whenever the nomadic horsemen feigned retreat to lure the more heavily armored Romans into an ambush. Until the advent of firearms, it is no accident that every army that defeated nomadic horsemen either adapted or independently devised the tactics first used by Alexander. Chinese

generals of the Han and Tang dynasties came up with comparable
formations against their nomadic foes, the Xiongnu and the Gök
Turks. The Han general Wei Qing, in addition, strengthened his
line by interspersing his infantry with squadrons of chariots acting
as platforms for crossbow men who laid down supporting fire.[10]
Song military experts wrote memoranda to their emperor advocating the same tactics against the Khitans, Tanguts, and Mongols.[11]
Byzantine military writers between the sixth and twelfth centuries
repeated the same recommendations, and they pointed out debacles
when commanders failed to follow these sound tactics.[12] As late as
the opening of the eighteenth century, Prince Eugene of Savoy, the
brilliant Habsburg commander and partner of John Churchill, the
Duke of Marlborough, applied the same principles when he was
battling Ottoman cavalry on the Hungarian plains.[13]

Alexander not only won victories against the Scythians but
also knew how to use them. Strategically, he thought in the long
term and devised a sound frontier policy to deal with the nomads.
He built highways and forts along the Jaxartes River, whereby he
sought to regulate the seasonal movement of nomadic pastoralists
across the frontier and to tax and direct trade with them. Alexander settled over twenty thousand of his Greek and Macedonian
veterans in Hellenic cities, invariably named Alexandria, in Sogdiana and Bactria, to provide manpower for his frontier army.[14]
The colonists were rewarded with generous grants of estates tilled
by the native agriculturalists. The colonists and their descendants
ruled from Hellenic cities as an elite supported by the rents and
labor services of their tenants. Alexander thus laid the foundation
of a future Greco-Bactrian kingdom that lasted for two centuries
after his death. Alexander's Greco-Bactrian cities soon prospered
on the growing trade of the Silk Road across Eurasia in the third
and second centuries BC.[15] French, Soviet, and Afghan archaeologists have excavated one such city near Ai-Khanoum, ancient Alexandria on the Oxus (and later the Greco-Bactrian royal capital
Eucratidia).[16] Excavations have yielded beautiful Greek sculpture,
Greek inscriptions, and a perfectly planned Greek city that have
awed archaeological enthusiasts and inspired a documentary.[17] These
Hellenized cities, notably Maracanda and Bactra (the future Samar-

kand and Balkh, respectively), survived and prospered even after new nomads, the Tocharians, overran the Greco-Bactrian kingdom in the later second century BC.

Alexander was an explorer as well as a conqueror, for he was accompanied by savants and engineers who measured the distances traversed and recorded anything of note. They clarified misconceptions about geography, classified flora and fauna, documented trade routes, and recorded the customs of many new peoples. Alexander revealed to the Greeks, for the first time, the immensity of India, the Eurasian steppes, and what might lie beyond, the land of the Seres, the people of the silk.[18] His successors, the Seleucid and Greco-Bactrian kings, maintained diplomatic missions at the court of the Mauryan emperor of India.[19] They also sponsored explorers who proved the Caspian and Aral Seas were inland salt lakes, charted the course of the Jaxartes River, and charted the passes over the Pamirs and Hindu Kush into the Tarim Basin and India. Alexander was hailed in history and legend as an explorer, whose longing to learn, called *pothos* by his biographer Plutarch, provided the information essential for the success of the later Silk Road. The results of this age of exploration initiated by Alexander can be seen five hundred years later in the world map drawn by Claudius Ptolemy.[20]

The Scythians across the Eurasian steppes benefited from the trade with the Greek cities and the courts of the successors of Alexander, the Diadochoi, who forged the Hellenistic world. The volume of trade can be sensed by the rise of imported wares found in the numerous kurgans of the fourth and third centuries BC. In turn, Scythian jewelry (with its distinct genius in rendering of animals), weapons, leather goods, and textiles were exported to the courts of Macedonian kings and Hellenized cities across the Near East. The Scythians, locked in a daily struggle of surviving on the steppes, gained vital foodstuffs, spices, and manufactured goods from this trade. The nomads of the central Eurasian steppes also learned how to use coins as money. The prime trade coins in international commerce of the Hellenistic Age were large, handsome silver tetradrachmae struck by Seleucid or Greco-Bactrian kings. Whenever these coins were in short supply, the nomads struck their own imitations as supplements.[21] Trade brought wealth and craftsmen so that elite Scythian warriors could commission lamellar armor and iron helmets, and elaborate body armor for their horses. Henceforth, heavily armored cavalrymen, armed with thrusting lancers, fought as shock troops in tandem with the traditional lightly armed horse archers who wore felt caps and leather jerkins. These so-called *cataphracti*, never numbering more than 10 percent of any nomadic army, delivered the decisive charge against foes who lost formation by pursuing Scythian horse archers. By this combination of firepower and shock actions, the Scythians, as well as later Sarmatians and Parthians, could defeat the more numerous armies of Hellenistic kings or imperial Rome. The Scythians thus devised their own tactics to counter those Alexander had devised against them. Hence, Scythian, and later Sarmatian, cavalry units were hired in large numbers as mercenaries in the Hellenistic royal armies and civic militias. Furthermore, as trade from the caravan cities of Sogdiana and Bactria extended ever farther east, Scythian lords grew rich in hiring out their warriors as guards, scouts, and interpreters. By the opening of the second century BC, the cultural and commercial ties between the Western and Central Eurasian steppes and the urban Hellenistic world had become so intertwined that the two worlds came to depend on each other in what has been dubbed the first era of a global economy.

Yet Alexander was not best remembered for his sound frontier policy against the Scythians, but rather for his dealings with such legendary peoples as the Amazons and the "Unclean Nations" (as designated in Greek and Latin texts) of Gog and Magog, who dwelled on the horizonless northern steppes. Immediately after Alexander's death, the historian Cleitarchus, writing at the court of King Ptolemy, circulated these fabulous tales that have captured the imagination of so many since. They quickly became the staple for popular works about Alexander, who was hailed as divine and the favored son of Zeus by his successors and their subjects. Six hundred years after Alexander's death, many of these tales were incorporated into the fictitious biography known as the *Alexander Romance*.[22] Composed in Greek during the later fourth century AD, the romance proved a bestseller in the Medieval world and inspired translations into Latin, Syriac, Armenian, Coptic, Ethiopian, and every major Medieval European vernacular as far as Iceland. In these later translations, each writer concocted new fabulous tales or embellished old ones, operating under the literary axiom that no writer deserves to write about Alexander unless he improves the story.[23] Alexander's dealings with the nomads became ever more fantastic and heroic with each retelling. The tales in these different versions of the romance fixed Medieval Christians' prejudices about steppe nomads.

Foremost, Alexander encountered the Amazons, the female warriors of Scythia, and this legend magnified his greatness over his ancestors Heracles and Achilles, each of whom had fought Amazon queens. Instead, Queen Thalestris, accompanied by three hundred of her Amazon warriors, visited Alexander in Hyrcania (northern Iran) because she desired to conceive a wondrous child with the Macedonian conqueror.[24] Thalestris, however, might have been a bit disappointed, because she towered over Alexander, who was rather short in stature. Quite likely she made the common error of mistaking Hephaestion, Alexander's taller best friend and alter ego, for the king himself. Later retellings of the legends report that she rode on a tiger, returned to her homeland, and gave birth to the child. Mother and child tragically died soon after. Many historians included the tale as fact. Onesicritus, an otherwise reliable historian who had accompanied Alexander, years later recited the incident from his history at the court of Lysimachus, a tough veteran general of Alexander who had turned himself into the king of Thrace and Western Asia Minor. Upon hearing the tale, the no-nonsense Lysimachus was amused and quipped that he could not recall why he had somehow missed the encounter.

The tale of Alexander and the Amazons might have been concocted from a mission sent by the Scythian king Pharasmanes, who ruled over the steppes around the Aral Sea. Pharasmanes offered a marriage alliance between his daughter and Alexander.[25] The Scythian king, like many others before him, sought to cement an alliance and win trading privileges with each new Great King. At the time, Alexander was already assuming the guise of the Great King to win the loyalty of his Iranian subjects. Hence, Alexander adopted Persian royal dress and court protocol, much to the resent-

ment of his Macedonian soldiers and Greek allies. He also kept a
harem so that he could link himself by marriage with prominent
Iranian families and vassal rulers. After capturing the Persian capital of Persepolis, Alexander married Barsine, the stunning Iranian
beauty who, along with her father, had once sought refuge at the
Macedonian court. Alexander, then fifteen years old, had been
so smitten by Barsine that he married her years later, once he had
overthrown the Persian monarchy. He also married two of Darius's
daughters, and his love match and principal wife, Roxane, daughter
of a Sogdian baron who ruled a strategic mountain fastness. Taking
Scythian brides would have been a sound way of securing valuable
allies north of the Jaxartes River. A dull but sensible political marriage alliance with a Scythian king was far less exciting than an
encounter with the Amazon queen. Even Plutarch felt so, although
he doubted the veracity of the story. The legend prevailed. Later
Greeks relished in deploring female warriors, outlandishly attired in
armor, riding alongside or fighting against Scythians. Greek storytellers even claimed, falsely, that the name of Amazon denoted the
practice of the warrior princesses surgically removing their right
breast so that they could, unimpeded, draw their bows.[26] Christian
Europeans inherited this prejudice so that they denounced later
Turkish and Mongol princesses as Amazons. With Alexander, the
Amazons were enshrined as the warrior princesses of the steppes.
In Homer's day, Greeks had believed that the Amazons dwelled on
the northeastern shores of Asia Minor (today Turkey), along the
Thermodon River (Terme Çayı), which arises in the Pontic Alps
and empties into the Black Sea midway between the modern Turk-
ish cities of Samsun and Ordu. Herodotus relocated the realm of
the Amazons to Scythia beyond the Caucasus Mountains. As later
Europeans gained ever more accurate knowledge of the Eurasian
steppes, the Amazons retreated to ever more remote regions. Yet
Medieval ethnographers and chroniclers of Christian Europe never
ceased to hope that these warrior maidens might be courted into
an alliance against the dreaded nomads of the steppes.[27] Once the
Amazons could no longer be found on the Eurasian steppes, the
Portuguese transferred them to Brazil.

Even more popular was Alexander as the architect of a fabulous wall and his Iron Gate to seal off the civilized world from the "Unclean Races" of Gog and Magog (rendered in later Greek as Goth and Magothy). The Gates of Alexander were most commonly located in the Caucasus, either at the Dariel or Derbent Pass, which Alexander never reached. In the many versions of the *Alexander Romance*, Alexander, cast as a virtuous Christian king, defeated these "Unclean Races" and pursued them for fifty days over the northern wastelands until he reached the great mountain range of the Caucasus (conceived as stretching from the Black Sea across the northern steppes to India).[28] As Alexander approached, the two separate chains of the Caucasus, by the power of God, miraculously moved toward each other to form a narrow pass, which Alexander blocked with a massive bronze gate. Thereafter, the accursed nomadic races of the steppes were condemned to dwell forever outside the civilized world until the end of time.[29] In the imagination of Greeks, Romans, and Medieval Christians, the Gates of Alexander symbolized the same barrier between civilized and barbarian nations as did the Great Wall for the Chinese. The megalomaniacal emperor Nero, a self-styled emulator of Alexander, briefly toyed with the idea of leading his own expedition to the famed Gates (as well as an expedition to find the sources of the Nile).[30] But Nero reconsidered, preferring a Greek trip where he could display his creative genius on the stage to the acclaim of adoring crowds. His eventual successor, the blunt and pragmatic Vespasian, instead sent engineers and legionary detachments to secure the Dariel and Derbent Passes, and diplomats with rich gifts to court the nomadic tribes on the Kuban steppes.[31]

The Jewish historian Flavius Josephus, writing in the later first century, identified the Scythians with the descendants of Magog of *Genesis*, who is described as a descendant of Noah's son Japheth. Josephus witnessed the invasion of Alans, who had crossed the Caucasus and wantonly devastated Armenia, Mesopotamia, and Media in 72 AD. Josephus was so shocked that he could only conclude the Sarmatian Alans were nothing more than Scythians.[32] At approximately the same time, the author of *Revelation*, drawing on Jewish apocalyptic texts, recast Gog and Magog from an impious individual and his land into two races who served Satan.[33] In the

final days, the "Unclean Races" of Gog and Magog would rise up
and wreak destruction on the world once Satan broke free from the
bonds of his imprisonment of one thousand years. Henceforth, to
Jews and Christians alike, all the Eurasian nomads were the children of Cain and the Devil's horsemen. Yet the Christians of Medieval Europe, as they gained more knowledge of the peoples on
the Eurasian steppes, were ever moving the homeland of these impious races farther east.[34]

In the *Koran*, Alexander, called Dhu al-Qarnayn or "the righteous king of the two horns," traveled east and erected a great
wall to shut out Gog and Magog, rendered in Arabic Yajuj and
Majuj.[35] In the Koranic tradition too, Yajuj and Majuj will burst
through the barrier in the final days, and bring about the ultimate
reckoning of Allah. Successive Medieval Muslim geographers and
chroniclers embroidered upon the legends of Alexander's Gate.[36]
The Turkish nomads were initially identified as an accursed race
sprung from Gog and Magog. Alexander, in his Islamic guise as
Dhu al-Qarnayn, had traversed the Far East, receiving the submission of the civilized lands of India, Tibet, and China. Then, at
God's command, Alexander constructed a great gate of brass and
iron to wall off the Turks forever in the land of darkness.[37] But as
ever more Turkish tribes embraced Islam from the tenth century
on, Muslim writers turned the children of Gog and Magog into
monstrous giants and relocated them in ever more remote northern frozen climes beyond the steppes.[38] Ahmad ibn Fadlan, envoy
of the Abbasid Caliph of al-Muqtadir, journeyed across the steppes
between the Aral and Caspian Sea to the Bulgar khan's settlement
at the juncture of the Volga and Kama Rivers. The Turkish khan
had recently embraced Islam, and had requested both teachers in
the true faith and an alliance with the caliph. Ibn Fadlan recalled
years later the bitter cold he and his attendants endured crossing the
steppes in 921/2. Once at the Bulgar capital, the khan showed ibn
Fadlan the bones of a giant who had terrorized the realm and was
captured and hanged.[39] The khan assured ibn Fadlan that the giant
was an escaped child of Gog and Magog who dwelled even farther
north where the winter was perpetual and where they were sealed
off by a great gate until Allah would release them at the end of days.

Ibn Fadlan, a polished courtier of Baghdad, must have shivered as he penned this memory.[40] By the thirteenth century, the legends were turned into a cosmic struggle in which the races of Gog and Magog toiled each day to undermine the Gate of Alexander, but during the night, Allah repaired the damage.[41] The hordes of Gog and Magog were condemned to a Sisyphean task until Allah, in the fullness of time, would release them in the final days.

In legends for the next fifteen centuries after his death, Alexander was remembered foremost as the pious defender of the civilized world from monstrous races and fabulous creatures of Inner Asia, India, and Ethiopia. None of these nations was more hostile to civilization than the Eurasian nomads. The legends cast the nomads as barbarians beyond the pale, beyond assimilation as civilized peoples, and beyond redemption by the God of Abraham. Yet these fears and prejudices hardly reflected reality on the northern frontiers of Alexander's empire. Alexander had pursued a pragmatic policy based on his own experience with and out of respect for his nomadic foes. He improved upon the frontier policy inherited from his Persian predecessors, and promoted and protected trade between the Scythians and his Greek cities of Sogdiana and Bactria. In so doing, he created the conditions for the development of the western half of the Silk Road, and so the first global trade network.

5

Modu Chanyu and the Great Wall of China

At age thirty-eight, Qin Shi Huang (221–210 BC) declared himself the first emperor of China. He had ascended the throne of the kingdom of Qin at age thirteen, and over two decades of tough campaigning, he defeated every rival king and ended the era of Warring States. Qin Shi Huang forged a new imperial state, China, named after his original realm.[1] He imposed cultural unity by ordering the destruction of all scrolls not in Chinese and imposing one language and one script of ideograms.[2] Three years before his death, he projected his supreme power granted under the Mandate of Heaven by constructing his stupendous Epang Palace.[3] Although only the massive forecourt was ever finished, the complex in its unfinished state still awed the court historian Sima Qian, who described it two generations later.[4] Even in death, Qin Shi Huang would not renounce his grip on power, because he was buried in a mausoleum beneath his palace with a life-sized terra-cotta army of six thousand warriors clad in lamellar armor, and chariots to command in the next world.[5] Each officer or soldier was carefully cast to represent an individual who had followed his ever victorious emperor in life. The discovery of his tomb in 1974 dazzled the world just as it must have dazzled his subjects. Later Han emperors had to content themselves with far fewer, and much smaller, terra-cotta warriors in their tombs, but Chinese rulers long followed the burial rites of Qin Shi Huang.[6]

Foremost, Qin Shi Huang marked off China as a single realm by tearing down the border walls between the former warring kingdoms, and by extending the northern defenses of the former kingdoms of Yan, Zhao, and Qin into a single system: the Great Wall. The Great Wall of China stretched over three thousand miles (or ten thousand *li*) from the ports on the Liaodong Peninsula near the border with Korea to the Yumen Pass, the gateway to Gansu (or Hexi) corridor, in the west.[7] The Great Wall immediately became the symbolic frontier between the civilized Han peoples of China and the nomadic barbarians, collectively called the Hu, who had menaced the rival Chinese kingdoms since the eighth century BC.[8] Meng Tian, Emperor Qin's top general, conceived of and executed the project. Each year, Meng Tian conscripted tens of thousands of peasants as well as mandarin critics of the emperor who had been sentenced to what was for them a lethal punishment of laboring on the Great Wall.[9] This first version of the Great Wall was not the grandiose walls to which millions of tourists on buses from Beijing flock each year and photograph. These masonry walls were built by the Ming emperors over sixteen centuries later. In the third century BC, Chinese workers raised ramparts of rammed earth shaped into great blocks from soil, lime, chalk, and binding material.[10]

The workers first excavated a fossa, or deep ditch, as the wall's first barrier, and the soil was used for making blocks of rammed earth. Workers also built wide platforms at regular intervals along the wall upon which they constructed timber or stone watchtowers. Behind the wall, Meng Tian had depots, headquarters, and highways constructed. Nor was the Great Wall continuous. Only the most vulnerable points, such as wide plains, mountain passes, and river crossings, required fortification. In place of walls across long sections of the system, Meng Tian incorporated natural barriers of mountains, rivers, and desert. Even so, Qin Shi Huang undertook the first of many stupendous building projects that have ever since distinguished China as the most effective, centralized state on the globe. Over the next five years, Qin Shi Huang mobilized laborers and resources equivalent to fielding an army one hundred thousand strong. The Great Wall awed Chinese and barbarians alike, conveying to them his universal rule under the Mandate of Heaven. Qin Shi Huang rightly took great pride in his wall. He ordered the construction of a grand highway from his capital, Xianyang, today in central Shaanxi province, to the first sections of wall built on the northern banks of the Ordos triangle.[11] After the first year of construction, in 214 BC, he conducted a tour of inspection of the wall, in what was yet another ostentatious display of his supreme power.

Qin Shi Huang was never so naive as to expect the wall alone could seal off China from nomads. Patrols, garrisons, and diplomacy would do this. Nor was the Great Wall just a prestigious warning to the hordes of northern barbarians, because for the past two centuries, nomadic raiders were more of a nuisance rather than a threat.[12] Instead, the Great Wall was an integral part of a well-thought-out policy of imperial expansion. To this end, the emperor Qin Shi Huang also imposed conscription on all his subjects, calling up for ten years of military service peasants who were relentlessly drilled to professional levels by the emperor's officers.[13] Peasant draftees joined units with rituals and symbols that inspired devotion to their emperor and comrades. They were generously rewarded upon honorable discharge with pensions and legal privileges. Qin and Han emperors could mobilize against the nomadic cavalry of the Xiongnu disciplined armies comprising three hundred thousand infantry and twenty thousand chariots. In 215 BC, Meng Tian fielded such an imperial army one hundred thousand strong (some of whom may well be depicted among the terra-cotta army in the emperor's mausoleum). Based on the terra-cotta statues from the emperor's tomb, Qin soldiers comprised overwhelmingly heavily armored infantry with pikes, and backed up by crossbow men and chariots. Qin and later Han armies lacked cavalry, because the small horses of China were only suitable for chariot teams rather than riding.[14] Meng Tian expelled the Xiongnu from their pastures in the upper valley and the great bend (often called the Ordos triangle) of the Yellow River.[15] He also cleared out other nomads to the northeast in the lands later known as the Sixteen Prefectures. Garrisons and villages of thirty thousand peasant colonists followed the advance of the imperial army. Once the new lands were consolidated behind the Great Wall, Meng Tian twice commanded expeditions three hundred thousand strong that attacked the Xiongnu, who had retreated to the steppes of Mongolia. The Qin army was the first Chinese army ever to march north from the wall, over three hundred miles (one thousand *li*) across the Gobi Desert, against nomads on the eastern Eurasian steppes. In logistics and planning, the Qin campaigns equaled the Scythian expedition of King Darius three centuries earlier. Meng Tian captured and deported thousands of prisoners, horses, and livestock, but he could not break the power of the Xiongnu.[16]

He was frustrated by the lack of conventional military objectives and the refusal of the Xiongnu to offer decisive battle. In crossing the Gobi, Meng Tian encountered grueling logistical problems, and his army sustained high casualties due to dehydration, disease, and desertion. It is a testimony to Chinese organization that Meng Tian and his army did not starve on the steppes, but they had to be sustained by a supply train of tens of thousands of bearers and thousands of carts. The Xiongnu easily spotted the ponderously advancing Qin army so that they always enjoyed the strategic initiative, and they could harass the invaders from afar. Twice Meng Tian scattered the Xiongnu and torched their encampments; each time he declared victory and withdrew to the wall. Yet Qin Shi Huang was perhaps too successful. By building the Great Wall, Qin Shi Huang ironically forced the barbarians to unite and attack China. At the time of the death of Qin Shi Huang, Chinese chroniclers report three barbarian tribes north of the wall: the Donghu, dwelling on the easternmost steppes; the Xiongnu, who had fled to central Mongolia; and to the west of the Xiongnu in the Tarim Basin and its adjoining steppes, the Yuezhi (later known as Tocharians or Kushans).[17] The Xiongnu were by far the weakest. Within a year of the emperor's death, a new chanyu or leader of the Xiongnu, Modu, seized power and went on to unite Iranian-, Tocharian-, and Altaic-speaking nomads into the first imperial confederation on the Eurasian steppes.[18] At his death, the Xiongnu Empire stretched 2,500 miles across the steppes, from Lake Baikal and the Altai Mountains, east to the Amur River, and south to the upper valley and the Ordos bend of the Yellow River.

The charismatic Modu Chanyu (209–174 BC), the first known conqueror of the steppes, so impressed the Chinese historian Sima Qian that, writing two generations later, he recorded anecdotes of the conqueror's bravery and genius in his monumental narrative account of the Han dynasty, Shiji, or Records of the Grand Historian.[19] Sima Qian possessed the same keen understanding of the nomadic barbarians of his day as did Herodotus of the nomadic Scythians.[20] Modu's father, Touman Chanyu, never trusted his precocious son, so he favored as his heir the pliant half brother of Modu. Touman even sent Modu as a hostage to the ancestral foe, the Yüeh-chih, in hopes that they would murder the young prince in reprisal for his raids against them. Instead, Modu charmed his hosts, ingeniously stole a horse, and escaped to the acclaim of the younger warriors among the Xiongnu. His father had no choice but to receive Modu back at court. Modu immediately formed a bodyguard of ten thousand warriors trained to shoot at anyone, including members of court, on his personal command. At a practice match, Modu deviously directed his bodyguard of archers to slay his own father. Acclaimed the new chanyu, Modu quickly dispatched his half brother, his stepmother, and all of their supporters.[21]

At his accession, Modu Chanyu, age twenty-four, and the Xiongnu faced the threat of extinction. The emperor Qin Shi Huang had driven the Xiongnu out of their rich pastures south of the Yellow River's great bend, constructed the Great Wall, and attacked across the Gobi. Modu Chanyu, the son of a father humiliated by defeats at the hands of the Qin army, had to rally his people lest they die of starvation or fall victims to their more powerful neighbors who were beyond the reach of the Qin armies. Foremost, Modu Chanyu aimed to recover the lost pastures south of the Yellow River and the vital northeastern Chinese provinces later dubbed the Sixteen Prefectures. Stock raising on the Mongolian steppes and hunting in the Siberian forests were insufficient to sustain the Xiongnu. They had to have access to millet and other produce of Chinese agriculturalists.

In 209 BC, Modu Chanyu grasped that true nomads were poor

nomads, but he also realized that the disparity in military power between his Xiongnu and the Qin Empire made the conquest of even the lost lands unlikely. At its height, in ca. 150 BC, the population of the Xiongnu Empire perhaps numbered one million, whereas the Han Empire of China totaled fifty-four million subjects.[22] Although later Chinese chroniclers reckoned the full levy of the Xiongnu at two hundred thousand, no chanyu ever mobilized so large a force. Modu Chanyu himself operated with far fewer horsemen, probably never more than twenty-five thousand. Modu Chanyu, however, overcame the odds against him due to his genius and the unexpected turn of events in China.

Modu Chanyu soon exploited the mobility of horse archers against a Chinese frontier army of infantry committed to defending cities and sown fields. He conducted lightning raids that netted huge profits in captives, livestock, and booty on a scale beyond previous brigandage or trade. He also lucked out because the death of Qin Shi Huang plunged China into political crisis. Neither of Qin's two sons who followed in quick succession could maintain the unity of the empire in the face of so many rebels. Modu Chanyu was thus free to raid at will until 206 BC, when the lord of Western Chu, Liu Bang, overthrew the last Qin ruler, Ziying, and reimposed unity. Four years later, he declared himself emperor under the throne name of Gaozu of Han.[23] The Han emperors were destined to rule for the next four centuries, and they founded the classic Confucian state.[24] But as a usurper, Gaozu had to check Xiongnu raiders and to restore order along the Great Wall if he were to win over his subjects to his claim to the Mandate of Heaven. In 200 BC, the emperor Gaozu suffered an embarrassing reverse at the hands of Modu Chanyu on a plateau near Mount Baideng (today Datong, Shaanxi).[25] Modu Chanyu had laid siege to the city of Taiyuan, but he retired to the steppes when the imperial army under Gaozu approached. Gaozu pursued too far into the steppes so that he was lured into an untenable position on the arid plateau without water and cut off from his supplies. Gaozu and his army narrowly escaped destruction by bribing the Xiongnu to let down their guard.

★ ★ ★

Gaozu could not afford any more such reverses. He had learned from bitter experience the difficulties of waging war on the steppes. He had suffered unsustainable logistical costs and high attrition among his soldiers and horses, who were not easily replaced. To be sure, Chinese rebels posed a far greater political threat to him than the Xiongnu, but the high cost of battling nomadic foes strained imperial fiscal and military institutions, and so risked yet more rebellions. Furthermore, victory on the steppes netted little of value to the imperial treasury. Campaigns beyond the Great Wall against the Xiongnu were at best preemptive strikes that gained neither rich booty nor new provinces profitable to tax. Imperial armies could be far more profitably deployed against Korea, with its lucrative mines, or the lands of the Yangtze basin rich in rice paddies and silk farms.[26] The clearheaded Gaozu calculated the advantages of peace over the ruinous costs of continuing frontier war. He opted for a tribute system (ho-ch'in), popularly known as the "Five Baits," whereby he could exit the war and still maintain the fiction of his celestial supremacy. His plan was to pacify the Xiongnu by addicting them to Chinese goods.[27] In 198 BC, the emperor Gaozu adroitly switched policy from confrontation to accommodation. He sent his polished diplomat Liu Jing, who negotiated the first treaty with the Xiongnu.[28] This treaty defined future relations between many a Chinese emperor and nomadic conqueror. Modu Chanyu received an alliance and a Chinese bride (hegin), and so he was hailed a brother of the emperor. In return for a nominal submission (a pledge of loyalty that carries no weight), Modu Chanyu could expect each year Han envoys arriving from the imperial capital of Chang'an (today Xi'an) to renew the treaty. They also conveyed precious gifts of silk, gold plate, jewelry, weapons, and spices, which he then handed out to members of court, the lesser kings (kuli), and his commanders in return for loyal service.[29] Furthermore, the Xiongnu were granted trading privileges along the Han frontier so that they readily obtained millet, rice, and finished goods vital for surviving on the steppes. Modu Chanyu and his successors, in turn, provided horses for the Han armies as well as felt, leather, and woolen goods. Henceforth, Modu Chanyu had the revenues to secure the loyalty of his own subjects and his vassal tribes, and so to impose order, for the first time, over the entirety of the eastern Eurasian steppes. And so, for a price, he also assured the timely arrival of caravans from the Tarim Basin that brought to the Han court jade and other exotic luxuries from the West. Both courts profited from the alliance, but this alliance depended upon both parties upholding their end of the bargain.[30]

For twenty-five years, Modu Chanyu must have basked in the aura of respectability whenever Han envoys showed up to utter polite greetings and to present Chinese princesses, along with their great troupes of eunuchs and servants, destined to be consorts of members of his royal family. Furthermore, no one doubted that Gaozu had admitted defeat, because he relinquished control over the Ordos triangle and the Chinese agricultural communities of the Sixteen Prefectures. Modu Chanyu regarded as invaluable these Chinese subjects whose produce and labor fed the Xiongnu. Over time, northern Chinese provincials and Xiongnu fused into members of a distinct frontier society that straddled the Great Wall. They lived in a symbiosis with each other, exchanged ideas and goods, and intermarried. Of mixed ancestry and culture, they would come to play a decisive role as interpreters and mediators between the world of the steppes and the Chinese Empire. Hence, future nomadic conquerors and Chinese emperors strove to control these frontier lands.

Modu Chanyu had gained far more from the treaty than Gaozu. Foremost, he was now free to subject all the tribes on the eastern Eurasian steppes, and weld them into an imperial confederacy. Upon concluding the treaty with the emperor Gaozu, Modu Chanyu turned next against the Yuezhi.[31] The Xiongnu feared most the Yuezhi, whose ancestors had taught the Xiongnu (and the Chinese as well) to use the horse and wheel in the Bronze Age. The Yuezhi were quickly brought to heel, as were other tribes speaking eastern Iranian dialects or the Tangut languages of Manchuria.[32] His own Xiongnu apparently spoke an Altaic language, which would have been related to modern Turkish and Mongolian, and so today the government of Ulan Bator claims Modu Chanyu and the Xiongnu as their progenitors. In grammar, syntax, and morphology, Altaic

languages differ radically from Indo-European languages and the
tonal languages of the Chinese and Tibetans. Yet for the first time,
Modu Chanyu overcame the ethnic and linguistic diversity that
had long divided the nomads on the eastern Eurasian steppes, and
so he added the warriors of all the tribes to his own. His military
power rested upon horse archers, but he adapted Chinese organization and writing, drew revenues from the subjected agriculturalists
in northern China, and exploited the caravan trade between the
Tarim Basin and China.[33] In constructing the first imperial order
on the Eurasian steppes, Modu Chanyu wrote the script for subsequent steppe conquerors from Attila the Hun to Genghis Khan.

Modu Chanyu grasped the need for the two pillars of every authoritarian regime, an army and bureaucracy. He looked to his more
wealthy and powerful rival to the south, Han China, for inspira-
tion. The Scythians and Sarmatians lacked both, and so their confederacies never attained the effectiveness of the Xiongnu Empire.

First, Modu Chanyu reorganized his warriors, who were tradi-
tionally marshaled by clan and family, into imperial units based on a
decimal organization.[34] This same organization was later used by the
Gök Turks and Mongols, the two most successful steppe barbarians
after the Xiongnu. Although the Xiongnu excelled in riding and
archery, they engaged in raiding their neighbors in bold acts of cattle rustling or wife stealing. Against Chinese settlements, Xiongnu
raiders operated in larger groups, but they too hardly constituted a
disciplined army. Modu Chanyu turned his warriors into soldiers.
He imposed discipline on them and a clear chain of command on
his officers, who were appointed and promoted on the basis of merit
and personal loyalty. Every able-bodied male Xiongnu had to become a soldier if Modu Chanyu were to match the Han armies.
With such an army, Modu Chanyu waged three decades of victorious campaigns against the Han Empire, to extort ever greater
sums of tribute, or against rival nomadic tribes, who were either
subjected or expelled. In response to Chinese aggression and the
Great Wall, Modu Chanyu forged the first nomadic imperial army
and his own strategy of imperial expansion.

Second, Modu Chanyu had to impose his undisputed rule over
his Xiongnu and the growing number of vassal tribes. He co-opted

family and clan leaders, whom he ennobled with high-sounding titles of Chinese origin, fancy gifts, and grants of pastures so they became, in effect, members of an imperial aristocracy.[35] Descent still counted, but so did the favor of and loyalty to Modu Chanyu. The top twenty-four were elevated to regional rulers or *kuli*. Above them, he appointed two deputies: the Wise King of the Left (East), designated the heir presumptive, and the Wise King of the Right (West), each with his own officials to collect tribute, levy warriors, and enforce law. Hence, Modu Chanyu could issue orders that were obeyed. None of the previous nomads, the Hu barbarians reported in Chinese chronicles since the eighth century BC, possessed any such organization.

The Chinese court feared, but perhaps secretly admired, the imperial administration created by Modu Chanyu, who attracted many willing mandarins to his service. The most infamous, the eunuch Zhonghang Yue, is still condemned in China today as a traitor.[36] Sent on a mission by the emperor Wen, in 174 BC, he defected to Jiyu, the son and successor of Modu Chanyu. He betrayed Chinese state secrets and advised his new barbarian master to reject Chinese gifts and to extort better terms by raiding. The eunuch renegade was hardly alone. Modu Chanyu and his successors could easily find numerous Chinese scribes to keep records on wooden tablets and to write up their demands as directives and laws. Modu Chanyu's officials devised their own script based on the Chinese ideograms imposed by the emperor Qin Shi Huang. Modu Chanyu's successors expanded and reformed this bureaucracy, and so they created an imperial institution with its own collective memory. It might well have persisted long after the fall of the Xiongnu Empire, and inspired the later Gök Turk and Mongol kaghans who appreciated the power of writing.[37] In the opinion of some scholars, Attila the Hun too might have inherited this respect for literate, foreign officials who could turn his commands into written words and record the tribute or levies of warriors owed. The Roman secretary Orestes, who headed Attila's bureaucracy, later, with the fall of his master's empire, promptly returned to imperial service and put his own son Romulus Augustulus on the throne as the last Western Roman emperor.[38]

To Modu Chanyu, Chinese ideograms were a form of drawing, for calligraphy was always appreciated by the Chinese elite. The first Chinese writing, preserved on the Oracle Bones during the Shang period, was designed for divination—a practice of the shamans revered by all steppe peoples.[39] Under the Emperor Qin Shi Huang and his Han successors, writing and calligraphy were put at the service of an emperor to enforce his Mandate of Heaven. Chinese ideograms painted on beautiful scrolls had the advantage that they could be read by literate officials who spoke mutually unintelligible languages. In contrast, the Scythians and Sarmatians on the central and western Eurasian steppes, as far as we know, never devised their own script based on the alphabets and cuneiform of their southern neighbors, the Greeks and Persians, respectively.[40] There are two possible reasons for this. First, a Scythian lord would have learned of writing from a Greek merchant, plying his wares, or from a curious traveler such as Herodotus who was taking notes. Merchants from the Persian Empire also would have employed alphabetic scripts for either Aramaic or one of the Anatolian languages. The alphabet was simple and easy to learn, but it hardly had the dignity of Chinese calligraphy or the advantage of Chinese ideograms that they could be read by those speaking mutually unintelligible languages. Furthermore, neither was used widely in divination nor associated with royal power. The Great King of Persia never prized calligraphy as did the Chinese emperor. King Darius himself confessed that he did not have time to learn literacy, for his scribes kept records in Aramaic and read to him, translating the Aramaic into spoken Persian.[41] Cuneiform, long the preferred writing of the Near East, was passing out of general use, and Persian kings limited its use to commemorative inscriptions. The Scythians never would have seen the great Achaemenid monuments, such as the trilingual inscription of the Behistun Rock, which narrated royal deeds in ornate cuneiform.

Second, Modu Chanyu must have been impressed by Chinese imperial officials versed in calligraphy and a canon of classics. Qin Shi Huang ruled China through such officials operating on the principles of the Legalist philosophy justifying that might makes right; his Han successors preferred the Confucian tradition.

The mandarins, whatever their philosophical leanings, upheld the emperor's Mandate of Heaven not just by writing administrative documents but also by propounding the principles of a sophisticated imperial ideology. Modu Chanyu was but the first of many nomadic conquerors to embrace Chinese political ideology and ceremony that cast him as the Son of Heaven. Finally, these mandarins were far more numerous than any of their counterparts who served kings and emperors in the Near East or in the Mediterranean world. This is illustrated by a single statistic about the Roman Empire of the Principate and the Chinese Empire of the Tang or Song dynasty. The two empires were comparable in size and population. The Roman emperor of the first and second centuries AD governed the most effective imperial order in the Western tradition before the modern era. He had one senior imperial official for every four hundred thousand subjects. Each senior official was expected to provide his own immediate staff from among his family members, freedmen, and slaves. The Chinese emperor of the Tang or Song dynasty appointed one senior official for every fifteen thousand subjects, and these officials were supported by an army of professional scribes, accountants, and lawyers.[42] In imperial China, Modu Chanyu could thus see numerous professional officials promoted by a rigorous examination system that required command of the classic texts and calligraphy. He also could buy these bureaucrats. No Scythian or Sarmatian ruler ever saw such a system.

For Modu Chanyu and his successors, their power rested on the flow of gifts from the Han emperor, and so they were keen to exploit rather than to destroy China. Yet their power was vulnerable, because Modu Chanyu had precipitated the reunification of China under effective Han emperors, who turned China into the most powerful bureaucratic empire in its day. In time, they would inevitably come to resent the humiliation and expense of paying tribute to mere Hu barbarians since each new chanyu would demand more gifts of silk. It is recorded that between 51 and 1 BC, the number of silk fabrics distributed as gifts to the Xiongnu court rose from eight thousand to thirty thousand pieces.[43]

The accompanying gifts of gold, silk floss, and rice were likewise increased. After over sixty years of peace and prosperity, the

emperor Wudi (141–87 BC) wearied of rendering ever more tribute to the arrogant barbarians, and so he chose war over diplomacy.
In so doing, he committed the Han dynasty to destroying the empire of the Xiongnu.[44] Yet, ironically, the centuries-long struggle
also destroyed the first Chinese Empire. For, during those same
sixty years, Modu Chanyu and his heirs too had forged a nomadic
empire that could match the Han Empire on nearly equal terms.

6

The Xiongnu and Chinese Emperors at War

After nearly ten years of captivity among the barbarian Xiongnu, Zhang Qian, envoy of the Han emperor Wudi, at last reached his destination, the distant western land of the Yuezhi (today Tajikistan). In 138 BC, the emperor Wudi had commissioned Zhang Qian to conclude an alliance with the Yuezhi, Tocharian speakers whom the Xiongnu had expelled from their homeland fifty years earlier.[1] Zhang Qian and his party, however, were captured by Xiongnu soon after they had passed through the Jade Gate. Zhang Qian, a gentleman and officer, won the favor of the Xiongnu ruler Jurchen, grandson of Modu Chanyu, and was treated as an honored guest until he managed his escape with his barbarian wife, their son, and the guide Ganfu. Zhang Qian was the first Chinese to penetrate so far west. He was impressed by what he saw. He was also disappointed because he failed in his mission. The emperor Wudi had ordered Zhang Qian on a daring mission to convince the Yuezhi to attack the Xiongnu from the west. The Yuezhi had close contact with Chinese civilization before their exodus to their new home in Ferghana. Zhang Qian had marveled at the magnificent beasts, which, at the gallop, sometimes sweat streams of blood because they were infected by a parasite. There alfalfa fields nourished the heavenly horses then prized as the finest cavalry horses in Eurasia.[2] But the Yuezhi showed no interest in taking on the Xiongnu again. In 128 BC, Zhang Qian set out for home, but he and his family were again captured by the Xiongnu. They were again treated honorably until they escaped soon after the death of Jurchen Chanyu. Three years later, Zhang Qian reached the Han court and reported his findings to an astonished Emperor Wudi, who had long ago given up his envoy for dead. From Zhang Qian, the Han court obtained its first accurate information about the Xiongnu, the Western Regions, the great kingdoms beyond, and the profits to be gained from the Silk Road.[3]

By the time Zhang Qian returned, the emperor Wudi had already declared war on the Xiongnu. The emperor had not taken the decision lightly. The historian Sima Qian reports a debate between a frontier official and general Wang Hui and the minister and Confucian scholar Kong Anguo. Wang Hui pressed for war, frustrated by the frequent violations of the treaty by the Xiongnu, whereas Kong Anguo urged caution, warning that war was unpredictable save for emptying the treasury.[4] The emperor Wudi, a nervous autocrat, feared that gifts to the barbarians could be viewed as a sign of weakness and spur on plots against him. The emperor Wudi had good cause for his suspicions. By all accounts, he lacked the commanding presence expected of an emperor. Disfigured from smallpox when a child, he was ugly and unassuming. Yet this retiring and taciturn ruler possessed a powerful intellect, thinking in farsighted strategic terms. In my opinion, today Wudi could outthink the best Russian chess masters by six moves in advance. He was the first Chinese ruler to pursue a long-term strategy that has characterized Chinese regimes ever since.

The emperor Wudi ordered his ministers to draft memoranda on how to defeat the nomads. They based their recommendations on a memorandum written a generation earlier by Chao Cuo, the minister of his grandfather, the emperor Wen, who had briefly considered, and then rejected, war against the Xiongnu. Wudi implemented many of these recommendations.[5] He rearmed his infantry with pikes and crossbows with improved triggers and fitted for shooting multiple bolts.[6] He replaced bronze weapons and armor with iron ones. Even more ambitious, he ordered the mounting of cavalry in place of chariots. Few Chinese at the time knew anything about horsemanship. The Chinese craftsmen would have to learn how to produce saddles, stirrups, and harnesses on short notice. The emperor would also have to overcome the prejudices of Chinese who long disparaged the leather trousers, boots, and kaftans of nomadic horsemen as barbarous garb. Furthermore, Chinese horses were too small and fragile to serve as cavalry mounts.[7] Wudi needed to acquire and breed the best horses of Eurasia, the heavenly horses from Ferghana. Among his priorities, Zhang Qian was to negotiate a trade deal with the Yuezhi to supply thousands of Ferghana horses to the imperial army. In preparing for war, Wudi had to put the empire's economy on a permanent war footing.

During a reign of fifty-four years, Wudi relentlessly waged a war against the Xiongnu on two fronts.[8] On the northern front, Wudi sought to reoccupy and colonize the upper valley and great bend of the Yellow River and the Sixteen Prefectures, which had been lost to Modu Chanyu a generation earlier. The Great Wall, once repaired and extended, provided bases where Han generals concentrated men, horses, and matériel for an invasion of the Xiongnu heartland. Wudi aimed to break the power of the Xiongnu forever by forcing them to decisive battle. In the second theater to the west, Wudi ordered the conquest and annexation of the Western Regions beyond the Jade Gate. Here, the Han army first garrisoned the narrow Gansu (or Hexi) corridor between the steppes to the north and Tibetan highlands to the south. Then followed the occupation and colonization of the caravan cities of the Tarim Basin.

The war on the northern front opened in 133 BC, while Zhang Qian was languishing as an honored guest of Jurchen Chanyu. The emperor Wudi prudently decided not to lead the army himself, and he entrusted operations to his veteran general Wang Hui.[9] Wang Hui planned an ambush outside of the city of Mayi (today Shaanxi) to annihilate the Xiongnu at a single stroke.[10] Outside the city, the peasants and their livestock were left unawares that they were the tempting bait for the approaching Xiongnu. But Jurchen Chanyu sensed the deception, refused to take the bait, and withdrew. For the next seven years, the Xiongnu raided the northern Chinese fron-

tiers in retaliation.[11] Han frontier armies failed to check Xiongnu
raiders, who easily escaped north across the Gobi.

In 127 BC, the Han general Wei Qing occupied the Ordos bend
and upper valley of the Yellow River and repaired the Great Wall.
The Xiongnu were again ruthlessly expelled, and one hundred
thousand Chinese colonists were settled.[12] Three times over the
next eight years, Han generals mounted major invasions across the
Gobi Desert, scattering the Xiongnu, and driving off livestock and
captives. Zhang Qian, returned to imperial service, was attached to
the imperial army, and he provided invaluable information on the
sources of water and routes across the Gobi Desert. In 119 BC, the
Han generals Wei Qing and Huo Qubing coordinated their strategy
to defeat and compel the new Xiongnu ruler Ichise Chanyu, the
brother of Jurchen and known as Yizhixie to the Chinese, to submit unconditionally.[13] Each general led a separate column of large
numbers of light cavalry into the Khangari Mountains.[14] They then
perfectly timed their attacks to converge on Ichise Chanyu's tent
city of Mobei, probably in the Orkhon valley (and close to Genghis Khan's capital, Karakorum). The stunned Xiongnu fled across
the Gobi, and Ichise Chanyu escaped to rally his people. For all its
strategic brilliance, the battle failed to end the war. Chinese losses
ran into the tens of thousands, while one hundred thousand horses
died from exhaustion and dehydration.[15] The generals Huo Qubing
and Wei Qing pressed operations and acquitted themselves well in
two lesser engagements. Huo Qubing encircled and destroyed a
Xiongnu army led by the Wise King of the Left. Meanwhile, Wei
Qing showed tactical finesse in defeating, for a second time, Ichise
Chanyu, in open battle. Wei Qing drew up in a tight formation his
chariots and heavy infantry armed with pikes and crossbows. They
presented an unbroken front against Xiongnu horse archers who
repeatedly charged, fired their arrows, and retired. The Chinese
infantry held their ground in perfect discipline. Toward dusk, and
under cover of a sandstorm, Wei Qing ordered his heavy cavalry
to flank and encircle the charging Xiongnu, and so won the day.
But Ichise Chanyu and many of the Xiongnu again escaped. These
Han victories, while costly, ended major Xiongnu raids for a decade.

In 121 BC, the emperor Wudi directed his army west for the

first time, to secure the Gansu corridor, and then to drive out the
Xiongnu from the Western Regions (Xiyu). Once again, Zhang
Qian provided vital information. General Huo Qing waged a campaign of maneuver, driving the Xiongnu out of the Gansu (Hexi)
corridor. The next spring, he marched from Longzi, defeating another Xiongnu detachment, and then advanced as far as Lop Nur,
seizing captives and livestock. Han armies methodically pacified
district after district of the Western Regions over the next thirteen
years. The eastern districts of the Tarim Basin just west of the Jade
Gate were organized into Chinese military provinces. The Great
Wall was extended to Dunhuang, the caravan city that yielded to
Sir Aurel Stein so many commercial and religious texts. In 115 BC,
Zhang Qian was again engaged as an envoy, this time to the Wu-
sun, Iranian speakers who were perhaps ancestors of the Alans.[16]
The Wu-sun, disaffected vassals of the Xiongnu, were courted into
an alliance against their overlords. In return for tribute payments
of silk, the Wu-sun patrolled the steppes just north of the Gansu
corridor. Between 108 and 101 BC, every oasis city of the Tarim
Basin submitted to Chinese rule; the principal caravan centers such
as Loulan and Turfan accepted Chinese garrisons.[17] With the revenues of the caravan cities lost, the Xiongnu chanyu was hard-
pressed to keep the loyalty of his western vassals, many of whom
defected from the confederacy.

The emperor Wudi and his generals learned the value of cavalry from three decades of experience in waging brutal frontier
warfare against an elusive mounted foe. Wudi was determined to
assure the supremacy of the imperial army by obtaining breeding
stock of Ferghana horses so that the imperial government would
no longer depend on horses obtained in tribute from nomadic allies. In 104 BC, he entrusted an army to Li Guangli, brother of the
emperor's favorite concubine, to march over one thousand miles
from the Dunhuang against the recalcitrant Sogdians, who were
called the Dayuan by the Chinese.[18] The Sogdians had refused to
provide Ferghana horses to the imperial army. Li Guangli, while
protesting his undying loyalty, was not up to the task. He botched
the expedition and lost most of his army in the Taklamakan Desert
before he ever reached his objective. In 102 BC, Li Guangli, thanks

to the pleadings of his sister before a skeptical emperor, obtained
an even larger army, one hundred eighty thousand strong. Only
a fraction of this expedition reached the Sogdian city Khodjend
(today Khujand in Tajikistan), the first major stop on the Jaxartes
River for caravans descending from the Pamirs and heading west.
Li Guangli cut off the city's water supply, and compelled the Sogdians to provide Ferghana horses. Out of the one hundred eighty
thousand who set out on the march, only one thousand cavalry
and ten thousand infantry managed to return to base the next year.
The war euphemistically called the War of the Heavenly Horses
epitomizes the determination of Wudi to win at any cost. For the
emperor, the loss of over two hundred thousand soldiers was acceptable in return for five thousand horses, which, in time, might breed
fifty thousand horses for the imperial army. Yet the experiment in
breeding never worked. The fodder fed to horses in China lacked
the selenium necessary for strong bones and muscles, so Chinese-
bred horses did not match those nurtured on the grasslands of the
Eurasian steppes. In the end, Wudi could never free the imperial
army from its dependence on horses provided by the steppe nomads.

Yet the war against the Xiongnu did not end with the Han conquest of the Western Regions. In his final years, Wudi witnessed
several embarrassing setbacks, including the defeat and capture of
the court favorite Li Guangli.[19] Li Guangli, ever the opportunist,
switched sides and married the daughter of Hulugu Chanyu, although he later ran afoul of his new master and was condemned to
commit suicide on the grounds of treason.[20] The later Han generals
failed to achieve the same success of earlier invasions of the Xiongnu
heartland, because the later chanyu Qiedi and Hulugu adopted a
scorched-earth strategy and evaded decisive battle. At no point did
Wudi consider negotiation and renewal of the tribute system. He
thus committed his successors the emperors Zhao and Xuan to another thirty years of prosecuting this ruinous frontier war. Wudi
also committed his successors to subjecting the resentful Tocharian
and Sogdian inhabitants of the Western Regions, who shared far
more in mores and outlook with the Xiongnu than the Chinese.
They chafed under the heavy taxation of the Han administration
that impaired their commerce. Chinese losses in men and horses

over the course of forty-five years were staggering. The expeditions against Mobei in 119 BC or Sogdiana in 102 BC alone totaled losses of over three hundred thousand men and tens of thousands of horses.[21] The Han treasury repeatedly faced crises; over half of the annual revenue (ten billion cash) was consumed in the campaign of 119 BC alone.[22]

Wudi waged his war against seven successive chanyu. Denied tribute from the Han emperor, and without the revenues from the caravan trade, each chanyu faced not just defeat but extermination. They would have preferred to return to the terms of the treaty of 198 BC, but they were denied this choice. So they could only fight on tenaciously. Three of them, Ichise, Qiedi, and Hulugu, displayed exceptional resilience and determination, and they inspired the Xiongnu to amazing defiance in the face of overwhelming odds. Chinese historians recording these events never comment on the courage and sufferings of the hated barbarians.[23] They report that in the campaigns of 124 to 119 BC, over three hundred thousand Xiongnu were slain or captured. If these figures are at all accurate, between one-quarter and one-third of the confederacy's population was lost due to direct Chinese military actions. Famine and disease carried off many more, because the same chroniclers report in glowing terms the millions of captured cattle, goats, sheep, and horses. The losses suffered by the Xiongnu, in modern terms, reached the level of genocidal.

War also revealed the political weakness of the confederacy despite the central administration forged by Modu Chanyu. The Xiongnu, like most nomadic peoples, practiced lateral succession.[24] Upon the death of a chanyu, succession did not pass automatically to the eldest son, but rather to the eldest, and most charismatic, of the adult relatives of the chanyu's generation. Kingship thus often passed from brother to brother, uncle to nephew, or cousin to cousin. Any transfer of power risked civil war. Under the hammer of repeated attacks by Han armies, rival candidates disputed, and even fought over, the right to succeed as chanyu. In 54 BC, civil war erupted among the Xiongnu, pitting Zhizhi Chanyu, who ruled over the northern tribes of the confederacy, against his brother Huhanye, who was recognized by the southern tribes dwelling north of the

Chinese frontier.[25] The Han emperor Xuan backed Huhanye, and awarded him a treaty and tribute. Huhanye eventually emerged the victor, and so at minimal cost, the emperor Xuan gained peace for the next sixty years. But later Han emperors failed to convert the benefits of peace into effective governing. In 9 AD, Wang Mang, an impoverished scion of the imperial house, ended his regency over a boy emperor and proclaimed himself emperor of a new Xin dynasty.[26] He vowed to restore the legendary prosperity of the Zhou dynasty, and so his officials feverishly searched texts for precedents for a program of radical reform. Wang Mang himself had cut an impressive figure during his three decades of imperial service. Confident, inventive, and affable, he charmed many at court, but he also aroused jealousy in many others competing with him for imperial favor.

Wang Mang immediately set to work reforming the fiscal and military institutions undermined by decades of corruption and frontier wars. In the boldness of his vision, Wang Mang has been aptly compared with the Roman emperor Diocletian (284–305), another brilliant, conservative reformer who rescued his empire from crisis.[27] Both rulers shared an understanding of the urgency for currency reform.[28] But Wang Mang went much further, overturning the established social order and seizing and redistributing so much private property that he has ever since been condemned or praised as the first proponent of state socialism. Wang Mang, unlike Diocletian (who retired after a successful reign of twenty years to cultivate his cabbage garden), was not favored by fortune. Wang Mang could never overcome the hostility of imperial officers and officials for his audacious seizure of power. His ablest general, Wang Chang, an astrologer turned soldier, failed to win the decisive Battle of Kunyang, and then died mysteriously while hunting. His other generals failed to win the decisive battle against the rebels led by Liu Xiu (and the future Han emperor Guangwu). Even Zhi Chanyu was not impressed.[29] As soon as the emperor's envoys appeared bearing the customary gifts, the chanyu objected to the new seal on the treaty in the name of the Xin rather than the Han Son of Heaven. Zhi Chanyu could read Chinese ideograms, and he doubted the legitimacy of the new regime in Chang'an. The Chinese envoys refused to use the original seal to authenticate the treaty, and then destroyed it in front of Zhi Chanyu. Zhi Chanyu was enraged and declared the treaty broken. He immediately ordered attacks along the Chinese frontier. Wang Mang, just as infuriated, declared war, but failed to take military action. Instead, Wang Mang resorted to duplicity, encouraging Xiongnu pretenders. Twice, Wang Mang even violated safe conduct pledges and seized high-ranking Xiongnu as hostages. Meanwhile, Wang Mang was battling pretenders of the Han dynasty and peasant rebels outraged over his sweeping reforms. He was compelled to withdraw the garrisons of the Western Regions to counter the threats within the empire. The Xiongnu promptly imposed their rule over the cities of the Tarim Basin for the next sixty years.[30] His dismal failure in checking the Xiongnu proved the final blow. Wang Mang died fighting in his palace against the forces of Liu Xuan. His body was mutilated and its head severed to be nailed to the city walls of Wancheng and later kept as a trophy in the imperial vaults. Liu Xuan, under the throne name of Gengshi, restored the Han dynasty.[31]

The new Han emperors and their historians condemned Wang Mang as an impious usurper who never enjoyed the Mandate of Heaven, but they quietly adopted his policy of dealing with the Xiongnu. Henceforth, the Han emperor showered titles and gifts upon any nomadic prince who would do his bidding. In contrast, early Han emperors had supported a single chanyu so that he could keep the tribes in line and assure trade. The emperors of this Latter or Western Han dynasty aimed to restore the northern frontier and control over the Western Regions. In 46 AD, the opportunity came with the outbreak of another civil war, this time between two first cousins.[32] Prince Bi of the southern tribes challenged the right to rule by his cousin Punu, son of Huduershidaogao Chanyu. The emperor Guangwu backed Prince Bi and the southern Xiongnu, and so committed the Han dynasty to yet another Xiongnu war of nearly sixty years. The Xiongnu confederacy thereafter permanently split into a northern and southern one under rival branches of the house of Modu Chanyu.[33] Chinese emperors henceforth distinguished between Inner Barbarians dwelling north of the Great Wall who were accorded a treaty and tribute from the remote

Outer Barbarians on the Mongolian steppes, who were perceived as the prime threat.[34] In effect, Han emperors drafted tribal regiments of the Inner Barbarians into the imperial army so that they were the equivalent of federate barbarian regiments of late imperial Rome.[35] This modified tributary system exalted the Han emperor over barbarian rulers, maintained the conceit of the primacy of the Middle Kingdom, and gained invaluable nomadic cavalry. Yet the chanyu of the Southern Xiongnu profited even more because he held the decisive military power along the Chinese northern and western frontiers. In time, any Xiongnu prince could turn himself into an emperor in North China should the power of the Han dynasty ever weaken.

The later Han emperors entrusted to their generals in the field far more independence of action in conducting campaigns and imposing settlements on the defeated. In part, these Han emperors were far more concerned about frontiers in Korea and the far southern regions. None of them enjoyed the long reign and indomitable will of Wudi, who kept an iron grip over strategy and his armies. Furthermore, Han generals needed the freedom of action if they were to impress and inspire the Xiongnu allies to follow. Victory in this second war, in many ways, was as much the victory of the Southern Xiongnu tribes as it was of the Han army. Promoting disunity among the Xiongnu complicated both diplomacy and strategy as each Xiongnu prince shifted his allegiance between the Han emperor and the chanyu of the Northern Xiongnu. At the end of this second war, Chinese chroniclers were bewildered by the number and diversity of tribes on the Eurasian steppes, counting at least one hundred twenty tribes.[36]

Two of the ablest Han generals delivered final victory against the Northern Xiongnu on the eastern steppes. Dou Xian directed a series of campaigns between 89 and 92 that finally broke the power of the Northern Xiongnu. He owed his position to his sister, the empress Xiaowen, who was married to the emperor Wen. Dou Xian brilliantly served three successive emperors, but he was recalled in disgrace just after winning the final victory because he was implicated in a plot masterminded by his sister, then dowager empress, against her young stepson, the emperor He, and his powerful eunuch minister, Zheng Zhong. Dou Xian was spared due to his loyal service, but other members of his family were executed.[37] Even so, Dou Gu won immortality among Chinese generals by his victory over the Northern Xiongnu at Yanran Mountain in 89 AD. He ordered a memorial inscription cut into the sandstone cliffs exalting his achievements in the traditional courtly poetry of the *Chu Ci*. Thereafter, the proverbial phase of praise of carving on a stone of Yanran was granted to a successful general. The location of the inscription was lost until it was rediscovered by a Mongolian travel writer in 2001.[38] Sixteen years later, a team of Mongolian and Chinese scholars returned to the site on the southeastern edge of the Gobi. They photographed, transcribed, and translated the inscription. They were astonished to discover that the brother-sister team of historians, Ban Gu and Ban Zhao, had faithfully recorded the text soon afterward. Their record, in turn, was incorporated and preserved in the *Hou Hanshu* (*Book of the Latter Han*) of the fifth century AD.

In the Western Regions, the equally brilliant general Ban Chao expelled the Northern Xiongnu and reimposed imperial rule between 75 and 102 AD.[39] Ban Chao, a Confucian mandarin from a family of historians, was assured that his deeds would be remembered in the most favorable light.[40] Even so, he proved to be an able general and adroit diplomat. Even more important, he never ran afoul of the two emperors he served or the scheming factions at the court of Luoyang. Ban Chao, appointed Protector General of the Western Regions in 91, wielded regal power. He signed treaties of alliance with nomadic allies, elevated and deposed dynasts who ruled the caravan cities, and directed expeditions into the Central Eurasian steppes. In the course of twenty-seven years, he acquired eight native wives to cement political alliances. Six of them survived to accompany Ban Chao to a comfortable, well-deserved, and all too brief retirement at Luoyang in 102. Today, Ban Chao is honored with a heroic statue in the city of Kashgar, at the eastern end of the Xinjiang Uyghur Autonomous Region of the Chinese People's Republic. He is rightly hailed as the founder of Chinese rule in the Western Regions, to the acclaim of Chinese residents and to the chagrin of Uyghur nationalists.

In 86, Ban Chao reached the banks of the Upper Jaxartes, and brought into submission Iranian-speaking nomads as far as the Aral Sea. He thus extended the Han Empire to its farthest limit. He now learned firsthand how the political geography of the lands beyond the Western Regions had changed since the visit of Zhang Qian over two centuries earlier. The Kushan emperor Vima Taktu, hailed as the great savior by his Greek subjects of Bactria, reigned as the Son of Heaven over a great empire stretching from the Jaxartes to the Ganges.[41] Ban Chao must have been awestruck by how the descendants of the Yuezhi, despised by Chinese and Xiongnu alike, had risen to imperial status. The Kushan emperor could correspond on terms of equality with the other Son of Heaven at Luoyang. He could also challenge Han authority in the Western Regions. To the west of the Kushan Empire ruled the Arsacid king of Parthia, known to the Chinese as Anxi. They were yet another steppe nomadic people who had turned themselves into masters of a powerful empire. They were also possible allies against the Kushans. Beyond Parthia lay an even greater imperial power, Daqin, the Roman Empire. In 97, out of curiosity and fear, Ban Chao acted as the proxy of his emperor He and dispatched as an imperial envoy Gan Ying to learn about these distant powers and, if possible, to secure commercial and military alliances.

The travels of Gan Ying excited the imagination of later Chinese historians who faithfully recorded his extraordinary tour of the Kushan and Parthian Empires.[42] Gan Ying, once he crossed the Jaxartes River, left the area of Chinese control.[43] He followed the caravan route to Bactra (Balkh), crossed the Hindu Kush, and visited Gandhara in the heart of the Kushan Empire. He descended to the middle Indus, and then traveled west to Areia (Herat) via the Bolan Pass into the Parthian Empire. After a journey of three months, he finally reached Tiaozhi (Characene) and Sibin (Susiana) in southeastern Iran today. As far as can be determined, he never saw the Tigris River or the Parthian capital of Ctesiphon. At Susa, Gan Ying likely spoke with members of the Arsacid court about Daqin. His Parthian informants discouraged him by exaggerating the dangers and the length of the journey to Daqin, which, they alleged, could only be reached by an ocean voyage of three months. They were referring to the trade route from Charax, on the Persian Gulf, around the Arabian peninsula, to ports on the Red Sea in Roman Egypt. They deliberately omitted mentioning a more direct overland route across the Fertile Crescent to Antioch in Roman Syria. Gan Ying, who was now nearly five thousand miles from home, feared, like many of his countrymen, venturing out to sea. He decided to retrace his steps and to report to Ban Chao his findings. Based on his informants, he brought back to his fellow Chinese the first description of the Roman Empire. The historians of the *Hou Hanshu* summarized the report as follows:

Their kings are not permanent. They select and appoint the most worthy man. If there are unexpected calamities in the kingdom, such as frequent extraordinary winds or rains, he is unceremoniously rejected and replaced. The one who has been dismissed quietly accepts his demotion, and is not angry. The people of this country are all tall and honest. They resemble the people of the Middle Kingdom and that is why this kingdom is called Da Qin [or "Great China"]. This country produces plenty of gold [and] silver, [and of] rare and precious [things] they have luminous jade, "bright moon pearls," Haiji rhinoceroses, coral, yellow amber, opaque glass, whitish chalcedony, red cinnabar, green gemstones, gold thread embroideries, rugs woven with gold thread, delicate polychrome silks painted with gold, and asbestos cloth. They also have a fine cloth which some people say is made from the down of "water sheep," but which is made, in fact, from the cocoons of wild silkworms. They blend all sorts of fragrances, and by boiling the juice, make a compound perfume. [They have] all the precious and rare things that come from the various foreign kingdoms. They make gold and silver coins. Ten silver coins are worth one gold coin. They trade with Anxi [Parthia] and Tianzhu [Northwest India] by sea. The profit margin is ten to one… The king of this country always wanted to send envoys to Han, but Anxi [Parthia], wishing to control the trade in multi-colored Chinese silks, blocked the route to prevent [the Romans] getting through [to China].[44]

Historians have long speculated about what would have happened if Ying Gan had pressed on, for he would have reached Rome in the year 98. He would have gained an audience from the emperor Trajan, arguably the greatest emperor after Augustus, who enjoyed the singular distinction of being more popular at his death than at his accession. Trajan would have been most receptive to an alliance against the Parthians, who challenged Rome for mastery of the Near East and charged outrageously high customs duties on silks carried by caravans bound for Rome.[45] The Han court, however, would have wanted an alliance against the Kushans. It is extremely unlikely that the negotiations would have resulted in any effective cooperation. When the two courts finally did exchange envoys in 166, they remained respectfully, and distantly, on cordial terms.[46]

The Han dynasty reached its apex at the opening of the second century AD, at the same time when the emperor Trajan had brought the Roman Empire to its greatest extent. Yet the Han court feared appointing effective protector generals who might challenge the dynasty's Mandate of Heaven. Within a generation of the death of Ban Chao, the Han armies were withdrawn from the Western Regions.[47] The greatest Kushan emperor, Kanishka I, soon asserted control over the Tarim Basin.[48] The Tocharian- and Iranian-speaking residents of the cities and the nomads of the Tarim Basin preferred Kushan hegemony over a Chinese one. Even more significantly, as Han power weakened from the mid-second century on, Xiongnu allies moved south of the Great Wall and settled in northern China. There, Xiongnu princes began to carve out their own states. In time, they would assume Chinese throne names and, with the aid of mandarin bureaucrats, rule as regional lords over the northern provinces of the former Han Empire.[49] Ultimately, Han victory proved to be Pyrrhic, for it ironically benefited the Xiongnu allies far more than the dynasty. In 220, the Han Empire did not so much fall as fragment for the next three hundred fifty years.[50] The wars between the Xiongnu and Han emperors also drove west Tocharian- and Iranian-speaking nomads to seek new homes in Transoxiana, Iran, and northern India. Foremost among these were the Kushans, descendants of the Yuezhi.

7

The Sons of Heaven and the Silk Road

Under a bright sun on an April day in 630, the mendicant monk Xuanzang, nearly thirty years old, stood in awe before the colossal statues of Gautama Buddha, Vairocana, and Sakyamuni, cut from the sandstone cliffs overlooking the Bamyan Valley on the road over the Hindu Kush into India.[1] Over a year earlier, Xuanzang had evaded imperial guards ordered by the Tang emperor Taizong to turn back all unauthorized travelers to the west. The emperor faced a possible war with the newest nomadic foes of China, the Gök Turks. But Xuanzang was determined to make his pilgrimage because he had been inspired by a dream from the Buddha. A learned man of a Confucian noble house, he vowed to visit the Buddhist monasteries to the west in search of manuscripts faithfully recording the Buddha's enlightened word so that he could translate the Tripitaka more accurately into Chinese.[2] He was a serious scholar concerned about the authenticity of the Buddhist doctrine that had been carried to China over five centuries earlier.[3] Over the past year, he had toured Buddhist monasteries of the Tarim Basin, conversed with Buddhist rulers, and found his way to Bamyan after overcoming privations and bandits.[4] Xuanzang would have gazed up at the decorated largest statues in the world, and yet he was even more impressed by the thousands of monks celebrating their faith, and the numerous richly painted cave monasteries that overlooked the valley. Soon after, Xuanzang crossed the Khyber Pass into northern India and spent the next fifteen years visiting the Buddhist shrines and collecting manuscripts.[5] When Xuanzang returned home in 645, he retired to a monastery, where he translated the *Mahaprajnaparamita Sutra* and, on the order of his emperor, composed a detailed account of the Western Regions. Xuanzang had moved through a cosmopolitan world of monasteries, caravan cities, and imperial capitals. Merchants from many lands traversed the Silk Road in search of profit, while missionaries of many faiths proclaimed their religion to converts. At the time of his death in 664, Xuanzang could not have anticipated that this world was soon to be violently overturned by the Arab armies fighting in the name of the Prophet Muhammad. What Xuanzang also did not know was this international world was also the creation of nomadic peoples whose ancestors had once dwelled on the western frontiers of his China: the Kushans.

During the first and second centuries AD, the Kushan emperors who styled themselves the Sons of Heaven, in the fashion of Han emperors, did more to promote the commerce of the Silk Road and the spread of Buddhism to East Asia than any previous rulers. They were descendants of Tocharian-speaking nomads who had dwelled in Gansu and had traded jade and horses with the Chinese since the Bronze Age.[6]

Modu Chanyu, ruler of the Xiongnu, out of personal hatred, attacked the Yuezhi, slew great numbers, seized livestock, and turned the skull of the Yuezhi king into a goblet.[7] His son Jiyu, known to the Chinese as Laoshang, expelled the Yuezhi from their ancestral grasslands by the mid-second century BC.[8] The Yuezhi first sought refuge in the upper Ili valley, and then moved west again into Sogdiana (Dayuan to the Chinese) and expelled the resident nomads, Iranian-speaking Sacae. The Sacae, over the course of the next fifty years, fled southwest first into the Parthian Empire, and then turned east, crossing the Hindu Kush and extinguishing the Greek kingdoms of northwestern India.[9] These refugee Sacae, often dubbed Indo-Scythians, ruled thereafter as satraps in the Sind and Gujarat.[10] The Jats, one of the favored martial castes of recruiting officers of the British Raj, today claim descent from the Sacae. Meanwhile, in Transoxiana, the Yuezhi, called by Greeks Tocharoi, pressed south from the middle Jaxartes. They overthrew the last Greco-Bactrian king, Heliocles (who might have fled to India), and took possession of Bactria (called Daxia in Chinese sources), where Zhang Qian found them in 126 BC.[11] Together, Tocharian newcomers and Iranian Sacae abruptly ended the political legacy of Alexander the Great in Central Asia and India, but not the cultural one. The Hellenic cities of Bactria and Northern India still flourished, and imparted to their new masters a delight in Hellenic literary and visual arts. The nomads themselves hardly turned out to be the dreaded Gog and Magog in the legends about Alexander the Great, because they quickly appreciated the high culture they found in their new homes.

Zhang Qian reckoned the might of the Yuezhi between one hundred thousand and two hundred thousand horsemen, but they still dreaded the Xiongnu and declined to enter into an alliance with the emperor Wudi.[12] For the Tocharian newcomers had imposed themselves on subject population ten times their number. They had to come to terms with Sogdian merchants, Greek residents of the cities, and native Iranian-speaking agriculturalists, all of whom paid tribute. Furthermore, the Tocharian tribes lacked political unity when Zhang Qian visited. In the early first century BC, Chinese sources report a confederation of five Yuezhi tribes each ruled by a dynast or *yabgu* (*xihou* in Chinese), a title later designating a subordinate Turkish kaghan.[13] Some of these Tocharian dynasts struck silver coins in their own names and based on Greco-Bactrian originals, but the Greek inscriptions are so blundered that the coins are illegible. The *yabgu* of the Kushan tribe (or Guishuang in Chinese) soon emerged as first among the Tocharian princes. The first Kushan *yabgu* known by name, Heraeus (ca. 1–30 AD), is only recorded on his large silver coins, tetradrachmae, that replaced those minted by the Greco-Bactrian kings that had circulated as the trade coin of Central Asia for two centuries. The face of a nomadic conqueror occupies the obverse of these first Kushan coins in place of the exquisite portraits of the heroic, clean-shaven

Greek rulers who had emulated the look of Alexander the Great.[14] The Greek artists designing the coins were hard put to render their Kushan lord according to the canons of their art. Heraeus is depicted sporting the diadem of Hellenistic kings, but his rough face with a drooping mustache shows his head with the ritual deformity practiced by many steppe nomads—a practice verified by skeletal remains from Scythian kurgans and descriptions of the later Huns, Turks, and Mongols.[15] On the coins' reverse, in place of the heroically nude divine protectors Zeus, Apollo, or Heracles, the *yabgu* himself, attired in felt cap, kaftan, and trousers, is astride a Ferghana horse. Heraeus (whose Tocharian name is unknown) is styled in Greek as tyrant rather than king. The title was meant to convey the sense of dynast, but it also denoted the true feelings of his resentful Greek subjects.

The successor and likely son of Heraeus, Kujula Kadphises (ca. 30–80), united the Tocharians in Transoxiana, and subjected Afghanistan and Gandhara so that he controlled the caravan routes through the Khyber and Bolan passes linking India to Central Asia. Kujula Kadphises was the first of seven remarkable Kushan rulers who transformed the Tocharians from nomadic warriors into the masters of one of the world's four mightiest empires by the early second century AD.[16] Kushan rulers had to win over their diverse subjects by a heady array of symbols and appeals. The second Kushan emperor, Vima Taktu (ca. 80–105), went so far as to emulate Alexander the Great, for his coins depict the royal portrait as a clean-shaven youth, wearing the diadem of Hellenistic kings, who was assimilated to the features of both Hellenic Helios and Persian Mithra.[17] Greek inscriptions on his coins' reverse hail the emperor, depicted as a mounted nomadic warrior, not as tyrant but rather as king of kings and great savior (*soter megas*), the traditional sobriquet accorded to royal benefactors of Greek cities.

The greatest Kushan emperor, Kanishka I (127–153), ruled a realm stretching from the caravan cities of the Tarim Basin across the Central Eurasian steppes, Transoxiana, and northern India to Pataliputra (today Patna) on the middle Ganges. Pataliputra had been the capital of the Mauryan emperors who had first united India three centuries earlier. Kanishka's empire matched that of the

Mauryan emperor Ashoka, who had embraced Buddhism, and it
anticipated the Moghul Empire of Akbar.[18] Yet the Kushan emperors failed to write their own history. Instead, chroniclers of the later
Han Empire, Greek and Roman authors, and Buddhist writers record their dealings with and opinions of the Kushan emperors. The
Kushan emperors, however, struck a remarkable series of coins in
gold and copper that reveal much about their aspirations and piety.

Kanishka corresponded as an equal with both the Han and
Roman emperors, each of whom sought from him a commercial
treaty and an alliance against common foes, either the Xiongnu
or the Parthians.[19] At court, Kanishka received Han envoys as the
Son of Heaven, in the Chinese manner. On his exquisite gold and
copper coins, he reveals himself as the heir of Persian Great Kings,
Greco-Bactrian kings, and Mauryan emperors. The coins proclaim him in the Bactrian language written in a Greek script King
of Kings, Kanishka the Great Kushan—a title of Persian monarchs
since Cyrus the Great.[20] Kanishka officially declared Bactrian, an
eastern Iranian tongue, the language of his court in place of Greek.
We now know this not only from his coins, but also from a monumental inscription found at Rabatak in Afghanistan in 1993, where
Kanishka dedicated a sanctuary to the Iranian goddess Nana on the
Silk Road and proudly listed his illustrious progenitors.[21] But the
coins record much more about Kanishka.[22] On the obverse of his
coins, Kanishka is depicted as a towering figure standing before a
Persian-style fire altar in an act of sacrifice. The stately, bearded
emperor is clad in felt cap, leather kaftan, leather belt, silk trousers
sewed with jewels and pearls, and leather riding boots. He wields
a ceremonial mace and long scepter, and included in each coin's
field is the emblem of the emperor's nomadic clan, called *tamgha*
by the Mongol khans or *tughra* by the Ottoman sultans. The coins
reproduced in miniature royal statues that graced every city of
Kanishka's realm. One such, with its head and arms missing, survives from Mathura.[23] This was the first time a great ruler was so
depicted, standing in the garb of an equestrian conqueror. The
image has long persisted from India to Britain. In a manuscript illumination overlaid by an encomium, Louis the Pious, Holy Roman

Emperor and son of Charlemagne, differs little in his symbolic pose from Kanishka on his coins.[24]

On the reverse, the coins reveal even more about the piety of Kanishka. Leading gods and goddesses of the Greek, Iranian, and Hindu pantheons are depicted and identified by name in the Bactrian language written in a Greek script. Foremost is the emperor's favorite goddess, Nana.[25] The most remarkable Kushan god is Oesho, with four arms and associated with the bull, who is a composite of Avestan Vayu, Greek Heracles, and Hindu Shiva.[26] Before him stands a heroic bull, Nandi, the vehicle of Shiva. Kanishka's son Huvishka, who appears with a halo on his coins, favored Hindu divinities. He is depicted on his coins often astride an elephant, making the royal progress among the sacred cities of Aryavarta, the heartland of the Vedic gods.[27] Kanishka I shared with his nomadic ancestors a pragmatic respect for all divinities whose rites and holy ones conferred legitimacy on their cults. Perhaps he too, like Napoleon, humored all the gods, but we shall never know his true religious sentiments because he never confided them to a biographer.

Foremost, Kanishka struck coins that are among the earliest depictions of the Buddha in human form. These rare ceremonial gold coins, struck at Pataliputra, depict a standing haloed Buddha, flanked by his name in the Greco-Bactrian script and the emperor's own clan emblem or tamgha.[28] Buddhist writers had no doubt as to what the coins only suggest, namely that Kanishka converted. They praise Kanishka as second only to the Mauryan emperor Ashoka, the first great ruler ever to embrace the teachings of Siddhartha Gautama. Whereas Ashoka elevated Buddhism to favored status in his empire, Kanishka turned Buddhism from an Indian faith into a world religion that today claims over 535 million adherents or 10 percent of the globe's population. Kanishka, just like all Kushan emperors, imposed order over the nexus of strategic central sections of the Silk Road. Over these routes, Buddhist missionaries trod from his realm to Han China. Nearly five centuries later, the Chinese pilgrim Xuanzang traversed this same path in reverse on his own spiritual quest to reach Sarnath, where the enlightened Siddhartha Gautama first preached under a bodhi tree.

Kanishka, however, was more than an admirer of Buddhism. He

patronized Buddhist monasteries, and constructed a great stupa, the domed monumental shrine of Buddhism, located near his palace at Purusapura (today Peshawar in Pakistan). Successive Kushan emperors enlarged the stupa until it rose to 55 feet in height. The ruins still impress the visitor, for the base measures 175 feet on each side as a perfect square, and it is oriented on the four points of the compass. The Chinese pilgrim Faxian, Xuanzang's predecessor writing over two centuries earlier, was likewise awed by the stupa.[29] Its copper-plated wooden tower was the tallest Buddhist building at the time. He reports that the *vindha*, the Buddhist monastery in the complex, was richly decorated with painted relief sculpture, and it housed many relics. A reliquary with three bone fragments of the Buddha was recovered in the excavations directed by David Brainerd Spooner in 1908–1909.[30] It has since been transferred to the Burmese monastery of U Khanti Hill in Mandalay.[31]

The stupa of Kanishka also housed golden leaves that recorded the rulings of the Fourth Buddhist Council held at Harwan in Kashmir.[32] Kanishka convened this council on the recommendation of his spiritual mentor Asvaghosa, who was the first scholar to translate the Buddha's teachings from the original vernacular Prakrit into classical Sanskrit. The council upheld the rulings of earlier councils in favor of Mahayana Buddhism or the Greater Vehicle. This was the Buddhism destined to win East Asia, for it taught that any believer, even one who had not taken ascetic vows, could attain enlightenment in a single lifetime, and so break dharma, the law governing the cycle of rebirths. Five hundred monks from the monasteries of Kashmir got to work compiling the Mahavibhasa under the direction of Asvaghosa. This compendium completed over a generation after the council summarizes in classical Sanskrit five centuries of learned commentaries on the faith.[33] For two years, in 632–633, Xuanzang assiduously studied with masters in the monasteries of Kashmir to perfect his understanding of these Sanskrit commentaries. By mandating that philosophical disputation should henceforth be written in Sanskrit, the council ensured that Buddhist thinkers could debate on equal terms with their rivals, the Brahmins, who upheld caste (*varna*), the Vedic cults and Sanskrit scriptures, and who demoted the Buddha to an illusionary avatar of Vishnu, the lord of creation. Over the centuries, Brahmins had transformed the spoken Sanskrit of the *Rig-Vedas* into a beautiful literary language ideal for expressing every subtle poetic or philosophical nuance. To be sure, the council had probably reasoned, Siddhartha Buddha had taught in Prakrit, but he must have surely contemplated in Sanskrit. At the same time, Buddhist missionaries in the cities of Bactria, Sogdiana, and the Tarim Basin commenced the translating of the Buddhist texts and commentaries into Tocharian and eastern Iranian languages. In time, they universalized the appeal of what had been an Indian religion. These translations removed the primacy of Sanskrit as language of the faith outside of India, and so stressed the message over the word. In this regard, Buddhism and Christianity share the same position on scripture. They have upheld the universal validity of their faith's message, which can be expressed in every language rather than in a single sacred one.

Kanishka was for Buddhists a second Ashoka, who had summoned the second Buddhist Council (which is considered by many to be the first historical council). He also has been compared to the Roman emperor Constantine, who summoned the First Ecumenical Council so that learned theologians could expound to him the fundamentals of the Christian faith and the reckoning of the date of Easter. Kanishka, like Constantine, also decisively transformed the visual presentation of his favored faith. The Kushan emperors were sophisticated in their aesthetic tastes, patronizing artists working in Hellenic, Central Asian, and Indian traditions. In the 1930s, French excavators at Begram, fifty miles north of Kabul in Afghanistan, found in two storerooms a cache of fabulous luxury items from Rome, China, and India. Among the objets d'art were glassware and jewelry from the Roman world, Chinese silks and lacquers, and carved ivories from India.[34]

Given the range of objects, the cache was initially interpreted as a treasury of the Kushan summer palace at Begram, the ancient city of Kapisa. Instead, the cache is far more likely the inventory of a merchant prince who supplied his royal customers along the Silk Road with exotic and prestigious goods. Even so, the Begram treasure attests to the eclectic tastes of Kushan elites. Alexander the Great settled Macedonian veterans in Kapisa, which was renamed the Hellenic city Alexandria in the Caucasus. It lay on the main route from Bactria, across the Persian satrapy of Paropamisadae, to Gandhara, the gateway to the Indus valley. The Kushan kings maintained one of their courts at Kapisa, where they attracted to their service artists and architects from across Eurasia.

During the reign of Kanishka, sculptors worked in two separate traditions, a Hellenic one in Gandhara and an Indian one of Mathura, the site of a Kushan palace, which has yielded many royal portrait statues that are a perfect blend of Indian and Greco-Iranian art. These sculptors created new visual arts that forever enriched Buddhism. In Gandhara, Greek-trained artists produced the first sculptures of the Buddha in human guise.[35] Previously, the Buddha was portrayed symbolically as a parasol conveyed in a cart.[36] Under the Kushan emperors, artists applied their genius to creating the likeness of the Buddha in his many guises, either carved out of living rock, or sculpted from stone blocks, or cast from gold, silver, or bronze. Relief sculpture and mural paintings in Buddhist sanctuaries henceforth greeted worshippers with beautiful visions of the Buddha's life, teachings, and ascent to nirvana. Some of the finest such relief sculptures of the Kushan era are still found on the monumental gateways (*torana*) of the great stupa at the monastery of Sanchi on a hilltop in the scrub forests of the central Indian district of Madhya Pradesh.[37] The complex is an architectural tour de force of Hellenic, Middle Eastern, and Indian traditions. The Kushan emperor Vasudeva, even though a devotee of Shiva, patronized the monastery. Remarkably, neither the Chinese pilgrim Faxian nor Xuanzang is reported to have visited the site, probably because Sanchi lay too far south of the Buddhist heartland in the Ganges. Each would have been dazzled by its beauty just as I was when I visited the complex in 2010. Sanchi remains to this day the most profoundly moving spiritual site I have ever experienced.

When Xuanzang entered India in 630, he traveled across a spiritual landscape filled with the most diverse of sanctuaries.[38] Buddhist, Hindu, and Jain temples coexisted side by side, and often shared many of the same worshippers. The Gupta emperors, who had succeeded to the Indian domains of the Kushans, had promoted the Brahmin caste and the Vedic cults in the fourth and fifth centuries, but the Buddhist monasteries remained equally pervasive and equally appealing to the masses thanks to the patronage of Kanishka and his successors. The commerce of the Silk Road, which soared under the protection of the Kushan emperors, enriched many families of the merchant caste, Vaishyas, who were attracted to Buddhism. Their success in business reflected well on their karma, and so their worthiness for nirvana. In thanks, they commissioned many of the rock-carved sanctuaries of Ajanta decorated with masterpieces of Buddhist religious painting inspired by Hellenic, Central Asian, and Indian traditions.[39] Xuanzang was amazed by the outpouring of such expressions of popular piety that have characterized Buddhism since the Kushan era. Xuanzang eventually found his way to Kannauj, home of the emperor Harshavardhana (605–647), who had reunited northern India after the fall of the Gupta dynasty. Harshavardhana, in policy and outlook, was the heir of the Kushan emperor Kanishka. He too was eclectic in his faith, honoring Shiva, but he also patronized Buddhist scholars and monks, because many members of the royal family, including his brother, were convinced Buddhists.[40] He warmly welcomed Xuanzang, and so together, monarch and monk exchanged spiritual views. The monarch was ever ready to discuss with scholars how to break the cycle of lives and achieve either moksha of the Hindus or nirvana of the Buddhists. To Xuanzang, Harshavardhana was a devout Buddhist in all but name. The emperor had raised thousands of stupas and hospices for pilgrims of all faiths along the banks of the Ganges. He outlawed animal sacrifice to the Vedic gods, one of the most objectionable Hindu practices to Buddhists. His charitable foundations and alms conformed to the best tenets of karma. Xuanzang witnessed at Kannauj a spectacular three-week festival that climaxed when Harshavardhana and his vassal kings paid obeisance before a life-sized golden statue of the Buddha. Xuanzang even offered to act as an envoy of Harshavardhana to convey greetings and gifts to his own emperor, Taizong.[41] To be sure, Xuanzang hoped to win back favor from Taizong because he had violated the imperial travel ban. Yet Xuanzang aimed for a far more significant success, namely bringing together the two greatest sovereigns, Harshavardhana and Taizong, who could assure the universal acceptance of the teachings of the Buddha. Such cooperation was never realized. Upon his return home, Xuanzang advanced the faith in China, but with the death of Harshavardhana, Buddhism waned in India until it was dealt a fatal blow by the Muslim army of Muhammad Ghor in the early thirteenth century.

The spectacular success of Buddhism as a world religion depended so much on the policies and patronage of the Kushan emperors of the second and third centuries AD. The proliferation of dedications of cave monasteries by successful merchants attest the prosperity of communities of Buddhist merchants along the Silk Road in the Tarim Basin, Transoxiana, and northern India for the next four centuries.[42] The success of the Kushan emperors, in turn, depended on the revenues gained from taxing commerce on the Silk Road. Under the peace imposed by the Sons of Heaven, Sogdian caravan cities, especially Samarkand and Bukhara, boomed, as did the new towns of Chorasmia (Khwarazm), in the lower valley of the Oxus between the Karakum and the southern shores of the Aral Sea. Once Kanishka extended his sway over the Tocharian-speaking cities along the northern route of the Tarim Basin, Kashgar, Kucha, and Turfan enjoyed one of the most prosperous eras in their long history. Meanwhile, the Indian subjects of the Kushan emperor prospered too because merchants of the Roman world pioneered a complementary ocean route to the ports of India. At the end of the second century BC, either a Greek merchant named Eudoxus of Cyzicus, or a skipper, Hippalus, discovered how to use the winds of the monsoon season to sail across the Erythraean Sea (the Indian Ocean).[43] These first voyages of discovery gave way to large-scale commerce once the emperor Augustus secured the Roman peace.[44] At Rome, the demand for Chinese silk, along with Indian pepper and beryls, soared. Demand often exceeded supply. Parthian officials drove up prices by levying high customs duties on caravans crossing their section of the Silk Road. Hence, Roman merchants sought more direct access to Chinese silk in the markets in the Kushan Empire. The geographer Strabo of Amasia, writing at the end of the first century BC, notes that each year in July, 120 merchantmen departed from the Roman ports of Berenice or Myos Hormos on the Red Sea. Favorable winds propelled the heavy ships

across the twenty thousand nautical miles of the Red Sea and Indian Ocean.[45] Three months later, the ships arrived at the ports of
either Barbaricum, at the mouth of the Indus River, or Barygaza,
at the mouth of Narmada River opposite Gujarat. There Roman
merchants exchanged luxuries and coins from the Roman world
for Chinese silk and lacquers, to the profit of the subjects of the
Kushan emperor.[46] From there, Roman ships often continued sail-
ing along the Malabar coast to Muziris (today Cranganore), in the
heart of the pepper plantations of Tamil Nadu, or farther south to
Taprobane (Sri Lanka), the source of emeralds and rubies.

Yet with the death of Vasudeva I (190–230), the Kushan Empire
rapidly declined. Foremost, the Kushans faced new and far more
dangerous rivals.[47] To the west, their foes the Parthians were overthrown by a vassal prince, the Sassanid shah Ardashir I, in 227. Ardashir and his even more brilliant son Shapur I (240–270) waged
wars of conquest under the banner of a resurgent Zoroastrianism to
restore the Persian Empire of the Achaemenid kings. Persian shahs
declared their intent to reconquer the Upper Satrapies, the heartland of the Kushan Empire. They also aimed to retake the Indian
lands that had once been Achaemenid satrapies. In a series of campaigns in 240–248, Shapur, during a time-out from attacking the
Roman Empire, ended the power of the Kushan Sons of Heaven
and imposed his suzerainty over the Upper Satrapies (Bactria and
Sogdiana) and Gandhara.[48] Over the next three generations, the
Sassanid shahs fought to impose direct rule over the cities and nomadic tribes of Transoxiana. To the south of the Hindu Kush, lesser
Kushan princes in Northern India reigned as vassals of the Shah,
but by the mid-fourth century they bowed to a new overlord, the
Gupta emperor, who styled himself the heir to the Mauryan leg-
acy.[49] In effect, the Sassanid shah of Iran and the Gupta emperor of
India partitioned the Kushan Empire.

Today, the Kushans are largely unknown not just because they
never wrote about themselves, but also because they do not fit neatly
into modern nationalist histories. They were far too tolerant and
eclectic in religion and culture for ardent Hindu nationalists. The
Kushans are disliked because they favored Buddhism even though
they also upheld dharma essential to the Hindu cults. As nomadic

invaders in India, they could never be accommodated within caste. Later Hindu writers deplored Kanishka for committing unspeakable atrocities against the sacred cities of Aryavarta, whereas they lauded Gupta emperors for sponsoring classical Sanskrit letters, Hindu art, and the Vedic cults. Sassanid shahs, who were militant Zoroastrians, and their Muslim successors, the Arab caliphs, preferred to forget the Kushan legacy. To fundamentalist Muslims of today, the Buddhist legacy of Central Asia created by the Kushans is unsettling. This hostility is epitomized by the Taliban's dynamiting of the two colossal rock-carved statues of the Buddha at Bamyan in 2001.[50] The statues so lovingly described by Xuanzang are now a mass of fragments that scholars and conservators are struggling to reassemble. The Taliban committed more than a savage act of vandalism; they committed a deliberate policy of rewriting their own history. The Taliban aimed for a cultural amnesia to remove the distressing fact that most Muslims of Central Asia today are descendants of people who were once Buddhists, compliments of the tolerant Kushan emperors who came from the Eurasian steppes. Even so, the commercial world of the Silk Road long prospered, and the new world religion Buddhism still endures, even after the Kushans have been long forgotten.

8

The Parthians, Nomadic Foes of Imperial Rome

In the failing light of June 3, 53 BC, Marcus Licinius Crassus, proconsul of Rome, realized that he had lost the battle.[1] Parthian horse archers surrounded his legionaries, who had closed ranks into a defensive square to await an opportunity to charge the mounted foe when the Parthians exhausted their supply of arrows. Their chance never came. Surena, the Parthian commander, had improvised a train of camels to keep his archers supplied. The Parthians, perhaps twenty thousand strong, were significantly fewer than the Romans, but they enjoyed decisive mobility on the rolling countryside to the northeast of Carrhae (today Harran) in Mesopotamia. Crassus had erred in departing from the main road, advancing across a swollen river late in the day. Centurions and legionaries fell out for a late lunch, but then Crassus ordered them back into formation to press on. The proconsul had received reports that the enemy were nearby. The hungry, thirsty legions blundered into a favorite ruse of encirclement used by nomadic horsemen. Crassus's cavalry was driven off in confusion, and his own son Publius fell in the retreat. The Roman legionaries doggedly stood their ground while their tormentors rained arrows on them. Toward evening, Crassus ordered a retreat to Carrhae that turned into a rout as the

Romans rushed to the safety of the city. The next morning, Crassus organized a breakout in three columns. Only the column under Gaius Cassius Longinus, a future assassin of Julius Caesar, reached the bridge at Zeugma over the Euphrates, and thus safety. Crassus and the other two columns were forced to surrender. Surena ordered Crassus beheaded, and the head was sent to Ctesiphon to serve as a prop as Pentheus's head in Euripides's *Bacchae*, to the amusement of his master, the king Orodes. Out of an army of forty-five thousand, twenty thousand Romans fell in battle; another ten thousand, along with their legionary eagles, were captured. The magnitude of the Parthian victory shocked Rome. Crassus failed in logistics and reconnaissance, and so deserves the blame for the defeat. But he, like many Romans, held the Parthians in contempt as effete and cowardly barbarians. The Parthians had proved otherwise, and they changed the course of Roman history. The death of Crassus left the two surviving triumvirs, Julius Caesar and Pompey the Great, as rivals destined to clash in a civil war that destroyed the Roman Republic.

The Arsacid kings of Parthia were descendants of Iranian-speaking nomads who had dwelled immediately east of the Caspian Sea.[2] Their tribe, originally called the Parni, had been members of the Scythian confederacy of the Dahae. In 247–246 BC, the princely brothers Arsaces and Tiridates seized the satrapy of Parthia from the Seleucid kings, the successors to Alexander the Great's Asian domains. The satrapy comprised the lands between the low mountain range of the Kopet Dag and the middle Oxus valley, on the border of Iran and Turkmenistan today.[3] The principal settlement, Nisa, remained the ancestral Parthian capital and royal cemetery for the next five centuries. From their new home, the princes and their followers took the new ethnic name of Parthians.

Within fifty years, four able Arsacid kings wrested from the Seleucid kings Iran and Mesopotamia, and so fell heir to the Achaemenid monarchy of Persia. In the summer of 139 BC, Mithridates I (171–138 BC) decisively defeated and captured the Seleucid king Demetrius II Nicator.[4] Mithridates occupied Media, Persia, and Babylonia—the heartland of the Achaemenid Empire—and assumed the title King of Kings.[5] Demetrius Nicator, ever irrepressible, soon won many friends at the Parthian court. At age fourteen, Demetrius had regained his throne from a usurper, and now the young king charmed his captors Mithridates and then his son and successor Phraates II. Demetrius was married to Rhodogune, a daughter of Mithridates, who overlooked the inconvenient condition that Demetrius was already married to a Ptolemaic wife. Twice Demetrius effected his escape in ingenious disguises; each time he was detected and returned to a gilded captivity, and his Parthian wife.[6] After just over ten years of captivity, Phraates released Demetrius to incite civil war in the Seleucid Empire, because Demetrius's brother Antiochus VII Sidetes had raised a large field army of Greek mercenaries and overrun Babylonia and Media.[7] In the spring of 129 BC, Phraates ambushed Antiochus and his royal bodyguard outside of Ecbatana (today Hamadan). Antiochus committed suicide; his Greek mercenaries offered their services to Phraates. Phraates succeeded beyond all expectation. By his unexpected victory, Phraates not only ended future Seleucid threats, but he also confirmed Parthian rule over Iran and Mesopotamia. The Upper Euphrates henceforth marked the western boundary of the Parthian Empire. Meanwhile, the ever-colorful Demetrius returned to his capital and plunged what was left of the Seleucid Empire into civil war.[8] As for the jilted Rhodogune, she lived on in legend as a valiant warrior princess neglected by her cad of a husband. She captured the imagination of French dramatists and painters in the seventeenth century. She is depicted on the canvas in the company of Cleopatra, both of whom shared the fate of marrying foreign husbands too ambitious for their abilities.[9] Pierre Corneille, a master of turning Classical legend into French drama, composed the tragicomedy *Rodogune* to the delight of the court of Louis XIV.[10] Unfortunately for Phraates, he did not long enjoy his victory. He fell fighting new invaders from the east, the Iranian Sacae, driven from their Sogdian homeland by the Tocharian-speaking Yuezhi. Antiochus's Greek mercenaries betrayed their new paymaster at the critical moment in the battle, and defected to the Sacae.[11] Fortunately for Phraates's successors, the Sacae turned southeast into the Helmand valley, and then crossed into India.

Mithridates II (124–87 BC), a cousin of Phraates II, transformed the Parthian kingdom into an empire. He adapted Seleucid and Achaemenid bureaucratic practices to tax a far greater state than any of his predecessors had ruled. The wealth of his empire lay in the cities of the Fertile Crescent stretching from the Red Sea to the Eastern Mediterranean, the cradle of Eurasian urban civilization.[12] Great Greek and Aramaic merchant families at Babylon controlled the banking and commerce of the Near East. Babylonia was the most densely populated region of the Near East outside of Egypt. The land was crisscrossed by an irrigation system that each year yielded windfall harvests of cereals, fruits, and vegetables.[13] Mithridates also controlled the central section of the Silk Road, and so he taxed caravans traveling between Palmyra and Maracanda (Samarkand) as they passed through his realm.[14] The route was both well-known and without an alternative. The Greek geographer Isidore of Charax a generation later described meticulously the distances between stations, water sources, and markets along the route.[15] Mithridates thus forged a bureaucratic empire that provided the revenues to hire horse archers from among nomadic allies on the central Eurasian steppes, and to reward a landed Parthian warrior caste that furnished heavy cavalry (*cataphracti*) under the terms of feudal arrangements.

Foremost, Mithridates, as a nomadic conqueror, needed legitimacy for his pretenses to being the newest King of Kings in the Near East. To this end, he took two measures, namely creating an ideology to exalt his kingship, and building a new capital to serve as the theater for the ceremonies of this ideology. Parthian silver coins, drachmae, provide our best guide as to how Mithridates shifted his stance from a nomadic warrior king to the Great King. On their silver coins, drachmae, Arsaces, eponymous founder of the dynasty, and his immediate successors are depicted as clean-shaven princes of the steppes clad in the bashlyk, a soft felt cap with flaps designed to protect the head from the extremes of temperature on the Eurasian steppes.[16] Mithridates presented a new portrait; he sports a long, neatly groomed beard, the mark of virility since the first conqueror Sargon of Akkad. Mithridates, on his earliest coins, wears the pearl diadem popularized by Alexander the Great and adopted by Hellenistic monarchs.[17] Then, on later coins, he exchanges the diadem for a tall, bejeweled tiara of the Great King of Persia. He is shown as clothed in silk ceremonial robes sewed with pearls and jewels.[18] On the reverse of his coins, Mithridates retains the conventional figure of his ancestor Arsaces, clad as a steppe warrior with bow and arrow, but henceforth, Arasces is enthroned in the fashion of a Near Eastern monarch rather than seated on the omphalos.[19] The Arsacid kings had adapted this reverse type from the Seleucid kings, devotees of Apollo, who had depicted on their coins the god as an archer seated on the omphalos, the stone at Delphi, representing the navel of the world. Engravers, trained in the Greek artistic tradition, cleverly refashioned a divine scene into a royal one. In keeping with their conceit as philhellenes, Parthian kings used Greek for their coin inscription. With Mithridates II, the coins proclaim each Arsacid ruler King of Kings.

A weathered rock relief, perhaps commissioned by Mithridates's son, survives at Behistun, which is on the western edge of the Iranian plateau, east of the Zagros Mountains, near the modern Iranian city of Kermanshah.[20] The limestone cliffs overlook the royal road from Ecbatana to Babylon so that any visitor could not fail to see the monumental reliefs carved on the cliffs. On his relief, Mithridates is attired in his new regalia, and accompanied with four loyal governors; the Greek inscription is mostly lost. The relief is but a modest version of the nearby awesome, trilingual inscription of Darius I, who in his relief receives twelve subservient rebel monarchs and lists his deeds. Even so, the casual visitor was expected to associate the two monarchs as the righteous King of Kings.

Like any ruler of nomadic origin, Mithridates appreciated the silk and exotic gifts that enhanced his prestige in the eyes of his subjects, and provided rewards to loyal Parthian nobles and vassal princes. At some date soon after 115 BC, the Chinese historian Ban Gu reports that a Parthian king, undoubtedly Mithridates, welcomed envoys of the emperor Wudi with an escort of twenty thousand horsemen, and then feted the envoys at his capital.[21] In return for the costly silks of China, Mithridates sent the envoys home loaded with gifts, including ostrich eggs, and accompanied by magicians, most likely Zoroastrian priests. Arsacid kings prized Chinese silk, rubies and emeralds of southern India, and pearls harvested from the Red Sea. All were necessary for the ceremonial costumes and display projecting the power of the Parthian monarch at his new capital, Ctesiphon. For Mithridates, just like Kublai Khan twelve centuries later, required a great city to awe his new subjects. Hence, Parthian Ctesiphon and Mongol Shangdu, better known as Coleridge's Xanadu, served the same purpose.

Mithridates chose to build his new capital at Ctesiphon, today twenty miles southeast of Baghdad. The city occupied an island and its opposite east bank in a sharp bend of the Tigris River, and it was directly across from the Greek city Seleucia ad Tigrim.[22] Mithridates likely never considered alternatives that were ruled by vassal princes: Persepolis, the Achaemenid ritual capital; Susa, the Persian administrative capital; or Charax, the leading port on the Persian Gulf. The Arsacid kings held their winter court at the palace in Ctesiphon, where they received foreign delegations. Successive Parthian kings and Persian shahs expanded and beautified the city, building additional palaces, a vast park housing caged lions and elephants, and a wide processional avenue that ended at a grandiose audience hall.[23] By the mid-fourth century AD, the city, its suburbs, and Seleucia had merged into a sprawling metropolitan center twice the area of imperial Rome. The markets of the Greek city Seleucia supplied the daily needs of the residents of the Twin Cities that might have peaked at over one million. The cosmopolitan city thrived and was graced with royal architecture that fused Hellenic and Near Eastern traditions. Merchants and craftsmen from across Eurasia flocked to the city. Scholars, religious thinkers, and philosophers found an exciting intellectual life in a city that was home to Zoroastrians, Christians, Jews, Manichees, Buddhists, and worshippers of the ancestral gods of many peoples.

Unfortunately, nothing of the Parthian city survives aboveground because the Sassanid shahs remodeled and built over the Parthian city between the third and seventh centuries AD. Yet the ruins of the Sassanid audience hall, dubbed in Arabic Tāq Kasrā, and later Persian Medieval accounts give us a glimpse of how envoys must have been awed as they made their way to the throne room of a Parthian king.[24] In the sixth century, envoys would have traveled down wide colonnaded boulevards, passing vast parks stocked with wild animals. Guards in ceremonial silver- or gold-plated armor lined the final approaches to the audience hall. Once inside, the envoys saw a vast rectangular hall supported by monumental baroque colonnades. The notables of court stood in ranks, arranged by their social rank and identified by their distinct robes and headdress. At the far end, under a great vaulted ceiling reaching 110 feet (30 meters), stood the shah's golden throne on a raised platform. At a lower level, to the right, behind, and to the left of the shah's throne, were lesser, empty ones representing the emperors of China, the Roman emperor, and the Hephthalites (the successors to the Kushans). Sassanid shahs were masters of diplomatic ceremony so that they undoubtedly articulated and innovated on earlier Parthian royal rituals. They upheld an ideology based on their Persian heritage and the Zoroastrian faith, whereas Parthian kings tolerated all faiths and styled themselves as patrons of Greek culture and cities. Even though only brief descriptions of the Parthian palace have survived, Mithridates and his heirs employed comparable rituals to promote their ideology as heirs of both the Persian Great King and Alexander the Great. Even more significant, Mithridates made Ctesiphon the imperial center of the Near East for the next seven centuries. Yet in constructing Ctesiphon, Mithridates unwittingly made his empire vulnerable to attack. At the end of his reign, Mithridates failed to perceive the danger posed by the Roman Republic. In 92 BC, his envoys abased themselves in supplication before L. Cornelius Sulla, the Roman governor of Cilicia (today southeastern Turkey). The proud Sulla, seated atop his tribunal, bestowed as a favor to Mithridates the friendship of the Senate and Roman people. Mithridates was outraged and ordered the envoys severely punished. The incident was the opening of a strategic clash between Parthia and Rome.

The later Parthian kings found their empire flanked by two dangerous rivals: Kushans to the east, and the Roman Republic to the west. Rome proved the deadlier foe. Parthian cavalry twice thwarted Roman invasions. At Carrhae, Parthian cavalry annihilated Crassus's legions; in 36 BC, they repelled an invasion by Mark Antony.[25] Once Augustus founded the Roman Empire, the balance of power shifted decisively in Rome's favor. Augustus transformed

the legions of the Republic into a professional imperial army un-
equaled on the battlefield and possessing superb engineering and
logistics. Augustus also hit upon a winning diplomacy against the
Arsacid king and thereby at minimal cost secured his eastern frontier on the Upper Euphrates River. Augustus avenged the defeat of
Crassus, at least to the satisfaction of his poets, and restored Roman
honor thirty-three years later, in 20 BC. He threatened the then
reigning Parthian king, Phraates IV, with an invasion if Phraates
refused to return the legionary standards and prisoners of Crassus's
army.[26] The imperial army would have easily marched down the
Euphrates and sacked the Twin Cities of Ctesiphon and Seleucia
ad Tigrim. Phraates folded. He could not possibly resist the imperial army under M. Vipsanius Agrippa, Rome's most talented commander and the emperor's devoted comrade in arms. Furthermore,
over the past thirty years, the Romans had mastered the art of fighting against Parthian horse archers.[27] The aged survivors of Crassus's
army returned home from a dreary exile on the edge of the Karakum Desert, where they had been posted to mount guard against
nomadic tribesmen. The legionary eagles were eventually housed
in a massive Temple of Mars Ultor (the Avenger) in the new forum
of Augustus. Poets, historians, and artists went to great lengths to
hail a diplomatic settlement as a victory. Augustus knew better.[28]
He had exploited Phraates's difficulties with rivals to his throne to
extort a symbolic concession. In return, Augustus sent a delegation
of senators who hailed Phraates as a friend of the Roman people.
They also conveyed many exotic gifts, foremost a renowned courtesan (hetaira), Musa Urania. The heavenly Musa (as Augustus had
anticipated) so dazzled Phraates with her charms and wit that the
smitten king made her his principal wife and consort.[29] She soon
bore Phraates a son. The king recognized his son, Phraates V, as his
heir in preference to his other sons who had been handed over as
hostages to Augustus. Musa intrigued incessantly. In 2 BC, she had
her husband poisoned and assumed the regency for her adolescent
son.[30] She wielded extraordinary power, for she is the only Parthian
queen whose portrait appears on coins. The Chinese historian Fan
Ye in the Hou Hanshu reports this as a curious fact based on travelers'
reports.[31] Mother and son botched a war in Armenia and were over-

thrown by the nobility, who then warred among themselves over the succession for the next thirty years.[32]

The emperor Augustus had discovered the Parthians' strategic weaknesses, which he could exploit to Rome's advantage. No Arsacid king could afford to risk his capital or Babylonia. Although the Parthians ruled a Near Eastern Empire, they remained children of the Eurasian steppes, and so prone to war over the choice of kings based on the principles of lateral succession. A Roman imperial army threatening to invade Babylonia and to incite civil war among family rivals could quickly compel any Arsacid king to negotiate. But the principles of lateral succession complicated the family politics of the Arsacid house. Each Arsacid king had to provide lesser realms for his brothers, nephews, or cousins. Armenia, vital to the defense of the Roman East, became the cockpit of wars because Arsacid kings sought to place their younger kinsmen on the Armenian throne.[33] Rome insisted that any king of Armenia owed his crown to the Roman people ever since the imperator Pompey the Great had restored King Tigranes the Great to his throne in 66 BC.[34] The proud Armenian nobles—nakharars, to use their Medieval name—shared with their Parthian counterparts the same martial ethos, passion for hunting, and keen sense of personal honor.[35] Most of them preferred an Arsacid prince as their king over any candidate dispatched from Rome, who aped the arrogant manners and dress of a Roman senator. Inevitably, Rome and Parthia clashed in seven major wars. Each time, the imperial legions eventually triumphed over the Parthian cavalry, and three times Roman legions sacked the Parthian capital of Ctesiphon.

Throughout this strategic rivalry, neither the Roman emperor (with the exception of Trajan) nor Parthian king aimed to destroy the other's empire, but rather they contested control over the strategic routes across Armenia and the grasslands of northern Mesopotamia between the Upper Euphrates and Tigris Rivers, known today by its Arabic name, al-Jazirah.[36] From Rome's perspective, the cities and irrigated fields of Mesopotamia could support Roman provincial administrations and legions. The high plateau of Armenia was best left to a vassal king, but any king acceptable to Rome was unpopular with his nobility. For the Arsacid king, his strategic task was far easier. In Mesopotamia, the Parthian king easily won over Aramaic-speaking princes of the cities, who doubled as tribal rulers of the surrounding Bedouin tribes.

For two generations, no Arsacid king dared to challenge the settlement of Augustus. In 53, a charismatic king Vologases I ended a generation of civil war, and placed his younger brother Tiridates on the throne of Armenia. In the autumn of 54, the new emperor at Rome, Nero, sent as commander of an expeditionary force Gnaeus Domitius Corbulo with instructions to oust Tiridates from Armenia.[37] Corbulo, hailed the finest of imperial commanders by the senatorial historian Tacitus, brilliantly accomplished his mission, and so earned the jealousy of Nero.[38] This War of the Armenian Succession (54–66) ended in a sensible settlement whereby Tiridates ruled in Armenia, but received his crown from Rome.[39] Nero hosted Tiridates at a spectacular celebration that magnified the power of Rome. During the festivities, Tiridates quipped that never was so malevolent a monarch, Nero, served by so noble a general, Corbulo.[40] Tiridates returned to rule Armenia as a dutiful Roman client, whereas Corbulo was later forced to commit suicide on orders of Nero or face trumped-up charges of treason.

Both Nero and Vologases had avoided direct conflict, but the later Flavian emperors took measures to ensure Roman supremacy in any future war with Parthia. Rome henceforth stationed legions on the Upper Euphrates, and built across Asia Minor depots, bridges, and highways.[41] In 113 AD, another Armenian crisis erupted when the Parthian king Osroes I crowned his nephew king of Armenia in violation of the settlement of 66. Osroes calculated that his opportunistic action might result at most in another proxy war in Armenia.[42] Instead, in the next year, the emperor Trajan, the greatest of all warrior emperors, took the field at the head of an expeditionary army of over one hundred thousand. Osroes was stunned by the speed and scale of Trajan's invasion. In the next two years, Roman legions overran Armenia and Mesopotamia. In 116, Trajan deployed the logistics and strategy perfected in the Dacian Wars. Two Roman columns, marching down the Tigris and Euphrates, converged to storm and sack first Seleucia ad Tigrim, and then Ctesiphon.[43] Osroes fled east over the Zagros Mountains.

Trajan reached the shores of the Persian Gulf, where he navigated the waters and contemplated repeating Alexander's march to India. But the emperor, age sixty-two, was weary from a life of tough campaigning. He received alarming news when he put ashore.[44] The Parthian client prince of Adiabene in northern Mesopotamia had rebelled. More bad news soon followed.[45] The Jews of Cyprus, Egypt, and Cyrenaica revolted under an obscure figure, Loukas, who claimed to be the Messiah of the House of David.[46] Trajan returned north to deal with these threats, but he died suddenly at the sleepy town of Selinus on the southeastern shore of Asia Minor on August 19, 117. His cousin and heir Hadrian, to his credit, judged his abilities correctly. He could not manage major rebellions and a war of conquest at the same time. He withdrew Roman forces to the west of the Euphrates, and concentrated the legions against the rebels. Armenia was returned to a client king.[47] King Osroes, amazed by his good fortune, rallied the Parthians, expelled the pro-Roman Parthian king in Ctesiphon, and recaptured Babylonia and Mesopotamia.[48] From the start, Trajan pursued a strategy of overthrow, aiming to annex as provinces Armenia and Mesopotamia and to impose a compliant king on the Parthian throne ruling over Babylonia and Iran. It is doubtful that the Arsacid monarchy could have survived as a great power had Trajan lived to consolidate his victory.

In withdrawing from Trajan's conquests, Hadrian has been praised by modern scholars for his prudence in recognizing that the empire was overextended.[49] Yet he acted more out of expediency than strategic design. At the time, the move was extremely unpopular and precipitated a plot by four of Trajan's senior generals. Subsequent events would prove that Trajan was correct, and Hadrian was wrong, on the imperial boundary in the Near East. Roman security in the East required control of the highways across Mesopotamia between the upper Euphrates and the Tigris. This meant future wars with the Arsacid kings were inevitable.

In 161, another able Parthian king, Vologases IV, challenged Rome's right to appoint the king of Armenia, when he received news of the accession of two untested emperors, Marcus Aurelius and Lucius Verus. The war initially went in favor of Vologases, whose horse archers destroyed a Roman legion, and expelled from Armenia the king C. Julius Sohaemus, a polished Roman senator widely unpopular among his subjects.[50] Two years later, veteran Roman commanders coordinated offensives in Armenia and Mesopotamia that reversed the situation. Lucius Verus, the indolent adoptive brother and son-in-law of Marcus Aurelius, was dispatched from Rome to oversee these operations. Lucius Verus, however, never made it to the field, but rather lingered in Antioch, capital of Roman Syria and third largest city of the empire. Lucius Verus preferred the pleasures of the city and the charms of his mistress, the courtesan Panthea, to the neglect of his wife, his co-emperor's daughter. The most talented among the commanders, C. Avidius Cassius, repeated Trajan's march into Babylonia and sacked Seleucia and Ctesiphon.[51] His victorious soldiers returned to Rome infected with a plague which has sometimes been classified as the first pandemic, which came out of China and swept Eurasia.[52] Avidius Cassius gained top honors for winning this war, but he later erred in staging a revolt against Marcus Aurelius, and was forced to commit suicide.[53] In 169, Lucius Verus, to the relief of Marcus Aurelius, died from the plague.

For Vologases, this war was almost as disastrous as the one against Trajan. Rome annexed the region immediately east of the Euphrates, Osrhoene, and so controlled the strategic crossings across the Euphrates. The kings of Osrhoene and Armenia were permitted to keep their thrones as friends of Rome.[54] Less than a generation later, the emperor Septimius Severus, in two successive Parthian Wars waged between a major Roman civil war, extended the Roman province of Mesopotamia to the Upper Tigris River, stationed two legions in the province, founded Roman colonies, and built highways. In the second war, Septimius Severus invaded Babylonia, and sacked Ctesiphon for a third time in January 198.[55] Henceforth, the Arsacid king faced the strategic nightmare that, in any future clash with Rome, the legions could easily invade from bases in northern Mesopotamia and sack the Twin Cities, the financial hub of the Parthian Empire.

For two generations, Rome and the Parthians had clashed over the mastery of the Near East, and in 200, Rome had emerged as the victor. During this period, the Arsacid king was hard-pressed to meet the threat from Rome as well as another one from the Kushan emperor to the east. Wars over the succession prevented kings Osroes and Vologases V from countering Trajan or Septimius Severus. In 214, the emperor Caracalla, son of Septimius Severus, marched east in yet another Roman invasion during a civil war between Arsacid brothers.[56] This time, the emperor acted out of impulse rather than strategic reasons. Caracalla, savage in nature and prone to fits of rage, longed to emulate Alexander the Great by conquering the Parthian Empire. He even proposed to marry the daughter of Vologases VI, one of the Parthian contenders. For, after all, Alexander had married Persian princesses. Caracalla and his court took over two years to reach the front, because they were too busy playing tourists among the celebrated Greek sanctuaries and cities. In 216, Caracalla waged a limited offensive across the Tigris, and withdrew to winter at Carrhae. On April 8, 217, the emperor was ignominiously murdered while relieving himself in the bushes near Carrhae on orders of his Praetorian prefect Macrinus.[57] Macrinus was declared the new emperor, and concluded with Artabanus V, the victor of the civil war, a peace confirming the *status quo ante bellum*.

Even though the assassination of Caracalla cut short the Roman invasion, the mere threat of a fourth sack of Ctesiphon fatally compromised Artabanus V. Ardashir, the Sassanid king of Persis, was emboldened to rebel against his Parthian overlord.[58] In 224, Ardashir defeated and slew Artabanus V. Three years later, he entered Ctesiphon, where he was crowned in the Parthian palace as King of Kings of a new Persian or Sassanid Empire. The Sassanid shahs, under the banner of a militant Zoroastrian, proved far more deadly rivals of Rome, for they aimed to restore the empire of the Achaemenid kings of Persia. For the next four centuries, Imperial Rome and Sassanid Persia fought themselves to mutual exhaustion in their struggle for the mastery of the Middle East.

It is often pointed out that Rome ironically undermined a Parthian rival to the benefit of a far deadlier foe, the Sassanid Persians. Hence, in the nationalist hagiography of Iran today, the Parthians are dismissed as interlopers who were neither victorious nor pious

Zoroastrians. Yet, in contesting Roman advances into the Middle East, the Parthians defined the eastern limits of Roman imperial power. They thus proved worthy imperial rivals to Rome. Even more significantly, the Parthians defined, for the first time, the geo-politics of the Middle East that have dictated the course of strategic rivalries in this region down to the present day. The Arsacid king drew on the resources of Iran and the Central Eurasian steppes to oppose a far stronger power, Rome. Rome, however, was a West-ern power based in the Mediterranean world, and she could not impose her hegemony over the entire Middle East in the face of an effective Iranian power, the Parthians. Any power with its base outside the Middle East faces the same challenge. Each succeeding Western power has to come to terms with the regime in Iran, which sees its legacy as including the historic lands of Iraq, Afghanistan, and Transoxiana. In the sixteenth and seventeenth centuries, the Safavid shahs of Iran similarly checked the Middle Eastern ambi-tions of the Ottoman sultans of Constantinople, whose empire was based in the Balkans and Anatolia. Since the nineteenth century, first the British and then the Americans have had to reckon with Iran in any strategic policy. And so the Parthians, the offspring of Eurasian steppe nomads, have left their imprint on the world poli-tics of today.

9

Heirs of the Xiongnu: The Northern Wei

From his palace, Wencheng (452–465), emperor of the Northern Wei, directed one of the most stupendous masonry projects of Buddhism—comparable to the colossal statues of the Bamyan at the other end of the Silk Road. During his reign, sculptors completed five of the cave monasteries at Yungang, near his capital, Pingcheng (Datong), in northern China, and today a United Nations Education, Scientific and Cultural Organization (UNESCO) World Heritage Site.[1] The complex eventually stretched nearly one-half mile, comprising fifty-three cave monasteries and fifty-one thousand niches for statues of the Buddha. The artists combined the traditions of Gandhara with those of China and the steppes to cut out of the sandstone cliffs the most beautiful Buddhist sculpture of China—for Emperor Wencheng was a most pious Buddhist. He also proved an effective, if ruthless, monarch, for he had succeeded his grandfather Taiwu by surviving the gruesome politics of the Wei court that shocked his Confucian officials. Even so, Buddhist writers remembered Wencheng fondly for his patronage of the faith.[2] As he supervised the massive project honoring the Buddha, the emperor Wencheng could take comfort that his monumental celebration of the faith had won him the karma

that perhaps would enable him to achieve nirvana in his own lifetime. His Buddhist subjects would have no doubts that their emperor was a Bodhisattva worthy of their obedience and reverence.[3]
The emperor Wencheng, under his personal name Tuoba Jun, betrayed his nomadic origins. He was the direct descendant of Tuoba
Gui (386–409), who had united northern China and took the Chinese throne name Daowu of the Wei dynasty.[4] The emperors of
the Northern Wei descended from nomads of the Tuoba clan of
the Xianbei tribe, once pastoralists of Inner Mongolia. Nomadic
in origin, the Tuoba were not bound by Confucian ideals. They
readily adopted anything of practical use. Wencheng was the first
among his dynasty to embrace Buddhism, whose worshippers so
obviously prospered in trade because of their piety.

Wencheng's immediate ancestors had hardly been favorable to
the teachings of the Buddha. His grandfather, the emperor Taiwu,
had embraced the Daoist beliefs that were so popular among many
of his Chinese subjects. He was the first of four emperors to per-
secute Buddhists in China.[5] Taiwu outlawed Buddhism, closed
its temples, and arrested its monks on grounds of treason. Daoist
priests encouraged these measures, for they had long looked with
suspicion on the mendicant Buddhist monks as rivals for the piety
of the masses.[6] Their misgivings were shared by the Confucian
mandarins at the Wei court, who dismissed Buddhism as an exotic
foreign superstition inconsistent with virtue.

Sogdian and Tocharian merchants from the Western Regions
had carried Buddhism to Han China in the first century AD.[7] Eastern Han emperors recognized and respected Buddhism as a legal
faith even though many Confucian officials and scholars objected.
The emperor Ming (57–75), who relentlessly waged war against
the Xiongnu for control of the Western Regions, granted permission for the construction of the first Buddhist temple, the White
Temple, near his capital, Luoyang.[8] The faith, however, was long
confined to the foreign merchants resident in China. Between the
early first and early fourth centuries AD, wealthy merchant families in the cities of Transoxiana and the Tarim Basin reconciled
their ancestral gods and rituals as previous incarnations of the Bud-

dha, and considered success in trade as a merchant's dharma. They expressed their thanks by endowing monasteries (*vihana*), which provided hostels for travelers, so that pilgrims such as Xuanzang in the seventh century could find food and lodging on their way from the Jade Gate to the Khyber Pass. Sir Aurel Stein found the treasure trove of commercial documents in the rock-carved monasteries of Mogao, decorated with magnificent fresco murals, near Dunhuang, the first major stop for caravans laden with Chinese silks heading west from the Jade Gate.

At the same time, these merchants, who were conversant in many languages, commissioned translations of Buddhist scriptures from Sanskrit into vernacular languages. Surviving Buddhist texts dating between the third and eighth centuries are translations in two distinct Tocharian languages at the northeastern cities of Karasahr (Chinese Yanqi) and Turpan, and the western city of Kuchea.[9] At Khotan, along the southern caravan route, the translations are in Sogdian.[10] In the later second century, the first translators of the Buddhist scriptures from Sanskrit into Chinese were An Shigao, styled a Parthian prince and likely a Sogdian speaker, and the Tocharian-speaking Kushan scholars Lokaksema (Zhi Loujiachen) and his student Zhi Yao.[11] At the opening of the fifth century, a number of major schools were busily translating Buddhist scriptures into Chinese. At the same time, the Chinese Buddhist monk Faxian, whose travelogue is the earliest to come down to us, toured India for fifteen years seeking out Sanskrit manuscripts.[12]

The Chinese warlords who succeeded to the Han Empire, and then the barbarian nomadic conquerors who carved out their own states in North China, were despised by Confucian elites as untutored men of talent without virtue.[13] These tough warrior kings found most appealing the vision of Mahayana Buddhism that all who pursued their allotted fate piously in this life according to the law of dharma might achieve nirvana and the end of the cycle of reincarnation. Filial devotion so important to both nomadic peoples and Chinese could also be expressed in the Buddhist concept of karma. The emperor Wencheng was not the first such ruler during this era of warring states to embrace Buddhism, but he proved the most important. He presided over the rewriting of the religious landscape of northern China for the next century and a half. In just over a generation after his death, over nine thousand Buddhist monasteries staffed by one hundred fifty thousand monks are reported in northern China.[14] In response to the rising popularity of Buddhism, Daoists devised new rituals to lure converts back.[15] They also presented their tenets of the way (*dao*) and detachment as the proper Chinese expressions of Buddhist dharma and nirvana. Despite three later persecutions, Buddhism, reconciled with traditional Chinese ancestor worship, was here to stay in China. At the same time, Buddhism gained many adherents among the nomadic tribes of the eastern Eurasian steppes who fought or allied with the later Northern Wei emperors.

The first Northern Wei emperors also remained faithful to their ancestral speech and mores, and so completed the process of transforming the society of Northern China since the late second century AD. Soon after defeating the Northern Xiongnu, Han emperors had steadily granted power to regional Chinese warlords who kept order along the Great Wall.[16] No charismatic chanyu emerged to reunite the nomadic tribes under his hereditary rule. Councils of the leading men, comparable to the later Mongol *kurultai*, governed most tribes, and they elected leaders only in time of war. Small-scale raiding became a livelihood rather than an act of policy by a chanyu to extort better treaty terms from the Han court.[17] With so many individual leaders to placate, the Han emperor soon found it more expensive to pay off many rulers rather than one powerful one. Later Han emperors thus turned to veteran Chinese governors, versed in frontier warfare, to check the habitual raiders who threatened to devastate and depopulate the lands south of the Great Wall. None of these nomadic invaders posed an existential threat, but instead, they contributed significantly to the rising fiscal demands by the Han court.[18] In 184, three Daoist brothers stirred the peasants in Central China to revolt against the oppressive taxes and labor services demanded by the Han emperor Ling. This Rebellion of the Yellow Turbans, so named because rebels sported yellow scarves, collapsed in the next year, but it sparked a spate of revolts and protests for the next twenty years.[19] Frontier warlords raised private armies and engaged nomadic tribal allies to put down Chi-

nese rebels. It was only a matter of time when an ambitious warlord
would turn his army against the Han emperor. In 220, the warlord
Cao Pi compelled the last Han emperor to abdicate and declared
himself the emperor Zihuan of the Wei dynasty.[20] The new emperor Zihuan was immediately challenged by rival warlords in the
south who carved out their own regional empires of the Shu Han
and Eastern Wu dynasties. The turbulent era is immortalized in the
Romance of the Three Kingdoms, the earliest of the four Chinese prose
masterpieces. For the next sixty years (220–280), the Three Kingdoms of Wei, Shu, and Wu battled it out for supremacy.[21] These
civil wars during this era of the Three Kingdoms were contemporary with those waged by the three regional states of the Roman
Empire.[22] Rome, however, quickly regained unity under the soldier emperor Aurelian in 274; China failed to achieve lasting unity
for the next three centuries despite a valiant effort by Sima Yan
(266–290), who, under the imperial name Wu, battled to restore
the grandeur and unity of Han China.[23]

   In 311, the southern Xiongnu under She Le Chanyu renounced
their allegiance to the Jin emperor Sima Chi (306–311) and audaciously sacked the former Han capital, Luoyang. The Xiongnu
burned the imperial palaces to the ground, and captured and executed the emperor himself.[24] The shock reverberated across East
Asia with the same horrified disbelief felt about the sack of Rome
by the Goths a century later.[25] A Sogdian merchant, in an unde-
livered letter found by Sir Aurel Stein, lamented the event to his
partners in Samarkand and reported that he had received no reports from his agents in Luoyang in the three years since the sack.
In his own language, the Sogdian merchant called the barbarians
Huna, most likely his generic name for nomads, but it might have
also rendered the spoken Chinese pronunciation of Xiongnu at the
time.[26] Five years later, the Xiongnu sacked the other Han capital
Chang'an. Meanwhile, the eastern Jin emperors Sima Rui (318–
323) and Sima Yan (325–342) relocated the capital south, twice,
and centered their lesser state on the rich lands of southern China.[27]

   During the two centuries following the sack of Luoyang, two
significant changes took place that have defined China ever since.
First, many Han Chinese relocated from the Yellow River (Huang

He),[28] the cradle of Chinese civilization, to the southern lands of the Yangtze rich in rice paddies and silk farms. They arrived in such numbers that they transformed the linguistic and ethnic map of southern China, for they assimilated or expelled many of the indigenous peoples. These southerners came to regard themselves as the true Han Chinese, and by the tenth century, they comprised the majority of Chinese speakers. Their emperors of the Jin dynasty claimed the Mandate of Heaven and employed Confucian professional bureaucrats chosen by merit. Simultaneously, later Chinese historians lamented the arrival of the so-called Five Barbarians (Wu Hu) into northern and western China. Foremost were nomadic tribes of Xianbei or Xiongnu origin who settled in the valley of the Yellow River and northeastern regions known as the Sixteen Prefectures. Tribal leaders who had often served under Chinese warlords were now emboldened to seize power in their own name and to carve out kingdoms under Chinese-sounding dynastic names. These rulers quickly adopted Chinese methods of government, but they and their tribesmen turned themselves into a military caste, intermarrying with their Chinese counterparts. Many of these states proved short-lived, because the successors of the founder often failed to reconcile the competing demands of their tribal warriors with the needs of their Chinese officials and subjects.[29] The most successful among the newcomers were the Xianbei, who had once been vassals of the Xiongnu. In large part, they owed their success to the lessons they learned from their predecessors, who had devised an imperial order based on Chinese administration, cities, and agriculture, but defended by a shield of nomadic horse archers.[30] Tuoba Gui (386–409) made his Tuoba clan the masters of the Xianbei, and then united most of northern China for the next one hundred fifty years, thereby ending this era of warring states later dubbed the Sixteen Kingdoms.[31] Under the Chinese throne name Daowu, Tuoba Gui proclaimed his dynasty to be the new Wei family, and so he claimed the legacy of the Chinese Wei emperors who had ruled so successfully over the northern half of the Han Empire in the third century.

During the fourth and fifth centuries, a distinct provincial Chinese society emerged that straddled both sides of the Great Wall.

The newcomers, especially the Northern Wei, changed their Chinese hosts in many ways. For example, the upper classes preferred ayran, the mix of yogurt, water, and salt, over proper Chinese tea. Riding, archery, and proficiency in arms were expected of every ruler, even those who mastered calligraphy and the Confucian classics.[32] The Chinese emperors of the Sui and Tang dynasties who would reunite China were themselves products of this martial provincial society. The newcomers retained the custom of steppes whereby women often fought alongside men.[33] Hence, in the lands of the Northern Wei arose the legend of the first woman warrior of China, Hua Mulan.[34] She took the place of her aged father and, disguised as a man, served in the army for twelve years and attained high rank. Upon discharge, she returned home and resumed her female identity, to the later shock of her comrades when they discovered that they had served under a woman. Hua Mulan, a most un-Chinese heroine, has been celebrated in ballads, romances, dramas, films, and TV series to this day.

Ironically, the Northern Wei emperors confronted new nomadic foes in Mongolia who shared a distant descent from the Xiongnu and whose monarchs were the first to use the title khan or kaghan. Rouran khans, whose ethnic origins and language are still disputed, were the first since Modu Chanyu to unite all the tribes on the eastern Eurasian steppes.[35] The ethnic name Rouran was of obscure origin; Chinese chroniclers disparagingly bestowed it on these nomadic foes to designate them as wanderers or servants of the Wei emperor.[36] When the Xianbei expanded into Northern China in the early fourth century, the Rouran tribes followed, settling on the steppes of Inner Mongolia, and in the Ordos bend and upper valley of the Yellow River. In the second and third quarters of the fourth century, a succession of able rulers had slowly united sundry tribes into a loose confederation that straddled both sides of the Great Wall. Their success came to the attention of the new Northern Wei emperor Tuoba Gui, or under his Chinese imperial name, Daowu, because he saw these same regions as the vital recruiting grounds for his own cavalry. In 391, civil war erupted between the two brothers Heduohan, ruling the western Rouran tribes (who was perceived as the greater threat by Tuoba Gui), and

Pihouba, overlord of the eastern tribes.[37] In 394, the Wei army intervened to tip the balance in favor of Pihouba, but the eventual
victor, Yujiulü Shelun, son of Heduohan, rallied the western tribes
and avenged his father by slaying his uncle Pihouba, his cousins,
and their supporters.[38] Then he and his followers had to flee across
the Gobi Desert to escape retaliation from a second Wei army in
399. The Wei emperor henceforth was master of the strategic borderlands on both sides of the Great Wall, but he had, just like the
first Chinese emperor Qin Shi Huang, compelled the nomads on
the eastern steppes to organize. Once on the Mongolian steppes,
Shelun relentlessly waged war to rebuild the second great nomadic
confederation.[39] He, just like Modu Chanyu, organized his diverse
warriors in units based on a decimal system and imposed strict discipline.[40] In 402, he assumed the title Khan of the Rouran. Shelun
and his successors subjected nomadic peoples who spoke diverse
languages, including Altaic dialects related to modern Mongolian
and Turkish, and eastern Iranian languages. Rouran power centered on the Orkhon valley in Mongolia, and hence they too are
claimed as progenitors of the modern Mongol nation. The Rouran
khans steadily extended their sway west to Lake Balkhash and the
Ili River. Yet this confederacy proved far weaker than the Xiongnu
confederacy of Modu Chanyu. The Rouran khan never imposed
effective authority over his vassal tribes because he faced Northern Wei emperors well versed in the same nomadic warfare. The
Rouran khans could never mount serious attacks against China and
so extort treaty terms from the Wei court as the Xiongnu had done.
Also, by their relentless drive to dominate the steppes as far as the
Altai Mountains, the Rouran khans drove Iranian-speaking tribes
such as the Chionites and Hephthalites into Transoxiana and the
Sassanid Empire of Persia. These migrations disrupted commerce
along the Silk Road.[41] Without the revenues from tribute or trade,
the Rouran khan could not sustain an administration comparable
to that of the Xiongnu or reward the loyalty of his subordinates
and warriors with Chinese silk, or feed his people with Chinese
produce.[42] The khans were too often beholden to their council or
kurultai. The Rouran khans had no choice but to encourage their

vassals to raid for a livelihood rather than out of a strategic policy. Inevitably, the Wei emperors would take action.

During the fifth century, the Northern Wei emperors waged a war against their distant nomadic kinsmen as ruthlessly as the Han emperors had against the Xiongnu.[43] The Northern Wei emperors were thus as much heirs to the Han emperors as they were to the Xiongnu chanyu. Tuoba Gui was no less determined than the Han emperor Wudi to crush the nomadic foe. Tuoba Gui sternly rebuked his Confucian ministers whenever they urged caution, favoring the virtue of peace over war with its high costs.[44] The emperor lectured them bluntly on how he knew how to wage war against nomads. Given the pattern of seasonal migrations, the Rouran were weakest in the early spring. During the winter, the Rouran moved to their southern pastures close to the Chinese frontier. Swift-moving, veteran imperial cavalry of horse archers could surprise Rouran encampments while the nomads were still enduring the long fasting of winter. Imperial cavalry could drive off horses and livestock, capture women and children, and scatter the warriors, who faced starvation on the steppes. Repeatedly Wei generals conducted such attacks. In 429, the Wei emperor Taiwu, better known by his personal name Tuoba Tao, planned a campaign that netted reportedly three hundred thousand prisoners and millions of horses and livestock.[45] Many captives were resettled along the northern frontiers as military colonists.

As long as Wei emperors maintained their frontier army and valued their ancestors' martial skill, they had the upper hand against the Rouran. Besides horse archers, the Wei emperors could field Chinese infantry armed with pikes and crossbows, engineers, and supply trains that followed the strike forces of light cavalry.[46] Their Chinese peasants raised the produce to sustain these armies; their Chinese craftsmen manufactured the arms and armor. At the same time, the Wei emperors warred against rivals in China, and expanded their domains from the frontiers of Korea west to the Jade Gate and Dunhuang at the western end of Gansu corridor.[47] Success in warfare gained the Wei emperors legitimacy in the eyes of their Chinese subjects and security for the caravans arriving from the west on the Silk Road. They practiced war most effectively; in the words of the elder Marcus Porcius Cato, "war sustained itself" (*bellum se ipsum alet*).[48]

The emperor Xiaowen (471–499), the grandson of Wencheng, renounced his family's military traditions and name, changing his personal name from Tuoba Hong to Yuan Hong.[49] In so doing, he identified himself with the "originators" (*yuan*), the first celestial emperors to rule with the Mandate of Heaven. Kublai Khan too would adopt the same impeccably Chinese name, but Kublai Khan never committed the fatal blunder of Xiaowen of renouncing his nomadic identity and skill in war. Xiaowen ascended the throne at age thirteen under the regency of his step-grandmother, the dowager empress Feng, who was the favored consort of his grandfather, Wencheng.[50] Chinese by birth, the dowager empress dominated palace politics through her network of clients: imperial eunuchs, mandarin officials, and spies. She had wielded influence at the court of the father of Xiaowen, the emperor Xianwen (465–471), who had also ascended the throne as a minor of eleven years of age. In contrast to imperial custom, Feng refused to join her deceased husband Wencheng by suicide, and instead advised her stepson, intrigued against his regent, and bribed officials. She was quite successful in selecting able generals who scored victories over rival warring states. To his credit, the young emperor Xianwen took seriously the Confucian virtues of statecraft. He cracked down on corruption, but in so doing, he clashed with his stepmother Feng. He also objected to her lover, a lowly official, whose brother was caught up in an ugly scandal at court.[51] Weary of the incessant scheming at court, Xianwen abdicated in favor of his minor son Xiaowen and retired to study philosophy. The dowager empress Feng promptly asserted control over her step-grandson Xiaowen, and five years later reportedly arranged for the poisoning of her annoying, bookish stepson.[52] Meanwhile, Xiaowen was given a proper Chinese education under the guidance of the dowager empress. He matured into an avid Buddhist and thoroughly Chinese ruler. He imposed a policy of assimilation, ordering intermarriage between his Xianbei and Chinese subjects, all of whom must dress in proper Chinese dress, assume Chinese names, and speak Chinese.[53] He removed his palace from the frontier city of Pingcheng (today Datong) on the border of Inner Mongolia to the Luoyang, the former Han capital, where he could rule as a proper Chinese emperor served by Confucian officials.[54] He even instituted land reform along the lines of the enigmatic emperor Wang Mang, whereby the imperial government confiscated private property and allotted the use of land according to each peasant family's needs. Inevitably, the proud Xianbei generals and warriors objected vociferously to these changes, and twice they plotted to assassinate the emperor. Even so, the successors of Xiaowen remained at Luoyang and ruled as Chinese emperors. In the generation after Xiaowen's death, the Wei Empire was rocked by revolts of both the Xianbei military caste and Chinese peasants. The Xianbei military elite resented their loss of rank, hated assimilation, and demanded a warrior emperor who would lead them to victory over the Rouran. Chinese peasants were outraged over corrupt officials who profited from land reform and demanded high taxes and labor services. In 535, a civil war over the succession resulted in the Wei Empire splitting into two warring lesser states. The senior line of eastern Wei emperors at Luoyang ended in 550, that of the western dynasty seven years later.[55]

The reign of Xiaowen also marked a turning point in the relations between the increasingly Sinified Wei emperors at Luoyang and the Rouran khans. They halted the expensive preemptive strikes against the Rouran tribes across the Gobi Desert. For such campaigns favored generals and warlords, both Xianbei and Chinese, on the northern frontier. Instead, Xiaowen and his successors deferred to their Confucian ministers, who favored the seemingly less costly and morally far more virtuous policy of the later Han emperors. They directed the gifts of the "Five Baits" to lesser khans who were encouraged to rebel against the Rouran khan.[56] Fifteen years after the demise of the Eastern Wei dynasty in 535, this policy succeeded far beyond expectations. Rouran vassals, the Gök Turks, overthrew their masters and forged the third great empire on the eastern steppes—to the dismay of all Chinese rulers, northern and southern.[57] In response to this new threat, in 581, the Chinese official Yang Jian at the court of Chang'an overthrew the then reigning Zhou emperor, a scion of a Wei military family. Yang Jian declared himself the emperor Wen of the Sui dynasty, and went on to reunite all of China.[58] The emperor Wen, a devout Buddhist and able general, was himself the product of the military aristocracy of the Northern Wei, for only rulers skilled in the warfare of the steppes could impose unity and keep the new nomadic foe at bay.

The Northern Wei are seldom recognized for their achievements, and they are too easily dismissed as yet one more foreign dynasty in the kaleidoscope of ephemeral kingdoms during the 360 years between the imperial greatness of the Han, and the even greater grandeur of the Sui and Tang dynasties. Yet these heirs of the Xiongnu, the Northern Wei emperors, contributed decisively to the making of the northern Chinese society of today. They wrote the Buddhist religious landscape of stupas and monasteries that persists to this day. During the first century of their rule, they brought peace and prosperity to their diverse subjects, and so they amassed the wealth that enabled emperor Wencheng to commission the statues and cave monasteries of Yangyang, still considered masterpieces of Buddhist art in China. Foremost, for a century, they governed effectively by balancing the interests of their military caste and warriors of the steppes with those of their Chinese subjects. This was no small achievement, and an important lesson for Kublai Khan, one of the greatest nomadic conquerors who would rule all China. These pragmatic rulers, scions of the Eurasian steppes, thus stand as worthy heirs to the imperial legacy of the Xiongnu.

In confronting the second nomadic confederacy of the Rouran khans, the northern Wei emperors achieved considerable success with far less resources than the Han emperors. The Wei emperors never controlled the rich southern lands of the Yangtze basin, the vital tax base of any Chinese regime. They also never exercised any authority over the caravan cities of the Western Regions beyond the Jade Gate. They instead based their power on invincible horse archers furnished by the nomadic tribes just north of the Great Wall, whom Chinese chroniclers disparagingly called Inner Barbarians. For a century, they waged the nomadic way of warfare, and so they strategically, and often tactically, outfought the Rouran on the eastern steppes. Yet the clash between Wei emperor and Rouran khan had unintended consequences. The Rouran khans were driven to expand their confederacy to gain ever more warriors so that they could resist the Wei emperors. For just like the chanyu of the Xiongnu, the khan of Rouran faced the threat of his people's starvation on the steppes should they be denied Chinese markets and produce. In their relentless westward advance to the Ural Mountains, the Rouran khans dislodged many tribes from their grasslands. They set off a series of migrations that triggered the eventual ethnic transformation of the peoples of the steppes from Iranian- to Turkic-speaking. The Altaic-speaking ancestors of the Huns of Attila might well have been pushed west to the grasslands north of the Caspian Sea, where they first came to the notice of the Romans.[59] At the same time, other tribes speaking eastern Iranian dialects, dubbed Huna in Sogdian documents and Indian chronicles, turned southwest, crossed the Jaxartes River, and sought new homes in Sogdiana, Bactria, and northern India.[60] They inevitably clashed with the Sassanid shahs and Gupta emperors. Foremost among these tribes of Huns were the Hephthalites, destined to succeed to the legacy of the Kushans.

10

The Hephthalites: Huns in Iran

At the end of the summer of 474, envoys from the Persian court of Ctesiphon stood before the Roman emperor Zeno in his palace on the Bosporus, at Constantinople, the New Rome.[1] They arrived with an urgent message from the regent Valkash that his brother, the Sassanid shah of Persia, Peroz, was a captive of the Hephthalites, the White Huns. They were a new and dangerous barbarous race on the northeastern frontier of Iran, and they shared the same name as the Huns who had compelled Zeno's predecessor Theodosius to construct the awesome walls to defend the city's four miles on the land side. Shah Peroz had been defeated and captured in a great battle at the hands of the Hephthalites, who overran Sogdiana and Bactria. These Huns now demanded an extraordinary ransom. The envoys would have subtly pointed out how Zeno could negotiate with his fellow monarch as an equal, whereas Huns invaded, plundered, and demanded tribute from their slave, the Roman emperor. The envoys might well have employed the polite phrase that God had created Rome and Persia as the two eternal eyes of the earth.[2] Over a century later, an exiled shah, Khusrau II, so appealed to the emperor Maurice Tiberius, who furnished money and soldiers to the young shah so that he could regain his throne.[3] The unpopular Zeno, a tough

Isaurian soldier from southern Asia Minor, had ascended to the throne only because he had married the empress Ariadne, the only daughter of Leo I, another blunt soldier emperor who had bribed his way to the throne.[4] Zeno knew what was expected even before the envoys requested it. He was to dispatch sealed sacks of centenaria, each representing one hundred pounds of gold, to help meet the ransom demands.

The Hephthalites were satisfied with the initial payment in Persian silver dirhems and Roman gold solidi, and so they released Shah Peroz on promise of paying the balance as soon as he returned to Ctesiphon. Peroz had to hand over his son Kavad as a hostage to guarantee prompt payment, because the shah was well-known for going back on his word. Ironically, years earlier, at his accession in 459, Shah Peroz had engaged the Hephthalites as allies in his war against his brother Hormizd for the Sassanid throne.[5] At the time, Shah Peroz considered these newcomers just one of a number of convenient barbarian allies. Peroz won the civil war, and was crowned King of Kings at Ctesiphon, but his new allies neither returned to the pastures north of the Jaxartes River nor accepted their status as dutiful subjects within the Persian Empire. Peroz erred in his dealings with the Hephthalites, but, in fairness, he was following a well-established policy of his ancestor Shapur II, acclaimed by many as the greatest of all shahs, who had quite successfully dealt with other Hun barbarians.

The origins of the Hephthalites are obscure, but they likely traced their descent to Iranian-speaking nomads driven out of the arid steppes of the Tarim Basin due to the wars between their more powerful neighbors and the emperors of China during the third and fourth centuries.[6] The Byzantine historian Procopius, writing in the sixth century, described the Hephthalites as White Huns because "They are the only ones among the Huns who have white bodies and countenances which are not ugly."[7] Procopius's remark still incites controversy, but Procopius was reporting what his informants had seen, and to them the Hephthalites were Europoid in appearance and quite unlike Attila's Huns. The silver coins minted by the Hephthalites offer no assistance as to their appearance because they are faithful imitations of Persian dirhems.[8] On the obverse, the royal crowned bust is that of the Sassanid shah, preceded by the tribal tamgha of the Hephthalites, while the reverse mint marks carry the names of Herat or Balkh, cities that fell into their hands after the defeat of Shah Peroz.

The Hephthalites were but one of a number of nomadic tribes called Huns who trekked west from their ancestral pastures until they reached the Jaxartes River during the fourth and early fifth centuries. The Jaxartes River marked the limits of the Sassanid Empire. The pastures and rich caravan cities to the south have always been an irresistible attraction to nomads. When the Hephthalites crossed into Ferghana by the opening of the fifth century, they were not the first Huns to cross, for their kinsmen, the Kidarites, known as Chionites to Classical authors, had already preceded them by two generations.[9] These first Huns, the Chionites, soon pressed south in search of fresh pastures and water in the direction of Bactria. Under the best of circumstances, the newcomers, perhaps between one hundred thousand and one hundred fifty thousand strong, would have proved an intolerable burden on the indigenous urban residents, peasants, and pastoralists of Transoxiana. But the Huns came well armed, fielding twenty thousand horse archers, who could take by force what they needed from unwilling hosts. The local Kushan princes (who ruled in the name of the shah) and the councils of merchant princes in the caravan cities could not resist the Chionites. They thus appealed to their overlord, the Sassanid shah. Shah Shapur II could not countenance so many uninvited settlers from the steppes. He broke off his war with the Roman emperor Constantius II, and hastened east to wage a winter campaign against the Chionites in 357–358.[10] The Chionites quickly submitted, and accepted a treaty dictated by the shah, whereby they were permitted to settle in Bactria in return for military service. Less than a year later, in 359, a large contingent of their horse archers under the command of King Grumbates marched over one thousand five hundred miles west to join Shapur's field army readying to invade Roman Mesopotamia.[11]

Ammianus Marcellinus, the last great historian of imperial Rome, recalled his encounter with the Chionites during this Per-

sian invasion of Mesopotamia. Ammianus, assigned to the staff
of Ursicinus, the senior cavalry commander of the Roman East,
was sent to reconnoiter the advance of Shapur's army. Years later,
Ammianus recalled with awe when he spotted the Persian army as-
sembling to cross the Tigris River. Atop a high point, Ammianus
could identify Shapur by his splendid regal dress and gilt helmet in
the shape of a ram. To the shah's left rode Grumbates, advanced
in years and with withered limbs, but with an impressive bearing
won by years of fighting.[12] The Persian army crossed the Tigris
near the ruins of Nineveh, and marched along the southern route,
aiming to cross the Euphrates at Zeugma. The prize was Antioch,
third city of the empire. The Romans had laid waste this route, and
so Shapur unexpectedly changed direction north against the fortress city Amida on the steep west bank of the upper Tigris River.
Ammianus narrowly escaped into the city after he was nearly slain
in a night skirmish with a detachment of Persian cavalry. Ammianus
endured the seventy-three-day siege, and narrowly escaped again
when the city fell. Thirty years later, he wrote one of our best descriptions of a siege in Antiquity.[13] The massive Ottoman walls of
well-fortified Amida (today Diyarbakir in southeastern Turkey) rest
on Roman foundations, and the eastern and southern approaches
built on steep slopes were most difficult to attack. Shapur twice
offered terms to the garrison. Ammianus reports that Grumbates
and three hundred of his Chionites volunteered to deliver the second offer. As Grumbates approached under a flag of truce, he and
his company were greeted by a hail of arrows and bolts shot from
Roman ballistae. Grumbates's son was pierced by a bolt and instantly killed. The enraged Grumbates vowed revenge, and Shapur pressed the siege to appease his ally. Ammianus recalls how the
Chionites lamented the unnamed son of Grumbates in a manner
reminiscent of Scythian customs. For a week, the body was conveyed on a funeral bier throughout the camp, and the Chionites
slashed their arms and offered locks of hair. The body was then cre-
mated and its ashes placed in a golden urn.[14] Shapur then deployed
the full might of the Persian siege train—towers, war elephants,
and finally a great ramp (*agger*)—that brought down a vast section
of the west wall. When Chionites and Persians burst through the

breach, they ruthlessly sacked the city. Shapur ordered the Roman commander and his surviving officers crucified. The survivors were deported to Persia. Shapur, however, immediately withdrew east of the Tigris because he had squandered the campaigning season to punish the defiant Roman garrison.

The Chionites returned to their new homes around Herat and Balkh, where Grumbates gave the ashes of his son a burial with proper nomadic rites. He had not wished to inter his son's body so distant from his homeland. The Chionites, or Kidarites, came to terms with their new neighbors and quickly adapted to the mixed economy of Bactria. They minted a series of gold and copper coins that imitated the previous issues of the Kushan princes, for they now acted as the shah's protectors over the former Kushano-Sassanid satrapy of Bactria.[15] But two generations later, these Huns were, in turn, forced to move again, first into their strongholds in the Kabul valley, and finally into northwestern India. The second wave of Huns had arrived: the Hephthalites.

The Hephthalites arrived in greater numbers, and they posed a far greater danger to the Sassanid Empire. They were likely primarily speakers of an eastern Iranian dialect, but they employed titles and personal names that betray familiarity with Turkish, Tocharian, and Chinese languages.[16] They undoubtedly comprised a polyglot confederation of tribes headed by a high king, called either khan or, in Sogdian, *khushnavaz*.[17] They too, like the Kidarites, had dwelled on the steppes of the Gansu corridor or Tarim Basin, where they learned political organization from both Chinese emperors and Rouran khans. Procopius notes with approval how they obeyed a single high king, followed his laws faithfully, and were honest in their dealings just like Sassanid Persians and Romans.[18] The Hephthalites were also expert in the lucrative dealings with cities that needed protection for their caravans. Once secure in Transoxiana, they, like the Kushans before them, switched to Bactrian, the eastern Iranian language of culture and commerce, as their preferred language. They valued access to the markets and products of the sedentary communities of Transoxiana, and quickly adapted to the conditions and languages necessary to engage in trade.

The arrival of the Hephthalites, first in Sogdiana and then Bactria, proved to be the dress rehearsal for the migration of the Seljuk Turks into the Islamic world in the eleventh century. Shahs Bahram V (420–438) and Yazdegerd II (438–457) had to shift their attention away from the ancestral rival Rome to cope with yet another nomadic threat posed by these Hephthalites on the northeastern frontier. Fortunately for the shah, the Roman emperor in Constantinople was likewise preoccupied with other Huns in Central Europe and the south Russian steppes.[19] The shahs could never quite dislodge the Hephthalites from Sogdiana, for the Hephthalites repeatedly switched from foes to allies, and back again. Today, museums proudly display their collections of magnificent silver plates depicting the equestrian shah at hunt.[20] Persian envoys conveyed these ceremonial plates along with many other gifts to appease the khan of the Hephthalites. Shah Peroz (459–484) engaged the Hephthalites as allies to retake his throne, and then he recovered Bactra (Balkh) from the Kidarites. He soon clashed with his dangerous allies, and twice he was defeated.[21] In a third battle, the Hephthalites surprised Peroz and his army outside of Herat in 484. Peroz fell fighting, and his body was never identified.[22] His death plunged the Sassanid Empire into crisis.

The Persian nobility acclaimed Peroz's younger brother Valkash, who had loyally administered the realm during Peroz's captivity two decades earlier. The mild-mannered Valkash hastily concluded a peace with the Hephthalites.[23] He recognized the loss of Transoxiana, Bactria, and Khurasan (northeastern Iran), and promised an annual tribute. But the tough border lords (*marzpans*) and Zoroastrian priests (*magi*) objected to so pacific, and pragmatic, a policy. To them, Valkash had signed away nearly half of the Persian Empire. They deposed Valkash four years later and elevated to the throne Kavad, the eldest of the surviving sons of Peroz. In 496, Kavad was, in turn, overthrown by a clique of aristocrats and priests who were this time outraged over the shah's encouragement of the Mazdakites, members of a radical movement calling for the reform of Zoroastrianism.[24] The goals of Mazdak and his followers are obscure. Since they lost, their writings were condemned to the flames, and we must depend on the reports of their hostile opponents. Modern historians have either condemned or praised

Mazdak as yet another forerunner of the revolutionary leaders of the proletariat. Zoroastrian writers cursed Mazdak of impiety and depravity, because they alleged that he proclaimed a communal society based on the sharing of land, wealth, and women. Yet calls for religious reform gained many adherents discontented over corrupt priests and royal agents exacting higher rents and taxes to fund the defense against the Huns. Shah Kavad initially welcomed the Mazdakites as a counter to the powerful landed families who monopolized military positions and the Zoroastrian hierarchy.

The council representing the seven leading families of the empire ordered Kavad imprisoned in the notorious Castle of Oblivion in southeastern Persia, and acclaimed as the new shah Kavad's younger brother Jamasp.[25] Kavad escaped his gloomy imprisonment either disguised as a woman (with the aid of his wife) or rolled up in a carpet (with the connivance of his sister).[26] He immediately fled to the Hephthalites. During his captivity, Kavad had gained many friends among the Hephthalites and learned their customs. For a price, Kavad obtained their assistance and recovered his throne eighteen months later.[27] In 498, Kavad crushed the great families, implemented sweeping fiscal and land reforms, and promptly jettisoned his Mazdakite allies in favor of an orthodox Zoroastrian clergy purged of foes and subservient to his will. Kavad was long despised as a despotic, suspicious shah, but he held on to power until his death.[28] Foremost, Kavad recognized that the Hephthalites were indispensable allies, and so increased the tribute of his uncle.[29] The Hephthalites received so much silver in tribute that they minted an extensive silver coinage based on Persian originals that greased the wheels of commerce across Transoxiana.[30] Later in his reign, Shah Kavad disengaged from fighting Rome and waged a desultory war against the Hephthalites, who practiced the time-honored policy of raiding disputed borderlands to extort better terms from the shah. In 513, Kavad and the Hephthalite khan concluded a peace that lasted for nearly two generations.[31]

At the start of the sixth century, the Hephthalites had succeeded to the political legacy of the Kushans in Transoxiana, Bactria, and northeastern Iran, and they were just as adept in promoting and profiting off the trade of the Silk Road. Between 493 and 513, Kashgar, Kuchea,

and Khotan, the principal oasis cities of the Tarim Basin, put themselves under the protection of the Hephthalites.[32] The Northern Wei
emperor and Rouran khan each sent delegations bearing costly gifts
and seeking trade agreements. In the throne room of Ctesiphon, the
shah Khusrau I placed a golden chair for the Hephthalites, thereby acknowledging that their khan was an equal to the emperors of Rome
and China, each of whom was awarded a similar throne.[33]

The Sassanid shahs after Peroz lavished gifts on the Hephthalites,
but they poured even more money and resources into constructing the Great Wall of Gorgan to check Hephthalite attacks from
Khurasan into northern Iran.[34] This brick wall stretches nearly
125 miles from the eastern shores of the Caspian to the Pishkamar
Mountains, and forts guarded the strategic passes. Even though
Classical writers never learned of this wall, later Persians concluded
that it must have been built by Alexander the Great as yet one more
Gate of Alexander (Sadd-i-Iskandar) that was intended to seal off
the hordes of Gog and Magog. The system required thirty-five
thousand soldiers to man the walls, forts, and signal towers as well
as to patrol beyond the frontier and intercept raiders. This wall is
longer than Hadrian's Wall (seventy-seven miles) and the Antonine
Wall (forty-four miles) combined, and it is the second-longest defensive works ever raised against nomadic invaders. This wall still
stands as a testimony to organization of the Sassanid state, and to
the threat posed by the Hephthalites for nearly a century.

The Hephthalites, however, never succeeded to the Kushan political legacy in India. Chinese chroniclers and Buddhist writers
in India may refer to sporadic attacks launched across the Hindu
Kush by the Hephthalites. Instead, three successive hordes of other
Huns—Kidarites, Alchon Huns, and Nezak Huns—crossed the
Hindu Kush from bases at Kabul or Ghazna in Afghanistan today.
They sacked Buddhist sanctuaries, and carved out short-lived kingdoms in Gandhara and the Punjab.[35] These Huns likely were operating on their own rather than acting as the vassals of the Hephthalites.
It is very unlikely that any of the rulers of these three Hun confed-
eracies ever obeyed the writ of the khan of the Hephthalites.

The Kidarites, dislodged from Bactria by both Shah Peroz and the
Hephthalites, first found refuge in their strongholds in the Kabul val-

ley, where they had long established a court at Kapisa (today Begram), the former summer capital of the Kushans. Already, in 437, an embassy from the Northern Wei court arrived at Kapisa and flattered the Kidarite king by saluting him the Son of Heaven of the Great Kushans (Da Yuezhi).[36] These Chinese envoys also reported to their master the emperor Dong Wan that the son of this king held court at Purusapura (today Peshawar, Pakistan). The Tocharian-speaking subjects of Kidarites would have pointed out to their Kidarite overlord the routes to the rich cities of Gandhara and the Punjab over which their ancestors, the Great Kushans, had once held sway. Therefore, already in the early fifth century, Kidarites were migrating into India, but they relocated their principal court to Gandhara after 484.[37] In their Indian domains, the Kidarites minted silver dirhems with the portrait and the name of their former overlord Shah Peroz, who is identified by name in the Indian Brahmi script rather than the Persian one. Some of these coins carry a facing portrait that gives us our first depiction of a Hun who has a round, clean-shaven face with almond eyes.[38] He would have looked perfectly at home among the nomads dwelling north of the Great Wall.

The Alchon Huns soon followed the Kidarites, first into the Kabul valley and then into India, where they incorporated the Kidarites into their own confederacy.[39] These Alchon Huns too comprised a polyglot group of tribes who were apparently set in motion by the advance of the Hephthalites. The ethnic name Alchon only appears on their coins, while Indian authors indiscriminately called all invaders from the north Hunas. These Huns too adopted the Bactrian language written in a Greek script, and the royal names on coins are of Iranian origin. The portrait on the coins of the first known ruler, Khingila, depicts a clean-shaven man in his prime wearing a simple conical crown.[40] Khingila had a Roman nose, almond eyes, and a high forehead that had been flattened by the ritual cranial deformity practiced by many steppe nomads. On their coins, his successors sport long drooping mustaches and wear more ornate crowns, but otherwise they all share the same physical traits complete with the flattened forehead. They all would have hardly stood out among the mixed populations of the Tarim Basin, as revealed by the DNA testing of the Tarim Mummies.

Later Buddhist authors of India universally decried these Huns as impious barbarians ignorant of the teachings of the Buddha. Just before the mid-fifth century, Mihirakula, the ruler of the Alchon Huns, sacked Taxila, the capital of the Punjab and renowned center of Buddhist learning since the Mauryan Empire. Many of Mihirakula's coins were found by excavators just above the debris of the final sack that leveled the city forever. Buddhist envoys and pilgrims from the Northern Wei court likewise lamented the wanton destruction committed by these Huns across Gandhara and the Punjab, and deplored their barbarous customs. A century later, the Chinese monk Xuanzang was told tales about how the cruel invader Mihirakula had ravaged all of India.[41] According to so many hostile accounts, the Alchon Huns can be dismissed as too few, and too destructive, to succeed to the Kushan legacy in India so that they always remained invaders. But the Alchon Huns have left no written records of their presence other than their coins, which testify to a sophisticated level of royal organization.[42] They, like their kinsmen the Hephthalites, must have adapted existing administrative and fiscal institutions to their needs, and promoted international commerce that brought the silver specie for their coinage. They remained animists, devoted to their shamans and the spirits of the eternal blue sky. Once securely in control, their rulers respected all faiths, and, at least in one case, an Alchon Hun monarch endowed a Buddhist monastery.

At the end of the fifth century, the Alchon Huns posed a deadly threat to the Gupta emperors, who had forged the second great Indian empire and sponsored Hindu cults and letters. The Huns overran the Doab and upper Ganges valley, and briefly threatened to overthrow Gupta rule over Aryavarta, the heartland of Hindu civilization. Yet, in the early sixth century, the kings of the Alchon Hun, Toramana and Mihirakula, each suffered a decisive defeat that ended their ambitions to forge a Hun Empire in India. In 510, the Gupta emperor Bhanugupta won a major victory over Toramana, who abandoned his campaign against the Gupta capital, Pataliputra. In 532, Mihirakula, after suffering a humiliating defeat, submitted to Yashodharman (ca. 515–545), the ruler of Malwa, who briefly reunited northern India after the fall of the Gupta Empire.[43] Each victor raised a grandiose memorial column to commemorate the battle. By the mid-sixth century, the Alchon Huns steadily withdrew to the valley of Kabul, where they regrouped with other tribes and soon returned under new rulers of the Nezak Huns.[44] These last of the Huns only carved out a regional kingdom in Gandhara at the end of the sixth century. They too struck a series of remarkable silver and copper coins inspired by Sassanid prototypes.[45] Each ruler is depicted sporting an elaborate crown that combined Persian lunar and solar symbols with the horns of the Indian water buffalo. None of the coins carries personal names, and each Nezak ruler is a ringer for a Cossack hetman. The Nezak Huns too were driven out of India into the Kabul valley, where Arab armies encountered them at the end of the seventh century.

None of the Hun confederations forged a lasting imperial state, and yet each played a significant role in the fragmenting of the Gupta imperial order, and the proliferation of the bewildering array of regional Buddhist and Hindu kingdoms for the next six centuries. In Hindu literature, all these Huns have been remembered as the Hunas, a valiant foreign warrior race, dwelling just beyond the Himalayas. In the Indian national epic *Mahabharata*, the Hunas join the righteous side commanded by Yudhishthira, the eldest brother and leader of the Pandavas, in the legendary war against their rival cousins, the Kauravas.[46] The Rajputs, a martial race admired by agents and officers of the British Raj, have sometimes claimed descent from the Huns.

Whereas the sundry Huns in India failed to build an empire, the Hephthalites north of the Hindu Kush proved to be too successful. The khans of the Hephthalites, who remain anonymous to this day, were worthy heirs to the Kushan Sons of Heaven, and they were so recognized by their foe, the Sassanid shahs. They posed an existential threat on the eastern frontier of the Sassanid Empire after 484. The shahs were already overtaxed in defending their western and northwestern frontiers. In 379, Shah Ardashir II had concluded an agreement with the Roman emperor Theodosius I to partition Armenia, the bone of contention for so many wars between the two imperial rivals.[47] The majority of the kingdom passed under Sassanid rule, and soon proved a poisoned gift. The Armenians were recalcitrant subjects who refused to abjure their Christian faith or to pay taxes to a heathen oppressor.[48] The shah also acquired the expensive task of garrisoning the Dariel and Derbent Passes through the Caucasus Mountains. In 395–396, a horde of Huns from the south Russian steppes crossed the Derbent Pass and pillaged across Armenia and Iraq, halting just north of Ctesiphon.[49] They then withdrew with a haul of booty and captives. Repeatedly, later shahs loudly requested subsidies from the Roman emperor to pay for the common defense against the nomads north of the Caucasus.[50] Each time, the emperor flatly refused, for any payment to the shah might be interpreted as tribute.

Facing nomadic foes on his northwestern and eastern frontiers, Shah Khusrau I (531–579), the son and successor of Kavad, was determined to avenge the humiliating defeats suffered at the hands of the Hephthalites, and to reestablish Persian power in Transoxiana. He found new allies in the Gök Turks, who had just arrived on the central Eurasian steppes north of the Jaxartes River. In 557, Shah Khusrau concluded an alliance with Ishtemi, the *yabgu* or subordinate kaghan of the Gök Turks of the West.[51]

Khusrau even sealed the deal by marrying a daughter of Ishtemi Kaghan—the first significant marriage of a Turkish princess to a sovereign of the Near East. Together, in 557–581, Persians and Turks overthrew and partitioned the Hephthalite Empire. Khusrau regained northeastern Iran and Bactria, but the Gök Turks occupied the cities north of the River Oxus. They thus gained the crucial caravan cities of Bukhara, Samarkand, and Kashgar. Shah Khusrau had indeed eliminated the menace of the Hephthalites, but he and his heirs henceforth faced a far more dangerous nomadic foe in the Turks, who were to transform forever the linguistic and ethnic identity of the nomadic peoples across Eurasia.

Meanwhile, as the Sassanid shahs battled the Hephthalites, "the White Huns," imperial Rome, the other eternal eye of the earth, faced other Huns, who arrived on the edge of the Roman world in 370. These Huns under the world-famous Attila, the Scourge of God, would forge one of the greatest of the steppe empires, and so determine the destiny of the Roman Empire, and the future of modern Europe.

11

Huns, Allies and Foes of Rome

In the summer of 375, a despairing King Ermanaric committed suicide as his final act of defiance after leading his people, the Greuthungi Goths, into a disastrous battle with a new foe: the Huns, horsemen who had swept out of the Eurasian steppes.[1] The precise location of the battle is unknown, but Goths and Huns clashed somewhere on the south Russian steppes between the lower Volga and Don Rivers. The Huns had suddenly appeared from the east beyond the limits of the world known to Goths and Romans. The newcomers had allied with the Alans, the Iranian-speaking nomads dwelling on the steppes north of the Caucasus Mountains, and together they had attacked the Goths repeatedly. In desperation, the Goths elected a new king, Vithimiris, who also went down in defeat in the next year. Their kinsmen, the Terving Goths, who dwelled to the southwest on the plains between the Dniester and lower Danube Rivers, sent reinforcements under their elected magistrate, Athanaric. He was bushwhacked by the Huns in a night attack on the Gothic camp, and withdrew. Athanaric might have then refortified the dilapidated Roman turf wall between the Prut River and the Greek city Tyras on the shores of the Black Sea as a barrier against the Huns.[2] If so, it was to no avail. In the early autumn of

376, Athanaric and his people quit their homes and fled en masse to the Lower Danube. There, they petitioned the Roman emperor Valens for permission to seek refuge within the Roman Empire.[3]

Two centuries later, the Gothic monk Jordanes, writing his people's history in Latin, explained away this humiliating defeat by inventing an invincible king of the Huns.[4] Jordanes also claimed that Ermanaric did not commit suicide. Instead, the jealous king ordered a grisly death for his beautiful young wife, falsely accused of infidelity. Her two aggrieved half brothers, clad in magical armor, attacked the tyrannical king while he slept. They hacked off the king's limbs, but the dying king cried out for help. His bodyguards, unable to penetrate the two assailants' armor, crushed them to death by hurling great stones. The legend lived on. In Norse verse and saga, they were remembered on under the names of King Jörmunrek, Queen Svanhild, and the brothers, Hamdir and Sörli, honored heroes received into Valhalla.[5]

The sober contemporary Roman historian Ammianus Marcellinus, however, described these extraordinary events accurately. He reported the newcomers, the Huns, as frightfully ugly. "From the moment of birth they made deep gashes in their children's cheeks,[6] so that when in due course hair appears its growth is checked by the wrinkled scars; as they grow older this gives them the unlovely appearance of beardless eunuchs. They have squat bodies, strong limbs, and thick necks, and are so prodigiously ugly and bent that they might be two-legged animals, or the figures crudely carved from stumps which are seen on the parapets of bridges. Still their shape, however disagreeable, is human..."[7] Ammianus Marcellinus was at a loss to account for these invaders who spoke an unintelligible language, but as a Roman officer, he appreciated their martial skills inasmuch as the Huns waged the nomadic way of war violently. In battle, Huns atop sturdy horses rained arrows from afar, and then closed and lassoed foes on foot and horseback. The helpless men were quickly dispatched and their heads severed as trophies. Unbeknownst to Ammianus, the Huns were the first Altaic-speaking nomads from Inner Asia to arrive in Eastern Europe, and they too, like their contemporaries the Rouran and Hephthalites, had long been on the move.[8]

News of the Hun victory alarmed the Roman imperial courts.

The Roman Empire was then informally divided between the emperor Valens, ruling the East from Constantinople, and his nephew, the Western emperor Gratian, at Milan. Since the treaty of 332, the Gothic tribes had patrolled the steppes stretching from the lower Danube to the Don Rivers as dutiful allies of Rome.[9] In return, the Goths received subsidies in gold and access to Roman markets on the Danube. The treaty marked the end of three generations of frontier wars between Rome and the Goths, who had the singular distinction of defeating and slaying in battle a Roman emperor, Trajan Decius, in 251.[10] The ancestors of the Goths had departed from Sweden in the second century AD, and settled on the Pontic-Caspian steppes.[11] There they had learned horsemanship from the Sarmatians, Iranian speakers who had succeeded the Scythians as the dominant nomadic people on the western steppes in the second century BC. The Huns now threatened to disrupt the network of alliances with Germanic tribes defending Rome's northern frontiers along the Rhine and Danube.

Perhaps as many as one hundred fifty thousand Goths stood on the northern banks of the Danube, imploring the emperor Valens to receive them into the empire.[12] Valens hesitated, and then accepted, settling the Goths as federates pledged to military service, in Moesia (today northern Bulgaria), on the Roman side of the lower Danube. Valens sorely needed soldiers, but his corrupt officials drove these desperate Goths, the future Visigoths, into rebellion the next year. The ferry crossing had been chaotic; the refugee camps overcrowded; hunger and disease forced Goths to sell children into slavery. Valens hurried west, and summoned his field armies to concentrate at Constantinople. Meanwhile, more Goths and even a contingent of Huns crossed the Danube to join the rebels. Under a scorching sun, on August 9, 378, the Goths defeated and slew Valens at Adrianople.[13] To rescue the Balkans, the emperor Gratian elevated an experienced officer, Theodosius, as Eastern emperor, who negotiated the return of the Goths to Moesia.[14] The emperor accepted the fact that the imperial army now depended on federate Germanic tribal armies. The Goths, in turn, learned that rebellion secured land and gold.

The Huns had set off a chain reaction that pushed Germanic

tribes to cross and seek new homes in the Roman Empire over
the next century, whereby they unwittingly toppled the Western
Roman Empire. Ammianus Marcellinus admitted that he did not
know from whence came these Huns. Their previous home lay east
of the Caspian Sea, on the arid grasslands of Kazakhstan, stretching
over five hundred thousand square miles between the Ural and Altai
Mountains.[15] The Huns dwelled well north of the Jaxartes River,
and beyond the western limits of China. Their remote ancestors
had likely dwelled much farther east on the Mongolian steppes,
where they once had been vassals of the chanyu of the Xiongnu.
During the third and fourth centuries AD, the Huns had limited
contact with Persian or Chinese civilizations. Other than sharing
what had become a generic name designating ferocious nomads,
Huns and Xiongnu had no direct connection. Although Huns and
Xiongnu each spoke an Altaic language and shared a common
way of life, the Huns spoke a Western Turkish dialect that had diverged from any common parent language they shared with the
Xiongnu centuries before.[16] Nor did the Huns ever adopt writing,
in contrast to the Xiongnu. The few Hun decorative arts found
in Central Europe exhibit no artistic similarities to those of the
Xiongnu.[17] In Attila's day, the Huns were still animists, worshipping
ancestral spirits invoked by shamans, and revering the eternal blue
sky Tengri.[18] They showed no familiarity with Buddhism, Manichaeism, or Christianity, which many nomads engaged in the trade
along the Silk Road had embraced. When they arrived in Europe,
the Huns, according to Ammianus Marcellinus, comprised tribes
who followed a collective leadership. In 395, two elected leaders,
Basikh and Koursikh, shared command of the Huns and Alans in
the daring raid across the Caucasus to plunder Roman Anatolia and
Persian Mesopotamia.[19] Therefore, the Huns, when they arrived in
Eastern Europe, were hardly the heirs to the imperial organization
of the Xiongnu confederacy, but they did prove quick studies and
learned much from imperial Rome.[20]

The ancestors of the Huns would have migrated west from the
eastern steppes for several reasons. Initially they might well have
been pushed into the central Eurasian steppes due to the fighting
between the Rouran khans and rival tribes. Far more pressing were

seasonal droughts and hard winters that would have driven them steadily ever west in search of water and green pastures. During twenty years of favorable weather, a population of any clan or tribe could double. Then, a sudden dry winter followed by a drought left nomads the stark choice of starving or leaving to find water. The Huns hardly assembled as a single nation of one hundred fifty thousand and headed west in a planned migration. Instead, far smaller groups, each representing a clan or *yurt* and comprising hundreds rather than thousands of individuals, set out on their own treks. Others soon followed as they received the news of the success of those who had departed. By 370, the Huns were settled in considerable numbers just north of the Caspian Sea when they learned of richer grasslands pierced by numerous broad rivers to the west occupied by Goths. Even then, the Huns allied with the Alans, inveterate foes of the Goths, to conquer the south Russian steppes.[21] After defeating the Goths, again a series of Hun wagon trains quickly migrated over the south Russian steppes. Once they reached the Carpathian Mountains, many Huns crossed into Central Europe, settling on the great Hungarian plain, while others traveled southwest into the grasslands north of the lower Danube valley, which the Visigoths had just vacated. Well before 400, Huns had reached the borders of the Roman Empire along the middle and lower Danube River.[22]

In the course of these migrations in the last quarter of the fourth century, the Huns allied with, subjected, or assimilated many other peoples, foremost Alans and the East Germanic tribes of Ostrogoths, Gepidae, and Herulians.[23] In Attila's day, many Huns bore Germanic or Iranian names, and within Attila's empire, perhaps only one in five could claim largely East Asian descent. When the Huns settled on the grasslands of Central Europe, they shared with imperial Rome a frontier of over one thousand miles along the Danube River from its great turn south near Budapest to its mouths emptying into the Black Sea. The Huns settled in considerable numbers on rich grasslands of Transylvania between the middle Danube and the western slopes of the Carpathian Mountains (today divided between Hungary and Romania). This area totaled but a fraction of the south Russian steppes. They also subjected many agriculturalists of diverse origin and language who lived in the rich river valleys. In Central Europe, Uldin, the first Hun king known by name, organized a loose Hun confederation comprising new and old nomadic groups, as well as many villages and towns in the former Roman province of Dacia (today Romania).[24] It is unknown what political ties linked Uldin and his western Huns with their kinsmen dwelling on the south Russian steppes, but clans of Huns continuously moved between the two regions.

The Huns forged a confederacy without any challenge from Rome, because the professional legions of the Principate no longer defended northern frontiers. Since 378, emperors recruited into their field armies ever more tribal regiments of German federates who served under their own commanders rather than veteran Roman officers.[25] Personal loyalty to the emperor turned German barbarians into imperial soldiers, because the mission of the imperial army had changed from defending the empire to defending the emperor against all enemies, domestic and foreign. The emperor Theodosius I, who came to terms with the Goths after the disaster at Adrianople, inspired loyalty among his Germanic officers and soldiers. But upon the death of Theodosius on January 17, 395, the Roman Empire was divided between his two young sons.[26] The retiring, weak-willed seventeen-year-old Arcadius succeeded in the East, while in the West reigned the gentle, pious eleven-year-old Honorius, who mistook his outbursts of obstinacy as courage. The two imperial courts, at Constantinople and Milan, not only were hostile to each other but also each perceived the Huns quite differently. The Eastern court dominated by the emperor's wife Eudocia and her professional civilian bureaucrats soon came to see the Huns as an existential threat.[27] In contrast, the Western court dominated by the *magister militum* Stilicho, who commanded the best Roman field armies, considered the Huns allies of convenience who would check barbarian federates, foremost the Visigoths resettled in Moesia by Theodosius.[28]

Stilicho also alienated both courts because he claimed that Theodosius on his deathbed had entrusted him with the guardianship of both young emperors.[29] Few at either court believed him. Stilicho, himself of Vandal origin and so barred from the imperial throne, later linked himself to the imperial family by marrying his young son to a daughter of Honorius, who distrusted and hated his general. In early 395, Alaric, a veteran officer of Theodosius, clamored for a Roman high command, and new lands for his people. When the Eastern court refused, Alaric assumed his second-best option as king of the Visigoths, and rampaged across the Balkans during the next three years.[30] He and his people had set out on a fifteen-year trek that took them to the gates of Rome. In 397, Stilicho intervened, and settled the Visigoths on Roman territory for a third time, in Epirus (northwestern Greece today).[31] Stilicho also placed in Constantinople a strong Gothic garrison under a loyal officer, Gainas, so that the generalissimo could dominate the Eastern court as well as the Western one. Stilicho had compromised the empire, while Gainas soon overplayed his hand. On July 12, 400, an ugly incident exploded into a general riot against the insolent Gothic soldiery.[32] At one of the city gates, a Gothic soldier took offense to the prayer of an elderly beggar woman, lamenting the presence of so many Arian barbarians in the capital. The Goth assaulted her, but a Roman came to the rescue and slew the Goth. The brawl quickly escalated in a rising of the city's population and the enraged citizens of Constantinople massacred Stilicho's Goths. Gainas fled north across the Danube and fell into the hands of Uldin, king of the Huns. Uldin severed and returned Gainas's head as a favor to Arcadius and a demonstration of Hun strength. The Eastern court got the message. Uldin was hailed a friend of Rome, and granted a treaty and subsidy in gold.[33]

Meanwhile, in Epirus, Alaric rearmed his warriors with Roman equipment and horses. In 402, the Visigoths marched west through the Balkans toward Italy, almost certainly to the relief of Arcadius's court. A terrified Honorius hastily relocated his court from Milan to Ravenna, a sleepy port on the Adriatic Sea and surrounded by malarial marshes.[34] For the next four years. Stilicho was hard-pressed to prevent Alaric from crossing the Alps, and so he transferred Roman field armies from Gaul to Italy.[35] Even now, Stilicho hoped to negotiate with Alaric rather than destroy the Visigoths. In 406, unexpectedly, another Gothic host, under Radagaisus, quit their home on the Hungarian grasslands, crossed the Alps, and advanced toward Rome. Uldin now rescued the Western court, and lent Stilicho a Hun army that intercepted and destroyed Radagaisus's army just north of Florence.[36] Stilicho also appreciated the Huns, for he retained a bodyguard of Huns after Uldin's warriors returned home. Stilicho also tacitly accepted Uldin's occupation of the province of Pannonia (today western Hungary), the fertile rolling plains west of the great bend in the River Danube. In late December 406, the Rhine froze. For months, endless wagon trains of Alans and Germanic tribes—Saxons, Franks, Burgundians, Sueves, and Vandals—crossed over the ice in a mass exodus into Roman Gaul.[37] By the spring of 407, barbarian tribes overran and settled in Gaul and Spain. In Britain, the Roman army mutinied and declared their commander Constantine emperor. Three years later, in 410, Constantine crossed the Channel, and he and his army were annihilated by forces loyal to Honorius.[38] Picts north of Hadrian's Wall, and Saxons, Angles, and Jutes from across the North Sea then descended on the undefended island province. Honorius rightly blamed Stilicho for these disasters, and he ordered his general arrested and executed in 408.[39] Stilicho's veterans promptly deserted to Alaric, whereupon the Visigoths entered Italy, besieged Rome three times, and captured the Eternal City on August 24, 410.[40] Even though Alaric, a Roman citizen and an Arian Christian, respected churches, and conducted organized blackmail rather than a sack, Christians and pagans alike took the event as a sign of divine punishment heralding the end of days. The next year, Honorius convinced Alaric's successor, Athaulf, who held captive the emperor's half sister Galla Placidia, to recross the Alps and restore order in Gaul and Spain.[41] In return, Athaulf's Visigoths received land and the rights to collect taxes in the Aquitaine as an act of hospitality (*hospitium*) at the expense of distraught Roman landowners. Athaulf made Toulouse his capital, and founded the first independent Germanic kingdom on Roman soil. By the death of Honorius on August 15, 423, the Western Roman Empire was fatally compromised and destined to fall. German barbarians, far better organized and armed than their forefathers, carved out their own kingdoms within the empire. To be sure, the imperial army and administration had failed, but so had Honorius and Stilicho, neither of whom had been up to the task of defending the empire. But foremost, the barbarians who invaded the Roman Empire did so to escape the fury of the advancing Huns.

Meanwhile, Uldin at least twice launched major attacks across the Danube River, devastating the provinces of Moesia and Thrace in search of booty, livestock, and captives.[42] The army of the Eastern Roman Empire could neither prevent nor punish these raids. During the second attack, in 408, the Praetorian Prefect Anthemius, regent for the boy emperor Theodosius II, resorted to massive bribery of Uldin's vassals to desert so that Uldin had to cut short his campaign. Yet the feckless Eastern emperors Arcadius and Theodosius II enjoyed crucial strategic advantages to weather the barbarian invasions triggered by the Huns.[43] A resolute empress advised each: Eudocia, the wife of Arcadius and the daughter of a leading Frankish general, and Aelia Pulcheria, the piously virtuous elder sister of Theodosius.[44] Just as important, each emperor was served by loyal, professional ministers and bureaucrats, who controlled policy and checked ambitious generalissimos who might scheme to dominate the court.[45] These same officials ensured the collection of taxes from the far wealthier eastern provinces, whereas after 406, Honorius was starved of manpower and money. Simultaneously, they faced no threat from the Persian shah, who was preoccupied defending his northeastern frontiers against the Hephthalites.[46] Therefore, while Uldin and his Huns ravaged the Balkan provinces with impunity, they lacked a fleet so that they could not invade the Asian provinces in concert with the Persians. But the greatest obstacle the Huns faced was the four miles of land walls of Constantinople, which turned the imperial capital into the strategic citadel blocking them from crossing the Bosporus.

The Praetorian Prefect Anthemius directed most of the nine-year construction of the Theodosian Walls, which were completed in 413.[47] The population of Constantinople, dedicated as the New Rome by Constantine in 330, grew tenfold within seventy-five years, from a city of thirty-five thousand to three hundred fifty thousand. The massive new walls enclosed a vast, densely settled area one and one-half miles beyond the original city walls.[48] The city was built on a triangular peninsula, with the Sea of Marmara along its southern arm, and its northern arm along the southern

shores of the estuary of the Golden Horn that emptied into the
Bosporus. Walls rising to between fifteen and twenty feet on the
edge of the shores protected these two sides. In addition, treacherous shoals and currents hindered any naval assault. It was the city's
land side, the western base of the triangle stretching between the
Golden Horn and the Sea of Marmara, that had no natural defense. Two points along the land side were particularly vulnerable:
the northeastern corner, where the ground dropped sharply to the
shore of the Golden Horn, and the so-called Middle Wall (Meso-
teichion) between the Gate of Charisius (today Edirne Kapı) and
the Gate of Saint Romanus (today Top Kapı). There a natural valley fell nearly one hundred feet, forming the two slopes of the bed
of the river Lycus, which had been enclosed and channeled as the
source of the city's numerous cisterns.

The Theodosian Walls comprised a succession of three defensive lines constructed of white limestone reinforced at regular intervals with layers of bricks and concrete which enclosed a dense
interior of bricks, stone, and concrete rubble.[49] The outermost obstacle was a fossa excavated from the bedrock to a depth of twenty
feet and a width of sixty feet.[50] This fossa was faced on either side
with masonry and brick walls, and above the eastern side rose a
six-foot wall two to six feet thick. Between this first line and the
Outer Walls stretched an open space of over sixty feet, the Para-
teichion, where attackers were exposed to murderous missile fire
from the defenders on the Outer Walls. The Outer Walls, the second line of defense, rose twenty-five feet high, and were two to
six feet thick.[51] At regular intervals, the wall was strengthened
by projecting towers of thirty feet that were designed to accom-
modate artillery. Behind the Outer Walls stretched another open
zone, the Periobolos, fifty to sixty-five feet wide.[52] On its eastern
side rose the awesome Inner Walls, forty feet high and thirteen to
fifteen feet thick, with towers at regular intervals soaring to sixty
feet.[53] Ten main gates, along with several smaller postern gates of
the Outer Walls, were massively fortified. All three walls rested on
deep masonry foundation so that they could not be undermined by
mining operations. To this day, the Theodosian Walls stand as the

most ambitious feat of military engineering ever built to defend a
city against nomadic foes.

The circuit of Constantinople's walls, nearly thirteen miles, is
comparable to that of the walls of Rome constructed by the emperor Aurelian in 271–275 in response to a Vandal invasion of Italy.[54]
Rome's walls, however, stand on no naturally defensible terrain,
and they straddle the Tiber so that they required triple the number
of defenders. Rome's single ring of walls was far less formidable.
The walls, originally sixteen feet high, were doubled in height and
strengthened with towers during the civil wars of the early fourth
century. Furthermore, Rome had to be supplied from its port of
Ostia, twenty miles away at the mouth of the Tiber, and the water
system fed by eleven aqueducts could be easily cut. Twice, in 410
and 455, the imperial capital fell to barbarian attackers: Alaric and
his Visigoths and Gaiseric and his Vandals, respectively. In the sixth
century, Rome endured three sieges and exchanged hands five times
during the war waged by the emperor Justinian to reconquer Italy
from the Ostrogoths.[55]

The Theodosian Walls have sometimes been dismissed as a fancy
prestige project to settle the nerves of the citizens and to awe the
Huns, who are sometimes wrongly demoted to a nuisance rather
than a threat. Instead, the walls stand as a testimony to the magnitude of the threat posed by the Huns in the fifth century. For
the next millennium, time and again, the walls thwarted every at-
tacker save on two occasions. On April 13–15, 1204, the Venetians
and members of the Fourth Crusade stormed the walls in reckless assaults against defenders who were too few and too demoralized.[56] On May 29, 1453, the Ottoman army of Sultan Mehmet II
numbering one hundred thousand overwhelmed the seven thousand heroic defenders under the last emperor of the Roman East,
Constantine XI, in three successive final assaults after a siege of
six weeks.[57] State-of-the-art Ottoman artillery had pounded large
sections of the ancient walls to ruins, and even then the final attack nearly failed.

The court of Theodosius II did not depend on the walls alone.
The prefect Anthemius directed an expansion of the river flotilla pa-
trolling the lower Danube, and repairs to the fortified cities along the

frontiers or at strategic points on the imperial highways. Diplomacy was just as important. In 412, a brief notice of one such embassy survives, headed by the historian Olympiodorus of Thebes, who set sail from Constantinople to Aquileia, from whence he crossed the Alps and made his way overland to the court of Charaton, who had succeeded Uldin as high king of the Huns.[58] Olympiodorus, accompanied by his prop, a talking parrot, and an ostentatiously large retinue, complained incessantly about the uncomfortable journey. He must have reached the main Hun encampment on the east bank of the Middle Danube, perhaps opposite Budapest. The purpose and outcome of his mission are unclear, because his detailed account is largely lost. Still the embassy underscores how the imperial government in Constantinople regularly dispatched embassies bearing letters of polite nothings about mutual interests and tribute euphemistically bestowed as gifts, to appease the Huns. At the same time, envoys from the court at Ravenna too crossed the Alps and arrived to beg for contingents of Hun warriors.[59]

In 420, the two brothers Rugila (whose name was also rendered as Rua or Ruga) and Octar succeeded jointly as high kings of the Hun Confederacy of the tribes dwelling on the steppes between the Rivers Danube and Volga.[60] They and their predecessors forged this confederacy by capitalizing on the exodus of so many Alans and Germanic tribes into the Roman Empire. The precise arrangements between the brothers are unknown, but each surely maintained his own retinue and vassal tribes. Rugila, the elder, resided at the main settlement east of Budapest. But the brothers cooperated to exact tribute and access to Roman markets from a reluctant imperial court at Constantinople, and to hire out Hun contingents to the Western court at Ravenna. In 422, Rugila personally led a massive raid into the Roman Balkans, captured and sacked cities, and brushed aside Roman resistance.[61] The Eastern Roman emperor Theodosius, who had recently attained his majority, had to treat for terms. He preferred to spend hours studying the mysteries of the Trinity and perfecting his calligraphy, so that he often deferred to his shrewd elder sister Aelia Pulcheria, his ministers, and his veteran general Aspar on foreign and military policies. Rugila secured a treaty with an annual subsidy of 350 pounds of gold.[62] Seven years later, Rugila was acclaimed by the leading princes as universal lord of the Huns after the death of his brother Octar. In 432, Rugila died without adult male heirs, and his nephews, Bleda and Attila, succeeded. Few at the time could have realized that the younger of the two would shake the Roman world to its very foundations.

When Bleda and Attila succeeded, the Huns had profoundly changed from their ancestors described by Ammianus Marcellinus two generations earlier. Ammianus, with a condescending disapproval, noted how Huns roamed over the steppes, and avoided entering buildings that would block out the view of the eternal blue sky. They lived virtually atop their horses rather than in cities. Yet for all of his prejudices, Ammianus wrote of a nomadic people who could endure the harsh life on the Eurasian steppes. In 432, the Huns now headed a great confederation in diversity and complexity that matched that of the Xiongnu. The high king of the Huns, perhaps called a khan, could summon thousands of horse archers from across the steppes, and field numerous warriors of many subject tribes. Few of the burials excavated in Hungary, Romania, or Ukraine have been conclusively identified as those of Huns, but several important ones included male skeletal remains with the ritual cranial deformity of the steppes.[63] Most of the graves have been classified as East Germanic based on jewelry and weapons comparable in workmanship to those found in contemporary Scandinavian graves of the Vendel period (400–600). All graves included Roman gold coins, plate, jewelry, glassware, or weapons. Whatever the precise ethnic ancestry of the deceased, they were members of the elite class within the Hun confederation who obtained many costly, exotic objects in war or trade.

The historian Priscus, who visited the settlement of Attila in 449, reports that, once he crossed the border, he passed settlement after settlement comprising tents and timbered structures.[64] He found lodging and hospitality in one such village ruled by the widow of Attila's brother Bleda. He was greeted by a leading Hun prince, Onegesius, whose settlement included a timbered bathhouse, comparable to those at Roman army posts. The architect, a Roman captive, had designed it, but instead of emancipation, the hapless man remained a slave and the bath's attendant, because Onegesius considered him too valuable to free. The Huns had found along both sides of the River Danube a martial frontier society, the product of a fusion of Roman soldiers, indigenous peoples, and barbarian newcomers since the second century AD.[65] One in four Roman provincials counted at least one immediate ancestor of barbarian origin. The general Stilicho was the son of a loyal Vandal officer; the Eastern commander Aspar was an Alan in origin. On the imperial frontier, men trained in the use of arms could just as easily serve under either a khan of the Huns or a Roman supreme commander (*magister militum*).

Priscus reports an exchange between himself and a wealthy Roman citizen of Viminacium (near modern Kostolac, Serbia) at Attila's settlement.[66] The incident reveals how readily the Huns assimilated captives, exiles, renegades, and voluntary immigrants from the Roman world. Priscus was surprised that the man was well-dressed in Scythian garb, and spoke perfect Greek. He had been taken prisoner in a raid, but his skill in arms and riding won him his freedom, a Hun wife, and admission into the ranks of Attila's trusted warriors. Priscus implored him not to forget his former life as a citizen living under the just laws of Rome. With tears in his eyes, the man admitted the achievement of Roman law in principle, but he deplored the application of the law in practice. He bemoaned the onerous taxes and arbitrary justice meted out by the emperor's officials and soldiers, whereas he had gained higher status and wealth in the service of Attila. Punishment by the Huns was swift and cruel, but at least it was impartially applied, and obedience and loyalty were well rewarded. The conversation captures well why so many Roman provincials felt no loyalty to rise to the defense of the emperor against the barbarians of the fifth century.

Therefore, Bleda and Attila inherited a powerful barbarian confederacy that could rival imperial Rome. All Romans ranked the Huns as the fiercest of barbarian warriors. What they could not anticipate was what these warriors could achieve under a charismatic conqueror soon to be known as the Scourge of God.

12

Attila, the Scourge of God

In the summer of 449, the Eastern Roman emperor Theodosius II dispatched to the court of Attila a mission headed by the senior official Maximinus and his friend the rhetorician Priscus of Panium. They were carrying a letter from the emperor in reply to Attila, who had charged the Romans with violating the treaty signed two years earlier.[1] Unbeknownst to Priscus and Maximinus, their interpreter Vigilas was on a secret mission from the emperor's eunuch minister Chrysaphius to suborn Attila's bodyguards to murder their master. Vigilas thought he was in league with a leading Hun, Edeco, who had headed Attila's legation to Constantinople, but Edeco himself was playing a double game to ferret out conspirators. The party traversed the desolate provinces of Thrace and Moesia, passing gloomy ruins of Roman cities sacked just years earlier by the Huns and now home to a handful of monks awaiting the Apocalypse.[2] Attila's men greeted them at the border, the juncture of the Margus (today Morava) and Danube Rivers. The next day the Roman envoys were received at the tent of Attila, for the restless king had journeyed south, and pitched his camp on the west bank of the Middle Danube. Edeco confided the details of the plot to Attila, and Vigilas was sent off on a fool's errand back

to Constantinople. Attila cleverly questioned Priscus and Maximinus, and determined that they were unwitting dupes, and so they
accompanied Attila back to his royal settlement on the east bank
of the Danube, perhaps near the Theiss River rather than opposite
the former Roman fortress Aquincum, today a suburb of Budapest.[3]
Attila's uncle Rugila had constructed a sprawling city of markets,
tents, and halls as the seat of the Hun confederacy. Priscus, a polished diplomat and careful observer, recorded a reception by Attila
in a great hall. At the festivities, Maximinus and Priscus sat at the
far end, while the envoys of the Western Roman emperor Valentinian III sat at the other.[4] Only noble warriors were seated in the
middle closest to Attila, whereas the slaves of the despised Roman
emperors were tolerated at the fringes of the feast. The scene inspired the Hungarian nationalist artist Mor Than to paint his "The
Feast of Attila" (1870), hanging today in the Hungarian National
Gallery in Budapest. The scene exalts Attila as the progenitor of the
Magyar kings of Hungary rather than recording the historical event.

During this visit, Priscus remembered vividly all that he saw,
and so he gives our sole contemporary description of Attila. "He
was a man born to shake the races of the world, a terror to all lands,
who in some way or other frightened everyone by the dread report
noised abroad about him, for he was haughty in his carriage, casting his eyes about him on all sides so that the proud man's power
was to be seen in the very movements of his body. A lover of war,
he was personally restrained in action, most impressive in counsel,
gracious to suppliants, and generous to those to whom he had given
his trust. He was short of stature with a broad chest, massive head,
and small eyes. His beard was thin and sprinkled with gray, his nose
flat, and his complexion swarthy, showing the signs of his origin."[5]

Attila, just like Genghis Khan, was every inch a charismatic
conqueror who inspired his warriors. He despised ostentation, and
never mistook ceremony for the reality of power. Throughout his
life, Attila remained modest in his dress and abstemious in his habits. At the banquet, Priscus recalls how Attila toasted with a simple wooden goblet and ate simple fare off his wooden plate.[6] The
riches and slaves he won were for rewarding his loyal followers.
Attila, shrewd, brave, and patient, shared the hardships of his men.

He possessed a keen sense of tactics and a strategic genius of the first order so that he turned the Hun confederacy into an empire.

In 434, the two brothers Bleda and Attila, in their mid-thirties, succeeded their uncle Rugila as joint rulers of the Hun confederacy.[7] According to the rules of lateral succession, the brothers were acclaimed by the council or *kurultai* of the clans' leading men, because they were the ablest mature members of the royal family of their generation. Bleda was slightly older, but Attila was the greater in deeds and words. For eleven years, the brothers ruled in an uneasy partnership, for each had his own jealous followers who incessantly argued and brawled with each other. Given the expanse of the confederacy, Attila ruled over the western tribes in Central Europe, while Bleda held sway over the eastern tribes on the south Russian steppes.[8] Yet they often acted in concert against the Eastern Roman Empire, and negotiated from horseback as partners with Roman envoys from Constantinople. In 445, Attila arranged for the murder of Bleda while hunting.[9] A long-simmering rivalry had erupted four years earlier. In 441, the Huns attacked the city of Margus, alleging the bishop had defiled a Hun cemetery near the city in search of treasures. The bishop fled to the Huns, where he cast the blame on his fellow citizens out of fear that they would turn him over to the Huns for punishment. The bishop swore that he would trick the garrison to sally out of the city so that the Huns could ambush them. He delivered on his word. Margus was taken and sacked.[10] To Bleda fell Zerco, a humpback jester of Moorish ancestry, who amused Bleda by his ugly countenance, ungainly gait, and babbling tongue.[11] Attila found Zerco repulsive, and the two brothers quarreled over the jester. Zerco even once escaped, was captured, and returned to Bleda. Bleda, who had a cruel streak of humor, married the dwarf off to a noble lady who had fallen into disfavor as a means to humiliate her family. For Attila, this was the final unforgivable act of cruelty. Once Bleda was killed, allegedly in a hunting accident, Attila was acclaimed the grieving brother and sole ruler. Yet the dispute over the jester concealed a deeper rivalry over who should succeed. Attila had at least three sons, and he favored Ernac as his successor, marking him out at feasts in the great hall.[12] Attila was determined to impose the hereditary succession of his house alone and so eliminated any rivals to his heirs. Therefore, in treaties with the Romans, Attila always insisted on the provision that Hun exiles of high rank be turned over to him. Attila executed at least two young royal Hun exiles handed over by Theodosius. The cravenly emperor Theodosius II even appeased Attila by ordering the execution of a number of Huns of high birth unwilling to leave Constantinople lest Attila claim treaty violations.

For fifteen years, Attila played a dual game of attacking the wealthier Eastern Roman Empire and providing Aetius, patrician and *magister militum* of the emperor Valentinian III, with Hun armies to secure the Roman West.[13] Attila timed his attacks precisely when Roman field armies were engaged on other distant frontiers, and he exacted the maximum terms from the feckless Eastern emperor Theodosius II. Attila displayed a keen sense of strategy, and an ability to gather and interpret reports about his foe. Attila also learned from Rome, for he was the only barbarian enemy of Rome who mastered siege warfare. He fielded a corps of Roman engineers and a supply train so that the Huns could wage winter campaigns. The Romans were shocked to see a barbarian army besiege, capture, and raze their cities. To be sure, the Huns fielded superb horse archers, but the subject Germanic tribes provided heavy cavalry and infantry to what was an imperial army.[14] Attila, like the Xiongnu chanyu or the Rouran khan, depended on the tribute rendered by the Roman emperors and the booty and captives gained in raids. Yet he was hardly the boss of a barbarian protection racket, for he maintained a secretariat staffed by Orestes, a Roman who chose to take Hun service. Orestes kept records and wrote diplomatic letters in Latin.[15] Attila sent out envoys who were able diplomats accompanied by skillful interpreters in Latin or Gothic. Since Attila died unexpectedly in his late forties, we shall never know whether he would have annexed and administered Roman provinces in the fashion of many steppe conquerors. Given time, he and effective heirs could well have learned to rule cities, tax sedentary subjects, and mint coins in the manner of contemporary Huns in Iran and northern India or the Tuoba Xianbe emperors of the Northern Wei in northern China.

Initially, Attila and Bleda were content to collect the annual tribute of 350 pounds of gold under the treaty their uncle Rugila had extorted from the Eastern emperor Theodosius II twelve years earlier. In 435, Attila demanded the return of exiles at the imperial court of Constantinople, and complained about trading rights accorded to Huns at Roman markets along the Danube.[16] Theodosius II, preoccupied with the Vandals in North Africa, dispatched envoys who concluded a new treaty at Margus, in Moesia, in 435.[17] Theodosius agreed not to receive Hun exiles or to ally with any foes of the Huns. He also doubled the annual subsidy to 700 pounds of gold and extended access to Roman markets. Border incidents continued. In 441, Attila seized on the one over the violations of Hun cemeteries by the Bishop of Margus to launch a six-year war, devastating the Balkan provinces almost to the suburbs of Constantinople.[18] The Huns sacked every major city along the imperial highways with the exceptions of Adrianople and Heraclea on the shores of the Sea of Marmara. Theodosius could do little, because the field army under the ablest general, Aspar, an Alan by descent, was campaigning against the Vandals who had captured Carthage in North Africa. Theodosius hastily concluded a peace with the Vandals, and recalled Aspar and his army in 442.[19] In the next year, Aspar suffered a decisive defeat in Thrace. The desultory war raged on, with more Roman setbacks. On January 26, 447, a major earthquake shook Constantinople, bringing down fifty-seven towers and a long section of the walls.[20] Theodosius, barefoot and dressed as a suppliant, headed a procession through the devastated city to implore God's protection lest Attila suddenly appear before the walls. Within sixty days, under damp, overcast winter skies, members of the circus factions (the clubs that backed chariot teams in the Hippodrome) feverishly repaired the walls.[21] But Theodosius lost confidence in the walls and his soldiers, so that he dispatched a senior general, Anatolus, to beg for terms. Attila dictated the most humiliating treaty ever imposed on the imperial government.[22] The annual tribute was tripled to 2,100 pounds of gold, and an additional 6,000 pounds for arrears, and yet thousands more to redeem Roman captives at an exorbitant rate. To be sure, these sums represented a fraction of the empire's wealth, but it was a significant proportion of the emperor's disposable income.

In twenty-eight years, between 422 and 450, Theodosius had paid in tribute to the Huns 18,500 pounds of gold.[23] Only two other payoffs, each a onetime payment to a Persian shah, matched this sum.[24] Furthermore, Attila insisted on prompt payment each year from his slave Theodosius. Finally, the Romans agreed to evacuate their fortresses and the civilian population at a distance of five days' journey (at least one hundred miles) from the lower Danube frontier. The Roman frontier in the Balkans had just collapsed.

On July 26, 450, the emperor Theodosius, age forty-nine, died after having been thrown from his horse days earlier.[25] His older sister Aelia Pulcheria, renowned for her intelligence and piety, secured the court. She quickly married and elevated to the throne Marcian, a senior Roman officer, who had the backing of the imperial army.[26] Marcian, a blunt Illyrian provincial, ended the tribute, ordered the recruitment of soldiers and repairs of the walls, and braced for the inevitable Hun invasion. It never came. Attila, while furious over Marcian's embassy that repudiated the treaty, turned his attention to the Western Roman Empire. Court intrigues at Ravenna during the summer of 450 offered him an opportunity to gain control over most of the Western Roman Empire.

From his accession, Attila had consistently honored an alliance with Flavius Aetius, *magister militum* of the Western army, and the dominant figure of the court of Emperor Valentinian III at Ravenna. Aetius, a provincial Roman in origin, was the son of a high-ranking officer of Stilicho. Between the ages of fifteen and twenty-five, he was sent as a hostage, first among the Visigoths, and then the Huns, from whom he learned their languages, archery, and horsemanship.[27] He encountered the leading Huns, and likely became a sworn brother, or, in Mongol terms, *anda*, to many of them. He met Attila already the most promising among the younger royal princes. On August 15, 423, the Western emperor Honorius, then thirty years old, died from a wasting disease. He left no sons. Castinus, a lackluster ex-general and scheming courtier at court, placed on the imperial throne Johannes, a meek and bookish bureaucrat.[28] The Eastern emperor Theodosius II refused to recognize Johannes and furnished his cousin Galla Placidia, the half sister of Honorius, and her young son Valentinian III with an army.

The Eastern army invaded Italy, and easily defeated the kingmaker and usurper in 425.[29] But Castinus had sent Aetius to the court of Rugila with ample gold to buy a Hun army. Aetius arrived three days late and missed the civil war so that, at the head of a Hun army, he extorted from an unwilling Galla Placidia command of a field army in Gaul.[30] Although the historian Procopius two centuries later hailed Aetius as "the last of the Romans," in truth, he was the first of the Medieval warlords.[31] For twenty-five years, Aetius controlled the best Western field army, which was stationed in Gaul.[32] He intrigued incessantly to achieve supreme military and civilian power in the Roman West. Aetius was not above masterminding the poisoning of a rival general, and mortally wounding another by cheating in single combat. Galla Placidia was eventually forced to retire into a private life of Christian charity, while her son Valentinian grew to fear and loathe his general, who pressed for an imperial marriage of his son to the emperor's younger daughter.[33] Yet Aetius delivered order in Gaul and Spain by employing his Hun allies to terrorize the Germanic and Alan federates settled within the Western Roman Empire. In 437, Attila obliged Aetius by lending a Hun army that wiped out the troublesome Burgundians settled around Worms in the Rhineland.[34] Later German, Anglo-Saxon, and Norse poets recast the mundane event into a heroic legendary tale about the ill-fated royal house of the Burgundians.[35] While Attila had ravaged the Balkan provinces of the Eastern Empire, Aetius stayed on respectful terms with Attila, but this alliance of convenience ended in the summer of 450. The empress Honoria, the older sister of Valentinian, was forced into a marriage with a boring elderly senator after she was allegedly caught in a scandalous sexual liaison with her chamberlain. She sent her signet ring and a message to Attila, imploring him to rescue her.[36] Attila chose to interpret the call for help as a marriage proposal, and demanded as the dowry Gaul and Spain, all that was left of the Western Empire outside of Italy. Aetius and Valentinian were both shocked, and flatly refused. To Attila, the refusal was an act of war, for as a son of the steppes, he expected such a marriage offer as a recognition that he was, after all, lord of all Huns and the equal of Roman emperors.[37] The Persian Great King, the Chinese emperor, and the Sassanid shah all offered daughters to the harems of nomadic conquerors, but Romans were strictly monogamous. Christian Roman princesses should not marry pagan, barbarian monarchs.

In the spring of 451, Attila marched rapidly west along the Danube, and descended into the Rhine valley, striking terror among Romans and Germans alike. Throughout the spring and summer, Attila waged a campaign of terror. He enrolled numerous Germanic allies, and divided his army into at least two columns. His army numbered at most fifty thousand men, and depended on speed and surprise.[38] The Huns quickly captured with siege engines Strasbourg, Worms, Mainz, Cologne, Trier, Metz, Reims, Tournai, Cambrai, Amiens, and Beauvais. The cities were ruthlessly sacked and burned; captives were herded together for the slave markets. The destruction across Roman Gaul was without precedent, and the Gauls long remembered how saints, such as Saint Geneviève of Paris, implored God's intercession to save their city from Attila's hordes. Aetius, with a field army of twenty thousand Romans, gained thirty thousand more men by engaging King Theoderic of the Visigoths, and the federate Alans settled near Orleans, and the Franks settled on the Lower Rhine.[39] In late summer, Attila put Orleans (Aurelianum) under siege, but Aetius arrived with his coalition army to raise the siege. Attila dared not risk an engagement near Orleans. He retired northeast in search of supplies and favorable terrain on the Catalaunian fields, between Troyes and Châlons.[40] There, in early autumn, Attila fortified his camp by circling his wagons into a laager and awaited Aetius. On the morning of the battle, Attila remained in camp because his shamans read unfavorable omens in the charred sheep bones.[41] In the afternoon, Attila suddenly issued forth from his camp, with his Huns and Alans occupying the center, and Germanic allies holding the flanks.[42] The Hun right wing rested on high ground overlooking the Marne River. Aetius placed his least reliable allies, Alans, in the center, and deployed Romans and Franks on his left to contest Attila's Germanic allies for the summit of the hill. The Visigoths on his right opposed their cousins the Ostrogoths on Attila's left. The battle lines looked more like a civil war among who's who in the barbarian world than a clash of empires. Attila's Huns drove back the Alans in Aetius's center, in what was likely a combined attack by horse archers and heavy cavalry. But the Romans and Franks gained the crest of the high ground and then wheeled into the right side of Attila's center. The Franks recklessly led the charge downhill, throwing their axes on the run. The Visigoths drove back the Ostrogoths on Attila's left, but King Theoderic fell in a failed counterattack against Attila, who had broken through Aetius's center. The inconclusive fighting raged on until dusk, when Attila retired to his camp, covered by the superb Hun archers. Later legends claimed the slain warriors still battled in the sky during the night. Attila feared a night counterattack, and prepared a funeral pyre of saddles so that he could immolate himself rather than fall into enemy hands. Aetius's forces were scattered over the battlefield. Aetius and Thorismund, the son of the fallen Theoderic, both lost their way back to their own lines. Aetius dared not press a night attack, for his army was exhausted.[43] The next morning, Aetius rejected Thorismund's proposal to storm the Hun camp. Aetius feared Attila might win a decisive victory or, even worse, suffer a crushing defeat. Politically, Aetius still needed Attila, for Aetius hoped to renew the alliance. First the Visigoths, then the Franks, and finally Aetius withdrew. Tactically the battle was a draw, but Attila held the field and retreated in good order, with his slaves and booty, across the Rhine. He could always recruit fresh forces in the winter. The war would go on.

In the following year, 452, Attila invaded Italy, but he halted and retired rather than press on to Rome.[44] Aetius and Valentinian were amazed. Legend soon supplied the answer: Pope Leo I had persuaded Attila to depart.[45] In that winter, Attila died unexpectedly from overindulgence at marriage festivities.[46] If Attila had not died so suddenly and realized his goals of an imperial marriage with Honoria, the course of events in the Western Roman Empire might well have turned out quite differently. The last Roman field army had sustained heavy casualties at Catalaunian Plains, and an imperial army of Huns under Attila could have restored order in Gaul and Spain. Attila and Honoria, and their heirs, might well have presided over a successful composite state of Romans and Huns not too dissimilar from that of the contemporary state of the

Northern Wei emperors. Instead, for the next fifteen years, Attila's sons fought over the succession, while the subject tribes rebelled in a bid for independence.[47] Attila's empire did not collapse so much as fragment, as was the case of so many steppe empires. On the banks of the Nedao River, a tributary of the Danube, a coalition of Germanic tribes defeated and slew Attila's eldest son, Ellac, in 454, just eighteen months after Attila's death.[48] The emperor Marcian had supplied gold and encouragement to the disaffected vassals, who soon fought among themselves. The Gepidae and Lombards fought over the great Hungarian plains between the middle Danube River and the Carpathian Mountains, while the Ostrogoths, then settled in the rolling plains of Pannonia (today Hungary west of the Danube), migrated south into the depopulated lands of the Roman Balkans.[49] Farther east, Attila's other two sons, Dengizich and Ernac, as allies of Rome, briefly ruled lesser groups of Huns residing between the lower Danube and Dnieper Rivers.[50] No charismatic ruler emerged to succeed Attila, and so to unite the nomadic tribes into an imperial confederacy. Instead, over the next century, newcomers, the Turkic-speaking Kutrighurs, Otrighurs, and Sabirs, steadily migrated out of the arid Kazakhstan steppes and settled across the south Russian steppes.

Meanwhile, the empress Honoria retired to a villa on the Bay of Naples, where she grew reconciled to the comfortable life of leisure with her elderly retiring husband. Aetius was fatally compromised, and he did not long survive Attila. In 454, the year after Attila's death, Aetius was cut down by his own master, Valentinian, at an audience.[51] In the next year, Valentinian too was dead, murdered by a cravenly ambitious senator who failed to prevent a Vandal sack of Rome.[52] A succession of phantom emperors followed for the next two decades. Edward Gibbon, with regard to one such emperor, Severus III, wrote, "History has scarcely deigned to notice his birth, his elevation, his character or his death."[53] Gibbon's obituary for Severus, with one exception, could be applied to the rest of the last emperors of the Roman West.[54] Barbarian generals who commanded the tribal regiments exercised real power.[55] In the final four years of the Western Roman Empire, Odoacer, a general of the former Hun Empire, gained power as *magister mili-*

tum at the head of a band of Attila's unemployed Germanic veterans. Odoacer elevated to the throne the last two Western Roman emperors. The second, Romulus Augustulus, was ironically the son of Attila's secretary Orestes, who had entered Roman service after Attila's death. In 476, Odoacer executed Orestes, forced the boy emperor Romulus Augustulus to abdicate, and ruled henceforth as king in Italy in the name of the Eastern emperor Zeno.[56] The Western Roman Empire had come to an ignominious end.

The meteoric career of Attila has inspired awe, wonder, and fear to this day. Even in his own lifetime, Attila was the stuff of legends. Priscus was told a legend about how Attila received the invincible sword of Mars from a shepherd who had stumbled upon it by accident, and so Attila could claim a universal kingship bestowed upon him by the eternal blue sky.[57] This particular legend gained currency among the Christian kings of Medieval Hungary, who claimed descent from Attila and the discovery of his lost sword in the eleventh century. This sword passed into the hands of the Dukes of Bavaria, then to the Habsburgs, and now it is on display in the Künsthistorisches Museum in Vienna. Ironically, the Ottoman sultans, the ancestral enemy of the Hungarians, too claimed Attila as a progenitor and a fellow *ghazi* warrior so that statues and displays of Attila are still found across Turkey today.

Medieval Christian writers cast Attila as the Scourge of God, a pitiless barbarian conqueror at the head of the hordes of Gog and Magog sent to punish a sinful world. To be sure, Attila ruthlessly sacked churches and slew priests and monks across the Balkans, Gaul, and northern Italy, but he waged the nomadic way of war in which those who resisted could expect no mercy. Yet Attila never persecuted his Christian subjects out of religious intolerance, and he welcomed loyal warriors and servants of many faiths. Quite in contrast, Arian Vandal and Visigothic kings in the Roman West fiercely persecuted their Catholic Roman subjects on several occasions.[58] Attila remained devoted to his ancestral spirits and scrupulously consulted shamans and seers, but he also respected the holy ones of other religions. Hence, the legend of Pope Leo, by his mere presence, impressing Attila to withdraw has a plausible ring. The

fateful meeting with Pope Leo might well have led Attila to make
up his mind whether to retreat or press on to Rome.

The Germanic peoples, many of whose ancestors were once subjects to Attila, celebrated him for centuries as a mighty lord, presiding over a great hall of heroes in the same fashion as their god
Odin (or Woden in Old English) held court at Valhalla. Priscus witnessed the celebrations held by Attila in his hall, and the account
reads as if it came right out of *Beowulf* or Norse saga.[59] In legend,
Atli, the Norse name for Attila, was extolled as a Great King, but
avaricious and lusting after the gold hoard of the Niflungs, the
treasure's original guardian dwarfs of the Rhineland. The Burgun-
dian king Gunnar, who is based on his namesake slain by the Huns
in 437, gained the hoard from his brother-in-law, Sigurd the dragon
slayer, by treacherously contriving the murder of Sigurd. Atli lured
Gunnar and his warriors to their destruction in a legendary last
stand fought within Attila's own great hall. Gudrun, sister of Gunnar and wife to Atli, avenged her family by slaying Atli and setting
the Hun hall ablaze.[60] In the *Nibelungenlied*, the Christian version of
the legend composed in the Middle High German verse, Etzel (Attila) is a sympathetic figure who presides over a court of the no-
blest of Germanic heroes. He is shocked that his wife Kriemhild
(Gudrun) arranged the attack on her brother Gunther (Gunnar) to
avenge herself against her own family for the murder of her first husband, Siegfried (Sigurd). Hildebrand, Etzel's master of arms, then cuts
down Kriemhild for violating the ties of kinship.[61] Based on Germanic
verse and Norse saga, Richard Wagner perpetuated the memory of
the legendary Attila in his four operas of *Der Ring des Nibelungen*.

Since the nineteenth century, the image of Attila and his hordes
of Huns sweeping across Europe still captures popular imagination
in novels, paintings, and films. The best known image of rampaging
Huns is still the painting by Alphonse de Neuville, the patriotic artist who illustrated the popular history of Medieval France of François
Pierre Guizot, which the author published in 1823. The illustration
combines the images of Attila's horsemen as harbingers of the Apocalypse and European fears of the Asiatic peril. It was to this image Kaiser Wilhelm II appealed when he exhorted German soldiers about to
embark for China at the port of Bremerhaven on July 27, 1900.[62] He

reminded the soldiers to avenge the atrocities of Attila and fight like Huns against the Boxers, Chinese rebels frustrated over decades of European imperialist oppression. The German expeditionary force arrived too late to participate in the relief of Beijing, where the foreign embassies had been besieged by the Boxers, but the Kaiser's words were turned against him. An unseen reporter had recorded the speech of Kaiser Wilhelm, notorious for his tactless, spontaneous remarks (to the angst of his ministers). The reporter then telegraphed the speech to newspapers across Europe and the United States. The public outcry, even among many Germans, surprised the Kaiser, because Attila, Etzel, was a respected king in German legend. In 1914, the British delighted in turning the Kaiser's own words against him, denouncing German soldiers rampaging across Belgium as the real Huns.[63] Even during the Second World War, Winston Churchill and Franklin D. Roosevelt in their communiqués to each other often referred to Germans as Huns. Two Hollywood epic spectacles, both released in 1954 and best seen in a drive-in theater, epitomize popular misconceptions about Attila and the Huns today. Anthony Quinn played the starring role in "Attila," but a stunning Sophia Loren as the empress Honoria stole the show.[64] In this less than historical epic, the best scenes are the Battle of the Catalaunian Fields and the meeting between Pope Leo and Attila. But Jack Palance wins honors as best Attila on the screen in "Sign of the Pagan."[65] Seven years later, he went on to play a just-as-menacing Ogatai Khan in "The Mongols," which was very loosely based on the Mongol invasion of Europe in the thirteenth century.

Yet Medieval legends and modern novels and film, however unhistorical and at times even silly, pay homage to a charismatic, barbarian conqueror who is widely perceived as altering the course of history. Attila and his Huns had terrorized the Roman world for nearly fifteen years, and earned a reputation comparable to that of Genghis Khan. In comparison to Genghis Khan, Attila counts far fewer lasting achievements.[66] Even so, Attila decided the destinies of the Roman world. His invasions forced an ineffective Western Roman court to turn to German tribal armies settled within the empire for defense. In so doing, Attila ensured that the Germanic kingdoms of the West would succeed Rome as the new order of Medieval Europe.[67] His wars in the Roman Balkans severed the strategic highways between Constantinople and Ravenna, and so led to the parting of the Western and Eastern Roman worlds that shared a common Classical, urban civilization. The Medieval West, aligned along the axis of Rome to London, would find its future among the Romanized, Celtic, and Germanic populations of Northwestern Europe. The Byzantine East, centered on Constantinople, also turned north and realigned itself with the Slavic peoples.[68] In the process, the modern boundaries between Western and Eastern Europe were born. Finally, for the Roman East, Attila compelled future emperors in Constantinople to perfect an artful diplomacy to undermine such confederations of steppe nomads from ever emerging in the future.

13

The Heirs of Attila and the New Rome

In early June of 626, the patriarch Sergius led a solemn procession atop the walls of Constantinople to ward off a new barbarous race, the Avars, who laid siege to the city.[1] Before the procession was carried the city's holiest icon, the Hodegetria, reputedly painted by Saint Luke and housed in the church to the Virgin Mary in the northeastern district of Blachernae.[2] The icon depicted Mary Theotokos, Mother of God, cradling the infant Jesus. Soldiers and citizens raised their voices in prayer for deliverance from these new Huns off the Eurasian steppes who were in league with the ancestral foe, the Sassanid shah of Persia. A Persian army of Shah Khusrau II was encamped at Chalcedon on the Asian side of the Bosporus opposite the city.[3] Only the imperial fleet prevented the Persians from crossing in force and joining their Avar allies in storming the land walls of Constantinople. For the first time, the citizens of the capital of the Roman Empire of the East endured a siege, for even Attila had not dared to approach the daunting Theodosian Walls. For two months, the Persians and Avars strove to take Constantinople. Then, news of the first victories arrived from the east. The emperor Heraclius had launched a daring counteroffensive against the Persian shah in Armenia and Iran.[4] The Avars and

Persians withdrew. Within three years, Heraclius smashed three Persian field armies, sacked the Persian capital Ctesiphon, and dictated a peace.[5] The Avar siege of Constantinople, however, marked a turning point in the relations between East Rome or Byzantium, and the northern steppe barbarians. For the next four centuries, the Byzantine emperor battled Turkish nomads and their Slavic allies who settled in the Balkans, while on the South Russian steppes, he courted the leading Turkish confederacy to check first the Sassanid shah, and then the Arab caliph.

Two generations earlier, the Avars, Turkish-speaking nomads, had fled west soon after Bumin Kaghan of the Gök Turks had overthrown the Rouran kaghanate in 552.[6] In 558, suddenly, twenty thousand Avar warriors and their families appeared on the steppes just northeast of the Caspian Sea.[7] They had fled swiftly across the vast steppes of Kazakhstan because Ishtemi, the brother and deputy (or *yabgu*) kaghan of Bumin, pursued the Avars, who, scions of the Rouran, had refused to accept defeat and to submit to the Gök Turks. When the Avars arrived, they found wide rivers, greener pastures, and a medley of warring nomadic tribes on the south Russian steppes. In the century after Attila's death, the Byzantine governor resident in Cherson, the principal Greek port on the southern shores of the Crimea, routinely sent envoys bearing gold and silk, to incite wars among Hun, Kutrighur, and Otrighur princes lest one of them unite the tribes and invade the imperial provinces in the Balkans.[8] The Avars, however, sent a large deputation directly to Constantinople. The Avar envoys excited awe and curiosity as they strode confidently into the throne room, sporting leather kaftans and felt caps; their long locks of hair were braided with wire-thin gold twists.[9] They introduced themselves to the emperor Justinian, then seventy-five years old. Justinian, who had lost none of his diplomatic acumen, immediately put the Avars on the imperial payroll, for he judged that they would soon be masters of the south Russian steppes. Today, Justinian is best remembered for his greatest achievements, his legal code and the church of Hagia Sophia, and for his notorious wife Theodora, the courtesan turned empress. But for thirty years, Justinian had labored to restore the Christian Roman Empire of Constantine. He had nearly bankrupted the empire in wars waged to recover Italy, Africa, and southern Spain from the Germanic invaders.[10] Justinian dared not risk the northern frontier by insulting the Avars. Ten years later, Justin II succeeded his uncle Justinian. He and his wife Sophia, a niece of Theodora, were hailed the honeymoon couple of a new golden age, for all in Constantinople despised Justinian for his endless wars, high taxes, and lurid scandals at court. The nervous, irritable Justin soon proved to be worse. He refused any more tribute under his uncle's treaties, first to the Kaghan Bayan, and then, in 572, to the Shah Khusrau I. Justin thus incited wars with both the Avars and the Persians.[11] For the next century, the Eastern Roman and Sassanid Empires were locked in nearly perpetual war that ultimately ruined both belligerents. At the same time, the imperial government could do little to defend either Italy or the Balkans. The emperor Justin soon after went mad. In 574, the empress Sophia prevailed upon her unbalanced husband to adopt as his heir the general Tiberius Constantine, who promised the kaghan an annual subsidy of 80,000 gold solidi (over 1,100 pounds) in return for a peace.[12] The Avars observed the treaty far more in the breach than the adherence. In 582, the kaghan made even higher demands from the next general acclaimed the emperor Maurice Tiberius. The kaghan demanded, received, and returned in contempt first an elephant and then a golden throne.[13] His final demand to increase the tribute was refused, and ignited a major war in the Balkans. From the start, Maurice Tiberius, while an able soldier, was at a disadvantage.

In 567, Bayan, kaghan of the Avars, had allied with the Lombards to exterminate their inveterate foe the Gepidae, who dominated the Hungarian grasslands between the Danube and the Carpathian Mountains. The Lombards received the booty, and thereupon invaded Italy and wrested control of half of the peninsula from the Byzantine emperor.[14] The Avars occupied the Hungarian grasslands, and Kaghan Bayan built his capital, the "Seven Rings," upon Attila's former settlement opposite Budapest. From there Bayan exercised a hegemony over the diverse tribes on the south Russian steppes as far as the Don River. The Avars initiated major ethnic changes that still define Central and Southeastern Europe. The last of the East Germanic tribes, the Lombards, forever departed the steppes to find new homes in northern Italy to which they gave their name, Lombardy. Henceforth, Turkish-speaking Avars, and then their Finno-Ugric-speaking successors, the Magyars, dwelled on the grasslands of Central Europe. Recent DNA testing of skeletal remains of Avars exhumed from graves in the Banat (where the Theiss River joins the Danube) has revealed that members of the elite classes of the Avar confederacy were descended from peoples of the Mongolian steppes.[15] Archaeology proves also that the Avars adhered to their ancestral ways, revering their shamans and honoring their ancestral spirits according to burial rites common on the Eurasian steppes.[16] The Avar kaghans soon found new allies among the numerous clans and families of Slavs who had migrated out of the forests of Eastern Europe to fill the lands vacated by German tribes in Central Europe between the Elbe and Vistula Rivers. Since the mid-sixth century, Slavic tribes had already crossed the Danube River and pressed south into the Balkan provinces of Moesia and Thrace (the future Bulgaria). True to steppe policy, the Avar kaghan raided to win captives and booty for his followers, but the Slavic tribes came to stay, and they turned the Balkans into a largely Slavic-speaking land over the coming centuries.[17]

The Avars proved almost as formidable as the Huns. A succession of warlike kaghans under the dynastic name Bayan timed attacks during the winter, when ice and snow blocked the imperial fleet on the Danube, or whenever they received news of the imperial army engaged in campaigns against the Persians. They also employed Roman engineers. In 579, Kaghan Bayan besieged Sirmium (today Sremska Mitrovica, Serbia), the strategic fortress on the Save River, by constructing a fortified bridge that cut off and forced the city to surrender after a siege of over three years.[18] Avar horse archers possessed superior mounts and saddles equipped with steel stirrups. An expert archer astride his horse could easily turn about in his saddle and fire deadly volleys at pursuing foes as they were lured into an ambush.[19] The author of the Byzantine military treatise *Strategikon* describes this frontier warfare between Byzantines and Avars.[20] Writing under the pseudonym of the emperor Maurice Tiberius, the veteran officer devotes most of his manual to how to battle the Avars and Slavs in the desultory fighting of raids, skirmishes, and ambushes. The imperial army came to depend ever more on mounted lancers and archers, who could move quickly to surprise and encircle the nomadic foe. Over the course of the sixth and seventh centuries, the very nature of this warfare disrupted urban life and agriculture to the benefit of Avar raiders and Slavic colonists. Together, pagan Avars and Slavs massacred, enslaved, or expelled the Christian provincial populations. The survivors fled to cities on the Dalmatian coast of the Adriatic Sea, or to Greek cities on the Aegean and Euxine shores.[21] In these cramped cities on the shores, the residents turned to their patron saints. At Thessalonica, the capital of northern Greece, citizens repeatedly beseeched their patron Saint Demetrius, from whose crypt flashed lightning and arose a foul-smelling sulfurous gas that drove off Avar hordes.[22] Witnesses swore that apparitions of the saint himself and a host of angels on the walls also warded off the attackers. By the late seventh century, the emperor had lost control over the interior of the Balkans, northern Greece, and even the Peloponnesus. There, Roman cities crumbled into ruins and were abandoned; roads, bridges, and aqueducts were never repaired and fell out of use. With the end of urban life, imperial institutions and Christianity disappeared for the next four centuries.

In 590, the emperor Maurice Tiberius gained an unexpected opportunity to reverse the strategic situation in the Balkans. The young Sassanid shah Khusrau II, named after his illustrious grandfather and rival of Justinian, appeared at Constantinople and pleaded for assistance against a usurper, the popular general Bahram Chobin, who had defeated the Hephthalites and then seized power in Ctesiphon.[23] Maurice Tiberius furnished men and money whereby Khusrau regained his crown at the price of concluding a treaty favorable to Constantinople. The emperor Maurice Tiberius thereupon transferred his field army to the Balkans, and waged a methodical war of pacification against the Avars for the next ten years.[24] The parsimonious emperor drove his army relentlessly, withheld pay, and, in the winter of 601–602, ordered them into makeshift winter quarters on the dreary Hungarian steppes. The soldiers mutinied under a centurion, Phocas, seized Constantinople, and butchered the imperial family.[25] Phocas, a usurper of low birth, proved incompetent and unpopular. Shah Khusrau declared war to avenge his murdered ally and patron Maurice Tiberius. Khusrau soon shifted from revenge to conquest when the disaffected Monophysites, Christian sectarians who were the majority of the population in Roman Syria and Egypt, welcomed the Persians.[26] The Avars resumed their attacks, and by 610, the Roman Empire of the East was on the brink of collapse. Heraclius, the son and namesake of the elderly, popular governor of Carthage, was invited to rescue the beleaguered capital. In the autumn of 610, Heraclius and the imperial fleet appeared in the Bosporus. Soldiers and citizens rebelled and slew Phocas, and hailed Heraclius as emperor.[27] In the next twenty-five years, Heraclius pulled off the greatest victory of any Roman commander in Rome's seven centuries of conflict against the Parthians and Persians.[28] It ended in the overthrow of Shah Khusrau and unconditional surrender of the Persians, who restored occupied provinces, captives, and the True Cross, which followed Heraclius in his triumphal entry into Jerusalem on his march back to Constantinople.

The war climaxed in the siege of Constantinople in the summer of 626. During the long summer, Avar warriors and their Slavic allies suffered grievously from disease and privations, and futile assaults on the outer defenses of the Theodosian Walls. The Avar kaghan was forced to retreat, and he never recovered from his loss of prestige among his vassal peoples.[29] Several years later, the Hun, Turkish, and Magyar tribes between the Dniester and the Don Rivers revolted. To the north, Slavic tribes, resentful of paying tribute in furs and slaves, also rebelled and declared the first Slavic state in Central Europe under their prince Samo.[30] The Avars retreated to the Transylvanian steppes, abandoning the Balkans and the south Russian steppes. They switched to raiding northern Italy and southern Germany, but the Frankish kings checked the Avars. In 791–796, Charlemagne, soon to be crowned Holy Roman Emperor, invaded the Hungarian steppes, sacked the "Seven Rings," and ended the Avar kaghanate.[31]

The collapse of the Avar confederacy brought no respite to Heraclius and his heirs in the Balkans, because they almost immediately faced the full might of the Arabic armies that overran Armenia,

Syria, Palestine, and Egypt in the name of Islam. The Byzantine emperor, who henceforth ruled a far lesser state centered on Asia Minor, could not expel the Slavs settled in the Balkans. Hence, the imperial government initially welcomed as allies against the Slavs the Bulgars, Turkic-speaking nomads, who were losers in the most recent tribal war on the south Russian steppes. In 681, the Bulgar khan Asparuh led his nation across the Dobruja and settled in Moesia, the same frontier lands where the Visigoths had settled three centuries earlier.[32] The Bulgars, however, quickly welded the Slavic clans of the Balkans and the nomads immediately north of the Lower Danube into the third barbarian confederation to challenge Constantinople. The Bulgar khans thus succeeded the Avar kaghans as the new Scourge of God. The most dreaded was Khan Krum, who surprised and slaughtered an imperial army under the emperor Nicephorus I in the Vorbina Pass in 811.[33] The emperor was slain in the rout, and his skull was gilded and decorated with jewels to serve as the khan's goblet at feasts whenever he received Byzantine envoys. Two years later, Krum slaughtered another imperial army under the emperor Michael I at Versinica. Michael was deposed by his officers of the eastern army, while Krum's horse archers ravaged across Thrace to the very walls of Constantinople, and then retired to sack Adrianople and enslave its inhabitants.[34] The next Khan Omurtag (814–831) obtained a favorable treaty marking off the "Great Fence of Bulgaria" as the southern boundary of the Bulgar Khanate.[35] The emperor Theophilus (829–842), in turn, preferred diplomacy to war so that he outfitted his throne room to awe the khan's envoys.[36] A golden tree stood near the throne; in its branches were steam-powered mechanical birds that chirped in unison. The throne's flanking golden lions simultaneously roared through the power of steam. Finally, the throne itself could be suddenly raised to a second level, where attendants quickly changed the emperor's ceremonial dress, while Bulgar envoys lay prostrate and facing the ground, reciting the khan's petition. When they rose again, they would see Theophilus, originally clad in a silk robe sewed with emeralds, now dressed in one sewed with dazzling rubies or diamonds. Yet such diplomatic ploys might have whetted the khan's appetite for more gold and silk rather than discouraged him.

What must have most impressed the khan's ambassadors was Hagia Sophia and an imperial mass held beneath its great dome that was pierced at its base by forty glass windows and seemed to float on a flood of light. Today even the casual tourist gapes in awe at the dome hovering seventeen stories above. To steppe nomads, the Dome of Heaven crowned what must have been the dwelling of the all-powerful god of the blue skies. In 866, Khan Boris, who had secretly accepted baptism two years earlier, ordered his subjects to embrace Orthodox Christianity.[37] From Byzantine missionaries, Boris received an autonomous church under its own patriarch, the Cyrillic alphabet and liturgy in Slavic, and a literate clergy who could keep records and turn a Bulgar khanate into a Christian kingdom. As a Christian Tzar, Boris fused Turk and Slav into a new Christian people, the Bulgarians, who entered the spiritual and cultural commonwealth of Byzantium, and so the new Christian world of Eastern Europe.

Tsar Symeon (893–927), Boris's second son, received a Christian education in Constantinople, where he drank deeply from the heady brew of Orthodox theology and Byzantine political ideology. For a generation, Symeon waged abortive wars against Constantinople, but not in the fashion of a nomadic conqueror, but rather as a Christian monarch who, in the second war, sought to marry himself into the imperial family.[38] Tsar Symeon was the first among future Slavic monarchs—Bulgarian, Serbian, and Russian—who have aspired to sit on the throne of Constantinople. This political legacy still influences Russian foreign policy today. In 895, during his first war against Byzantium, Symeon even outmaneuvered the emperor Leo VI in Byzantine diplomacy.[39] Leo VI incited the Magyars, Finno-Ugric speakers of the forest who had adopted the nomadic way of life, to attack the Bulgarians from the north.[40] Symeon, however, convinced the even fiercer Pechenegs farther east to invade the homeland of the Magyars. Driven from the south Russian steppes, the Magyars crossed the Carpathian Mountains during the winter of 895–896 and settled on the Transylvanian grasslands.[41] Western European chroniclers dreaded these newest barbarian marauders as Hunni (and so Hungarians), or Ougri (and so ogres). The Magyars, like the Avars before them, raided widely across Italy and Germany for the next sixty years, until they suffered a decisive defeat at the hands of Otto the Great, Holy Roman Emperor, on the banks of the Lech in August 955.[42] In 972, Geza, the Arpad khan of the Magyars, and his queen Sarolt together accepted baptism and the spiritual authority of the Pope, although they and their nation still practiced ancestral rites. Their son, the saintly King Stephen, turned the pagan Magyars into Christian Hungarians.[43] Within a century, Hungary ceased to be an extension of the Eurasian steppes, and became a land of cities, villages, and ranches, and so the bastion of Latin Christendom against future invaders from the east. As a consequence of the migration of the Magyars, the Bulgarian Tsar lost control over the steppes north of the Danube, and ruled henceforth a Slavic Balkan kingdom, which Byzantine emperors incorporated into the empire in the late tenth and eleventh centuries.[44] But the ethnic lines of today's southeastern Europe were defined, although Ottoman rule would later complicate the mix.[45] The Hungarians still dwell on the Pannonian and Transylvanian grasslands; Roman provincials speaking Latin or Illyrian languages retreated to the mountain zones, where they reemerged as Romanians or Albanians. The south Slavs—Slovenes, Croatians, Serbians, and Bulgarians—settled in the lands north of the treaty line negotiated between the Bulgar khan and Byzantine emperor in 814–816. The lands to the south of the boundary have remained Greek in language and Orthodox in faith.

Meanwhile, on the south Russian steppes, the emperor in Constantinople sought allies among the most powerful of the nomadic confederacies between the sixth and eleventh centuries. The emperor Justin II received an embassy from Ishtemi, *yabgu* of the Western Gök Turks, who demanded as his any tribute paid by the imperial government to the Avars, who were, after all, his slaves.[46] Justin adroitly evaded any payouts, but he sacrificed a lucrative trade agreement for importing silk. The Western Turks continued to press west, reaching the great bend of the Don River and threatening the imperial port of Cherson in the Crimea. The emperor Tiberius Constantine sent the next mission to Tardu, the son and successor

of Ishtemi, to arrange an alliance and an alternate route across the
steppes to the cities of Transoxiana and so to the markets of the
Silk Road now controlled by the Western Turks. Tardu, suspicious
of Byzantine duplicity, greeted the imperial envoy as the one who
spoke ten tongues and a single lie. He gestured by raising his fin-
gers to his mouth, and likely nodding his head backward, today the
gesture of refusal among modern Turks. A generation later, the political situation had changed for emperor and kaghan.[47] The Tang
emperor Taizong waged a war of conquest against the Eastern Turks,
while the Western Turks warred among themselves over the succession. In 625, the emperor Heraclius concluded an alliance with
Western Turkish tribes soon to be known as the Khazars.[48] Their
ten thousand horse archers under their commander Ziebel proved
decisive in the victory over Sassanid Persia.

The Khazars initially headed a confederation of ten tribes who
dwelled on the steppes along the northern shores of the Caspian Sea
and constructed market towns of tents and cabins along the lower
Volga River. Under able kaghans, scions of the royal Ashina family
of the Gök Turks, the Khazars expanded to the west, to the lower
reaches of the Dnieper River, and south to the northern foothills
of the Caucasus.[49] The Caspian became a veritable Khazar Sea, a
popular designation still used by the Turks of Inner Asia today. The
Bulgar tribes either retreated northeast to the middle Volga valley,
where they accepted the Khazar kaghan as their overlord, or migrated southwest into the Roman Balkans. The Khazars proved invaluable allies to Constantinople for over two centuries. In just four
years after his victory over Persia, Heraclius saw his work undone
by Arab tribal armies united under the banner of Islam. The Arabs
toppled the Sassanid Empire and overran Byzantine Syria, Egypt,
and North Africa. A new world power, the Caliphate, emerged,
aiming to conquer Constantinople, which Arab armies twice besieged and failed to capture in 671–674 and 717–718.[50] At the same
time, Arab armies repeatedly crossed the Caucasus Mountains to
win the south Russian steppes for Islam. Byzantine emperor and
Khazar kaghan allied against the common foe. During the seventh and eighth centuries, the Khazars beat back repeated Arab
attacks, and in turn attacked Muslim military colonies in Armenia

and Azerbaijan.[51] On a single occasion, a kaghan was compelled to embrace Islam as the price of a treaty, but he renounced the faith as soon as the Muslim army withdrew from the steppes.[52] The Khazars thus acted as a shield for Constantinople that ensured Byzantine mastery over the Black Sea and access to vital trade routes north to the Baltic Sea and east across the Eurasian steppes. Without the Khazar alliance, the Byzantine Empire might not have survived.

Byzantine emperors recruited many Khazar horse archers into the imperial army. The emperor Justinian II, the last of Heraclius's dynasty, proved too arbitrarily autocratic even by Byzantine standards so that in 695 he was deposed and mutilated to disqualify him from the throne. His nose was slit. Justinian, now nicknamed Rhinometus or the Slit Nose, was banished to Cherson, but the ex-emperor ten years later escaped to the Khazar court.[53] The kaghan likely viewed the emperor's disfigurement, which Justinian concealed with a golden nose, as a ritual of bravery. He furnished Justinian with an army, and his sister as a wife who was renamed the new Theodora. Justinian regained his throne, but his excessive acts of vengeance ensured a second deposition, and execution.[54] Henceforth, those deposed Byzantine emperors who were spared execution were awarded the retirement program of castration, blinding, and consignment to a remote monastery.

Even Justinian Rhinometus must have been impressed by the ceremony of the Khazar court.[55] The kaghan ruled as the Son of Heaven; the silk ceiling of his great tent was embroidered with the sun, moon, and stars of the firmament against a blue background. An army of servants catered to his every need, and ritual dictated every act that betrayed familiarity with Chinese practices. A large harem of beautiful, exotic concubines proclaimed the kaghan's virility and lordship, for no one woman was worthy to be his wife and queen. The kaghans, preoccupied by ritual, appointed the supreme commander or bek (Turkish for *lord*), and they rewarded tribal leaders and warriors with gifts gained from trade and war. The emperor Leo III, a tough Anatolian general who had seized the throne and defeated the Arabs in their final siege of Constantinople, married his son Constantine V to a Khazar princess renamed Irene of Khazaria.[56] She popularized Khazar court protocol and her fa-

vorite silk dress with floral patterns (*tzitzakion*), for in Turkish, her
name, Tzitzak, meant "flower princess." The Byzantine court also
adapted the Khazar bridal competition whereby the most beautiful woman was chosen to be the imperial spouse.[57] The Byzantines
added a test on Classical mythology and a golden apple to the winner in imitation of the Judgment of Paris.

The Khazar kaghans could maintain such an opulent court because their tent encampment at Atil soon emerged as the nexus of
trade routes linking the lands around the Baltic and Caspian Seas,
as well as caravans crossing the Caucasus to Baghdad and the cities
of Iran, and across the Eurasian steppes to the cities of Transoxiana and the Tarim Basin.[58] Arab travelers and geographers of the
tenth century report Atil straddled both banks of the Volga River
and was partitioned into quarters for each community of foreign
residents. According to one such report, the palace was located
on an island in the middle of the river, and it was connected to
both banks by a number of pontoon bridges.[59] International trade
brought many foreign merchants who settled permanently at Atil,
where they engaged in marketing Chinese silk, Indian spices, and
Persian cottons in exchange for slaves, furs, and timber destined
for the cities of Eastern Islam. Among the merchant families were
members of prominent Jewish banking houses in Baghdad, Cairo,
and Cordova. From them, the Khazar court learned of Judaism,
and converted to the faith by the opening of the ninth century. The
Khazars gained familiarity with Muslim silver coins, dirhems, and
minted their own imitations (called in contemporary records *yar-
maqs*). Two of these, bearing Kufic inscriptions, have surfaced in the
Spillings Hoard found on the Swedish island of Gotland and carry
the profession of faith altered from Muhammad to Musa (Moses)
as God's prophet.[60] The coins are dated by the Islamic calendar to
the year 837/8 AD, so the court had embraced Judaism before this
date. The Khazar kaghan might have opted for Judaism because
adopting either Islam or Orthodox Christianity could lead to political clashes with Byzantium or the Caliphate.[61] Far more significant
appeals were a universal, omnipotent God easily equated with the
Tengri of the eternal blue sky, Judaism's ritual purity, and its stress
on the written word.[62] In the cosmopolitan markets of Atil, Jewish

merchants and bankers, versed in many written languages and with wide-flung business connections, were welcomed by a court that had grown dependent on the profits of international trade. It was long debated whether the Khazars contributed significantly to later Jewish communities in Russia after the collapse of their kaghanate in 965. Recent DNA testing indicates that this is not the case,[63] but the Khazars contributed significantly to the formation of the early Russian state of Kiev.[64]

The conversion of the Khazars to Judaism cooled relations between Atil and Constantinople from the mid-ninth century on. The Khazar kaghan politely refused overtures to embrace Orthodox Christianity, and tolerated all faiths practiced by the diverse peoples of his confederacy. The imperial government thus sought out new allies among the foes of the Khazar kaghan, foremost the Pechenegs, Turkish nomads recently arrived from the Kazakhstan steppes, and the Rus, Swedes who had crossed the Baltic Sea and followed the Volga River to trade at Atil.[65] Each could be a dreaded foe, and an even more frightening ally. Even so, emperors recruited warriors of each race into the imperial army. The Pechenegs, organized into eight hordes (or armies in Turkish), had migrated across the northern edge of the south Russian steppes so as to avoid the pastures of the Inner Tribes of the Khazar confederacy. They expelled some vassals of the Khazar kaghan, notably the Magyars, and subjected many others. By 860, the Pechenegs ruled a rival confederation of the nomadic tribes between the Don and Dniester Rivers, and they could easily threaten the Byzantine cities of the Crimea.[66] Nearly a century later, Constantine Porphyrogenitus, an affable and learned emperor, wrote a practical treatise on the governing of the empire, *De Administrando Imperio*, in which he advised his young son Romanus never to endanger the alliance with the Pechenegs, for they were by far the most formidable of all the empire's neighbors.[67]

By 860, many Rus, Swedish merchant princes and warriors, had shifted their primary trade route away from the Volga and the Caspian Sea eight hundred miles west, to the Dnieper and the Black Sea, so that they could trade directly with Constantinople.[68] For over one hundred fifty years, the Rus had traded in the market

towns along the Volga River with the permission of the Khazar
kaghan. They had to pay the costs of dealing with merchants of
diverse nationalities who were the essential middlemen. The Rus,
well-armed Viking warriors from Scandinavia, provided the slaves
destined for Muslim harems, barracks, and plantations by raiding
the Slavic tribes of the Russian forests. In exchange, the Rus acquired numerous Muslim silver coins, Chinese silks, and exotic
goods of every description. The most remarkable item is a bronze
statuette of the Buddha from Gandhara that dates to the sixth century.[69] It was unearthed in excavations at Helgö, a Swedish market
town on Lake Mälaren. A Rus merchant on the Volga likely acquired it as a conversation piece to settle a debt with a merchant in
one of the Khazar market towns. In 921/2, Ahmad ibn Fadlan, a
jurist in Islamic law, visited the Khazar court at Atil as the envoy
of the Abbasid caliph al-Muqtadir. In his account, ibn Fadlan was
fascinated by the tall, fair-haired Rus, and so reports their methods of trade and a Viking ship burial on the banks of the Volga that
was spectacularly re-created in the film "The Thirteenth Warrior"
(1999).[70] The Rus, however, were profoundly influenced by their
hosts. The Rus prince at Atil, styled kaghan, was enthroned on a
tribunal surrounded by bodyguards and concubines of his harem.
He donned the silk robes and jewelry gained in trade to project
his wealth and power.[71] A generation later, the Byzantine historian Leo the Deacon gives the earliest description of a Rus prince,
Sviatoslav of Kiev, who parlayed with the emperor John Tzimisces
on the banks of the Danube.

> After the treaties were arranged, Sphendosthlavos [Sviatoslav]
> asked to come and speak with the emperor [John Tzimisces].
> And the latter came without delay on horseback to the banks
> of the Istros [Danube], clad in armor ornamented in gold, ac-
> companied by a vast squadron of armed horsemen adorned
> with gold. Sphendosthlavos arrived sailing along the river in
> a Scythian light boat, grasping an oar and rowing with his
> companions as if he was one of them. His appearance was as
> follows: he was of moderate height, neither taller than average,
> nor particularly short; his eyebrows were thick; he had grey

eyes and a snub nose; his beard was clean-shaven, but he let the hair grow abundantly on his upper lip where it was bushy and long; and he shaved his head completely, except for a lock of hair that hung down on one side, as a mark of nobility of his ancestry; he was solid in the neck, broad in the chest and very well articulated in the rest of his body; he had a rather angry and savage appearance; on one ear was fastened a gold earring, adorned with two pearls with a red gemstone, between them; his clothing was white, no different from that of his companions except in cleanliness. After talking briefly with the emperor about the reconciliation, he departed sitting on the helmsman's seat of the boat. Thus the war of the Romans with the Scythians came to an end.[72] This Scandinavian ruler of Kiev had sported the garb of the Eurasian steppes, because his forefathers had learned from the Khazars their dress, mores, cuisine, and court protocol.

During the early ninth century, the Rus founded fortified settlements at Novgorod (in Old Norse, Holmgard) and Kiev (ON Koenugard) to open a new route down the Dnieper to the Black Sea and Constantinople. At the opening of the twelfth century, an unknown monk in the Cave Monastery outside of Kiev composed the *Russian Primary Chronicle*. The chronicler struggled to reconcile legends and early documents into a coherent narrative. He reports that in 862, warring Slavic tribes agreed to invite a Viking sea king, Rurik (ON Erik), to rule over them and to establish laws.[73] Rurik, who resided in the Norse market town of Novgorod, exercised authority over the Norse settlements along the river routes linking the Baltic and Black Seas. His jarls, or earls, Askold (ON Höskuld) and Dir (ON Dýr), administered Kiev on the Dnieper, from whence they launched the first Rus naval attack on Constantinople in 860.[74] Rurik's successors turned themselves into territorial monarchs ruling from Kiev. They subjected the Slavs of the forests, built towns, and exacted tribute in furs and slaves. Commercial and military expeditions required organization, because Rus ships had to navigate seven hundred miles of the Dnieper to the Black Sea, and then another five hundred miles along the western shores of the Black Sea to the Bosporus and Constantinople. In its lower reaches, the Dnieper turns south, dropping over 160 feet through nine granite outcrops stretching over fifty miles. The nine rapids and numerous small islands make the Dnieper unnavigable so that the Rus had to make a portage by dragging their ships over an improvised roadway.[75] Since Rus ships were vulnerable to Pecheneg attacks, the Rus had to cooperate with the Pechenegs.

The Rus, as Vikings, also found the Theodosian Walls challenging rather than daunting. Three times in the tenth century, Rus fleets attacked the city.[76] Each time, the Rus were repelled by imperial warships armed with siphons squirting out steams of liquid incendiaries known as Greek fire.[77] Each time afterward, the prince of Kiev negotiated a favorable commercial treaty. Thereafter, many Scandinavian merchants in the capital and warriors in the service of the emperor accepted baptism. In 957, Queen Olga (ON Helga), regent for her son Prince Sviatoslav (ON Sveinheld), was inspired by a mass in Hagia Sophia to convert on the spot.[78] Her son Sviatoslav, an obdurate pagan, instead saw Constantinople as a prize. In 965, he allied with the Pechenegs to sack Atil and topple the Khazar confederacy.[79] Two years later, he invaded Bulgaria, and steadily advanced on Constantinople.[80] In 970–971, the emperor John Tzimisces drove the Rus back into Dorystolum on the lower Danube, and compelled the Rus to withdraw to Kiev.[81] The Pechenegs turned on their allies the Rus as they were negotiating the Dnieper Rapids. The Rus were slaughtered in droves, and Sviatoslav's skull joined the Pecheneg kaghan's tableware.

The ill-advised Balkan campaigns of Sviatoslav ended in catastrophic defeat and the destruction of a generation of Rus warriors. The Byzantine emperor John Tzimisces, received in triumph as the savior of Christendom, promptly annexed a devastated Bulgaria.[82] The Pechenegs were the real winners because they henceforth dominated the steppes from the lower Danube to the lower Volga Rivers. For the emperor in Constantinople, the Pechenegs had grown too powerful, and he found new allies in Turkish tribes, the Cumans, migrating west from the steppes of Kazakhstan, and, surprisingly, from the Rus too.[83] The greatest of Byzantine warrior emperors, Basil II, the Bulgar-slayer, turned to Prince Vladimir of

Kiev during a civil war in 989.[84] Vladimir furnished Basil with six thousand elite Varangian warriors wielding double-headed axes, who surprised and slaughtered the rebel army. Henceforth, the Varangians, mercenaries recently arrived from Scandinavia, served as the imperial bodyguard, and left their runic graffiti carved on the city's monuments, including the Hagia Sophia. In return, Vladimir converted to Orthodox Christianity and received the emperor's sister Anna as his bride.[85] The Russian chronicler reported a later legend, that is probably true, that Vladimir was convinced to embrace Orthodox Christianity after holding a debate among the theologians of the leading monotheistic faiths.[86] The final choice came down between Orthodoxy and Sunni Islam. The Byzantine missionary won over Vladimir by demonstrating God's omnipotence through icons, and affirming that as Christians, the Rus could still drink vodka, essential for surviving brutal Russian winters.

Just like Tsar Boris of Bulgaria, Vladimir gained an autonomous church with its own patriarch, the Slavic liturgy, and a clergy who could staff a royal bureaucracy. Within a generation, Scandinavian nobles and Slav subjects turned into Russians, who were Slavic in speech, Orthodox in faith, and Byzantine in culture. Russian princes built domed churches and palaces that transformed Norse towns into Christian Russian cities.[87] Russian peasants with improved plows and oxen relentlessly pushed south and southeast to put under cultivation the black earth of the mixed steppe and forest zones of the middle Dnieper and the upper reaches of the Don and Donets Basin. Pechenegs, Bulgars on the Volga (who had embraced Islam in the early tenth century), and later Cumans were all alarmed by the advance of Kievan Russia that threatened their way of life. Furthermore, Russian Christian princes ceased to be trading partners because they refused to sell their Christian Slavic subjects as slaves. Denied a market in Slavic slaves, Turkic-speaking nomads raided Russian villages and towns for captives. Turk and Russian quickly became sworn enemies, and the resulting desultory frontier warfare defined the future of Russia.[88]

Meanwhile, in Constantinople, the emperor Alexius Comnenus, the most intelligent man ever to sit on the imperial throne, forestalled a Pecheneg migration into the Balkans and so won the final

Byzantine triumph over nomadic foes. In 1091, Alexius allied with the Cumans, Kipchak Turks from the Kazakhstan steppes, and together they annihilated the Pechenegs in a great battle at Levounion, near the mouth of the Hebrus River (the modern Maritsa), which empties in the Aegean Sea.[89] The Cumans went on to forge the fourth great nomadic confederacy on the south Russian steppes, but Alexius did not have to deal with this threat because Russian princes henceforth battled the nomads. Cumans and Russians warred among themselves and against each other for the next two hundred fifty years. An unknown author was inspired to compose the first Russian heroic lay about Prince Igor of Novgorod-Seversk, whom the Cumans defeated in 1185.[90] The epic, while composed in prose, has a poetic cadence rich with alliteration and assonance so that the language conveys magnificent images of nature and omens foreshadowing Igor's defeat.[91] Prince Igor is exalted as an exemplary Orthodox prince who urges unity in the face of the Cumans. He is defeated and captured, but soon escapes. Meanwhile, Yaroslavna, Igor's wife, atop the city walls of Putivi, delivers the most moving passages as she laments to the winds and rivers for cruelly abandoning her husband at the decisive moment. This powerful epic epitomized how the frontier wars defined the Russians in the generations before the Mongol invasion. The epic, long forgotten, was rediscovered in a monastic library in 1795. It inspired the Russian music, poetry, and paintings of the nineteenth century, foremost the opera "Prince Igor" composed by Alexander Borodin, and completed and performed by Nikolai Rimsky-Korsakov in 1890.

For six centuries, the emperor of New Rome, Constantinople, forged a subtle Byzantine diplomacy against the nomads of the western Eurasian steppes that is still the envy of geopolitical policy makers today.[92] The imperial government countered the Bulgars and Slavs who invaded the Balkans, and eventually won their spiritual loyalty within a wider Orthodox commonwealth. Byzantine missionaries scored their greatest success by converting the Russians, who fell heirs to the imperial legacy as the Third Rome. Foremost, successive emperors repeatedly signed and broke a bewildering web of alliances with the Avars, Khazars, Magyars, Pechenegs, and Cumans. They thereby saved Constantinople from facing a mighty nomadic confederacy under a new Scourge of God. For all its successes against Turkic-speaking nomads from the north, the Byzantine Empire was toppled suddenly, unexpectedly, and decisively by other nomads from the east, the Seljuk Turks fighting in the name of Allah and his Prophet Muhammad. These newcomers were scions of the Eastern Gök Turks, who had overthrown the Rouran khanate and challenged Tang China.

14

Turkish Kaghans and Tang Emperors

The beautiful Orkhon valley in Mongolia has been the sacred land of eastern nomads from time immemorial. There, in 732, the Bilğe Kaghan of the Eastern Turks carved on a monumental monolith his heroic deeds next to his future funerary tumulus.[1] He also set down warnings to his fellow Turks learned from the humiliating servitude to the Tang emperors of China for two generations. He branded those Turks traitors who had accepted as their kaghan the Chinese emperor Taizong, and who fought for this Chinese kaghan in distant wars. He complained that too many Turks had become addicted to silk and luxuries brought by Chinese envoys and merchants in return for tribute of thousands of horses. He warned against adopting Chinese ways and giving up the martial ethos of their ancestors to become the docile slaves of a Chinese emperor. Above all, the Turks must not build cities in the Chinese fashion. They must shun buildings that enclosed the sky, and ride free over the steppes and sleep in the felt tents of the *yurt*. The words of Bilğe Kaghan rang true for any nomads who confronted urban civilizations on the edges of their world, but especially for the Turks who suddenly appeared on the eastern steppes in the mid-fifth century and founded three great kaghanates that challenged Tang China.

The Turks, who gave their name to the Altaic languages that came to be spoken by the majority of the Eurasian nomads, were reportedly refugees from the steppes north of the Gansu corridor.[2] In the fourth century, the Rouran kaghan settled them as vassals along the eastern foothills of the Altai Mountains and on the steppes immediately to the east, which were watered by Lake Issyk and its tributaries. They were thus a vassal tribe on the western fringes of the kaghanate.[3] They called themselves the Gök Turks or Celestial Turks, and they soon became renowned as miners and smiths, manufacturing the finest iron weapons, tools, furniture, and the first iron stirrups that revolutionized warfare among the nomads. The Buddhist pilgrim Xuanzang later marveled at a well-wrought Turkish bedpost at the court of one of his hosts.[4] Expertise in metalworking brought wealth to the Gök Turks, who long revered these mines as ancestral caves worthy of sacrifice. To the north of the Gök Turks dwelled the Kyrgyz, who were also expert miners and blacksmiths, and so rivals to any ambitious ruler of the Gök Turks.

In 551, Bumin, prince of Gök Turks and a member of the Ashina clan, revolted against his overlord, the Rouran kaghan Yujiulü Anagui. After years of loyal service battling the Rouran kaghan's foes, Bumin respectfully requested a Rouran princess as his bride, but Yujiulü Anagui refused any such marriage, contemptuously dismissing Bumin as a slave of smiths.[5] Thereupon, Bumin turned to the Western Wei court, ever ready to incite war among the Rouran kaghan's subjects. Bumin received a Chinese princess as his bride and the silk and gifts whereby he rallied numerous Turkish-speaking tribes and overthrew the Rouran kaghanate.[6] Yujiulü Anagui went down in defeat in a great battle and committed suicide. Bumin assumed the title of kaghan and declared a new Turkish kaghanate. Within a year, in 552, Bumin too died, but his two able sons succeeded, Issik and then Mukan Kaghan, who turned the Gök Turk confederacy into the third nomadic empire on the Eurasian steppes.[7] Bumin also designated his younger brother Ishtemi as *yabgu*, or deputy kaghan, over the steppes to the west. Ishtemi relentlessly pursued the defeated Rouran, who fled west and eventually set-

tled in Central Europe as the Avars.[8] He subjected the tribes west
of the Altai Mountains to the lower reaches of the River Don. In
557–558, he concluded an alliance with the Sassanid shah Khusrau
I, and together they defeated the Hephthalites, whom Ishtemi regarded as allies of the Rouran kaghan. Henceforth, Ishtemi ruled
as protector of the Sogdian caravan cities north of the River Oxus
and in the western Tarim Basin.[9] Ishtemi, the most successful of
nomadic conquerors since Modu Chanyu, felt entitled to demand
tribute from the emperor Justin II in return for opening routes of
the Silk Road to Byzantine merchants.[10]

Four generations later, on his memorial inscription in the Orkhon valley, Bilğe Kaghan revered the brothers Bumin and Ishtemi as
his progenitors and as models of fraternal cooperation whom future
generations of the Ashina clan should follow. Kaghan Bumin, as
head of the Ashina clan, claimed to rule by the mandate of Tengri,
supreme god of the sky.[11] He claimed as his own the sacred Orkhon valley and the mountain Ötüken in the range of the Khangai
in Mongolia today. This magnificent landscape surely must have
sprung from the union of Tengri and mother earth Umay in an act
of creation. There, beside the banks of the snow-fed Orkhon River,
tribal and clan leaders met in assembly to proclaim kaghans, ratify
treaties, and declare war. Successive Turkish and Mongol kaghans
would gather there all their subjects dwelling within the felt tents
to proclaim their universal lordship.[12] Many future dynasties of
Turkish rulers traced or invented a descent from the Ashina clan.
They also revered the wolf as the sacred animal, because Bumin
and his sons circulated the aetiological myth of descent from a
she-wolf.[13] Chinese soldiers dreaded Turkish armies carrying their
golden standards of the wolf, for the Turks, in the words of Bilğe
Kaghan, fought as if wolves descending on a flock of sheep.[14] Even
today, the wolf is the totem of Turkish nationalists in the Middle
East and Central Asia.

The brothers Bumin and Ishtemi did far more than replace one
nomadic confederacy with another. They initiated changes in language and warfare that still dictate the lives of the peoples of the
Eurasian steppes and those of their neighbors living in the civilizations of Europe, the Islamic world, India, and China. Between

the sixth and eleventh centuries, the Turks expelled or assimilated Iranian-speaking nomads and so forever changed the linguistic and ethnic makeup of the steppe nomads. The Turkish languages today, classified as a branch of the Altaic language family, might have emerged in the first century BC, but its earliest written records are the inscriptions of the Orkhon valley eight centuries later.[15] All Turkish languages share vowel harmony (in which the vowels of each word must belong to only one of two classes), an agglutinative morphology (in which the meaning of root words is changed by attaching suffixes), and a paratactic word order (without conjunctions and subordinate clauses governed by a relative pronoun). Speakers of Turkish languages within the same branch can still understand each other with a high degree of intelligibility. All five modern branches of Turkish can be traced back to the language of the Orkhon inscriptions nearly thirteen centuries earlier. The distribution of today's Turkish language is a direct result of the migrations and conquests during the Middle Ages. Over half of today's Turkish speakers belong to the Oghuz branch, residing in Turkey, Azerbaijan, northwestern Iran, and Turkmenistan. The Seljuk Turks planted this language in these lands between the tenth and thirteenth centuries. Kipchak Turkish prevails across the central Eurasian steppes and Transoxiana, and this branch is represented today by Kazakh, Uzbek, and Kyrgyz. With their conversions to Islam from the tenth century on, Oghuz and Kipchak Turkish-speakers borrowed extensively from Arabic and Persian vocabulary and grammar. Until recently they used the Arabic script, which has been replaced by the Roman or Cyrillic alphabets. The Uyghurs, whose ancestors settled in the Tarim Basin in the ninth century and eventually embraced Islam, still employ the Arabic script. Their distinct language has been heavily modified by Tocharian, Sogdian, Arabic, Persian, Chinese, and even Russian. The Uyghurs, perhaps twelve million strong, are fast becoming a minority within their own homeland due to ruthless policies of the regime in Beijing. In the central and eastern Siberian forests, the speakers of the northeastern branch likewise face pressure to adopt Russian. Finally, the Lir or most western branch of Turkish languages, with one exception, has gone extinct.[16] It included the languages of the Bulgars, the Pechenegs, and perhaps the Khazars, whose descendants were assimilated by Slavic speakers. The rapid expansion of Turkish speakers across the steppes facilitated communication and trade among tribes, and so the easy exchange of ideas, material goods, and technology. Merchants and Sufi mystics from the Caliphate who had mastered a Turkish vernacular could readily persuade their hosts to embrace Islam as they traveled from tribe to tribe.

By the early seventh century, the Gök Turks devised an alphabetic script based on the Tocharian and Sogdian alphabets, which in turn were based on Brahmi and Aramaic scripts brought to the Tarim Basin by Buddhist missionaries during the Kushan Age.[17] This Turkish script visually resembles Norse runes, and hence it was fitting that a Danish philologist, Vilhelm Thomsen, deciphered these Turkish runes.[18] Over two hundred inscriptions survive; most are from the heartland of the three successive Turkish kaghanates, but examples have surfaced among the Bulgars in the Balkans and the Hungarians in Central Europe. The alphabet was widely known until it was replaced by the Arabic script in the tenth and eleventh centuries. With writing, Turkish rulers could keep records and commemorate their achievements in monumental inscriptions. Poets and storytellers could transmit in writing across time and space the traditional values and deeds of their ancestors so that even today all Turkish speakers feel a kinship and shared history going back to the Gök Turks. The adoption of writing was no small achievement. Chinese historians credit the Xiongnu with adapting Chinese characters to their own language, but no examples of this writing survive. Between the first and sixth centuries, nomadic peoples are not known to have committed their own languages to writing, although many were familiar with Chinese, Sogdian, and Tocharian writing systems. In adapting writing for their own language, the kaghans of the Gök Turks ensured a cultural and ethnic unity across the Eurasian steppes, and their distant successors, the Ottomans, would make Turkish one of the three great literary languages of the Islamic world. Today, in the garden of Ankara's Museum of Anatolian Civilizations stands a perfect replica of the monumental inscription of Bilge Kaghan in a proper recognition of the common origin of all Turkish languages.

The Gök Turks owed their success to their skill and ferocity in waging war. Between the first and fifth centuries, Turkish tribes devised superior leather saddles, and stirrups, first of leather toe lops and then a metal stirrup.[19] The innovations changed tactics. Perhaps as early as the fourth century, Eurasian nomads used a leather toe loop so that a warrior could ride his horse high rather than on its back. They devised better wooden-leather saddles, and by the early sixth century, metal stirrups had come into wide use. The military author of the *Strategikon*, writing in the late sixth century, reports that Byzantine heavy cavalry had already modified their tactics by the adoption of the steel stirrup.[20] Hence, from the sixth century on, Turkish horse archers proved far more deadly than their Iranian predecessors, because they could direct their horses and fire with deadly accuracy. The Turks were armed with superior composite bows, and they were superb metallurgists, manufacturing superior helmets, chain or lamellar armor, and edged weapons. The Turks, experts in a pastoral way of life, bred the finest of Eurasian horses for endurance and speed. Henceforth, Turkish horse archers were seldom defeated by armies of the urban, literate civilizations until the advent of handheld firearms. Even foes of the nomads acknowledged that the tactical balance on the battlefield had shifted decisively to the Turkish horse archers in the fifth and sixth centuries. The Byzantine author of the *Strategikon* and the Tang general Li Jing almost simultaneously recommended similar tactics against Turkish horse archers.[21] Byzantine, Chinese, and Muslim rulers, whose armies, depending on heavy cavalry, equipped with metal stirrups and charging with leveled lances, recruited numerous Turkish horse archers as supporting light cavalry. They drew the obvious conclusion that if they could not beat the Turks, then hire them.[22] The prolific Muslim theological writer al-Jahiz in the early ninth century noted with regret how Turks outclassed the best of Arabic horsemen. He noted that "Neither the Kharijites [Muslim sectarians] nor the Bedouins are famous for their prowess as mounted bowmen. But the Turk will hit from his saddle an animal, a bird, a target, a man, a crouching animal, a marker post, or a bird of prey stooping on its quarry. His horse may be exhausted from being galloped and reined in, wheeled to the right and left, mounted and dismounted; but himself goes on shooting, loosening ten arrows before the Kharijite has loosened one. He gallops his horse up a hillside or down a gully faster than the Kharijite can make his go on the flat. The Turk has two pairs of eyes, one at the front, and the other at the back of his head."[23]

Yet for all the Turks' prowess in war, the first Turkish kaghanate founded by Bumin and Ishtemi, and the succeeding second Turkish and Uyghur kaghanates, shared the same fate. Since the Turks practiced lateral succession, each of the three kaghanates was plagued by civil war in the second or third generation.[24] Given the great size of a Turkish kaghanate, each kaghan had to parcel out territories to his kinsmen under lesser titles so that in a civil war, each claimant could count on the support of his tribes. The Tang emperor Taizong (626–649) exploited a civil war to end the first Turkish kaghanate. The second kaghanate too fell because of civil wars in the generation after Bilğe Kaghan wrote his warnings. A century later, the Uyghur kaghanate collapsed when Kyrgyz tribesmen, on the invitation of a claimant in a civil war, invaded and sacked the Uyghur capital.

In all three cases, charismatic Turkish rulers forged an imperial kaghanate because of political disunity in China. But the geographic and demographic facts had not changed since the third century BC. China sustained a population of forty-five to fifty million, whereas all the nomads east of the Altai Mountains and north of the Great Wall numbered at most one million.[25] To be sure, most Turkish adult males were seasoned warriors, but a united China under an able emperor possessed the manpower and wealth to defeat the nomads. The Turkish nomads depended just as much as the Xiongnu had on Chinese foodstuffs and manufactured goods if they were to survive on the Mongolian steppes. On his monumental inscription, Bilğe Kaghan stressed how good kaghans gained access to Chinese markets and secured prosperity for their people, while bad ones fought among themselves and neglected the welfare of the people.[26] His younger brother Prince Kül Tegin and his senior commander Tonyukuk admonished the same on their monumental inscriptions in the Orkhon valley.[27]

Strategically, Bumin and his three sons could easily raid south of the Great Wall, because they faced little opposition from the regional dynasts of North China. They could camp on the grasslands of Inner Mongolia and the Ordos triangle, which provided vital fodder and fresh water for their men and horses exhausted from crossing the Gobi. Upon reaching the middle Yellow River, a Turkish army threatened the great Chinese capital cities Luoyang and Chang'an, or the rich northeastern provinces known as the Sixteen Prefectures. In 581, the strategic situation abruptly changed. Duke Yang Jian, scion of a distinguished family that had served both Han and Northern Wei emperors, deposed the last Northern Zhou emperor, and assumed the throne name Wen of the Sui dynasty.[28] In the next eight years, the veteran northern general-turned-emperor reunited China and vowed to restore the boundaries of the Han Empire. For the Gök Turks, the timing could not have been worse. In 581, Tardu (576–603), the son of Ishtemi and the senior member of the Ashina clan, ruled in splendid isolation over the Western kaghanate from his encampments on Lake Issyk and the Talas River. But he longed to add the eastern one to his realm. On the eastern steppes, Amrak, a grandson of Bumin, immediately was challenged and forced to abdicate in favor of his cousin, the short-lived Ishbara (581–587).[29] In 589, Ishbara's son and successor Bagha Kaghan plunged the kaghanate into another succession crisis when he fell in battle in Iran, slain by an arrow shot from the bow of the legendary Persian hero and warlord Bahram Chobin.[30] Bahram Chobin then seized Ctesiphon and proclaimed himself Shah of Persia, but he missed capturing the legitimate Sassanid heir Khusrau II. Khusrau fled to Constantinople and returned to recover his throne with a Roman army furnished by the emperor Maurice Tiberius. Bahram Chobin escaped to live a life of exile among the Gök Turks.[31] So ended the first Turkish attempt to conquer Iran. In 599, Tardu realized his long-cherished ambition and briefly reunited the two kaghanates. But many princes of the eastern Turks refused to recognize him. Five years later, in 603, he died soon after a military debacle in China. With his death passed political unity of the Turks forever. Throughout these kaleidoscopic turns of fortune, the emperor Wen adroitly backed a host of pretenders and rebel vassal princes in a bewildering web of alliances whereby he undermined Turkish power for two decades.[32] The situation briefly changed yet again in 618 at the death of the tyrant emperor Yang, whose death signaled a second civil war in China. But the Gök Turks were in no position to exploit the disorder to their long-term advantage. Another veteran general, Li Yuan, quickly seized the imperial throne as the emperor Gaozu of the Tang dynasty. Gaozu reunited China, and built upon the successes of the Sui emperor Wen.[33]

The Sui and first Tang emperors, who were linked by matrimonial ties, hailed from the frontier society of northern China. While educated in calligraphy and the Confucian classics, they were Buddhists and skilled in riding, archery, and the art of war. Collectively, they reformed and increased the imperial army, mounting ever more cavalry on steeds obtained from the Turks.[34] They also expanded and repaired the Great Wall and Grand Canal in stupendous projects involving over a million laborers, while in southern China, peasants vastly increased cultivation of rice and silk.[35] In the words of the first Tang emperor, Gaozu, imperial policy aimed to compel the submission of all barbarian peoples of the four directions who flanked the Middle Kingdom.[36] Sui and Tang emperors could routinely field and supply armies of one hundred fifty thousand, and river flotillas on the Grand Canal could convey men, horses, and supplies to the northern frontiers in a matter of weeks. The Sui and Tang emperors could maintain under arms professional armies totaling over one million men or the equivalent of the total population of the steppe nomads east of the Altai Mountains and north of the Great Wall.

Rival Turkish kaghans during their wars of succession readily submitted to the Chinese court and rendered tribute in horses in return for titles, Chinese brides, and silk.[37] Losers fled as exiles to Chang'an, while the victors repudiated their oaths of allegiance and raided the frontier lands. Yet each contender never amassed enough wealth to placate his supporters, and so the elites of all three Turkish kaghanates proved far more recalcitrant than their counterparts of the Xiongnu Confederacy.[38] In 626, Illig Kaghan of the Eastern Gök Turks commanded a great raid that briefly threatened the Tang capital of Chang'an.[39] Illig Kaghan wished to avenge his earlier defeat at the hands of the emperor Gaozu's second son, Li Shimin, who had surprised the kaghan's camp under the cover of a thunderstorm. The raid, however, backfired. Illig Kaghan unwittingly triggered a palace coup that placed his nemesis, Prince Li Shimin, on the imperial throne.

For eight years, Crown Prince Li Shimin and his elder brother, Li Jiancheng, had clashed in a bitter rivalry that split asunder the Tang court and compromised defense against Turkish raiders. Each brother enlisted retainers, generals, and officials, and disputed assignments of commands and policies, because the emperor Gaozu had invested each son with the power to issue imperial edicts in his own name. Li Shimin proved an abler general and intriguer, advocating strong action against the Turks, while Li Jiancheng supported their father, Gaozu, who contemplated the unpopular move of abandoning the capital and relocating to southern China.[40] The struggle climaxed in 626 with the raid of Illig Kaghan. Li Shimin outmaneuvered Li Jiancheng, who was alleged to be committing adultery with their father's concubines in a sordid plot to seize the throne. Before Li Jiancheng could answer the charges, he was ambushed and shot dead by an arrow from the bow of Li Shimin. Li Shimin promptly seized power; two months later, he coerced his father to abdicate in his favor as the emperor Taizong, age twenty-seven.[41]

No emperor of China was ever more skillful in fighting steppe nomads than Taizong. The new emperor retaliated not with a counterattack but with an invasion to conquer both Turkish kaghanates. Taizong, a master strategist, cut a very different figure from his distant predecessor, the retiring Han emperor Wudi. Taizong reveled in battle, and often led his men in the decisive attack. He publicly announced his preference for a free life on the steppes over the regimented rituals and mores of the Tang court. He possessed the charismatic personality that inspired Chinese frontier warlords and Turkish princes alike. Nearly a quarter of known officers of Taizong were of foreign origin.[42] Taizong personally attended to their wounds in battle, rewarded their bravery, and enriched their families. One of his Turkish generals, Qibi Hebei, was proudly steadfast to his emperor. He was remembered for cutting off his ear to demonstrate his loyalty either when his tribe was discussing rebellion or when he was mourning the death of Taizong.[43] He and fellow Turkic officers committed suicide to join their lord Taizong in death. Two others of the Ashina clan were accorded the high honor of their own tombs within the emperor's burial complex, Zhaoling. Even Bilğe Kaghan on his memorial inscription grudgingly recognized Taizong's charisma, because Bilğe Kaghan complained how Taizong seduced the Turks into fighting his battles in the Tarim Basin and Korea.[44] In character, Taizong must have resembled the Roman emperor Theodosius the Great, a gifted general who commanded the loyalty of his Gothic soldiers.[45]

Taizong, like the patient Han emperor Wudi, thought in long-term strategy. Tang historians record a number of debates over policies toward the nomads.[46] The Confucian mandarins of the great southern houses, headed by the minister Wei Zheng, held the Turks in contempt as faithless barbarians best expelled or massacred.[47] As virtuous gentlemen who had passed the imperial examination in Confucian classics, they alone should set policy. Even more significantly, they also wrote the regime's histories. Northern generals and officials, often of mixed ancestry, urged pragmatic policies based on experience. Some favored the assimilation of Turks, who, upon adopting Chinese and a sedentary way of life, could join the Han community. Others, including the emperor Taizong himself, believed the Turks could be accommodated as loyal pastoralists within the empire.[48] The same debate still persists in China today. The fact that Taizong could preside over and profit from these heated quarrels marked him as an exceptionally clearheaded ruler, because each side was just as prone to the sins of favoritism and patronage to win over the emperor.

In 629, Taizong declared war on the Eastern kaghanate. In the next year, his two best generals, Li Jing and Li Shiji, each crossed the Gobi, united near the Iron Gate (in the Hisar range in modern Uzbekistan), and surprised the Gök Turks in their encampment.[49] Illig Kaghan was captured, spared, and pensioned off to a comfortable retirement spent hunting in a deer park. The Eastern Turkish kaghanate collapsed; thousands of Turks were resettled as military colonists in northern China. In the next five years, both generals deployed the same tactics to secure the cities of the Tarim Basin, which were reorganized into the Four Garrisons.[50] Furthermore, Taizong, just like his distant predecessor Wudi, took measures to secure stocks of horses to breed in China, but these efforts could never supply all the necessary mounts for the imperial army, and the system was abandoned after Taizong's death.[51] In 641, Taizong was hailed as kaghan by the Turks of the eastern steppes, and he assigned Chinese military governors over the tribes, which were grouped into territorial prefectures.[52] At his death, Taizong was the mightiest sovereign on the globe. The Byzantine emperor and Sassanid shah each appealed to him for assistance against their new foe, the Arabs. Even after Taizong's death, his son the emperor Gaozong pressed the conquest of the steppes and brought the Chinese Empire to its greatest extent ever. In 657, six years after Taizong's death, the Turks of the Western Kaghanate too accepted the Tang emperor as their kaghan.[53] The imperial peace brought prosperity across the central and eastern steppes. Under the Tang peace, trade along the Silk Road flourished. The caravan cities of the Tarim Basin and Transoxiana also profited from supplying Chinese provincial governors, their courts, and garrisons. Sir Aurel Stein revealed this cosmopolitan world when he uncovered the stunning cave frescoes and commercial documents of Dunhuang.

Yet victory came at a high price for the imperial treasury.[54] The frail Gaozong, ailing in his later years, was taxed to govern the steppes and to check new foes, the Tibetans and the Goguryeo kingdom (today Korea and Manchuria). In 655, he married as his consort and empress Wu Zetian, a concubine of his father.[55] For the next thirty years, she dominated the court, first as regent for her failing husband, then for minor stepsons or their sons, and finally as empress of a new Zhou dynasty, until she was forced to abdicate in 705. She is still the only woman ever to rule China in her own right. She is the most celebrated member of the Tang dynasty, inspiring a spate of modern biographies and TV miniseries in China and Korea. Misogynist Confucian ministers loathed her and circulated lurid tales of sexual escapades, sale of favors, and evil spells she cast over her gullible husband. Yet Wu Zetian, born into a rich family, had received the finest education, and possessed a keen wit. She was so hated by the Confucian elite because she outclassed her

male rivals in court politics. She was accused of suffocating her infant daughter in order to frame her rival, minister Wang, but Wu
Zetian turned the charge against Wang for allegedly poisoning
her infant. Both had lied. The infant likely died of crib death.[56]
She appointed able generals who defended the Tarim Basin against
the Tibetans, and conquered the Korean Goguryeo Kingdom, the
graveyard of previous Sui and Tang armies.[57] She calculated that
both regions yielded revenues for the imperial treasury, whereas direct rule over the Eurasian steppes was a fiscal loss. When the Eastern Turks, and then the Western ones, renounced their allegiance,
she resorted to the tested diplomacy of the Five Baits.

In 682, Ilterish Kaghan emerged from his mountain fastness to
head a successful revolt against the Chinese. He proclaimed a second Turkish kaghanate on the Mongolian steppes, but Tonyukuk,
a talented warrior of the Ashina clan, was its true architect.[58]
Tonyukuk served as counselor and commander to four successive
kaghans for nearly fifty years. His last master and son-in-law, Bilğe
Kaghan, exalted among his counselors Tonyukuk, who fulminated
against adopting corrupting Chinese ways and foreign faiths. Under
Tonyukuk's guidance, the Gök Turks once again subjected the
tribes between the Altai and Khingan Mountains, and reclaimed
the sacred landscape of the Orkhon valley.[59] At his death in 726,
Tonyukuk received a magnificent funeral with horse and human
sacrifices, and his body was interred in a tumulus in the Orkhon
valley.[60] His tumulus was marked by a monolith carved in Turkish
runes praising his deeds. His funerary complex is the first of three
such ones in the Orkhon valley now recognized as World Heritage sites. The other two, also with an inscribed monolith, are for
the brothers Bilğe Kaghan (717–734) and Prince Kül Tegin. Together, for fifteen years, the two inseparable brothers extended the
kaghanate to its farthest limits.

Tonyukuk, Bilğe Kaghan, and Kül Tegin, the three who forged
the second kaghanate, succeeded because indifferent emperors
reigned in China after Empress Wu Zetian's abdication. The self-
indulgent emperor Xuanzong (717–756) presided over a decadent
court, lingering for days in the largest harem of any Chinese emperor.[61] In fairness, Xuanzong was an astute and learned man who

presided over a brilliant cultural flowering. He initially entrusted
policy to able ministers, and he was well served by the mandarin
officials who administered the provinces. He was just simply not
up to governing a great empire. Therefore, he invested power in
venal favorites at court and military governors on the frontiers,
who recruited private armies. Many of the frontier warlords were
of barbarian origin themselves so that they prized Turkish horse
archers, and signed alliances with Turkish kaghans. As imperial
demands soared, peasants groaned over onerous taxation and conscription. In 751, two imperial field armies were all but annihilated in two decisive defeats, one in Nanzhao (today Yunnan), and
the other in Ferghana.[62] In December 755, widespread discontent exploded in a popular rebellion headed by An Lushan, commander of the field army on the northeast frontier.[63] An Lushan,
himself of Sogdian and Turkic origin, had been the emperor's
favorite and most successful general, so his disloyalty unnerved
Xuanzong. In the next year, An Lushan captured both capitals,
while Xuanzong fled south and abdicated in favor of his more resolute son, the future emperor Suzong.[64] The An Lushan Rebellion
raged for over seven years across northern and central China, and
nearly toppled the Tang dynasty. Even though the rebellion failed,
the Tang dynasty was broken.[65] The Tang court defeated the rebels
in large part because they summoned new allies from the steppes, the
Uyghurs, who had just forged the third great kaghanate on the
eastern Eurasian steppes.

The second Turkish kaghanate too fell because of a civil war
within a decade after Bilge Kaghan wrote his warnings. In 744,
Qutlugh Bilge Köl, ruler of the vassal tribe of Uyghurs dwelling
on the steppes just north of the Tarim Basin, rebelled, defeated and
slew the last Gök Turk kaghan, and proclaimed the third Turkish
kaghanate on the eastern steppes.[66] Qutlugh Bilge Köl extended his
sway over the eastern nomadic tribes so quickly because the emperor
Xuanzong neglected affairs of state. During the An Lushan Rebellion, Tang emperors repeatedly drew on Uyghur horse archers,
and in return, Uyghur kaghans received record-breaking strings
of cash—the copper coins of China—bolts of silk, and foodstuffs.[67]
They also sold horses to the imperial army at exorbitant prices.[68] For

the next century, Tang emperors, for a price, summoned Uyghur horse archers against all foes, foreign and domestic. The balance of power shifted decisively to the Uyghurs who propped up the Tang dynasty.

The political balance shifted because Uyghur kaghans demanded and received Chinese brides who were high-ranking daughters of the emperor. Five of the Uyghur kaghans married imperial Tang princesses, each of whom was accompanied by a caravan of attendants, scribes, craftsmen, musicians, and entertainers.[69] The Uyghur kaghans eagerly adopted Chinese protocol, titles, and rituals to exalt themselves over the ancestral assembly or *kurultai*. Matrimonial ties and kinship linked the Uyghur and Tang imperial families, and so the Chinese wives wielded great influence over their Uyghur husbands. They refused to join their deceased husbands in the tumulus, and they even avoided slashing their cheeks as a sign of mourning. The last Tang princess, who adopted the lofty Turkish name Kün Tengride Ülüg Bulmış Alp Küçlüg Bilge Kaghan, survived her husband and the kaghanate, and so she comfortably retired to the Tang court.

Qutlugh Bilge Köl too made his principal settlement in the sacred Orkhon valley, but his son and heir Bayanchur Kaghan turned this settlement into a Chinese-style city, Karabalghasun, the predecessor of the Mongol capital Karakorum. The city flourished as a nexus of international trade, and the surrounding arable lands were put under intensive cultivation to support a growing population.[70] Muslim visitors from the Caliphate marveled at the size and diversity of the city, and the range of products available in its markets. Sogdian- and Tocharian-speaking merchants and monks settled permanently in Karabalghasun, bringing their mores, aesthetics, and faiths of Buddhism, Manichaeism, and Nestorian Christianity. Even more than their predecessors the Gök Turks, Uyghur kaghans appreciated the power of writing in statecraft. They continued the use of Turkic runes for public inscriptions, but they conducted diplomatic correspondence in Chinese, and commercial transactions in Sogdian. Sogdian-speaking officials who staffed the kaghan's literate bureaucracy devised a new alphabet based on the Brahmi script employed in the cities of the Tarim Basin.[71] Five centuries later,

Kublai Khan ordered his Uyghur officials to adapt this script to the Mongol language. Nor were the other lessons in state-building lost on the Mongol khans.

On November 20, 762, Bögü Kaghan, called Yingyi in Chinese accounts, captured Luoyang in the name of his ally, the Tang emperor Suzong.[72] The ancestral capital of Han China thus suffered for a second time a sack by barbarians during a Chinese civil war. Bögü Kaghan, however, did not loot and leave, but instead lingered near Luoyang, where he met Sogdian-speaking Manichaean missionaries with whom he conversed at length during nocturnal feasts in his tent. The missionaries accompanied the kaghan back to Karabalghasun, where Bögü Kaghan proclaimed Manichaeism as the official faith of his nation. There is no reason to reject this story as legend, even though the Uyghurs were long familiar with this faith prevalent in Transoxiana, the Tarim Basin, and northern China. These mendicant monks impressed the kaghan, who admired their learning and the prosperity of their coreligionists engaged in commerce. The faith, while an imperially recognized religion in China, never won over a Chinese emperor. Many Chinese would have viewed Manichaeism as a pale imitation of Buddhism or Daoism, the two most popular faiths among the Chinese masses. Manichaeism, just like Judaism for the Khazars, offered an advantage that it was not the faith of a neighboring imperial rival, but this advantage was likely a benefit rather than a reason for the kaghan's conversion.

The prophet Mani (216–274) was born on the Roman side of the frontier in northern Mesopotamia (today Iraq), but he preached his new interpretation of the faith of Abraham in cosmopolitan cities of Sassanid Mesopotamia. Christians condemned his teachings as a heresy of the Devil that had even seduced Saint Augustine for a time.[73] Later Muslim theologians dismissed Mani as a painter who peddled a muddled version of Zoroastrianism. But the Mani Codex, discovered in Egypt in 1969 and now housed in the library of the University of Cologne, has revolutionized our understanding.[74] Mani proclaimed himself the prophet to his divine twin Jesus, and experienced mystical trances whereby he ascended to Heaven. His followers later claimed that he was the Paraclete promised by Saint Paul, and others identified him with previous religious teachers. He was credited with performing miracles, healing the sick, and even teleporting. Therefore, Manichaeism was far from a Christian heresy, but rather an independent religion of Abraham. Mani was inspired by a heady brew of Christian, Zoroastrian, and Buddhist beliefs. He taught a strict dualism, and so the truly enlightened or "elect" strove to detach themselves from corporal corruption and seek liberation with the divine. Manichaean ascetics lived on the charity of the "auditors," who had heard the message, but could not achieve enlightenment in their lifetime. Instead, the auditors discharged their allotted tasks in this world, and supported the elect in the hopes of enlightenment in a future life. In its message and organization, the new region shared similarities with Buddhism, which many merchants along the Silk Road from Ctesiphon to Luoyang had embraced. Yet Mani taught a stark dualism of a perpetual cosmic struggle between lightness and dark, a concept inspired by Zoroastrianism. As a mystic, he thought and taught in allegorical metaphors, drawing on diverse myths as imperfect glimpses of a single divine reality. For strict Christians with a fixed canon, Mani was a Gnostic, who employed the condemned scriptures of other faiths. He also rejected the wrathful God of the Old Testament in favor of the merciful one of the New Testament. Yet the appeals of Mani were universal and flexible. Sogdian and Tocharian merchants, Turkish nomads, and Chinese urban dwellers could readily adapt their ancestral myths to Mani's cosmology. For Turks in particular, the supreme god of Mani was readily identified with Tengri of the eternal blue sky.

Mani taught and wrote in Aramaic, the lingua franca on the Silk Road second only to Sogdian, so that his teachings were widely circulated across Eurasia even during his lifetime.[75] He did write a single treatise in Persian, which he dedicated and presented to Shah Shapur I. The shah politely received the work, and just as politely declined to convert. Mani, however, ran afoul of the Zoroastrian clergy, and they convinced Shah Bahram I to cast Mani into prison, where he was still allowed to receive and instruct his disciples in the

manner of the last days of Socrates. His followers, however, dignified him as a martyr, crucified on orders of the shah.

For a century, the Uyghur kaghans followed the tenets of Mani,
while later Tang emperors, in a bid for popularity, rescinded the
legal status of foreign faiths, and the emperor Wuzong waged fierce
persecutions of both Manichaean and Buddhist monks and sanctuaries in 840–843.[76] Save for the Uyghur kaghans, Manichaean missionaries failed to convert great sovereigns who would advance the
faith.[77] The success of Manichaeism was linked to the fate of the
Uyghur kaghanate, and so the faith waned and finally disappeared
in the centuries after the collapse of the kaghanate.

The vassal tribes envied the prosperity of the Uyghur kaghans,
while later Tang emperors resented the humiliating alliances and
gifts. As Bilge Kaghan had warned, cities made Turks vulnerable.
In 840, the Kyrgyz Turks, resentful vassals to the northeast of the
Altai Mountains, invaded during a civil war, sacked Karabalghasun, and sent the last kaghan's head to the Tang court.[78] The Kyrgyz
Turks had attacked, if not with the approval of, certainly to the
delight of the Tang government. The Kyrgyz ravaged the Orkhon
valley, and retired to their ancestral steppes with a haul of booty
and captives. The Uyghur survivors found refuge in the cities of
the Tarim Basin, where their Turkish language would eventually
prevail. Their descendants intermarried with their Tocharian and
Sogdian hosts, and adopted Buddhism. For clearly, the god of Mani
had failed them. The sudden exodus of the Uyghurs opened the
eastern steppes to the Mongols, who claimed as their own the sacred Orkhon valley.

The Tang Empire, however, lost its most valuable ally. Without
the Uyghur alliance, the Tang court lost any chance of reasserting
its influence in Central Asia against the rising power of Islam. In
less than two generations, in 907, the last Tang emperor, Zhaozang,
was compelled to abdicate.[79] China descended into yet another violent era of warring states. Simultaneously, the fall of the Uyghur
kaghanate ended unity on the central and eastern steppes for the
next four centuries. During these centuries, the Turkish nomads
were transformed by encountering a new monotheistic creed and
civilization, Islam and the Caliphate.

15

Turks and the Caliphate

O n July 22, 838, the Byzantine emperor Theophilus clashed with the northern column of a two-pronged Abbasid invasion of Asia Minor outside of Dazimon.[1] The fortress city guarded a strategic pass between the central Anatolian plateau and the northern coast of the Black Sea. Today it is the Turkish city of Tokat, renowned for its Ottoman baths and many shops in its beautiful bedestan. Theophilus planned to defeat the smaller Muslim army, and then swing southwest to intercept the main army under Caliph al-Mu'tasim. Initially, the battle went in favor of the Byzantines. On the wings, imperial heavy cavalry repelled and pursued a new foe, mounted Turkish horse archers. But the Byzantine cavalry lost formation, fell into an ambush, and was driven off the field in disorder. Theophilus bravely steadied his infantry. The Turkish cavalry surrounded and shot arrows into the densely packed Byzantine foot soldiers, who by late afternoon were on the verge of panic, when a thunderstorm suddenly broke. The Turkish bows were drenched by the downpour and lost their tension.[2] The Turks fell back, and Theophilus withdrew to his camp as evening fell, and then retreated to Constantinople. The battle was a tactical draw. The caliph al-Mu'tasim, however, advanced unopposed across

Anatolia and sacked the provincial capital Amorium, also the ancestral home of the imperial family. Then, under a relentless summer
sun, the caliph withdrew, but many of his soldiers and captives died
of thirst in the blistering heat.[3] The battle was the first between a
Byzantine army and Turkish cavalry. The near defeat so unnerved
Theophilus that in the next year, the emperor sent envoys to Louis
the Pious, the son of Charlemagne.[4] Louis claimed to be the rightful
Holy Roman Emperor, but Theophilus swallowed his pride, for he
knew that he was the true Roman emperor. Theophilus appealed
to Louis for aid on the basis of their common Christian faith. The
alliance never happened. Fortunately for Theophilus, the caliph
was satisfied to win prestige as the Sword of Islam and planned no
future campaigns. But the appeal was not forgotten.

The Battle of Dazimon announced to the Christian world that
Turkish cavalry, as the caliph's allies or slave soldiers, was now the
decisive arm in Muslim armies for the next millennium. Byzantine
emperors and generals, who had faced such foes on their northern frontier, henceforth had to battle Turkish horse archers in the
caliph's employ along the eastern frontier to defend the imperial
heartland of Anatolia. The caliph, however, and his military governors at Merv in Khurasan had long respected the valor of Turkish
horse archers during the fighting for control of Transoxiana, which
the Arabs called the same in their own language: Mawarannahr,
"that which lies beyond the river."[5] For the Turkish peoples of the
central Eurasian steppes, the distant clash at Dazimon was but one
incident on their journey from dreaded barbarians, to convenient
allies and slaves, to full members of the community of Islam (*umma*).

The Western Turkish tribes asserted their independence late in
the reign of the empress Wu Zetian (690–705), but they failed to
forge an imperial confederacy.[6] The tribes on the far western steppes
north of the Caspian Sea and stretching to the great bend of the
River Don had already formed their own confederation.[7] They were
always beyond the reach of Chinese armies. Their kaghan Tong
Yabgu, who may be the Ziebel named in Byzantine sources, concluded an alliance with Heraclius against the Sassanid shah Khusrau
II in 630.[8] The leading tribe of this confederation, the Khazars, asserted dominance soon after the mid-seventh century. To the im-

mediate east of the Khazars, around the Aral Sea, dwelled Oghuz Turkish tribes.[9] But on the central Eurasian steppes of Kazakhstan, Turkish-speaking tribes of the former Western kaghanate contended for supremacy. Rival rulers styled themselves as *yabgu*, and so deputies of whoever was kaghan of the eastern Turks and controlled the sacred heartland of the Orkhon valley. The Karluks proved the most successful. They held sway over a regional confederation of three tribes centered on Zhetysu, "the land of the seven rivers," the grasslands watered by the River Ili and the six lesser tributaries of Lake Balkhash in southeastern Kazakhstan today.[10] They pitched their tents at a summer encampment on the shores of Lake Issyk, near the thermal waters of the thousand springs. In winter, they encamped on the Talas River near the modern city of Taraz. They also roamed over the pastures of Ferghana, home to the finest steeds of Eurasia, and longed to extend their sway over all of Transoxiana. Many other Turkish-speaking tribes and clans had long settled on the grasslands surrounding the caravan cities of Transoxiana. They traded their horses, salted meat, dairy goods, hides, and woolens for foodstuffs and finished products of the Iranian-speaking agriculturists and urban dwellers. In Transoxiana, Turk and Iranian thus shared a distinct frontier way of life.[11]

The Tang court, however, never renounced its claims to hegemony over the Karluks or the caravan cities of Transoxiana, but it had to fight off an even more deadly enemy, the Tibetans under the monarchs of the Tarlung dynasty. These Tibetan monarchs aspired to rule the cities of the Tarim Basin and to tax the caravans bound for China.[12] Tang military governors of the Four Garrisons, who ruled as independent warlords, set policy, signed alliances, and hired Turkish horse archers. They battled the Tibetans for control of the oasis cities, and the routes over the Pamirs into Ferghana and Transoxiana. The Karluks repeatedly switched allegiances from Chinese vassal to Tibetan ally.[13] The struggle became even more complicated as armies of the Umayyad caliphs steadily campaigned to reach the Jaxartes River.

Within a decade of the Prophet Muhammad's death, his first two caliphs ("successors") repeatedly defeated both Byzantine and Sassanid armies, and conquered a world empire stretching from Libya to western Iran.[14] At the death of Muhammad and each of the first two rightly guided or Rashidun caliphs Abu Bakr (632–634) and Umar (634–644), the leading Muslims convened and elected a new caliph, passing over the Prophet's cousin Ali, married to Fatima, Muhammad's only daughter.[15] In 656, the Arab army in Egypt mutinied, marched on Medina, and slew third caliph Uthman and his wife during their prayers. The unruly soldiers then offered the office of caliph to Ali. Ali was immediately opposed by the powerful governor of Damascus, Muawiya, a kinsman of Uthman. Muawiya won the civil war when extremist assassins who rejected both rival caliphs thrust a poisoned dagger into the skull of Ali as he prayed in the great mosque of Kufa, in lower Iraq. Ali's partisans, the Shi'a, refused to accept as caliph Muawiya, who was recognized by the Muslim majority or Sunni.[16] Muawiya founded a hereditary monarchy at Damascus, and so removed political power from the Holy Cities of Mecca and Medina. He and his successors, the Umayyad caliphs, followed the commandment of the Prophet to conquer Rum, the Arabic name for the Byzantium Empire. Twice Umayyad armies failed to capture Constantinople by siege, and thereby fatally compromised the dynasty.[17] Meanwhile, on the frontiers, Umayyad governors directed a second wave of conquests of North Africa and Spain in the West, and of Eastern Iran, the Sind, and Transoxiana in the East.

As soon as Arab armies reached the Oxus River in 671, the Umayyad governors at Merv found the cosmopolitan caravan cities filled with merchants and missionaries traveling the Silk Road a prize too tempting to resist. They repeatedly raided across the river to loot Buddhist, Zoroastrian, and Manichaean sanctuaries.[18] These governors set policy, struck Sassanid-style silver coins in their own names, and waged campaigns in the name of holy war (jihad) to preoccupy their unruly regiments of Bedouins lest rival clans within each regiment settle ancestral vendettas among themselves.[19] Umayyad governors recruited many Iranians from Khurasan, former heartland of the Parthians, to serve as infantry and engineers. These Iranian soldiers were among the first converts (mawali) to Islam, because the "people of the book" (dhimmi)—Jews, Christians, and Zoroastrians—were tolerated but forbidden the use of

arms and horses. Iranian soldiers proved more reliable than Arab
Bedouins, because as converts, they gave their steadfast loyalty to
the rightful caliph.[20] Qutayba ibn Muslim (700–715), governor of
Khurasan, shifted from raiding to conquering the lands south of the
Jaxartes River.[21] When Qutayba ordered conversion by the sword,
he drove the Iranian urban populations to summon as their liberators Turgesh Turks dwelling on the steppes north of the Jaxartes
River. The Turgesh Turks were foes of Karluks and nominal allies
of the Tang emperor of China. For thirty years, Suluk, *yabgu* of the
Turgesh, outfought the caliph's governors.[22] He inflicted the first
humiliating defeats Arab horsemen suffered at the hands of a foe
superior in their own tactics of scorched-earth. Suluk was never
defeated in battle, and he was only felled by an aggrieved rival in
748. It had taken thirty years of relentless campaigning and concil-
iatory policies toward the indigenous populations to secure Muslim
rule throughout Transoxiana.

In 749, Abu al-Abbas, governor of Khurasan, raised the black flag
of rebellion against the Umayyad caliph Marwan II.[23] At the head
of the eastern army, Abu al-Abbas swiftly marched across Iran and
defeated Marwan at a battle on the banks of the Great Zab River in
northern Iraq on January 25, 750. Marwan died an exile in Egypt
eight months later, and Abu al-Abbas, who claimed descent from
the youngest uncle of Muhammad, was hailed caliph of a new
Abbasid dynasty. The victor lured the surviving Umayyad princes
to a feast of reconciliation, but during the height of festivities, the
new caliph ordered his guards to club the guests and throw carpets over the bleeding guests. He and his courtiers finished dining
seated on the carpets over the bodies of the dying princes. Remains
of the Umayyad caliphs, save for Umar the Pious, were exhumed
and scattered to the four winds.[24] Henceforth, the new caliph was
known as as-Saffah, "the bloodthirsty." A single Umayyad prince,
Abd al-Rahman, escaped the massacre and found his way to Spain,
where the Arab army there proclaimed him emir of Cordova.[25]
To his credit, Caliph as-Saffah opened the bureaucracy, army, and
court to loyal Muslims of all backgrounds, and so the Caliphate was
transformed from an Arabic into an Islamic Empire.[26] His successor,
al-Mansur, founded a new capital at Baghdad, the Muslim succes-

sor to Sassanid Ctesiphon, and henceforth the economic, political, and cultural axis of the Caliphate shifted to Iran, and the Abbasid court steadily adapted Persian rituals, institutions, and aesthetics.[27] During the ninth century, Persian savants and artists at Baghdad pioneered the synthesizing of Islam with the learning of Persia, India, and Greece into the intellectual and artistic civilization of the eastern lands of the Caliphate.[28]

The new caliph faced not only a hostile Umayyad emir in Spain but also Alid pretenders and Shi'ite mystics.[29] The former aspired only to put a descendant of Ali and Fatima on the throne, but Shi'ite sectarians elevated Muhammad's cousin and son-in-law Ali to a spiritual authority second only to the Prophet himself. Ali and his descendants each was hailed mahdi, an enlightened one, who would herald the end of days and vindication of the true believers over both unbelievers and the impious.[30] Caliph as-Saffah, in a bid for legitimacy, directed his governors on distant frontiers to take the initiative in pressing holy war. Meanwhile, the Tang emperor Xuanzong, also in a bid for popularity, instructed his frontier governors to do the same.[31] In 749, an exiled Sogdian prince convinced Gao Xianzhi, the Tang governor general of the Western Regions, to expel the legitimate Ikhshid ruler in Shash (today Tashkent, Uzbekistan), capital of Ferghana. In the next year, a Chinese army captured Shash, beheaded the Ikhshid king, and looted the city. But the king's son fled to Samarkand, where he appealed to Ziyad ibn Salih, the Abbasid governor of Transoxiana, to drive out the Chinese invaders.[32] Gao Xianzhi and Ziyad ibn Salih, each a veteran commander, appreciated the heavenly horses of Ferghana. Each also valued Turkish allies.[33] In 751, Ziyad ibn Salih at the head of an army of thirty-five thousand advanced north from Samarkand to expel the Chinese from Ferghana. Gao Xianzhi departed from the oasis city Kuchea in the Tarim Basin, crossed the Pamirs, and entered the Talas valley. He commanded ten thousand veteran Chinese infantry armed with pikes and crossbows and twenty thousand Karluk horse archers. Ziyad ibn Salih had slightly greater numbers, but Gao Xianzhi possessed the better officers and superior cavalry. In July, the two armies clashed along the banks of the Talas River at an unidentified site on the border between present Kyrgyzstan

and Kazakhstan. Although the Chinese heavy infantry held fast in
the center, their Karluk allies deserted at the decisive moment and
delivered victory to the Muslims. The Tang army was annihilated,
but the Muslims sustained heavy casualties.[34] Abbasid caliph and
Tang emperor chose not to renew this distant frontier war. For the
emperor Xuanzong, the defeat was the second such debacle in the
same year, and it fueled popular resentment that exploded in the An
Lushan Rebellion. Later Tang emperors entrusted the defense of
the Tarim Basin to Turkish allies and steadily withdrew to the Jade
Gate. The Chinese emperor's armies did not return to the Western Regions until the Ming emperors. For the caliph as-Saffah, the
battle netted him immense prestige as the defender of Dar-al-Islam.
Later Muslim historians exaggerated the scale of the victory and
reported an implausible legend that Chinese captives were put to
work manufacturing the first paper in the Islamic world.[35] Yet the
Abbasid caliphs accepted the Jaxartes River as the northeastern limit
of the Islamic world for the next two centuries. The true victors,
however, were the Turks, who henceforth were rid of Muslim and
Chinese interference, and so they could gleefully battle each other
over blood feuds, grazing rights, and caravan routes.[36] Far more
important, the Turks could encounter Islamic civilization on their
own terms, whereby they could embrace Islam and still retain their
language and way of life. In so doing, they forged a distinct Turkish Muslim identity that is still shared by Turkish speakers today.

The Abbasid caliphs pursued the frontier policy similar to that
of their distant Achaemenid and Sassanid predecessors. Therefore,
Muslim governors along the same frontier stretching from the Caucasus to the Pamirs launched military demonstrations, courted favorable Turkish kaghans, and manipulated tribal rivalries, but they
added a new twist to the frontier policy. They incited intertribal
warfare among the Turks so that the losers would be sold off as
slaves to Muslim merchants, who supplied an ever-expanding demand for labor within the Caliphate between the seventh and tenth
centuries. By 800, Baghdad boasted over one million residents,
and populations in cities across Iraq, Iran, and Transoxiana soared
as Eurasia recovered from the devastation of two centuries of pandemic.[37] Under the peace of the caliphs, irrigation systems in Iraq

and Egypt, commercial farming, and trade in foodstuffs rose to feed the growing population.[38] For the next three centuries, the demand for laborers by the Islamic world fueled the slave trade across the Eurasian steppes[39] and Eastern Europe, whereas, in contrast, today the European Union draws many laborers, either as immigrants and guest workers, from the Islamic world. Tens of thousands of Turks were sold in the slave markets of Bukhara, Samarkand, Merv, and Balkh each year. Many Slavs, sold off by the Rus to the Khazars, left Atil for the cities and plantations of Iraq and northern Iran. Bantu-speaking slaves from East Africa were prized as agricultural laborers who turned the malarial marshes of lower Iraq into arable grain fields, orchards, and cotton plantations.[40] In 869, many mal-treated black slaves, called Zanj in Arabic, joined a popular upris-ing of varying dissidents under a former Abbasid official, Ali ibn Muhammad, who proclaimed an egalitarian vision of Islam. This rebellion raged on for nearly fourteen years and disrupted the sup-ply of foodstuffs to Baghdad. Turkish slaves, however, were valued primarily as soldiers, especially adolescent males, who were circum-cised, given Muslim names, and enrolled into a ruler's elite units. While these slave soldiers faithfully served their masters, most of them retained their Turkish speech and martial ethos.

Merchant princes first employed Turkish slaves, called *ghilman* (singular *ghulam*) or mamluks, as military escorts for their cara-vans traversing the Silk Road.[41] The Abbasid caliphs at Baghdad, their military governors, and their hereditary regional deputies or emirs quickly adopted the practice. In 836, the caliph al-Mu'tasim switched his residence to Samarra, a city nearly eighty miles north of Baghdad.[42] Today, Shi'ites revere the city where the last visible imam disappeared in 873 and has been followed by a succession of hidden imams, the last of whom will announce the end of days.[43] Caliph al-Mu'tasim also reformed his Turkish slave soldiers into an elite bodyguard of ten thousand (*haras*).[44] Two years later they proved their worth in the campaign against the Byzantine emperor Theophilus, but the Turkish soldiery soon terrorized Samarra, and, with the death of Caliph al-Mutawakkil in 861, dominated the court politics.[45] The caliph's bodyguard surpassed the better-known Praetorian Guard of Rome as kingmakers, deposing and execut-

ing no less than four caliphs in eight years. Meanwhile, hereditary
emirs outside of Iraq asserted their independence, collecting revenues, administering justice, and hiring their own Turkish slave
soldiers during the ninth century.[46] Sunni emirs professed loyalty
to an Abbasid caliph, who reigned solely as a religious authority
of Sunni Islam. They included the caliph's name on their coins
and documents and at high Friday prayers. In turn, the caliph issued fatwas, empowering emirs with powers to act as his deputies.
Foremost were the Samanid emirs of Bukhara, descended from a
distinguished family of Persian converts, who ruled Transoxiana
and eastern Iran from the late tenth century. The Samanid emirs
organized massive raids north of the Jaxartes, enslaving thousands
of Turks.[47] They entrusted frontier defense and distant provinces to
loyal mamluk officers of Turkish origin, who, in time, asserted their
independence. The situation on the central Eurasian steppes grew
ever more chaotic after the fall of the Uyghur kaghanate, because
many vassal tribes migrated west and clashed with their kinsmen,
Karluks, Turgesh, and Oghuz Turkish tribes dwelling on the central Eurasian steppes. Brutal tribal wars peaked between the mid-
ninth and mid-tenth centuries, and the defeated invariably ended
up as slaves in the Islamic world.[48] Yet despite, or perhaps because
of, the misery, atrocities, and deaths from the slave trade, many
Turkish nomads learned of Islam.

Many Muslim merchants settled in the caravan cities of the Tarim
Basin, and the principal settlements on the Eurasian steppes, especially around the Aral Sea, the well-watered region of Zhetysu between Lakes Balkhash and Issyk.[49] They intermarried with Turks,
and brought silks, spices, fine cottons and linens, and well-wrought
material goods. Their success in commerce must have impressed
their Turkish hosts as the blessing of the God of Islam. Turkish warriors returning from service in the armies of the caliph or his emirs
likewise brought silver coins, weapons, fine cottons and linens, and
well-wrought household goods that enriched the lives of their kin
and clan. They also brought home tales of the awesome Muslim
cities, the power of the caliph, and plunder and honor won from
defeating the caliph's foes. For these veterans, the God of Islam, invoked before battle, was the god of victory. Fighting as *ghazi*, holy

warriors in the name of jihad, came naturally to Turkish warriors bred on the harsh conditions and warfare of the Eurasian steppes.

In Islam, the believer has immediate and direct access to God by prayer and accepting Muhammad's five pillars of the faith.[50] Muslim worship, public or private, needs only an appropriate space to pray. Turkish warriors would have seen their Muslim comrades place their kilims on the ground, turn in the direction of Mecca, and solemnly bow and rise to offer their prayers to the sky above in submission to Allah. A mosque constitutes such a space oriented in the direction of Mecca, and offering a glimpse of the beauty of paradise, but it is not, in itself, sacred like a Christian church. Worship does not require a mosque; it can be performed anywhere, for faith resides in the heart of the believer. Turkish nomads observing Muslim merchants or warriors at prayer, especially in the early morning or late evening, instinctively felt the same deep spirituality whenever they themselves offered prayers to Tengri, lord of the eternal blue sky. Today the powerful spirituality of early Islam is still evoked in the great summer mosques when the roof is rolled away so that all within the mosque have a clear vision of the firmament during evening prayer. While prayer is offered communally, it is mystical and personal at the same time as each individual enters his own communion with God. Upon completing communion, each worshipper may then rise and serenely depart. I have witnessed this beautiful spiritual experience at a summer mosque of the Sufi order Naqishbandi at Menzil in eastern Turkey. Even though a nonbeliever, I too was enraptured by the moment, and felt whisked off to the dawn of Islam, when the Prophet Muhammad, a merchant and warrior, directed his first followers to behold the evening stars and pray to Allah, creator of the universe.[51]

In the company of Muslim merchants, many Sufi mystics arrived at Turkish encampments and settlements along the Silk Road. Sufis, whose name designated their simple woolen garment (suf), would have awed Turks as Muslim shamans. Sufis preached a mystical personal union with God through dance, poetry, and song so that Turkish shamans could readily adapt their rituals and folk traditions to the glorification of Allah.[52] Sufis, just like shamans, attained ecstatic experiences in trances (sometimes induced by the smoking of hashish) to ascend to the other world. Shamans, however, induced trances so that they could enter the spirit world, confront demons, and effect cures of the sick.[53] Shamans ascended to the heavens to glimpse the incomprehensible power of the eternal God. Even so, for Turkish nomads, Sufi and shaman were but two different types of mentors, or *hoca*; each communicated with the divine in his own way. Muslim geographers and chroniclers, however, were often scandalized when they reported how Muslim Turks after conversion regularly consulted their shamans, who were believed to shape-shift into wolves or birds of prey to battle demonic spirits of disease. Only Turkish tribes or clans settling in the vicinity of the cities of Transoxiana acquired over time the conventional beliefs and practices of Islam of the medresse. Even today, many Muslim nomads of the steppes still cherish their ancestral practices and trust their shamans. When Tsarina Catherine the Great (1762–1796) ordered her officials to classify her nomadic subjects by religion, her officials were frustrated because they found few Turkish nomads practiced Islam as they had learned it from textbooks.[54] Instead, they classified nomads by language and ethnicity, and so drew the boundaries of the future Soviet, and then modern republics of Inner Asia.

By the early tenth century, Muslim historians report the first mass conversions of Turkish tribes on the western and central Eurasian steppes. Shortly before 921/2, the kaghan of the Bulgars and his nation on the middle Volga embraced Islam en masse, and he sent envoys to Caliph al-Muqtadir, requesting alliance and Muslim imams to instruct him in the new faith.[55] The Bulgars, vassals of the Khazars, had learned of Islam from merchants settled among their encampment for over a century. The caliph sent his accomplished diplomat Ahmad ibn Fadlan, who penned an insightful account of the mores of the Khazars, Bulgars, and Rus living in the northern lands of darkness. Ibn Fadlan's travels, along with the Anglo-Saxon epic *Beowulf*, inspired the novel of Michael Crichton and the movie spectacle "The Thirteenth Warrior" (1999).[56] In 956, Oghuz tribes on the steppes of Kazakhstan, including the ancestors of the Seljuk Turks, embraced Islam. Many of their warriors had served as allies or mercenaries in the armies of the Samanid emirs of Bukhara.[57] Four years later, Satuk Bughra Khan compelled two hundred thousand tents (or *yurt*) of the Karakhanid confederacy, which then dominated the old Karluk heartland of Zhetysu and Ferghana, to convert en masse.[58] Satuk, when a boy of twelve, had been converted by a Sufi mystic, and he concealed his faith until six years later, when he overthrew his father. For two decades, he zealously promoted Islam, obtained a fatwa from the caliph, and built the first mosque in his capital of Kashgar. The later Ottoman historians hailed Satuk as the first Muslim ruler of the steppes, who waged jihad and forged a Turkish state. Therefore, by year 1000, Islam had spread across the western and central Eurasian steppes and was no longer the religion of the majority of the inhabitants within the boundaries of the Caliphate under Harun al-Rashid (786–809), who in his own day and ever since has been revered as presiding over the Golden Age of Classical Islam.

By converting to Islam, the Turkish nomads also gained access to the high civilization of Eastern Islam created by the Samanid emirs. Nasr ibn Ahmad (864–892) united eastern Iran and Transoxiana, and waged war against Turkish nomads north of the Jaxartes River.[59] In 875, he received a fatwa from the Caliph al-Mutamid, for his family, descended from an early Iranian convert Saman Choba of Balkh, had long loyally served the Abbasid court. He and his heirs were not the first, but they were the most important patrons who made Persian letters, arts, and architecture the high culture of Eastern Islam. They built the skylines of Merv, Bukhara, Samarkand, and Balkh with the towering minarets of medresses and mosques that transformed these cities into Muslim ones. Unfortunately, few Samanid monuments have survived, but the family mausoleum at Bukhara escaped destruction by the Mongols. Built by Nasr's brother and successor Ismail, the mausoleum is the oldest and among the finest examples of Islamic architecture of Inner Asia.[60] The building measures over thirty feet in height, and tapers in the form of the cube resembling the Kaaba of Mecca. It is mounted by an octagonal squinch dome measuring twenty-three feet in diameter, flanked by four smaller decorative domes. The decorative patterns of the bricks are an eclectic synthesis of styles from across Western and Inner Asia. Any Turkish nomad visiting Bukhara in the ninth century would have gazed upward in awe at the mausoleum's dome.

At the opening of the tenth century, Turkish visitors would have encountered comparable architecture in every caravan city of Transoxiana. Families of merchants and craftsmen organized in guilds, and even peasants of the surrounding villages had embraced Islam for generations. Medresses replaced Buddhist and Christian monasteries as schools of learning, and provided soup kitchens for the poor. Everywhere, Turkish visitors would have seen the rich social and cultural life of Muslim cities.[61]

The Samanid court also sponsored the creation of a distinctly Persian literature in the tenth century. Scribes and scholars adapted Persian, an Indo-European language enriched with many Arabic loan words, to the Arabic script. Persian quickly emerged as the language of poetry and belles lettres, while Arabic was reserved for religious and scholarly works.[62] Sir Richard Burton, the volatile and brilliant explorer, linguist, and rogue, declared Persian the Italian of the Middle East, which one could learn in an evening.[63] The greatest of Persian poets, Hakim Abu'l-Qasim Ferdowsi Tusi, composed the national epic of the heroes of Iran before the Arabic conquest, the *Shah-nameh* or the "Book of Kings."[64] Simultaneously, scholars translated into Persian Arabic medical, mathematical, and scientific texts.

Hence, Turkish khans of Kashgar aspired not only to the political but also to the cultural legacy of the Samanid emirs. These khans learned from the Samanid emirs how to promote a distinctly Turkish Islamic culture throughout their confederacy in the tenth and eleventh centuries. They built the first medresses and domed mosques beyond the borders of the Caliphate. The khans patronized poets and scholars writing works in Turkish recorded in the Arabic script. Foremost was the meticulous polymath Mahmud ibn Hussayn al-Kashgari, whose life spanned virtually the entire eleventh century; he died at the age of ninety-seven in 1102.[65] He composed the first comprehensive dictionary of the Turkish language, in which he recorded numerous verses of traditional lyric poems and epics. Mahmud also drew the first map of the Turkic tribes, today housed in the National Library in Istanbul. Mahmud laid the foundation for all future writers to create a literature that in diversity and beauty would match Arabic and Persian. His writings delighted later Ottoman scholars who assiduously collected, edited, and transmitted his works. They were also inspired to follow his example, composing compendiums summarizing and cataloging all knowledge. The Turkish literary and visual arts promoted by the khans of Kashgar thus provided a model for all future Turkish conquerors of the steppes who aspired to forge a Muslim state and culture.

The spiritual and cultural lives of the Turkish nomads were forever transformed, because no matter how heterodox their beliefs and practices, they were members of the *umma*, the Muslim community of believers. When the Seljuk Turks burst into the Islamic world in the mid-eleventh century, they were perceived not as hordes of Gog and Magog but rather as Muslim warriors waging the steppe way of war in the name of the Sunni Caliph of Baghdad. The horsemen of the Seljuk Turks did not herald the Apocalypse. Instead, they revived Muslim power, dominated the battlefield for the next millennium, and changed the world from Britain to India.

16

The Seljuk Turks and Their Sultanate

Late in the afternoon, August 26, 1071, the Byzantine emperor Romanus Diogenes lost control over his infantry attempting to wheel about and return to the camp. In the morning, he had sought to force a decisive battle against the Seljuk Turks under their sultan Alp Arslan on the rolling plains just west of the fortress at Manzikert.[1] The emperor Romanus IV, a leading general, had ascended to the throne three years earlier, pledging to end Turkish attacks. At Manzikert, Romanus fielded an army forty-five thousand strong, but it comprised Pecheneg and Norman mercenaries and ill-trained provincial infantry. Alp Arslan commanded twenty thousand expert Turkish horsemen, veterans of battles from Transoxiana to Anatolia. This time the Turks fought not as allies of the caliph but as the soldiers of jihad, holy war, against the unbeliever under their own sultan. The day before the battle, the Pechenegs learned they were kinsmen of the Seljuk Turks and deserted. In the morning, Romanus drew up his battle line in a classic formation to counter horse archers. He commanded the infantry in the center, while strong cavalry detachments guarded the infantry's flanks and rear. Romanus sent word south of his position to a secondary column stationed north of Ahlat on Lake Van to force march and take the Turks in the flank or rear. Romanus conducted a measured advance, but failed to lure the Turks into charging his infantry. The secondary column never appeared. Late in the afternoon, Romanus ordered a halt and withdrawal. At that moment, the rear guard cavalry under the emperor's brother-in-law Andronicus Ducas, and then the Norman knights, treacherously galloped off the field, while the panicked infantry cried out that the emperor had been slain. Alp Arslan saw his chance and led a furious charge into the disordered Byzantine ranks. Thousands of Byzantines were cut down in flight. The Turks captured the emperor and his camp. Today Manzikert is the sleepy Turkish town of Malazgirt, its Medieval fortress converted into an outside café. On an eastern rise overlooking the town stretches a long stadium.[2] Its entrance is flanked by two monoliths that recall far more the monolith in "2001: A Space Odyssey" (1968) than the Pillars of Asia. Signs greet visitors proclaiming fanciful historical myths. Each year Turkish nationalists descend on the site to celebrate the Seljuk victory. The jingoist slogans and rituals aside, the battle was decisive, for it signaled the collapse of Byzantine power in Asia Minor and its settlement by the Turks.

The Battle of Manzikert marked the climax of a long march of the Seljuk Turks westward from their original home on the steppes to the north and west of the Aral Sea to a new homeland in central Anatolia. The ancestors of the Seljuk Turks were members of a loose Oghuz confederation who had migrated from farther east to the arid steppes of Kazakhstan during the eighth and ninth centuries.[3] Their rulers styled themselves as *yabgu* rather than kaghan, because they were resentful vassals of the Khazar kaghan. Oghuz Turks bred horses, sheep, and hybrid camels, which were a cross between the two-humped Bactrian camel and the single-humped dromedary of the Near East.[4] These hybrid camels, sure-footed on the ice and inured to the winter cold on the steppes, were prized as the beast of burden on the Silk Road.

The Oghuz Turks also prospered off the slave trade. Each year, thousands of Slavic slaves (dubbed Saqaliba in Arabic sources) were herded from Atil or Bulgar on the River Volga across the steppes

to the markets of Khwarazm, which straddled the rich valley of the
lower River Oxus (Amu Darya) emptying its waters north into the
Aral Sea. From the Khwarazmian cities of Jurianiya and Kath, the
unfortunate souls were driven south to the markets of Bukhara,
the Samanid capital and cultural center of Muslim Transoxiana.[5]
The Abbasid diplomat Ahmad ibn Fadlan marveled at the comeli-
ness of these fair-haired, fair-skinned, blue-eyed Rus warrior merchants, Scandinavians from the far north who sold great numbers
of Slavs destined for the Islamic slave markets.[6] In early March of
922, Ahmad ibn Fadlan and his party traversed this route north to
visit the court of the kaghan of the Bulgars on the middle Volga
River. Years later, ibn Fadlan in his journal still felt exhausted from
the bitter cold and deep snow as his party covered great distances
from dawn to dusk for fifteen days until they reached winter settlements of Oghuz Turks, whom he called in Arabic Ghuzz Turks.[7]
Ibn Fadlan reports how he and his companions, sons of the sunny
skies of Baghdad, had to bundle up in multiple layers of clothing,
and wear the felt caps and jackets, sheepskin cloaks, and leather boots
of nomads.[8] The ever-perceptive ibn Fadlan gives our best report
on the customs of the Oghuz Turks before they converted to Islam.
The envoy's Oghuz hosts, long familiar with Muslim merchants,
greeted their guests in Arabic with the profession that there is no
God but Allah and Muhammad is His prophet. Ibn Fadlan, however, realized that the greeting was uttered out of politeness rather
than conviction. For Oghuz Turks happily invoked the Muslim
God along with their traditional prayers to the lord of the universal sky, Tengri. The success and survival of ibn Fadlan's company
depended on the hospitality of the Oghuz Turks, who lent horses,
camels, and money on the solemn word that the Arab visitors would
repay in full once their mission was accomplished.[9] Among the
Turks, such gift exchanges sustained caravans crossing the steppes,
and so assured the delivery of linens, cottons, dried fruits, grains,
and well-wrought weapons and tools from the Islamic world that
were vital to life on the steppes. Woe to any guest, Turk or foreign
merchant, who failed to keep his word, for the malefactor was tied
to the branches of two different trees, and then the branches were
released to spring back to their original position, tearing the man

asunder.[10] One's word was his bond, and any faithlessness endangered all and merited the harshest of punishments.

Ibn Fadlan's Turkish hosts also expected rich gifts of silk and silver, and news about Baghdad, the fabled city of the caliph. Ahmad ibn Fadlan, piously fastidious about cleanliness, deplored the miserable lives of these nomads who were, in his opinion, little better than the animals they herded. He was also shocked by the immodesty of the women, who were unveiled and unashamed to relieve themselves in the presence of their menfolk and guests. Ibn Fadlan's host laughed at his guest's embarrassment, and replied through a translator that his wives allowed no other man near them, and they were more faithful than Muslim women, veiled and covered, who seduced other men.[11] Brutal winters on the steppes permitted no privacy for families huddled together within their felt tents for months. In many ways, the lives of these Oghuz Turks resembled those of the Scythians described by the Greek historian Herodotus over thirteen centuries earlier. Ibn Fadlan reports the sacrifice of horses, which were propped up in the air on poles around the tomb of a deceased lord. Shamans, in dreams or trances, confirmed that the sacrificed horses carried the deceased to the ancestors.[12] The Turks, just like the later Mongols, had taboos on washing, especially during the winter months, and often they allowed their clothes to rot and fall off.[13] During his brief stay, ibn Fadlan was both fascinated and repelled by the habits of the Oghuz Turks. The polished Abbasid courtier could never have conceived that just three generations later, the descendants of these nomads, under their own sultan, would enter the city of Baghdad in triumph as the saviors of Islam.

Perhaps a generation after ibn Fadlan had visited, Dukak, leader of an obscure clan of the Oghuz Turks, led his people in a gradual trek from the northern shores of the Aral Sea east in the direction of the greener pastures around Lake Issyk.[14] His followers merely numbered one hundred horsemen, one thousand five hundred camels, and fifty thousand sheep. Twenty years later, in ca. 985, Dukak's son Seljuk settled his people around Jand or Yenikent, "new settlement," on the lower Jaxartes (Syr Darya), with the permission of the Iranian-speaking shah of Khwarazm, who was a vassal of the Samanid emir of Bukhara.[15] Seljuk and his followers were obligated to defend Khwarazm against Turkish marauders from the north. They also embraced en masse Islam, and Seljuk was revered thereafter for leading his nation into the community of believers (*umma*) so that his followers henceforth adopted the ethnic name of Seljuk Türkmen. He bestowed Muslim names on his three sons: Arslan Isra'il, Mika'il, and Musa.[16] Seljuk, reportedly living over a century, proved a worthy nomadic ruler, increasing the prosperity and numbers of his people. Within a generation of Seljuk's death, his heirs turned a tribe on the remote fringes of Transoxiana into the arbiters of the Muslim world.

In 1005, the exile Isma'il Muntasir, the last Samanid emir, was murdered by his Arab hosts near Merv. His death ended five years of pyrrhic victories to restore the Samanid emirate.[17] In 999, the Bughra khan Ahmad Arslan had defeated and captured Isma'il Muntasir, who was compelled to relinquish Bukhara and Samarkand. Isma'il, however, soon escaped prison, recruited Oghuz Turkish horse archers, and raised abortive revolts in Khwarazm and Khurasan.[18] The sudden collapse of Samanid power ignited petty wars across Transoxiana and eastern Iran, as local dynasts and civic elites settled by force long-standing quarrels with neighboring rivals.[19] Two great rivals, the Karakhanids and the Ghaznavids, each claimed the Samanid legacy. The Bughra khan ruled from Kashgar the powerful Karakhanid confederacy of nine inner tribes that was the first Muslim Turkish state on the central Eurasian steppes.[20] He also held sway over the western cities of the Tarim Basin, Kuchea and Khotan, home to many Turkish speakers who followed Buddhism or Islam. The most powerful of the Bughra khans, Ali Tigim (1020–1034), nearly realized his dream of claiming the Samanid political legacy, for he had secured the caravan cities of the Tarim Basin.[21] But Ali Tigim faced rivals within his own family because the descendants of Khan Ahmad Arslan had parceled out appanages to all members of the royal family so that each Bughra khan invariably faced challengers from among his kinsmen. He also faced a deadly rival in the Ghaznavid sultan Mahmud.

The Ghaznavid sultans, descendants of Turkish slave soldiers or mamluks in Samanid employ, opposed the Karakhanids, whom they dismissed as nomadic interlopers. Ghaznavid sultans, although

Turkish in origin, were Persian in speech and patrons of Muslim poets, artists, and architects.[22] Persian Muslim jurists and bureaucrats administered the realm; the Ghaznavid sultans also received firmans, or edicts ruling on administrative or judicial matters, that designated them deputies of the Abbasid caliph.[23] Foremost, the Ghaznavid sultans were zealous Sunni Muslims who waged jihad against the unbelievers in northern India. The emir Sebüktigin, who founded the Ghaznavid state, was born on the steppes around Lake Issyk. At age twelve, in ca. 965, he was captured and sold into slavery in Bukhara.[24] His master, Alp Tigin, also a Samanid mamluk of Turkish origin, recognized the brilliance of Sebüktigin, to whom he married his daughter.[25] In 977, Sebüktigin succeeded his father-in-law to the lordship of Ghazna, in central Afghanistan. Hailed as the lion of Ghazna, Sebüktigin gained control over the strategic passes across the Hindu Kush, and repeatedly raided the Punjab and Kashmir, sacking Buddhist monasteries and Hindu temples. His Turkish horse archers, either mamluks or mercenaries just off the steppes, perfected tactics to counter Indian infantry and war elephants. They also learned about the size and wealth of India—invaluable knowledge for all future Muslim conquerors of the subcontinent. During his reign of two decades, Sebüktigin turned his own realm, the ancient Bactria of diverse faiths since the Kushan era, into the Muslim land of Afghanistan today. His son and successor, Mahmud (997–1030), was even more ambitious, for he aspired to dominate all of Eastern Islam. Mahmud, the hammer of the infidels, waged seventeen campaigns against the Punjab and Kashmir, or one Indian campaign every second year for a generation.[26] In his most daring raid, in 1024, Mahmud sacked the celebrated temple of Shiva at Somnath in Gujarat. The shrine was stripped of its gold and silver objects, and its great silver lingam of Shiva was smashed to bits. The silver was later melted down and recast to adorn the minbar of the sultan's mosque in Ghaznva. Muslim chroniclers magnified the glorious feats of Mahmud, while Hindu writers deplored his iconoclastic atrocities, which Hindu nationalists still condemn today.

Simultaneously, Mahmud battled his Karakhanid rivals for supremacy over Khurasan, Khwarazm, and Transoxiana. The three sons of Seljuk fought as allies on both sides, repeatedly switching allegiances, and even backing the shah of Khwarazm's brief bid for independence.[27] The eldest brother, Arslan Isra'il, exercised supreme authority, but his younger brothers, Mika'il and Musa, each commanded his own warriors. All three brothers recruited many more Oghuz clans and tribes who migrated off the steppes into Transoxiana during the desultory fighting. The Seljuk Turks swelled from a modest tribe into a consortium of many tribes under independent leaders clamoring for fresh pastures, booty, and glory. Each of Seljuk's sons was constantly taxed to discipline and direct his warriors toward a common goal. The sultan Mahmud grew alarmed over the rising numbers of Seljuk Turks. In 1029, he treacherously seized and imprisoned Arslan Isra'il, who soon died in captivity, and then Mahmud scattered the Seljuk Turks across Khurasan.[28] Mahmud's treachery backfired. By 1035, the brothers Chaghri and Tughrul Bey, sons of Seljuk's second son, Mika'il, had rallied their followers and gained mastery of Khurasan, once the heartland of the Parthians.[29] The new Ghaznavid sultan, Masud, was compelled to recognize the fait accompli in exchange for Seljuk promises of loyalty. The fraternal team of Chaghri and Tughrul Bey, just like previous ones among the Turkish nomads, worked in tandem to forge a Muslim Turkish state in Khurasan along Samanid lines.[30] Professional Iranian bureaucrats governed the cities; councils of elders administered the villages. Any corrupt official was severely punished. The brothers imposed strict discipline over their tribal regiments, which protected caravans from the chaotic fighting between Ghaznavids and Karakhanids, much to the approval of merchant princes. The brothers piously patronized mosques and medresses, and so won praise from Islamic jurists (ulema).

In 1037, Tughrul Bey declared himself sultan at Nishapur, after audaciously raiding to the very walls to Ghaznva.[31] An enraged Masud, campaigning in India, declared war on his unruly Seljuk vassals. On May 23, 1040, the armies of Sultan Masud and of the brothers Tughrul Bey and Chaghri clashed in a decisive battle at Dandanakan, to the west of Merv (today in Turkmenistan).[32] The Seljuk army of twenty thousand horse archers encircled and annihilated the Ghaznavid army of fifty thousand, complete with sixty

Indian war elephants. For weeks, the Seljuks had retreated west from Merv in the direction of Sarakhs, a caravansary on the eastern border of modern Iran. Masud's army suffered from harassing attacks of Turkish horse archers, who laid waste the land and poisoned the wells. The Ghaznavid soldiers, dehydrated and demoralized, broke ranks and fled before the hail of Turkish arrows, while their own stampeding elephants, maddened by wounds, rampaged among the Ghaznavid infantry. Masud escaped across the Hindu Kush to Lahore, where he was to seek his political future in northern India.[33] The Seljuk victory proved a decisive turning point.

In the next several years, Chaghri secured the lands of eastern Islam to the banks of the Jaxartes (Syr Darya) and the western slopes of the Hindu Kush. The Bughra khan in Kashgar acknowledged Seljuk overlordship and renounced his claims to Khwarazm.[34] The fame of Tughrul Bey raced across the Eurasian steppes so that nomadic Turkish warriors flocked to Khurasan to take service with the legendary Turkish sultan. Just two years after the victory of Dandanakan, the first of these Türkmen bands raided into Armenia, recently annexed by the Byzantine Empire.[35] Meanwhile, Tughrul Bey relentlessly marched west across northern Iran with the aim of liberating Baghdad from Buyid rule. For nearly a century, Buyid emirs, who were Shi'ite sectarians of Persian origin, exercised power over western Iran and Iraq.[36] They reduced the Abbasid caliph to a pitiful figurehead so as to placate the large restive Sunni populations. After fifteen years of hard fighting, Tughrul Bey overthrew the three Buyid emirates. In December 1055, Tughrul Bey at the head of his army entered Baghdad to the cheers of the Sunni residents who detested the ignominious Buyid rule. A nervously grateful caliph, al-Ka'im, bestowed supreme command of his armies and a daughter in marriage on his Turkish sultan.[37] Tughrul Bey quickly discovered ruling a great empire was far more daunting than winning it. Possession of Baghdad conferred legitimacy on Tughrul Bey and his heirs, but the city was nearly 1,800 miles from the strategic northeastern frontier on the Jaxartes River. Beyond the frontier, great Seljuk sultans in Baghdad had to cultivate alliances with the Turkish tribes of Kazakhstan and Zhetysu, who furnished fresh recruits to the sultan's army.[38] But Tughrul Bey, as the defender of the faithful, inherited an even more important priority, the war against the Fatimid caliphs of Cairo, who controlled the Levant and the Holy Cities of Mecca and Medina. In 909, the hidden imam, Abu Abdallah al-Shi'i, emerged out of the deserts of Maghreb, the far Muslim West, and announced that he was the true expected one and caliph, al-Mahdi.[39] He claimed direct descent from Ali and Fatima, the only daughter of Muhammad, through their younger son, the martyred al-Husayn, and then from Isma'il ibn Jafar, the seventh and last visible imam on earth. Their rivals, the Twelver Shi'ites of Eastern Islam, instead followed the descent of Isma'il's younger brother Musa, whose line ended with the twelfth visible imam, Hujjat Allah al-Mahdi, who went into hiding at Samara in 873/4.[40] The Seveners or Isma'ilites professed a radical theology to bring about the Apocalypse through violent means. Isma'ilites often penetrated urban guilds as a cover to set up networks of secret societies that sent out hit squads targeting Sunni rulers and theologians. Abu Abdallah called for the cleansing of a decadent Islam that inspired puritanical Berber tribesmen to wage holy war. In the next sixty years, Berber armies in the name of their Fatimid caliph swept across North Africa, conquered the wealthy Nile valley, and occupied the Holy Cities of Mecca and Medina.[41] At their capital, Cairo, from 973 on, the later Fatimid caliphs aimed to take Baghdad and unite all Islam. Yet they also shifted from leaders of a revolutionary movement to monarchs of a bureaucratic state headed by viziers and professional officials.[42] Fatimid armies comprised disciplined regiments of Berber cavalry, Armenian mercenaries, and slave soldiers of Slavic or black African origin.[43]

In 1055, Tughrul Bey, as defender of Sunni Islam, fought a pitiless war against the soldiers of the heretical Fatimid Caliph across the strategic grasslands of al-Jazirah, "the island," today the borderlands straddling the frontiers of Syria, Turkey, and Iraq. In 1057–1058, Fatimid forces even occupied Baghdad, where for forty consecutive Fridays, muezzins from atop the city's tiled minarets summoned the faithful to midday prayer in the name of the Fatimid caliph.[44] Meanwhile, the rival Abbasid court desperately held out in the palace until Tughrul Bey's warriors retook the city.

Sultan Tughrul Bey, and his nephew and successor Alp Arslan

(1063–1072), the son of Chaghri, faced two additional threats. First, their unruly Seljuk tribesmen found the humid heat of Iraq debilitating. They also could not find pastures in southern Iraq, a land of sown fields and orchards crisscrossed with canals. Baghdad, the jewel of Islam, offered too many attractions and vices to tribesmen who inevitably haggled and clashed with residents in the marketplaces. Urban residents and peasants alike found their Turkish protectors hard masters, and both sultans feared seething resentment among the Arab populations could burst into rebellion.[45] Therefore, the sultans stationed their tribal regiments in the al-Jazirah, where they found ample pastures and fresh water for their herds and flocks. Beyond, to the north, lay the high plateau of Armenia, and to the west of the Taurus Mountains the grasslands of central Anatolia, which were the provinces of the Byzantine Empire. The lure of raiding these Christian lands proved irresistible to Seljuk Turks, and both sultans encouraged these attacks to avert a second threat. In 1001, the warrior emperor Basil Bulgaroctonus signed a treaty with the Fatimid caliph al-Hakim recognizing the formal partition of Syria and Mesopotamia (northern Iraq).[46] The Fatimid caliph pledged to protect Christian pilgrims leaving Antioch, in Byzantine territory, on their way to Bethlehem and Jerusalem. To Tughrul Bey and Alp Arslan, the emperor in Constantinople was still held in awe as the greatest of Christian monarchs, and equal to the caliph or the emperor of China. They feared the alliance of Constantinople and Cairo would prove too powerful. Little did they know that the Byzantine Empire had long passed its apex and was racked by succession crises, rival factions of bureaucratic and military elites, and widespread discontent in the countryside over oppressive taxes and buyouts of peasant lands by "powerful ones" (*dynatoi*).[47] The Armenians settled along the empire's eastern frontier were further alienated by the suppression of their national church in favor of the imperial Orthodox one. The inept heirs of Basil II, habitually short of money, debased the coinage and slashed military budgets, while corrupt officials raided the treasury and thwarted any reforms.[48]

Therefore, neither Tughrul Bey nor Alp Arslan ever planned to overthrow the Byzantine Empire, pace the claims made in the jingoistic signs that welcome visitors to the great stadium in modern Malazgirt today. At most, they directed Seljuk bands to distract the Byzantine army from assisting the Fatimid army in Syria. But these Turkish raiders found little effective resistance, and grasslands of central Anatolia and Armenia that were similar to their original homeland of the Eurasian steppes. At Manzikert, Alp Arslan had redeployed his army from Syria based on reports of possible Byzantine operations against Turkish bases near the Armenian cities Ani and Kars.[49] He was stunned by the size and determination of Romanus's army, and he offered to negotiate, but Romanus flatly refused. Romanus could not easily levy another such field army, and he needed a decisive victory if he were to intimidate scheming, corrupt bureaucrats of Constantinople into implementing much-needed reform. The battle should have ended in a draw. Romanus was instead betrayed, and his inexperienced infantry then panicked.

Alp Arslan survived his victory at Manzikert by just over a year, for on November 25, 1072, he was felled by an assassin's dagger while campaigning on the Jaxartes River.[50] His son and successor Malik Shah was preoccupied with battling the Fatimids for control of Damascus and Jerusalem, and checking the return of his Ghaznavid foes from India. He had no time for exploiting his father's victory in Byzantine Asia Minor. Instead, independent bands of Seljuk Turks migrated with their families into Anatolia and carved out their own lordships.[51] In northeastern Asia Minor, the *ghazi* warrior Malik Danishmend ruled his own emirate in the Iris valley (today Yeşil Irmak) from the citadel of Niksar (Classical Neocaesarea).[52] Suleiman ibn Qutalmish, a descendant of Seljuk's oldest son, seized the cities of Nicaea (Iznik) and Iconium (Konya), declaring himself the sultan of Rum (Arabic for Rome).[53] Suleiman's capable heirs eventually united Muslim Asia Minor and laid the foundations of modern Turkey.

These Seljuk warlords succeeded because their followers found the rolling grasslands of Anatolia, called in Turkish *ova*, ideal for herding their animals. They were inured to the deep winter snows and blazing summer heat of Anatolia, whereas earlier Arab military colonists settled on the plateau's southern edge by Abbasid caliphs abandoned their settlement after enduring a single winter.[54] Seljuk

Turks, in contrast, discovered in Anatolia a fragment of their ancestral home on the Eurasian steppes ringed by mountain ranges cutting it off from the warm waters of the surrounding seas. By their very way of life, they steadily turned Anatolia from a land of farming to one of stock raising over the next three centuries. It has only been put back under the plow in the last two generations. Christian agriculturalists, dwelling in the deep river valleys, quickly came to terms with the conquerors, selling their produce for the leather and woolens of the nomads, and rendering tribute to their Seljuk lords resident in cities.[55] For three centuries, Byzantine, Crusader, and Seljuk armies waged desultory wars of attrition over the peninsula that tipped the ecological balance in favor of the nomadic way of life. The fighting ruined the irrigation systems and the Roman system of roads, bridges, and depots. Twenty-five years after the Battle of Manzikert, Byzantine guides were bewildered by how drastically conditions had changed. They could not locate highways and cisterns, and so the leaders of the First Crusade suspected them as perfidious Greeks in league with the Turks.[56]

The fighting also undermined imperial institutions and the Orthodox Church. Prelates, nobles, and their families fled to Constantinople. The imperial government compensated aristocratic refugees with hereditary titles and new lands in the Balkans, while prelates in the capital continued to collect tithes from their sees, which they never again visited.[57] Seljuk Turks blockaded cities in Asia Minor so that Christian residents were compelled to surrender on terms. A Turkish court and its garrison, served by Persian and Apostate Christian officials, ruled from the citadel of each major city, while the cathedral was converted into the principal mosque (*ulu camii*). Many Christians fled to the cities on the Aegean and Euxine shores, to which the imperial fleet could bring supplies and reinforcements. To be sure, the Turks massacred populations that resisted, enslaved thousands, and targeted monasteries for destruction.[58] Even so, most Christians bowed to their new masters. Over these three centuries, many Christians learned Turkish to communicate with their overlords and to bargain with their nomadic neighbors.[59] Some Christians remained true to their faith but gave up the Hellenic tongue for Turkish written in the Greek alphabet.[60] By the mid-thirteenth century, as hopes of deliverance by the emperor's army faded, many Christians turned to Islam.

The sultans of Konya built medresses, minarets, and mosques, thereby transforming the urban skyline of Anatolia from a Christian to a Muslim one.[61] Christian merchants and craftsmen learned Turkish and Arabic and embraced Islam so that they could compete with their Muslim competitors. Ambitious young men entering the army or bureaucracy had to become Muslims. On the countryside, impoverished, illiterate parish priests ministered to their demoralized peasant congregations.[62] Christians adopted not just the Turkish language but many other Turkish manners and material culture. They added yogurt and spices to a Mediterranean grill diet, and they adapted nomadic styles to their jewelry, dress, ceramics, and carpets. In Anatolia of the early thirteenth century, many Christians were ready to seek spiritual solace in Islam if the new faith could be reconciled with their ancient traditions. Jalal ad-Din Muhammad Rumi (1207–1273), Persian poet and Sufi mystic, built the spiritual bridge whereby Anatolian Christians crossed over to Islam.[63] He was the son of a theologian and jurist of a medresse in Balkh, and at age twelve, he and his family fled west to escape the Mongols, eventually settling in Konya. In 1244, at age thirty-seven, Jalal ad-Din experienced a mystical conversion upon an encounter with a celebrated ascetic. He promptly reorganized members of the Mawlawiyya order resident at his family's medresse in Konya, who are today world-famous as the Whirling Dervishes. In his poetry, Jalal ad-Din stressed the oneness of God, and His universal love of humanity.[64] Theological debates and nuances among faiths paled into insignificance in comparison to the joy of celebrating the love of God. His followers, in wide flowing white kaftans and tall turbans, danced in a circular movement with one outstretched hand pointing to the sky and the other to the earth, symbolizing the mystical union of God and worshipper. Jalal ad-Din and his followers codified a folk Islam of the Eurasian steppes for Anatolian Christian villagers. Tales abounded celebrating how the charismatic poet and spiritual mentor inspired entire villages of Christians to convert. Today this poetry, music, and dance, which I have witnessed, are still deeply moving. To Christians, long bereft of spiritual fulfillment, the performances and message were awesome, and easily reconciled to the music, festivals, and rules of hospitality of traditional Anatolian village life. In his lifetime, Jalal ad-Din was already acclaimed the Mevlana, "the master," and his funerary memorial, Yeşil Türbe in Konya, is the most revered shrine and the premier pilgrimage site of Muslim Turkey.[65] Within a generation of the death of the Mevlana, Anatolia had become Turkey, the seat of a new civilization, Muslim in faith, Persian in aesthetics and letters, Turkish in speech, and forever linked by ethos and way of life to the ancestral Turkish homeland on the Eurasian steppes.

The Seljuk Turks achieved a remarkable success in assimilating the conquered. In 1071, Byzantine Anatolia comprised at least twelve million Greek- and Armenian-speaking Christians, whereas the newcomers, arriving in two waves, first in the eleventh and then in the thirteenth century, totaled at most five hundred thousand.[66] Yet in three centuries, the Anatolian Christians acquired the language, faith, and identity of their conquerors. The Seljuk Turks' achievement is all the more remarkable when compared to that of their distant kinsmen, the Turks who simultaneously crossed into India. Between the eleventh and sixteenth centuries, successive Turkish conquerors built Muslim empires, centered on Lahore or Delhi and embracing the valleys of the Indus and Ganges Rivers. In power and wealth, Muslim rulers of India far surpassed their contemporaries in Anatolia, but they depended on immigrants of Turkish soldiers from the steppes, and Iranian officials and savants. Even though Islam gained many converts, the masses of India adhered to their ancestral faith and accommodated the newcomers as members of yet one more caste. The Hindu populations proved too numerous and too wedded to their ancestral cults. They ultimately accommodated the newcomers as a separate caste within a broader Hinduism so that they turned Islam into an Indian religion.[67]

Finally, the Battle of Manzikert profoundly altered the course of history for the Christian world. Romanus Diogenes too did not long survive his defeat at Manzikert. Once brought as a captive before Alp Arslan, Romanus was magnanimously released by the sultan not out of mercy for the defeated, as later Muslim legends claim, but on the promise of a ransom of 1.5 million gold nomismata and

an annual tribute of three hundred sixty thousand.[68] Alp Arslan
shrewdly calculated an emperor returned in disgrace was far more
useful than a captive. Romanus returned to his capital to find his
stepson Michael Ducas enthroned and guided by his mentor, the
historian philosopher Michael Psellus. Romanus had little support
and abdicated on promise of a safe retirement into a monastery, but
the new emperor's uncle John Ducas reneged on the agreement. He
ordered Romanus blinded.[69] The torturers botched the blinding
three times, to the horror of a crowd of onlookers who bewailed
the pathetic fate of so brave an emperor. In prison, Romanus suffered a lingering death months later due to the inevitable infec-
tion. The self-proclaimed genius Michael Psellus, who recorded
imperial events since the death of Basil II, had ruined his lazy, me-
diocre protégé Michael Ducas. Neither was up to the task of rou-
tine governing. Together, emperor and counselor, who repudiated
Romanus's treaty with Alp Arslan, were incapable of coping with
the triple threat of Normans in southern Italy threatening to invade the Balkans, Pecheneg hordes restless to cross the Danube, and
Seljuk Turks overrunning Asia Minor. In 1078, the parsimonious
Michael VII Ducas, nicknamed Parapinaces (the "quarter pincher"
for debasing the gold currency), was forced to abdicate as the empire
plunged into a four-year civil war.[70] In the opinion of Sir Steven
Runciman, "The state of the Empire in 1081 was such that only a
man of great courage or great stupidity would have undertaken its
governance."[71] Fortunately, a man of great intelligence, the general
Alexius Comnenus, seized the throne and rescued the empire on
the brink of collapse. Alexius Comnenus was also most fortunate
because his daughter the princess Anna Comnena penned a history
narrating his thirty-seven-year reign. She lauds her father's bravery,
but she stresses even more his artful diplomacy. With a careful eye
for detail, Anna Comnena rightly emphasizes the achievements of a
father whom she idealized, but she also wrote out of frustration. She
turned to history, because her retiring husband Bryennius Caesar
thwarted her ambitions to ascend to the throne in her own right.
He reported his wife's plotting to his brother-in-law John Comnenus, and so Anna was forced into private life.[72] Anna, of course,
blamed her younger brother rather than her retiring husband. She

followed the time-honored tradition of Greek historians, namely, those who fail to make history find solace in writing it.

During the first five years of his reign, Alexius drove back a Norman invasion of the Balkans, and granted trade concessions to the Venetian Republic in return for naval assistance.[73] He then cleared the Aegean of Turkish pirates based at Smyrna (today Izmir), and courted the Cumans into an alliance to defeat Pecheneg invaders in 1091. The survivors among the Pechenegs were settled throughout the Balkans as colonists. Their young men were recruited into the mounted imperial police who patrolled the highways. The next year, Alexius conducted sweeping monetary and fiscal reforms.[74] Yet for all his successes, Alexius knew that he still must expel the Seljuk Turks from Asia Minor. Alexius, desperate for mercenaries, remembered the appeal of his predecessor Theophilus 250 years earlier. He implored Pope Urban II and the leading Frankish princes to send him several thousand heavily armored knights.[75] Even the haughty Anna Comnena, well-known for her disdain of the rude Westerners, grudgingly acknowledged that charging Frankish knights at full gallop and with leveled lances could sweep all before them on the battlefield and even burst through the walls of Baghdad.[76] But at Clermont, on November 27, 1095, Pope Urban called for the liberation of Jerusalem. Tens of thousands, princes, knights, and commoners, across Western Europe assumed the cross, shouting, "God wills it."[77] Alp Arslan had unwittingly triggered a Christian holy war. Seljuk warlords in Anatolia and Syria could hardly restrain their Turkish warriors from attacking Christian pilgrims making their way to Jerusalem. In the next year, instead of mercenaries, Alexius received the First Crusade, and half the armed might of Latin Christendom that came first to save and then to destroy Byzantium.

17

The Legend of Prester John
and the Gurkhans of Cathay

On November 18, 1145, Hugh, Bishop of Jabala in the Crusader Principality of Antioch, entered the papal palace at Viterbo, north of Rome. Pope Eugenius III, who was planning a great crusade of Christian kings to rescue the hard-pressed Crusaders in Outremer, had relocated to the pleasant Tuscan town because the radicals led by Arnold of Brescia controlled the Eternal City and declared a commune. Fortunately, we have an eyewitness account of this meeting from an accomplished churchman and writer, Otto of Freising, a great-nephew of the future Hohenstaufen Holy Roman Emperor Frederick Barbarossa.[1] Bishop Hugh pleaded the case for the Christians in the Crusader states. His sovereign prince, Raymond of Antioch, was desperate for a new crusade to check the Turkish emir Zengi, who had stormed the city of Edessa the previous year and now targeted Antioch.[2] But Hugh also brought exciting news of a powerful Christian priest-king in the East who had just smitten the Saracens in a climactic battle. This Christian potentate Prester John vowed to reach Jerusalem next. He had marched his host to the Tigris but failed to find a crossing and so withdrew into Inner Asia. Yet Christians clung to the hope that Prester John would soon return. Bishop Hugh, however, wanted to dispel hopeful tales then circulating among Christians in Western Europe that this mighty king would soon return and deliver Jerusalem. For centuries, this king was identified with Saint John, rumored to have escaped death and was even now walking the earth until the Apocalypse.[3] This king might have also descended from one of the Magi or one of the wealthy kings of India converted by Saint Thomas, the doubting apostle of Acts and the patron saint of the Christian churches of the East. He wielded an emerald-tipped golden scepter and commanded innumerable legions. His wondrous realm stretched across the distant eastern lands filled with fabulous animals, great riches, and pious Christians. Bishop Hugh succeeded in his immediate task. Pope Eugenius III inspired Kings Louis VII of France and Conrad III of Germany to assume the cross in the next year.[4]

This Second Crusade ended in dismal failure before the walls of Damascus in 1148.[5] King Conrad of Germany returned home in disgrace. He was never crowned Holy Roman Emperor and thereafter battled unruly Welf vassals who challenged the Hohenstaufen right to rule.[6] The failure was just as humiliating for King Louis. His wife, Queen Eleanor of Aquitaine, divorced her dull husband upon their return.[7]

Louis had grown suspicious over Eleanor's alleged intimacy with her uncle Raymond of Antioch. Eleanor soon married the dashing Henry Plantagenet, Count of Anjou, Duke of Normandy, and heir to the English throne. Henry II and Eleanor, the tempestuous couple celebrated by troubadours, ruled the greatest realm in Latin Christendom since Charlemagne, and outshone their monkish liege lord Louis VII. With the failure of the Second Crusade, hopes of the return of Prester John again ran high. Twenty years after Hugh's report, a purported Latin translation of a letter from Prester John to the Byzantine emperor Manuel Comnenus circulated across Western Europe.[8] The letter was a clever conceit to extol the realm of Prester John as a vision of the Paradise to come rather than a correspondence between two Christian autocrats. Over one hundred manuscripts of the Latin version have survived. Throughout the next two centuries, the letter was translated into

every European vernacular. Each copyist had no business record-
ing the letter unless he improved upon it. The power of Prester
John grew ever greater, his realm ever wider with each retelling.
Seventy-two kings served him daily. He ruled the kingdom of the
Three Indies, vaguely conceived as Ethiopia, India, and Inner Asia.
He guarded the tomb of Saint Thomas in India, and, foremost,
he succeeded to Alexander the Great as the guardian against the
hordes of Gog and Magog beyond the deserts and steppes of Inner
Asia. These rumors were retold and believed ever more enthusias-
tically in an era of depressing wars among Christian kings. Today
such reports, claims, and visions might be grist for the mill of so-
cial media, but at least the Medieval tales disseminated apocalyptic
hopes rather than the absurd conspiracy theories of today's media.
Pope Alexander III, a shrewd diplomat versed in theology and
canon law, decided to write to Prester John in the autumn of 1177.
Just several months earlier, Pope Alexander had reconciled with the
Holy Roman Emperor Frederick Barbarossa at the cathedral of San
Marco in Venice, and so ended eighteen years of warfare between
Pope and German emperor.[9] Alexander III hoped that a favorable
reply from Prester John would inspire the Christian kings of Europe to assume the cross in a Third Crusade. On September 27,
1177, a delegation headed by the Pope's physician Master Philip set
sail from Venice bound for the court of Prester John. The hapless
envoys arrived in Outremer, and then disappeared into Asia, never
to be heard from again. Pope Alexander truly believed that a great
sovereign ruled in Inner Asia, and in his letter claims that Master
Philip, when in the East, had spoken with wise elders who knew of
Prester John's realm firsthand.[10] The letter also set diplomatic protocol for future papal correspondence with Mongol khans in the
next century. Alexander opened with salutations and urged Prester
John to embrace the true faith by acknowledging the primacy of
Saint Peter's successors at Rome. Then followed an appeal to unite
in a common war against Muslims. The reply never arrived. Ten
years later, Saladin, sultan of Egypt and Syria, annihilated the Crusader army at Hattin, and recaptured Jerusalem.[11] New crusades of
kings and princes followed, and failed, while Christians fervently
prayed for the return of Prester John.

The immediate events that fired Christian hopes of deliverance by Prester John occurred on the Eurasian steppes. These events heralded major political and military changes that anticipated the arrival of the Mongols a century later. On September 9, 1141, Yelü Dashi, Gurkhan of the Khitans, defeated the Seljuk sultan Ahmad Sanjar in a great battle at Qatwan just outside of Samarkand. By this victory, Yelü Dashi secured the caravan cities of Transoxiana and the central Eurasian steppes, the heartland of the Turkish Karakhanids who had embraced Islam two centuries earlier.[12] The Khitans were neither Muslims nor Christians but rather Buddhists and shamanists from the borderlands of northern China. Nestorian monks in the cities of Transoxiana, grateful for his religious tolerance, baptized Yelü Dashi as one of their own and spread rumors of his impending arrival as Prester John ruling the kingdom of Cathay. Within months, these reports raced two thousand miles over the Silk Road to the ports of Outremer, where Bishop Hugh learned about Prester John from informants claiming direct knowledge. Even more significantly, the Khitan victory over Sultan Sanjar shattered the unity of the Seljuk sultanate.[13] Thereafter, Turkish rulers waged ruinous, desultory wars among themselves to gain supremacy over the lands of Eastern Islam.[14] Across the Muslim world, the imams preached doom for the sinful, and the pious trembled at an impending Khitan invasion of Dar al-Islam. These barbarian nonbelievers must surely be the hordes of Gog and Magog foretold in the *Koran* because they had just overwhelmed the best army of the Abbasid caliph.

Yet the barbarian victor, Yelü Dashi, a scion of the royal house of the Khitans, halted his advance west after he received the submission of the cities of Samarkand and Bukhara.[15] The threat of a barbarian invasion quickly faded. Yelü Dashi was himself an exile who had fled from his homeland in northern China fifteen years earlier. The Khitans, a Mongolian-speaking people, long dwelled on the grasslands of the upper Liao River that stretch east to the wooded mountainous regions of Manchuria.[16] The Khitans, named in Chinese chronicles since the fourth century AD, exchanged furs, flax, honey, timber, and horses for Chinese silk, foodstuffs, and finished goods.[17] During the ninth century, Khitan tribal leaders warred among themselves for the rank of Great Khan, and so each khan rendered homage to either the Uyghur kaghan or the Tang emperor whose patronage could tip the balance in conflicts with rivals.[18] In 901, a charismatic warrior, Yelü Abaoji, then age thirty-one, was acclaimed khan of the Yila, a leading tribe of the eight Khitan tribes.[19] Later historians hailed Abaoji as the greatest descendant of the legendary progenitors, a warrior astride a white stallion and lady in an ox-drawn cart, who met and married atop the sacred mountain Mu-yeh, where their cult statues were long venerated with sacrifices of a horse and ox.[20] These mysterious ancestors were avatars of the lord of the sky and mother earth, and their eight sons were the ancestors of the eight Khitan tribes. Abaoji's mother, Yaonian Yanmujin, is claimed to have witnessed in a dream the sun fall from the sky into her bosom to impregnate her.[21] Her son was to be a marvel, both as a warrior and as a shaman who could foresee the future. In 903, the Khitan Great Khan of the Yaolian clan appointed Abaoji as his supreme commander (*yüyu*). Within a year, Abaoji overthrew his master, and then battled his way to the rank of Great Khan in 907.[22] Yet Abaoji proved to be far more than another warlord. He turned the Khitans from a federation of tribes into imperial conquerors who founded an effective state in northern China that was heir to the Northern Wei and Tang dynasties.

In the year 907, the general Zhu Wen dispensed with ruling through puppet emperors, and deposed the last Tang emperor, the teenager Ai, who was quietly murdered afterward.[23] Zhu Wen (907–912) declared himself the emperor Taizu of a new Liang dynasty, but he faced too many rivals among dynasts of the Tang military elite who also aspired to the imperial throne.[24] The ailing Zhu Wen, notorious for indulging his prodigious sexual appetite in his summer palace at Luoyang, neglected affairs of state, and so fell victim to an assassination plot of his third son, Zhu Yougui.[25] Zhu Yougui, in vain, battled his irate older half brother Zhu Youwen and rebel military governors.[26] Later Neo-Confucian historians lamented the next dismal fifty years of disunity as the era of the Five Dynasties and Ten Kingdoms (907–960).

Abaoji as Great Khan of the Khitans deftly exploited Chinese disunity, for he commanded the most formidable cavalry in East Asia. He organized his veteran warriors into regiments who, along with their families, were based in separate military encampments (*orda*).[27] Abaoji, in the guise of an early Tang warrior emperor, subjected the tribes on the eastern steppes as far as the Altai Mountains, and recruited yet more horse archers. He invited the Uyghurs to return to their ancestral home, and to rebuild their capital, Karabalghasun, which the Kyrgyz Turks had sacked in 840.[28] But the Uyghurs declined the offer, preferring the comforts of urban life in the Tarim Basin so that the sacred Orkhon valley passed from the Turks to the Mongols. Abaoji initiated the conquest of the sixteen frontier prefectures of northeastern China. In 916, Abaoji proclaimed himself emperor of the Liao dynasty, and assumed the Chinese throne name Taizu. For the next two centuries, he and his heirs would rule an empire embracing northern China, southern Manchuria, and the Mongolian steppes.

Quite in contrast to previous nomadic conquerors, the Liao emperors were recognized as members of a legitimate Chinese dynasty, and so they were accorded official dynastic histories.[29] They, however, adapted rather than embraced Chinese civilization. In the year 1000, the Khitans numbered at most seven hundred fifty thousand souls, of whom thirty thousand warriors were assigned to the military encampments.[30] They were outnumbered by their Chinese subjects by a factor of twenty. From the start, Abaoji employed Chinese mandarins to administer the Chinese provinces, and adopted many Chinese court rituals and bureaucratic procedures.[31] But he kept the Chinese mandarins at a distance lest the Khitans, just like their predecessors, the Northern Wei, would be assimilated into the Han people. Abaoji ordered the creation of a Khitan script based on Han characters for use in royal correspondence and records. The Khitan script of 378 characters, later modified into one of 370 characters, prevented the mandarin bureaucrats from monopolizing imperial records.[32] The Khitan emperors also employed a separate legal code for each of their diverse subjects, and they divided the realm into five great prefectures, each with its own capital and administration.[33] The principal capital was Shangjing on the eastern steppes of Inner Mongolia (in today's banner or district of Bairin),

where the Great Khan could reward loyal tribal khans with titles,
silk, and marriageable princesses in the best tradition of the Five
Baits. Regional capitals were established at Zhongjing (Ningcheng),
Dongjing (Liaoyang), Xijing (Datong, Shaanxi), and, in the south,
Nanjing (Beijing), the last destined to become the royal metropolis
of northern China. Finally, just like the Northern Wei emperors,
the Liao emperors embraced Buddhism, which was easily reconciled to their ancestral Khitan gods and shamans.[34] They ordered
the translations of the principal Buddhist texts into their own language. Foremost, they tolerated all faiths within their empire, re-
versing the hostility of the later Tang emperors to foreign faiths.

The later Mongol khans learned from their Khitan subjects these
lessons in statecraft for governing China, but the Khitan emperors,
unlike their Mongol successors, never aspired to rule over all of
China for two reasons. First, Khitan emperors were always hard-
pressed to appease both their nomadic warriors and their Chinese
subjects, and this juggling act limited their imperial ambitions. In
916, when Abaoji declared himself the emperor Taizu, he also proclaimed his eldest son, Yelü Bei, as his successor.[35] With the utmost
reluctance, the notables of the national assembly, the *kurultai* of the
later Mongols, consented to strict hereditary succession over traditions of lateral succession. Much to the resentment of the proud
Khitan warlords, Yelü Bei received the education of a refined Chinese gentleman, mastering the Confucian classics, calligraphy, and
painting at the expense of the martial arts. In 926, upon Abaoji's
death, the dowager empress Shulü Ping refused to join her deceased
husband Abaoji. Instead she cut off her right hand for ritual burial
with her husband's body. For the next twenty-five years, she dominated the court in the fashion of Mongol empresses of the thirteenth
century. Twice she provoked succession crises to put her candidate
on the throne.[36] In 953, she was finally forced to abdicate and to
retire into a gilded exile. The strong-willed empress championed
the martial ways of the steppes so that she rigged the election of
her younger son, Yelü Deguang, as Abaoji's successor under the
Chinese throne name of Taizong (927–947).[37] Yelü Deguang did
not disappoint his mother or his supporters, because he conquered
the remaining sixteen prefectures and the lower Yellow River val-

ley, the cradle of Chinese civilization.[38] He also briefly occupied
the former Tang capital, Kaifeng, at the nexus of four major canals
and boasting perhaps a half million residents. But these successes
of Yelü Deguang committed later Khitan emperors to consolidat-
ing and defending rather than expanding their Chinese domains.
Out of necessity, later Liao emperors turned their nomadic confederation into a Chinese bureaucratic state based on predictable
revenues gained in taxation rather than the plunder of conquests.[39]

Second, the later Khitan emperors faced two powerful rivals for
the mastery of China. In significant ways, the political division of
China in 960 resembled the one following the collapse of the Han
Empire. In the far west, Xi Xia emperors, Tangut speakers and descendants of Tibetan highlanders, ruled over Gansu and the Ordos
triangle, thereby controlling and profiting off the trade along the
strategic corridor of the Silk Road.[40] Xi Xia tribesmen had long
served as frontier guards (*jiedushi*) of Tang emperors, and their
leaders styled themselves as "dukes" (*li*) within the Tang military
hierarchy.[41] They intermarried with Chinese colonists, Turkish nomads, and Tocharian-speaking residents of the caravan cities of the
Tarim Basin. In 954, the dynast Li Yixing (954–967) consolidated
these Sinified lands into a single realm and assumed the royal title
of "he who has pacified the West." He promptly acknowledged the
suzerainty of the Song emperor Taizu of southern China so that
Li Yixing was granted the Song imperial title Xia. Thereafter, he
ruled as an independent sovereign in splendid isolation.[42] His heirs
maintained this precarious independence by adroitly exploiting the
rivalry between their two more powerful neighbors, the Liao and
Song emperors. The Sinified Xi Xia rulers too successfully played
the dual role of Han emperor and nomadic khan.

Meanwhile, the Song emperors forged a Neo-Confucian state
in southern China, home to over two-thirds of the Han people,
estimated at 120 million strong in the year 1000.[43] This empire
was rich in rice paddies and silk farms, and trade was facilitated by
the Grand Canal stretching from Kaifeng to Hangzhou. The Song
emperors saw themselves as the true heirs of the Han and Tang
dynasties. Ironically, Khitan successes compelled many aristocrats,
merchants, and peasants to flee North China to Song domains,

where their reports of Khitan atrocities galvanized the southern
Chinese to resist the barbarian interlopers. In 960, Zhao Kuangyin,
a warlord of frontier forces (*jiedushi*), seized Kaifeng and declared
himself emperor Taizu (960–976) of a new Song dynasty.[44] This
emperor Taizu, the third to take the name in the tenth century,
imposed unity over southern China and forged an imperial order
based on Neo-Confucian precepts.[45] He aimed to break the power
of the Tang regional elites who had monopolized office and ruled
as regional hereditary dukes (*li*). Civilian bureaucrats henceforth
were chosen by merit upon passing an examination system based
on the Confucian classics. The wide dissemination of block printing of Confucian classics enabled many men of humbler origin to
study the texts, pass the examinations, and so enter imperial service.[46] Mandarin officials from the highest to lowest levels shared
a set of philosophical precepts that put correct rule (*zheng*) at a pre-
mium. All were expected to master the canonical texts in order
to achieve harmony with the way (*dao*), especially the proper conduct and veneration of the ancestors. Even the Song emperor, if he
were to retain the Mandate of Heaven, had to obey the same ideals. Therefore, later Song emperors, their courtiers, and officials
all preferred diplomacy and peace over war, and they subordinated
generals, officers, and soldiers to the civilian officials. Furthermore,
Song emperors of the eleventh century elaborated ritual and protocol at court to elevate themselves above their officials and subjects.[47]
Yet at the same time, they demonstrated their proper conduct by
undertaking projects to promote the welfare of their subjects. State
monopolies in manufacturing ceramics and iron have been praised
as veritable prototypes for economies to scale in the later industrial revolution.[48] International commerce linking ports of southern China to those of Chola India and Fatimid Egypt boomed.
Simultaneously, Song emperors incorporated non-Han peoples in
the far south, and they sponsored Han colonists to expand the arable portions of these new lands.

Yet for all their successes, the Song emperors lacked the military
means and will to restore the northern frontier of the Great Wall.
Foremost, the Song could never mount sufficient cavalry in quality or quantity to match the horse archers of the Khitan Liao em-

perors.[49] In 1005, the Song emperor Zhenzong negotiated with his Liao counterpart Shengzong the Treaty of Chaoyuan, whereby the two monarchs agreed to the permanent partition of China. Zhenzong, although he retained Kaifeng, renounced claims to the sixteen prefectures and agreed to an annual subsidy of one hundred thousand taels of silver and two hundred thousand bolts of silk in return for Shengzong's nominal submission.[50] Shengzong emerged from these negotiations as the winner, because he gained access to a revenue stream of gifts to reward his vassals. He and his successors repeatedly renegotiated the terms to their advantage. The Song court neither forgot nor forgave this expensive humiliation to purchase peace from the Khitan emperor so that Song diplomats clandestinely backed Khitan rebels and sought out other barbarian allies. They found their instrument in an ambitious Khitan vassal, Wanyan Aguda (1114–1123), chieftain of the Jurchens, a Tangut-speaking people of the Manchurian forests who had settled on the eastern steppes and adopted the nomadic way of life.[51] Wanyan Aguda loathed his Liao master, the emperor Tianzuo (1101–1128). Tianzuo, while on a royal progress, had humiliated the proud Wanyan Aguda when he refused to join other Jurchen chieftains in a degrading dance to amuse the Khitan court.[52] In the autumn of 1114, Wanyan Aguda rebelled, and defeated a Khitan army. Early the next year, Wanyan Aguda exchanged envoys with the Song court in the first of seven diplomatic missions crossing the Bohai Gulf (the northwestern arm of the Yellow Sea).[53] In 1121, the Song emperor Huizong and Wanyan Aguda concluded the so-called "Alliance Conducted at Sea" that stipulated joint military operations against the Khitans, and the return to Song control all lands south of the Great Wall.[54] Huizong and his diplomats at Kaifeng congratulated themselves on destroying the hated Khitan invader at minimal cost, but the agreement turned out to be a blunder. Huizong overestimated the ability of his army, and underestimated that of Wanyan Aguda. The Song army lacked the cavalry and logistics to wage offensive operations, and failed to take any of its objectives. Wanyan Aguda, who had declared himself the emperor Taizu of the Jin dynasty, quickly overran the Khitan Empire. Tianzuo, while wickedly clever in humiliating his vassal, was not up to the task of

defeating him in battle. Contrary to Song expectations, the Jurchens were not simple barbarians satisfied with looting and leaving. Wanyan Aguda refused to hand over the sixteen prefectures
to Song control. In 1125, Wanyan Sheng (1123–1135), brother and
successor of Wanyan Aguda, captured Tianzuo, and ended the Khitan Empire.[55] Two years later, in 1127, Wanyan Sheng invaded the
lower valley of the Yellow River, occupied Kaifeng, and captured
Huizong and his court.[56] A younger son of Huizong, Gaozung
(1127–1162), escaped and retreated to Hangzhou, the cosmopolitan
metropolis at the southern terminus of the Grand Canal. There he
consolidated his hold over the southern domains of the Song Empire. Gaozung, however, formally accepted the loss of the northern lands, including the capital Kaifeng, by the treaty of Shaoxing
in 1141.[57] He also agreed to pay Wanyan Hela, the third Jurchen
emperor known by his Chinese throne name as Xizong, an annual
subsidy of two hundred thousand taels of silver and two hundred
fifty thousand bolts of silk. The emperor Huizong and his diplomats had substituted one nomadic foe with a far more dangerous
one who had seized the capital of Kaifeng and lands of the lower
Yellow River.

The sudden collapse of the Khitan Empire had long-term consequences for both China and the Eurasian steppes. Any chances of
restoring the unity of the Middle Kingdom were gone. Song emperors henceforth accepted partition, and so they were forced on
the defensive. The Song army fortified the Yangtze and its tributaries in a succession of fortified lines to check nomadic invaders.[58]
The imperial navy launched river flotillas to support this Maginot
line, and squadrons to guard the ports, to suppress pirates, and to
protect overseas commerce. Beyond their northern fortifications,
Song diplomats looked for yet another barbarian ally to rid them
of the one they had summoned to destroy the Khitans.

The Jurchen emperors too accepted partition, and they set in motion two important events that transformed the Eurasian steppes.
First, since Jurchen emperors enjoyed their role as Chinese emperors of the Jin dynasty, they exercised a far looser hegemony over
the nomadic tribes of Mongolia.[59] Jurchen emperors, in contrast to
their Khitan predecessors, came to despise their nomadic kinsmen

and neighbors. They promoted tribal and clan warfare rather than courting the kaghans and tribes on the eastern Eurasian steppes.[60] Their contempt was quickly returned with fear and loathing from their nomadic vassals. By inciting wars among the tribes during the next two generations, the Jin emperors unwittingly created the conditions for the rise of Genghis Khan.

The Jurchen emperors also drove Yelü Dashi and his Khitans west into the Islamic world, and thereby contributed to the making of the legends about Prester John. Yelü Dashi of history is in many ways far more remarkable than his counterpart Prester John of legend. In 1125, Yelü Dashi, when he decided to retreat west, was age thirty-seven and an accomplished minister and general.[61] He had attained the highest Confucian degree (*jinshi*), mastered Chinese and Khitan calligraphy, and excelled in riding and archery. He fought bravely for his emperor, Tianzuo, until he was captured, and released on the promise to take service with the Jurchen conqueror.[62] Yelü Dashi, however, soon defected, allegedly fearing punishment because he had bested his Jurchen commander, Nian Han, in a board game. Yelü Dashi soon realized serving Tianzuo again was a lost cause. On an evening in 1125, he and a small band of followers slipped out of Tianzuo's encampment in Inner Mongolia and headed west for the Liao military settlement at Kedun, one of the Khitan desert fortresses near the archaeological site of Chin Tolgoin Balgas in central Mongolia, 145 miles west of Ulaanbaatar.[63] From there, Yelü Dashi recruited ten thousand warriors from among the Tatars and Turkish tribes dwelling on the Mongolian steppes to the north as far as the Orkhon valley. Initially, Yelü Dashi posed as a loyal subordinate of his emperor, Tianzuo, so that he won over the Liao military governor and the vassal kaghans. During the next six years at Kedun, Yelü Dashi fought an uneven defensive war against the superior Jurchens. He failed to lure both the Xi Xia and Song emperors into an alliance against the common foe of the Jurchens, because his would-be allies viewed him as little more than a leader of nomadic brigands.[64]

On May 13, 1130, Yelü Dashi sacrificed a gray ox and white horse to the ancestral progenitors and announced his bold plan to march over two thousand miles west to the grasslands around Lake

Issyk, to where many Khitans had already fled as immigrants or mercenaries serving the Eastern Karakhanid kaghan of Balasagun.[65] These central Eurasian steppes had been the extreme western edge of the Tang Empire four centuries earlier, but now Muslim Turkish kaghans ruled as resentful vassals of the Seljuk sultan Sanjar. Yelü Dashi gambled on the long shot of recruiting more warriors and gaining Ferghana's heavenly steeds that sweat blood for his war against the Jurchens. He had to cut short his first western expedition, return to Kedun, and drive off a Jurchen attack. In commemoration of this victory, either in 1131 or 1132, Yelü Dashi was acclaimed by his followers as Gurkhan or Universal Khan.[66] Yelü Dashi also assumed the Chinese throne name of Dezong so that Chinese chroniclers recognized him as a legitimate emperor, albeit a provincial one, ruling as the Western Liao Son of Heaven. His followers henceforth were known as the Karakhitans, "Black Khitans," whose ethnic name Christian chroniclers turned into Cathay, the European name for northern China. The conquest of the central Eurasian steppes proved costly, because Khitan expeditions from Kedun had to cover great distances over arid terrain that took a hideous toll on men and horses. The Turkish kaghans on the central steppes and the Uyghur rulers of Khotan and Kashgar in the Tarim Basin opposed Yelü Dashi and conspired to hire away Khitan warriors as mercenaries for their own conflicts. In 1134, Yelü Dashi received an unexpected stroke of good luck. He entered Balasagun on invitation of the feckless Eastern Karakhanid kaghan, long weary of the burdens of the crown.[67] Yelü Dashi assumed absolute control of this kaghanate. He built his own Chinese-style capital near Balasagun, from whence he steadily subjected the Turkish tribes north of the Jaxartes River (Syr Darya).[68] He also defeated another Jurchen army under his former commander, Nian Han, in a decisive battle in the desert to the west of Kedun in 1137.[69] His military achievements to date had been extraordinary, and Yelü Dashi is more than worthy to enter the hall of great nomadic conquerors. Over the course of twelve years, Yelü Dashi boldly, even recklessly, fought his way west over three thousand miles from his homeland in China to the Central Eurasian steppes around Lake Issyk, where he established a new Chinese bureaucratic state, the

Karakhitan Empire. Despite repeated defeats, he proved a resilient, charismatic Gurkhan who rallied warriors to win the battles that mattered. Yet his greatest victory was yet to come.

Yelü Dashi, once master of Balasagun, inevitably clashed with the ruler of Eastern Islam, the Seljuk sultan Sanjar, because Yelü Dashi quickly became entangled in the web of local conflicts among the rival Muslim rulers of Bukhara, Samarkand, and Khwarazm. In the summer of 1141, the sultan Sanjar marched east with an army of fifty thousand in response to appeals from his vassals about Khitan and Karluk attacks along the caravan routes.[70] The sultan aimed to restore order in Transoxiana, and to reckon with the new ruler at Balasagun, Yelü Dashi, whose kingdom posed a serious threat on the northeastern border of Dar al-Islam. At the same time, Yelü Dashi and the Khitan army crossed the Jaxartes in response to an appeal from Atsiz, shah of Khwarazm, who never forgave the execution of his son on orders of Sanjar. Accounts of the great battle survive from both Muslim and Chinese sources. The meticulous Persian historian Atâ-Malek Juvayni, writing at the Mongol court of Tabriz in the thirteenth century, drew on eyewitness accounts, while the Chinese Chronicle of the Liao (*Liao Shi*) provides details of the Khitan army. The two armies, each perhaps fifty thousand strong, clashed at Qatwan, eight miles outside of Samarkand, on September 9, 1141.[71] Each army employed the same nomadic tactics, but the Khitan horse archers, along with their Karluk allies, proved superior in archery and mobility. The Seljuk army was encircled and annihilated. Sultan Sanjar escaped, but Yelü Dashi captured the sultan's harem and treasury.

By his great victory at Qatwan, Yelü Dashi extended his realm, from the western slopes of the Altai Mountains across the central Eurasian steppes to the Oxus River (Amu Darya). Henceforth, he also exercised a hegemony over the caravan cities of the western Tarim Basin. If Yelü Dashi had then marched another two thousand miles west and entered Jerusalem, as Christians hoped, they would have been disappointed. Yelü Dashi would have tolerated and accommodated his far more numerous Muslim subjects, pursuing a policy that was not unlike one of his Mongol successors.[72] Although he professed Buddhism, he tempered his faith with Con-

fucian teachings and Khitan animist beliefs. In the tradition of the
Liao emperors, he respected the faiths of all his subjects: Christian,
Manichaean, and Muslim. To be sure, he wielded no magical scepter like Prester John, and hardly marked the coming of the Last
Judgment. Instead, he was a pragmatic, farsighted emperor ruling
in the style of the Tang emperor Taizong, and inspiring the loyalty of his nomadic warriors in the manner of the Northern Wei
emperor Tuoba Gul. His successors would rule just as judiciously
over Central Asia for the next century.[73]

Once the initial shock of the defeat of Seljuk sultan Sanjar had
passed, Muslims were puzzled by what to make of these new invaders from the steppes. After the caravan cities of the Transoxiana
submitted, Yelü Dashi and his heirs were content to rule a distant empire on the northeastern edge of the Islamic world.[74] This
Karakhitan realm, in a number of ways, approximated the Hephthalite Empire of seven centuries earlier. The Khitans thus did not
turn out to be the scions of Gog and Magog of the Apocalypse,
but rather they brought peace and prosperity along the Silk Road.
Karakhitan emperors allowed their Muslim vassals to retain their
titles and courts; they never interfered in the administration of
sharia in Muslim cities. For Muslim jurists and theologians, tolerant Karakhitan rule posed a dilemma, because it was inconsistent
with the teachings of the *Koran* that nonbelievers, especially Buddhists, who were scorned and considered heathens (*gavur*), should
rule over Muslims. Even more puzzling to Muslims, Karakhitan
emperors, in contrast to Turkish kaghans, never showed any interest in converting to Islam. Instead, the Karakhitan emperors had
brought their own civilization from northern China.[75] They possessed a veteran field army of forty thousand horse archers, and numerous officials trained in both Chinese and Khitan languages and
bureaucratic procedures. These imperial servants ensured the primacy of the Han literary canon and imperial institutions of the Liao
state of northern China.[76] Muslims were tolerated and protected, but
they enjoyed no special status over Khitan subjects of other faiths.
What Muslims at the time could not have realized was that this orderly Karakhitan rule was a preview of Mongol rule yet to come.
Popular perceptions of the Karakhitans varied across the Islamic

world.[77] In the Middle East, rulers, theologians, and historians soon dismissed the Karakhitans as restless marauders intent on plunder and slaves and little else. They perceived the Frankish Crusaders as far more dangerous foes because the Franks fought to take the Holy City of Jerusalem, and threatened Cairo and Damascus. In the lands of Eastern Islam, many Muslims too soon viewed Karakhitan rule with indifference. Muslim merchants, travelers, and pilgrims who visited the caravan cities of Transoxiana and the Tarim Basin seldom commented on the Karakhitan overlords because ordinary life had changed so little. Therefore, few Muslims were prepared to confront the far greater shock when Genghis Khan burst into the Islamic world.

Meanwhile, Christian Europe still blissfully pinned hopes on Prester John. In the spring of 1221, an excited Jacques de Vitry, Bishop of Acre, penned effusive letters to Pope Honorius III, King Henry III of England, and Duke Leopold VI of Austria, reporting news of the expected savior from Inner Asia.[78] At the same time, the members of the Fifth Crusade were bogged down in the flooded fields of the Egyptian Delta in a doomed advance to capture Cairo.[79] In 1217, the Crusaders had invaded Egypt to win Jerusalem on the banks of the Nile with a strategy of exchanging Cairo for the Holy City. In the face of yet another failed crusade, Jacques de Vitry proclaimed that David, Prester John's son, or perhaps his grandson, had just defeated the Saracens in another great battle and was even now on the march to Jerusalem. Once again, a French bishop seized upon the garbled reports of Nestorian monks about great events in Central Asia, but this time, the deliverer turned out not to be a grandson of Prester John, but rather the greatest of all conquerors of the steppes, Genghis Khan.

18

From Temujin to Genghis Khan

In the spring of 1206, the khans and princes of all the tribes of the eastern steppes gathered in the Orkhon valley beneath the sacred mountain Khairkhan, today designated a World Heritage Site.[1] Their retinues and subjects filled the tent cities along the riverbanks. Voices in every dialect of Turkish, Mongol, and Khitan reverberated in the valley verdant with grasses so vital for the grazing herds. For days, wrestling matches, horse races, and archery contests thrilled onlookers, while sacrifices and feasts were offered to Tengri, the lord of the eternal blue sky. Shamans emerged from their trances induced to see into the other world and offered predictions of an imperial future. This was the greatest *kurultai* ever held. Before the assembly of lords and warriors, Temujin, then forty-four years old, was acclaimed Genghis Khan, perhaps designating him the "mighty lord," but more aptly rendered as "oceanic or universal lord."[2] No one could have predicted this future for the boy Temujin, born of a second wife to a khan of a lesser clan of an obscure Mongol tribe, Tayichiud, in the Onon valley. After nearly thirty years of fighting, he imposed a unity among those dwelling in the felt tents for the first time in nearly four centuries. Temujin, ever after known as Genghis Khan, turned the Mongol tribes into a nation, and won for them a world empire.

Temujin's nation, the Mongols, were comparative newcomers on the eastern Eurasian steppes, for their ancestors had long dwelled to the north in the Arctic forest of the taiga, where they pursued hunting, fishing, and trapping. Between the late tenth and early twelfth centuries, Mongolian-speaking clans settled the Orkhon valley and eastern steppes of Mongolia abandoned by the Uyghurs surviving the sack of their capital, who had migrated to the cities of the Tarim Basin.[3] The Mongols spoke a distinct Altaic language that had diverged from Turkish seven or eight centuries earlier.[4] The language of Genghis Khan, dubbed Middle Mongolian by philologists, is well-known because his grandson Kublai Khan commissioned his Uyghur scribes to invent a script to record in Mongolian Genghis Khan's deeds in the so-called *Secret History of the Mongols* and law code (*yassa*), as well as his own decrees.[5]

Mongolian, a typical agglutinative language, employs suffixes to designate grammatical functions of nouns and verbs. It shares with Turkish the rules of vowel harmony, but vowels are grouped into three classes rather than the two classes of Turkish. In Genghis Khan's day, Mongols had already borrowed numerous Turkish words for objects, diet, and activities associated with the nomadic way of life. Also the language already betrayed influences from the tonal languages of Tibetan and Chinese. Mongols were adaptable, adopting words, concepts, and material culture from their neighbors. They had to be, because they were always a minority on the eastern Eurasian steppes. At the death of Genghis Khan, Mongolian speakers numbered at most one million.[6] Their modern descendants total six million or are six times as many, and they are evenly split between the Mongolian Republic and Inner Mongolia under Chinese jurisdiction. In contrast, today seventy-eight million or thirteen times as many individuals speak Turkish languages, of whom nearly half reside in the Republic of Turkey. Most likely, three-quarters of the warriors who loyally followed Genghis Khan were Turkish rather than Mongolian speakers. Yet to the world, they were all feared as Mongols.

Once on the steppes, the Mongols adapted a nomadic way of

life learned from their Turkish kinsmen and neighbors, because intermarriage, often conducted by ritual raids to steal wives, was always a common practice among nomadic tribes. The Mongols also claimed the sacred landscape of Mount Khairkhan and the Orkhon valley as their own. In 1162, Temujin was born into this world of incessant clan and tribal warfare. In this world, the Mongols were neither numerous nor remarkable.[7] Their kinsmen to the immediate southwest, the Keraits, were wealthier, for they roamed the far more temperate grasslands between the Sayan and Altai Mountains. The Turco-Mongolian Naimans just east and south of the Altai Mountains were more powerful; the Merkits south of Lake Baikal were fiercer; the Tatars on the steppes southeast of the Mongols were the wealthiest of all the tribes and allied to the Jin emperors, themselves descendants of Jurchen barbarians from Manchuria. The Jin emperor who ruled over northern China and the steppes south of the Gobi had long incited wars among the nomadic tribes.[8]

The *Secret History* alone records the travails of Temujin's early life, but so many of the incidents are more the stuff of epic rather than history. Temujin was the first son of Yesügei, a lesser khan of the minor Mongol clan Tayichiud, and his second consort, Hoelun, in 1162.[9] His father, Yesügei, smitten by her beauty from afar, had abducted Temujin's mother, Hoelun, from her husband, Chiledu, when the newly wedded couple were en route to the husband's Merkit encampment. The Merkits did not forget or forgive the abduction, but Yesügei kept his lovely prize.[10] Hoelun later claimed that her son Temujin was born holding a blood clot in his right hand—an omen Hoelun never quite fathomed.[11] For all the tales of Temujin's precociousness, he was merely the son of the second consort. Sochigel, the principal wife, had two sons, Begter and Belgutei, who took precedence in the clan, and Begter was the eldest and presumed heir.[12] At age nine, Temujin was betrothed to Börte, a slightly older girl of the nobler Onggirat clan, and, as was customary, Temujin was to labor for his in-laws until the couple was of age for marriage. The marriage sealed an important alliance for Yesügei, who removed Temujin as a rival to Begter.[13] Upon concluding the marriage contract, Yesügei set out for his encampment in the Onon valley, but he chanced upon a band of Tatars, who offered hospitality. One of his hosts recognized Yesügei as marked for death over a vendetta, so he administered a slow-acting poison in Yesügei's food. Temujin was summoned home, but his father had already passed away.[14]

The clan's *kurultai* dispossessed Temujin, still age nine, abandoning his family without horses or stock animals, because the impoverished clan could ill afford to feed the two widows, Sochigel and Hoelun, and their eight young children, Temujin and his five siblings and his two half brothers. Hoelun immediately took charge.[15] The family eked out an existence in the forests along the valleys of the Onon and Kerulen Rivers. Temujin matured into a wily, resourceful adolescent, dubious of any ties except loyalty demonstrated by deeds. He expected, even anticipated, betrayal throughout life, and so survived the treacherous politics of the Eurasian steppes. He also gained a sense of his destiny, and the favor of Tengri, eternal lord of the blue sky. Hence, he would never accept anything less than primacy over those he led. At age fourteen, in 1176, he and his younger brother Khasar stalked and murdered their older half brother Begter, who would have succeeded to the leadership of the family and even taken Hoelun as his consort.[16] Begter calmly accepted his death, uttering the prophetic words that "without me you have no companions but your shadow."[17] Soon afterward, Hoelun exclaimed the same words, for she instantly surmised the dastardly deed committed by her two sons. She cursed her sons as bloodstained wolves. Since such acts of homicide within any tribe were a communal pollution in the eyes of the gods, Temujin's clan, the Tayichiud, tracked down and captured Temujin, who had fled into the northern forests. The clan punished him by imprisoning him in a cangue. The cangue was a solid wooden wheel in two movable halves with an opening in the center for the victim's neck. The prisoner's arms were bound to the cangue by iron handcuffs, so he was utterly helpless. Yet the humiliating punishment did not break Temujin's will. Remarkably, he escaped due to the aid of a kindly couple of elderly servants who had been entrusted to care for the prisoner. Temujin never forgot their courageous act.[18]

Temujin escaped to rule over a clan comprising little more than a single *gers* and his immediate family: his mother and stepmother, his five younger siblings, the younger half brother, Belgutei, and his closest companions, Boorchu and Jelme, destined to be two of the leading generals of the Mongol imperial army.[19] Even more surprising, Börte had faithfully waited for her groom the past seven years, and her father, Dei Seichen, honored the betrothal when Temujin reached sixteen years of age.[20] His father-in-law, who had no love for Temujin's own clan, saw in his son-in-law a brave and cunning warrior. Two years later, in ca. 1180, Temujin presented the bridal gift of Börte, a magnificent sable cloak, as a gift to Toghrul, Ong Khan of the Keraits, so that Temujin could renew a family tie with this old friend of his father. Toghrul accepted Temujin as a vassal and the leader of his own clan.[21] Temujin also swore an oath of brotherhood (*anda*) with Jamuka, a boyhood friend of the Jadaran clan and rising warrior in the service of Toghrul Khan.[22] Contrary to the intimations of our main sources, the *Secret History*, the Chinese accounts, and the two Persian historians Atâ-Malek Juvayni and Rashid al-Din, Temujin was the lesser partner in each transaction.[23] Together Jamuka and Temujin attracted the bold and ambitious among the young warriors.

The Merkits settled their score with Temujin's family over the kidnapping of Hoelun by abducting Börte in a dawn attack on Temujin's encampment. While Temujin and his companions galloped off into the early light, Börte remained behind to be taken prisoner, and so distracted her husband's pursuers.[24] In 1181, Temujin and his new allies surprised the Merkit camp in the Khilok valley in a night raid and rescued Börte.[25] Soon after, Börte bore a son, Jochi; Temujin always accepted the boy as his son, although Jochi was almost certainly the son of his mother's captor, Chilger Bökh,[26] given the length of her captivity. The daring rescue, which is celebrated at length in the *Secret History*, won Temujin instant fame among the Mongol clan leaders and the jealousy of Jamuka. Tensions mounted as Temujin outshone his immediate superior, Jamuka, in raids against the Tatars. Perhaps within a year of Börte's rescue, Jamuka expelled Temujin from his encampment, although Temujin later claimed that he left of his own accord. Thereupon, with the approval of his overlord Toghrul, his clans proclaimed Temujin their khan. Temujin thus repudiated his oaths of brotherhood and fealty to Jamuka.[27] Jamuka, in turn, claimed the greater title gurkhan, for he commanded far more numerous and distinguished clans and boasted of a superior descent of the white bones from nobler Mongol progenitors. The ailing Toghrul, if not encouraging, did not discourage this clash between his two leading vassals. The Jin and Song emperors initially must have dismissed the clash as another civil war among Mongol clans aggrieved over petty slights. But Temujin and Jamuka each sought out ever more allies. Over the course of the next two decades, the conflict escalated until every tribe on the eastern steppes, and even many Mongol tribes of the taiga, were embroiled in a general war. The emperors of the three Chinese empires then could not resist interfering in a conflict that conveniently pitted the tribes against each other. The Jin and Song courts backed different contenders as alliances and the fortunes of war repeatedly shifted.

For over ten years, Temujin and Jamuka clashed in running battles and raids on encampments, but neither could nor desired to achieve all-out victory. Their followers sought honor, booty, and slaves, and the fighting seldom ended in pursuit of the scattered foe. Furthermore, even in war, the bonds of brotherhood still counted for both Temujin and Jamuka. In 1195, Jamuka gained a decisive edge and overran the Kerait encampment so that Toghrul Khan fled as an exile to Gurkhan Yelü Zhilugu of the Karakhitans.[28] In 1197, Temujin rallied his clans and gained the backing of the Jin court so that he reversed the situation and restored Toghrul Khan to the Kerait throne.[29] The desultory fighting climaxed in 1202 when Temujin and Toghrul Khan decisively defeated Jamuka at the head of a coalition of disaffected Mongols, Merkits, Naimans, and Tatars near the foothills of the Khingan Mountains.[30] For the moment, Temujin controlled the steppes between the Onon River and Khingan Mountains. Temujin ruthlessly massacred the Tatars in revenge for their poisoning of his father.[31] All Tatar males taller than the wheel of a *gers* were executed, while the women and children were enslaved. Envoys of the Jin emperor Zhangzong hailed the victory, and conferred on Toghrul the rank of wang, "king," a coveted title within the Chinese hierarchy of allies.[32] Yet fancy imperial titles could not assuage Toghrul's fear and resentment of his overmighty vassal Temujin. The new Wang Khan, egged on by his son Senggum, fatally blundered by allying with Jamuka.[33] In 1203, Toghrul Khan suddenly turned on Temujin. In a surprise attack, he and Jamuka won a hard-fought battle, scattering Temujin's warriors. Toghrul Khan, however, halted any pursuit because his son Senggum had been struck in the head by an arrow. His new ally, Jamuka, also wanted to humble rather than destroy Temujin, for Jamuka had his own political scheme. Jamuka hoped to turn Temujin into an ally who would counter Toghrul Khan in his own bid for supremacy over the Mongol tribes. Temujin escaped to Baljuna, a lake on the swampy eastern edge of Mongolia. Only a handful of companions stood by Temujin, and they faced a bleak exile on the northern fringe of the steppes, where grasslands give way to the taiga.[34] For the rest of his life, Temujin remembered those warriors who stood by him in defeat and shared the privations during that dark summer. But Toghrul Khan and Jamuka soon quarreled, and Temujin rallied his warriors and audaciously captured the Kerait encampment.[35] Toghrul fled west, but fell into the hands of the Naimans, who failed to recognize the Wang Khan and slew him.[36] The surviving Keraits bowed to Temujin as their khan. If not earlier during this long conflict, certainly by now Temujin started to reorganize his warriors into tactical units drilled by his faithful companions and organized without regard to kinship.

The ever-resilient Jamuka organized another coalition of Naimans, Merkits, and fugitive Mongols to stop Temujin. In the spring of 1204, Temujin summoned a national *kurultai* that declared his foes rebels and traitors, because Jamuka's newfound allies, the Naimans, were ancestral enemies of the Mongols. In a brilliant campaign of speed and maneuver, Temujin brought his foes to decisive battle near the future site of Karakorum in the autumn of 1204. Temujin smashed Jamuka's army.[37] Only the Naiman prince Kuchlug escaped the catastrophe, eventually seeking refuge at the court of the gurkhan of the Karakhitans.[38] Jamuka himself fled the battlefield, but soon after, he was betrayed by his companions. Even though Temujin still feared his rival and former friend, he long wrestled with the decision to order the execution of his *anda*, for it was tantamount to fratricide.[39] According to the *Secret History*, Temujin even implored Jamuka to join his circle of comrades, but Jamuka proudly declined, accepting that he alone had broken the oaths of *anda*. To be sure, the dramatic scene has been embroidered by the *Secret History*, but without a doubt, Temujin reluctantly and sadly made one of the most difficult decisions in his life: the execution of his childhood friend and blood brother. Temujin graciously granted Jamuka his final request for a noble death and burial. Jamuka was wrapped in a carpet, laid on the ground, and trampled by Mongol horsemen lest any blood were shed that might bring down divine retribution on the Mongol nation. Jamuka was given an honorable funeral and burial on a high point, where, as he had promised in his final words, his guardian spirit would protect his friend Temujin and his progeny.[40] Temujin now faced no serious rival on the eastern Eurasian steppes.

The next year, 1205, Sübetei, the brother of Jelme and Temujin's finest general, defeated and massacred the Merkits, who still defied Temujin.[41] Sübetei acted on direct orders from Temujin, who wanted not only to pay back a vendetta but also to send a stern warning to any would-be rebels. By the end of the year, all the tribes of the eastern steppes had acknowledged Temujin as their lord. In May 1206, Temujin summoned the *kurultai* that acclaimed him Genghis Khan. Even at the pinnacle of his success, Temujin showed restraint in accepting his lordship. He praised at length each of his brothers and companions to whom he owed his success.[42] He singled out many individuals, whatever their rank or clan, who had done favors for him in the past. All were richly rewarded. To be sure, Temujin demanded absolute loyalty, but he generously shared his successes with all who loyally served. All present were inspired by his display of greatness, and few, if any, had doubts that they had just elected the greatest khan ever to rule on the Eurasian steppes.

Temujin, ever after known as Genghis Khan, had just united the tribes of the eastern Eurasian steppes for the first time in four hundred years. Only an exceptional ruler such as Genghis Khan could have pulled off such an extraordinary achievement. In retrospect, his spectacular rise to power can too easily be seen as inevitable because of the favorable accounts of the *Secret History*, Persian court historians, and Chinese accounts written with the advantage of hindsight. Instead, each of the previous imperial confederations of steppe nomads had risen primarily through the actions of exceptional leaders. Yet even such leaders were hard-pressed to maintain the unity of their confederations, and their heirs soon warred among themselves. Therefore, it would be unfair to censure the emperors of the three warring Chinese states for not grasping that domination of the nomads by a Sinified emperor of North China had just abruptly ended. Nor could they have dreamed that Genghis Khan would achieve the unimaginable of winning the greatest world empire ever ruled by a nomadic conqueror.[43]

Genghis Khan himself never mistook ceremony for the reality of power.[44] He was unimpressed by Chinese pomp, and he could never have played the role of the Son of Heaven in the fashion of his grandson, Kublai Khan, who ruled over all of China. Genghis Khan, just like Attila, was modest in personal habits and dress, sharing the hardships and simple food with his men. He looted fabulous riches and took innumerable slaves, but he gave them away to his followers. By the end of his reign, Genghis Khan maintained a harem comprising four camps (ordu), each of forty women, but these consorts and concubines were trophies or gifts to seal a political alliance. He cherished Börte as his wife and counselor.[45] Only their children and grandchildren were destined to inherit under the rules of lateral succession.

By all accounts, Genghis Khan possessed a commanding presence: he was tall, with a full beard, and penetrating catlike gray eyes. The Khitan noble Ila Ahai, an envoy of the Jin emperor, was so impressed by Genghis Khan's bearing that he abandoned his master and declared his loyalty to the Mongol khan.[46] Many Khitan, Uyghur, and Chinese generals and officials were equally so inspired to join his court. We are fortunate to possess a portrait of Genghis Khan, the first of any conqueror of the steppes. This Chinese painting is based on an ink sketch commissioned by Kublai Khan fifty years after his grandfather's death.[47] The portrait's features convey the charismatic personality that so impressed his grandson, Kublai Khan. Throughout his life, Genghis Khan relentlessly campaigned, sustained two near fatal wounds, and died from the exertions of his last war on August 25, 1227. He was restless, perceptive, and quick to learn from his foes. He had honed his skills in cunning and deception to survive the treacherous world of raids and plots on the steppes. At a very young age, he had learned to trust only the few who acted loyally rather than the many who spoke promises. He never tolerated those who flattered him or sought to capitalize on their kinship or high rank. He could stage fits of rages to cow sycophants or to intimidate suspected traitors into confessing. His suspicious nature served him well as general and ruler, but he tempered it with praise and rewards to the loyal, whose successes he never envied. Hence, he was a terror to his enemies and a benefactor to his people.[48]

Genghis Khan has also been hailed for his tolerance of the faiths of all his subjects, but he shared the pragmatic spiritual beliefs of all nomads.[49] He was devoted to his ancestral spirits. Before any campaign, he engaged shamans who could read the future in the charred shoulder bones of sheep. Among many tribes of the eastern Eurasian steppes, shamans were as respected as khans, and in some cases, charismatic individuals combined both roles. Temujin had long depended on the shaman Kokchu for sage advice and insight into the future until the shaman dared to plot treachery soon after his acclamation. Genghis Khan ordered an honorable ritual execution.[50] Kokchu too was wrapped in a carpet and trampled under the hooves of the horses ridden by the household guards. Genghis Khan thereafter only consulted shamans who dared not challenge his authority. He also treated prophets, ascetics, and mystics of other faiths as blessed ones with insights into the divine. In May 1222, Genghis Khan received into his camp south of the Hindu Kush the renowned Daoist monk Qiu Chuji. According to his biographer, Li Chi Chang, the serene Qiu Chuji was summoned from China to Samarkand, and then he was escorted to the Mongol camp. Khan and sage discussed the matter of immortality and just life. Genghis Khan was so impressed that he corresponded with Qiu Chuji thereafter and extended numerous benefits to him and his disciples.[51]

Genghis Khan, just like the earlier Turkish khans, was willing to consider a new divine power if its holy ones could demonstrate its power. Genghis Khan favored Nestorian monks because they tended the sick during plagues.[52] Turkish mothers since the sixth century had tattooed crosses on their children's foreheads to ward off disease.[53] Genghis Khan shared with his fellow Mongols the view that the sign of the cross was an apotropaic device against disease and a symbol of the divine blessing of the world's four quarters. Furthermore, Christian monks could consume meat and fermented drink, the staples of the nomadic diet. He appreciated the deep spirituality of Buddhist monks, even though they were vegetarians.[54] Foremost, Buddhist monks, while vegetarians, blessed those of his subjects in military and merchant careers for following their dharma of upholding the Mongol order. Genghis Khan could only conclude that so many merchants who flocked to his court had prospered because of their Buddhist faith. His encounter with Islam came much later in life. In 1222–1223, Genghis Khan toured the caravan cities of Transoxiana and eastern Iran, which his warriors had so ruthlessly sacked just years before.[55] He could not help but be impressed by medresses with tiled minarets and richly decorated domed mosques whose fountains offered a glimpse into paradise. Through interpreters, he conversed with Sufi mystics and imams. He discovered that he approved of many of the practices of Islam, although he found incomprehensible the Muslim's duty to make a pilgrimage to Mecca, and he was deeply suspicious of the allegiance of Sunni Muslims to the caliph in Baghdad as the successor of Muhammad, whom Genghis Khan considered one more shaman.[56]

He tolerated and respected the many faiths of his subjects, but he never showed the slightest inclination to convert to any of them. These faiths of other nations were merely ancient expressions of the universal power of Tengri, lord of the eternal blue sky. He also insisted that all clergy obey his laws, which were recorded in his law code, *yassa*, the first one known from a nomadic conqueror.[57] The khan's law took precedence over any sacred law. In their dealings with the Pope of Rome and the caliph of Baghdad, Genghis Khan and his heirs insisted that spiritual leaders must first recognize the Mongol khan and his law as absolute if they were to receive any protection or patronage. In his mind, Genghis Khan simply concluded that his authority must be far superior to all others because his successes marked him alone as enjoying divine favor.

Genghis Khan forged a Mongol nation devoted to him in the crucible of war. To this day, the Mongols still see him as the greatest of conquerors, favored by Tengri, and the khan who inspired their ancestors to acts of epic bravery that forever changed the world. From hard experience, Genghis Khan learned to read the loyalty and ability of men so that he judged and promoted each on the basis of merit. He held his councils of war as informal and frank discussions, eliciting honest advice from his trusted commanders. He consulted and inspired, listened and commanded. His ability to lead is the rare exception in history. He prized and rewarded ability, and the genius of his senior commanders reflected his own genius. His capacity to lead is best seen in the careers of his trusted "four dogs of war," four of the best generals in the Mongol army.[58] None of them was a kinsman; two of them were not even a Mongol by birth. Sübetei and his older brother Jelme were sons of a humble blacksmith of the forest people who pledged the boys to the service of Yesügei, Temujin's father.[59] At a comparatively late age, the teenage boys had to master archery, horsemanship, and strategy. Kublai hailed from similarly obscure origins, and rose in rank due to exceptional bravery. Jebe, of the Besud clan, was a deadly foe turned companion. In the so-called Battle of the Nine Arrows in 1201, Jebe shot an arrow that lodged into Genghis Khan's neck. Jelme drew it out and sucked out the poison from Temujin's veins. Afterward, the captured Jebe bravely admitted the deed, but instead of punishing him, Temujin took Jebe into his service.[60] Temujin renamed the bold warrior Jebe, "the arrow," in place of his former name. Jebe would prove to be a brilliant strategist. All had stood by Temujin during the dark days after the defeat in 1204. The *Secret History* lauds them in epic verse when Jamuka replies to his Naiman ally Tayang Khan's inquiry about the identity of these foes on the battlefield. "These are the Four Dogs of my *anda* Temujin. They feed on human flesh and are tethered with iron chains. They have foreheads of brass, their jaws are like scissors, their tongues like piercing awls, their heads are iron, their whipping tails swords. They feed on dew. Running they ride on the back of the wind. In the day of battle, they devour enemy flesh. Behold, they are now un-leashed, and they slobber at the mouth with glee. These four dogs are Jebe, and Kublai, Jelme, and Subotai."[61] They were appropri-

ately named, because the Mongols employed in war Tibetan mas-
tiffs bred as ferocious guard dogs.

Sübetei has been hailed as the greatest of the four, fighting in
over sixty-five battles in twenty major campaigns. He improved on
tactics, employing encirclement and continuous frontal attacks in
successive waves rather than the feigned retreat and ambush.[62] Strategically, he operated over wide fronts hundreds of miles in length
so that he could move swiftly and strike terror before he concentrated his forces for the decisive battle. Tsarist and Soviet military
theorists intensively studied Sübetei's campaigns, from which they
drew lessons of strategic maneuver and concentration of force. The
Soviet Marshal Mikhail Nikolayevich Tukhachevsky, nicknamed
the "Red Napoleon," credited Sübetei for his own strategy of deep
battle with which the Red Army countered the Wehrmacht's Blitzkrieg in the Second World War.[63] Tukhachevsky, however, ran afoul
of his paranoid master, Stalin. The marshal was denounced, arrested
by the NKVD,[64] convicted in a show trial, and shot in the back
of the head in 1937. His family suffered the same fate.[65] Sübetei,
however, was entrusted with independent campaigns by his master
Genghis Khan, and served with equal distinction under Genghis
Khan's son Ögedei. Sübetei died at age seventy-two, honored and
celebrated in epic verse.[66] His descendants just as loyally and honorably served the later khans. The contrast cannot be more stark
between the two autocrats in their treatment of their subordinates.
Genghis Khan employed terror against foes; Stalin against his own.

Genghis Khan exceeded all previous conquerors in placing bravery and loyalty above all other considerations. He accepted many
defeated nomads into the Mongol nation. His bodyguard and army
were organized without considerations of clan or nation. All served
as Mongols who drank fermented mare's milk, *qumis*, and accepted
the salt of the Great Khan. In turn, Genghis Khan accepted them
into both his service and the Mongol nation. Therefore, Genghis
Khan reorganized the tribal armies into an imperial one based on
units of ten and commanded by officers of proved loyalty and bravery.[67] Only after he had been declared Genghis Khan could Temujin
reorganize his warriors into an imperial army. Quick to innovate,
Genghis Khan in his later offensive campaigns also mastered lo-

gistics and siege warfare on a scale no previous nomadic conqueror ever achieved.[68] He and his heirs also drafted the subject peoples as auxiliaries who served as infantry, archers, or heavy cavalry. With each conquest, the imperial Mongol army gained in strength and diversity. Yet his officers, drawn from Genghis Khan's bodyguard, even imposed strict discipline and drill on vassal and allied units.[69] Even by the standards of his time, Genghis Khan was pitiless in waging war. He committed far more massacres than any previous conqueror of the steppes, and he is perhaps exceeded only by his emulator, Tamerlane.[70] After 1206, he applied the massacres so common on the steppes on a grand strategic level to conquer the cities of Northern China and the lands of Eastern Islam. Muslim, Christian, and Chinese writers condemned as acts of barbarism his policy of massacres and wanton destruction of cities and cultivated fields. Yet Genghis Khan deliberately struck terror into the hearts of their foes by slaughtering villagers and urban populations that showed the slightest resistance. Terrified refugees fleeing the Mongol advance spread reports that often shocked enemies into immediate surrender. His sons and grandsons conducted the same gruesome strategy in their conquests of Russia, the Islamic world, and China. Genghis Khan remained a son of the Eurasian steppes. War was for him personal, a matter of bravery and honor. At times, grief and wrath swelled up into uncontrollable rage whenever one of his kinsmen fell in battle. In 1217, he ordered the massacre of a recalcitrant forest people who had slain his adopted son Boroghul in a skirmish.[71] Five years later, in 1221, Genghis Khan committed two grisly atrocities to settle a blood feud committed by determined foes. In April, the Mongol army massacred the entire population of Nishapur, the famed caravan city of northern Iran, in retribution for the death of Genghis Khan's son-in-law Tokuchar the year before.[72] Even more ghastly, months later, Genghis Khan ordered the extermination of all living creatures in the valley of Bamyan.[73] In the fighting to capture the strategic valley, the khan's favorite grandson, Mutugen, fell, pierced by an arrow. The ruined settlements were never reoccupied, and the desolate landscape bore witness to all future travelers of the terrible grief and wrath of the Great Khan. For Genghis Khan, these massacres avenged a blood feud on a colossal scale rather than served as a calculated act of terror, although the results differed little from his deliberate acts of genocide. Genghis Khan never changed his outlook that war was bound up with his personal honor and survival of his family. Such had been the case for all previous conquerors from the steppes. But Genghis Khan possessed in his army a most lethal instrument to exact his vengeance on a scale that even shocked Chinese, Muslim, and Christian contemporaries who were accustomed to the brutalities of war, which today would be condemned as war crimes.

Yet to his warriors and his nation, Genghis Khan was hailed the greatest of rulers who embodied the virtues long prized in a ruler and first recorded on the Turkic monumental inscriptions of the Orkhon valley. In 1206, Temujin had ensured his fame in poetry and legend. Yet in the next twenty years, he would achieve far more than in the previous forty. That year, the Jin emperor Zhangzong and court realized that they now faced war, but they could not fathom the ferocity and genius of their opponent.[74] They meticulously mobilized for war against the upstart khan of the Mongols. They did not have to wait long.

19

Genghis Khan, the World Conqueror

In February 1220, after a siege of only fifteen days, the leading citizens of Bukhara opened the gates and surrendered their city to Genghis Khan.[1] Only the garrison of veteran Turkish slave soldiers in the citadel held out, but these mercenaries were quickly overcome and massacred. In a brilliant strategic maneuver of deception, Genghis Khan and his youngest son, Tolui, had crossed the Jaxartes River (Syr Darya), while two other Mongol columns attacked Otar on the middle Jaxartes River and Khojend in the Ferghana valley, thereby confusing Muhammad Shah, the master of Khwarazm, as to Mongol intentions. Audaciously, Genghis Khan and Tolui at the head of fifty thousand horse archers headed southwest into the desolate Kizil Kum, moving swiftly from oasis to oasis. The Mongols then suddenly emerged from the desert to take the city of Bukhara by surprise from the southwest.[2] Genghis Khan's Chinese engineers immediately set to work battering the walls. The citizens of Bukhara were stunned because for the first time a nomadic army possessed engines that undermined walls. Refugees flocking into the city from the countryside reported that the Mongols had spared those villages that instantly submitted, but they destroyed those that resisted. Terror paralyzed the defenders;

the patricians of the city soon treated for terms. The Persian historian Atâ-Malek Juvayni, writing in the reign of Genghis Khan's grandson Hulagu, preserves or perhaps re-creates the proclamation of Genghis Khan, who spared the city from a sack, but deplored the great ones who had misled the people into committing the sin of resisting.[3] Hence, the rich would have to surrender all their wealth in an organized shakedown rather than a wanton sack. Even so, craftsmen, physicians, and scribes were deported to Karakorum; provisions and war matériel confiscated; and young men conscripted into the Mongol army for its next operation, the assault of Samarkand, Bukhara's sister city in the Zeravshan valley 160 miles directly east of Bukhara.[4]

Bukhara was the jewel of eastern Islam. The city lay on the Zeravshan River arising in the Pamirs and flowing west to join the middle course of the great Oxus River on its northwestern journey to the Aral Sea. Bukhara was thus always a major destination for caravans arriving from Kashgar after crossing the Pamirs or caravans arriving from Merv to the west. The Samanid emirs, deputies of the Abbasid Caliph in Baghdad, had adored the city with masterpieces of Iranian architecture during the ninth and tenth centuries.[5] The Naqshbandi sufi order had flourished in this city since the twelfth century and its inspired holy ones had carried mystical Islam to the Turkish tribes of the central steppes.[6]

Even though Bukhara under the Karakhitan rulers had lost its primacy as the political capital and hub of international trade of Transoxiana, the city was still revered as the spiritual and cultural center of Eastern Islam. Its surrender was symbolic, but symbolic victories can be just as decisive as strategic ones in war.

Genghis Khan, now nearly sixty years old, must have been awed, and perhaps a bit unsettled, by what he saw. Bukhara lay at the extreme western edge of his world. He was familiar with the grandeur of the imperial cities of northern China, but Bukhara's architecture was new and alien to him. The minarets of the medresses with blue glazed tiles dominated the skyline. Genghis Khan looked up 150 feet in wonder to view the Kalyan minaret, then just a century old, that towered over the religious heart of the city and gave a commanding view of the entire plain.[7] He must have been amazed into reverence, for he ordered the minaret spared, but he directed his soldiers to level the surrounding complex with its great mosque because he mistook it for a palace of Muhammad Shah.

Over the next two years, the Mongols captured every major city on the Silk Road in Transoxiana, Afghanistan, Khurasan, and northern Iran.[8] These victories stunned the world. Yet for all the brilliance, Genghis Khan did not wage this campaign as part of a grand strategy of world conquest. The vision of world conquest was a result not a cause of this campaign. Hence, it is often argued that the Mongol Empire started with the accession of Ögedei, for he framed the strategic plans of a world conquest.[9] But, in my opinion, this view is misleading. The spectacular victories in 1220–1221 confirmed to, perhaps even inspired, Genghis Khan that the conquest of the world by the Mongols was not only possible but their destiny. Ögedei implemented the plans Genghis Khan would have pursued if he had lived longer. Hence, the triumphant entrance into Bukhara marked a turning point. For Genghis Khan, it gave him a new sense that his army could conquer any foe on the Eurasian continent. Yet this war that put the Mongols on the path to world conquest arose over an unanticipated, sordid, even trivial incident.

Fifteen years earlier when Temujin had been proclaimed universal lord, he had no plans for world conquest, and the fabled caravan cities of Muhammad Shah's realm were far beyond the limits of the world known to Mongols.[10] Temujin, now Genghis Khan, had more immediate concerns. Foremost, he had to make his power effective, and legitimate, after three decades of incessant fighting among the tribes. At the great feasting of the *kurultai*, Genghis Khan ostentatiously rewarded and promoted loyal officers (*noyan*) and warriors. He presided over rites to the ancestral spirits, invoking their protection for his warriors soon to set out on raids against recalcitrant forest tribes or border towns of the Jin Empire.[11] All these celebrations required the blessing of the leading shaman Kokchu, whose father, Monglik, was shaman to Temujin's father, Yesügei. Kokchu wielded great influence over the Mongols, because he was widely believed to ascend on a gray horse to the other world. In his mystical trances, he had long foretold the universal lordship of Temujin. The wily Kokchu, in effect, gave Genghis Khan his legitimacy in the eyes of many of the tribes, but Kokchu wanted more than spiritual authority. Within days of the celebrations, he conspired to overthrow Temujin.[12] The ever-watchful Börte detected the traitors, and then warned her husband, who promptly summoned and arrested Kokchu. The shaman was executed in the customary fashion. Kokchu was wrapped in a carpet and trampled by Mongol horsemen lest the ancestral spirits be offended by the shedding of the blood of a holy one. Relations between khan and shaman had perhaps never been more than superficially cordial. After this incident, Temujin politely consulted diverse spiritual figures, but he took every measure to ensure that his authority was absolute.

Genghis Khan also took practical measures to consolidate his power. During the years immediately following the great *kurultai*, he steadily turned his warriors into an imperial army. Genghis Khan revolutionized the warfare on the steppes, first seen among the Scythians and Xiongnu, and tactically perfected by the Turks. He imposed discipline and organization that made the Mongol army into the finest of steppe armies, and one of the greatest fighting forces of all time. Genghis Khan organized his army into tactical units of ten, a method of reckoning employed on the steppes since the Xiongnu.[13] The cavalry was based on an *arban* of ten men, who were, in effect, a military *yurt* or a band of brothers in arms. The ten *arbanlar* were grouped into a formation of hundred men known as *jaghun*; ten *jaghunlar* were grouped into a *mingghan*, a unit of one thousand men. Ten *minggahanlar* comprised a *tumen* of ten thousand men at a full strength. The *tumen* was a strategic unit that could operate as a column of a greater expedition (*ordu*) or as an independent army so that its strategic function was comparable to the corps of Napoleon's Grande Armée.[14] In organizing his army, Genghis Khan broke with previous practice of grouping units by clan, tribe, and language. Instead, his men were recruited into units without regard to origin, language, or religion; they were selected on the basis of their merit and loyalty.[15] Officers and men ceremoniously pledged their life and honor to Genghis Khan because they accepted their salt from the Great Khan, and they toasted him by drinking his fermented mare's milk *qumis* (or *kumis*). On the Eurasian steppes, warriors had long paid homage to their lord by accepting his salt, an invaluable commodity obtained in trade from the sedentary civilizations. Drinking of fermented mare's milk (*qumis*) had long sealed oaths of brotherhood (*anda*) among warriors or signaled the submission of a ruler's envoys to an overlord.[16] Genghis Khan applied these traditional acts of homage to his entire army. Every warrior henceforth became sworn brothers (*anda*) to their lord Genghis Khan so that acts of disobedience were punished with the utmost severity.

Within this army of devoted warriors, Genghis Khan selected an even more elite force, his bodyguard (*kashik*) of ten thousand men, many of whom were appointed training officers at all levels for the *tumenler*.[17] From the *kashik*, Genghis Khan and his heirs drew accomplished generals and subordinate officers based on loyalty and talent. Genghis Khan thus could dispense with clan and tribal leaders, who might challenge his authority. He entrusted command only to those men of proved loyalty, foremost his "four dogs of war," who had shared his early adventures and dangers: Jebe, Sübetei, Jelme, and Bo'orchu. Within perhaps five years, Genghis Khan had transformed the Mongol and Turkish warriors of the eastern Eurasian steppes into an army imperial in its loyalty, and professional in its discipline, tactics, and ethos. His sons and grandsons would expand and improve this superbly disciplined army.[18] Genghis Khan created an imperial army that outmatched every opponent of the Eurasian continent for the entire thirteenth century. At his death in 1227, the Mongol army numbered 129 *tumenler* or 129,000 horsemen—an extraordinary mobilization of manpower from a population of the Mongolian homeland that perhaps totaled between seven hundred fifty thousand and one million souls.[19]

Genghis Khan trained his imperial army so that he could maintain his authority across the eastern Eurasian steppes in the fashion of previous nomadic conquerors. The desultory fighting of the past thirty years disrupted trade with the cities of the Jin and Xi Xia Empires. Genghis Khan, just as much as Modu Chanyu, depended on this trade for silk, manufactured goods, and foodstuffs to sustain his people and his own power.[20] Incessant raiding among the tribes had diminished the flocks and herds of livestock so essential to the nomadic way of life. As Great Khan, Temujin immediately approved great raids by his vassals, who seized great numbers of

stock animals, plunder, and skilled captives in the Chinese borderlands. On the strategic level, in 1206, Genghis Khan was planning
a far more ambitious reckoning with his ancestral foe, the Jurchen
emperors of the Jin dynasty who had incited warfare among the
tribes and backed foes of Genghis Khan. Genghis Khan aimed to
wrest the prefectures of northern China, and impose his hegemony
over the rump Jin Empire. But first Genghis Khan had to control
the Ordos triangle, and so the entrance into the middle and lower
Huang He, the heartland of the Jin Empire. The sinified Tangut-
speaking emperors of the Xi Xia controlled this strategic region
along with the Gansu corridor and the caravan cities of the eastern
Tarim Basin. Genghis Khan was kept informed about Jin and Xi
Xia courts by leading Khitans, Chinese, and Uyghurs who sought
Mongol service.[21] Genghis Khan soon learned that the Xiangzong,
who had seized the throne of the Xi Xia in 1206, warred against
the Jin emperor Wanyan Yongji, who reigned under the Chinese
throne name Xingsheng (1208–1213).[22] Furthermore, many Khitans, Chinese, and Uyghurs were ready to welcome a Mongol army
that would overthrow the usurper Xiangzong.

In the spring of 1209, Genghis Khan attacked the Xi Xia in his
first campaign waged outside of Mongolia. His army swiftly covered
over 650 miles, including the final stretch of two hundred miles
across the Gobi, to surprise the Xi Xia army. But Tangut generals, following the precepts of the memoranda presented to the Han
emperor Wudi over thirteen centuries earlier, fortified the passes
and they evacuated the civilian population behind city walls.[23] The
campaign soon stalled until reinforcements arrived from Mongolia so that Genghis Khan defeated the Xi Xia field army in a war
of maneuver and skirmishing in late summer. In October 1209,
Genghis Khan laid siege to Ningxia, the Xi Xia capital, but the
Mongol army was inexperienced in siege warfare and suffered grievously from privation and disease.[24] After a grueling siege of three
months, Genghis Khan ordered the diversion of dammed waters
to undermine the city walls, but the defenders sabotaged the operation so that waters instead flooded the Mongol camp. Genghis
Khan, in frustration, negotiated. In January 1210, Genghis Khan

accepted the submission of Xiangzong as a vassal, who sealed the deal with promises of a marriage alliance and tribute.[25] The treaty held for the next fifteen years. Strategically, Genghis Khan henceforth gained free passage through Xi Xia domains to attack the Jin Empire. Even more important, Genghis Khan learned hard lessons in logistics and siege warfare. He immediately recruited a corps of Chinese engineers which accompanied the Mongol army on every future expedition.

In March 1211, Genghis Khan summoned another national *kurultai* on the banks of the Onon River and in view of the holy Khenti Mountains.[26] In a magnificently staged spectacle, Genghis Khan harangued the Mongol nation in arms, denouncing the arrogant envoys of the Jin emperor Xingsheng who demanded Genghis Khan, just like his forefathers, render tribute to their golden emperor reigning in Zhongdu. The summoned nation of the Mongols roared its objections and declared war on the Jin emperor. Thereupon, Genghis Khan withdrew into solitude to consult the ancestral spirits and Eternal Blue Sky for three days. On the fourth day, he emerged to announce that victory was assured by divine favor. For Genghis Khan, a successful war against the Jin would be the capstone of his career. He would live on in legend as the greatest conqueror of the steppes, surpassing the deeds of his Xiongnu, Rouran, Turkish, and Uyghur predecessors. Genghis Khan dispatched twenty thousand horsemen to guard the western frontiers, while he himself commanded the rest of the national levy, reportedly sixty-five thousand strong, in an invasion of northern China.[27] From the start, Genghis Khan planned a war of conquest with the ultimate objective the cities and fields of the Yellow River (Huang He). To many observers, Genghis Khan's war appeared to be an act of folly. At best, the Mongol invasion would end up as another great raid with hauls of captives and booty, followed by posturing between Mongol Khan and the Jin emperor that would end up in a treaty restoring trade between the steppes and the cities of northern China. The Jin emperor Xingsheng ruled domains in wealth and population that were twenty to thirty times greater than that of Mongolia.[28] He could field and maintain an army of five hundred thousand men, including one hundred twenty thousand cavalry.[29] Yet the vacillating Xingsheng, seventh of the Jurchen emperors, was no match to Genghis Khan. His generals directed operations; most of the army was committed to garrisoning cities. The best of the cavalry units comprised tribal regiments of Khitans and Turks long disaffected with Jin rule. They were weary of the onerous drafts of their warriors to fight incessant wars against the Song Empire.[30] The Öngüt Turks, who patrolled the arid steppes of Inner Mongolia north of the Great Wall, promptly went over to Genghis Khan and opened the way to China.[31] As soon as the Mongols broke through the defenses of the Great Wall in June 1213, many Chinese and Khitan subjects of Xingsheng welcomed the Mongols.[32] The princely brothers Ila Ahai and Tuka, former envoys of the Jin court, had switched their allegiance to Genghis Khan a decade earlier. They now persuaded many of their leading countrymen to embrace the Mongol cause. Once in northern China, Genghis Khan divided his army into columns that swept Jin domains, defeated Jin armies in detail, and accepted the surrender of many towns on terms over the next year. The indecisive Xingsheng desperately tried to negotiate, but Genghis Khan refused.[33] Genghis Khan was determined to bring down the Jin house. He laid siege to Xijing (today Dotong in Shanxi), the western capital of the Jin Empire. Late in 1212, Genghis Khan himself was seriously wounded in the knee by an arrow during the siege.[34] He turned over command to his youngest son, Tolui, but Tolui failed to press the siege and lost the initiative. A detachment of Jurchen soldiers slipped past the Mongol siege works and occupied the strategic Juyong Pass, thereby threatening to cut off the besieging Mongols from their lines of communication to their homeland. Tolui might have raised the siege and withdrawn, except the ever-bold Jebe retook the pass in a daring night attack.[35] Xijing was doomed and fell soon after. In the autumn of 1213, the Mongol horsemen appeared before the walls of Zhongdu, the principal Jin capital. On September 13, 1213, the Jin general Hushahu murdered his discredited master in Zhongdu and declared a princely cousin of the emperor, Wanyan Xun, as the next emperor, Xuanzong (1213–1224).[36] The treacherous Hushahu was soon murdered by officers loyal to the former emperor, and to the relief of the new one. Xuanzong, however, could neither oppose the Mongol army nor offer acceptable terms to Genghis Khan. In the summer of 1214, Xuanzong quit Zhongdu, and relocated his court to Kaifeng in the lower valley of the Yellow River.[37] Meanwhile, Genghis Khan first blockaded and then besieged Zhongdu.[38]

Zhongdu, the Xanadu of Western travelers and poets, boasted one million residents, spacious parks, the fabled Daning Palace, and the beautiful artificial Taiye Lake, around which Kublai Khan would later center his palace when he rebuilt Zhongdu as his summer capital. Zhongdu was massively fortified, and defied the Mongol army for nearly a year. Genghis Khan had to fight off a major Jurchen relief expedition; his Mongols suffered from disease and the heat of summer, and then the blistering winter in 1214–1215. On May 31, 1215, the city fell to the Mongols only because Khitan officers of the Jin garrison betrayed the city by handing over the Lugao Bridge, vital to the defense of the southern approaches of the city.[39] The siege had proved costly. In retaliation, Genghis Khan ordered his first large-scale massacre of a civilian population, and his horsemen were even directed to destroy the crops by riding over the cultivated fields of the surrounding countryside. Mongol warriors spent over a month looting Zhongdu and massacring its population.[40] Allegedly sixty thousand virgins cast themselves from the walls to escape the ravages of the Mongol barbarians. Later visitors still reported hills of bleached bones around the city and a land drenched in a foul stench arising from the tens of thousands of decomposed bodies of unburied victims. To be sure, massacre was long the fate of the defeated on the steppes, but Genghis Khan deliberately ordered the destruction of Zhongdu and a massacre on such a scale to terrorize the remaining cities of northern China into surrender. The Jin court at Kaifeng was powerless to recover its capital, and the emperor Xuanzong braced for the inevitable Mongol invasion of the valley of the Huang He. But the invasion never came.

In the spring of 1216, Genghis Khan retired to Mongolia, and he entrusted the pacification and organization of the Chinese conquests (today Shanxi, Hebei, and Shandong) to his viceroy (*guo-wang*) Mukali.[41] Genghis Khan, just like previous nomadic conquerors, planned to rule northern China through mandarin officials. He also could not afford to leave Xuanzong in Kaifeng, where the Jin emperor might parley with the Song emperor Lizong to make common cause against the northern barbarians. The Song court, however, failed to perceive a Mongol threat, but instead pursued a policy of pitting Jurchens against Mongols and applauded the defeat of the hated Jurchens.[42] At this point, the Song court calculated correctly. While Genghis Khan waged war with tactical and strategic brilliance, as yet he pursued a traditional policy of gaining mastery over the borderlands of northern China. He did not contemplate a conquest of Song China, let alone world conquest. Instead, Genghis Khan prepared for a methodical conquest of the remaining Jin domains, and for another grueling siege of a Jin capital, Kaifeng. But a series of unforeseen circumstances diverted Genghis Khan's attention to the west and ultimately brought him before the walls of Bukhara. He would not return to face his Jin rival until nine years later, near the end of his life.

Rebellions on the western and northwestern regions of his empire erupted in 1217. First, Genghis Khan swiftly punished an incipient revolt among his ancestral foes the Merkits by virtually exterminating the tribe.[43] Meanwhile, Boroghul, an adopted son of Genghis Khan, was slain in an unsuccessful expedition against the Kori-Tumar forest peoples. Boroghul, a captive Jurchen infant whom Genghis Khan's mother, Hoelun, had reared, had risen to high rank in the imperial guard. The wrathful Genghis Khan immediately turned the full might of the Mongol army against the rebels. He exacted a fierce vengeance.[44] One hundred Tumar captives were sacrificed to the spirit of Boroghul. The Oriats peoples of the forest and nomadic Kyrgyz were terrorized into submission upon hearing the news of these Mongol atrocities.[45] They dutifully furnished warriors to the imperial army. Genghis Khan now extended his sway far across the central Eurasian steppes to the pastures watered by the lower Yenisei and Irtysh Rivers. Immediately to his west lay the Karakhitan Empire.

Zhilugu, Gurkhan of the Karakhitans (1178–1211), had preferred to rule peacefully from Balasagun over the central Eurasian steppes,

Transoxiana, and Western Tarim Basin, but he faced repeated challenges from his unruly Muslim vassals.[46] The ailing Gurkhan himself, who doubled as the Chinese emperor Tianxi of the Western Liao dynasty, was content to draw revenues from his diverse subjects who were taxed and administered by Chinese-trained bureaucrats. The Gurkhan, however, had received the refugee prince Kuchlug years earlier. Kuchlug, the indomitable warrior of the Naimans and implacable foe to the Mongols. Kuchlug had refused to submit to Temujin in 1204. He and his followers had fled west to the court of Gurkhan Zhilugu.[47] Kuchlug rose in the Gurkhan's favor, winning a marriage to a daughter of Zhilugu and conveniently converting from Nestorian Christianity to Buddhism in 1210.[48] Kuchlug rallied numerous dissidents and exiles who detested Temujin turned Genghis Khan. He also intrigued with the Gurkhan's vassal Muhammad Shah of Khwarazm to overthrow his father-in-law, and then to partition the Karakhitan domains with Muhammad Shah.[49] In 1211, Muhammad Shah revolted, crushed the Karakhitan army, and secured the cities of Transoxiana (Mawarannahr). Meanwhile, Kuchlug ambushed and captured the Gurkhan while on a hunting expedition.[50] Thereafter, Kuchlug ruled through his father-in-law as a figurehead until his death in 1213, whereupon Kuchlug ruled as Gurkhan in his own right.[51] Kuchlug willingly signed off on the cities of Transoxiana, because he intended to turn the rest of the Karakhitan state into a base to oppose Genghis Khan. From Balasagun Kuchlug could draw upon the Turkish nomadic horse archers of the central Eurasian steppes and the wealth of the western and southern caravan cities of the Tarim Basin. In effect, he ruled a provincial Chinese bureaucratic state which he hoped would give him the means to confront Genghis Khan. But as a zealous convert to Buddhism, Kuchlug foolishly persecuted his Muslim subjects, even crucifying a defiant iman of Khotan.[52]

Genghis Khan received many appeals from Uyghurs and Khitans against the tyrant Kuchlug, who, it was feared, was organizing an army to challenge Genghis Khan's supremacy over Mongolia. In 1218, Genghis Khan decided to act decisively. Jebe, with two crack *tumenler* (twenty thousand horsemen), invaded the Karak-

hitan Empire, and the Mongols were hailed as liberators by the outraged Muslim subjects of Kuchlug.[53] Jebe took the city of Kashgar
by surprise. Kuchlug barely escaped from the city, and fled into
the Pamirs. But he was ignominiously recognized and captured by
a hunter who turned him over to Jebe. Jebe ordered the Naiman
prince beheaded.[54] By this single short campaign, Genghis Khan
extended his sway over large swaths of the central steppes to the
banks of the Jaxartes River (Syr Darya) and the Aral Sea. He now
shared a frontier with Muhammad Shah, deeply suspicious of his
new neighbor to the northeast.

Muhammad Shah suspected the imperial ambitions of Genghis
Khan, and he provoked an incident that resulted in the first Mongol invasion of the Muslim world and the collapse of his own
Khwarazmian Empire. In 1215, three Bukharan merchants outfitted
a caravan and traveled to Karakorum so that they could present rich
gifts to Genghis Khan and then sell luxuries to the Mongol elite
at high prices.[55] The savvy Persian merchants had received news
of Genghis Khan's capture of Zhongdu and the fabulous wealth in
the storerooms of Karakorum. They were well rewarded for their
generous gifts and polished ways. Three years later, in 1218, they
returned home accompanied by three Mongol envoys who carried
a letter from Genghis Khan to Muhammad Shah. Two versions of
the letter are reported by Juvayni and Rashid al-Din, respectively.
Each version is a polite request for trade, but Juvayni stresses that
Genghis Khan addressed Muhammad Shah as an inferior prince.[56]
Muhammad Shah must have flown into rage over the Mongol
khan's pretensions. At the same time, he feared that Genghis Khan
would not be satisfied with his conquests in distant China, but he
would look to the west next.

Meanwhile, in the same year, a Mongol caravan arrived at Otrar
(or Urtar) on the upper Jaxartes River. The governor Inal Khan,
perhaps acting on orders from Muhammad Shah, seized the goods
and executed the merchants and an envoy of Genghis Khan on
grounds that they were Mongol spies.[57] The accusation was plausible,
if not true. Genghis Khan immediately demanded compensation.
Muhammad Shah refused to pay, and so Genghis Khan promptly

declared war. Muhammad Shah has been criticized for foolishly precipitating a war that released a whirlwind of destruction on the Islamic world, but at the time he had a reasonable expectation that he could defend his realm.[58] Muhammad Shah has been unfairly portrayed as haughty and incompetent by hostile sources, Mongol and Islamic alike. Yet he viewed the Mongols as barbarians content to loot and leave just like previous nomadic invaders from the steppes.[59] Far more important were his plans to conquer the eastern lands of Dar al-Islam and to subordinate the Abbasid Caliph in Baghdad so that he could rule as the legitimate Turkish sultan over Sunni Islam. Muhammad Shah, himself Turkish in origin, employed Persian ministers and promoted the high culture of eastern Islam, but he based his field army on Kipchak and Cuman mercenaries and *ghilman*, slave soldiers.[60] With good cause, Muhammad Shah feared the expansion of Mongol power across the western Eurasian steppes and the loss of access to the recruiting grounds of Kipchak Turks. Furthermore, he had also easily smashed the Karakhitan army so that he dismissed the Mongols as similar pagan barbarians. He had no experience in confronting a Mongol army with a strategic and logistical speed hitherto unknown. Instead, Muhammad Shah shared with his Muslim contemporaries a far greater fear of the Crusading Franks bent on capturing the great cities in the heartland of Islam. In the spring of 1219, members of the Fifth Crusade, who had already captured the port of Damietta, the gateway to Egypt, threatened to advance on Cairo.[61] Rumors circulated alleging that the Emperor Frederick II, *stupor mundi*, was about to arrive with a vast host to command the final advance. Muslims feared Frederick as the greatest of Christian kings, and respected him as a civilized foe fluent in Arabic and conversant in Islamic theology.[62] But Frederick proved a no-show. The Crusaders, bogged down in the canals of the Egyptian Delta, stalled, and withdrew in defeat. Frederick's repeated excuses to postpone his promised crusade earned him the ire and excommunication of Pope Gregory IX.[63] Instead, the Mongols unexpectedly burst into the Islamic world from the northeast.

In the spring of 1219, Genghis Khan, at age sixty, had meticulously planned and led his third and by far most audacious offensive

campaign. He summoned virtually the entire levy of the Mongol
nation as well as Khitan and Uyghur allies, and, of course, his Chinese engineering and medical corps. His army might have totaled
as many as one hundred fifty thousand men, and over one million
mounts. The expedition posed unprecedented strategic and logistical challenges.[64] Well in advance, Genghis Khan ordered the routes
across the steppes cleared so that his army could move swiftly over
three thousand miles from Karakorum to the grasslands of the
Irtysh valley. Each Mongol warrior was accompanied by as many
as ten remounts so that fodder and water were essential if the Mongol army were to cover the distance at forty miles per day. Within
ten weeks, at the end of the summer, Genghis Khan had reached
the Jaxartes River (Syr Darya), to the dismay of Muhammad Shah,
who was still mobilizing his ponderous army.

On the Jaxartes River, Genghis Khan boldly divided his smaller
army into three strategic columns.[65] While Genghis Khan and his
youngest son, Tolui, with the main force moved against Bukhara,
his other sons commanded the two other columns. His sons Chagatai, the most aggressive, and Ögedei, the most judicious, attacked
Otrar on the middle Jaxartes River.[66] When the city fell, the Mongols massacred the population. The Khwarazmian governor Inal
Khan, who had provoked the war, was cruelly punished. Molten
silver was poured down the throat.[67] Farther east in Ferghana, the
Great Khan's eldest son, Jochi, besieged and captured Khujand.[68]
Within months, in early 1220, the Mongols had overrun the northeastern defenses of Muhammad Shah, and so they ravaged at will all
of Transoxiana, Afghanistan, and northern Iran. Mongol columns
captured every major city on the Silk Road from Samarkand to Tabriz, either by siege or voluntary submission, in less than two years.[69]
Everywhere the Mongol army was invincible, while Muhammad
Shah's mercenaries and slave soldiers deserted or surrendered after
token resistance, only to be promptly massacred by their captors.

From Bukhara, Genghis Khan advanced on Samarkand, and
within a month the citizens of this fabled city, celebrated for its
lush gardens and fountains, surrendered. Once again, the residents
were ordered to evacuate the city. Samarkand was then plundered;
the Turkish garrison was slaughtered; thirty thousand artisans and

skilled residents were deported to Mongolia.[70] The fall of Samarkand, a capital of the Karakhitan and Khwarazmian states, marked the collapse of Muhammad Shah's realm. Muhammad Shah fled west into Khurasan, but before he could rally his soldiers, Jebe and Sübetei arrived in hot pursuit with two *tumenler* of twenty thousand men.[71] Muhammad Shah narrowly escaped to a small island opposite Abeskun on the southern shores of the Caspian Sea, where he died a broken man by the end of the year. Meanwhile, Jebe and Sübetei relentlessly rode west across northern Iran, invaded Christian Armenia and Georgia, and then crossed the Derbent Pass onto the Pontic-Caspian steppes, where they defeated a joint Cuman-Russian army on the banks of the Kalka River on May 31, 1223.[72] Soon after, they rejoined their master in Central Asia, flush with victories and carrying information invaluable for the future conquest of the distant western lands.

Meanwhile, within a year of the surrender of Bukhara, Genghis Khan crossed the Oxus River (Amu Darya). Balkh immediately submitted, but Tolui stormed Merv, and punished the defiant residents, reputedly numbering seven hundred thousand, by ordering their massacre.[73] Herat, yet another famed oasis city of the Silk Road in Hari valley, suffered an equally gruesome fate six months later in the autumn of 1221.[74] Farther west in Khurasan, Genghis Khan just as ruthlessly punished the rebels of Nishapur, home of the poet Omar Khayyam. Nishapur, which had submitted to Jebe and Sübet the year before, renounced its fealty once the Mongols rode west. Tokuchar, son-in-law of Genghis Khan, fell in a skirmish during an abortive attack by the Mongols to retake the city.[75] In April 1221, the Mongols stormed into the city and massacred the population. Muslim chroniclers report grisly scenes of pyramids of human heads; even dogs and cats were slaughtered. Bamyan, however, suffered the most frightening fate of all. There, six centuries earlier the Chinese monk Xuanzang had reverently gazed upward to the two colossal statues of Buddha as Vairocana and Sakyamuni. During the savage fighting in the strategic valley, Mutugen, Genghis Khan's favorite grandson, was killed by an arrow. The vengeful Great Khan ordered all living creatures in Bamyan slain. The city was leveled to the ground, cursed and forever abandoned.[76]

In 1221, cities in Afghanistan and Khurasan resisted on the false hopes that Jalal al-Din, the dashing son of Muhammad Shah, would soon arise and smite the barbarians. From the outset, Jalal al-Din had vehemently objected to his father's strategy of trusting to fortified cities and avoiding battle with the Mongols.[77] When Muhammad Shah opted for an obscure exile on the shores of the Caspian Sea, his son rallied forces in Khurasan and fought his way east to Ghazna, where he summoned reinforcements from his vassals in northern India.[78] Genghis Khan, however, once again outmaneuvered his Khwarazmian foe, surprising Jalal al-Din before he could marshal his forces. In November 1221, Jalal al-Din retreated across the Hindu Kush. Genghis Khan followed. On the banks of the middle Indus north of Multan, Genghis Khan smashed the motley forces of Jalal al-Din, who only avoided capture by swimming across the Indus. Genghis Khan chose not to pursue the fugitive prince without a kingdom into India, and he retired to the winter pastures just south of the Hindu Kush.[79]

In the next year, 1222, Genghis Khan shifted from conquest to consolidation. Over the next eighteen months, he toured the cities of Khurasan and Transoxiana. Just as in China, Genghis Khan understood that he could only administer these new provinces by co-opting Persian officials and imans, and by recognizing the legal status of Islam.[80] He had little time to perfect a new central administration for the lands of eastern Islam, because he was pressed to return to Mongolia. When he finally reached Karakorum in 1225, eight years had passed since his departure. He still had to reckon with the Jin emperor in Kaifeng, and the new emperor of the Xi Xia Aizong who repudiated his Mongol alliance.[81] Before Genghis Khan could complete his campaign against the Xi Xia, he died in August 1227, at the age of sixty-five.

The Khwarazmian campaign of Genghis Khan had changed the world. To the shock of the Islamic world, Genghis Khan and his Mongols, unexpectedly and swiftly, captured and sacked the great cities of Eastern Islam. Some of the caravan cities, such as Bamyan and Urgench, never recovered and lie in ruins to this day. Prosperity returned to the other cities of the Silk Road during the next two generations under Mongol peace imposed by Great Khan Öge-dei, and then by Hulagu and his heirs, who ruled as the Ilkhans of Iran.[82] The sudden collapse of the Khwarazmian Empire struck terror in the hearts of Muslims who saw the new invaders as the sons of Gog and Magog come to announce the end of the world as foretold in the *Koran*. Muslim rulers were stunned and uncertain how to act.[83] Imans fervently urged true believers to return to the moral strictures of the *Koran* lest they risk a catastrophic end of days wrought by these unclean peoples of the steppes. Genghis Khan also triggered a major migration west within the Islamic world that redrew linguistic and religious boundaries that still determine the Middle East today. Genghis Khan unintentionally hastened the shift of the central steppes and Transoxiana, today represented by the nation states of Kazakhstan, Kyrgyzstan, Turkmenistan, and Uzbekistan, from Iranian- to Turkish-speaking lands.[84] Numerous Persian refugees fled the great cities of Transoxiana and Khurasan west to Syria and Anatolia.[85] Among them was the family of Bahā ud-Dīn Walad, a jurist and mystic of Balkh, who ultimately set-tled in Konya, capital of the Seljuk sultanate of Rum.[86] His son, Jalāl ad-Dīn Mohammad Rūmī, who succeeded to the family medresse, turned out to be the Mevlana. The Mevlana, inspired poet and founder of the Mevlevi order of Whirling Dervishes, ini-tiated the conversion of Byzantine Christian Anatolia into Muslim Turkey. Many Turkish tribes too fled west into Anatolia. Among them was an obscure tribe dwelling near Merv who were reput-edly the ancestors of the Ottomans.[87]

Meanwhile, in Acre, on the distant shores of the Levant, Bishop Jacques de Vitry hailed garbled reports about Genghis Khan's vic-tories as proof that David, the son, or perhaps the grandson, of Prester John, was on the march with a great host to join members of the Fifth Crusade and smite the Muslims.[88] Disquieting reports arrived soon after about the Mongols wreaking havoc in Christian Georgia and Armenia, and then defeating the Russian princes.[89] But these reports were dismissed as God's punishment of George IV for his failure to come to the aid of the Crusaders, and the Or-thodox Russian princes, who were, after all, obdurate schismatics refusing to acknowledge the spiritual authority of the Pope. Latin

Christendom instead eagerly anticipated the imminent arrival of
the Mongols as the warriors of Prester John. But their hopeful expectations turned to shock and horror dashed twenty years later
when the Mongols invaded Central Europe.

Before embarking on his Khwarazmian campaign, the *Secret
History* reports a tempestuous meeting between Genghis Khan and
his four sons over the succession.[90] Jochi, encouraged by his father,
claimed the right to speak first, but he was immediately challenged
by Chagatai, who cast aspersions on his brother's paternity. Ögedei,
always the favorite and slightly inebriated as usual, urged reconciliation. The youngest son, Tolui, remained inconspicuously in the
background. Genghis Khan, saddened and dismayed, had to implore his sons to stand together for the sake of the Mongol nation.
He nominated Ögedei to succeed as Great Khan. In contrast, the
two Persian chroniclers Juvayni and Rashid al-Din each reports
dignified, sober deliberations on the matter, but they are unclear
as to the precise date of these discussions.[91] Most likely, Genghis
Khan, when he prepared for his Khwarazmian campaign, raised the
issue of succession lest his sons quarrel should he fall in the forth-
coming campaign.

The fighting in Khwarazm soon confirmed in Genghis Khan's
mind that Ögedei should succeed as the Great Khan. While Genghis Khan and his youngest son, Tolui, with the main army overran
Transoxiana, Afghanistan, and Khurasan, Genghis Khan ordered
his three older sons, Jochi, Chagatai, and Ögedei, to unite their
armies and to besiege Urgench, the principal city of Khwarazm,
which lay at the mouth of the Jaxartes River as it emptied into the
Aral Sea.[92] Urgench (also known as Gurganj), renowned for its silks,
was a favorite residence of Muhammad Shah. The garrison heroically defended Urgench for seven months, between October 1220
and April 1221. Jochi and Chagatai repeatedly quarreled over operations and the ultimate fate of the city so that Genghis Khan finally had to appoint Ögedei as supreme commander.[93] Jochi, who
was promised the city, wanted to capture Urgench intact, and thus
profit off its silk plantations, whereas Chagatai delighted in press-

ing the siege at all costs and punishing the city as a deliberate act of terror, and to the annoyance of his brother Jochi. Ultimately, Chagatai prevailed. During the siege, the Mongols chopped down the groves of mulberry trees, the source of nourishment for the silkworms, to construct siege engines. Finally, Ögedei diverted the Syr Darya to undermine the walls. When the Mongols burst in the city, they massacred the population. Many Mongols took sadistic pleasure by disemboweling citizens suspected of having swallowed their jewelry or pearls.[94] The city was abandoned, and the diverted Syr Darya flowed into the Caspian Sea for the next three hundred years until the course shifted again to the Aral Sea. The city never recovered; today the site is ruins. A successor city was built on a different site but this city too was abandoned when the river again changed course in the time of Tamerlane.[95]

When Genghis Khan returned to his capital Karakorum in 1225 he must have sensed his mortality and so he urged his sons to accept as Great Khan their brother Ögedei, who was the third son of Genghis Khan and Börte. The eldest brother, Jochi, for all his loyalty, could never wash away the taint of a dubious parentage. To Jochi, Genghis Khan promised the western steppes still to be conquered and destined to be called the Golden Horde. Jochi's son Batu succeeded to this realm because Jochi predeceased his father by a matter of months.[96] Second son Chagatai, notorious for his hot temper, received the central Eurasian steppes, along with the cities of the Tarim Basin and Transoxiana. He and Ögedei remained on good terms, and they died within weeks of each other. To Tolui, the youngest, went Mongolia and the sacred Orkhon valley, seat of the national *kurultai*.[97] Genghis Khan reasoned that under the amiable Ögedei the brothers, each provided with *ulus* or a nation of warriors, would cooperate and press his vision of world conquest. Genghis Khan would not have been disappointed, for he had chosen well.

20

Batu and the Devil's Horsemen

On May 31, 1223, Mstislav the Bold, Prince of Novgorod, led a coalition of the Russian princes and Kaghan Koten of the Cumans across the Kalka River against a new foe, two *tumenler* of Mongol cavalry (twenty thousand strong). This new foe drew together rival Russian princes, and Cumans, who had dominated the western steppes for the past 150 years. The Russians and Cumans had inflicted a minor defeat on the invaders on the banks of the lower Dnieper, and then crossed in force, perhaps sixty thousand strong, to chase the elusive horsemen.[1] For nine days, the Russians and Cumans pursued the Mongols, who feigned retreat across the Pontic-Caspian steppes, luring their pursuers to the banks of the Kalka, a small river in Ukraine emptying into the Sea of Azov.[2] On the morning of the battle, Mstislav ordered his Cuman allies to cross the river first, while the Russian knights and infantry followed. The Cumans fell into a classic trap. Sübetei and Jebe, the two ablest generals of Genghis Khan, attacked as the Cumans emerged from the riverbank. The Cumans turned and fled into the Russian ranks, spreading panic. Mstislav could not rally the Russians, who faced murderous volleys of Mongol arrows for the first time. The Russians raced back to their fortified camp, and Mstislav surrendered three days later. The Mongols promptly slaughtered many of their captives, although Prince Mstislav escaped.[3] Modern Russian and Soviet historians have remembered the disaster as marking the beginning of Russia's three centuries under the Tartar yoke.[4] The Medieval *Chronicle of Novgorod* lamented, "In such a way did God bring confusion upon us, and an endless number of people perished. The evil event came to pass on the day of Jeremiah the prophet, the 31st day of May. As for the Tatars, they turned back from the Dnieper, and we know neither from whence they came nor whither they have now gone. Only God knows that, because He brought them upon us for our sins."[5]

The fear of these newest Devil's horsemen quickly passed, and so the Russians and Cumans resumed their frontier wars against each other. Meanwhile, Jebe and Sübetei rejoined Genghis Khan and the main Mongol army on its return march to Karakorum. In just over two years, they had covered over five thousand miles, riding from Nishapur to Tabriz in northern Iran, crossing the Caucasus Mountains, battling their way as far west as Kiev and the Genoese colony of Kaffa in the Crimea, and finally returning east after defeating the Bulgars on the middle Volga.[6] In the course of their spectacular march, they had also twice defeated the armies of King George IV of Georgia, and a coalition of Cumans and Alans on the Kuban steppes.[7]

Genghis Khan hailed his daring generals, but he was unable to exploit their victories. Only twelve years later, in 1235, at a *kurultai* held outside of Karakorum, did the new Great Khan Ögedei authorize a campaign against the western lands.[8] Batu was to command, for he was the son of Jochi, to whom Genghis Khan had assigned the task of conquering the western lands as far as the hooves of the Mongol horses had trodden. In February 1227, Jochi had died; Genghis Khan then had died less than eight months later, in August. Six more years had passed before Ögedei permitted his nephew Batu to lead the imperial army west. There were sound strategic reasons for the delay.

At his acclamation on September 13, 1229, Ögedei at age forty-three faced daunting challenges both within the empire and on its distant frontiers. Foremost, he had a great empire to organize. His reign of twelve years proved decisive in converting Genghis Khan's conquests into the tribute-paying provinces of a well-administered empire.[9] Ögedei codified and promulgated his father's laws as the *yassa*, and he ordered the compilation of the *Secret History*. He insisted that the future khans, his son Güyük and his nephew Möngke, master writing and at least have a familiarity with the canon of Chinese texts.[10] Khans henceforth had to govern as well as conquer. Ögedei applied his genius to administration, selecting ministers with the same skill that his father possessed in choosing his generals. Ögedei took to heart the admonishment of his mandarin adviser Yelü Chucai that China, although conquered from horseback, could not be ruled from horseback.[11] He chose exceptionally loyal and able ministers for each of three great regional divisions of the empire, the Muslim lands, the caravan cities of Central Asia, and the Northern Chinese prefectures—staffed by Persians, Uyghurs, and Chinese or Khitans, respectively. Local tax farmers collected the tribute in silver, but they answered to imperial officials.[12] The silver currency was vastly extended by the issuing of paper currency backed by silver, and later, in China, by silk.[13] Fiscal demands drove economic recovery and prosperity as Ögedei's subjects had to earn hard currency to pay taxes. Simultaneously, he imposed order across the entire Eurasian steppes for the first time, a *pax Mongolica*. Trade revived and boomed along the caravan cities of the Silk Road from Tabriz to the Jade Gate, with a new extension taking caravans to the burgeoning capital of Karakorum.

Ögedei, who loved pomp and circumstance, turned Karakorum into a capital where he could preside over ceremonies that projected his universal power.[14] The city, located on the steppes in former Kerait territory, emerged as the financial center of Eurasia and an international market in every luxury. It was massively fortified with black masonry walls (hence its name naming "Black Stones"), but lacked a large agricultural hinterland so that its population had to be sustained by imported foodstuffs. The city possessed a palace, artificial lake, and gardens in the Chinese manner, and bureaucratic offices, but two-thirds of the city comprised warehouses and workplaces for the thousands of captive craftsmen who supplied the court and army.[15] The city, despite its fortifications, was always vulnerable, for Ögedei failed to heed the words of Bilğe Kaghan of the Gök Turks, if he had ever read them, that nomads must not build cities.

Ögedei even in his lifetime was criticized for being profligate and lazy, although his spending habits went a long way to stimulating the recovery of prosperity in the lands devastated by his father. So often Ögedei falls short in comparison to his father.[16] Even his portrait commissioned by Kublai Khan seems to lack the strength of character and commanding eyes of his father. In personal habits, he was a contrast to his abstentious father.[17] Ögedei was notoriously addicted to *qumis*, and his alcoholism aggravated his poor health, and contributed to his premature death. At best, he was probably a mellow, functional alcoholic. The feasting at his coronation, in contrast to that of his father, Genghis Khan, degenerated into an orgy of drunkenness for weeks. Ögedei opened the storerooms of Karakorum, indiscriminately handing out pearls, gold, and silk in acts of unrestrained generosity to his fellow Mongols without regard to merit or rank. His father rewarded the loyal and able; Ögedei bought popularity.

For all his personal failings, Ögedei proved an able khan, and he implemented the strategic vision of his father, Genghis Khan, directing the final conquests of the Xi Xia and Jin Empires. Kaifeng fell in 1234, and the reign of Jin emperors ended, but his erstwhile ally the Song emperor Lizong conveniently discarded his treaty of alliance and seized from the Mongols Kaifeng and the historic Han capitals Luoyang and Chang'an in the valley of the Yellow River.[18] In 1235, Ögedei faced a new war in China against Song emperor Lizong. Even though Ögedei never commanded in person, he entrusted expeditions to his seasoned generals and the new generation of imperial princes.[19] Foremost, Ögedei fostered cooperation within the imperial family in pursuing conquest. His obstreperous son and heir Güyük repeatedly clashed with his cousin Batu, who was senior in rank and in command of the western campaign. Their clash climaxed in an acrimonious shouting match during a victory celebration at Saray when Güyük contemptuously belittled Batu's achievements and stormed out of the event.[20] Ögedei recalled his son to Karakorum, and sternly censured Güyük, stressing that Batu alone merited the praise for the subjection of the Russian princes.

Ögedei would tolerate no rivalries within the family that threatened imperial unity. In this regard, he took to heart the warnings of his father, and again, if he could read the Turkish runes, the same warnings of Bilğe Kaghan carved on his memorial inscription of the Orkhon valley nearly five centuries earlier.[21]

In 1235, Ögedei summoned a *kurultai* near Karakorum, and raised the issue of war. Ögedei preferred to reckon with the Song, and retake Kaifeng, but Batu and Sübetei, then sixty years old, pushed for the long-delayed western expedition.[22] The Mongols knew little about Orthodox Russia or Latin Christendom other than that these were lands of cities, towns, and rich fields of grain. Immediately to their west on the Pontic-Caspian steppes, Mongols would face formidable nomadic foes the Cumans (more properly called Kipchak Turks) and the Bulgars. Ögedei relented and agreed to the western expedition, although he sent a major force against China that failed to retake Kaifeng.[23]

Ögedei assigned to Batu perhaps half of the national levy along with numerous allies, who totaled one hundred fifty thousand horsemen, and the corps of Chinese engineers.[24] The ailing Sübetei, unable to ride due to his great size, accompanied in a chariot as the senior strategist, because he knew the routes, terrain, and foes to the west. This expedition might have even exceeded Genghis Khan's campaign against Khwarazm. A train of innumerable pack animals and remounts followed Batu's horde. The rapid march of Batu's host across four thousand miles of steppes was an awesome spectacle, and reports of the Mongols' approach terrorized the Kipchak Turks, who either submitted or fled.

Batu, at age thirty, commanded perhaps the greatest Mongol expedition to date, for he was recognized as the most charismatic of Jochi's sons, all of whom deferred to their brother. In the next seven years of hard campaigning, Batu proved an indomitable general, every inch the equal of his grandfather. A decade later, the papal envoy Giovanni da Pian del Carpine, en route to the Great Khan, spent months at Batu's encampment on the lower Volga River. Friar Carpine was awed by Batu's presence, and judged the khan a shrewd and experienced warrior and the most deadly of foes who inspired devotion among his men.[25] Batu's three brothers, the eldest, Orda, and the two younger ones, Berke and Horde, accompanied. Ögedei also insisted the rising princes of the other imperial houses serve in this great expedition. His own two sons, Güyük and Kadan, Baidar, the son of Khan Chagatai, and Möngke, eldest of the four sons of Tolui, served; each would distinguish himself commanding independent columns over the next seven years. It was a testimony to Batu that he kept his brothers and cousins, each jealous of the others and eager for glory, focused on the enemy.

Given the scale of operations, from the start, Batu planned to operate in several columns that would strategically encircle and converge on an enemy. In the summer of 1236, the Mongol army swept across the western steppes between the Volga and Ural Rivers, where the Kipchak Turks submitted and joined the Mongol army.[26] In the autumn of 1236, Batu and Sübetei, with a column of thirty-five thousand veteran horsemen, crossed the middle Volga, ravaged the lands of the Bulgars, and sacked their capital. The destruction of Bulgar, the leading Muslim city on the western steppes since the early tenth century, was both a punishment and a warning to others.[27] The Bulgars arrogantly refused to submit, confident in their valor because they had defeated Sübetei's army on its return march twelve years earlier. Other Mongol columns swept across the steppes to the west and southwest. Those Kipchaks who dwelled west of the lower Don River (dubbed Polovtsians by the Russians or Cumans by the Western Europeans) fled west to seek asylum from King Bela IV of Hungary.[28] On the grasslands of the Kuban, to the southwest of the lower Volga, the Alans were overwhelmed in a single battle, and the survivors escaped into the Caucasus Mountains.[29] Within six months, Batu had subdued the entire of the western steppes, and enrolled into the imperial army numerous horsemen from his new subjects.

In the next year, 1237, Batu sent envoys to the Russian cities, demanding their submission, and refitted and drilled his army on the lower Volga River. Suddenly, in November, he launched a daring winter campaign when the frozen marshes and rivers of Russia acted as highways. Batu surprised the Russian princes, who were in comfortable winter quarters. The Mongols, however, were impervious to the cold and ready to ride their sturdy mounts that could forage beneath snow. Yuri II, Grand Prince of Vladimir-Suzdal, who aspired to a hegemony over his rival Orthodox princes, contemptuously rejected Batu's demands of submission, and he called upon his rival princes to join in a grand alliance against the heathen invaders.[30] But the jealous princes could not mobilize their armies until the next spring. Furthermore, each Russian prince would defend his own realm rather than cooperate with rival princes. For Batu, it was simply a matter of reducing cities and towns defended by wooden stockades. The Mongols employed captives to construct fosse and palisade to cut off a town. The Chinese engineers then bombarded the town walls by launching from mangonels or trebuchets incendiaries of fire lances or iron grenades; within days, the city was ablaze.[31] Engineers and craftsmen in the khan's employ had also altered the formula of black gunpowder to ignite in a single explosion. Assorted metal projectiles were propelled by black gunpowder fired from iron tubes; many were operated by a single man.[32] The noise and smoke demoralized the defenders, whose own artillery lacked the range to return fire. Therefore, the Mongols timed their final assault during the height of confusion, and so captured and sacked a city at little cost to themselves. Batu could repeat this pattern of attack across Russia for the next three years. Batu opened his Russian campaign in December 1237, when he laid siege to Ryazan, a leading city of central Russia on the Oka River.[33] Prince Yuri, who coveted the city, sent no help—a selfish act all too common among the Russian princes. Within five days, Chinese engineers and captive laborers ringed Ryazan with siege works. Ryazan's wooden walls were set ablaze by incendiaries hurled by Batu's artillery. On December 21, 1237, the Mongols stormed into Ryazan, massacred the population, and burned the city to the ground. The ferocity and speed of the destruction of this venerable city stunned the Russian princes.[34]

Batu and Sübetei, whose scouts covered great distances quickly, had accurate reports as to the state of the defenses of Russian towns and the whereabouts of Russian armies. In the winter months of early 1238, Batu swept north to capture and sack Moscow, then a minor city, but on the strategic nexus of Russia's waterways.[35] The city of Vladimir, then the greatest of the Russian cities, was their next objective. Prince Yuri II and his army were outmaneuvered, defeated in detail, and driven into Vladimir. On February 8, 1238, the last day of Lent, Batu's sappers breached the walls of Vladimir. The Mongols poured into the city, reduced it to ashes, and slaughtered the population.[36] Yuri II escaped the massacre and raised a new army, but on March 4, 1238, Yuri and his army were annihilated at the Battle of the Sit River.[37]

Batu then divided his army into columns, each of two or three *tumenler* (twenty thousand to thirty thousand men strong) so that the Mongols sacked fourteen major Russian cities over the next two years.[38] Only Novgorod and Pskov in the far northwest escaped destruction because an early spring thaw turned dirt roads into rivers of mud. The fighting climaxed in the winter campaign of 1240, when Batu targeted the last serious foe, Prince Danylo of Halych, known by his Western contemporaries as Daniel of Galicia, who ruled the cities of Kiev, Chernigov, and Pereyaslav.[39] In November 1240, Batu opened another one of his winter campaigns by laying siege to Kiev, mother of Russian cities and home to the holiest icons and churches of Orthodox Russia. The garrison of one thousand men, commanded by *voivode* of Dmytro, a vassal of Prince Danylo, refused to surrender, even though he could expect no assistance.[40] Meanwhile, Prince Danylo appealed in vain for help from King Bela IV of Hungary. On November 28, Batu positioned his artillery against the walls of Kiev, and then on December 6, 1240, the Mongols breached the walls and stormed the city. The garrison and population, numbered at fifty thousand, were slaughtered; only two thousand escaped the carnage. Remarkably, the *voivode* of Dmytro, who was wounded in the final fighting, was spared for his bravery. Kiev's nobles, however, were executed by the customary trampling by the hooves of Mongol horses.[41] The capture of Kiev was far more a symbolic than a strategic victory because the destruction of so renowned a city sent a wave of terror across Christendom. Kiev's beautiful churches were famous among all Christians, and the city's princely and noble houses were long linked by marriage to all the courts of Christian Europe.

Across Russia, organized resistance simply collapsed. Everywhere, the Mongols were free to range widely over the countryside, burning villages and sown fields, and enslaving tens of thousands of peasants. Terrified refugees fled west into Poland and Hungary, spreading tales of Mongol atrocities.[42] To the Russians, the savage horsemen must be Ishmaelites, the unclean descendants of Ishmael, the son of Abraham and his Egyptian concubine Hagar. Since the seventh century, Orthodox writers accepted as truth the apocalyptic sermon of Pseudo-Methodius, a mystic writing in Syriac, who identified the Ishmaelites as Jews, Arabs, and Scythians.[43] As these tales of horror raced across Western Europe, they became ever more frightening with each retelling. The Mongols ceased to be viewed as the soldiers of Prester John; instead they must be the children of Gog and Magog heralding the end of days. By the time these rumors reached the shores of England, the chronicler Matthew Paris, comfortable at his desk in Saint Albans Abbey, misconstrued the tribal name Tatars as Tartars and applied it to all Mongols, whom he turned into creatures of Tartarus, Classical hell, and so the Devil's horsemen.[44] The name has stuck ever since.

In just four years, Batu had conquered the principalities of Orthodox Russia, and for the next three centuries, Russian princes saluted Batu and his heirs as Tsar, the Slavic for Caesar, and so the secular lord of the Orthodox world. Batu significantly contributed to forging the future ideology and institutions of autocratic Russia.[45] The Russian princes, long in awe of the power of the Tartar Khan at Saray, fused Mongol ritual and institutions to those of their Byzantine heritage. Batu also unwittingly shifted the political axis from Kiev to Moscow. The Grand Princes of Muscovy steadily extended their political influence because they dutifully acted as the revenue agents who collected and delivered the tribute that the Russians owed to Batu's heirs.[46] Repeated failure to shake off the Mongol hegemony in the fourteenth and fifteenth centuries sharpened Russian hatred of any foreign rule. It took the military revolution in Europe of the sixteenth century to alter the balance of power between Tartar Khans and Moscow's Grand Princes. Ivan IV, the Terrible (1547–1575), who first assumed the title Tsar, initiated a Russian tradition that has endured to this day, namely the mastering and improving of the newest military technology.[47] Ivan adopted the most current European artillery and handheld firearms so that his army could batter down the city walls and check the nomadic cavalry charge. His conquest of the middle and lower Volga signaled a new power on the march across the steppes: imperial Russia. With the fall of Kazan in 1552 and Astrakhan in 1556, Ivan IV ended the slave markets that had supplied Islamic regimes with mamluks. Tsar Ivan IV and his heirs were determined to end the nomadic threat forever.[48] They directed the most successful of European expansions overland, across the forests and steppes of Eurasia, while the maritime European powers expanded across the oceans of the world.[49] Russia's rulers never forgot nor forgave the Mongols, who alone hold the honor of conquering Russia. None of the Western invaders since—the Poles, Swedes, French, or Germans—have overcome the autocratic Russian regimes forged in response to the Mongols.

With the capture of Kiev, Batu had secured the Pontic-Caspian steppes, subjected the Russian principalities, and reigned as the unchallenged Khan of the western steppes. Batu, however, immediately set out to carry Mongol arms into the unknown lands of Latin Christendom and so to reach the western shores of the great ocean that encircled the world. Batu seized on several pretexts for his invasion of Central Europe, foremost the reception of fugitive Cumans (deemed rebellious subjects) and the murder of Mongol envoys by King Bela IV of Hungary.[50]

While the monarchs of Western Europe failed to heed the warnings about the Mongols, Batu and Sübetei meticulously collected information from spies, captives, and merchants about the situation to the west. They planned a coordinated two-pronged attack against Poland and Hungary during the early winter months of 1241, just weeks after their capture of Kiev.[51] Batu commanded the main army that formed the southern column with Hungary as its objective. Sübetei commanded the northern column of two *tumenler* (twenty thousand horsemen) with the strategic mission to invade Galicia and distract the German and Polish princes from coming to the aid of the main foe, King Bela IV of Hungary. Batu's older brother Orda, and Baidar, son of Khan Chagatai, each commanded one of the *tumenler*. In early February 1240, Sübetei crossed the frozen Vistula, and divided his army into two raiding columns that devastated southern Poland and southeastern Silesia.[52] At the Battle of Chmielnik, on March 18, 1241, Prince Baidar crushed the army of Duke Boleslav V of Cracow, "the Chaste," who was the brother-in-law of King Bela IV.[53] No sooner was the battle joined than Duke Boleslav fled the field, thereby panicking the rest of his army, which was slaughtered by the Mongols. Cracow was abandoned; the Mongols burned the empty city on March 24, 1241.[54] Refugees streamed west, spreading yet more stories of Mongol atrocities. Henry II, "the Pious," Duke of Silesia (1238–1241), hastily rallied Polish princes and the Teutonic Knights to defend his realm. The impatient duke, however, blundered into risking battle before the arrival of the army of his brother-in-law, King Wenceslaus I of Bohemia, which was perhaps a day's march away. On the plains of Liegnitz (modern Legnica), April 9, 1241, Orda Khan, commanding ten thousand Mongols, encircled and annihilated an army of twenty thousand Germans, Poles, and Teutonic Knights.[55]

Prince Henry was slain in the rout. The Mongols brandished his head atop a spear before the walls of Liegnitz and Breslau, to the horror of the defenders. The carnage on the field of Liegnitz was frightening; Western chroniclers report that Sübetei carted off nine sacks of ears taken from the slain.[56] Sübetei had accomplished his mission brilliantly, for his northern column defeated two armies that would have joined King Bela in Hungary. Immediately after their victory at Liegnitz, Sübetei and Orda withdrew south, crossed the Mehadia Pass, and joined the other three Mongol columns commanded by Batu, Baidar, and Güyük that were converging on Hungary.[57]

Batu had executed a masterful strategy whereby he denied Bela IV reinforcements from neighboring monarchs, and compelled the Hungarian king to abandon the grasslands of Transylvania. Bela was forced to make a stand on the western banks of the Tisza (or Theiss) River, some one hundred miles east of his capital, Buda. On April 10, 1241, Batu reunited his four columns on the east bank of the river Mohi or Sajo, a tributary of the Tisza River, and just opposite the camp of King Bela.[58] The two armies were evenly matched. Medieval chroniclers report eighty thousand Hungarians faced seventy thousand Mongols, although many modern scholars would reduce the numbers by half or two-thirds.

King Bela had summoned his kingdom's feudal levy, and he had confidence in his knights and crossbow men even though none of them had experience fighting nomadic cavalry. Bela, suspicious of the loyalty of his Cuman allies, had treacherously ordered them slain, thereby foolishly depriving his army of the light cavalry who could have matched the Mongols.[59] Batu had every reason to be confident of victory, and concealed most of his army from Bela's view so that the Hungarian king was unsure of Mongol strength and intentions. Five miles upstream from the camps was a bridge over the Sajo River; Bela ordered Prince Kalman of Slavonia with a company of crossbow men to secure the bridge on the evening of April 10, 1241.[60] In the darkness, the Hungarians surprised a Mongol detachment guarding the bridge, and the crossbow men drove off the Mongols. Kalman then withdrew his main force, unaware that a major Mongol column was advancing to cross the bridge at dawn. Batu, upon learning of the defeat, ordered his cavalry to ford on either side of the bridge, while he deployed his artillery to drive the Hungarian crossbow men off the bridge. The Mongols attacked soon after dawn on April 11, 1241.[61] They seized the bridge, and then marched swiftly to surprise the Hungarian army in camp, which was ringed by a laager of wagons. King Bela hastily ordered his army to meet the Mongols, but the Hungarians were quickly outflanked and driven back into their camp.[62] Bela and his knights fought valiantly and inflicted heavy casualties on those Mongols who dared to risk close-order fighting. But the Hungarian infantry soon broke and ran. Many fugitives were blocked by the laager and fell in the camp; those who broke free were hunted down and slaughtered by pursuing Mongol horsemen. When Bela ordered his knights to withdraw, they too became entangled in the laager and fell fighting in the camp.[63] The carnage was dreadful. Hungarians of all ranks fell in great numbers, and the kingdom's military power was broken for a generation, but Mongol losses too were heavy.[64]

Bela lost the battle of Mohi strategically when he failed to secure the bridge over the Sajo River. Tactically, the feudal levies of the Hungarians were completely outclassed by the veteran cavalry of the

Mongol Empire. Bela lacked the disciplined infantry who could support his knights in a formation comparable to those recommended by Maurice Tiberius against the Avars or Li Jin against the Gök Turks. King Bela miraculously escaped from the confused fighting in the camp. He fled to Pest, thence to the court of Duke Frederick II of Austria, and finally to Zagreb on the Dalmatian coast.[65] He wrote letters, imploring the Holy Roman Emperor Frederick II and Pope Gregory IX for reinforcements, especially crossbow men, who alone could repel a Mongol charge.[66] Meanwhile, in the Hungarian camp, Batu seized the royal seals found on the body of Bela's chancellor. Batu thereupon issued bogus decrees ordering peasants not to flee, but to remain in their villages.[67] Throughout the summer, the unopposed Mongols ravaged the kingdoms of Hungary, Croatia, Serbia, and Bulgaria, rounding up thousands of captives, who were deported to Mongolia. Then, suddenly, by the end of summer, Batu withdrew east to his encampment at Saray on the lower Volga.[68] The threat to Latin Christendom had suddenly passed. His cavalry horses had consumed the fodder of the Hungarian plains, and reconnaissance detachments that had reached as far as Vienna and the Dalmatian coastal towns reported a dearth of pastures to sustain the army.[69] In a tactical sense, Batu had achieved his immediate mission of punishing Bela for his alleged murders of Mongol envoys and his asylum granted to Cuman refugees. Yet the scale of Batu's operation points to a far greater strategic objective than a punitive expedition. Logistics compelled Batu's withdrawal; politics at Karakorum turned his attention away from Christian Europe.

Christendom was spared a new Mongol onslaught due to fortuitous circumstances. On December 11, 1241, Ögedei died, a victim of his own alcoholism, although rumors of poison circulated widely.[70] Perhaps weeks later, his older brother Chagatai, khan of the central steppes, too had passed away. All the sons of Genghis Khan were now gone, and their sons, grandsons of Genghis Khan and cousins to each other, would inevitably dispute the succession to the imperial throne. Within six weeks, the unsettling news of these deaths reached Batu at his winter encampment on the Volga. Ögedei's widow, Töregene Khatun, who despised Batu, intrigued to put on the throne her son Güyük, the least favored son of the deceased Great Khan and no friend to Batu.[71] Batu postponed any plans of a new offensive in the west, and sought allies in the *kurultai* that would elect the new Great Khan. Batu could not have anticipated that the election would be held five and a half years later. Nor could he have imagined that he would never return to his homeland or campaign in Europe again. During the decade following the death of Ögedei, two succession crises brought the empire to the brink of civil war.[72] Each election put on the imperial throne a short-lived Great Khan, Güyük and Möngke. Despite plans to renew the war in the far west, each of these khans instead deployed the imperial army against far wealthier opponents, the Islamic Middle East and Song China. Latin Christendom ultimately escaped the Mongol yoke due to its strategic insignificance and poverty in the eyes of the Mongols.

Many historians have pointed out that circumstances also spared Batu from almost certain defeat if he had pushed into Central Europe in 1242. Later Western envoys sent to the Mongol court, especially Giovanni da Pian del Carpine (who doubled as a spy), boasted that Christian knights and crossbow men would prevail over Mongol horsemen.[73] Most Christians at the time were not so sanguine, and these later claims can be dismissed as special pleading. Modern scholars, with the benefit of hindsight, have often argued that the Mongols had reached the limits of their logistics and communications at the Battle of Mohi. Future conquests in Central and Western Europe were thus beyond their military capacity. The Christian monarchs and nobles of the thirteenth century had erected formidable masonry castles across Europe.[74] King John of England, for example, nearly went bankrupt building castles in Normandy, although his efforts came to naught when he lost the duchy in 1204.[75] Foremost, Batu would have faced Frederick II, Holy Roman Emperor, King of Germany, and King of the Two Sicilies (*Regno*), the greatest monarch in Christendom since Charlemagne.[76]

As to logistical obstacles and castles, Batu would have faced strategic problems no more daunting than those faced by Kublai Khan in his conquest of Song China. The Mongol imperial army would have had to recruit many local allies, expand its siege train, and reorganize its logistics to pursue a slow and methodical conquest of Central Europe and Italy. Therefore, Batu would have had to alter his strategy and the pace of conquest, and he needed the full might of the imperial army. As to Frederick II, he was indeed a worthy foe. Frederick II fielded the best army in Christendom, including numerous crossbow men, dreaded by the Mongols, and superb light cavalry of loyal Saracens (recruited from his military colony at Luceria).[77] If he could have drawn up his army in a tight formation on terrain of his own choosing, he had reasonable prospects of victory. But Frederick had far more pressing priorities. Frederick would have seen any war with the Mongols as a distraction from his prime aim of asserting his authority over the Papal States and communes of northern Italy.[78] He flatly refused assistance to Bela IV in 1241.[79] He admired Mongol discipline and tactics, and he ordered the princes and nobles of the Holy Roman Empire to evacuate the population behind walled cities, harvest and stockpile crops, and avoid open battle with the Mongols should they return the next year.[80] He planned typical defensive measures of a monarch who viewed the Mongols as marauders intent on loot and captives rather than conquest, although in later letters, Frederick expressed fears that the Mongols just might march on Rome. For Batu sent envoys to demand that Frederick submit lest the emperor risk defeat, capture, and demotion to the falconer of the Khan.[81] When Batu rode west in 1236, Frederick was warring with the Guelph communes of the Lombard League headed by Milan and supported by Pope Gregory IX and the maritime republics of Genoa, Pisa, and Venice. Frederick, who was willing to recognize papal authority in Central Italy, was determined to fight this war in northern Italy to the finish and then to reimpose imperial control over the all-too-independent communes.[82] As Batu overran the cities of Russia, Frederick won a decisive victory over the Lombard civic pikemen at Cortenuova in 1237—avenging the defeat his grandfather had suffered at the hands of the Lombards sixty years earlier at Legnano.[83] Yet Milan refused to negotiate, and Frederick could reach no accommodation with Pope Gregory IX. Instead, on February 22, 1240, Gregory led a solemn procession through the streets of Rome in supplication of Saints Peter and Paul, which climaxed in the declaration of

Frederick as a heretic and unworthy of his crowns.[84] For the first time, Gregory preached a crusade against a Christian monarch. His successor, Innocent IV, even more relentlessly pursued the political crusade that ended in the destruction of the Hohenstaufen imperial monarchy in Germany and Italy twenty-eight years later.[85] In 1242, Batu would have faced no united resistance in either Central Europe or Italy, and many German princes and Lombard communes could well have come to terms with Batu out of hatred of the Hohenstaufen emperor.

In the summer of 1241, Pope Gregory IX responded to King Bela's appeal, and proclaimed a crusade against the Mongols.[86] The project, however, languished with the death of Gregory and his short-lived successor, Celestine IV, in the autumn of the same year. For the next twenty months, the pontifical throne was vacant as Frederick intrigued to rig the election in his favor.[87] In June 1243, the newly elected Pope Innocent IV had even less desire than Frederick to direct a crusade against the Mongols. He aimed to support the Lombard communes to check Frederick in northern Italy, and he called upon the princes of Germany to rebel against the Anti-Christ Frederick.[88] In December of 1244, during the second year of his pontificate, Innocent quit Rome and relocated the Papal Curia to Lyons, under the protection of the saintly King Louis IX of France.[89] From there, he wrote letters, missives, and encyclicals to move the German princes to rebellion. He would not return to Rome until six years later, after the death of Frederick.

At a great ecumenical council that gathered at Lyons in the spring of 1245, Innocent IV addressed the Mongol threat, among many other pressing issues. He preferred diplomacy to war in dealing with the Mongols.[90] He sent the first European envoys to the Mongol court in an effort to convert the Great Khan. His Franciscan and Dominican friars carried papal letters extolling the true faith of the cross and the blessings of peace, but no reports survive of negotiations for an alliance against the Muslims. Yet, in his heart, Innocent must have nursed high hopes of converting the Great Khan and turning the Mongols into a mighty Crusader army that would smite the infidels and recapture Jerusalem for Christendom, for the third and last time. But such an alliance never came about.

21

The Mongol Sack of Baghdad

On February 13, 1258, Hulagu, grandson of Genghis Khan, and his Mongols entered the city of Baghdad in triumph. The Abbasid Caliph, al-Musta'sim Bilah, successor of the Prophet Muhammad and spiritual leader of Sunni Islam, had agreed to surrender the city on terms three days earlier.[1] But Hulagu did not honor the terms and ruthlessly sacked the city for forty days. The gentle Caliph, far more expert in pious calligraphy rather than war, had blundered into war on advice of his vizier Ibn al-Alkami.[2] On January 29, 1258, the Mongol army arrived beneath the walls and laid siege to the city. Within a week, Hulagu's Chinese and Iranian engineers breached the outer walls. On February 5, the Caliph initiated negotiations for a surrender on terms, but Hulagu, no friend of Islam, was determined to destroy the city as a deliberate act of terror. He also wanted to remove the spiritual center of Sunni Islam which he perceived as an intolerable threat to Mongol authority.[3] The Caliph was forced to witness the sack of his capital. Then he was rolled up into a carpet and trampled by the Mongol cavalry lest Mongol swords shed the blood of a ruler and offend Tengri, lord of the blue sky. Marco Polo, however, repeats a sensational, and most improbable, tale that Hulagu taunted the Caliph to feast on his gold which he had refused to spend on soldiers. Hulagu thereupon starved the Caliph to death by locking al-Musta'sim in his treasury.[4] The population of Baghdad, reportedly numbering eight hundred thousand souls, was indiscriminately slaughtered. Later accounts speak of three mounds of skulls—one of men, one of women, and one of children—piled upon the plain while the city burned.[5] Hulagu himself was a shamanist. Out of respect to his two Nestorian Christian wives, Hulagu spared the Nestorians who had sought refuge in their churches.[6] The Mongols wantonly destroyed mosques, medresses, and libraries. The Tigris River ran red with blood and black with ink. The cultural loss is incalculable because Baghdad had been the intellectual center of the Islamic world for four centuries.

The sack of Baghdad shocked the Islamic world, for Muslims everywhere trembled in terror from the reports of the ferocity and speed of the Mongol attack. Muslim chroniclers and theologians were at a loss to explain why Allah had permitted the sack; many accused the Christian residents of betraying the city and then joining in the rampage and rapine.[7] The massacre of the Muslims of Jerusalem by the Franks of the First Crusade 160 years earlier paled in comparison to the destruction of Baghdad and cruel murder of the Caliph.[8] The Mongols, not the Franks of the coast, were henceforth dreaded as the deadliest foes of Islam. Even today, many scholars consider Hulagu's invasion a catastrophe that forever changed the political and cultural axis of the Islamic world. For the Christian Europeans, who so gleefully celebrated the news of the sack of Baghdad, the equivalent would have been Batu's capture of Rome and execution of Pope Innocent IV. Significantly, Berke, the younger brother and successor of Batu as Khan of the Golden Horde, was enraged when he received the news of the sack. He threatened to march his army over the Caucasus and invade Iran to punish his cousin Hulagu. Six years earlier, Berke had embraced Islam after he had conversed with Muslim merchants in Bukhara. He henceforth allied with the Mamluk sultan against Hulagu.[9] For the first time, a Mongol khan placed his faith above family. His reaction already pointed to the eventual breakup of the Mongol

Empire, as the khans of the three western *ulus* would eventually convert to Islam and go their own way as regional rulers.[10]

Hulagu, the third son of Tolui and the Kereyid princess Sorghaghani Beki, invaded the Abbasid Caliphate as the deputy khan of his elder brother Möngke, proclaimed Great Khan seven years earlier in 1251.[11] The election of Möngke unexpectedly transferred the khanate from the house of Ögedei to the house of Tolui, the youngest of Genghis Khan's sons, who had been entrusted with the Mongol homeland and the regency that had elected Ögedei Great Khan.[12] In 1232, Tolui, after two days of binge drinking of *qumis*, staggered out his tent in a stupor and dropped dead.[13] Ögedei was delighted to seize his deceased brother's domains and warriors, and he incessantly pressured Tolui's widow, Sorghaghani Beki, to marry his repugnant son Güyük.[14] She adamantly refused, protesting the need to rear her four sons, and she nursed ever after a grudge against Ögedei for usurping her husband's heritage. Her revenge would come nineteen years later.

With the sudden death of Ögedei, his widow Töregene Khatum administered the empire as regent for the next five years, deliberately postponing the *kurultai* until she could assure an overwhelming majority to elect Güyük in 1246.[15] She and her son shared an antipathy toward Batu, whom they envied for his successes and disparaged due to his origins. Töregene halted future campaigns against Christendom lest they bring yet more distinction to Batu. She was widely believed to be plotting to have Batu poisoned.[16] Such unfounded accusations were often made against haughty queens who wielded power in their own right, but Batu took the rumors seriously. Töregene purged the court at Karakorum, and cashiered any *noyans* and generals who were not devoted to her.[17] Yet, for all her skill in intrigue, Töregene placed on the throne a son who proved an ingrate and a suspicious ruler with the personal failings of his father without his father's skills in governing.[18] Ögedei himself had always considered Güyük unfit to rule, and he had preferred as heir one of his grandsons, Shiremun.[19] To his credit, Güyük appreciated the power of ceremony. The Franciscan friar William of Rubruck, envoy of King Louis IX of France, witnessed Güyük's coronation at Karakorum on August 24, 1246. William was stunned by the opulence of the ceremonies, and the presence of thousands of envoys and rulers from across Eurasia who had trekked to Karakorum to offer obeisance to the new Great Khan.[20] Yet, after a reign of eighteen months, on April 20, 1248, the Great Khan Güyük suddenly died before he could lead an expedition against the Abbasid Caliphate. Just before his death, Güyük nearly clashed in a civil war with his cousin Batu, who had refused to attend Güyük's election and coronation.[21]

Batu, who was content to rule the western *ulus* in splendid isolation, needed powerful allies for his own protection against his implacable foes Töregene and Güyük. He soon found them among the other two imperial houses of Chagatai and Tolui. The sons of Chagatai loathed their cousin Güyük as a sybarite addicted to alcohol, but they resented even more the arbitrary power Töregene enjoyed at court. Baidar, Chagatai's second son, admired Batu as his commander and comrade in the western campaign, and Batu, in turn, praised and rewarded Baidar for his victory at Chmielnik.[22] Batu found another invaluable ally in Sorghaghani Beki, who was delighted to cooperate with Batu against the widow and son of Ögedei.

Before departing on his expedition against Baghdad, Güyük ordered his cousin Batu to journey to Karakorum and to render homage. Batu, forewarned by Sorghaghani Beki of Güyük's intention to arrest him, marched east with an escort of thirty-five thousand warriors.[23] Before the fateful meeting could take place, Güyük died under mysterious circumstances, most likely a victim of his heavy drinking. Sorghaghani Beki, with the support of Batu, outmaneuvered Güyük's widow Oghul Qaimish, and seized the regency.[24] Sorghaghani Beki, a Nestorian Christian, was an illustrious Kereyid princess and the favorite daughter-in-law of Genghis Khan. She had reared four sons—Möngke, Kublai, Hulagu, and Arigh Börke—all of whom were accomplished, intelligent men worthy of imperial rule. Sorghaghani Beki, just like Töregene, postponed the *kurultai* for nearly four years until she was assured of an overwhelming majority to elect Möngke, the fourth of the Great Khans, on July 1, 1251.[25]

Möngke, age forty-two at his accession, seemed a most promising khan, because he was circumspect, intelligent, and supported

by three able younger brothers. Yet he too was the product of the
deadly intrigue necessary to win election in the *kurultai*. Purges
inevitably followed; princes of the houses of Ögedei and Chagatai
were arrested and charged with treason when they showed up late
to offer their homage.[26] Möngke delighted in avenging his mother
against her rival, the fallen Oghul Qaimish, who was tortured, in
violation of Mongol law, and gruesomely executed after a show
trial.[27] Möngke rotated generals and *noyans* based on their loyalty,
and he planned imperial strategy based on his need to win fame and
to enrich his supporters. On his mother's advice, he had journeyed
to Saray to reward his cousin Batu with virtually unlimited powers over the Mongol West.[28] He also innovated on imperial ritual
at Karakorum to assert his legitimacy and universal lordship. The
Parisian goldsmith Guillaume de Boucher, who had been captured
at Belgrade ten years earlier, designed a gigantic bejeweled silver
tree that stood at the entrance of the palace's main hall.[29] William
of Rubruck, the Franciscan missionary at the Great Khan's court,
was amazed by the ceremonial prop. At the tree's base stood four
silver lions, each encasing a pipe, and each operated by a concealed
servant to pour *qumis*, fermented mare's milk, into a silver basin.
Within the tree's trunk, each of four pipes rose to the tree's top
and terminated as the mouth of a silver serpent, each spewing forth
a different alcoholic beverage. A silver angel atop the tree blew a
trumpet via a pipe operated by a hidden servant, whenever servants
needed to replenish the pipes with the drinks. Cupbearers scooped
up the drinks from the basins in ornate goblets, rushed to deliver
the drinks to guests, feasting in the palace, who had a direct view
of the silver tree. So Möngke hosted feasts for distinguished visitors
who were suitably awed by the spectacle. The Mongols had learned
well the power of ceremony. Four centuries earlier, the Byzantine
emperor Theophilus had equipped his throne room with similar
contraptions in gold to impress barbarian envoys from the steppes.
Möngke, the Great Khan of all the peoples who dwelled within
felt tents, now employed a similar prop to cow vassal rulers or their
envoys from the sedentary civilizations.

Möngke strove to implement his grandfather's vision of world
conquest. Within a year of his election, Möngke summoned a

kurultai which approved that the imperial army should ride against the Abbasid Caliphate and Song China.[30] Hulagu, Tolui's third son, was to command a great expedition to complete the conquest of the Islamic world. There remained much to be done in the former Khwarazmian Empire. Genghis Khan had appointed in the cities *darughachi*, officials who had acted as agents for the Gurkhan in the Muslim cities of his empire, as well as stationed Mongol garrisons.[31] The imperial Mongol army, however, departed in 1223, and the Great Khan's Muslim subjects resented pagan rule and revered as their spiritual lord either the Abbasid Caliph in Baghdad or the Grand Master of the Nizarite sectarians in his mountain fastness of Alamut. Furthermore, Jalal al-Din, the irrepressible son of Muhammad Shah, raised fresh forces in the Punjab, crossed the Hindu Kush, and raced across Iran to Hamadan in 1225. There, he rallied his Turkish servitors.[32] Jalal al-Din, although he aimed to restore Khwarazm, clashed with the Seljuk Sultan Kayqubad of Konya, the Ayyubid emirs of Syria and Iraq, and Queen Rusudan of Georgia.[33] The chaotic fighting disrupted trade along the Silk Road from Tabriz to Nishapur so that the new Great Khan Ögedei was determined to restore order. In 1230, he sent his *noyan* Chormaqan, a veteran officer of Sübetei and Batu, along with thirty thousand horsemen drawn from the allied tribes of Uyghurs, Karluks, and Turkmen from the Tarim Basin, to deal with Jalal al-Din, while a counterpart, the *noyan* Mönggerdü, was sent to defend the passes over the Hindu Kush into the Punjab.[34] Jalal al-Din, however, turned out to be more a nuisance than a threat, because the Seljuk Turks had already inflicted a decisive defeat on the Khwarazmian army before the Mongols arrived. In the next year, the Chormaqan crushed Khwarazmians near Ganja in Azerbaijan. The fugitive Jalal al-Din fled west only to be murdered ignominiously by an assassin in the pay of the Seljuk Sultan.[35] Thereupon, Chormaqan took up residence at Tabriz, and quartered his provincial field army called in Mongolian *tammachis* on the grasslands of Azerbaijan. The Mongol *noyan* in Tabriz ruled henceforth as a veritably independent viceroy over the Mongol domains in Transcaucasia and Iran for the next twenty years.

Some ten thousand unemployed Turkish mercenaries, protesting

their loyalty to the deceased Jalal al–Din, made for the grasslands
of the al-Jazirah, where they hired themselves out to the Ayyubid
emirs warring among themselves over the cities in Syria and Iraq.[36]
The Ayyubid Sultan of Egypt as–Salih Avyub redirected these rapacious Khwarazmians against Jerusalem, which his predecessor
had signed away to the Christians fifteen years earlier. On July 15,
1244, the Khwarazmians stormed the Holy City, massacred both the
garrison and the Christian population, and then retired to northern Iraq.[37] Sultan as-Salih soon after annihilated these dangerous
allies. When the news of the Khwarazmian capture of Jerusalem
reached Pope Innocent IV, he preached a new, Seventh, Crusade at
the Council of Lyons in the spring of 1245. The saintly King Louis
IX of France assumed the cross and vowed to win back Jerusalem
on the banks of the Nile. Four years later, Louis sent out his own
envoy, the Flemish Franciscan William of Rubruck, to broker an
alliance with the Great Khan against the common foe, the Ayyubid Sultan of Egypt.

Meanwhile, Chormaqan imposed order over the Muslim provinces of the Mongol Empire and ensured the predictable collection
of taxes. He died just months before his master Khan Ögedei, and
he was succeeded by his talented lieutenant Baiju, another veteran
officer of Batu. On his own initiative, Baiju exploited a civil war
within the Seljuk Sultanate of Konya, and invaded Anatolia.[38] On
June 26, 1243, Baiju crushed the army of Sultan Kay-khusraw I at
the Battle of Köse Dağ in eastern Anatolia, and then stormed the
cities of Sivas and Kayseri.[39] The sultan agreed to submit and pay
an annual tribute to the Great Khan. Baiju unknowingly determined the future of Anatolia for the next two centuries, because
under the Mongol overlordship the Seljuk Sultanate dissolved into
a bewildering array of petty warring states, the *beybeylikler*, from
which emerged a new Muslim power, the Ottomans.[40] The Ayyubid
princes of Syria and Mesopotamia followed suit and rendered submission to the Mongols. As for Baiju, a mere *noyan*, he had won the
singular distinction of breaking the power of a dangerous Muslim
foe and extending the empire's boundaries. Furthermore, Christian sovereigns hastened to protest their eternal loyalty to the Great
Khan, notably Queen Rusudan of Georgia, Emperor Manuel of

Trebizond, King Hethum of Cilician Armenia, and Prince Bohe-mond VI of Antioch.[41] To the regent, Töregene Khatum, Baiju had overstepped his authority. He was relieved and replaced by a more compliant *noyan*, Eljigidei, but the Great Khan Möngke restored Baiju to favor and his old command at Tabriz.[42] Möngke needed such experienced officers for his plans to conquer the Islamic West.

In October 1253, Hulagu, at the head of perhaps seventy-five thousand warriors and a corps of Chinese engineers, set out in the footsteps of his grandfather across three thousand miles of the Eur-asian steppes for the Jaxartes River (Syr Darya).[43] His most trusted Naiman general Kitbuka, a Nestorian Christian, with a *tumen* (ten thousand strong) had departed six months earlier, and cleared the steppes so that the main army had sufficient water and fodder.[44] Hulagu advanced slowly and deliberately. Contingents sent by Batu and his Chagataid cousins joined his army en route so that it might have totaled one hundred fifty thousand when Hulagu entered Samarkand in the autumn of 1255. Speed and strategic surprise were not essential because Hulagu's ultimate objective, Baghdad, lay one thousand five hundred miles to the southwest of the Jaxartes River. Instead, Hulagu staged a magnificent pageant of Mongol military might; rumors raced ahead of his host, awing Mongol vassals into obedience, and confounding foes.[45] On January 1, 1256, Hulagu crossed the Oxus River (Amu Darya), and quickly marched across northern Iran, receiving submissions of cities and summoning al-lies from among Christian vassals and the Seljuk Turks.

In November 1256, Hulagu and eighty thousand Mongols laid siege to Maymun-Diz, atop Mount Shatan, which was a residence of Rukn ad-Din, inspired iman and Grand Master of the Shi'ite sectarians known as the Assassins.[46] After a bombardment of ten days, Rukn ad-Din was frightened into surrendering his residence and castles, foremost the impregnable castle of Alamut, "the Eagle's Nest," nestled in the Elburz mountains south of the Caspian Sea.[47] Since the twelfth century, Grand Masters at Alamut commanded a network of spies and assassins, who were sent out as hit squads on suicide missions to remove opponents, Muslim, Christian, or Mon-gol. The assassins acquired their name from hashish, for the trainees were fed a steady diet of hashish.[48] In an intoxicated state, they were sent into shaded courtyards, and into the arms of beautiful women taught to respond to every whim. These aspiring Shi'ite martyrs easily mistook the delightful experience as a glimpse of the promised paradise, and so they gladly accepted death and entrance into paradise as the price of assassinating the foes of their Grand Master. Hulagu ordered the surrendered fortresses razed to the ground, the Assassins executed, and the library of priceless Shi'ite manuscripts torched, much to the approval of Sunni theologians.[49] The young Grand Master Rukn ad-Din, having outlived his usefulness after he had handed over all the Assassin castles, was deported to die a pitiful death at Karakorum.[50] By his destruction of the Assassins, Hulagu assured his unquestioned authority and personal security as the future Ilkhan of Iran.

Hulagu next targeted al-Musta'sim, the Abbasid Caliph of Baghdad, who ruled an inconsequential regional state in lower Iraq that was nominally a vassal of the Mongol Empire. But the Abbasid Caliph as the successor of the Prophet Muhammad alone conferred legitimacy on the numerous rulers of Sunni Islam. In March 1257, while his army was still in winter quarters in Azerbaijan, Hulagu sent from Hamadan an ultimatum to al-Musta'sim, who haughtily refused submission or negotiations.[51] The irresolute Caliph, with no sense of statecraft, listened to his manipulative Vizier Ibn al-Alkami and veteran Turkish generals who urged resistance. They convinced him that a mighty coalition of Sunni rulers would march to the rescue of Baghdad and drive the infidel Mongols back into the depths of Inner Asia. Throughout 1257, Hulagu rested and refitted his men and their horses, summoned Christian and Seljuk allies, and planned a winter campaign, thereby avoiding the scorching summer heat of Iraq. In January 1258, Hulagu suddenly descended upon Iraq. Hulagu's army advanced in two columns on either side of the Tigris River, while a secondary column of allied forces advanced from the northwest.[52] The Mongol army easily brushed aside the Caliph's Turkish cavalry, who retreated into Baghdad. Hulagu's Chinese engineers diverted the waters of the Tigris to flood the irrigated fields and undermine the city's walls.[53] On January 29, 1258, the Mongols converged on Baghdad. The Caliph al-Musta'sim immediately grasped the grim reality that his capital would soon fall, and that there was no mighty army of righteous Muslims marching to the rescue. The Caliph turned to the Catholicus Makikba, Patriarch of the Nestorian Christians resident in the city, to negotiate terms of surrender on February 5, 1258.[54] But Hulagu reneged on the terms; he sacked the city, massacred its inhabitants, and executed the Caliph. With the destruction of Baghdad, Hulagu had every reason to expect the western lands of Dar al-Islam would easily fall to Mongol arms.

In early 1259, Hulagu launched another lightning winter campaign, across the grasslands of al-Jazirah. His ultimate objective was Cairo, but Hulagu first had to subdue the quarrelsome Ayyubid emirs of Syria and the proud Christian nobles of Outremer who still held the Levantine ports after the loss of Jerusalem in 1244.[55] The number and speed of Hulagu's horsemen stunned the Muslims and Christians alike, and so later Islamic chroniclers report countless Mongol horsemen wreaking havoc in advance of the Apocalypse. Hulagu handily defeated the army of Ayybuid emir al-Kamil II, who had renounced his loyalty to the Great Khan and his intent to come to the aid of the Abbasid caliph. Hulagu then stormed and sacked the emir's capital Mayyafariqin (today in southeastern Turkey).[56] The pitiful emir was tortured, compelled to eat his own flesh, and then decapitated. Thereupon the Mongols brandished the emir's head stuck atop a lance before cities of the al-Jazirah whose inhabitants invariably surrendered.[57] Crossing the upper Euphrates, Hulagu next reckoned with the Ayyubid sultan al-Nasir Yusuf, ruler of Aleppo, Homs, and Damascus, and so master of Muslim Syria. The sultan, a Mongol vassal, repeatedly failed to render tribute or to respond to Hulagu's summons. Al-Nasir Yusuf fled his kingdom, abandoning the cities to their fates.[58] After a siege of five days, Hulagu easily took Aleppo on January 25, 1260.[59] The news of the fall of Aleppo, the seat of Ayyubid power in Syria that had defied Byzantine and Crusader armies, frightened the other Syrian cities to open their gates to the Mongols. In March, Hulagu's senior general Kitbuka, commanding a secondary column, pressed south, entering Damascus in the company of his Christian allies Prince Bohemond VI of Antioch and King Hethum of Cilician Armenia.[60] Then Kitbuka sent detachments of Mongol horsemen that

reached the walls of Gaza on the shores of the Mediterranean Sea.
The road to Cairo appeared to be open. Yet Hulagu had already
outrun his logistics, and just weeks after this capture of Aleppo,
he withdrew his army north, first to Ahlat on the northern shores
of Lake Van, and then to the grasslands of Azerbaijan.[61] The arid
terrain of the Levant during high summer provided insufficient
fodder and water for the Mongols' Eurasian horses, which might
have numbered between one-half to one million steeds. The hard
marching over dusty, rough roads ruined the hooves of many of
the mounts so that his army was exhausted by the beginning of
the summer of 1260, and in need of rest and refitting. Hulagu also
faced the daunting task of crossing the deserts of the Sinai Peninsula. No army has ever successfully invaded Egypt without a fleet
to convey provisions and water. In 1260, only the Venetian Republic possessed such a fleet, and the Republic of Saint Mark had
commercial ties with the Mamluk regime in Cairo.[62] The Christian
barons of Outremer still controlled the Levantine ports even after
the loss of Jerusalem. They were in no mood to treat with Hulagu
because the Mongols had sacked Sidon in retaliation for an ugly
clash with the Crusaders.[63] Finally, Hulagu most likely had limited
information about the Mamluk Sultan Qutuz, who would prove
the most formidable of Muslim opponents.

At Tabriz, before Hulagu could organize an invasion of Egypt in
the next year, he received the disturbing news that after the death
of his brother Great Khan Möngke on August 11, 1259, his youngest brother, Arigh Böke, had been elected Great Khan by an un-
representative *kurultai* at Karakorum.[64] Meanwhile, his brother and
best friend Kublai challenged the election, and the imperial army
declared him Great Khan on May 5, 1260. Hulagu suspended any
future operations against Cairo, and immediately sent envoys to
his brother Kublai, offering his support in the coming civil war.[65]
Hulagu, however, had every intention of resuming the campaign
against Cairo, for he had detached a force under his trusted general Kitbuka with orders to approach the Crusaders of Outremer,
who controlled the Levantine ports, and the Venetians for the fleet
needed to invade Egypt. Just like his uncle Batu fifteen years earlier, logistics compelled Hulagu to break off a victorious campaign,

but the politics of lateral succession denied him the chance to return and complete his conquest.

Hulagu had sent to Sultan Qutuz the usual ultimatum demanding capitulation, which the Mamluk sultan immediately rejected.[66] Not only was Sultan Qutuz confident in his Turkish slave soldiers, but he postured as the defender of Islam. Mamluk sultans were elected by a consortium of Kipchak generals who monopolized military power in Egypt. Young Kipchak males were enslaved and sold in the thousands by Batu and his heirs to the Venetians. Venetian ships then transported the young men to Egypt, where they were drilled into the finest of cavalry.[67] On May 2, 1250, the Turkish slave soldiers murdered their master, Sultan Al-Mu'azzam Turan-Shah, who was the last of the successors of the chivalrous Saladin.[68] They had grown impatient with the indifferent leadership of the Sultans As-Salih Ayyubid and Turan-Shah, father and son, against King Louis IX and his French Crusaders, who had captured the port of Damietta and threatened to advance on Cairo.[69] The Mamluk generals elected as sultan one of their own, Izz al-Din Aybak, who first checked the Crusaders at Mansurah, and then compelled Louis to surrender on April 5, 1260.[70] Louis ransomed his army to the tune of four hundred thousand livres tournois, equivalent to a third of the annual revenue of the French monarchy.[71] The Mamluks had scored the greatest victory ever won over the Crusaders, and they were not about to bow to the heathen Mongols.

As soon as Sultan Qutuz learned of the Mongol withdrawal, he swiftly crossed the Sinai at the head of twenty thousand horsemen in July. The Frankish nobles of Outremer met in high council at Acre and declared neutrality, for they saw no difference between a Mamluk or Mongol overlord. They did, however, offer Qutuz access to provisions and water, as well as free passage through the kingdom.[72] Undoubtedly, the Frankish nobles calculated that the Mamluks and Mongols would battle themselves to mutual destruction. Meanwhile, Kitbuka, commanding perhaps twenty thousand men, many of whom were Armenian and Georgian allies, hurried south from his base at Baalbek in the Bekaa valley to intercept the Mamluk army.[73] The two evenly matched armies clashed at the village of Ain Jalut in the Jezreel valley, in the Galilee, on

September 3, 1260.[74] Baybars, the leading emir, knew the terrain and so drew up the Mamluk army. He deployed a weak force
on rising ground, while he concealed the bulk of the Mamluk
army in the hills above. Meanwhile, Sultan Qutuz held his bodyguard in reserve. Kitbuka launched a classic Mongol attack against
Baybars's screening force, who retreated to the high ground, luring the Mongols into an ambush by the main Mamluk army. Even
so, the Mongols fought ferociously. Twice, Sultan Qutuz rallied
the Mamluks in the name of Islam, and he even removed his helmet to dispel the rumors in the ranks that he had fallen. Sultan
Qutuz won the battle by leading his bodyguard in a final, desperate counterattack that drove the Mongols off the high ground. Kitbuka fell fighting, and the Mongols, despite heavy losses, retired in
good order. The Mamluks, however, held the field and a strategic
victory. For the Muslims, the seemingly impossible had just happened. A Mongol army had been defeated. The Mamluk sultans
of Cairo were hailed the guardians of Islam.

It is still debated whether the Mamluk army could have with-
stood the full might of the Mongol army. Hulagu, just like his
uncle Batu, had to forfeit a victory due to a succession crisis, because Kitbuka commanded merely a detachment of the Mongol
army. Yet Ain Jalut proved decisive because the Mongols tacitly accepted its outcome as marking their western boundary. The Sunni
West was saved; Shi'ite Islam had been dealt a grievous blow;
the Crusaders, who were accused of praying for Mongol victory,
were compromised in the eyes of the Mamluks, who, in the next
thirty years, stormed all the remaining Crusader strongholds in the
Levant.[75] Meanwhile, the first Mongol civil war put on the throne
Kublai Khan, who had a far more ambitious plan: the conquest of
Song China. Soon after the victory at Ain Jalut, Baybars arranged
the assassination of his master and was acclaimed the new Mamluk sultan.[76] In the next year, the alleged Abbasid heir Abu'l-Qasim
Ahmad al-Mustansir, who had escaped the Mongol sack of Baghdad, arrived at Cairo. Baybars declared him Caliph and Cairo as
the new capital of Sunni Islam.[77] Baybars then braced for the return
of the Mongols, but they never came. .

22

Kublai Khan and the Unification of China

Kublai Khan was the most able and perceptive ruler among all of the descendants of Genghis Khan. He is remembered for his opulent summer palace at Shangdu, described by Marco Polo, and the Xanadu of Western literature and pop culture.[1] The Chinese to this day loathe and fear his memory because, alone of all the steppe conquerors, he invaded and ruled their Middle Kingdom. The Mongols do not particularly revere him as their national hero, either; this honor belongs to his grandfather, Genghis Khan. It is thanks to Marco Polo that the memory of Kublai Khan endures to this day, but for the wrong reason. Marco Polo cast Kublai Khan as an omnipotent, generous sovereign ruling the fabulously rich kingdom of Cathay, which was the destination of envious European travelers, merchants, and discoverers for centuries.[2] Kublai Khan instead should be remembered as the unifier of China and the architect of the political and cultural order of East Asia today. Marco Polo, among his many anecdotes about Kublai Khan, recalls Mongol banknotes printed on paper.[3] Foreign merchants arriving in Kublai's domains had to exchange their gold and silver coins for paper money. Marco Polo was amazed that these banknotes were accepted throughout Chinese markets. Polo's de-

scription matches the surviving notes. In 1260, Kublai Khan issued two different series of the banknotes. The first, backed by silk,
failed, but the second, in two separate issues and backed by silver,
succeeded. Kublai Khan devised a fiduciary currency to finance
his conquest of Song China, the construction of his two capitals,
Shangdu and Dadu, and innumerable projects to win his acceptance as the Son of Heaven by his Chinese subjects. He displayed
a talent unique among nomadic conquerors in adapting Chinese
fiscal and administrative instruments to rule and exploit his Chinese domains.[4] Even though Kublai Khan spoke at most a rough
colloquial Chinese and never mastered Chinese characters, he still
took to heart the warning of his uncle Ögedei's Confucian minister Yelü Chucai, namely that China could be won on horseback,
but it could not be ruled from horseback.[5]

The Mongol conquest of Song China was the most important
event on the globe during the thirteenth century. Kublai Khan
united China for the first time in over four centuries, and without
the unification by the Mongols, China most likely would have remained a divided land of warring realms, and so would never have
emerged as the world power it is today. In his own day, Kublai
Khan, as Great Khan and Emperor Shizu of China, must be credited with two extraordinary achievements. First, he forged a new
imperial army, recruiting Chinese infantry, expanding the corps
of engineers, and launching a fleet on the Yangtze and its tributaries that was vital for the rapid supply and movement of his army.
Mongol cavalry alone, even if accompanied by a corps of Chinese
engineers, could never have won the strategic war of sieges to break
through Song fortifications. In contrast, Batu and Hulagu, for all
their successes, waged the nomadic way of war with the imperial army forged by their grandfather Genghis Khan. Second, and
even more important, Kublai Khan also departed from his grandfather's vision of world conquest. Kublai Khan strove to win over
the Chinese of the Song Empire, who numbered perhaps fifty
million inhabitants. He forbade massacres to terrorize his foes into
surrender, and instead courted Song mandarins, generals, and soldiers to defect to his service.[6] Kublai Khan, declaring himself the
emperor Shizu, postured as the Son of Heaven come to restore the

empire of the Tang. Kublai Khan aimed for a single orderly world empire entrenched in China and ruled justly by the military caste of Mongols. To implement such a bold vision, Kublai Khan had to change the attitudes and institutions of both Mongols and Chinese.[7] Ultimately, he failed to transmit his vision either to the Mongols or to the Chinese, but his aim was daring, even noble, so much so that Marco Polo grasped the essence of Kublai's vision and cast the Mongol khan as the benevolent lord of Cathay.

At the *kurultai* summoned in 1252 to determine strategic priorities, the new Great Khan Möngke turned to his younger brother Kublai, then thirty-seven years old, to command the army that would be sent against Song China, the most formidable foe of the Mongol Empire.[8] At the same time, Hulagu was to march with the other half of the national levy against the other major foe, the caliph of Baghdad. Möngke delegated well. Kublai not only could win the war but also could win the hearts of the Chinese population. Kublai, who had never served on the western expeditions, gained his military experience in the Chinese and Korean campaigns of Ögedei. Kublai long admired Chinese political institutions and cultural achievements. For over two decades, he successfully governed a subordinate realm (best characterized as an appanage) of the northern China prefectures by employing mandarin officials.[9] He secured his realm by settling Chinese soldiers as farmers, who suppressed brigands and would-be rebels, and contributed to the restoration of prosperity. To his Chinese subjects, Kublai ruled in accordance with the Confucian virtues, the Mandate of Heaven, and the divine mission to promote the peace and welfare of his subjects.[10]

In 1253, Kublai was instructed to wage a major campaign against the Dali kingdom, which comprised the modern Chinese province of Yunnan. Since the tenth century, the monarchs of the Duan family ruled over the Bai people of Yunnan, who spoke a distinct Tibeto-Chinese tongue, but had long come under strong Chinese cultural influence.[11] The Duan monarchs acknowledged as their overlord the Song emperor, who, in turn, conferred on Duan dynasts imperial titles, silk, and Chinese princesses as brides. The Duan monarchs also sponsored as the state religion tantric Bud-

dhism since the tenth century so that they had important ties with
the great Buddhist monasteries of Tibet. If Möngke were to conquer Song China, he had to control the kingdom's capital, Dali,
and highways, which offered access to the upper reaches of the
Yangtze River.[12] For this expedition, Kublai was assigned the best
tumenler in the Mongol army, as well as numerous Chinese infantry regiments and the corps of engineers.[13] Kublai also had superb
generals in Bayan, from a distinguished Mongol clan that had long
served the family of Genghis Khan, and Uriyangkhadai, the son of
Sübetei.[14] The logistics of this expedition were daunting because
Kublai had to march his army of perhaps one hundred thousand
men over seven hundred miles south across the rugged terrain to
reach Dali on the Yunnan plateau. Kublai's officers, however, perfected the logistics to sustain Mongol cavalry operating far from
the Eurasian steppes, thereby overcoming the logistical barriers
that had checked Mongol armies in Central Europe and the Middle East. In 1253, three Mongol columns converged on the capital,
Dali, which surrendered immediately. Kublai appointed as vassal king Duan Xingzhi.[15] Uriyangkhadai was then detached with
a force to complete the pacification of the Yunnan plateau and to
secure the southern frontiers as far as Tufan and Annam (North
Vietnam) over the next three years.[16] In 1257, Möngke was ready
to move against the Song.

In October 1257, the Great Khan Möngke opened his first campaign against Song China.[17] Many must have viewed the Great Khan
as foolhardy, because the Mongols would invade the most densely
populated region on the globe, where rice paddies, canals, and cities
impeded the mobility of the Mongol cavalry. Yet he fielded ninety
thousand veteran Mongol horsemen and excellent generals, foremost his brother Kublai. Möngke restricted plundering and massacres to win over the Chinese. Even so, over the next two years,
Möngke and Kublai together waged a series of desultory sieges that
exacted a high death toll on the Mongol armies. On August 11,
1259, Möngke died of cholera while besieging Diaoyu, a supporting
fort just east of Hochwan.[18] His sudden death plunged the empire
into its fourth succession crisis, and the first Mongol civil war. The
Mongol army was stalled north of the Yangtze River when Kublai

Khan learned of the death of Möngke on September 1. He assumed that a *kurultai* would soon convene to elect him Great Khan, so he continued to press the war. He crossed the Yangtze in force, against the advice of his generals, and laid siege to the fortress of Ochou.[19] The Song court offered a treaty, along with annual payments of silk and silver, if Kublai would withdraw north of the Yangtze, but Kublai, confident of victory, rejected the terms.[20] Weeks later, in October, Kublai was surprised to learn that his younger brother Arigh Böke had rigged a hastily summoned *kurultai* at Karakorum to elect himself as Great Khan.[21] Thereupon, Kublai broke off the campaign in China and withdrew north of the Yangtze. On May 5, 1260, Kublai concentrated his army at Kaiping (destined to be his summer palace, Shangdu), and presided over his own *kurultai* that proclaimed him the Great Khan.[22] Arigh Böke claimed the legitimacy of a *kurultai* at Karakorum; Kublai, however, commanded the majority of the Mongol nation then fighting in China, even though he held the first *kurultai* outside the homeland.

Arigh Böke enjoyed the support of princes of the houses of Ögedei and Chagatai long resentful of their Toluid cousins with their haughty bearing and Chinese ways.[23] Hulagu, however, stood by Kublai and deployed his great army to Azerbaijan to check Berke, Khan of the Golden Horde, lest he declare for Arigh Böke.[24] Kublai possessed the decisive advantages of the wealth and resources of China. Kublai immediately ended trade to Karakorum so that the Mongol capital, facing starvation, welcomed Kublai as their Great Khan. In November 1261, Kublai decisively defeated Arigh Böke at Shimultai on the Chinese-Mongolian border, and he followed up with another victory ten days later on the western slopes of the Khingan Mountains.[25] By these victories, followed by a severe winter, Kublai convinced most of the princes and tribes to accept him as Great Khan. Arigh Böke fled west to his ally Alghu, the Chagataid khan whose realm on the central Eurasian steppes was known as the Blue Horde, but Alghu switched his allegiance to Kublai.[26] In 1263, Arigh Böke, deserted by his allies, surrendered himself to Kublai Khan at Kaiping. In a tearful exchange, Kublai forgave his brother, who retired into a gilded captivity and died three years later among rumors of poison.[27] In the same year, both

Khan Berke and Alghu Khan passed away. The ever-loyal Hulagu
had died the year before, and his body was accorded a spectacular
Mongol funeral, complete with human sacrifices, on Shahi Island
in Lake Urmia (today in Azerbaijan).[28] In 1266, Kublai had outlived
all his brothers and cousins, and so he reigned as the Great Khan of
all the Mongol domains for the next twenty-eight years. Yet Kublai
Khan compromised the unity of the empire, because he conceded
independence to his younger kinsmen in their domains in exchange
for acknowledging him as Great Khan. But Kublai Khan was now
free to pursue his strategic priority: the conquest of Song China.

  With the surrender of Arigh Böke, Kublai Khan opened negotiations with the Song court in the hopes of gaining by diplomacy
a formal submission and the promise of annual tribute in silk and
rice.[29] Kublai Khan wished to spare the imperial army from the ar-
duous fighting in southern China. During the civil war, the Song
army had recaptured the fortresses that the Mongols had taken in
1257–1259, but otherwise had accomplished little. It behooved the
Song court to come to terms with Kublai Khan as had their predecessors with the Khitans and Jurchens. Song China, for all its prosperity, suffered from political weakness that greatly aided Kublai
Khan. Confucian ministers controlled a vast bureaucracy and directed policy.[30] They also monopolized access to the emperor, who
was hard-pressed to obtain accurate information about the state of
the empire. Song emperors after Xiaozong (1162–1189), proved an
unimpressive lot, who lacked the will and ability to govern. Furthermore, the mandarins subordinated, distrusted, and despised
the military elite because they had not mastered the canon and so
could never be gentlemen of virtue. It is no surprise that many Song
officers defected to Kublai Khan.[31] Finally, the mandarins shared
the dream of reuniting the Middle Kingdom so that they refused
to come to terms with Kublai Khan. But the Song army, for all its
technological advantages, was not up to the task of defeating the
Mongol imperial army.

  When Kublai Khan opened negotiations, a new emperor reigned
in Hangzhou: the youthful Duzong, nephew and adopted son of
Lizong.[32] A dissipated young man, who seldom roused himself from
the pleasures of his harem, Duzong entrusted governance to his

senior mandarin officials, foremost Jia Sidao, a master of patronage and intrigue and the younger brother of the emperor Lizong's
favorite concubine.[33] Jia Sidao as chancellor was an expert in fi-
nances, reforming land tenure, taxation, and the paper currency.
He commanded widespread support among the mandarin elite and
landed classes, and he refused any terms that implied the subordi-
nation of the Song emperor to a barbarian monarch. He entrusted
the defense of the realm to professional officers who assured him
the northern frontier was impenetrable by the northern barbarian horsemen. In 1268, Kublai Khan reluctantly resumed the war
against the Song after a hiatus of seven years.

In 1268, the Song army was perhaps the most formidable ever
faced by the Mongols, for it comprised thirty thousand cavalry,
perhaps six hundred thousand infantry, and large river flotillas and
coastal fleets.[34] The Song army, while lacking experience in large-
scale military operations, was more than capable of defending the
long line of frontier fortresses north of the Yangtze. Although the
Song court had repeatedly slashed the military budgets and neglected dredging the Grand Canal, Song garrisons were well pro-
visioned with stores of rice and salted fish that could last for years.
River flotillas could run any blockade and bring reinforcements and
supplies to beleaguered garrisons. Jia Sidao thus opted for a strategy of attrition and stalemate, followed by negotiations and a treaty
similar to those granted to the Khitan and Jurchen foes.[35] Based on
centuries of dealings with nomads of the steppes, Jia Sidao calculated that there was no reason to risk the imperial army in a decisive battle. The Mongol threat might well disappear in the usual
kaleidoscopic civil wars among brothers and cousins.

Kublai Khan, however, could ill afford a war of sieges, because he
needed to deploy many of his Mongol horse archers against Kaidu
Khan, who contested the mastery of the Eurasian steppes.[36] Therefore, Kublai Khan expanded and reformed the imperial army, recruiting tens of thousands of Chinese infantry and launching river
fleets manned by his Chinese subjects and commanded by former
Song officers. Finally, Kublai Khan recruited ever more engineers,
notably Persians and Arabs, who constructed superior mangonels
and torsion trebuchets, which could hurl the Chinese explosive

shells at a far greater range and with deadly accuracy.[37] Kublai Khan thus embarked on this war as the unifier rather than the invader of the Middle Kingdom, and the composition of his imperial army matched his pretensions. Kublai Khan conquered southern China with a largely Chinese army, fighting a war very different from those waged by previous conquerors of the steppes.

In 1268, Kublai Khan reopened the war by laying siege to the twin fortress cities of Fengcheng and Xianyang on the Han River, a northern tributary of the Yangtze.[38] The cities were the keystone of a line of fortifications along the Yangtze that shielded the Song capital of Linan (modern Hangzhou). The well-provisioned fortresses defied Mongol assaults for over five years. So long as these fortresses held, the Song court refused to negotiate with Kublai Khan. Kublai entrusted operations to his best generals, Bayan, a veteran of the Dali and earlier Chinese campaigns, and the Song deserter Liu Cheng.[39] Liu Cheng proved indispensable because of his knowledge of Song military doctrines and his own expertise in naval warfare. At his direction, the Mongol army raised fortifications to blockade the twin fortress cities, and then Liu Cheng launched a massive fleet of paddle-driven ships on the Yangtze River to intercept supplies.[40] In early 1269, Kublai Khan's flotilla repelled a Chinese relief expedition in the first Mongol naval victory.[41] In the next year, Kublai Khan ordered the construction of another seven thousand ships, and this navy defeated repeated relief fleets sent by the Song court over the next three years. In December 1272, Kublai Khan finally broke the stalemate when the Persian engineers Ismail and Ala al-Din arrived, compliments of his nephew the Ilkhan Abaqa. The Muslim engineers constructed state-of-the-art mangonels and trebuchets. After a relentless bombardment of several days, the artillery breached the walls of Fengcheng.[42] The Mongols stormed into the city and, out of frustration and fear (and almost certainly in violation of Kublai Khan's orders), massacred the garrison and population. In January 1273, Bayan concentrated on the fortress Xianyang next. The Song general Lü Wenhuan held out for two months in the hopes of reinforcements that never arrived. He surrendered Xianyang on terms on March 2, 1273, and so avoided a massacre of the population.[43] With the fall of Xianyang, Kublai Khan entrusted the war to Bayan, and returned to his capital, Dadu, to order his new realm. The war was all but won. Jia Sidao desperately tried to negotiate, but Kublai Khan refused any terms except unconditional surrender.[44] The Mongol cavalry under Bayan, once through the network of fortresses, regained strategic mobility. In 1274–1275, the Mongol armies under Bayan overran southern China, secured the Grand Canal, and occupied the ports, thereby cutting off the Song capital, Linan.[45] Numerous mandarin officials and generals surrendered and entered the service of the Great Khan. On August 12, 1274, the premature death of the emperor Duzong, a victim of his own excesses, plunged the dynasty into a succession crisis. The grand empress dowager Xie immediately put on the throne her four-year-old grandson, Gong. Jia Sidao was blamed for the defeat; he had alienated many at court for his failure to negotiate a truce or to defeat the Mongol army on the battlefield. He was arrested, stripped of office, banished, and finally quietly executed.[46] Although Jia Sidao proved incompetent as a general, he had conducted bold fiscal and land reforms that had financed the cost of defense. On January 18, 1276, the grand empress dowager Xie and her grandson the emperor Gong entered the camp of Bayan outside Linan and surrendered.[47] Kublai Khan generously received the young emperor at Dadu and pensioned him off as the Duke of Ying.[48] Song loyalists under the chief minister Lu Xiufu fled south and organized resistance. On March 19, 1279, Lu Xiufu and the last of the Song loyalists were defeated at the naval Battle of Yamen.[49] Lu Xiufu, realizing the battle was lost, took up the last Song boy emperor, Huizong, and leaped into the sea at the mouth of the Xi River in Guangdong. Kublai Khan was now the undisputed emperor of China.

Yet Kublai Khan was not satisfied with ruling the Middle Kingdom. In the later years of his reign, Kublai Khan suffered a number of humiliating defeats that shattered the aura of Mongol invincibility, because he imbibed too deeply the heady brew of Tang imperial claims. He aimed to extend his Mandate of Heaven over all the neighboring peoples who dwelled across the East China Sea on the islands of Japan and in Southeast Asia. He must have also had confidence that, if he could create an imperial army capable of conquering southern China, he should be able to launch fleets that could land Mongol armies in Japan or Java. In this endeavor, Kublai Khan failed, because his Korean and southern Chinese subjects could not construct seaworthy transports and warships.[50] They were ungainly, too long, and prone to capsize in the slightest of rough weather. In contrast, the cities of the Hanseatic League in the thirteenth century launched cogs that regularly sailed the stormy North Atlantic to Iceland or Greenland.[51]

In 1273, Kublai Khan imposed his control over Korea, and dispatched Chinese officials to conduct a census and to assess taxes.[52] Kublai Khan secured Korea as the base for constructing a fleet for an invasion of Japan. He seized as a pretext for war the murder of Mongol envoys who had demanded submission and tribute from the Shogun Hojo Tokimune.[53] Kublai Khan also wished to assert the pretenses of Tang emperors as overlords of Japan long perceived as a wealthy prize. Since the seventh century, Japanese craftsmen forged the finest steel weapons of Asia, and the islands were renowned for their bounty of silk, rice, and fish.[54] In 1274, the Koreans duly launched a fleet of eight hundred vessels, including numerous horse transports, which were barely seaworthy for the crossing of 110 miles to the Japanese home island of Kyushu. The expedition numbered fifteen thousand Mongol, Jurchen, and Chinese soldiers, along with eight thousand Korean auxiliaries and seven thousand Korean sailors.[55] In November 1274, the expedition sailed from Korean ports to the islands of Tsushima and Iki and then landed at Hakata, the main port of the bay of the same name on the eastern shore of Kyushu.[56] The Mongol cavalry, supported by artillery, easily repelled the Samurai warriors who fought as individual swordsmen on foot on November 19, 1274. In the evening, a violent storm arose, and the Koreans persuaded the Mongols to embark on the ships to ride out the storm, but the fleet failed to reach the open waters in time. Several hundred vessels were smashed against the rocky shores of Hakata Bay, and at least thirteen thousand soldiers and sailors drowned.[57] Perhaps nearly 45 percent of the expedition did not return. When the surviving ships reached Korea, the dismayed Kublai Khan was determined to avenge his first defeat ever. But he was too preoccupied with his war against the Song to commit the money, manpower, and matériel for a second naval expedition.

As soon as the dowager empress Xie and her five-year-old grandson, the emperor Gong, submitted, Kublai Khan ordered the construction of a fleet in the Korean and southern ports of China. Seven years after the first expedition, in 1281, Kublai Khan launched another naval expedition totaling one hundred forty thousand men in a two-pronged invasion of Kyushu.[58]

A smaller fleet set sail from Korean ports; this expedition totaled forty thousand sailors and soldiers. The second expedition, reported as comprising one hundred thousand Chinese soldiers and sailors under the Song general Fan Wenhu, was scheduled to depart from the Chinese ports of Quanzhou and Suzhou and to rendezvous with the smaller expedition at Hakata on the island of Kyushu. Unknown to Kublai Khan, the Shogun Hojo Tokimune had strengthened the defenses of Hakata by constructing a wall around the entire bay.[59] The expedition from the Korean ports set sail first, and landed at Munakata, just to the north of the bay of Hakata, on June 24, 1281. The larger expedition under Fan Wenhu, which had suffered repeated delays due to logistical problems, arrived weeks later at the southern end of Hakata Bay.[60] The Japanese samurai held the fortifications between the two Mongol camps, and Fan Wenhu failed to fight his way to Munakata. Once again, the Mongols embarked upon their ships but failed to reach open waters to ride out a typhoon on the evening of April 15–16, 1281.[61] The Divine Wind, Kamikaze, dashed the invaders' ships against the shores. The losses in ships and men were staggering; one-third of the northern force and one-half of the southern force were lost at sea. Overall Mongol losses were light, because Koreans, Jurchens, and Chinese comprised the overwhelming majority of soldiers and sailors. Kublai Khan, however, could ill afford the setback, for he had lost face in the eyes of his Korean and Chinese subjects, who had paid the heavy costs of defeat in money and blood. Undeterred, Kublai Khan ordered a third expedition, but his ministers convinced him to abort the operation.[62] Kublai Khan had simply overreached the logistical, fiscal, and military capacity of his empire. The two defeats ended hopes of Mongol sea power.

For the Japanese, the gods had sent the Kamikaze, the divine wind
that promised to protect Japan as inviolate forever—a conviction
held by the Japanese down to 1945.

In Southeast Asia, Kublai Khan again aimed to extend his sway
over lands that Han and Tang emperors had once claimed as tributary provinces. In part, Kublai Khan was lured by the Tang imperial
pretenses to pursue these ill-advised wars, but also, Kublai Khan
declined markedly in his health and mental faculties after the death
of his beloved principal wife and empress, Chabi, in 1281.[63] She
had exercised a much-needed restraint on her husband, whose im-
pulsive actions and outbursts of anger led to poor decisions. Kublai,
who always enjoyed feasting, indulged himself in drink and food.
He gained so much weight that he could no longer ride, but he
was conveyed on a dais atop a team of elephants.[64] He was afflicted
by gout and rheumatism, and seldom held audiences, preferring
to communicate his decisions through his wife Nambui, a distant
relative of Chabi who succeeded to the role of first consort.[65] He
suffered yet more grievous blows with the death of his son and heir
Zhenjin in 1285, and the passing of many of his senior ministers.[66]
For the thirteenth century, Kublai Khan at age seventy-eight had
simply lived far too long, and he overreached his own capacity and
that of his empire by waging wars in Southeast Asia.

Furthermore, Kublai Khan's army was not up to the task of hack-
ing through and fighting in the humid jungles of Burma, Annam
(today northern Vietnam), Champa (southern Vietnam), or Java.
Roads were few and constantly in need of repair. Foremost, Southeast Asia lacked the network of canals so vital for Mongol logistics in China. The dense jungles negated the use of cavalry, and
the Mongol composite bows, because the bowstrings lost tension
due to the perpetual humidity. Campaigning during the monsoons was impossible, but even during the rest of the year, soldiers
were plagued by diseases, lack of potable water, and the relentless,
sweltering humidity. Mongols and Chinese alike must have been
unnerved by the sudden and complete darkness of the jungle with
the onset of night.[67] Finally, they confronted war elephants. Marco
Polo, while on his first fact-finding mission for Kublai Khan, questioned participants in the ferocious frontier battle between Kub-

lai Khan's soldiers and the Burmese under King Narathihapate of Pagan in 1277. He reports how the Mongol horses were terrified by the scent of two thousand war elephants.[68] The Mongols withdrew to the line of the jungle, dismounted, and halted the attacking elephants by releasing a hail of arrows along with missiles launched by the field artillery. In three costly wars waged over the decade of 1277–1287, Mongol armies toppled the kingdom of Pagan, but failed to impose control over northern Burma.[69] Farther east during the same period, Kublai Khan waged three unsuccessful campaigns to subject Annam and Champa.[70] Perhaps the most costly fiasco was the naval expedition Kublai Khan ordered in 1292–1293 against King Kertanegara of Singhasari on the island of Java.[71] Kertanegara had refused to render tribute to Kublai Khan, and he had allegedly mutilated Mongol envoys. The Mongol expedition suffered from a divided command and the lack of a clear strategic objective. Upon their return to the Mongol court at Dadu, two of the three commanders, Shi-bi and Ike Mese, suffered the lash or public reprimand, respectively, along with the loss of one-third of their property. The third, Gaoxing, who had urged caution throughout the campaign, was spared and rewarded for saving the survivors.[72] Yet the ailing Kublai Khan knew that he alone was ultimately at fault for the ill-advised expedition, so he later restored his disgraced generals to favor. Raden Wijaya, a Javanese prince of Singhasari, had simply outwitted and outfought the Mongols.[73] He initially allied with the Mongols to dispose of his rival, and then he turned on his allies and overran the Mongol camp in a surprise attack. The survivors escaped to their ships and set sail for the port of Quanzhou in southern China. The Mongol fleet suffered further losses at sea due to Javanese attacks and storms, but it reached Quanzhou in June 1293, from which it had departed seven months earlier.[74] Out of an expedition of thirty thousand men and one thousand ships, nearly two-thirds were lost. Fortunately, Kublai Khan died before he could launch a second Javanese expedition. The defeats in Southeast Asia, just like those in Japan, marked not only the limits of Kublai Khan's rule, but also those of China down to this day.[75]

In 1274, Marco Polo was presented by his own father and uncle to the Mongol court when Kublai was at the pinnacle of his career. By then, Kublai Khan ruled in two capacities as both Great Khan of the Mongols and Chinese emperor under the throne name Shizu, first of the Yuan dynasty. During a reign of nearly thirty-five years, Kublai Khan juggled these two roles. His successes and failures as Great Khan and Chinese emperor mark him as the leading world figure of the thirteenth century who forever changed the course of history. In each capacity, Kublai Khan faced stiff opposition.

Although Kublai Khan won the Mongol civil war, he only ruled effectively the Mongolian homeland and China, because his younger kinsmen reigned in their domains as independent rulers in all but name. Each of the other khans pledged an ill-defined loyalty to Kublai as Great Khan, who, in return, invested them with titles, gifts, and sovereignty over their *ulus*. Over the course of the fourteenth century, the later rulers of these Mongol realms would inevitably part ways with the heirs of Kublai Khan. Mengu-Timur, the grandson of Batu, had supported Arigh Böke, but upon his accession as Khan of the Golden Horde in 1266, he renewed his loyalty to Kublai Khan. Mengu-Timur thereafter was free to wage campaigns in Central Europe on his own initiative and to tax the lucrative slave trade bound for Kaffa and Tana, at the ports of the Genoese and Venetians, respectively.[76] Abaqa, Ilkhan of Iran and son of Hulagu, always stayed on excellent terms with his uncle Kublai Khan.[77] The courts of Dadu and Tabriz exchanged polite embassies of goodwill and shared breakthroughs in military technology, medicine, astronomy, and geography, as well as spices and improvements in daily life and diet.[78] Abaqa's heirs maintained these close ties down to the end of the dynasty in the mid-fourteenth century. On the central Eurasian steppes, Kublai Khan faced a resolute foe who contested Kublai's lordship over the Mongol nation: Kaidu Khan, the grandson of Ögedei, and his legendary daughter, the warrior princess Khutulun.[79] Kaidu refused to journey to Karakorum to bow in obedience to Kublai Khan. Kaidu aimed to restore the house of Ögedei to its rightful place as the senior one among the descendants of Genghis Khan. He waged a traditional war of raids across the Eurasian steppes and northern Transoxiana against any who supported Kublai Khan. At one point, he even threatened to capture Karakorum and the sacred heartland of Mongolia. Father and daughter were warriors who sought loot, captives, or tribute to exalt their fame and to enrich their followers. Therefore, they championed the nomadic way of life and opposed the autocratic khan in Dadu, who ruled in the manner of a Chinese emperor. Kaidu never relented, and he died in 1301, seven years after Kublai's death. His daughter Khutulun, who would have pressed her father's cause, was denied the khanate by her jealous, less valorous brothers.[80] They made their peace with Temür Khan, the grandson and heir of Kublai. Yet throughout his reign, Kublai was compelled to defend the Mongolian homeland, and he had to devise imperial policies carefully lest he alienate his Mongol subjects suspicious of their khan who favored Chinese ways.

As emperor of China, Kublai Khan learned invaluable lessons on how to turn his personal rule into a hereditary monarchy backed by an imperial army and bureaucracy that could assure an orderly transfer of power from one generation to the next. Kublai had witnessed the fundamental weakness that plagued the Mongol Empire with repeated succession crises and a civil war. Simply put, only the *kurultai* of the Mongol nation could elect the Great Khan. But any elections risked a civil war among brothers or cousins, each basing his claim to the throne on the principles of lateral succession. Such had been the fate of every nomadic confederacy since the Xiongnu. Kublai Khan wanted to impose hereditary succession, but he had to move cautiously lest he be perceived by the Mongols as an aspiring Chinese autocrat who had deserted the traditional mores of the steppes.[81] Throughout his long reign, Kublai always paid homage to this Mongol heritage whenever he was adapting Chinese institutions or courting his Chinese subjects. He ultimately aimed to transform the Mongols into an imperial military caste, committed to maintaining and governing the empire and his rule over sixty million Chinese subjects.[82]

Kublai Khan needed legitimacy in the eyes of his Chinese subjects, but Chinese accounts prefer to give undue credit to the Daoist recluse and sage Liu Bingzhong for advising Kublai on what policies to pursue.[83] Yet in many cases, Liu Bingzhong easily convinced a Mongol ruler who had already made up his mind. Hence, Liu Bingzhong is credited with suggesting to Kublai that he adopt the

name Da Yuan, "the Great Originators," for his new imperial family.[84] The name referred to the crucial Confucian text *Yijing* (*The
Book of Changes*), specifically the passage *da zai qian yuan*, "Great is
the heavenly and primal." Kublai Khan coupled the words *Da* (*great*)
with *Yuan* (*primal* or *origin*) to coin the name in Chinese "The Great
Originators." This name linked the foreign emperors of the Yuan to
the *qian* (Heaven) of that passage, making them literally "the Sons
of Heaven." Hence, the name was impeccably Chinese so that the
Mongol khan appeared to be accepting Chinese values and culture
even though he did so on his own terms. Henceforth, Kublai Khan
reigned under the Chinese throne Shizu, and he groomed his heir,
Zhenjin, the son of his principal wife and confidante, Chabi, as the
next emperor of China. Zhenjin was entrusted to mandarin tutors,
who inculcated in him the Confucian virtues expected of the Son
of Heaven.[85] The Mongol prince, while trained in the art of war,
also had to master Chinese characters and the canon of Confucian
classics so that he could converse and socialize with his mandarin
ministers and bureaucrats. Kublai was heartbroken when Zhenjin
predeceased his father by eight years. Kublai declared his son the
posthumous Chinese emperor Wenhui Mingxiao, and he ordered
the appropriate memorial temple tablets for his son to be commissioned in the Chinese fashion.[86] Kublai then hastily promoted his
grandson Temür Khan, then a young man of twenty-one, to succeed as the next Chinese emperor Chengzong.[87] In each case, Kublai dictated his choice of heir to the *kurultai* to establish a precedent
of strict hereditary succession to the khanate.

Kublai also appreciated his need for Chinese-style capitals if he
were to govern the Han peoples as their emperor. Kublai never ruled
from a single capital, for he, like all previous Mongol khans, toured
his empire in a series of royal progresses. Instead of moving among
Mongol encampments, he traveled between great Chinese-style
cities. In 1252, while prince of the northern Chinese prefectures,
Kublai, reportedly on the advice of Liu Bingzhong, transformed
Kaiping, located in Inner Mongolia, into his summer residence,
Shangdu, the Xanadu of Western poets and novelists.[88] Marco Polo,
who visited the city in 1275, marveled at the lake, woodlands, and
pastures stocked with exotic game and fish. The inner, or "forbid-

den," city of Shangdu was a paradise in the original sense of the Greek because it is comparable to similar complexes of palaces and hunting grounds of the Great King of Persia.[89] Behind the walls of the inner city of Shangdu, members of the imperial family lived as a *yurt*, surrounded by the wagon homes (*gers*), where males learned the bow and the horse, and females the domestic skills necessary to survive on the steppes. Even within the Chinese-style city of Shangdu, the Mongol imperial family learned the ways of their steppe homeland. In 1266, two years after winning the civil war, Kublai Khan ordered the construction of a second, even more impressive, Chinese-style capital, called Khanbaliq ("Khan's capital") by the Mongols and Dadu ("Great City") by the Chinese.[90] Dadu was constructed on the site of Zhongdu, the former central capital of the Jin Empire that Genghis Khan had razed to the ground nearly twenty years earlier. At the center of its "forbidden city" was the enchanting Lake Taiye, the grandiose imperial palace and many lesser ones, and sprawling parks and hunting grounds. Dadu, although its buildings possessed many decorative elements from Eastern Iranian art, was laid out according to a Confucian grid plan, but with unusually wide avenues for grandiose parades of horsemen. Kublai Khan symbolized the move of his court from Karakorum by transferring the monumental fountain and silver tree of Möngke to Dadu.[91] Marco Polo was dazzled by the city's diverse inhabitants from every corner of Eurasia, and he enthusiastically assured his readers that golden-clad palaces were on every street corner.[92] The exaggerations of Marco Polo aside, Dadu was unlike any imperial capital in Chinese history. The cosmopolitan population and architecture had no precedent. Dadu also lay far north of the traditional capitals of the Yellow River and, more important, the great cities on the Yangtze River, the heartland of Han civilization since the fifth century. Kublai Khan later ordered an extension of the Grand Canal constructed across Shandong from Jingning north to Linjing, from whence luxuries, silk, and rice from southern China could be conveyed by river transport to the vicinity of Dadu.[93] The project took five years to complete and employed tens of thousands of peasant laborers. Its upkeep was a major item on future imperial budgets.

Dadu provided Kublai Khan with the palace and administrative offices where he could hold court and confer with his mandarin ministers in the guise of the Yuan emperor of China. Kublai Khan built eight temples near his palaces in Dadu, where the rites of ancestor worship were performed in the Confucian way. Within each ancestral temple, memorial tablets in Chinese ideograms were commissioned for either an ancestor or predecessors: Hoelun and Yesügei (honored together in a single temple), and Genghis Khan, Jochi, Chagatai, Ögedei, Tolui, Güyük, and Möngke.[94] Significantly, his uncle Jochi and his father, Tolui, were both retroactively elevated to Great Khans, and Tolui was accorded even the Chinese temple name of Ruizong. Kublai Khan commissioned the painting of portraits of his predecessors from Genghis Khan on depicted as both Chinese sage and Yuan emperor.[95] Even the most hostile of Confucian mandarins would have grudgingly acknowledged Kublai Khan's piety. Kublai patronized the performers of Chinese theater and dance and the authors of novels, but Confucians would have dismissed these activities as beneath the higher arts of calligraphy, painting, and composing of philosophical treatises.[96] Kublai Khan courted rather than exalted the Confucian mandarins, and so he could never gain their loyalty.

Kublai Khan employed Chinese officials, but he dispensed with the Song examination system. Kublai Khan based appointments on loyalty and merit, and he preferred Uyghur, Persian, and Arab officials, as well as European adventurers such as Marco Polo.[97] Foremost among these ministers was his Muslim chancellor Ahmad Fanakati, who hailed from the town Fanakat in Transoxiana. Devoted to Kublai Khan, Ahmad administered the census and taxes of southern China, expanded imperial revenues from state monopolies, and cracked down on tax evasion by the landed classes.[98] The Confucian mandarins despised him as the epitome of the agents of Mongol oppression, accusing him of ruthless punishments and corruption.[99] Ahmad, however, was envied and hated for his success in implementing his master's will. The revenues raised by Ahmad were largely expended on projects that promoted the welfare of Kublai Khan's Chinese subjects. Ultimately, Ahmad ran afoul of rivals in the lurid intrigues at court, and fell victim to an assassin.[100] Kublai

Khan confiscated Ahmad's vast fortune, and had charges of corruption and witchcraft retroactively lodged against the dead minister. An equally efficient, and hated, chancellor Sanga, a Uyghur by birth, succeeded.[101] Yet the documentary sources record that Kublai Khan granted remission of taxes to villages suffering from the ravages of war or natural disasters. He lessened the harsh penalties meted out to peasants under Chinese law, and he sponsored numerous public projects to promote trade and agriculture.[102] The Neo-Confucians, especially of southern China, resented the loss of their primacy. Many refused service under Kublai Khan, and preferred to retire to private life, where they pursued painting, calligraphy, and the writing of philosophical and moral treatises. Mandarins who found their way to the Mongol court would have been scandalized by the gargantuan feasting and heavy drinking. Marco Polo delights in reporting these ostentatious feasts hosted by Kublai Khan, with generous plates of meat and freely flowing *qumis*, rice wine, mead, and even imported grape wine.[103] Guests dined to the sound of the heavy rhythm of Mongol music, repetitive to Chinese ears, followed by acrobats and dancers rather than a refined Chinese opera. To mandarins of Song China, Kublai Khan, for all of his veneer as Chinese emperor, behaved as an uncouth barbarian in his personal habits. Those mandarins who did take service with Kublai Khan had to compete for the Yuan emperor's favor with barbarians who spoke no Chinese. They resented the fact that their mastery of the Confucian canon, possession of the *jinshi* decree, and political connections at court no longer assured them and their families the high office and privilege that they saw as their birthright. Many must have served Kublai Khan out of a sense of resignation, for they had no other option once the Song were gone.

Although Kublai Khan respected Confucianism and Daoism, he tolerated all the faiths of his empire. He particularly protected the legal status of Muslim medresses and mosques since so many of his top ministers were Muslims.[104] Nestorian Christians believed that he would embrace Christ. Marco Polo too clung to high hopes that the Great Khan was on the verge of converting to Catholic Christianity.[105] Kublai Khan was at heart an eclectic monotheist in his beliefs. He revered Tengri of the eternal blue sky, and, significantly,

he preferred to be laid to rest with the traditional rites of his ancestors and in the sacred land beneath the sacred mountain Burkhan
Khaldun.[106] He also leaned toward Buddhism, because he could easily reconcile his animist faith with the teachings of the Buddha. In
1260, Kublai Khan appointed the ascetic monk Drogön Chögyal
Phagpa as guoshi or minister over the Buddhist monasteries of
Tibet, Mongolia, and the northern Chinese prefectures.[107] Five years
later, Kublai Khan expanded the competence of Drogön Chögyal
Phagpa to include the imperial administration of Tibet. Under the
direction of Drogön Chögyal Phagpa, the hierarchy of the Sakya
School ruled Tibet in the interests of the Yuan dynasty, and forged
close links with many Mongol princes, who embraced Buddhism
and generously showered their patronage on Tibetan monasteries.
Kublai Khan's policies favorable to Buddhism would ultimately
align Mongolia spiritually and culturally with Tibet. Finally, Kublai Khan turned to his spiritual mentor Drogön Chögyal Phagpa to
devise a phonetic alphabet known today as the "Square Script" for
writing Mongolian. Kublai Khan aimed to bestow literacy upon
the Mongols, who in time would create their own literature written in their own distinct alphabet.[108] The new alphabet of forty-one
letters was intended to replace the Uyghur one, which was ultimately derived from the Aramaic script, and the Chinese ideograms
that had previously been used to render Mongolian. Kublai Khan
learned from his Chinese officials the power of literacy in keeping
records. Kublai Khan, however, deliberately chose not to use Han
characters, in contrast to previous Liao, Jin, and Xi Xia emperors
who employed scripts based on Chinese characters. Kublai Khan
wanted future Mongols to create their own literary culture rather
than be assimilated into the Chinese one. Therefore, Kublai Khan
ordered that his decrees and laws be promulgated in Mongolian,
and translations into Mongolian be made of many Chinese works,
especially manuals on practical subjects. He erected monumental
inscriptions of his edicts in Mongolian followed by a Chinese translation, to the horror of the Confucian mandarins.[109]

Throughout his reign, Kublai Khan feared assimilation. He depended on one hundred fifty thousand Mongols and foreigners

in his service to govern a Chinese population of sixty million, of whom fifty million resided in the former Song Empire. From the start, Mongol rule bred resentment among mandarins and Chinese peasants alike. Despite all of Kublai Khan's efforts to promote the peace and prosperity of Chinese merchants, craftsmen, and peasants, he never won their loyalty, but rather a tacit resignation because there was no other option to his orderly rule. Chinese secret societies plotting to overthrow Yuan rule proliferated with the death of Kublai Khan.[110] Zhu Yuanzhang, a Buddhist monk of one such secret society, raised a great rebellion and expelled the Mongols in 1368.[111] Under the throne name Hongwu, he proclaimed a new Ming dynasty, razed the palace at Dadu, and built over its ruins the new Chinese capital, Beijing. The Mongols fled back to their homeland and would never again challenge China. The Ming emperors made sure of this by rebuilding the Great Wall with brick and stone, not so much as a barrier but as a monument to fear and loathing of the Mongols, the only nomads who had ever dared to rule China.[112]

23

Papal Envoys, Missionaries, and Marco Polo

In 1274, after a journey of over three years, a most enterprising young Venetian merchant, Marco Polo, reached the summer palace of Kublai Khan at Shangdu, immortalized in the poetry of Samuel Coleridge as Xanadu. Twenty-five years later, Marco Polo vividly recollected his initial awe of Shangdu while languishing in a Genoese prison. He dictated his memories to a fellow prisoner, Rustichello da Pisa, an accomplished composer of Arthurian romances. Rustichello composed in the northern French tongue (langue d'oeil), the widely known language of commerce and crusading, so it can never be determined how much he edited and embroidered Marco Polo's dictation in the Venetian language.[1] Yet Marco Polo's description of the Mongol summer capital rings true. The surrounding wall of the palace complex he saw was a perfect square measuring four miles on each side.[2] The main palace itself was a gilt-domed building of bamboo, mounted on the wheels of a huge *gers*, which could be dismantled and moved. Years later he still marveled at the gilt decorations of the palace. The grounds of the inner city had sprawling parks and woodlands filled with beautiful animals and a huge lake. The palace itself in opulence and size exceeded anything he had ever seen. Marco Polo had traveled in the company of his father and uncle, Niccolo and Maffeo, to find their fame and fortune, and so they took service with Kublai Khan for the next seventeen years.[3] Marco's anecdotal travelogue, best known as *Book of the Marvels of the World*, is often so difficult to verify that some scholars even suspect Marco invented the entire journey.[4] Yet despite his exaggerations and mistakes, Marco Polo was the first European traveler to record his experiences in East Asia.[5] His sensational reports about Kublai Khan's fabled kingdom of Cathay so excited the imagination of readers that Marco Polo shaped European perceptions of East Asia for the next seven centuries. The Polos, however, followed well-established routes of the Silk Road to reach the Mongol court, and avoided crossing the vast Eurasian steppes. The Polos were hardly the first Christian Europeans to make a journey to the court of the Great Khan. Earlier European travelers could and did make the trek across the Eurasian steppes. These accounts by travelers to the Mongol court reshaped European notions of the world, because they brought back the first accurate information since Antiquity about the peoples of the Eurasian steppes.

The three best accounts that speak to us today about the lives of nomadic peoples were penned by a papal envoy, a missionary, and the astute merchant prince Marco Polo. Each set forth with very different aims, but each man's view of the world was profoundly changed by the experience. Fortunately, each author took the time to write an account of his experiences. Numerous envoys, vassal rulers, and merchants flocked to the Great Khan's court, but they chose not to write down their experiences or, if they did, they do not survive.[6] Giovanni da Pian del Carpine and his colleague Friar Benedict each wrote up a report for Innocent IV.[7] Giovanni del Carpine composed by far the most insightful analysis about the military power and intentions of the Mongols. He closed with recommendations on how to oppose the next invasion by the Mongols.[8] His was a diplomatic report to Pope Innocent IV, and not unlike a report submitted to modern state departments. He included a wealth of information on the geography, fauna, and flora of the Eurasian steppes and the customs and diet of the Mongols. This information, however, was background to the military analysis. The work was well-known as attested by the number of surviving manuscripts. The Dominican encyclopedist Vincent of Beauvais incorporated virtually all of Giovanni's account into his *Speculum Maius*.[9] The missionary William of Rubruck, a Franciscan friar and chaplain to Queen Marguerite of France, penned some of the most insightful observations about daily life among the Mongols during his visit in 1253–1255.[10] William needed to learn about the peoples he wished to convert. Several years after his return, William of Rubruck met in Paris Roger Bacon, the renowned English scholastic, who included William's description of the Mongols in his *Opus Majus*.[11] William's own work thereafter sank into obscurity for the next three hundred years. Fathers Giovanni and William both wrote in Latin so that their reports circulated among the literate prelates and princes of Europe.

Marco Polo, however, wrote his account as a bestseller to recover the fortune he had made in the service of Kublai Khan and lost on his return voyage.[12] His bad luck is our good fortune. If Polo had returned to Venice with his wealth intact, he would never have written such an account, because he would have been reluctant to betray trade secrets to would-be competitors. Rustichello da Pisa, who translated Marco's recollections into French, ensured the widest circulation of the work. In the prologue of *Marvels of the World*, Marco Polo exhorts a secular readership—the princes, knights, merchants, and craftsmen of Europe—to revel in the wonders which he himself saw in the east.[13] Hence, the *Marvels of the World* has survived in many translations and over 150 known manuscripts. Furthermore, Marco Polo inspired a new genre of travelogue for a wider readership.[14] Ironically, of the three accounts, the most sensational work proved the most influential and long-lasting.

In 1245, Pope Innocent IV, resident in Lyons, sent out four missions to Asia. Two of the missions traveled to the Mongol courts in the hopes of achieving peace with the Great Khan and perhaps sealing an alliance against the Muslims who had recaptured Jerusalem in 1244. The other two were instructed to open negotiations for reunion with the churches of Eastern Christendom.[15] Innocent IV had very limited information about the Mongols. A refugee Russian bishop, Peter, about whom virtually nothing is known, had witnessed Mongol rampages across Russia and advised the Papal Curia.[16] A Hungarian Dominican friar, Julian, had filed a report of his journey across the Pontic-Caspian steppes to convert the Kipchak Turks just before Batu invaded and ended the mission.[17] Innocent turned to Franciscan or Dominican mendicant friars to serve as his envoys. For a generation, the friars had served as papal emissaries on delicate missions such as collecting tithes or negotiating with the secular princes of Europe. They were known for their observant reports to the Holy See. Saint Francis of Assisi and Saint Dominic each had founded an order of wandering friars who recognized no authority other than the Pope and pledged themselves to poverty and service in imitation of Christ.[18] They enthusiastically, sometimes with bigoted zeal, preached to convert the heathen and heretic. Dominicans conducted investigations into the heretic Cathars of southern France, and the lax Christians, Jews, and Muslims of Spain.[19] These investigations provided the legal precedent for the later Inquisition. Saint Francis, ever the zealous proselytizer, accompanied the Fifth Crusade and secured an interview with al-Kamil in a vain effort to convert the Ayyubid sultan of Egypt.[20] Pope Innocent IV knew his envoys could be trusted to represent the Holy See faithfully, for they could be neither bribed nor intimidated.

For the prime mission to the Mongol court, Innocent IV chose fellow Italian Giovanni da Pian del Carpine, a native from a small town outside of Perugia, and an early disciple of Saint Francis.[21] Friar Giovanni had considerable experience in Germany and Spain, and he was well-known at the courts of Prague, Breslau, and Cracow, and so he had an entrée to the courts of the Orthodox Russian princes. He was entrusted with two objectives, initiating serious talks about reunion with the churches of Orthodox Russia and opening diplomatic relations with the Great Khan.[22] If Innocent had possessed accurate information about the distances and dangers of the journey, he would not have chosen Friar Giovanni, who was at least sixty years old and overweight. The hardships of traversing the Eurasian steppes nearly proved too much for the gentle friar, who repeatedly complained of his ordeal.[23]

★ ★ ★

Giovanni da Pian del Carpine set forth from Lyons on Easter, April 16, 1245, and made his way across Central Europe. At Prague, he was joined by Friar Stephen, compliments of King Wenceslaus of Bohemia, and then he traveled to Breslau, where the Polish friar Benedict joined the company that now totaled ten members.[24] From Breslau they headed to Cracow, and thence to Kiev, where they entered into promising talks with the Russian boyars and prelates about reunion, but the Russians would make no final commitment until Prince Daniel Romanovich returned from the court of his overlord, Khan Batu.[25] The mission did not set out for the steppes until February 3, 1247, after they had secured Mongolian mounts that could survive the extremes of winter. For the corpulent Father Giovanni, who customarily rode a donkey at an easy pace, the hard riding on a horse was excruciating. Sixteen days later, after crossing the steppes in the dead of winter, the mission reached the town of Kaniev on the Dnieper River (today in Ukraine), where they obtained fresh mounts and provisions.[26] They set out again, traveling southeast toward the Sea of Azov, and soon stumbled upon a Mongol encampment. Friars Giovanni and Benedict recall with terror this first encounter with nomadic horsemen. The Mongol horsemen rushed out of their camp, surrounded the small company, and demanded to know the envoys' purpose and to receive precious gifts.[27] Friar Stephen, too ill to travel farther, was left behind as a hostage along with several servants. Father Giovanni and the rest of the mission persevered on fresh mounts and with Mongol guides, so that they next arrived at the camp of Qurumshi, a cousin of Khan Batu, who also demanded rich gifts and inquired as to Giovanni's purpose.[28] Giovanni and his companions tactfully conformed to Mongol protocol, kneeling three times and not touching the threshold of Qurumshi's tent lest they displease Tengri of the eternal blue sky.[29] Qurumshi sent the Christians on their way with fresh mounts and new guides. Father Giovanni and company reached the camp of Batu on the lower Volga River on April 4, 1246, just shy of one year from when Father Giovanni had departed from Lyons. They at last stood on the western edge of the Mongol Empire.

From a distance, Father Giovanni was awestruck by Batu's sprawling tent city along the banks of the Volga River, sixty-five miles north of the Caspian Sea and destined to become Saray, the capital of the Golden Horde. They were received into the tent of Batu, a richly furnished linen one that had been the property of King Bela IV of Hungary. Batu treated his unexpected guests to a banquet, but the monks could not partake of the strong drinks and meat served on exquisite golden plate because it was Lent.[30] Father Giovanni keenly observed Batu, judging him an exceptionally brave and cunning prince whose bearing commanded respect from his warriors. He would be a deadly foe should he return to Europe.[31] Conforming to Mongol protocol, Giovanni had Innocent's letter translated from Latin, via Russian- and Persian-speaking translators, into Mongolian.[32] Batu Khan listened politely, and circumspectly. His enemy Güyük was soon to be enthroned as the next Great Khan, and Batu could ill afford a diplomatic misstep. Since the Pope's letter was addressed to the Great Khan, Batu adroitly dodged any decision by recommending the envoys journey to Karakorum and see the Great Khan himself. Batu Khan furnished the envoys with fresh horses, provisions, guides, and a pass to travel along the imperial postal route.[33]

On April 8, 1246, Giovanni da Pian del Carpine and his companions departed for Karakorum, taking the southern route across the Eurasian steppes. The friars with Mongol guides and escorts rode all day, sometimes with as many as three changes of mounts per day, and often traveling into the night. Sometimes they rode for several days from one relay station to the next. Each dawn, they were aroused from their sleep, devoured a gruel of boiled millet, and rode until evening, when they camped and partook of a simple fare of broth and partially cooked leg of mutton.[34] They covered over three thousand miles in 106 days, at an average of thirty miles per day, to reach the summer encampment of Güyük, just a half day's ride south of Karakorum, on July 22, 1246.[35] The route took the travelers along the edges of the Karakum Desert, with views to the south of the shores of the Caspian and Aral Seas, across the fertile grasslands watered by the tributaries of Lake Balkhash, and finally over the Altai Mountains onto the steppes of Mongolia.

The great distances, endless seas of grass, and ever-distant horizon unnerved Father Giovanni, and shattered his worldview forever. The first European to traverse the Eurasian steppes, Father
Giovanni beheld landscapes beyond anything he had ever experienced before and nothing like what he had learned from reading
the fabulous tales handed down since Antiquity. In his account, he
dwells on the terror of the loneliness of minuscule humans on the
vast Eurasian steppes. It was all too easy to become disoriented and
lost, and starve to death.

The papal envoys arrived in time to witness the enthronement
of Güyük as the Great Khan on August 24, 1246. The humble
friar must have struggled to conceal his bewilderment and awe, for
over three thousand representatives of kings, princes, and peoples
across Eurasia attended and offered their obeisance to the new Great
Khan.[36] At that moment, he must have grasped for the first time the
immense size and diversity of the Mongol Empire and the awesome
might of the Great Khan. In Mongol eyes, Latin Christendom was
an inconsequential place on the edge of the great ocean encircling
the inhabited earth. To his credit, Giovanni kept his wits and noted
the Mongol's salient customs and ways of war, which he later wrote
up in his final report. Remarkably, Father Giovanni also overcame
his prejudices, and noted that many of their habits and diet, while
repugnant to Europeans, were born out of the necessity of surviving on the steppes.[37] He singled out for praise the Mongols' worship
of a single God, and the long-suffering character of both men and
women.[38] Yet he reassured his readers, and himself, that Christian
knights could defeat these Devil's horsemen of the Great Khan, but
he must have known that this was special pleading.[39]

The new khan was unimpressed by the Pope's appeal not to war
on Christians, and he was amused by the shabbily dressed friars
who were the least important of over three thousand envoys from
across Eurasia. They brought no worthy gifts, for what costly gifts
they had were long handed out to Batu and lesser Mongol princes.
After patiently listening to the two papal bulls read by translators,
Güyük agreed to dictate his reply in Mongolian, which, with the
aid of two scribes, was faithfully translated into Latin.[40] The final
version, in Latin, Arabic, and Mongolian, has survived in the papal

archives.[41] The Great Khan Güyük informs Pope Innocent IV that the eternal lord of the universe obviously entrusted the sovereignty of the world to Genghis Khan and his heirs. If the Pope and the kings of Europe desire peace, they are admonished to journey to Karakorum and render their submission. With Güyük's reply in hand, Fathers Giovanni and Benedict were granted permission to depart on November 13, 1246. Neither friar in his account records the details of the six-month winter journey back to the encampment of Batu, which they reached on May 25, 1247.[42] Giovanni only remembers endless frozen wastes, blizzards, and sleeping on the ground covered by snow and under the nocturnal skies of winter. They reached Kiev on June 10, 1247, sixteen months after they had initially departed from the Russian city. There they found Father Stephen, recovered and ready to return home.[43] Their amazed Russian hosts greeted the two friars as if they had returned from the dead. On October 2, 1247, the friars entered Cologne, where Fathers Giovanni and Benedict dictated their reports. In early November 1247, Giovanni da Pian del Carpine stood before Pope Innocent IV, over two and a half years from when he had departed.[44] Innocent IV was overjoyed to greet Giovanni, and he was most pleased with the report. He rewarded his envoy with an archbishopric, because Giovanni da Pian del Carpine was the first European to bring back accurate reports about Eurasian nomads since Herodotus penned his account of the Scythians.[45] Yet the report's conclusion was most disheartening. In his letter, Güyük curtly answers Innocent's appeals point by point, and concludes with the demand to submit before any alliance could be discussed. Innocent IV only saw a bleak future of another Mongol invasion of Europe.

The other three missions were even less successful. The two missions seeking reunion with the eastern churches returned with little to show for their efforts.[46] Innocent received equally distressing news from the other mission he had sent to the Mongols. The Dominican friar Ascelin of Lombardy headed a mission to the Mongol *noyan* Baiju in Iran. This company of five included the Dominican friar Guichard of Cremone, who had been stationed in Tiflis (today Tbilisi) for five years, so Ascelin was likely served by competent interpreters speaking Georgian and Persian. The friar Simon of

Saint Quentin wrote the account of the mission in his *Historia Tartarorum*, but the work does not survive except for citations by Vincent of Beauvais.[47] Ascelin took passage by sea to Trebizond (today Trabzon) on the southern shores of the Black Sea, and then traveled through Christian Georgia to Baiju's encampment.[48] He and his companions observed little of nomadic life, and had even less interest in describing it. Ascelin found Baiju's main encampment on the Aras River in Azerbaijan in 1247. Ascelin lacked the diplomatic manners of Giovanni da Pian del Carpine, for he tactlessly refused to genuflect before the image of the khan, and dismissed Mongol etiquette, which he found demeaning to the Holy Father at Rome. These negotiations did not end well. Baiju, to his credit, contained his ire toward the presumptuous Dominican friar.[49] The obstinate friar was lucky that the Mongols took seriously the inviolate status of envoys. Ascelin was ordered to return with Baiju's reply, a missive that demanded the submission of Pope Innocent and the Christian kings of the West.[50] Two Mongolian envoys, Aïbeg and Serkis, accompanied Ascelin, who reached Lyons in the late summer of 1248. The disappointed Pope could only issue an unenforceable papal bull, pleading that the Mongols should stop killing Christians. The Mongol envoys returned home with Innocent's reply dated November 22, 1248.[51] Thereafter, the Holy See suspended diplomatic approaches and braced for the inevitable Mongol invasion. But it never came.

The Great Khan Güyük died on April 20, 1248, before he could lead the imperial army in a second invasion of Central Europe. Surprisingly, the Mongols soon initiated the next diplomatic exchange with Latin Christendom. The new *noyan* of Iran, Eljigidei, sent a Nestorian Christian envoy named David to King Louis IX, whom the Mongol envoy found at the Cypriote port of Limassol in December 1248.[52] King Louis, who was preparing to invade Egypt, gleefully received an offer of alliance from Eljigidei, who, on his own initiative, was planning an attack on Baghdad. In reply, Louis dispatched as his ambassador to Güyük Khan André de Longjumeau, a Dominican friar who was conversant in Arabic and Syriac, and had met David in the Armenian city of Kars several years earlier.[53] Longjumeau's party set sail for Antioch on February

16, 1249, carrying letters from King Louis and rich gifts. It took over a year for Louis's envoys to traverse Iran and Transoxiana, cross the Jaxartes, and reach Karakorum. Once at Karakorum, André de Longjumeau learned that Güyük Khan was dead, rumored to have been poisoned by Batu Khan's agents. The regent Oghul Qaimish, the principal consort of Güyük, was busy scheming to rig a *kurultai* to elect her son Shiremun the next Great Khan.[54] She summarily dismissed the French envoys with the usual ultimatum ordering King Louis to submit. In 1251, André de Longjumeau returned to find King Louis at Caesarea, recently released by his Mamluk captors on promise of paying an enormous ransom.[55] Louis must have been crestfallen to receive more bad news, namely that there would be no Mongol alliance against the Muslims. André de Longjumeau wrote a detailed report of the mission, but the little that survives are brief citations by later chroniclers. What turned out to be far more important, André of Longjumeau met the Flemish Franciscan William of Rubruck. André lamented to William about the plight of the many German captives enslaved by Batu and who were without any spiritual comfort.[56] The earnest William of Rubruck was inspired to declare himself the Apostle of the Tartars, for he promised to bring comfort to the enslaved Christians and to convert the heathen Tartars. William of Rubruck, the missionary, would write the second, and in many ways the most perceptive, account of the Mongols.

William of Rubruck was probably in his thirties when he accompanied Saint Louis IX on the ill-fated Seventh Crusade that ended in debacle in 1250.[57] Friar William had heard reports about the mission of Giovanni da Pian del Carpine, and he likely read Giovanni's account. Once he was convinced of his calling to bring Christianity to the Mongols, William approached King Louis, but the king was not keen on pursuing yet another diplomatic mission to the Mongol court. Louis only agreed to entrust William with a polite letter to Sartaq Khan, the son of Batu, requesting that William be permitted to preach Christianity to the Tartars. Since Sartaq was rumored to be a Christian, Louis calculated that the request would be readily granted. Neither Louis nor William dreamed that William's small company of missionaries would repeat the trek across the Eurasian steppes to the Mongol court. Louis's letter proved indispensable, because Mongol khans and princes all misinterpreted the letter as commissioning William as the envoy of the French king. Hence, William was granted the inviolate status and liberty of an envoy, and so he was escorted to Karakorum, even though William always protested that he was not an envoy. Otherwise, in his own account, William admits that he would have never reached the camp of Batu on the lower Volga, let alone the court of the Great Khan Möngke.

On May 7, 1253, William set sail from Acre to Constantinople, where he conferred with Count Baldwin of Hainault, a vassal of the Latin emperor Baldwin II.[58] Baldwin of Hainault had married a Cuman princess, a daughter of Cuman kaghan Saronius, whose people had found refuge from the Mongols in the Latin Empire. Baldwin probably knew sufficient Turkish from his wife so that he could communicate with the Mongols directly. As an envoy of Baldwin II, he had just returned from the courts of Saray and Karakorum, so he could provide William with information about the political climate at both courts. William's party then sailed across the Black Sea and landed at Soldaia (today Sudak), a Genoese commercial port on the southern shores of the Crimea, on May 21, 1253. The notables who governed the city as vassals of the Batu advised William of Rubruck that he should represent himself as if he were an envoy without admitting it. They also gave him practical advice on how to reach the encampment of Sartaq on the Pontic-Caspian steppes, because many Genoese merchants engaged in the slave trade knew the way.[59] Two weeks later, on June 1, 1253, William of Rubruck, so informed, departed for the steppes. In retrospect, he was angry with himself for choosing to travel by ox-drawn carts rather than on horses. He more than doubled his time in travel, and repeatedly faced problems crossing rivers.[60] Yet the carts were often the only source of shade from the unrelenting summer sun on the treeless, flat grasslands.[61] Once at the encampment of Sartaq, William Rubruck presented the letter and costly gifts of Louis IX. Sartaq Khan could not help but conclude that William was another Latin envoy, and so instructed him to journey to Saray, and confer with his father, Khan Batu.[62] William immediately departed for Saray with an uneasy feeling about the future of his mission. First, Sartaq Khan, who inclined toward Nestorian Christianity, identified himself first and foremost as a Mongol.[63] Mongols practiced many faiths, and Sartaq was no different. To the dismay of William, Mongols considered no faith superior to the other, but all reflected a truth about Tengri, the lord of the eternal blue sky. Second, William already found himself at a disadvantage, because his interpreter, Omodeo, a Syrian Christian, whose native language was Arabic, was not up to the task of explaining in broken Turkish sophisticated theological arguments.[64] As the journey progressed, William grew ever more frustrated with Omodeo, whom he accused of being habitually drunk on *qumis*. Omodeo, in turn, finally refused to translate any religious arguments, because the task was beyond his capacity.[65] In contrast, Giovanni da Pian del Carpine had skillfully avoided this problem by sticking to immediate diplomatic concerns without raising issues of doctrine and conversion.

It took William's party over five weeks to travel from Soldaia to Batu's encampment on the Volga. At the Don River, the guides provided by Sartaq negotiated for a ferry to convey the carts across the river, but not the oxen or horses.[66] The guides promptly returned to Sartaq's camp, while William wasted three days seeking new teams of oxen from villagers on the eastern bank of the Don. Father William, just like Father Giovanni, expressed his awe of the endless grasslands, with forests to the north, and at times glimpses of the Black Sea to the south. The broad expanse of the Don River amazed him, for it was far wider than the broadest part of the Seine near Paris.[67] As soon as he was on the steppes, William repeatedly expressed his bewilderment and fear as he crossed an alien world.

In early July, Batu received friar William of Rubruck, whom Batu too viewed as yet another papal envoy, the second in seven years.[68] After Batu entertained the Latins, he then sent them on their way to Karakorum on September 16, 1253. During his stay at Saray, William explained details of court protocol. The Mongols always pitched their tents facing south, and family members, vassals, and guests were seated on the right (west) or left (east) based on a strict hierarchy of their rank and sex.[69] This orientation was at least as early as the time of the Xiongnu, who viewed the world from the same northern perspective looking south. William too avoided breaking taboos such as crossing over the threshold of Batu's tent. He was pleasantly surprised how much he enjoyed *qumis*, and approved of Batu maintaining three thousand white mares celebrated for the quality of their milk.[70]

William of Rubruck, along with a fellow Franciscan Bartholomew of Cremona, the interpreter, and a servant, crossed over three thousand miles of the Eurasian steppes in 111 days, reaching Karakorum on January 4, 1254.[71] Father William had to leave his French secretary, Gosset, and several servants behind as sureties for their proper conduct. Batu had issued William the imperial passport so that William's company and its Mongol escort could obtain fresh mounts and provisions at each station. Before their departure, the Mongol guide ensured the Latins were properly attired in felt caps, fur-lined boots, trousers, and coats. He also sternly warned that should the friars lag behind, they were on their own if they got lost, because only the fittest deserved to survive the rigors of travel in winter.[72] They endured the same hard riding over the same route as had Giovanni's party seven years earlier. But once at Karakorum, they were generously received by the new Great Khan Möngke, a most intelligent and tolerant ruler, who had directed his armies against the Caliphate of Baghdad and Song China rather than Latin Christendom.[73] Möngke too assumed that Father William was an ambassador of the French king. But the khan was long baffled as to the purpose of William's visit, because the Latin holy man showed little interest in war or politics. The interpreter, Omodeo, could not or would not explain how William wished to comfort Christian captives and preach to the Mongols.[74] It was only when William gained the friendship of the Parisian master goldsmith Guillaume de Boucher that he could communicate with Möngke effectively through Guillaume's adopted son, who was fluent in Mongolian.[75]

From the start, William of Rubruck discovered that he was out of his depth. He wrote the later chapters of his account to justify why his mission had failed. He never located the German slaves because they had been resettled near the Altai Mountains, where they mined iron and forged weapons for the Great Khan. During his six months at Karakorum, he baptized only six individuals as Catholic Christians. He vents his ire and disgust on the Nestorian Christians, who had initially welcomed him and offered their church in Karakorum for Catholic services.[76] Even so, William remained a thoughtful observer, for he describes the operation of Möngke's silver tree designed by Guillaume de Boucher. He also was the first Westerner to record a Buddhist prayer summoned by bells. But as the months wore on, William became ever more frustrated by the tolerant, heterodox, cosmopolitan society of the Mongol capital. The inflexible William simply lacked the tact and linguistic skills to convince anyone to convert. He could make no sense out of Buddhist doctrines, and dismissed Buddhists as heretical Manichees because the two shared a belief in transmigration of souls.[77] The later pages of his account are marred by his unfair criticisms of Nestorians, and his tedious claims that holy water and Catholic rites administered by him were the only cures against disease. His disappointment climaxed in a debate mandated by the Great Khan, who summoned Christians, Buddhists, and Muslims to argue the validity of their respective faiths.[78] William admitted no one was convinced by the debate. Each group offered up platitudes and declarations of faith, while the amused Mongols toasted points with *qumis* so that the event quickly became just another drinking bout at the Great Khan's court.

After six months, William had overstayed his welcome. Möngke summoned William, and put it to the Franciscan what he wanted to do. William cryptically answered that he wanted whatever pleased the Great Khan. Thereupon, Möngke sent William on his way back to Batu, with a letter to King Louis IX, on July 10, 1254.[79] The contents, as reported by William, suggest the original was not unlike the ultimatum sent by Güyük to Innocent IV. Friar Bartholomew chose to remain in Karakorum on grounds of age and illness. William of Rubruck retraced his route to the court of Batu at Saray, where he arrived on September 14, 1254.[80] His scribe, Gosset, rejoined the mission, and William, with Batu's passport, traveled southwest, crossed the Derbent Pass, and spent Christmas at Nakhchivan (today in Azerbaijan). He finally reached Cyprus in July 1255, only to discover that King Louis and Queen Marguerite had returned to Paris. His order appointed him to a lectureship in theology at Acre.[81] He was languishing as a lecturer and longing to return to Paris when he composed his itinerary in the summer of 1255. His report was his passport back to Paris. William repeatedly wrote letters to Queen Marguerite, imploring her to approach her husband to recall him. William explained that, out of a sense of obligation, he must personally deliver the report into the hands of the king. He finally succeeded after two years, and returned to the comforts of the court of Paris.[82] His account provided the best description of the customs of nomadic peoples to date. It also recommended that in the future, the Holy Father of Rome must send an archbishop, along with a staff of priests and friars with the requisite languages, if he wished to gain converts. In 1289, Pope Nicholas IV sent such an archbishop, Giovanni da Montecorvino, who arrived at the Mongol court five years later in 1294. Consecrated the Archbishop of Khanbaliq,[83] Giovanni da Montecorvino earned the confidence of Yuan emperor Temür, the grandson and successor to Kublai Khan. The Catholic community prospered under Mongol protection, but it never amounted to more than thirty-five thousand souls. Most converts were among the foreigners in the employ of the Mongol khan or Turkish and Mongol Nestorian Christians.[84] Few if any Chinese were among the converts. The mission disappeared with the collapse of the Yuan dynasty in 1368.

While European diplomats and missionaries returned home with disappointing results, European merchants venturing into the Mongol Empire came home with fabulous windfalls and reports of even more opportunities for profit. The Great Khans Möngke and Kublai together greatly extended the Mongol Empire, and they united more of Eurasia under a single sovereignty than ever before or since. During the second half of the thirteenth century, these two Mongol khans imposed a *pax Mongolica* over the Eurasian steppes, the cities of the Silk Road from Tabriz to Dadu, and China. Mongol courts required luxuries and foodstuffs, and so this demand fueled the rapid expansion of international trade across the continent. Saray on the lower Volga River succeeded to the commercial role of the earlier Atil of the Khazars. Genoese and Venetian merchants, based in their colonies on the southern shores of the Crimea, exploited

the trade in slaves, furs, and products of the forest, which khans of
the Golden Horde received in tribute from their Turkish and Russian subjects. In turn, the Italians supplied Saray with vendibles of
every description. Likewise, Tabriz, seat of the Ilkhans of Iran, attracted European merchants keen on acquiring silks and spices at
rock-bottom prices. The most lucrative markets were the most distant, the Mongol capitals of Shangdu and Dadu.[85]

In 1254, the brothers Niccolo and Maffeo Polo departed Venice
in search of business opportunities in the Levant and the Aegean
world. At the time, Niccolo's wife, Nicole Anna Defuseh, was with
child, a son, Marco, whom Niccolo would only meet fifteen years
later. The Polo brothers followed in the footsteps of many Venetian merchants seeking to profit off the trade in the Latin Empire
and Outremer.[86] They traveled first to Acre, the seat of Outremer,
but soon decided to quit the port for Constantinople, "Queen of
Cities," then ruled by Baldwin II, a French count declared Latin
emperor. Members of the Fourth Crusade had captured Constantinople, the historic capital of the Byzantine or Eastern Roman Empire, in 1204. Frankish emperors ruled, but the Venetians controlled
the banking and shipping in the city.[87] Shortly before the Byzantines recaptured their capital in 1261, the Polo brothers hit upon a
get-rich-quick venture. They exchanged all their merchandise for
gems, sailed to Soldaia on the southern shores of the Crimea, and
then made their way to the court of Khan Berke at Saray.[88] They
presented the gems to Khan Berke, who was most pleased. The khan
rewarded the brothers and permitted them to trade in the markets
of Saray, where they quickly reaped profits double the value of the
gems. With a keen sense for profit, the brothers Polo took their
leave of Saray a year later, and under the khan's protection, joined
a caravan crossing the steppes and Karakum Desert to Bukhara.[89]

In Bukhara, over the next three years, the Polo brothers learned
Persian, or more likely Sogdian, the eastern Iranian language still
widely used in commerce. They gained an intimate knowledge
of the trade in high-value commodities. They mastered the art of
working patronage among the merchant princes who governed the
city. An envoy of Hulagu en route to Kublai Khan (whom Marco

Polo never names) invited the brothers to join his mission so that a year later, perhaps in 1264, the Polo brothers presented themselves to Kublai Khan.[90] They offered costly gifts; they also impressed the khan by their respectful manner. The Polo brothers were the first Latins Kublai Khan had seen, although his brother Möngke would have related his opinion of William of Rubruck. Kublai Khan, just like his brother Möngke, saw European visitors as sources of information, and so he questioned the Venetians intensively. In 1266, Kublai Khan summoned the brothers to his presence and commissioned the Venetians to return home as his emissaries and to request from the Pope that one hundred men learned in Christianity be sent to Dadu. This odd request might have originated from the khan's fascination with the religions of the empire. Perhaps he had just witnessed a spectacular display of miracles performed by Buddhist monks, and so he desired to test Christian holy men next. If so, he shared the tolerant henotheistic views of his brother Möngke, who had staged the debate among Christians, Buddhists, and Muslims for the same reason. Once again, the Polo brothers, merchants by vocation, trod the Silk Road as the emissaries of a Mongol khan. Kublai Khan invested the Polo brothers with the golden tablet that charged Mongol officials to provide fresh horses and provisions without cost. A Mongol lord, Koeketei, accompanied them, but he fell ill and had to remain behind. It took the brothers over two years to traverse the domains of Kublai Khan and the Ilkhan Abaqa.[91] When they reached Acre, in late 1268, they learned that the papal throne was empty, and the College of Cardinals was deadlocked over electing a successor. They booked passage to Venice, where Niccolo met, for the first time, his precocious son of fifteen years of age, who had been reared by his maternal relatives after the premature death of his mother.[92] Marco Polo never reports the reunion with his father or how father and son quickly bonded over the next two years. Impatient to return to Dadu, Niccolo and Maffeo, along with seventeen-year-old Marco, set sail to Acre, and started the journey back to Dadu. Fortunately, they were quickly recalled, because the college elected Teobaldo Visconti, then the papal legate in the East, as Pope Gregory X on September 1, 1271. Gregory X, the last pope seriously committed to crusades, granted

the Polos a papal letter to Kublai Khan, and assigned two Dominican friars, who soon tired and turned back several months later.[93]
Once again, the Venetian merchants, eager for fame and fortune,
traveled the next three years as envoys of both Pope Gregory X and
Kublai Khan, for they still possessed the khan's golden passport.

The goal of the Polos was profit. To be sure, they were pious
Christians, but they were circumspect, polite toward those of other
faiths they encountered, and they themselves did not proselytize.
They came with the practical skills of business. Foremost, they did
not depend on interpreters, in contrast to papal envoys and missionaries. Marco Polo had an exceptionally retentive memory, and
there is no reason to reject his claim to know four languages.[94]
These were most likely his native Venetian tongue, Persian (likely
an eastern dialect still used in commerce and culture in the lands
of Eastern Islam), Turkish (likely the Uyghur dialect), and finally
Mongolian. He seems never to have learned Chinese, and he makes
no reference to Chinese characters, but neither did other European
travelers of the thirteenth and fourteenth century.[95] When Niccolo Polo presented Marco to Kublai Khan, Marco likely could
speak in Mongolian the polite phrases required by court etiquette.
On his travels from Baghdad to Khotan, Marco, between ages
seventeen and twenty, was constantly exposed to speakers of Persian and Turkish. His father and uncle could assist and encourage
him given what they had learned in Bukhara. Persian is an Indo-
European language, so its system of verbs and syntax are related to
Western European languages. Sir Richard Burton, the celebrated
explorer of the Victorian era and connoisseur of the bizarre in his
day, claimed Persian was the Italian of the Middle East. A clever
linguist could learn the language in an evening's study. Turkish,
an agglutinative language, posed a far greater challenge, but Marco
was adept in learning new languages so that he then attained some
fluency when the Polos reached Khotan in the Tarim Basin. The
Polos traversed the caravan cities along the northern rim of the
Taklamakan Desert, where Turkish was the dominant language of
commerce. They then spent a year at Campçio (today Zhangye)
in the Gansu corridor, resting or, more accurately, seeking future
business opportunities.[96] For well over a year, Marco encountered

many Uyghurs, from whom he learned Turkish. Once the Polos set out for the Mongol court in 1274, Marco could, through Turkish, gain familiarity with the related language of Mongolian, especially since he journeyed first across the eastern steppes to Karakorum, before he arrived at Shangdu, the summer palace of Kublai Khan in Inner Mongolia. Literacy and command of languages were the passports for the Polos in the Great Khan's service. They would be the most useful as the khan's emissaries, officials, and fact finders.

The Polos did not cross the vast expanses of the Eurasian steppes; instead, they joined caravans on the Silk Road. These caravan cities were well-known to merchants of the Islamic world. Benjamin of Tudela a century earlier, and Ibn Battuta a century later, recorded the cities and commerce along the Silk Road.[97] Neither work was known in Latin Christendom. For Europeans, Marco's account was a revelation. In *Marvels of the World*, Marco narrates his experiences in five books, dealing with the Middle East, Mongolia, Cathay, Mangi (southern China), and India and covering twenty-five years. He writes a discursive narrative, often including places he did not visit, because he could not pass up a story that would thrill his readers, such as the demise of the Assassins of Alamut or the gardens of Samarkand.[98] On the whole, it is possible to follow his itinerary. Once the Polos had crossed the Upper Euphrates River, they traveled by caravan to Baghdad, and thence to the port of Hormuz on straits between the Persian Gulf and Indian Ocean. Unable to book passage on a ship, the Polos joined another caravan heading for Balkh on the Oxus River, and crossed the Pamirs via the Tera Pass to reach Kashgar and then Khotan.[99] He reports the marvels that he witnessed with the interest of a merchant. Near Taican, where the Polos spent time resting, he describes the salt mines at Kamul. He explains in detail how asbestos is manufactured, and he dispels the myth cherished by the Europeans that a salamander was the source of the product.[100] The Polos also took their time traveling along the Silk Road rather than using the rapid travel afforded by the Mongol postal and relay system. Again, moneymaking dictated their choice. They took extended rest stops along the way, where they investigated future business possibilities. Hence, Marco dwells on each city's silks, cottons, spices, or gems—high-priced commodities easily transported and lucrative to market.

When at last Marco Polo reached noble Khotan, the first city on the edge of the Tarim Basin, he encountered a strange world unknown to Europeans. His tone and perspective noticeably change from just reporting the extraordinary to delight his readers to appreciating and approving of what he witnessed. He reports carefully the practices and beliefs among Buddhists.[101] Some he abhors such as cremation, but he comes to appreciate and even admire the morality of Buddhist monks, and their teaching on the soul and achieving union with the single divine entity. He also overcomes his distaste for idols, statues of the Buddha, and sees their function in Buddhist worship. Even more important, Marco Polo forever changed the European perspective on the Mongols. For Marco Polo, the Mongols were not the Devil's horsemen, but rather the finest of warriors. Hence, Marco Polo narrates a very different Mongol history for his European readers, praising the spectacular successes of Genghis Khan.[102] Prester John is demoted to a lesser king defeated and humbled by Genghis Khan.[103] Many of Marco's readers must have been shocked to read Marco's favorable comparison of Genghis Khan to Alexander the Great.[104] Even more shocking are his rhapsodies about Kublai Khan as the greatest, most just, and most beloved sovereign of the world.[105] Previous Westerners reported Mongol Khans as arrogant despots demanding that the Pope and Western kings journey to Karakorum and submit. Instead, Marco paints the enduring image that the Khan's palaces at Shangdu and Dadu were the most splendid in the world. The Mongol capitals were transformed from the seat of a dreaded foe to a most desirable destination. Even more significantly, he admires the prowess of Mongol horsemen, even warning that they should not become too accustomed to the luxuries lest they risk the loss of their martial virtues.[106] Throughout his second and third books, Marco writes from the Mongol perspective rather than a Western one. For Marco Polo, the conquest of Eurasia by the Mongols created a far more unified and better world, and it was maintained, along with all the trading opportunities, by the Mongol imperial army. He embraces the *pax Mongolica*, and only later, as emissary in the service of Kublai Khan, does he note in passing the dreadful costs paid by the conquered of Mangi (southern China).

In 1274, Kublai Khan must have been surprised, and pleased, to receive the Polos, who had departed eight years earlier.[107] The Venetian brothers were not accompanied by Christian holy men, but Kublai Khan seemed not to mind, and instead he gladly received Marco as courtier and official. Marco Polo surely did not rise to the high favor at the Mongol court he claims, for he was merely one of many foreigners who served the Great Khan. Even so, the young Venetian must have impressed the Great Khan with his mastery of languages, accounting, and winning ways. Kublai Khan soon after sent Marco Polo as a fact finder about the salt monopoly in the southwestern regions of China and borderlands of Burma and Annam.[108] The distance was a journey of six months from Dadu, and Marco returned with a detailed analysis of the Great Khan's revenues. Thereafter, he had the confidence of Kublai Khan, and so secured a succession of lucrative missions for the Great Khan over the next sixteen years.[109] These missions took him to the jungles of Burma and Annam, the great cities and canals of the Yangtze, and finally the ports of the Indonesian islands and the Malabar coast of India. With each mission, Marco Polo delights his readers with even more marvels, such as the hunting of lions in Southeast Asia or the incomprehensible size of the cities of southern China or the construction of cargo ships used in the Indian Ocean.[110]

By 1292, Kublai Khan was long failing, and the Polos had grown anxious over their position and wealth in the event of the Great Khan's death and a succession crisis. Marco Polo was now thirty-eight years old, and his father and uncles were in their early sixties. They were ready to return to Venice. Kublai Khan repeatedly refused to give the Polos leave because the loyal, experienced Venetians were too valuable. Again, the Polos exploited an unanticipated diplomatic opportunity to obtain permission to travel home at the Great Khan's expense.[111] An embassy from Arghun, the Ilkhan of Iran, had suddenly arrived, requesting a marriage alliance. Kublai Khan obliged his great nephew, and arranged for him a bride, Kököchin, an illustrious Mongol princess of age seventeen. Since Kublai Khan was warring with Kaidu Khan on the central steppes,

the delegation would travel by sea. The Polos were the ideal emissaries to accompany the young princess. Marco Polo, in his khan's
service, had already visited the ports of Indonesia and the Malabar coast of India. In his account, Marco expresses his joy because
the mission enabled him to learn the sea routes for future business
opportunities. The Great Khan was convinced; the Polos were allowed to leave. In 1292, the Polos set sail from the Chinese port of
Quanzhou and reached Venice four years later. They were among
the eighteen out of the original six hundred passengers to survive
the voyage.[112] They did deliver the bride, but not to the intended
groom because Arghun had died, and so Kököchin was wedded to
Arghun's son, Mahmud Ghazan, a convert to Islam.[113] But on their
overland journey from Hormuz to Tabriz, and thence to Trebizond,
the Polos lost most of their fortune to rapacious brigands and mis-
haps. When they reached the port of Trebizond and took passage
for Venice, they had little left of the fortune they had amassed in
the Great Khan's service.[114] Hence, Marco Polo had to write a bestseller if he were to recover his fortune lost on his way home. In the
Western tradition, Marco Polo assured the memory of Kublai Khan
and his golden palace of Xanadu, the name coined from Marco's
name for Shangdu. Hence, Samuel Coleridge, in an opium dream,
beheld a vision of Polo's Xanadu. He awoke to compose a poem,
but the vivid images escaped him before he finished, because he
was interrupted. In "Citizen Kane" (1941), the opulent California
estate of Charles Foster Kane is named after Coleridge's Xanadu.
Inevitably, Marco inspired many imitators who strove to outdo
him by writing their own versions of *Marvels of the World*. Among
these, the most successful was an author claiming to be an English
knight, Sir John Mandeville.[115] Sir John penned a fantastic travelogue of his supposed adventures in the mid-fourteenth century.
Even though Sir John never ventured farther east than the shores
of Normandy, he shrewdly cashed in on Polo's success. Sir John
shamelessly plagiarized many of Polo's descriptions, but Sir John
had a gift for storytelling equal to that of Sir Geoffrey Chaucer.
Sir John, unlike Marco Polo, populated his distant eastern realms
with monstrous races and fabulous creatures of Antiquity in which
European readers still wanted to believe.[116] What was far more im-

portant, learned Europeans sought to comprehend a new conception of the world revealed by Marco Polo. The world was not, as
Medieval maps had depicted, an orderly one of three equal conti-
nents surrounding the Mediterranean Sea with Jerusalem standing
in the center. The Italian cartographer Giovanni Battista Ramusio
claimed that his Fra Mauro Map of 1453, which was the first effort to render the known world to scale, was based on one brought
back by Marco Polo.[117] Christopher Columbus acknowledged that
he was inspired to sail west to Cathay after reading *Marvels of the
World*.[118] Marco Polo excited the Western imagination about East
Asia down to this day, and so Europeans dared to undertake one
of the greatest ventures: to sail the oceans in search of the fabled
Xanadu of Kublai Khan. In so doing, they launched the Age of
European Discovery, and the global economy of today.

24

Tamerlane, Prince of Destruction

O n June 19, 1941, Soviet anthropologists under the direction of Professor Mikhail Gerasimov were commissioned to exhume the body of Timur, known in the West as Tamerlane, the Prince of Destruction.[1] They were motivated by scientific curiosity and racial theory to prove Tamerlane a Mongolid barbarian conqueror.[2] In Russian and Soviet historiography, Tamerlane was long loathed as a pitiless, fanatical Muslim invader even more so than either Genghis Khan or Batu, who were at least tolerant shamanists. Timur was condemned for perpetuating the Tartar yoke by restoring Tokhtamysh, Khan of the White Horde (although these historians conveniently omitted the fact that Timur later returned to punish his wayward vassal to the ultimate benefit of the Grand Princes of Moscow).[3] Hence, Professor Gerasimov set out to prove the racial inferiority of the Mongolid ruler. Furthermore, the Soviet leadership inherited the Tsarist policy of denigrating Tamerlane lest his memory act as a rallying cry among Muslim Turkish-speakers in Central Asia against the rule by Moscow. Upon exhuming the body four days later, the scientists were surprised to find that Timur was of mixed ancestry, although they did verify literary sources that reported that Timur had sustained an injury in his right leg and hand, and walked with a limp. Based on their findings, portraits of the fearsome conqueror have been reconstructed because no contemporary images exist. Hours after the exhumation, Soviet news agencies reported that the Wehrmacht had just invaded the Soviet Union. Rumors immediately circulated that Tamerlane had cursed all those who would disturb his remains, and for five years, many Soviet citizens likely believed this curse.[4] Tamerlane's remains were interred after the examination, and rest in his mausoleum, Guri Amir, the tomb of the Grand Emir.[5]

Guri Amir still stands in Samarkand, in the Republic of Uzbekistan. The stately azure domed maqbarasi has been heavily restored by the Turkish-speaking Uzbeks, who proudly hail Timur as their progenitor and are eager to lure tourists to the final resting place of the celebrated conqueror. Visitors are still awed by the beautiful gilded paintings combining the best of Iranian and nomadic decorative arts, and the türbe of Timur, his sons, grandsons, and spiritual mentor Sayyid Baraka, which are memorial markers (for the actual remains in simple shrouds lie below the floor in the Muslim tradition). Guri Amir still conveys the power, and dignity, of the last great conqueror from the Eurasian steppes. Yet it also stands as testimony to a most unusual conqueror. Timur, while he reveled in campaigning with his nomadic warriors, also delighted in pursuing his aesthetic and intellectual interests at his capital, Samarkand, during the brief respites between campaigns. Tamerlane was as much a product of the high civilization of Eastern Islam as the Eurasian steppes. He poured his wealth and patronage into beautifying Samarkand, which still stands as an architectural jewel of Eastern Islam.[6] Furthermore, Tamerlane, while he based his power on nomadic horse archers, conceived of his empire in terms of cities, yielding tribute, and governed by his kinsmen or loyal lieutenants.[7]

The fascination with Tamerlane has long survived his death, and he shares with Attila the Hun and Genghis Khan an infamy as a ruthless barbarian conqueror. Although Tamerlane styled himself as the Sword of Islam, he sacked numerous Muslim cities, and he slaughtered many more Muslims than victims of other faiths.[8] Ironically, Tamerlane was most respected by contemporary Western Europeans, who never experienced the fury of Tamerlane's hordes.

At a safe distance, the Pope and princes of Latin Christendom saw in this conqueror a possible ally against the Ottoman sultans who threatened Constantinople and the Christian kingdoms of the Balkans. The Castilian nobleman Ruy Gonzalez de Clavijo journeyed to the court of Tamerlane as the envoy of his king Henry III, who fancied himself a Crusader pledged to battle the Ottomans in the Balkans rather than in Outremer, which had been lost over a century earlier. Clavijo and his party were accompanied by Tamerlane's envoy, whom the conqueror had sent to sound out alliances with the Christian princes of the far west. It took nearly sixteen months for Clavijo to find Tamerlane, and in September 1404 the Spanish diplomat at last arrived in Samarkand.[9] Clavijo was awed by what he saw. Gangs of laborers raised splendid domed buildings; orchards and fountains offered glimpses of Muslim paradise; and the size and wealth of Samarkand far exceeded any European city.[10] Tamerlane generously received the Christian envoys even though they were the least important among those seeking an audience with the Grand Emir. The observant Clavijo penned our best description of Tamerlane, noting his physical deformity, his powerful intellect, and his charismatic manner.[11] Based on Clavijo's portrait, the Elizabethan dramatist Christopher Marlowe wrote a play, *Tamburlaine the Great*, that has influenced subsequent Western perceptions of Tamerlane that were immortalized in the poem by Edgar Allan Poe.[12] Marlowe's play is more legend than fact, with wild fantasies about Tamerlane's conquering Africa and Babylon and filled with Classical allusions about monstrous races and beasts. Marlowe painted Tamerlane as the Prince of Destruction, a mighty and yet sadistic conqueror whose physical deformity marred his character. Marlowe's Tamerlane, the incarnation of unrepentant evil, delights in breaking his word and overthrowing every moral principle. The play shocked Elizabethan audiences. His critics seized upon it as proof of Marlowe's own amorality, and so persuaded the Privy Council to issue a warrant for Marlowe's arrest, but Marlowe was killed in a tavern brawl before the warrant could be executed.[13] The play was deemed so offensive to Baroque and Victorian sensibilities that it was not produced again until the late twentieth century, when it was successfully adapted for the tastes

of modern audiences fascinated with sinful tyrants delighting in
the sadistic humiliation of their victims.[14]

The historical Tamerlane, however, is even more extraordinary
than the Tamerlane of legend, for his career inspired Muslim historians and biographers of his day to record his deeds. Their accounts
in turn inspired an unknown author to compose the purported
memoirs of Timur, *Tuzk-e-Taimuri*, which the scholar Abu Taleb
Hosaini presented to the Mughal emperor Jahan in the seventeenth
century.[15] It is an entertaining work of fiction rather than fact, but
many anecdotes ring true in the spirit of Tamerlane's character,
if not in the actual deeds. During his siege of Damascus in 1401,
Tamerlane received and conversed with the city's most celebrated
resident, the historian Ibn Khaldun, who penned the definitive
analysis of the political rise and fall of Islamic dynasties.[16] Ibn Khaldun was impressed by Tamerlane's mastery of history and statecraft,
even though he deplored the cruel fate of his adopted city at the
hands of Tamerlane's warriors. Based on contemporary accounts,
two accomplished historians recorded the deeds of Tamerlane, who
is thus the best known of all the conquerors of the steppes. Twenty
years after Tamerlane's death, Sharif ad-Din Ali Yazdi, an Iranian historian and scholar of wide-ranging interests, composed the
Zafarnama (*Book of Victories*), more a panegyric than a biography.[17]
The historian was a native of the caravan city of Yazd, which had
prospered under Mongol rule, and he penned his work in honor of
his patron, Tamerlane's grandson Ibrahim Sultan. The finest surviving manuscript of the *Zafarnama* is illustrated with beautiful miniature paintings of the notable incidents of Tamerlane's life.[18] The
historian Yazdi conveys Tamerlane's humanity, praising his subject's virtues and minimizing his atrocities as acts of policy. Yazdi
dwells on incidents revealing Tamerlane's character, such as Tamerlane's inconsolable grief for the premature death of his favorite son,
Jahangir, his summary execution of corrupt officials in the interests of justice, and above all, his charismatic, even reckless, bravery on the battlefield. In 1379, against the pleadings of his officers,
Tamerlane accepted, before the walls of Urgench, single combat
with Yusuf Sufi, ruler of Khwarazm, who never expected Tamerlane to accept the challenge.[19] Within easy bowshot of the Khwaraz-

mian archers on the city walls, Tamerlane defiantly called out the cravenly Yusuf Sufi. When his challenger failed to leave the city, Tamerlane heroically galloped back to his siege works to the cheers of his men. For Yazdi, Tamerlane remained a heroic conqueror, a pious patron of Muslim arts and letters, and a serious intellectual who debated on equal terms with the most accomplished scholars of his day. In contrast, the Arabic historian Ahmad ibn Arabshah writes from the perspective of the victims, and his history's title betrays this perspective: *Aja'ib al-Maqdur fi Nawa'ib al-Taymur* (*The Wonders of Destiny of the Ravages of Timur*).[20] As a boy of thirteen, Arabshah and his family fled from their native Damascus when Tamerlane invaded Syria. Arabshah took service with the Ottoman Sultan Mehmet I, the son of the ill-fated Bayezit Yildirim, who was defeated and captured by Tamerlane at Angora in 1402. In 1425, Arabshah returned to his native Damascus, where he completed his history a decade later. Arabshah despises Tamerlane for his low birth, and repeatedly denounces Tamerlane as a sadistic tyrant and deplores the conqueror's gruesome massacres. Yet at the conclusion of his history, even Arabshah must grudgingly concede the virtues and accomplishments of Tamerlane, but Arabshah never ceased to despise the conqueror as a barbarian and sacker of cities. To him, Tamerlane was always the Prince of Destruction rather than the Sword of Islam.

In 1336, Timur was born to Taraghai, a lesser emir of the Turkish-speaking tribes comprising the Barlas confederation, and his consort Tekina Khatun.[21] His parents pitched their tents on the grasslands of Mawarannahr (Transoxiana) near the city of Kesh (today Shahrisabz), fifty miles southeast of Samarkand, which was then in the Chagataid khanate. Timur later favored Kesh as his place of birth, constructing a magnificent palace, Ak Saray ("White Palace"), and complexes of mosques and medresses.[22] Modern Shahrisabz, now a UNESCO World Heritage Site, attracts thousands of tourists each year to see Tamerlane's birthplace. The Uzbeks have erected a monumental bronze statue of their national hero Tamerlane amid the ruins of Ak Saray to greet the visitors.

The tribes of the Barlas confederation claimed descent from Mongol regiments settled in Mawarannahr by Chagatai, second

son of Genghis Khan.[23] Later historians claimed that the family of
Timur descended from a loyal *noyan* of the Great Khan himself.
Tamerlane, just like his exemplum Genghis Khan, was born into
a turbulent world of perpetual raids among rival clans and tribes.
The Chagataid Khanate, the central *ulus* of the Mongol Empire,
had fragmented into a kaleidoscope of city-states in Mawarannahr
and unruly Turkish-speaking tribes on the central Eurasian steppes
who protested a nominal allegiance to the Chagataid khans who
ruled from Samarkand. To the west, the Ilkhanate had collapsed
into a constellation of warring regional states under Turkish warlords.[24] In Mawarannahr, wealthy merchant princes dominated
the caravan cities, notably Bukhara, Samarkand, and Balkh, and
they patronized mosques and the high Persian culture of Eastern
Islam.[25] Turco-Mongolian emirs, who commanded tribal regiments
of horse archers recruited from the pastures surrounding the cities, exercised military power. These emirs warred with each other
over personal rivalries and trade routes in the name of the distant
Chagataid khans. On the central Eurasian steppes, the tribes adhered to traditional nomadic ways and resented demands from
Chagataid khans in Samarkand. These emirs ruled virtually independently on the grasslands of Ferghana (the lower Jaxartes valley),
Moghulistan (between the Tien Shan Mountains and Lake Issyk),
and Semirechye (the lands south of Lake Balkhash and along the
banks of the Ili River). In 1347, the Chagataid khanate, called by
European chronicles the "Middle Empire" (*Medium Imperium*), divided into two competing khanates.[26] In the Western Khanate,
Bayan Quli (1348–1358) ruled as a figurehead dominated by his
leading emir and kingmaker, Abdullah ibn Qazaghan (1358–1359),
who ruled the powerful clan of Qara'unas.[27] In 1359, ibn Qazaghan
was deposed by the rebel Barlas and Suldus tribes led by the emirs
Hajji Bey and Buyan Suldus, respectively.[28] Thereafter, the Western Khanate lapsed into anarchy as each rival emir declared his
own puppet Chagataid khan. Meanwhile, in the Eastern Khanate
of Moghulistan, Tughluq Temür (1359–1370) imposed himself as
khan over the tribes.[29] In 1360, he exploited the political confusion
of the Western Khanate, and invaded Mawarannahr and captured
Samarkand. Tamerlane, then age twenty-four, promptly submitted

to Tughluq Temür, who deposed Hajji Bey and appointed Tamerlane emir of the Barlas tribes.[30]

In 1360, Tamerlane had already established his reputation as a warrior in the seasonal raids and retaliatory attacks of nomadic warfare.[31] As emir of the Barlas tribes, Tamerlane drilled his warriors to the standards of the horsemen of Genghis Khan and extended his sway over the tribes of Mawarannahr. He made common cause with Husayn, the son of Abdullah ibn Qazaghan and emir of the Qara'unas.[32] Tamerlane and Husayn, sworn brothers since their youth, shared a friendship comparable to that of Temujin and Jamuka. Tamerlane married Aljaz Turkhan Agha, sister of Husayn, but her early death contributed to the waning of the friendship between the two men. Together, Tamerlane and Husayn raided the camps of rival tribes and lent their swords to their overlord Tughluq Temür, Khan of Moghulistan, or to lesser rulers of Mawarannahr and Iran. In 1362, while in the mercenary service of the emir of Sistan, Timur sustained a wound from an arrow to his right hip, and when the bones knitted, his hip and femur fused so that he walked thereafter with a pronounced limp, dragging his right leg.[33] He also sustained an arrow wound in his right hand. He must have battled pain throughout his life. Yet Tamerlane never failed to fight in the forefront of his warriors due to his injuries, and if anything, his followers viewed his deformity as proof of their lord's courage. When Clavijo met Tamerlane, then age sixty-seven, the Castilian envoy noted the pronounced height of Tamerlane's left shoulder from decades of dragging his right leg. By then, Tamerlane also suffered from boils and sores, and he lost mobility so that he was often conveyed by a litter, even on campaign.[34] Yet he never lost his iron will, exceptional discipline, and boundless energy to the day of his death. In 1405, he could still command and inspire his army to trek across the winter snow fields and ice of Central Eurasia in a surprise attack on Ming China.

In 1363, Tamerlane and Husayn joined hands to oust the oppressive Ilyas Khoja, son of Tughluq Khan, who ruled as his father's governor of Samarkand.[35] Ilyas Khoja fled to Moghulistan, where he eventually succeeded to his father's throne. Meanwhile, Tamerlane and Husayn soon fell out and clashed for mastery over the tribes of Mawarannahr over the next seven years. In 1370, Tamerlane decisively defeated and captured Husayn at Balkh. Tamerlane avoided the odium of executing his former sworn brother, and instead handed Husayn over to a subordinate, Kay Khusrau, who quietly murdered Husayn to avenge a blood feud.[36] Tamerlane thereupon entered Samarkand in triumph, and proclaimed himself Grand Emir and protector of the Chagataid khan Soyurgatmish (1370–1384). Tamerlane married Saray Mulk Khanum, the widow of Husayn and a direct descendant of Genghis Khan.[37] Given her ancestry and prestige, she conferred legitimacy upon Tamerlane. Until her death thirty-five years later, she presided over the court of Samarkand as the principal wife and confidante of her husband, even though they never had children and Tamerlane took other wives with whom he fathered children.[38]

In 1370, Tamerlane, age thirty-four, had achieved mastery over the tribes of Mawarannahr and the caravan cities of Samarkand, Bukhara, and Balkh, so that he possessed the wealth and manpower to restore the empire of Genghis Khan. Even more important, Tamerlane had the vision and charismatic leadership skills to do so. To his northeast reigned the khans of Moghulistan, who resented their loss of Samarkand, and they commanded the tribes dwelling on the steppes stretching from the Upper Jaxartes (Syr Darya) and Tien Shan to Lake Balkhash. As late as 1397, Tamerlane still had to wage one more campaign to chastise his recalcitrant vassal khan in Moghulistan.[39] To the northwest, the independent dynast Husayn Sufi ruled Khwarazm, which had once been within the Chagataid khanate. Khwarazm straddled the fertile valleys of the lower Amu and Syr Darya Rivers that emptied into the Aral Sea. The principal cities, Kart and Urgench, were celebrated for their cotton and silk plantations, while the deltas sustained great herds of cattle, and flocks of sheep grazed on the grasslands surrounding Urgench and Kart. Merchants from Saray and Bulgar on the Volga brought furs, honey, flax, timber, and slaves from the distant forest regions of Russia. Tamerlane claimed both Moghulistan and Khwarazm as his domains.[40] To his immediate west, the Ilkhanate of Hulagu had fallen in 1353. In its place ruled rival Turkish and Iranian dynasts and the Christian kings of Georgia. Farther west, the Ottoman sultans aspired to unite Anatolia, and the Mamluk sultans of Cairo, implacable foes of the Mongols, aimed to occupy the Levant and retake Baghdad. On the Pontic-Caspian steppes from the Dniester to the Volga, the heirs of Batu partitioned and fought over the khanate of the Mongol west and the hegemony over the Russian principalities. Finally, in 1368, the armies of the Ming emperor of China, Hongwu, stormed the Mongol capitals of Dadu and Shangdu (the Xanadu of Marco Polo), and ended Mongol rule over the Middle Kingdom.[41] The last Yuan emperor, Toghon Temür, retreated to Mongolia, where he and his heirs fought an unequal struggle against the imperial armies of China. Tamerlane, as Grand Emir, saw both the Ilkhanate and Batu's khanate as domains within his reach. But Tamerlane rendered a respectful homage to the Ming emperor Hongwu as the successor of Great Khan Kublai until he was ready to march east against China.

Tamerlane, convinced of his imperial destiny, consulted his court astrologers with the same respect and frequency that Attila the Hun or Genghis Khan had paid to their shamans.[42] They hailed him the Lord of the Fortunate Conjunction, but Timur never permitted ill forecasts to sway his decisions to fight on the eve of battle. He communicated this sense of destiny to his warriors, ninety thousand to one hundred thousand strong, recruited from the steppes of Mawarannahr. He imposed, for the last time, on nomadic warriors the discipline and organization of the Mongol imperial army so that his *tumenler* were the equal of those of Genghis Khan.[43] Tamerlane replaced clan and tribal leaders with officers promoted from his kinsmen and loyal comrades. At the head of such a devoted field army, Tamerlane could campaign relentlessly for months over great distances and under adverse conditions to achieve strategic surprise. Tamerlane was just as innovative as Genghis Khan in the art of war. He added to his army a corps of Iranian engineers and a siege train. In 1399, he returned from India with an elephant corps that proved decisive at the Battle of Angora.[44] His governors or vassal princes of Ferghana, Moghulistan, Khwarazm, Khurasan, and Azerbaijan served along with their horse archers, while infantry was recruited from the subject populations to assault and gar-

rison cities.[45] But the decisive arm of Tamerlane's army remained
his horsemen of Mawarannahr.

In 1381, Tamerlane crossed the Oxus River and marched against
Ghiyas ad-Din Ali, the ruler of Herat.[46] Herat, boasting over four
hundred thousand residents, was home to celebrated poets, min-
iaturist painters, and theologians. Its clay brick domed mosques,
medresses, and minarets faced with glazed blue tile dominated the
surrounding arid landscape. Its markets were filled with silks, cotton textiles, metalwork, and exotic objects traded along the Silk
Road. Today, Herat is a shadow of its former self. In 1885, the British demolished the historic monuments to deny them to the Russians, who never arrived. Warlords and the Taliban have plundered
the remaining treasures and museums in the past two decades.[47]
Ghiyas ad-Din Ali meekly submitted and ransomed his city. Tamerlane carried off savants and craftsmen, and carted off the city's treasures, which were displayed in a spectacular triumphal return to
Samarkand.[48] Two years later, the citizens of Herat rebelled, and
Tamerlane dispatched his son Miranshah, who ruthlessly massacred
the population, piling skulls of the decapitated in huge towers as
warnings to would-be rebels.[49]

The capture of Herat was a turning point, for it opened the first
of six major campaigns waged outside of Mawarannahr over the
next thirty-five years. In the manner of previous conquerors from
the steppes, he was ever in need of booty and slaves to reward
his warriors, so he was a consummate practitioner of the principle "war sustains itself" (*bellum se ipsum alet*).[50] But Tamerlane also
aimed to reunite the empire of Genghis Khan. In two successive
campaigns, in 1381–1384 and 1386–1389, Tamerlane overran the
domains of the Ilkhanate of Hulagu, receiving the submission of
many famed cities along the Silk Road, and regional Turkish and
Iranian dynasts.[51] In the spring of 1382, Tamerlane subdued the
Mazandaran, the fertile land between the southern shores of the
Caspian Sea and the Elburz mountains, whose ruler, Amir Wali,
threatened Tamerlane's hold over the cities of northern Iran.[52] Then
in the next two years (1383–1384), Tamerlane turned southeast,
and conquered the Helmand valley, Zaranj, which he sacked and

razed to the ground, and Kandahar, thereby securing Afghanistan and the strategic Bolan and Multan passes, which are the gateways to the middle Indus valley.[53] Tamerlane devastated the surrounding countryside and massacred defiant populations to terrify other cities into surrender. As another grim warning, he ordered two thousand prisoners immured alive within a tower of Isfizar, a small town south of Herat.[54] Then, in autumn 1384, he suddenly turned west again, raced across northern Iran, and entered unopposed Sultaniya (today Soltaniyeh), the former capital of the later Ilkhans and equal in splendor to Herat.[55] The dusty modern village of Soltaniyeh, northwest of Tehran, still possesses the mausoleum complex of Ilkhan Ojeytu, a UNESCO World Heritage Site, as a reminder of its glorious past.[56] Sultan Ahmad Jalayir fled from Sultaniya to Baghdad, where he intrigued to regain his ancestral throne for the next fifteen years in league with Qara Yusuf, chieftain of the Kara Koyunlu (Black Sheep Turks).[57] These Shi'ite Turkmen tribes, who dominated eastern Anatolia, Azerbaijan, and northwestern Iran, proved implacable foes to Tamerlane.

Tamerlane followed up his capture of Sultaniya with the occupation of Tabriz, the first and principal capital of the Ilkhans.[58] In just four years of spectacular campaigning, Tamerlane emerged as the political heir of Hulagu, but success also advanced his borders to those of three rivals: the Mamluk sultan Sayf ad-Din Barkuk (1382–1405), the Ottoman sultan Murad I (1360–1389), and, by far the most dangerous, Tokhtamysh (1376–1395), heir to the Mongol *ulus* of Batu, with pretenses to the title of Great Khan.[59] Three times, Tamerlane had backed the exile Tokhtamysh to recover his throne of the White Horde in 1376–1378.[60] In 1380, Tokhtamysh reunited the legacy of Batu and took the crown of the Golden Horde.[61] Tamerlane expected loyalty from his vassal Tokhtamysh, who was five years his junior. Tokhtamysh, proud of his descent from the Great Khan, must have despised the lame conqueror of lowly origin. Tokhtamysh certainly underestimated the Grand Emir. In 1385, the khan crossed the Derbent Pass and sacked Tabriz at the head of fifty thousand horsemen. Tokhtamysh acted out of a mixture of alarm and confidence.[62] He viewed with suspicion Tamerlane's conquest of Azerbaijan, which Tokhtamysh's predecessors had long coveted. Tokhtamysh was confident due to his victories over the Russians three years earlier.[63] The khan of the Golden Horde, however, provoked a ruinous war over the mastery of the western Mongol domains for the next decade.

In the next spring, in 1386, Tamerlane launched his second western campaign to regain Iran and Azerbaijan in the next three years. He quickly retook Tabriz, and then punished erstwhile allies of Tokhtamysh. Tamerlane's wrath fell first on King Bagrat V of Georgia (1355–1393), and then Qara Yusuf. As the Sword of Islam, he proclaimed jihad against Christian Georgia.[64] Tamerlane sacked Tbilisi (Tiflis) on November 21, 1386. King Bagrat was compelled to submit and to convert to Islam, but Bagrat renounced Islam as soon as Tamerlane withdrew.[65] Tamerlane returned to ravage Georgia in the spring of 1387, and twice again in later years. Tamerlane then crushed the Kara Koyunlu (Black Sheep Turks) and secured the cities of western Iran. When Isfahan, which had surrendered on terms, revolted, Tamerlane returned, stormed the city, and slaughtered the population, although craftsmen were deported to Samarkand. Tamerlane ordered twenty-eight towers of human heads, each of one thousand five hundred, stacked before the city's walls for a total of forty-two thousand citizens.[66] Meanwhile, during the same summer of 1397, Tokhtamysh retired north of Caucasus, boldly marched his army across the central Eurasian steppes, crossed the Jaxartes River, and invaded Mawarannahr.[67] Tamerlane hastily withdrew east and raised the siege of Bukhara by Tokhtamysh, who escaped north. For the next three years, Tamerlane had to stamp out revolts in Azerbaijan, Khurasan, and Moghulistan.

In the winter of 1390–1391, Tamerlane planned his most daring campaign to date against Tokhtamysh. In April of 1391, Tamerlane departed from Tashkent with his entire field army of one hundred thousand, or ten *tumenler*, in a campaign comparable in strategic surprise, speed, and logistics to Genghis Khan's campaign of 1219–1221.[68] His horsemen, with numerous remounts, advanced swiftly over pastures cleared of all inhabitants and livestock, pressing seven hundred miles north to the Upper Tobol River. Then Tamerlane swept west, traversing another one thousand miles along a ten-mile front, driving his men at a relentless pace in early summer.

Tamerlane surprised Tokhtamysh, whose hastily assembled army was crushed in a savagely fought battle on the banks of the Kondurcha River, a tributary of the Volga, on June 18, 1391.[69] Tokhtamysh's cavalry on the right flank had nearly won the battle. But Tokhtamysh threw away victory when he fled with his banner before Tamerlane's furious charge in the center. The Kipchak Turks were cut down in flight. Tokhtamysh escaped, abandoning his tent, his harem, and treasure. Tamerlane, however, withdrew to winter in Tashkent, cognizant that the new Mamluk sultan Barkuk was threatening the western frontiers.

Tamerlane, upon his return to Samarkand in the winter of 1391–1392, quickly planned and launched a new western expedition against Iran and Iraq (1392–1397). In the spring of 1392, Tamerlane opened his fourth campaign by subjecting rebels in the mountainous region of Mazandaran along the southern shores of the Caspian Sea.[70] In 1393, Tamerlane returned to ravage Georgia, then subjected Fars, and in August expelled from Baghdad sultan Ahmad Jalayir, former ruler of Sultaniya, who fled to the court of Mamluk sultan Barkuk. In 1394, Barkuk marched the Mamluk army into Syria, and concentrated at Aleppo, while Tamerlane again devastated Armenia and Georgia. Tokhtamysh, acting in concert with Barkuk, crossed the Derbent Pass and ravaged Shirwan in Azerbaijan.[71] Tamerlane retaliated the next spring. After wintering his army in Azerbaijan, he crossed the Caucasus in early spring, and on the banks of the Terek River annihilated the army of Tokhtamysh on April 15, 1395.[72] In the course of the battle, many of Tokhtamysh's allies on his left wing deserted to Tamerlane. Tokhtamysh fled north, and then east into the steppes, where he died an exile in 1406. Tamerlane ravaged the steppes of the Kuban, sacked the Genoese port of Kaffa, and then turned east, ravaging the steppes of the lower Volga and sacking both Saray and Astrakhan. He installed a Chinggisid puppet, Khan Temür Qutlugh, to rule over a ruined Golden Horde.[73] In spring 1396, Tamerlane withdrew forever from the Pontic-Caspian steppes and retired south over the Caucasus. Tamerlane ravaged the lands of the Circassians and Alans, and the kingdom Georgia, once again in the name of jihad. In 1396,

Tamerlane returned to Samarkand in triumph with immense hauls of booty and captives, and so he initiated a great building program in his capital over the next two years.[74] Tamerlane had waged a brilliant campaign and broken the power of the Golden Horde, but he failed to leave any imperial administration. His vassal Khan Temür Qutlugh (1395–1401) was hard-pressed to impose his authority over the Kipchak and Uzbek tribes, so that the khanate fragmented into the khanates of Astrakhan, Kazan, and the Crimea in the fifteenth century. The khanates of Kazan and Astrakhan fell to the Tsar Ivan IV, the Terrible (1533–1584). The Tartar khans of the Crimea escaped Russian rule by submitting to the Ottoman Porte.[75]

In 1398, Tamerlane suddenly shifted his strategic direction against the sultanate of Delhi, which was then ruled by the ineffectual Nasir ad-Did Mahmud Shah II (1393–1413).[76] The Tughluq Sultans had ruled over the Indus valley, Doab, and upper Ganges for nearly sixty years. They were members of the third dynasty of Turkish sultans to rule Delhi ever since Qutb ud-Din Aibak had captured the city and entrenched Muslim power in the Doab, the fertile lands between the Indus and Ganges Rivers. Successive Turkish rulers, however, depended on Persian officials and Turkish warriors to rule over a vast subject Hindu population. Ultimately, the Turkish invaders failed to transform India into a Muslim land in the same way as their western kinsmen did in Anatolia. The climate and terrain could not sustain the horses vital for Turkish cavalry; the Muslims remained too few in numbers; and the Hindus accommodated the members of the new faith of Islam as just one more caste. Furthermore, no Muslim sultan in Delhi could ever subject the proud Hindu warriors, the Jats and Rajputs, and so they had to co-opt rather than rule their Hindu vassals.

In many ways, Tamerlane and Nasir ad-Din Mahmud Shah were unlikely foes, for they shared the same culture, faith, and court language that should have enabled them to reach an understanding. But Tamerlane was determined to win booty, slaves, and glory for his warriors and the abject submission of the sultan.[77] The sultans of Delhi had repeatedly repelled Mongol attacks.[78] In 1299, the generals of the Khilji sultan Ala-ud-Din ambushed a Mongol army, and publicly executed the Mongol prisoners by decapitating the soldiers and ordering the officers trampled by elephants.[79] The Chagataid khan Tarmashirin avenged the defeat in 1327 when he invaded the Punjab, sacked Multan, and compelled the Tughluq sultan to ransom his capital, Delhi.[80] Tamerlane thus saw the sultanate of Delhi as part of the Mongol imperial legacy to which he was heir.

In March 1398, Tamerlane departed Samarkand at the head of ninety thousand men, and he paused to hold court and receive envoys at Kabul in April.[81] Then Tamerlane crossed the Khyber Pass and descended into the Land of the Five Rivers, penetrating to the Sutlej River by October. He detached his general Pir Muhammad against Multan.[82] This strategic city fell only after a six-month siege. In the name of jihad, Tamerlane waged a gruesome war of destruction, sacking temples and massacring populations during the height of the monsoons. In December, when the monsoons relented, Tamerlane reunited his army and invaded the Doab, compelling Mahmud Shah to fight for his capital, Delhi. On December 17, 1398, Tamerlane crushed the Tughluq army outside of Delhi under dark skies and against the dire predictions of his astrologers. Tamerlane, who faced long odds, ordered the massacre of tens of thousands of captives lest they rebel and pillage the camp during the battle.[83] In this battle, Tamerlane displayed his greatest tactical genius to date. He countered the sultan's armored elephant corps, supported by infantry, in the center, by preparing the battlefield with trenches and caltrops to lame the beasts. Tamerlane directed his men to shoot the mahouts, and to open ranks should any elephants reach their battle line, thereby offering lanes for the beasts to rush harmlessly off the battlefield. Those elephants reaching Tamerlane's center encountered a stampede of camels bearing burning stacks of hay so that these elephants turned about, and plunged into the ranks of the Tughluq army. Tamerlane's cavalry then charged and swept the enemy wings, and put the Tughluq army to flight. Tamerlane promptly occupied and looted Delhi in a three-day orgy of rapine and massacre.[84] Tamerlane, however, did not stay long in India. He received submissions from Indian princes over the next several weeks, and then withdrew. On his retreat in early 1399, Tamerlane plundered at his leisure Hindu temples and Muslim mosques so that he entered Samarkand with a dazzling array of spoils, including captured elephants. With the profits of this expedition, Tamerlane initiated another major building program at Samarkand, including a major restoration and refurbishing of *ulu camii*.[85] Tamerlane basked in the jubilant acclaim of the city's residents, and he ostentatiously rewarded his warriors who had waged a lightning campaign of nearly three thousand miles.

Tamerlane returned to Samarkand after an absence of eighteen months to receive news of threats on his western border posed by the Mamluk sultan Nasr ad-Din Faraj (1399–1412) and the Ottoman sultan Bayezit Yildirim (1389–1402). The two implacable foes had put aside their differences to oppose Tamerlane. The new Ottoman sultan Bayezit Yildirim disputed the eastern lands of Anatolia and the al-Jazirah so that he and Tamerlane had long exchanged acrimonious letters, each accusing the other of bad faith.[86] In 1394, the then Mamluk sultan Barkuk had supported Sultan Ahmad Jalayir to recover Baghdad, while Tamerlane was waging his campaign against the Golden Horde.[87] Tamerlane also received disturbing reports about his son Miranshah, who ruled from Sultaniya the western domains as his father's deputy.[88] Miranshah was married to Khanzada, the reluctant widow of Tamerlane's first and favorite son, Jahangir, who had died prematurely in 1376. She reported the decadent behavior of her despised husband and the corrupt practices of the prince's officials. Furthermore, the indolent Miranshah had failed to retake Baghdad from Ahmad Jalayir. Tamerlane, after a respite of only four months, summoned his field army, and appointed his grandson and heir presumptive Muhammad Sultan as viceroy of Mawarannahr.[89] In April 1399, Tamerlane marched west on his sixth great campaign of seven years (1399–1404) across Khurasan and Iran to winter in Azerbaijan and Qarabagh, the rich grasslands on the upper Aras River. At Sultaniya, Tamerlane executed corrupt officials, relieved his son Miranshah of his princely throne, and commissioned him as an officer so that he could learn self-discipline and the art of war.[90] On news of Tamerlane's approach, Sultan Ahmad Jalayir fled for the court of Bayezit Yildirim, and Baghdad surrendered.[91] In the course of subsequent fighting in 1400–1402, Baghdad changed hands four times, endured two sieges, and suffered another dreadful sack.[92] Baghdad, while of limited strategic value, was too symbolic as the former capital of the Abbasid Caliphate to ignore.

In the first two years of this campaign, Tamerlane aimed to subject the grasslands of the al-Jazirah and eastern Anatolia, which were homes to the Black Sheep Turkmen cavalry of his redoubtable foe Qara Yusuf. In 1400, Tamerlane invaded eastern Anatolia along the northern invasion route taken by the Mongol army in 1243. In August 1400, Sivas, home to beautiful Seljuk mosques and medresses, surrendered after a brief siege; the Muslim population was spared, but the Christians were enslaved.[93] Tamerlane had promised not to shed the blood of the three thousand men of Sivas's Armenian garrison, so they instead were buried alive in a hollow. Tamerlane then turned his army southeast, marching via Malatya and Gaziantep, to arrive before Aleppo, the Mamluk capital of northern Syria, in October 1400.[94] The Mamluk court at Cairo was stunned, and could not mount an expedition into Syria, so Aleppo fell after a brief siege and suffered a four-day massacre.[95] Tamerlane then swiftly marched against Damascus, before the Mamluk court could reinforce the garrison. Between January and March 1401, Damascus endured a siege as Tamerlane negotiated with the city's elders for a surrender.[96] The youthful Mamluk sultan Faraj briefly appeared with a relief expedition, but he retired, abandoning the city to its fate. During negotiations, Ibn Khaldun slipped over the city walls, and sought an audience with Tamerlane, who was delighted to converse with the celebrated historian.[97] Tamerlane promised to spare the city's religious scholars and sent the artful courtier Ibn Khaldun on his way. Ibn Khaldun, as much a master of court intrigue as dynastic history, made his way to Cairo, where he wrote apologetic letters justifying his high opinion of the Prince of Destruction. When the Damascenes were unable to pay a ransom of ten million dirhems, Tamerlane ordered the sack of the city on March 17, 1401.[98] To the shock of the Islamic world, the great dome of the Umayyad mosque collapsed; the mosque's interior was gutted by fires. The mosque today is a heavily restored Ottoman version of the sixteenth century.[99] Tamerlane then retired across the Euphrates to punish Baghdad, which had risen against the Timurid garrison. In June 1401, Baghdad suffered a second Mongol sack on orders of Tamerlane.

Again the Islamic world reeled from reports of yet another Mongol atrocity. Each of Tamerlane's soldiers had to present two heads of the citizens, and so many captives were massacred lest Tamerlane's soldiers fail to have the required heads and risk their master's wrath. The skulls, numbering ninety thousand, were then piled into 120 gruesome pyramids in a macabre reenactment of Hulagu's sack in 1258. Tamerlane again retired to winter in Azerbaijan, and in spring 1402 invaded Anatolia for a second time. This time, he was determined to reckon with sultan Bayezit Yildirim.

The Ottoman sultan Bayezit Yildirim had been too distracted by his campaigns in the Balkans to respond to Tamerlane's invasion of Anatolia in 1400. On September 25, 1396, he had defeated a crusade led by Sigismund, King of Hungary and future Holy Roman Emperor, at the Battle of Nicopolis.[100] Bayezit, hailed as the Sword of Islam, had ordered the ghastly slaughter of thousands of prisoners. In fulfillment of his vow to Allah, he constructed Bursa's *ulu camii*, the serenely beautiful great mosque with twenty domes.[101] The sultan then resumed his siege of Constantinople, because he knew that the Byzantine emperor Manuel II was the architect of the crusade to rescue the dying Byzantine Empire.[102] But the Theodosian Walls defied the Ottoman army, and the Venetian and Genoese fleets supplied and reinforced the imperial capital. The city's citizens once again paraded the icon of Mary Theotokos, the Hodegetria, atop the walls and implored God's intercession. Their prayers were seemingly answered when Tamerlane and his horse archers crossed the Euphrates.

Tamerlane advanced swiftly across central Anatolia, along the southern banks of the Halys River (today Kizil Irmak), feinting toward Tokat, the fortress guarding the strategic pass into northern Anatolia.[103] Bayezit broke off his siege of Constantinople, transported his army to Asia Minor, and marched east over fields and grasslands torched by Tamerlane's army. Bayezit's army arrived on the battlefield of Angora (today Ankara), famished and exhausted, on July 20, 1402. Tamerlane had occupied the field first, and his engineers diverted the course of the Çabuk Çayı so that the Ottoman army was denied water at the height of the summer heat.[104] Tamerlane, commanding a cavalry army of perhaps one hundred thirty-five thousand men, with an elephant corps from India, forced Bayezit, commanding perhaps eighty-five thousand, to risk battle. The Timurid elephant corps smashed through the Ottoman infantry center (which had occupied a ridge), while Tamerlane's cavalry flanked the Ottoman army. The Ottoman army collapsed, although the Serbian knights under Prince Stefan Lazarevic fought desperately to rescue the sultan. Bayezit was captured, and died of illness en route to Samarkand. The ever-hostile Arabshah reports that the Ottoman sultan, bound as if a bird, was compelled to witness Tamerlane's victory celebrations. Rumor turned a metaphor into the legend of the hapless sultan conveyed in an iron cage to Samarkand. Instead, Tamerlane, according to the historian Yazdi, ordered Bayezit carried in a regal litter—a courtesy extended to defeated sovereigns who had submitted.[105]

News of Tamerlane's victory at Angora raced across the Islamic world and Christendom. The Mamluk sultan Faraj sent envoys, offering submission and acknowledging the superiority of Tamerlane—a triumph that had eluded Hulagu and all subsequent Mongol Ilkhans. The rival Popes at Rome and Avignon and the monarchs of Europe hastened to seek alliances with Tamerlane, while Venice, Genoa, and the Byzantine emperor promised naval assistance should the Grand Emir invade the Ottoman Balkans.[106] Tamerlane, however, was content to plunder the rich cities of Asia Minor and reward his warriors rather than press west. He targeted the defiant Hospitallers and, in a supreme feat of engineering, breached the walls and captured their island castle in the bay of Smyrna (today Izmir, Turkey). The Christian fleet arriving too late to raise the siege was greeted with a ghastly bombardment of the severed heads of the knights. The demoralized Christians turned about and set sail west, spreading rumors of the invincibility of Tamerlane.[107] In the next year, Tamerlane withdrew east of the Euphrates, punished Georgia once again, and arrived in triumph at Samarkand in 1400.

The Western campaign of 1399–1404 was a strategic masterpiece on par with his campaign against the Golden Horde in 1395–1397. He had outmaneuvered both the Mamluk and Ottoman sultans, and inflicted a decisive defeat on Bayezit. With the death of Bayezit, Tamerlane partitioned the Ottoman sultanate between Bayezit's two sons, Suleiman, ruling the European provinces from Edirne, and İsa Çelebi, who at Bursa held sway over Anatolia.[108] The Ottoman Empire lapsed into civil war for the next decade. Yet just like his campaigns that broke the Golden Horde and the sultanate of Delhi, victory over the Ottoman sultanate netted Tamerlane no strategic gains. Tamerlane accepted protests of loyalty from the sons of Bayezit and the lords of Anatolia (beylikler), but he left no imperial administration. Instead, he looted famed cities, showered his warriors with booty and slaves, and left. The Byzantine emperor, reduced to ruling little more than his capital of Constantinople, gained a respite for the next fifty years. It took the genius of Sultan Murad II to restore Ottoman power, defeat yet another crusade sent to rescue Constantinople, and bestow a brilliant heir, Mehmet Fatih, who not only conquered Constantinople but forged the imperial Ottoman state, the Porte, destined to dominate the Islamic world for the next five centuries.[109]

In 1405, the ever-restless Tamerlane, sixty-eight years of age, set out from Samarkand on his seventh and last great campaign for the conquest of China. Although Tamerlane had previously exchanged diplomatic niceties with the Ming emperors Hongwu (1369–1398) and Yongle (1402–1424), he resented Ming pretensions to universal lordship.[110] The Grand Emir, after subduing the three western ulus of Genghis Khan's empire, dreamed of adding the fourth ulus of Mongolia and China, the realm of Kublai Khan. He also looked suspiciously from afar at the return of Chinese armies to the Tarim Basin. Tamerlane, just like he had supported Tokhtamysh to regain his throne, now championed the cause of Örüg Temür Khan (1402–1408), ruling in northern Mongolia and the Yuan pretender to the Chinese throne. In December 1404, the Castilian nobleman Ruy Gonzalez de Clavijo witnessed Tamerlane fly into a rage against the Ming ambassador.[111] The Grand Emir likely staged the drama to declare war, and ordered the hapless ambassador and his retinue cast into prison. He immediately ordered his army to concentrate at Tashkent for its first winter campaign—a decision often criticized by modern scholars.[112] Tamerlane, however, timed his invasion to surprise the Chinese garrisons in the Tarim Basin and seize the winter stores so that his army would have reached the Gansu corridor in the spring, where he expected to rendezvous with his ally Örüg Temür Khan. In January 1405, Tamerlane's army crossed the Pamirs in exceptionally low temperatures and heavy snows. The exertions of the crossing proved too much. At Otrar, Tamerlane died of fever on February 17, 1405.[113]

Tamerlane died at a most auspicious moment, invincible and indomitable to the end. Early in the campaigning season, Tamerlane might well have surprised the Chinese garrisons in the Tarim Basin. He might have even rallied support from the Mongol tribes against the Ming emperor Yongle. But he might just as well have gone down in ignominious defeat once he ventured beyond the Jade Gate into China, because he lacked the imperial army of Kublai Khan. His horse archers alone could never have conquered the Middle Kingdom. Fate kindly assured that he would be forever remembered as the invincible Lord of the Auspicious Conjunction and the Prince of Destruction. Yet his imperial legacy did not long survive his death, for his heirs lacked the charisma and character to inspire his warriors to new feats of conquest. His three grandsons, Muhammad Sultan, Khalil Sultan, and Shahrukh Mirza, warred over the succession rather than collaborated to maintain and expand the empire.[114] The Timurid Empire soon fragmented, and declined to a regional power in the fifteenth century. At the same time, a revolution in military technology produced new weapons, first artillery and then handheld firearms, that ended the dominance of the nomadic horse archer forever. Tamerlane unknowingly represented the climax and end of the Eurasian nomads' military dominance of over two millennia. But while the equal to Genghis Khan on the battlefield, Tamerlane, quite unlike the Great Khan, failed to forge enduring institutions, nor did he leave brilliant heirs. Perhaps it is fitting to conclude with the words of the Roman historian Livy, who judged Rome's greatest foe, Hannibal, as a general who, with the favor of the gods, could win great victories, but he did not know how to use them.[115] The same may be said of Tamerlane.

Epilogue

Nomadic Conquerors: Achievements and Legacies

For over two millennia, the nomadic horsemen of the Eurasian steppes proved among the most deadly warriors on the battlefield. They can be credited with initiating two military revolutions, the horse-drawn light chariot of the Bronze Age, and cavalry. Every state that ever confronted nomadic horse archers had to field chariots or cavalry. Extraordinary rulers could weld these warriors into disciplined soldiers who could win empires. Among them, three conquerors stand out as the greatest: Attila the Hun, Genghis Khan, and Tamerlane. On the battlefield, they displayed tactical and strategic genius of the highest order. They excelled in the nomadic way of war and learned from their foes to win spectacular victories over more numerous foes. Each led by example and inspired his warriors. Yet these conquerors could never have succeeded without the skills and devotion of their nations, and the unique way of life that sustained the nomads. Theirs was no small achievement, but what were the consequences?

Among these three conquerors, only Genghis Khan founded an empire that endured after his death, thanks to the extraordinary genius of his three grandsons: Batu, Hulagu, and Kublai Khan. Mongol imperial rule defined the thirteenth century across Eurasia and laid the foundations for the modern world. Foremost, Kublai Khan, by his conquest of the Song, assured the future unity of China. Attila and Tamerlane failed to leave political legacies because their empires fragmented soon after their deaths. Even so, Attila sounded the death knell of the Western Roman Empire by decisively tipping the balance in favor of the Germanic tribes who would create the Christian kingdoms of Medieval Europe. Tamerlane, after reuniting three of the four khanates of the Mongol Empire, undermined the possibility of a revival of that same Mongol Empire. He weakened the power of the Golden Horde, and shifted the balance of power to the rising Russian principality of Moscow. He provoked the resurgence of the Ottoman and Mamluk sultans, whose capitals at Constantinople and Cairo became the new axes of Sunni Islam. Even in Iran, he indirectly assured the rise of the Shi'ite Safavid shahs. These consequences, even though unintended, were crucial in making the modern world.

The lesser-known barbarian conquerors and their peoples too altered their world. King Darius of Persia and Alexander the Great learned that the nomadic Scythians were beyond their reach, and so they devised a diplomacy to court and restrain these northern barbarians. The first emperors of China had to do the same, for they faced a more formidable foe in the Xiongnu. Modu Chanyu, the first known conqueror from the steppes, forged the first confederation of nomadic tribes to match the power of the Han armies for nearly two centuries. When the Han emperor Wudi shifted from diplomacy to war, he created the long-term strategic thinking of Chinese rulers ever since. Likewise, Byzantine emperors in Constantinople devised their duplicitous Byzantine diplomacy to counter each new Turkish kaghanate. Other nomadic barbarians carved out their own empires within the urban civilizations of the Middle East and China. Parthians, Kushans, Hephthalites, the Northern Wei, and Jin emperors each founded imperial orders based on nomadic horse archers. Tughrul Bey and Alp Arslan restored the power of the Caliphate, conquered new lands for Islam, and created the first Turkish sultanate in the Islamic world. Bumin, the legendary progenitor of the Turks, initiated the rapid expansion of

KENNETH W. HARL

Turkish tribes who made the entirety of the western and central Eurasian steppes their homeland.

Yet none of these steppe empires endured once the charismatic line of rulers ended. Successive imperial confederations dissolved into civil wars. Even the Mongol khans could not maintain a single empire beyond three generations. Even though nomadic peoples built few cities and left little writing, they gave to us the horse, spoke-wheeled vehicles, saddles and stirrups, the composite bow, riding trousers, belts and boots as the masculine garb, yogurt, and ayran. They played a crucial role as transmitters of knowledge, religions, goods, and technology across Eurasia from one civilization to the next. By inclination, they were monotheists who worshipped foremost the eternal blue sky so that they readily adapted and spread many monotheistic creeds. They showed exceptional tolerance and pragmatism. Women were accorded important social, spiritual, political, and even military roles. To be sure, it is important not to exaggerate their role as transmitters of technology and ideas. But Mongol khans demanded accurate maps to facilitate conquest. Mongol courts patronized astronomers and mathematicians who could calculate festivals and determine the will of the stars. Foreign merchants carried technology, crops, textiles, and skills across Eurasia. Even if no nomadic ruler premised these exchanges on a policy to promote a global economy, the consequences were still no less important. The Mongols, the last of the nomadic conquerors, perhaps played the most decisive role by transmitting papermaking and block printing, and gunpowder. The first, papermaking and block printing, expanded the dissemination of knowledge on a previously unknown scale. The second sparked the gunpowder revolution. Europeans combined the black powder with their bronze casting techniques to manufacture cannons. They quickly devised guns mounted on oceangoing vessels and sailed to seek the fabled land of Cathay. In so doing, they mastered the world's oceans. The global economy of the modern age was thus born thanks to the Mongol legacy.

* * * * *

Glossary

Abbasid Caliphate (749–1258), the hereditary dynasty of Caliphs, established by as-Saffrah (750–754), and from 762 on resident at Baghdad. Mongol Ilkhan Hulagu ended the dynasty with the sack of Baghdad in 1258.

Achaemenid (descendants of Achaemenes). The royal family of the Great Kings of Persia (559–329 BC).

Afanasievo culture (3300–2500 BC) is the archaeological culture on the steppes and grasslands west of the Altai Mountains in southern Siberia. The Afanasievo people were genetically and linguistically immigrants of Yamnaya Indo-Europeans who became the ancestors of the Tocharian speakers of the Tarim Basin.

Ahura Mazda, the supreme god of creation in Zoroastrianism.

Alans were Iranian-speaking Sarmatians who settled on the steppes north of the Caucasus in the first century BC. In 375, many Alans submitted to the Huns, while others, along with Goths, migrated west. These Alans entered the Roman Empire as allies of the Vandals in 406–407.

Altaic Languages. A family of languages with common agglutinative grammar and syntax, vowel harmony, and vocabulary. The major branches are Finno-Ugric, Turkic, Mongolian, and Tungusic. The Korean and Japanese languages may also be branches of this language family.

Amber Road, overland routes between the lands of the Baltic and the lands of the Mediterranean and Black Seas since the Bronze Age (2200–1500 BC) over which amber and the products of the northern forests and Arctic lands were exported south. Pliny the Elder (23–79) first described the route in his *Natural History*.

An Lushan Rebellion (755–762) was raised by the Tang general An Lushan (of mixed Sogdian-Turkish origin) against the emperor Xuanzong (712–756).

The revolt, even though it failed, wrought great destruction throughout China, and compelled the emperor to withdraw garrisons from the Western Regions (Tarim Basin).

Anatolian Languages, the first language family to diverge from Proto-Indo-European in ca. 4000–3800 BC. Speakers of these languages who migrated into Asia Minor in ca. 2500–2300 BC were ancestors to the historic languages of Hittite (Neshite), Luvian, and Palaic.

anda is a sworn blood brother in Turkish and Mongolian society.

Andronovo culture (2000–1450) is the archaeological complex of sites on the Middle Eurasian steppes (today Kazakhstan) that was home to the Indo-Aryan-speaking nomads whose descendants migrated into the BMAC of Transoxiana.

Arsacid (descendants of Arsaces) is the royal family of the Kings of Parthia (246 BC–227 AD).

Aryan < Sanskrit arya, "noble." (1) Designation of related languages that has been replaced by Indo-European languages. (2) Speakers of Sanskrit who entered India in ca. 1500–1000 BC.

Aryavarta, "Aryan homeland," comprises the lands of the Upper Indus and Ganges Rivers that are home to the sacred cities of Hinduism.

Ashina < Sogdian "blue," designates the royal clan among the Gök Turks descended from the brothers Bumin (551–552) and Ishtemi (553–575).

Avars founded the first confederation of Turkish-speaking tribes on the eastern Eurasian steppes (557–798). They are known as Juan-Juan or Rouran in Chinese sources. In 551–552, Bumin, Kaghan of the Gök Turks, overthrew the Rouran Kaghanate (330–551). The Avars, kinsmen of the Rouran, migrated west to establish a new kaghanate on the Pannonian plains (580–796).

Avesta, the compilation of the sacred texts of Zoroastrianism. The Persian language of the texts known as Avestan shares close similarities to the Sanskrit of the *Rig-Vedas*.

Bactria, today northern Afghanistan, the fertile region of the upper Oxus River (Amu Daryu); the principal city Bactra (Balkh) has been the nexus of routes of the Silk Road between Central Asia and India.

Balghasun (or Karabalghasun), capital of the Uyghur Kaghanate (744–840). The city was sacked by the rebel Kyrgyz tribes from the upper Yenisei valley, and abandoned in 840.

Bamyan Buddhas were two colossal statues Vairocana (175 feet high) and Sakyamuni (120 feet high) carved out of living rock in 507 and 554, respectively, in the Bamyan Valley, 140 miles northwest of Kabul. They were destroyed by the Taliban in March 2001.

bashlyk is the distinctive nomadic felt cap.

BMAC, Bactria-Margiane Archaeological Complex (2300–1700 BC), was the agricultural culture centered on the lower Oxus valley revealed by archaeology that was in contact with Sumer and Meluhha. The earliest Indo-Iranian speakers migrated there from the lower Volga River.

Brahmi, the oldest alphabetic script employed in India, and based on Aramaic scripts of the Near East. The earliest inscriptions using the script date from the reign of Ashoka (268–232 BC).

Brahmin, in Hinduism, the first or priestly caste; see *varna*.

Caliph is the successor to the *umma* (community of Muslim believers). The first four Rashidun Caliphs were elected by a college. In 661, Muawiya (661–680) established the first line of hereditary caliphs.

caravansary, walled quarters, stables, and storage rooms constructed and maintained by the Turkish Muslim rulers, for the benefit of caravans. The upkeep of the caravansaray was paid by the profits of a foundation (*vakif* in Turkish; *waqf* in Arabic).

caste. See *varna*.

cataphracus (plural *cataphracti*), "lancers," heavily armored shock cavalry wearing chain mail or lamellar armor. This heavy cavalry, first attested among the Sarmatians, was adopted by the Romans in the reign of Hadrian (117–138).

Cathay. Medieval European name for China; it was derived from a misunderstanding of Khitan, Mongolian-speaking nomadic rulers of northern China who ruled as the Liao dynasty (907–1125).

Centum Languages are those western language families that evolved out of Proto-Indo-European in 3000–2500 BC. These language families share common changes in sound and morphology. These include the language families of Celtic, Italic, Germanic, and Balkan Indo-European languages (the putative mother language for later Greek, Macedonian, Phrygian, Illyro-Thracian languages, and possibly Armenian).

Chagataid are descendants of Khan Chagatai (1226–1242), second son of Genghis Khan and rulers of the central Eurasian steppes and Transoxiana.

chanyu, "son of endless sky," was the title of the ruler of the Xiongnu reported by Han and Song Chinese sources. In the early fifth century AD, the title was abandoned, and steppe nomadic rulers henceforth styled themselves as khan.

Chinggisids are descendants of Genghis Khan (1206–1227).

Cumans, Ghuzz or Western Turkish-speaking nomads and scions of the Kipchak Turks, migrated from the central Eurasian steppes, into the Pontic-Caspian steppes in the eleventh century. At the Battle of Leveunium (1091), in alliance with the Byzantine emperor Alexius I (1081–1118), they annihilated the Pechenegs. Also called Polovtsy or Polovtsians.

cuneiform, the first writing system, devised by the Sumerians in ca. 3500–3100 BC. The wedge-shaped writing was inscribed by a stylus on wet clay.

dharma, in Hinduism, the moral law that dictates the cycle of reincarnation.

dhimmi, in Islam, members of protected religious communities of the book, who practiced their faith upon payment of a special tax (*jizya*). They were originally Jews and Christians; later Sabians (polytheists of Harran) and Zoro-astrians were so protected.

digvijaya. The ceremonial royal progress made by an Indian maharaja atop an elephant.

Doab, the fertile lands between the Punjab and the upper Ganges and Yammu Rivers; Delhi and Agra are in the Doab.

Fatimid Caliphate (909–1171), Shi'ite Caliphs who claimed descent from Fatimia, daughter of the prophet Muhammad and wife of Caliph Ali (656–661). In 969, the Fatimid Caliphs ruled from Cairo, in Egypt, and protected the Holy Cities of Medina and Mecca.

Finno-Ugric Languages constitute a family of the Altaic languages. The language family includes Magyar (Hungarian), Estonian, Finnish, and the Samoyedic languages of Siberia.

Five Dynasties and Ten Kingdoms (907–960) were the rival kingdoms ruling in China between the Tang (618–907) and Song Dynasty (960–1279).

foederatus, plural *foederati*, "federates," barbarian military units commanded by their own leaders who fought as allies of the Roman Empire in the later fourth and fifth centuries AD.

Gansu (or Hexi) Corridor, the narrow zone between the Eurasian steppes and the Tibetan highlands that connects China with the Tarim Basin.

ger. Portable home mounted on wheels and made of felt over lattice frame. See *yurt*.

ghazi, the heroic, nomadic warrior prized by Turks.

Ghaznavid (963–1186), a dynasty of Turkish slave emirs, who ruled from Ghazna (Afghanistan) over Transoxiana and Iran, and raided northern India.

ghulam (plural *ghilman*), "possession," Arabic word for slave soldiers, usually of Turkish origin. See **mamluk**.

Ghurid Sultans (1148–1210), of Iranian origin, used Turkish mamluks and tribal regiments to establish the first Muslim sultanate in northern India. They clashed with the rival Khwarazmian Shahs for control of Transoxiana and Iran.

Ghuzz Turks, speakers of Western Turkish or Oghuz languages, who emerged on the central Eurasian steppes between the ninth and eleventh centuries. They included Seljuk Turks, Cumans, and Kipchak Turks.

Gog and Magog, figures (or nations) in Ezekiel, Revelation, and the *Koran*, whose arrival marked the great wars leading to the final days of the Apoca-lypse. Since the fifth century, Christian, and then Muslim, writers identified them with the nomadic invaders of the Eurasian steppes.

Gök Turks, "sky Turks," overthrew the Rouran Khanate in 551–552. Khan Bumin established the senior Gök Turk Kaghanate (551–744). His brother Ishtemi (551–575) established the junior Western Turk Kaghanate (553–659) on the central and western Eurasian steppes. In 681, after ending the Tang Chinese overlordship, the Western Kaghanate was reconstituted as the Confederation of the Ten Arrows (On Ok Turks).

Golden Horde (1240–1502), the Western Mongol *ulus* established by Khan Batu; see also **Jochids**.

Gupta Empire (320–550), the second great empire of India founded by Chandragupta I (319–335). The Gupta emperors patronized Sanskrit letters, and Hinduism, and ended Kushan rule in northern India.

Han Dynasty ruled imperial China as the Former or Western Han (206 BC–9 AD), and then as the restored Later or Eastern Han (25–220). The usurper Wang Mang, who overthrew the Former Han dynasty, failed to establish his own Xin Dynasty (9–25).

Hephthalites, "White Huns," were Tocharian-speaking nomads, driven from the eastern Eurasian steppes by the Northern Wei emperors of China and Rouran kaghans. They founded an empire embracing the western Tarim Basin, Transoxiana, and northern India in 408–560.

Hexi corridor; see **Gansu corridor**.

Hinayana Buddhism, "the Lesser Wheel," represents those Buddhist ascetics who rejected the doctrines of Mahayana Buddhism, and adhered more closely to the teachings of Siddhartha Gautama (563–483 BC).

Huns, the first Altaic-speaking nomads who conquered the Pontic-Caspian steppes in ca. 375, and, under Attila (434–453), forged a great barbarian empire from the Rhine to the Volga River that challenged the Roman Empire. The Huns were probably descendants of subject or allied tribes of the Northern Xiongnu.

Ilkhan, "loyal khan," title granted by Kublai Khan to his brother Hulagu (1256–1265) in 1260. It was carried by his descendants the Ilkhanates (1265–1353), who ruled over Iran, Iraq, and Transoxiana.

Indo-Scythians; see **Sacae**.

Jade Gate. The name for the strategic Yumen Pass on the Silk Road that connects the Tarim Basin to China.

Jazyges (or Iazgyes) were Sarmatians who settled as allies of Rome on the eastern Pannonian grasslands west of Dacia in the mid-first century AD.

jihad, in Islam, holy war.

Jin Dynasty; see **Jurchens**.

Jinshi, the highest level of mandarin officials in the Song examination system (960–1279).

Jochids are the descendants of Jochi, first son of Genghis Khan and Börte (1181–1227). Jochi was considered the illegitimate son of a Merkit captor of Börte. Batu (1227–1256), son of Jochi, founded the Western Mongol *ulus* or Golden Horde.

Jurchens were Tungusic-speaking peoples of Manchuria who overthrew their overlords the Khitans, and ruled northern China under the Chinese dynastic name Jin, "golden," (1115–1234). The Jurchen emperors exercised a loose hegemony over the Mongol tribes.

kaghan ("khan of khans") denoted in Turkish a great royal figure ruling over many subordinate khans.

Karakhanid Kaghanate (840–1212) was a Turkish confederation on the central Eurasian steppes that ruled Transoxiana from Kashgar and Samarkand. They converted to Islam in 934.

Karakhitans (1123–1218) were the Sinicized Khitans who migrated to the central Eurasian steppes and so escaped the rule of the Jurchens. In 1141, Kara-Khitan Kaghan Yelü Dashi (1124–1143) defeated the Karakhanids and Seljuk Sultan Ahmad Sanjar (118–1153) near Samarkand—a victory that gave rise to the legend of Prester John. Also called the Western Liao; see also **Khitans**.

Karakorum, located on the Orkhon River, was built by Great Khan Ögedei (1229–1241) as the political capital of the Mongol Empire in 1225–1260.

karma, in Hinduism and Buddhism, the individual merit acquired by an individual by meritorious deeds.

kashik (or *kheshig*), the bodyguard of 10,000 of the Great Khan of the Mongols.

khan ("king") was the Turco-Mongolian royal title.

Kharosthi is the Northern Indian alphabet, based on the Aramaic alphabet of the Near East, used to write Sanskrit and vernaculars of Sanskrit.

khatum ("lady"), Mongolian queen.

Khazars, members of the Ashina clan and Western Turk Kaghante, established their own Kaghantate (ca. 670–967) over the Pontic-Caspian steppes. The Khazar court converted to Judaism in the late eighth century. In ca. 965–967, the Khazar capital of Atil was sacked by Prince Sviatoslav of Kiev (964–972) and the Pechenegs.

Khitans were Mongol-speaking conquerors who ruled northern China under the Chinese dynastic name of Liao (907–1125). They were overthrown by their vassals the Jurchens.

Khwarazm (or Khwarezm) is the fertile delta lands of the lower Oxus River (Am Darya) flowing into the Aral Sea; the lands have been home to important caravan cities since the fifth century BC.

Khwarazmian Shahs (1077–1231) were Persian-speaking Sunni Muslim rulers appointed as governors of Khwarazm by the Seljuk Sultans. After 1156, the Khwarazmian Shahs clashed with the Ghurids over domination of former Ghaznavid lands in Iran and Transoxiana.

Kipchak Turks, Ghuzz or Western Turkish-speaking nomads who dominated the central Eurasian steppes in the eleventh through early thirteenth centuries. They submitted to Mongol Khan Batu in 1238–1241, and constituted the majority of tribes of the Golden Horde.

kshatriya, in Hinduism, the second caste of warriors; see *varna*.

kurgan is a stone-and-earth tumulus raised as a monumental grave on the Pontic-Caspian steppes and central Eurasian steppes from the Bronze Age to the thirteenth century AD. The kurgans of Scythians, between the sixth and fourth centuries BC, have yielded the richest burial goods.

kurultai (or *khuriltai*) was the national council of Mongols summoned to elect the khan or to declare war or to conclude peace.

Kushans were the Tocharian-speaking emperors who forged an empire embracing the Central Eurasian steppes, Transoxiana, and nothern India (30–230). They promoted Buddhism, and trade along the Silk Road. See also **Yuezhi**.

lamellar armor was an armor of overlapping plates sewed together, and often worn as a second protective armor over chain mail armor.

Liao Dynasty; see **Khitans**.

limes, originally, designated a Roman military highway. The term came to designate the political and cultural boundary between imperial Rome and the foreign peoples (*gentes externae*).

magister militum, "master of the soldiers," supreme commander of field armies in the Roman Empire. From the reign of Constantine I (306–337), commanders of the cavalry (*magister equitum*) and infantry (*magister peditum*) commanded regional field armies. After 395, the supreme commander of both arms was henceforth designated *magister militum*, one for the Western and one for the Eastern Roman Empire.

Magyars are Finno-Ugric-speaking nomads who migrated from the Siberian forests east of the Urals to the Pontic-Caspian steppes in the ninth century. In 896, they settled on the Pannonian grasslands; they are the ancestors of the Hungarians.

Mahayana Buddhism, "of the Greater Wheel," was the school that emerged in India in the first century BC, stressing the divine status of the Buddha, Siddhartha Gautama (563–483 BC). The schools of Mahayana Buddhism today are in East Asia (Tibet, Mongolia, China, Korea, and Japan).

Mamluk, Arabic "servant." (1) Turkish slave soldier in Islamic world. (2) Dynasty of Turkish slave soldiers that ruled Egypt (1250–1517). (3) Dynasty of Turkish slave soldiers that ruled the Delhi Sultanate (1206–1290).

Manichaeism, the dualist, monotheistic faith proclaimed by the prophet Mani (216–273), in Sassanid Mesopotamia. The faith was popular among Sogdian merchants of the Silk Road; Tengri Bögü, Kaghan of the Uyghurs (759–779), converted to Manichaeism in 763.

Mauryan Empire (322–185 BC), the first empire of India, established by Chandragupta (320–298 BC). The emperor Ashoka (268–232 BC) converted to Buddhism.

Mawarannahr, "land beyond the river," the Arabic name for Transoxiana.

maya, in Hinduism, the illusion of the physical world.

Meluhha is the Sumerian name for the earliest urban civilization of India known as the Indus Valley Civilization (2600–1700 BC). Possibly the term is related to Sanskrit Mleccha designating foreign-speaking non-Aryans.

Ming Dynasty (1368–1644) was founded by emperor Hongwu (1368–1398), who expelled the Mongols. The Ming was the last native dynasty of imperial China.

Mitanni were Indo-Aryan speakers who migrated from Transoxiana into northern Mesopotamia in the sixteenth century BC, where they established a kingdom over Hurrian- and Amorite-speaking populations. Their language is closely related to Sanskrit and Avestan Iranian.

Nestorian Christianity (Church of the East), the Christian confession that followed the teachings of Patriarch Nestorius of Constantinople (429–431), who taught that Mary gave birth only to the Man Jesus rather than Man and God. The Nestorians, condemned at the Third Ecumenical Council (431), spread their faith across the Silk Road, converting Turkish and Mongol tribes.

Northern Wei Dynasty (386–535) were Sinicized nomadic rulers of northern China and the Gansu corridor. They promoted Buddhism and the Silk Road. They were Turkish-speaking Tuoba, the royal clan of the Xianbei tribes.

Oracle Bones were inscribed divination bones of the Shang Dynasty (1600–1046); they are the first examples of Chinese writing.

ordu ("horde"), Turco-Mongolian army or military encampment.

Orkhon Inscriptions are the earliest memorial inscriptions in Turkish (722), celebrating the deeds of Bilge Kaghan (716–734) of the Gök Turks, and his minister Tonyukuk (646–726). A distinct runic alphabet is used.

Parthians were an Iranian-speaking tribe that were welded into a kingdom, and then a Near Eastern Empire by the Arsacid kings (246 BC–227 AD).

Pechenegs (or Patzinaks) were Turkish-speaking tribes whose confederation dominated the Pontic-Caspian steppes west of the Don River from ca. 860 to 1091.

Prakrit was the vernacular language of India that evolved out of Sanskrit after 600 BC. Buddhist texts were written or translated into Prakrit.

Proto-Indo-European (PIE) is the reconstructed mother language of the Indo-European languages in ca. 6000–5000 BC.

Qin Dynasty (221–206 BC) was founded by Qin Shi Huangdi (257–210 BC), when he unified China in 221 BC.

Qing Dynasty (1644–1911), the last imperial dynasty of China founded by the Manchu conquerors.

qumis, Turkish *kumis*, Mongolian fermented mare's milk; nomadic beverage of choice.

Rabatak (Afghanistan) is the site where a Kushan royal inscription in the Bactrian language was discovered in 1993. The Kushan emperor Kanishka I (127–147) gives his genealogy and names the tutelary gods of the empire.

Rajputs ("sons of the king") were the kshatriya or warrior caste who dominated Western India between the ninth and twelfth centuries.

rammed earth is a construction technique using earth, gravel, lime, and clay. The Qin and Han emperors employed this method to build the Great Wall. The construction is simple, but labor intensive.

Rashidun Caliphs (634–661), the first four elected caliphs from among the immediate associates of Muhammad: Abu Bakr (634–636), Umar I (636–644), Uthman (644–656), and Ali (656–661).

Rashtrakuta (753–982) were Prakrit-speaking kings who united most of southern and central India (or Deccan). They favored Hinduism.

Rig-Vedas, the earliest religious texts of Hinduism. The hymns, written in Sanskrit, have been dated as early as 1500 BC and as late as 600 BC.

Roxolani were Sarmatians who settled on the grasslands between the Carpathian Mountains and the Black Sea in the first century AD.

Sacae (Sakai) were an eastern branch of the Scythians dwelling on the central Eurasian steppes. In 145–135 BC they migrated across Sogdiana and Bactria into the Helmand valley, and then via the Bolan Pass into India in the early first century BC, where they were known as the Indo-Scythians.

Samanid (819–1005) was the family of Iranian emirs who ruled from Bukhara eastern Iran and Transoxiana as the representatives of the Abbasid Caliphate. They defined the visual arts and letters of Eastern Islam.

Sangha, the community of Buddhist believers (laity and ascetics) established by Siddhartha Gautama (563–483 BC).

Sanskrit, the sacred literary language of Hinduism.

Sarmatians were the Iranian-speaking nomads who succeeded the Scythians on the Pontic-Caspian steppes between the third century BC and the third century AD. There tribes included the Alans, Roxolani, and Jazyges.

Sassanid (or **Sasanian**) was the dynasty of Zoroastrian Shahs of the Neo-Persian Empire (227–651).

Satem Languages, the eastern branch of language families that evolved out of Proto-Indo-European in ca. 3000–2500 BC. The language families share sound changes and morphology. These include the Balto-Slavic and Indo-Iranian language families.

satrapy, a province of the Persian empire (550–329 BC), ruled by a satrap; Darius I (521–486 BC) organized the empire into twenty satrapies.

Scythians, "shooters," the general name applied by Classical Greeks to the Iranian-speaking nomads on the Eurasian steppes.

Seljuk Turks, the Ghuzz or Western Turks who founded the Seljuk Sultanate (1055–1194) that revived the power of Abbasid Caliphate. Seljuk Turks settled in Asia Minor after the Battle of Manzikert (1071).

Shah-nameh ("Book of Kings") is the Middle Persian national epic composed by Abu'l-Qasim Ferdowsi Tusi (ca. 940–1020).

shaman is a mystic prized for his insights gained by contact with the spiritual world through trances often induced by hallucinogens, notably hashish.

Shang Dynasty (ca. 1600–1046 BC) is the first historical dynasty of China, centered in the lower and middle Yellow River.

Sharia, Muslim religious law based on the *Koran*.

Shi'ia; Shi'ite < Arabic "partisan" is the sectarian school of Islam that desired a descendant of Ali (656–661) as the rightful Caliph and so upholds the authority of Ali.

Silk Road (German *Seidenestraße*), the network of caravan routes across Central Asia that linked China with Europe and the Mediterranean world. The German explorer Ferdinand von Richthofen coined the term in 1877.

Sintashta culture (ca. 2050–1900 BC) is an archaeological culture of the ancestors of the Indo-Aryan speakers on the lower Volga and Ural Rivers. The Indo-Aryans bred the ancestor of the modern horse, and perfected the light chariot.

Strategikon, Byzantine military manual, attributed to the emperor Maurice Tiberius (582–602), with sound recommendations for countering nomadic cavalry.

Sogdiana (or **Sogdia**) was lands of northern Transoxiana and the Ferghana valley; the Sogdians spoke an eastern Iranian language that was long the commercial language of the Silk Road.

Song Dynasty (960–1279), reunited most of China as the successors of the Tang emperors, and promoted Confucian traditions and perfected the bureaucratic state. The Khitans, and then Jurchens, denied the Song the recovery of northern China.

spolia are architectural elements or sculpture of older buildings recycled into new buildings.

sudra, in Hinduism, the fourth caste of laborers or peasants; see ***varna***.

Sufi < Arabic *suf* woolen garment; Muslim mystic who follows the Sunni tradition.

Sui Dynasty (581–618), reunited China and founded the third great imperial order; they were immediately succeeded by the Tang Dynasty.

Sunni, "the orthodox," Muslims who accepted the Umayyad Caliphate of Muawiya (661–680). The majority of Muslims follow Sunni Islam and the authority of the *Koran* first defined by the uncreated word of God by theologians of Baghdad in the ninth century.

Suren, the hereditary commander of the Drangiana and Arachosia (today western Afghanistan and Pakistan). The Suren had the right to crown the Arsacid King of Parthia. The exploits of the Suren might have inspired the legendary Rustam of the Medieval Persian epic *Shahnameh*.

sutra is a Buddhist sacred text of aphorisms.

taiga is the forest zone of Siberia.

Tang Dynasty (618–907), founded by emperor Gaozu (618–626), was the greatest imperial family of Classical China.

tantric is the higher moral and mystical interpretation of traditional village rites in either Hinduism or Buddhism.

Tarim Basin comprises the valleys of the tributaries of the Tarim River between the Tien Shan and the Tibetan highlands. The central zone comprises the Taklamakan Desert, and the eastern end is dominated by the salt depression of the Lop Nur. Today known as Xinjiang or Eastern Turkestan, the region was home to caravan cities on the Silk Road.

Ten Arrows (On Ok); see **Gök Turks**.

Tengri, the sky god, and progenitor of mankind in Turkish and Mongol polytheism, which is sometimes designated Tengrism.

Three Kingdoms (220–280), the period of political division (Wei, Shu, and Wu) in China after the fall of the Eastern Han dynasty.

Tien Shan ("Celestial Mountains") define the northern boundary of the Tarim Basin (today Xinjiang).

Timurids (1405–1506) are the descendants of Tamerlane (1370–1405), who ruled over Iran and Transoxiana.

Tocharian (Greek Tocharoi) is the name given to two, possibly three related Indo-European languages spoken in the Tarim Basin and used to translate Buddhist texts between the sixth and ninth centuries AD. The ancestors of the Tocharians migrated from the original Indo-European homeland on the Pontic-Caspian steppes to the Altai Mountains and then Tarim Basin in ca. 3700–3500 BC.

Toluids are the descendants of Tolui (1227–1229), the fourth son of Genghis Khan.

Transoxiana, the lands between the Oxus (Amu Darya) and Jaxartes River (Syr Darya); in Antiquity known as Bactria and Sogdiana.

tumen. Mongol military unit of 10,000 men.

tundra is the Arctic zone of Siberia.

Tungusic Languages are a branch of the Altaic language family, and are today spoken in Manchuria and eastern Siberia.

türbe (plural *türbeler*), the memorial tomb to a pious Muslim ruler or mentor (*hoca*).

ulema, the religious community of Muslim scholars who interpret *sharia*.

ulus, "nation," Turco-Mongolian nation, designating related tribes.

Umayyad Caliphate (6561–750), the first hereditary line of Caliphs established by Muawiya (661–680) and ruling from Damascus.

umma, in Islam, the community of believers as proclaimed by the prophet Muhammad (575–634).

Upper Satrapies. The Greek designation of the satrapies of Bactria and Sogdiana (Transoxiana) in the Achaemenid Empire of Persia (550–329 BC).

Uyghurs (744–840), Turkish-speaking nomads who founded the third Turkish confederation on the eastern Eurasian steppes. They converted to Manichaeism in 763.

vaishya, in Hinduism, the third caste of merchants; see *varna*.

varna, Sanskrit word ("outward appearance") that designated the original four castes of Indo-Aryan society described in the *Rig-Vedas*: Brahmins (priests), kshatriyas (warriors), vaishyas (merchants), and sudras (laborers). Only the first three castes were considered twice-born; the sudras represented the subjected populations.

vihara ("secluded place"), the community of Buddhist ascetics.

Warring States (481–221 BC) were the kingdoms in the period of political disunity in China following the collapse of effective rule by the Zhou Dynasty.

Western Regions (Xiyu), the designation by the Han and Tang emperors of their provinces in the Tarim Basin.

White Huns; see **Hephthalites**.

Xi Xia were Sinicized Tanguts who had settled in Gansu and Western China in the tenth century as nominal vassals of the Song emperors. With Jingzong (1038–1048), Xi Xia monarchs ruled as Chinese-style emperors who favored Buddhism (1038–1227).

Xia Dynasty (ca. 2100–1600 BC) is the legendary first dynasty of China.

Xinjiang (formerly Sinkiang) or Eastern Turkestan; see **Tarim Basin**.

Xiongnu (220 BC–53 BC), Altaic-speaking nomads, who forged the first nomadic confederacy on the eastern Eurasian steppes. In 56–53 BC, the Xiongnu divided into the southern and northern Xiongnu.

yabgu (plural *yabgular*), the subordinate of a khan or kaghan; among the Khazars, the leading commander of the army.

Yamnaya (3300–2000 BC) is the archaeological culture on the Pontic-Caspian steppes. It was the original home of Indo-European-speaking nomads who created the nomadic way of life, invented the *gers*, and began the domestication of the horse.

yassa, customary Mongol law codified by Genghis Khan (1206–1227); it exalted the authority of the Khan over all other legal and religious authorities.

Yuan Dynasty (1279–1368), "originators," was the Chinese dynastic name adopted by Kublai Khan (1260–1294) and his successors who ruled China and the Mongolia.

Yuezhi. The Chinese name for Tocharian-speaking nomads who dwelled on the central Asian steppes north of the Tarim Basin. In 155 BC, the Xiongnu drove the Yuezhi west into Ferghana, where Zhang Qian visited them in 128 BC. These Tocharian speakers, called Da Yuezhi (Great Yuezhi) were the ancestors of the Kushans. See also **Kushans**.

yurt designates the residence and social bonds of the kinship group of a *ger*. See *ger*.

Zhou Dynasty (1045–256 BC) was the second imperial dynasty of China, ruling in the early Iron Age. After 481 BC, Zhou emperors lost control over their vassals, and China lapsed into a period of Warring States.

Zoroastrianism is the monotheistic religion of the Iranians, based on the *Avesta* and so the teachings of Zoroaster, who might have lived in the sixth century BC. The Sassanid Shahs favored Zoroastrianism as reformed by Kartir in the third century AD.

Bibliography

Primary Sources:

Ammianus Marcellinus. *The Later Roman Empire (A.D. 354-378)*. Translated by Walter Hamilton. New York, NY: Penguin Books, 1986.

Arabashah, Ahmed ibn. *Tamerlane, or Timur the Great Amir*. Translated by J. J. Saunders. Lahore: Progressive Books, 1976.

Carpini, Giovanni di Plano. *The Story of the Mongols Whom We Call the Tartars*. Translated by Erik Hildinger. Boston, MA: Branden Books, 1996.

Carpini, John of Plano. *Mission to Asia*. Translated by Christopher Dawson. Toronto: University of Toronto Press (Medieval Academy of America), 1980.

Comnena, Anna. *The Alexiad*. Translated by E. R. A. Sweter. New York, NY: Penguin Books, 1960.

Dawson, Christopher, trans. *Mission to Asia*. Toronto: University of Toronto Press, 1980.

Ferdowsi, Abolgasem. *Shahnameh. The Persian Book of Kings*. Translated by Dick Davis. New York, NY: Penguin Books, 2006.

Gonzalez de Clavijo, Ruy. *Embassy to Tamerlane, 1403-1406*. Translated by Guy Le Strange and introduction by Caroline Stone. Kilkerran: Hardinge Simpole Ltd., 2006.

Gordon, C. D. *The Age of Attila: Fifth-Century Byzantium and the Barbarians*. Ann Arbor, MI: University of Michigan Press, 1972.

Herodotus. *The Histories*. Revised edition. Translated by Aubrey de Selincourt. London/New York, NY: Penguin Books, 1972.

Hill, J. E. *Through the Jade Gate to Rome: An Annotated Translation of the Chronicle of the Western Regions in the Hou Hanshu*. Charleston, SC: Book Surge Publishing, 2009.

Hirth, F. *China and the Roman Orient: Researches into their Ancient and Medieval Relations as Represented in the Old Chinese Records*. Chicago, IL: Ares Press, Inc., 1975; reprint of Shangai-Hong Kong, 1885.

Ibh Fadlan, *Ibn Fadlan and the Land of Darkness: Arab Travellers to the Far North*. Translated by Paul Lunde and Charlotte Stone. London/New York, NY: Penguin Books, 2011.

Juvayni, Ala al-Din Ata-Malik. *History of the World Conqueror from the Text of Mirza Muhmmmad Qazvin*. Translated by John A. Boyle. Manchester: Manchester University Press, 1958.

Levi, Scott C. and Ron Sela. *Islamic Central Asia: An Anthology of Historical Sources*. Bloomington, IN: Indiana University Press, 2010.

Lewis, Geoffrey, trans. *The Book of Dede Korkut*. New York, NY: Penguin Books, 1974.

Li, Rongxi, trans. *The Great Tang Dynasty Record of the Western Regions*. Berkeley, CA: Numata Center for Buddhist Translation and Research, 1995.

Mandeville, John. *The Travels of Sir John Mandeville*. Translated by C. W. R. D. Moseley. New York, NY: Penguin Books, 1983.

Maurice. *Stratekigeon: A Handbook of Byzantine Military Strategy*. Translated by G. T. Dennis. Philadelphia, PA: University of Pennsylvania Press, 1986.

Polo, Marco. *The Description of the World*. Translated by Sharon Kinoshita. Cambridge/Indianapolis, IN: Hackette Publishing Company, 2006.

Polo, Marco. *The Travels of Marco Polo, the Venetian*. Translated by Thomas Wright. London: George Bell and Sons, 1907.

Procopius. *History of the Wars*. 7 volumes. Translated by H. B. Dewing. Cambridge, MA: Harvard University Press (Loeb Classical Library), 1914–1940.

Pseudo-Callisthenes. *The Greek Romance of Alexander*. Translated by Richard Stoneman. London/New York, NY: Penguin Books, 1981.

Rubruck, William de. *The Mission of Friar William of Rubruck: His Journey to the Court of the Great Khan Möngke, 1253-1255*. Translated by Peter Jackson. Indianapolis, IN: Hackett Publishing, Inc., 1990.

The Russian Primary Chronicle: Laurentian Text. Translated and edited by Samuel Hazzard Cross and Olgerd P. Sherbowitz-Wetzor. Cambridge, MA: The Medieval Academy of America, 1973.

The Secret History of the Mongols. The Origin of Chingis Khan. Expanded Edition. Translated by Paul Kahn. Boston, MA: Cheng and Tsui Company, 1998.

Secret History of the Mongols, and Other Pieces. Translated by Arthur Waley. London: Allen and Unwin, 1963.

Sima Qian. *Records of the Grand Historian: Qin Dynasty*. Translated by Burton Watson. Hong Kong/New York, NY: Columbia University Press, 1993.

Skeleton, R. A., Thomas E. Marston, and George D. Painter. *The Vinland Map and the Tartar Relation*. New Haven, CT: Yale University Press, 1963.

Tacitus. *Annals of Imperial Rome*. Translated by Michael Grant. London/New York, NY: Penguin Books, 1975.

Yap, Joseph P., trans. *The Western Regions. Xiongnu and Han. A Collection of Chapters from the Shiji, Hanshu and Hou Hanshu*. Middletown, DE: Joseph P. Yap, 2019.

Yezdi, Sarfuddin Ali. *Political and Military Institutes of Tamerlane Recorded by Sharfuddin Ali Tezdi*. Translated by James Davy. New Delhi: Idarah-I Adabiyat-I Delhi, 1972.

Zahir al-Din. *The History of the Seljuk Turks: The Saljuq-name of Zahir al-Din Nishpuri*. Edited and translated by Edmund Bosworth. London/New York, NY: Routledge, 2000.

Zenkovsky, Serge A. *Medieval Russia's Epics, Chronicles, and Tales*. Revised Edition. New York, NY: E. P. Dutton, 1974.

Secondary Works:

Abu-Lugbod, Janet L. *Before European Hegemony: The World System A.D. 1250-1350*. Oxford: Oxford University Press, 1989.

Agusti, Alemany. *Sources on the Alans: A Critical Compilation*. Leiden: Brill Academic Publishers, 2000.

Alam, Muaffer and Sanjay Subramanyam, eds. *Mughal State, 1526-1750*. Oxford: Oxford University Press, 2011.

Allsen, Thomas T. *Culture and Conquest in Mongol Eurasia*. Cambridge, MA: Cambridge University Press, 2001.

Allsen, Thomas T. "Mongols as Vectors of Cultural Change." In *Cambridge History of Inner Asia: The Chinggisid Age*. Edited by Nicola di Cosmo, Allen J. Frank, and Peter B. Golden. Cambridge, MA: Cambridge University Press, 2009, pp. 135–156.

Allsen, Thomas T. "The Rise of the Mongolian Empire and Mongolian Rule in North China." In *The Cambridge History of China*. Volume 6. *Alien Regimes and Border States, 907-1368*. Edited by Herbert Franke and Denis Twitchett. Cambridge, MA: Cambridge University Press, 1994, pp. 321–413.

Amitai-Press, Reuven. *Mamluks and Mongols: The Mnngol-Ilkhanid War, 1260-1281*. Cambridge, MA: Cambridge University Press, 1995.

Angold, Michael. *The Byzantine Empire, 1025-1204: A Political History*. London: Longman, 1984.

Anthony, David W. *The Horse, the Wheel, and Language: How Bronze-Age Riders from the Eurasian Steppes Shaped the Modern World*. Princeton, NJ: Princeton University Press, 2007.

Bachrach, Bernard S. *A History of the Alans in the West from Their First Appear-

ance in the Sources of Classical Antiquity through the Early Middle Ages. Minneapolis, MN: University of Minnesota Press, 1973.

Badian, E. "Alexander in Iran." In *The Cambridge History of Iran.* Volume 2: *The Median and Achaemenid Periods.* Edited by Ilya Gershevitch. Cambridge, MA: Cambridge University Press, 1985, pp. 420–501.

Bagley, Robert. "Shang Archaeology." In *The Cambridge History of Ancient China from the Origins of Civilization to 221 B.C.* Edited by Michael Loewe and Edward L. Shaughnessy. Cambridge, MA: Cambridge University Press, 1999, pp. 124–231.

Bailey, H. W. "Khotanese Saka Literature." In *The Cambridge History of Iran.* Volume 3 (2): *The Seleucid, Parthian and Sasanian Periods.* Edited by Ehsan Yarshater. Cambridge, MA: Cambridge University Press, 1983, pp. 1230–1243.

Baldi, Philip. *An Introduction to Indo-European Languages.* Carbondale, IL: Southern Illinois University Press, 1983.

Barefield, Thomas J. *The Perilous Frontier: Nomadic Empires and China, 221 B.C. to A.D. 1757.* Oxford: Blackwell Publishing, 1989.

Bausant, A. "Religion under the Mongols." In *The Cambridge History of Iran.* Volume 5: *The Saljuq and Mongol Periods.* Edited by J. A. Boyle. Cambridge, MA: Cambridge University Press, 1968, pp. 538–549.

Beckwith, Christopher I. *Empires of the Silk Road: A History of Eurasia from the Bronze Age to the Present.* Princeton, NJ: Princeton University Press, 2009.

Benjamin, Craig. *Empires of Ancient Eurasia: The First Silk Roads Era 100 BCE-250 CE.* Cambridge, MA: Cambridge University Press, 2018.

Bielenstein, Hans. "The Institutions of Later Han." In *The Cambridge History of China.* Volume 1: *The Ch'in and Han Empires, 221 B.C.-A.D. 220.* Edited by Denis Twitchett and Michael Loewe. Cambridge, MA: Cambridge University Press, 1986, pp. 491–519.

Bielenstein, Hans. "Wang Mang, and the Restoration of the Han Dynasty, and Later Han." In *The Cambridge History of China.* Volume 1: *The Ch'in and Han Empires, 221 B.C.-A.D. 220.* Edited hy Denis Twitchett and Michael Loewe. Cambridge, MA: Cambridge University Press, 1986, pp. 223–316.

Biran, Michal. *The Empire of the Qara Khitai in Eurasian History: Between China and the Islamic World.* Cambridge, MA: Cambridge University Press, 2003.

Bivar, A. D. H. "The History of Eastern Iran." In *The Cambridge History of Iran.* Volume 3 (1): *The Seleucid, Parthian and Sasanian Periods.* Edited by Ehsan Yarshater. Cambridge, MA: Cambridge University Press, 1983, pp. 181–231.

Bivar, A. D. H. "The Political History of Iran under the Arsacids." In *The Cambridge History of Iran.* Volume 3 (1): *The Seleucid, Parthian and Sasanian Periods.* Edited by Ehsan Yarshater. Cambridge, MA: Cambridge University Press, 1983, pp. 100–115.

Bodde, Derk. "The State and Empire of Ch'in." In *The Cambridge History of China.* Volume 1: *The Ch'in and Han Empires, 221 B.C.-A.D. 220.* Edited by

Denis Twitchett and Michael Loewe. Cambridge, MA: Cambridge University Press, 1986, pp. 20–102.

Bosworth, C. E. "The Early Ghaznavids." In *The Cambridge History of Iran*. Volume 4: *From Arab Invasion to the Saljuqs*. Edited by R. N. Frye. Cambridge, MA: Cambridge University Press, 1975, pp. 162–197.

Bosworth, C. E. *The Ghaznavids 994-1040*. Edinburgh: Edinburgh University Press, 1998.

Bosworth, C. E. *The Islamic Dynasties: A Chronological and Genealogical Handbook*. Edinburgh: Edinburgh University Press, 1967.

Bosworth, C. E. "The Political and Dynastic History of the Iranian World (A.D. 1000-1217)." In *The Cambridge History of Iran*. Volume 5: *The Saljuq and Mongol Periods*. Edited by J. A. Boyle. Cambridge, MA: Cambridge University Press, 1968, pp. 1–202.

Boyle, J. A., "Dynastic and Political History of the Il-Khans." In *The Cambridge History of Iran*. Volume 5: *The Saljuq and Mongol Periods*. Edited by J. A. Boyle. Cambridge, MA: Cambridge University Press, 1968, pp. 303–421.

Brian, Michael. "The Mongols of Central Asia from Chinggis Khan's Invasion to the Rise of Temür: The Ögedeid and Chaghandaid Realms." In *The Cambridge History of Inner Asia: The Chinggisid Age*. Edited by Nicolas di Cosmo, Allen J. Frank, and Peter B. Golden. Cambridge, MA: Cambridge University Press, 2009, pp. 46–66.

Brook, Levin Alan. *The Jews of Khazaria*. 2nd edition. New York, NY: Rowman and Littlefield, 2009.

Bulliet, Richard W. *The Camel and the Wheel*. New York, NY: Columbia University Press, 1990.

Bulliet, Richard W. *Cotton, Climate and Camels in Early Islamic Iran: A Moment in World History*. New York: Columbia University Press, 2009.

Burns, T. R. *Barbarians Within the Gates of Rome*. Bloomington, IN: Indiana University Press, 1994.

Burns, T. R. *A History of the Ostrogoths*. Bloomington, IN: Indiana University Press, 1984.

Bury, J. B. *History of the Later Roman Empire* 2 vols. New York, NY: Dover, 1958.

Bury, J. B. *The Invasion of Europe by the Barbarians*. New York, NY: Russell and Russell, 1963.

Cahen, Claude. "The Mongols in the Near East." In *A History of the Crusades*. Edited by Kenneth W. Setton. Madison, WI: University of Wisconsin Press, 1969, Volume II, pp. 715–734.

Cahen, Claude. *Pre-Ottoman Turkey: A General Survey of the Material and Spiritual Culture and History c. 1071-1330*. Translated by J. Jones-Williams. London: Sidgick and Jackson, 1968.

Cahen, Claude. "Tribes, Cities and Social Organization." In *The Cambridge His-*

tory of Iran. Volume 4: *From Arab Invasion to the Saljuqs.* Edited by R. N. Frye. Cambridge, MA: Cambridge University Press, 1975, pp. 303–328.

Cahen, Claude. "The Turkish Invasions: The Selchükids." In *A History of the Crusades.* Edited by Kenneth W. Setton. Madison, WI: University of Wisconsin Press, 1969, Volume I, pp. 135–176.

The Cambridge History of Ancient China from the Origins of Civilization to 221 B.C. Edited by Michael Loewe and Edward L. Shaughnessy. Cambridge, MA: Cambridge University Press, 1999.

The Cambridge History of China. Volume 1. *The Ch'in and Han Empires, 221 B.C.-A.D. 220.* Edited by Denis Twitchett and Michael Loewe. Cambridge, MA: Cambridge University Press, 1986.

The Cambridge History of China. Volume 2. *The Six Dynasties, 220-589.* Edited by Albert E. Dien and Keith N. Knapp. Cambridge, MA: Cambridge University Press, 2019.

The Cambridge History of China. Volume 3, Part 1. *Sui and T'ang China, 589-906.* Edited by Denis Twitchett. Cambridge, MA: Cambridge University Press, 1979.

The Cambridge History of China. Volume 5, Part 2. *Sung China, 960-1270.* Edited by John W. Chaffe and Denis Twitchett. Cambridge, MA: Cambridge University Press, 2015.

The Cambridge History of China. Volume 6. *Alien Regimes and Border States, 907-1368.* Edited by Herbert Franke and Denis Twitchett. Cambridge, MA: Cambridge University Press, 1994.

The Cambridge History of Iran. Volume 2: *The Median and Achaemenid Periods.* Edited by Ilya Gershevitch. Cambridge, MA: Cambridge University Press, 1985.

The Cambridge History of Iran. Volume 3 (1): *The Seleucid, Parthian and Sasanian Periods.* Edited by Ehsan Yarshater. Cambridge, MA: Cambridge University Press, 1983.

The Cambridge History of Iran. Volume 3 (2): *The Seleucid, Parthian and Sasanian Periods.* Edited by Ehsan Yarshater. Cambridge, MA: Cambridge University Press, 1983.

The Cambridge History of Iran. Volume 4: *From Arab Invasion to the Saljuqs.* Edited by R. N. Frye. Cambridge, MA: Cambridge University Press, 1975.

The Cambridge History of Iran. Volume 5: *The Saljuq and Mongol Periods.* Edited by J. A. Boyle. Cambridge, MA: Cambridge University Press, 1968.

Canepa, Matthew P. *The Two Eyes of the Earth: Art and Ritual Kingship between Rome and Sasanian Iran.* Berkeley, CA: University of California Press, 2009.

Chaffee, John W. "Reflections on the Sung." In *The Cambridge History of China.* Volume 5, Part 2. *Sung China, 960-1270.* Edited by John W. Chaffe and Denis Twitchett. Cambridge, MA: Cambridge University Press, 2015, pp. 1–18.

Chambers, James. *The Devil's Horsemen.* New York, NY: Athenaeum, 1975.

Chang, Kwang-Chih. *Shang Civilization*. New Haven, CT: Yale University Press, 1980.

Chaussende, Damien. "Western Jin." In *The Cambridge History of China*. Volume 2. *The Six Dynasties, 220-589*. Edited by Albert E. Dien and Keith N. Knapp. Cambridge, MA: Cambridge University Press, 2019, pp. 70–95.

Chittick, Andrew. "The Southern Dynasties." In *The Cambridge History of China*. Volume 2. *The Six Dynasties, 220-589*. Edited by Albert E. Dien and Keith N. Knapp. Cambridge: Cambridge University Press, 2019, pp. 237–272.

Clements, Jonathan. *Wu: The Chinese Empress Who Schemed, Seduced and Murdered Her Way to Become a Living God*. San Bernardino, CA: Beacon Books, 2007.

Crews, Robert D. *For Prophet and Tsar: Islam and Empire in Russia and Central Asia*. Cambridge, MA: Harvard University Press, 2006.

Cribb, Joe and Georgina Herrmann, eds. *After Alexander: Central Asia before Islam*. Oxford: Oxford University Press, 2007.

Crone, P. and G. M. Hinds. *God's Caliph: Religious Authority in the First Centuries of Islam*. Cambridge, MA: Cambridge University Press, 1980.

Crummey, Robert O. *The Formation of Muscovy, 1304-1613*. New York, NY: Longman Grioup, 1987.

Cunliffe, Barry. *The Scythians: Nomad Warriors of the Steppe*. Oxford: Oxford University Press, 2019.

Curta, Florin and Roman Kovaley, eds. *The Other Europe in the Middle Ages: Avars, Bulgars and Cumans: East Central and Eastern Europe in the Middle Ages, 450-1450*. Leiden: Brill Academic Publication, 2007.

Curtis, V. S. and S. Stewart, eds. *The Age of the Parthians*. London: I. B. Tauris, 2007.

Dale, Stephen F. *The Muslim Empires of the Ottomans, Safavids, and Mughals*. Cambridge, MA: Cambridge University Press, 2010.

Dale, Stephen. "The Later Timurids, c. 1450-1526." In *Cambridge History of Inner Asia: The Chinggisid Age*. Edited by Nicola di Cosmo, Allen J. Frank, and Peter B. Golden. Cambridge, MA: Cambridge University Press, 2009, pp. 1999–220.

Dardess, John. "Shun-ti and the End of Yüan Rule in China." In *The Cambridge History of China*. Volume 6. *Alien Regimes and Border States, 907-1368*. Edited by Herbert Franke and Denis Twitchett. Cambridge, MA: Cambridge University Press, 1994, pp. 561–586.

Daryaee, Touraj. *Sasanian Persia: The Rise and Fall of an Empire*. New York, NY: J. B. Taurus & Co., Ltd., 2009.

Davis, R. H. C. *The Medieval Warhorse: Origin, Development, and Redevelopment*. London: Thames and Hudson, 1989.

de Crespigny, Rafe. "History: Wei." In *The Cambridge History of China*. Volume 2. *The Six Dynasties, 220-589*. Edited by Albert E. Dien and Keith N. Knapp. Cambridge, MA: Cambridge University Press, 2019, pp. 1–49.

de Crespigny, Rafe. "History: Wu." In *The Cambridge History of China*. Volume 2. *The Six Dynasties, 220-589*. Edited by Albert E. Dien and Keith N. Knapp. Cambridge, MA: Cambridge University Press, 2019, pp. 50–65.

de Rachewiltz, Igor. *Papal Envoys to the Great Khans*. Stanford, CA: Stanford University Press, 1971.

Debevoise, N. C. *A Political History of Parthia*. Chicago, IL: Chicago University Press, 1938.

di Cosmo, Nicola. *Ancient China and Its Enemies: The Rise of Nomadic Power in East Asian History*. Cambridge, MA: Cambridge University Press, 2002.

di Cosmo, Nicola. "The Northern Frontier in Pre-Imperial China." In *The Cambridge History of Ancient China from the Origins of Civilization to 221 B.C.* Edited by Michael Loewe and Edward L. Shaughnessy. Cambridge, MA: Cambridge University Press, 1999, pp. 885–966.

di Cosmo, Nicola, Allen J. Frank, and Peter B. Golden. *The Cambridge History of Inner Asia: The Chinggisid Age*. Cambridge, MA: Cambridge University Press, 2009.

Dien, Albert J. "Eastern Wei-Northern Qi." In *The Cambridge History of China*. Volume 2. *The Six Dynasties, 220-589*. Edited by Albert E. Dien and Keith N. Knapp. Cambridge, MA: Cambridge University Press, 2019, pp. 184–209.

Dien, Albert J. "Western Wei-Northern Zhou." In *The Cambridge History of China*. Volume 2. *The Six Dynasties, 220-589*. Edited by Albert E. Dien and Keith N. Knapp. Cambridge, MA: Cambridge University Press, 2019, pp. 210–236.

Donner, Fred M. *The Early Islamic Conquests*. Princeton, NJ: Princeton University Press, 1981.

Dresden, Mark. "Sogdian Language and Literature." In *The Cambridge History of Iran*. Volume 3 (2): *The Seleucid, Parthian and Sasanian Periods*. Edited by Ehsan Yarshater. Cambridge, MA: Cambridge University Press, 1983, pp. 1216–1229.

Duchesne-Guilliemin, J. "Zoroastrian Religion." In *The Cambridge History of Iran*. Volume 3 (2): *The Seleucid, Parthian and Sasanian Periods*. Edited by Ehsan Yarshater. Cambridge, MA: Cambridge University Press, 1983, pp. 866–908.

Dunlop, D. N. *The History of the Jewish Khazars*. Princeton, NJ: Princeton University Press, 1954.

Dunnel, Ruth. "The Hsi Hsia." In *The Cambridge History of China*. Volume 6. *Alien Regimes and Border States, 907-1368*. Edited by Herbert Franke and Denis Twitchett. Cambridge, MA: Cambridge University Press, 1994, pp. 154–214.

Eberhard, Wolfram. *Conquerors and Rulers: Social Forces in Medieval China*. Leiden: E. J. Brill, 1965.

Ebrey, Patrick. "The Economic and Social History of Later Han." In *The Cambridge History of China*. Volume 1: *The Ch'in and Han Empires, 221 B.C.-A.D. 220*. Edited by Denis Twitchett and Michael Loewe. Cambridge, MA: Cambridge University Press, 1986, pp. 649–725.

Eilers, Wilhelm. "Iran and Mesopotamia." In *The Cambridge History of Iran*. Volume 3 (1): *The Seleucid, Parthian and Sasanian Periods*. Edited by Ehsan Yarshater. Cambridge, MA: Cambridge University Press, 1983, pp. 481–504.

Elverskog, Johan. *Buddhism and Islam on the Silk Road*. Philadelphia, PA: University of Pennsylvania Press, 2010.

Emmerick, R. E. "Buddhism among Iranian Peoples." In *The Cambridge History of Iran*. Volume 3 (2): *The Seleucid, Parthian and Sasanian Periods*. Edited by Ehsan Yarshater. Cambridge, MA: Cambridge University Press, 1983, pp. 949–964.

Emmerick, R. E. "Iran Settlement East of the Pamirs." In *The Cambridge History of Iran*. Volume 3 (1): *The Seleucid, Parthian and Sasanian Periods*. Edited by Ehsan Yarshater. Cambridge, MA: Cambridge University Press, 1983, pp. 263–278.

Endicott-West, Elizabeth. "The Yüün Government and Society." In *The Cambridge History of China*. Volume 6. *Alien Regimes and Border States, 907-1368*. Edited by Herbert Franke and Denis Twitchett. Cambridge, MA: Cambridge University Press, 1994, pp. 587–615.

Farmer, J. Michael. "History: Shu-Han." In *The Cambridge History of China*. Volume 2. *The Six Dynasties, 220-589*. Edited by Albert E. Dien and Keith N. Knapp. Cambridge, MA: Cambridge University Press, 2019, pp. 66–69.

Ferrill, Arther. *The Fall of the Roman Empire: The Military Explanation*. London: Thames and Hudson, 1986.

Foltz, Richard. *Religions on the Silk Road: Premodern Patterns of Globalization*. 2nd edition. London: Palgrave Macmillan, 2010.

Fowden, Garth. *From Empire to Commonwealth: Consequences of Monotheism in Late Antiquity*. Princeton, NJ: Princeton University Press, 1993.

Franke, Herbert. "The Chin Dynasty." In *The Cambridge History of China*. Volume 6. *Alien Regimes and Border States, 907-1368*. Edited by Herbert Franke and Denis Twitchett. Cambridge, MA: Cambridge University Press, 1994, pp. 265–320.

Franke, Herbert. "The Forest Peoples of Manchuria." In *The Cambridge History of Early Inner Asia*. Edited by Denis Sinor. Cambridge, MA: Cambridge University Press, 1990, pp. 400–423.

Franke, Herbert and Denis Twitchett. "Introduction." In *The Cambridge History of China*. Volume 6. *Alien Regimes and Border States, 907-1368*. Edited by Herbert Franke and Denis Twitchett. Cambridge, MA: Cambridge University Press, 1994, pp. 3–42.

Franklin, Simon and Jonathan Sheppard. *The Emergence of the Rus, 750-1200*. New York, NY: Longman Group, 1996.

Fuller, J. F. C. *The Generalship of Alexander the Great*. New York, NY: Minerva Books, 1960.

Frye, Richard N. *The Heritage of Persia from Antiquity to the Turkish Expansion*. Princeton, NJ: Markus Wiener Publishers, 1996.

Frye, R. N. "The Political History under the Sasanians." In *The Cambridge*

History of Iran. Volume 3 (1): *The Seleucid, Parthian and Sasanian Periods.* Edited by Ehsan Yarshater. Cambridge, MA: Cambridge University Press, 1983, pp. 116–180.

Frye, R. N. "The Samanids." In *The Cambridge History of Iran.* Volume 4: *From Arab Invasion to the Saljuqs.* Edited by R. N. Frye. Cambridge, MA: Cambridge University Press, 1975, pp. 136–161.

Gabriel, Richard A. *Genghis Khan's Greatest General: Subotai the Valiant.* Norman, OK: University of Oklahoma, 2004.

Garsoïan, Nina. "Byzantium and the Sasansians." In *The Cambridge History of Iran.* Volume 3 (1): *The Seleucid, Parthian and Sasanian Periods.* Edited by Ehsan Yarshater. Cambridge, MA: Cambridge University Press, 1983, pp. 568–592.

Golas, Peter J. "The Sung Fiscal Administration." In *The Cambridge History of China.* Volume 5, Part 2. *Sung China, 960-1270.* Edited by John W. Chaffe and Denis Twitchett. Cambridge, MA: Cambridge University Press, 2015, pp. 139–213.

Golden, Peter. *Central Asia in World History.* Oxford: Oxford University Press, 2011.

Golden, Peter B. "Inner Asia c. 1200." In *The Cambridge History of Inner Asia: The Chinggisid Age.* Edited by Nicolas di Cosmo, Allen J. Frank, and Peter B. Golden. Cambridge, MA: Cambridge University Press, 2009, pp. 9–25.

Golden, Peter B. "The Karakhanids and Early Islam." In *The Cambridge History of Early Inner Asia.* Edited by Denis Sinor. Cambridge, MA: Cambridge University Press, 1990, pp. 343–370.

Golden, Peter B. "The Peoples of the South Russian Steppes." In *The Cambridge History of Early Inner Asia.* Edited by Denis Sinor. Cambridge, MA: Cambridge University Press, 1990, pp. 256–283.

Golden, Peter B. et alii, eds. *The World of the Khazars.* Leiden: Brill Academic Publication, 2007.

Goldsworthy, A. K. *The Roman Army at War 100 B.C.-A.D. 200.* Oxford: Oxford University Press, 1996.

Golombek, Lisa and Maria Subtelny, eds. *Timurid Art and Culture: Iran and Central Asia in the Fifteenth Century.* Leiden: E. J. Brill, 1992.

Gordon, Stewart. *When Asia Was the World: Traveling Merchants, Scholars, Warriors, and Monks Who Created the "Riches of the East."* Philadelphia, PA: Da Capro Press, 2008.

Graff, David A. "The Art of War." In *The Cambridge History of China.* Volume 2. *The Six Dynasties, 220-589.* Edited by Albert E. Dien and Keith N. Knapp. Cambridge, MA: Cambridge University Press, 2019, pp. 273–296.

Graff, David A. *Medieval Chinese Warfare, 300-900.* New York, NY: Routledge, 2002.

Graff, David A. and Robin Higham, eds. *A Military History of China.* Lexington, KY: University of Kentucky Press, 2012.

Greenfield, J. C. "Aramaic in the Achaemenian Empire." In *The Cambridge History of Iran*. Volume 2: *The Median and Achaemenid Periods*. Edited by Ilya Gershevitch. Cambridge, MA: Cambridge University Press, 1985, pp. 698–713.

Grousset, René. *The Empire of the Steppes: A History of Central Asia*. Translated by Naomi Walford. New Brunswick, NJ: Rutgers University Press, 2010.

Guisso, Richard W. K. "The Reigns of Wu, Chung-tsung and Jui-tsung (684-712)." In *The Cambridge History of China*. Volume 3. Part 1. *Sui and T'ang China, 589-906*. Edited by Denis Twitchett. Cambridge, MA: Cambridge University Press, 1979, pp. 290–332.

Gupta, Parmeshwari Lal and Sarojini Kulashreshtha. *Kuṣāna Coins and History*. Delhi: D. K. Printworld, Ltd., 1994.

Halperin, Charles J. *Russia and the Golden Horde: The Mongol Impact on Medieval Russian History*. Bloomington, IN: Indiana University Press, 1995.

Hansen, Valerie. *The Open Empire: A History of China to 1600*. New York, NY: W. W. Norton and Company, 2000.

Hansen, Valerie. *The Silk Road: A New History*. Oxford: Oxford University Press, 2012.

Harl, Kenneth W. *Coinage in the Roman Economy 300 B.C.-700 A.D.* Baltimore, MD: Johns Hopkins University Press, 1996.

Hartman, Charles. "Sung Government and Politics." In *The Cambridge History of China*. Volume 5, Part 2. *Sung China, 960-1270*. Edited by John W. Chaffe and Denis Twitchett. Cambridge, MA: Cambridge University Press, 2015, pp. 19–138.

Haw, Stephen G. *Marco Polo's China: A Venetian in the Realm of Kublai Khan*. London/New York, NY: Routledge, 2006.

Headrick, Daniel R. *The Tools of Empire: Technology and European Imperialism in the Nineteenth Century*. Oxford: Oxford University Press, 1981.

Heather, Peter. *Goths and Romans*. Oxford: Oxford University Press, 1991.

Hildinger, Erik. *Warriors of the Steppes: A Military History of Central Asia 500 B.C. to 1200 A.D.* Cambridge, MA: Da Capro Press, 1997.

Hodgson, M. C. S. "The Isma'ili State." In *The Cambridge History of Iran*. Volume 5: *The Saljuq and Mongol Periods*. Edited by J. A. Boyle. Cambridge, MA: Cambridge University Press, 1968, pp. 422–482.

Hocombe, Charles. "Eastern Jin." In *The Cambridge History of China*. Volume 2. *The Six Dynasties, 220-589*. Edited by Albert E. Dien and Keith N. Knapp. Cambridge, MA: Cambridge University Press, 2019, pp. 96–118.

Hocombe, Charles. "Eastern Jin." In *The Cambridge History of China*. Volume 2. *The Six Dynasties, 220-589*. Edited by Albert E. Dien and Keith N. Knapp. Cambridge, MA: Cambridge University Press, 2019, pp. 237–272.

Hocombe, Charles. "Foreign Relations." In *The Cambridge History of China*.

Volume 2. *The Six Dynasties, 220-589.* Edited by Albert E. Dien and Keith N. Knapp. Cambridge, MA: Cambridge University Press, 2019, pp. 297–308.

Hocombe, Charles. "The Sixteen Kingdoms." In *The Cambridge History of China.* Volume 2. *The Six Dynasties, 220-589.* Edited by Albert E. Dien and Keith N. Knapp. Cambridge, MA: Cambridge University Press, 2019, pp. 119–144.

Holt, Frank L. *Alexander the Great and Bactria: Formation of a Greek Frontier in Central Asia.* Leiden: E. J. Brill, Mnemosyne Supplement, 1988.

Hopkirk, Peter. *Foreign Devils on the Silk Road: The Search for the Lost Treasures of Central Asia.* London: John Murray, 1980.

Hopkirk, Peter. *The Great Game: The Struggle for Empire in Central Asia.* New York, NY: Kodansha America Inc., 1990.

Hsiao Ch'i-ch'ing. "Mid-Yüan Politics." In *The Cambridge History of China.* Volume 6. *Alien Regimes and Border States, 907-1368.* Edited by Herbert Franke and Denis Twitchett. Cambridge, MA: Cambridge University Press, 1994, pp. 490–560.

Hucker, Charles. *China's Imperial Past: An Introduction to Chinese History and Culture.* Stanford, CA: Stanford University Press, 1995.

Hyun, Jin Kim. *The Huns, Rome, and the Birth of Europe.* Cambridge, MA: Cambridge University Press, 2013.

Hyun Jin Kim, F. J. Vervaet, and S. F. Adali, eds. *Eurasian Empires in Antiquity and the Early Middle Ages: Contact and Exchange Between the Graeco-Roman World, Inner Asia, and China.* Cambridge, MA: Cambridge University Press, 2017.

Isaac, Benjamin. *The Limits of Empire: The Roman Army in the East.* 2nd edition. Oxford: Clarendon Press, 1993.

Jackson, Peter. *The Delhi Sultanate: A Political and Military History.* Cambridge, MA: Cambridge University Press, 1999.

Jackson, Peter. "The Mongol Age in Eastern Inner Asia." In *The Cambridge History of Inner Asia: The Chinggisid Age.* Edited by Nicolas di Cosmo, Allen J. Frank and Peter B. Golden. Cambridge, MA: Cambridge University Press, 2009, pp. 26–45.

Jackson, Peter. *The Mongol Conquest of the West, 1221-1410.* London: Pearson Longman, 2005.

Jackson, Peter. *The Mongols and the Islamic World from Conquest to Conversion.* New Haven, CT: Yale University Press, 2017.

Johnson, Douglas L. *The Nature of Nomadism: A Comparative Study of Pastoral Migrations in Southwestern Asia and Northern Africa.* Chicago, IL: Chicago University Press, 1969.

Keay, John. *India: A History.* New York, NY: Grove Press, 2000.

Keightley, David N. "The Shang: China's First Historical Dynasty." In *The Cambridge History of Ancient China from the Origins of Civilization to 221 B.C.* Edited by Michael Loewe and Edward L. Shaughnessy. Cambridge, MA: Cambridge University Press, 1999, pp. 232–291.

Kelekna, Pita. *The Horse in Human History*. Cambridge, MA: Cambridge University Press, 2009.

Kelly, Christopher. *The End of Empire: Attila the Hun and the End of Empire*. London/New York, NY: W. W. Norton and Co., 2009.

Kennedy, Hugh. *The Armies of the Caliphate: Military and Society in the Early Islamic State*. London/New York, NY: Routledge, 2001.

Kennedy, Hugh. *The Great Arab Conquests: How the Spread of Islam Changed the World We Live In*. Philadelphia, PA: Da Capro Press, 2007.

Kennedy, Hugh. *The Prophet and the Age of the Caliphate: The Islamic Near East from the Sixth to the Eleventh Century*. 2nd edition. London: Pearson Longman, 2006.

Khodrakovsy, Michael. *Russia's Steppe Frontier: The Making of a Colonial Empire, 1500-1800*. Bloomington, IN: Indiana University Press, 2002.

Kinoshita, Hiromi and Jane Portal, eds. *The First Emperor: China's Terracotta Army*. London: British Museum, 2007.

Kohl, Philip L. *The Making of Bronze Age Eurasia*. Cambridge, MA: Cambridge University Press, 2007.

Kuhn, Dieter. *The Age of Confucian Rule: The Song Transformation of China*. Cambridge, MA: Harvard University Press, 2009.

Kurz, Otto. "Cultural Relations between Parthia and Rome." In *The Cambridge History of Iran*. Volume 3 (1): *The Seleucid, Parthian and Sasanian Periods*. Edited by Ehsan Yarshater. Cambridge, MA: Cambridge University Press, 1983, pp. 559–567.

Kuzmina, E. E. *The Prehistory of the Silk Road*. Edited by Victor H. Mair. Philadelphia, PA: University of Pennsylvania Press, 2008.

Kwanten, Luc. *Imperial Nomads: A History of Central Asia, 500-800*. Philadelphia, PA: University of Pennsylvania Press, 1975.

Lambton, A. K. S. "The Internal Structure of the Saljuq Empire." In *The Cambridge History of Iran*. Volume 5: *The Saljuq and Mongol Periods*. Edited by J. A. Boyle. Cambridge, MA: Cambridge University Press, 1968, pp. 203–282.

Lang, David M. "Iran, Armenia, and Georgia." In *The Cambridge History of Iran*. Volume 3 (1): *The Seleucid, Parthian and Sasanian Periods*. Edited by Ehsan Yarshater. Cambridge, MA: Cambridge University Press, 1983, pp. 505–536.

Lange, Christian and Songül Mecit, eds. *The Seljuqs: Politics, Society, and Culture*. Edinburgh: Edinburgh University Press, 2012.

Lee, Jen-der. "Women, Families, and Gendered Society." In *The Cambridge History of China*. Volume 2. *The Six Dynasties, 220-589*. Edited by Albert E. Dien and Keith N. Knapp. Cambridge, MA: Cambridge University Press, 2019, pp. 443–459.

Lewis, Archibald R. *Nomads and Crusaders, A.D. 1000-1368.* Bloomington, IN: Indiana University Press, 1991.

Lewis, Mark E. *China between Empires: The Northern and Southern Dynasties.* Cambridge, MA: Cambridge University Press, 2009.

Lewis, Mark E. *China's Cosmopolitan Empire: The Tang Empire.* Cambridge, MA: Cambridge University Press, 2009.

Lewis, Mark E. *The Early Chinese Empires, Qin and Han.* Cambridge, MA: Harvard University Press, 2007.

Lieu, Samuel N. C. *Manichaeism in the Roman Empire and Medieval China.* Tubingen: J. C. R. Mohr, 1992.

Lincoln, W. Bruce. *The Conquest of a Continent: Siberia and the Russians.* Ithaca, NY: Cornell University Press, 1994.

Liu, Xinru. *The Silk Road in World History.* Oxford: Oxford University Press, 2010.

Loewe, Michael. "The Former Han Dynasty." In *The Cambridge History of China.* Volume 1: *The Ch'in and Han Empires, 221 B.C.-A.D. 220.* Edited by Denis Twitchett and Michael Loewe. Cambridge, MA: Cambridge University Press, 1986, pp. 103–222.

Loewe, Michael. "The Structure and Practice of Government." In *The Cambridge History of China.* Volume 1: *The Ch'in and Han Empires, 221 B.C.-A.D. 220.* Edited hy Denis Twitchett and Michael Loewe. Cambridge, MA: Cambridge University Press, 1986, pp. 463–490.

Macartney, C. A. *The Magyars in the Ninth Century.* Cambridge, MA: Cambridge University Press, 1930.

MacKerras, Colin. "The Uighurs." In *The Cambridge History of Early Inner Asia.* Edited by Denis Sinor. Cambridge, MA: Cambridge University Press, 1990, pp. 317–342.

Magdalino, P. *The Empire of Manuel I Komnenos 1143-1180.* Cambridge, MA: Cambridge University Press, 1993.

Mair, Victor, ed. *Contact and Exchange in the Ancient World.* Honolulu, HI: University of Hawaii Press, 2006.

Mallory, J. P. *In Search of the Indo-Europeans: Language, Archaeology, and Myth.* London: Thames and Hudson, 1989.

Mallory, J. P. and Victor H. Mair. *The Tarim Mummies: Ancient China and the Mystery of the Earliest Peoples from the West.* London: Thames and Hudson, 2000.

Mallowan, Max. "Cyrus the Great (558-529 B.C.)." In *The Cambridge History of Iran.* Volume 2: *The Median and Achaemenid Periods.* Edited by Ilya Gershevitch. Cambridge, MA: Cambridge University Press, 1985, pp. 392–419.

Mansvelt Beck, B. J. "The Fall of Han." In *The Cambridge History of China.* Volume 1: *The Ch'in and Han Empires, 221 B.C.-A.D. 220.* Edited by Denis

Twitchett and Michael Loewe. Cambridge, MA: Cambridge University Press, 1986, pp. 317–376.

Manz, Beatrice, F. "Temür and the Early Timurids to c. 1450." In *Cambridge History of Inner Asia: The Chinggisid Age*. Edited by Nicola di Cosmo, Allen J. Frank, and Peter B. Golden. Cambridge, MA: Cambridge University Press, 2009, pp. 182–198.

Manz, Beatrice F. *The Rise and Rule f Tamerlane*. Cambridge, MA: Cambridge University Press, 1989.

Marozzi, Justin. *Tamerlane, Sword of Islam, Conqueror of the World*. Cambridge, MA: Da Capo Press, 2006.

Marshall, Christopher. *Warfare in the Latin East*. Cambridge, MA: Cambridge University Press, 1991.

McDermott, Joseph P. "Economic Change in China, 960-1279." In *The Cambridge History of China*. Volume 5, Part 2. *Sung China, 960-1270*. Edited by John W. Chaffe and Denis Twitchett. Cambridge, MA: Cambridge University Press, 2015, pp. 321–436.

Meaenchen-Helfen, Otto J. *The World of the Huns: Studies in Their History and Culture*. Edited by Max Knight. Berkeley, CA: University of California Press, 1973.

Melyukova, A. I. "The Scythians and Samartians." In *The Cambridge History of Central Asia*. Edited by D. Sinor. Cambridge, MA: Cambridge University Press, 1990, pp. 97–117.

Millar, Fergus. *The Roman Near East 31 B.C.-A.D. 337*. Cambridge, MA: Harvard University Press, 1993.

Millward, James A. *Eurasian Crossroads: A History of Xinjiang*. New York, NY: Columbia University Press, 2007.

Mirsky, Jeanette. *Sir Aurel Stein, Archaeological Explorer*. Chicago: Chicago University Press, 1977.

Morgan, David. *The Mongols*. Cambridge, MA: Harvard University Press, 1986.

Motte, Frederick W. "Chinese Society under Mongol Rule, 1215-1368." In *The Cambridge History of China*. Volume 6. *Alien Regimes and Border States, 907-1368*. Edited by Herbert Franke and Denis Twitchett. Cambridge, MA: Cambridge University Press, 1994, pp. 616–664.

Motte, Frederick W. *Imperial China, 900-1800*. Cambridge, MA: Harvard University Press, 1999.

Muir, William. *The Mamluke or Slave Dynasty of Egypt*. Amsterdam: Oriental Press, 1968.

Muller, Shing. "Northern Material Culture." Dien, Albert J. "Eastern Wei-Northern Qi." Hocombe, Charles. "Eastern Jin." In *The Cambridge History of China*. Volume 2. *The Six Dynasties, 220-589*. Edited by Albert E. Dien and Keith N. Knapp. Cambridge, MA: Cambridge University Press, 2019, pp. 384–417.

Narain, A. K. "Indo-Europeans in Inner Asia." In the *New Cambridge History of Inner Asia*. Edited by Denis Sinor. Cambridge, MA: Cambridge University Press, pp. 151–176.

Oblensky, Dimitri. *The Byzantine Commonwealth: Eastern Europe, 500-1453*. Creswood, NY: St. Vladimir's Seminary Press, 1982.

O'Connor, Jane. *The Emperor's Silent Army: Terracotta Warriors of Ancient China*. New York, NY: Viking Press, 2002.

O'Flynn, John Michael. *Generalissmos of the Western Roman Empire*. Edmonton: University of Alberta Press, 1983.

Okladnikov, A. P. "Inner Asia at the Dawn of History." In *The Cambridge History of Inner Asia*. Edited by Dennis Sinor. Cambridge, MA: Cambridge University Press, 1990, pp. 41–96.

Ostrer, Harry. *Legacy: A Genetic History of the Jewish People*. Oxford: Oxford University Press, 2012.

Parry, V. J. and M. E. Yapp, eds. *War, Technology, and Society in the Middle East*. Oxford: Oxford University Press, 1975.

Peacock, Andrew and Sara Nu Yildez, eds. *The Seljuks of Anatolia: Court and Society in the Medieval Middle East*. London: I. B. Tauris, 2012.

Pearce, Scott. "Northern Wei." In *The Cambridge History of China*. Volume 2. *The Six Dynasties, 220-589*. Edited by Albert E. Dien and Keith N. Knapp. Cambridge, MA: Cambridge University Press, 2019, pp. 155–183.

Petrushevsky, L. F. "The Socio-Economic Condition of Iran under the Il-Khans." In *The Cambridge History of Iran*. Volume 5: *The Saljuq and Mongol Periods*. Edited by J. A. Boyle. Cambridge, MA: Cambridge University Press, 1968, pp. 483–528.

Piggott, Stuart. *The Earliest Wheeled Vehicles from the Atlantic Coast to the Caspian Sea*. Ithaca, NY: Cornell University Press, 1983.

Pohl, Walter. *The Avars: A Steppe Empire in Central Europe, 567-822*. Ithaca, NY: Cornell University Press, 2018.

Portal, Jane. *Terra Cotta Warriors, Guardians of China's First Emperor*. Washington, DC: National Geographic, 2001.

Pourshariati, Parvaneh. *Decline and Fall of the Sasanian Empire: The Sasanian-Parthian Confederacy and the Arab Conquest of Iran*. New York, NY: J. B. Taurus & Co., Ltd., 2008.

Prawdin, Michael. *The Mongol Empire*. 2nd edition. Translated by E. and C. Paul. New York, NY: The Free Press, 1961.

Ratchnevsky, Paul. *Genghis Khan: His Life and Legacy*. Translated by Thomas N. Haining. Oxford: Blackwell Publishing Ltd., 1991.

Reder, Ellen and Michael Treiser. *Scythian Gold*. New York, NY: Harry N. Abrams, Inc., 1999.

Rice, Tamara Talbot. *The Scythians*. London: Thames and Hudson, 1958.

Rice, Tamara Talbot. "The Scytho-Sarmatian Tribes of South-Eastern Europe," in *The Roman Empire and Its Neighbors*, by Fergus Millar, 2nd edition. New York, NY: 1981, pp. 281–294.

Rice, Tamara Talbot. *The Seljuk Turks*. London: Thames and Hudson, 1961.

Rickerman, E. "The Seleucid Period." In *The Cambridge History of Iran*. Volume 3 (1): *The Seleucid, Parthian and Sasanian Periods*. Edited by Ehsan Yarshater. Cambridge, MA: Cambridge University Press, 1983, pp. 3–20.

Roemer, H. R. "The Successors of Timur." In *The Cambridge History of Iran*. Volume 6: *The Timurid and Safavid Periods*. Edited by Laurence Lockhart. Cambridge, MA: Cambridge University Press, 1986, pp. 98–146.

Roemer, H. R. "Timur in Iran." In *The Cambridge History of Iran*. Volume 6: *The Timurid and Safavid Periods*. Edited by Laurence Lockhart. Cambridge, MA: Cambridge University Press, 1986, pp. 42–97.

Rossabi, Morris. *Khubilai Khan, His Life and Times*. Berkeley, CA: University of California Press, 2009.

Rossabi, Morris. "The Reign of Khubilai Khan." In *The Cambridge History of China*. Volume 6. *Alien Regimes and Border States, 907-1368*. Edited by Herbert Franke and Denis Twitchett. Cambridge, MA: Cambridge University Press, 1994, pp. 414–489.

Runciman, Stephen. *A History of the First Bulgarian Empire*. London: G. Bell and Sons, 1930.

Sadao, Nishijima. "The Economic and Social History of Former Han." In *The Cambridge History of China*. Volume 1: *The Ch'in and Han Empires, 221 B.C.-A.D. 220*. Edited by Denis Twitchett and Michael Loewe. Cambridge, MA: Cambridge University Press, 1986, pp. 545–607.

Saunders, J. J. *A History of Medieval Islam*. London: Routledge and Kegan Paul, 1963.

Saunders, J. J. *The History of the Mongol Conquests*. Philadelphia, PA: University of Pennsylvania Press, 1991.

Schafer, Edward H. *The Golden Peaches of Samarkand: A Study in T'ang Exotics*. Berkeley, CA: University of California Press, 1963.

Schottenhammer, Angela. "China's Emergence as a Maritime Power." In *The Cambridge History of China*. Volume 5, Part 2. *Sung China, 960-1270*. Edited by John W. Chaffe and Denis Twitchett. Cambridge: Cambridge University Press, 2015, pp. 437–525.

Sellwood, David. "Parthian Coins." In *The Cambridge History of Iran*. Volume 3 (1): *The Seleucid, Parthian and Sasanian Periods*. Edited by Ehsan Yarshater. Cambridge, MA: Cambridge University Press, 1983, pp. 279–299.

Shaban, M. A. *The Abbasid Revolution*. Cambridge, MA: Cambridge University Press, 1970.

Shaughnessy, Edward L. "Western Zhou History." In *The Cambridge History of Ancient China from the Origins of Civilization to 221 B.C.* Edited by Michael

Loewe and Edward L. Shaughnessy. Cambridge, MA: Cambridge University Press, 1999, pp. 292–351.

Shavegan, M. R. *Arsacids amd Sasanians: Political Ideology in Post-Hellenistic and Late Antique Persia*. Cambridge, MA: Cambridge University Press, 2011.

Shufen, Liu. "The Southern Economy." In *The Cambridge History of China*. Volume 2. *The Six Dynasties, 220-589*. Edited by Albert E. Dien and Keith N. Knapp. Cambridge, MA: Cambridge University Press, 2019, pp. 33–354.

Silverberg, Robert. *The Realm of Prester John*. Athens, OH: Ohio University Press, 1996.

Sinor, Denis, ed. *The Cambridge History of Early Inner Asia*. Cambridge, MA: Cambridge University Press, 1990.

Sinor, Denis. "Establishment and Dissolution of the Türk Empire," *The Cambridge History of Early Inner Asia*. Edited by Denis Sinor. Cambridge, MA: Cambridge University Press, 1990, pp. 285–316.

Sinor, Denis, "The Hun Period." In *The New Cambridge History of Inner Asia*. Edited by Denis Sinor. Cambridge, MA: Cambridge University Press, 1990, pp. 177–205.

Skaff, Jonathan K. *Sui-Tang China and Its Turko-Mongol Neighbors: Culture, Power, and Connections, 580-800*. Oxford: Oxford University Press, 2012.

Smail, R. C. *Crusading Warfare*. Cambridge, MA: Cambridge University Press, 1956.

Somers, Robert M. "The End of the T'ang." In *The Cambridge History of China*. Volume 3. Part 1. *Sui and T'ang China, 589-906*. Edited by Denis Twitchett. Cambridge, MA: Cambridge University Press, 1979, pp. 682–789.

Sulimirski, T. *The Sarmatians*. Southhampton: Thames and Hudson, 1970.

Sulimirski, T. "The Scyths." In *The Cambridge History of Iran*. Volume 2: *The Median and Achaemenid Periods*. Edited by Ilya Gershevitch. Cambridge, MA: Cambridge University Press, 1985, pp. 149–199.

Sulimirski, T. and T. Taylor. "The Scythians." In *The Cambridge Ancient History*. Volume III, Part 2. Edited John Barodman et alli. Cambridge, MA: Cambridge University Press, 1991, pp. 547–590.

Szádeczky-Kardoss, Samuel. "The Avars." In *The Cambridge History of Early Inner Asia*. Edited by Denis Sinor. Cambridge, MA: Cambridge University Press, 1990, pp. 206–228.

Talbot Rice, Tamara. *The Scythians*. London: Thames and Hudson, 3rd edition, 1961.

Tarn, W. S. *The Greeks in Bactria and India*. Third edition revised by Frank L. Holt. Chicago, IL: Ares Publishers, 1984.

Thapar, Romila, *Early India from the Origins to A.D. 1300*. Berkeley, CA: University of California Press, 2002.

Thapar, Romila. *A History of India*. 2 volumes. London/New York, NY: Penguin Books, 1990.

Thompson, E. A. *The Huns*. Oxford: Blackwell Publishers, Ltd., 1996.

Thorpe, Robert L. *China in the Early Bronze Age: Shang Civilization*. Philadelphia, PA: University of Pennsylvania, 2006.

Twitchett, Denis. "Hsüan-tsung, (reign 712-56)." In *The Cambridge History of China*. Volume 3. Part 1. *Sui and T'ang China, 589-906*. Edited by Denis Twitchett. Cambridge, MA: Cambridge University Press, 1979, pp. 333–463.

Twitchett, Denis and Klaus-Pieter Tietze. "The Liao." In *The Cambridge History of China*. Volume 6. *Alien Regimes and Border States, 907-1368*. Edited by Herbert Franke and Denis Twitchett. Cambridge, MA: Cambridge University Press, 1994, pp. 43–153.

Twitchett, Denis and Howard J. Wechsler. "Kao-tsung (reign 640-81) and the Empress Wu, the Inheritor and the Usurper." In *The Cambridge History of China*. Volume 3. Part 1. *Sui and T'ang China, 589-906*. Edited by Denis Twitchett. Cambridge, MA: Cambridge University Press, 1979, pp. 242–289.

Vásáry, István. *Cumans and Tatars: Oriental Military in the Pre-Ottoman Balkans, 1185-1365*. Cambridge, MA: Cambridge University Press, 2005.

Vásáry, István. "The Jochid Realm: The Western Steppes." In *The Cambridge History of Inner Asia: The Chinggisid Age*. Edited by Nicolas di Cosmo, Allen J. Frank and Peter B. Golden. Cambridge, MA: Cambridge University Press, 2009, pp. 67–88.

Veith, Veronika. "The Eastern Steppe: Mongol Regimes After the Yuan (1368-1636)." In *Cambridge History of Inner Asia: The Chinggisid Age*. Edited by Nicola di Cosmo, Allen J. Frank, and Peter B. Golden. Cambridge, MA: Cambridge University Press, 2009, pp. 157–181.

von Gabain, A. "Irano-Turkish Relations in the Late Sasanian Period." In *The Cambridge History of Iran*. Volume 3 (1): *The Seleucid, Parthian and Sasanian Periods*. Edited by Ehsan Yarshater. Cambridge, MA: Cambridge University Press, 1983, pp. 613–624.

Vyrnos, Speros. *The Decline of Medieval Hellenism in Asia Minor and the Process of Islamization from the Eleventh through the Fifteenth Century*. Berkeley, CA: University of California Press, 1964.

Waldron, Arthur. *The Great Wall of China: From History to Myth*. Cambridge, MA: Cambridge University Press, 1990.

Wang, Helen. *Money on the Silk Road. The Evidence from Eastern Central Asia Including a Catalogue of the Coins Collected by Sir Aurel Stein*. London: The British Museum Press, 2001.

Wang Tseng-Yü. "A History of the Sung Military." In *The Cambridge History of China*. Volume 5, Part 2. *Sung China, 960-1270*. Edited by John W. Chaffe and Denis Twitchett. Cambridge, MA: Cambridge University Press, 2015, pp. 214–249.

Walker, Annabel. *Aurel Stein, Pioneer of the Silk Road*. Seattle, WA: University of Washington Press, 1995.

Watson, William. "Iran and China." In *The Cambridge History of Iran*. Volume 3

(1): *The Seleucid, Parthian and Sasanian Periods.* Edited by Ehsan Yarshater. Cambridge, MA: Cambridge University Press, 1983, pp. 537–558.

Watt, W. Montgomery. *Muhammad, Prophet and Statesman.* Oxford: Oxford University Press, 1975.

Weatherford, Jack. *Genghis Khan and the Making of the Modern World.* New York, NY: The Three Rivers Press, 2004.

Wechsler, Howard J. "The Founding of the T'ang Dynasty: Kao-tsu (Reign 618-26)." In *The Cambridge History of China.* Volume 3. Part 1. *Sui and T'ang China, 589-906.* Edited by Denis Twitchett. Cambridge, MA: Cambridge University Press, 1979, pp. 150–187.

Wechsler, Howard J. "T'ai-tsung (reign 626-49), the Consolidator." In *The Cambridge History of China.* Volume 3, Part 1. *Sui and T'ang China, 589-906.* Edited by Denis Twitchett. Cambridge, MA: Cambridge University Press, 1979, pp. 188–241.

Whitby, Michael. *The Emperor Maurice and His Historian Theophylact Simocattta on Persian and Balkan Warfare.* Oxford: Clarendon Press, 1988.

Whitefield, Susan. *Aurel Stein on the Silk Road.* Chicago, IL: Serindia Publications, 2004.

Whitefield, Susan. *Life along the Silk Road.* Berkeley, CA: University of California Press, 1999.

Whittlow, Mark. *The Making of Byzantium, 600-1025.* Berkeley, CA: University of California Press, 1996.

Widengren, G. "Manichaeism and Its Iranian Background." In *The Cambridge History of Iran.* Volume 3 (2): *The Seleucid, Parthian and Sasanian Periods.* Edited by Ehsan Yarshater. Cambridge, MA: Cambridge University Press, 1983, pp. 965–999.

Wright, Arthure F. "The Sui Dynasty (581-617)." In *The Cambridge History of China.* Volume 3. Part 1. *Sui and T'ang China, 589-906.* Edited by Denis Twitchett. Cambridge, MA: Cambridge University Press, 1979, pp. 48–149.

Xinru Liu. *The Silk Road in World History.* Oxford: Oxford University Press, 2010.

Xiong, Victor Cunbui. "The Northern Economy." In *The Cambridge History of China.* Volume 2. *The Six Dynasties, 220-589.* Edited by Albert E. Dien and Keith N. Knapp. Cambridge, MA: Cambridge University Press, 2019, pp. 309–329.

Yarshater, E., ed. *The Cambridge History of Iran.* III: *Seleucid, Parthian, and Sasanian Periods.* Cambridge, MA: Cambridge University Press 1983.

Yarshater, Ehsan. "Mazdakism." In *The Cambridge History of Iran.* Volume 3(2): *The Seleucid, Parthian and Sasanian Periods.* Edited by Ehsan Yarshater. Cambridge, MA: Cambridge University Press, 1983, pp. 991–1026.

Yu Ying-shih. "Han Foreign Relations." In *The Cambridge History of China.* Volume 1: *The Ch'in and Han Empires, 221 B.C.-A.D. 220.* Edited by Denis

Twitchett and Michael Loewe. Cambridge, MA: Cambridge University Press, 1986, pp. 377–463.

Yu Ying-shih. "The Hsiung-nu." *The Cambridge History of Inner Asia*. Edited by Denis Sinor. Cambridge, MA: Cambridge University Press, 1990, pp. 118–150.

Yu Ying-shih. *Trade and Expansion in Han China*. Berkeley, CA: University of California Press, 1967.

Zakaria, Rafiq. *Razia, Queen of India*. Oxford: Oxford University Press, 1966.

Zarrineus, 'Abd al-Husain. "The Arab Conquest of Iran and Its Aftermath." In *The Cambridge History of Iran*. Volume 4: *From Arab Invasion to the Saljuqs*. Edited by R. N. Frye. Cambridge, MA: Cambridge University Press, 1975, pp. 1–56.

Zeimal, E. V. "The Political History of Transoxiana." In *The Cambridge History of Iran*. Volume 3 (1): *The Seleucid, Parthian and Sasanian Periods*. Edited by Ehsan Yarshater. Cambridge, MA: Cambridge University Press, 1983, pp. 232–262.

Notes

Prologue: Attila on the Road to Rome

1   See Judith Herrin, *Ravenna: Capital of Empire, Crucible of Europe* (Princeton, 2020), pp. 1–16.

2   See Christopher Kelly, *The End of Empire: Attila the Hun and the Fall of Rome* (New York/London), pp. 224–226.

3   See Hyun Jin Kim, *The Huns, Rome and the Birth of Europe* (Cambridge, 2013), pp. 37–42, who argues convincingly for the Huns inheriting imperial institutions, including diplomatic protocol, from the Xiongnu.

4   See Yu Ying-shih, *Trade and Expansion in Han China: A Study in the Structure of Sino-Barbarian Economic Relations* (Berkeley, 1967), pp. 36–54.

5   See Mark Edward Lewis, *China between Empires: The Northern and Southern Dynasties* (Cambridge, 2009), pp. 73–85.

6   See J. B. Bury, *History of the Later Roman Empire from the Death of Theodosius I to the Death of Justinian*, Volume I (New York, 1958), pp. 289–290. The precise intentions of Honoria in appealing to Attila are still uncertain.

7   For Attila ruling a steppe confederation from the Middle Danube to the Volga Rivers, see Hyun Jin Kim, *The Huns, Rome and the Birth of Europe* (Cambridge, 2013), pp. 43–60, supporting the older opinions by E. A. Thompson, *The Huns* revised edition (Oxford, 1999), pp. 177–185, and Otto J. Maenchen-Helfen, *The World of the Huns: Studies in Hun History and Culture* (Berkeley, 1973), pp. 94–129. For a revisionist opinion, diminishing the significance of the Huns, see Peter Heather, *The Fall of the Roman Empire: A New History of Rome and the Barbarians* (Oxford, 2006), pp. 329–332 and 360–366. See R. Lindner, "Nomadism, Huns, and

Horses," *Past and Present* 92 (1981), pp. 1–19, who argues the Huns, once settled on the Hungarian grasslands, lacked sufficient pastures to maintain a large army of horse archers. Attila, however, was in the position of the Ottoman sultans of the sixteenth through eighteenth centuries, who could summon large cavalry forces from the Tatars of the Crimea and the South Russian Steppes. See Rhoads Murphy, *Ottoman Warfare, 1500–1700* (New Brunswick, NJ, 1999), pp. 160–161.

8   See G. Turville-Petre, *The Heroic Age of Scandinavia* (London, 1951), pp. 27–37, and Jan de Vries, *Heroic Song and Heroic Legend* (Oxford, 1962), pp. 44–71, for Attila in the Norse cycle of the Volsungs (in saga and Eddic poetry) and the Middle High German epic *Nibelungenlied*.

9   See H. M. D. Parker, *A History of the Roman World, A.D. 138 to 337*, second edition (London, 1958), p. 147. The citizens attributed the defeat of Maximinus to intervention of their god Belenus, who was sometimes identified with Apollo.

10   See Thompson, *Huns*, pp. 158–159.

11   *Ibid.*, pp. 160–161.

12   See John Michael O'Flynn, *Generalissimos of the Western Roman Empire* (Alberta, 1983), pp. 190–191, and Bury, *History of Later Roman Empire*, I, p. 295.

13   See Maenchen-Helfen, *World of the Huns*, pp. 137–138.

14   Kelly, *End of Empire*, pp. 262–264, Thompson, *Huns*, pp. 160–163, and Bury, *History of Later Roman Empire*, I, pp. 295–296.

15   See Bury, *History of Later Roman Empire*, I, pp. 295–296.

16   See Gerard Friell and Stephen Williams, *The Rome that Did Not Fall: The Survival of the East in the Fifth Century* (London/New York, 2005), p. 87.

17   See Kelly, *End of Empire*, p. 263. The next morning, Attila's bodyguard slew Ildico immediately inasmuch as they expected foul play. Ildico lived on in legend as Gudrun of Norse poetry and saga, and Kriemhild of the *Nibelungenlied*.

18   See Maenchen-Helfen, *World of the Huns*, pp. 142–149. The rebellion is better characterized as a Hun civil war among Attila's sons Ellac, Dengizich and Ernak. Ellac fell fighting on the Nedao River against a coalition of Germanic vassals headed by Andaric, King of the Gepidae.

19   See chapter 5.

20   Herodotus, *Histories* IV. 1–205; Penguin translation, Herodotus, *Histories*, translated by Aubrey de Selincourt (New York), pp. 217–280. Herodotus based his account on eyewitness reports of Greeks who traded and lived among the Scythians.

21   Ammianus Marcellinus 31. 2. 1–12; Penguin translation, Ammianus Marcellinus, *The Later Roman Empire (A.D. 354–376)* (New York, 1986), pp. 411–412. See Thomas S. Burns, *Rome and the Barbarians, 100 B.C.–A.D. 400* (Baltimore, 2003), pp. 1–40, for critique of the stereotypical images of barbarians in Greek and Roman sources.

22   The reaction of Zhang Qian was incorporated in the *Hanshu* 6. 1. See Joseph P. Yap, ed. and trans., *The Western Regions, Xiongnu and Huns: A Collection of Chapters from the Shiji, Hanshu, and Hou Hanshu* (Independent Publication), pp. 275–276. For the reaction of Ahmad ibn Fadlan, see Ibn Fadlan, *Ibn Fadlan and the Land of Darkness: Arab Travellers in the Far North*, translated by Paul Lund and Caroline Stone (New York, 2012), pp. 25–39.

23   See E. Denison Ross and Vilhelm Thomsen, "The Orkhon Inscriptions: Being a Translation of Professor Vilhelm Thomsen's Final Danish Rendering," *Bulletin of the School of Oriental Studies, University of London* 5 (1930), pp. 861–876.

24   See Paul Kahn, trans., *The Secret History of the Mongols: The Origin of Chingis Khan*, revised edition (Boston, 1988), pp. ix–x. The second Great Khan Ögedei (1229–1241) commissioned the work in Mongolian shortly after the death of his father, Genghis Khan. The text, however, only survives in later Chinese redaction rather than in the original Mongol language.

1 The Peopling of the Eurasian Steppes

1   See Annabel Walker, *Aurel Stein: Pioneer of the Silk Road* (Seattle, 1995), pp. 136–171.

2   See J. P. Mallory and Victor H. Mair, *The Tarim Mummies: Ancient China and the Mystery of the Eastern Peoples from the West* (London, 2000), pp. 230–255.

3   See James A. Millward, *Eurasian Crossroads: A History of Xinjiang* (New York, 2007), pp. 322–332, for the competing political claims and separatist aspirations of the Uyghurs.

4   See Walker, *Aurel Stein*, pp. 41–70.

5   See Sven Hedin, *Durch Asiens Wüsten. Drei Jahre auf neuen Wegen in Pamir, Lop-nor, Tibet und China*, 2 vols. (Leipzig, 1899). Hedin subsequently mounted expeditions to Tibet in 1904–1907. He fell into disrepute by his admiration of, and correspondence with, Adolf Hitler, although Hedin later came to criticize National Socialism and the Third Reich.

6   See Ferdinand von Richthofen, "Über die zentralasiatischen Seidenstrassen bis zum 2. Jh. n. Chr," *Verhandlungen der Gesellschaft für Erdkunde zu Berlin* 4 (877), pp. 96–122.

7   See Walker, *Aurel Stein*, pp. 164–171. See analysis of the documents by Imaeda Yoshiro, "Provenance and Character of Dunhuang Documents," *Memoirs of the Toyo Bunko* 66 (2008), pp. 81–102.

8   This language family is by convention denoted as Tocharian, even though speakers of the language did not define themselves as such. The term is based on Greek Tokharoi, which designated the inhabitants of Sogdiana and Bactria in the Kushan era. For the decipherment of the language, see J. P. Mallory, *In Search of the Indo-Europeans: Language, Archaeology and Myth* (London, 1998), pp. 56–63.

9   See Philip Baldi, *An Introduction to the Indo-European Languages* (Car-
     bondale, 1983), pp. 142–150, and Mallory and Mair, *Tarim Mummies*,
     pp. 299–304.

10   Many scholars of the nineteenth and early twentieth century employed
     the term Aryan (from Sanskrit *arya* or "noble") to denote the language
     family now designated Indo-European. Nazi ideologues identified lan-
     guage with race and so forever discredited the term Aryan.

11   See Michael Palencia-Roth, "The Presidential Address of Sir William
     Jones: The Asiatick Society of Bengal and the ISCSC," *Comparative Civ-
     ilizations Review* 56 (2007), pp. 21–39, for analysis of Jones's method and
     conclusions. For the text of the address, see Sir William Jones, "The
     Third Anniversary Discourse: On the Hindus, 1786," in *The Works of
     Sir William Jones*, Volume 3 (Bengal, 1977), pp. 24–46.

12   See Bedřich Hrozný, *Die Sprache der Hethiter: ihr Bau und ihre Zugehörig-
     keit zum indogermanischen Sprachstamm* (Leipzig, 1917), the groundbreaking
     work in the decipherment of Hittite. For the distribution of the Hittite
     (more properly called Neshite), Luvian, and Palaic languages in Anatolia,
     see Trevor R. Bryce, *The Kingdom of the Hittites*, 2nd edition revised (Ox-
     ford, 2005), pp. 10–20, and David W. Anthony, *The Horse, the Wheel, and
     Language: How Bronze Age Riders from the Eurasian Steppes Shaped the Mod-
     ern World* (Princeton, 2002), pp. 41–47 and map, fig. 3.1.

13   Trevor R. Bryce, *Life and Society in the Hittite World* (Oxford, 2002), pp.
     57–60, for the adaptation of cuneiform script, which was ill-suited to
     express the diphthongs of Hittite, an Indo-European language.

14   See Mallory and Maier, *Tarim Mummies*, pp. 63 and 184–185.

15   See Folke Bergman, *Archaeological Researches in Sinkiang, Especially in the
     Lop-Nor Region*, Volume 1 (Stockholm, 1939), pp. 51–332, for his exca-
     vations of Xizhoe Cemetery in 1934. For discussion and analysis of the
     finds, see Victor H. Mair, "The Rediscovery and Complete Excavation
     of Ördek's Necropolis," *Journal of Indo-European Studies*. 34 (2006), pp.
     273–318.

16   See Mallory and Maier, *Tarim Mummies*, p. 191.

17   See *ibid.*, pp. 181–183.

18   See *ibid.*, pp. 230–252. For analysis of DNA evidence, see F. Zhang, C. Ning,
     and A. Scott, "The Genomic Origins of the Bronze Age Tarim Basin Mum-
     mies," *Nature* 599 (2021), pp. 256–261.

19   See Anthony, *Horse, Wheel, and Language*, pp. 285–287.

20   See René Grousset, *The Empire of the Steppes: A History of Central Asia*,
     translated by Naomi Walford (New Brunswick, N.J., 2010), pp. 50–53.

21   For the catalog of frescoes, see Roderick Whitfield and Anne Farrer, *Caves
     of the Thousand Buddhas: Chinese Art from the Silk Route* (London, 1990).

22   See Anthony, *Horse, Wheel, and Language*, pp. 65–75.

23   See J. P. Mallory, *In Search of the Indo-Europeans: Language, Archaeology and*

Myth (London, 1989), pp. 143–185, who rules out the thesis of Russell Gray and Quentin Atkinson, "Language-Tree Divergence Times Support the Anatolian Theory of Indo-European Origin," *Nature* 426 (2003), pp. 435–439, who proposed Anatolia as the homeland, based on a statistical compilation of similar sounds mapped as if they were genetic codes. This is a flawed approach; neither scholar is a linguist nor archaeologist. Such word lists, without studying grammar, syntax, or isoglosses, have no linguistic or cultural context. An Anatolian homeland for PIE makes no sense because cuneiform texts reveal that the speakers of Anatolian languages were the elite ruling a majority of non-Indo-European Hattians. It would turn the speakers of PIE into the earliest agriculturalists, who, from at least 3000 BC, are known to speak non-Indo-European languages such as Hattian and Hurrian. Also, there is no evidence for horses in Anatolia until the Anatolian speakers brought the horse with them from the steppes.

24 See Anthony, *Horse, Wheel, and Language*, pp. 18–21 and 193–223, and Philip L. Kohl, *The Making of Bronze Age Eurasia* (Cambridge, 2007), pp. 137–144.

25 See Anthony, *Horse, Wheel, and Language*, pp. 134–159.

26 See *ibid.*, pp. 21–38, and for Baldi, *Indo-European Languages*, pp. 14–22.

27 In the early first millennium BC, the initial hard labial sound *p* in Germanic languages shifted to a fricative *f* sound in the first Germanic consonantal shift, the so-called Grimm's law. The linguist Jacob Grimm first noted this linguistic rule. He is, however, far better remembered for his compilation of fairy tales rather than his linguistic law. See Baldi, *Indo-European Languages*, pp. 129–139.

28 See Anthony, *Horse, Wheel, and Language*, pp. 63–77.

29 See *ibid.*, pp. 193–201, and map, fig. 10. 2.

30 See *ibid.*, pp. 135–190.

31 See *ibid.*, pp. 300–317.

32 See *ibid.*, pp. 340–349.

33 See Kohl, *Making of Bronze Age Eurasia*, pp. 57–85.

34 See Bryce, *Kingdom of Hittites*, pp. 12–14.

35 See *ibid.*, pp. 21–43, and Seton Lloyd, *Early Highland Peoples of Anatolia* (New York, 1967), pp. 38–56, for the Assyrian merchant communities (*karum*), and their commercial records in the Akkadian language and written in the cuneiform script on clay tablets.

36 See Bryce, *Kingdom of Hittites*, pp. 64–100.

37 See Anthony, *Horse, Wheel, and Language*, pp. 39–48, and Baldi, *Indo-European Languages*, pp. 151–164.

38 See *ibid.*, pp. 307–311, and J. P. Mallory, *In Search of the Indo-Europeans: Language, Archaeology and Myth* (London, 1980), pp. 56–63.

39   See Mallory and Mair, *Tarim Mummies*, pp. 270–273, and Mallory, *Indo-Europeans*, pp. 58–59.

40   See Anthony, *Horse, Wheel, and Language*, pp. 27–30, for diverging into the Centum and Satem branches of Indo-European languages.

41   See Baldri, *Indo-European Languages*, pp. 130–132.

42   *Ibid.*, pp. 144–145.

43   *Ibid.*, pp. 55–56.

44   For Corded Ware culture, see Anthony, *Horse, Wheel, and Language*, pp. 360–382. For DNA analysis documenting the migration of Yamnaya populations into Europe, see Morton E. Allentoft *et al.*, "Population Genomics of Bronze Age Eurasia," *Nature* 552 (2015), pp. 167–172.

45   See Nicholas Patterson *et al.*, "Ancient Admixture in Human History," *Genetics* 192 (2012), pp. 1065–1093, and David Reich, "Ancient DNA Suggests Steppe Migrations Spread Indo-European Languages," *Proceedings of the American Philosophical Society* 162 (2018), pp. 39–55. The small percentage of Neanderthal DNA was passed into the general European populations via the hunter-gatherers.

46   Mallory, *Indo-Europeans*, pp. 363–370.

47   See Mallory, *Indo-Europeans*, pp. 30–35 and 66–75. I accept the position that Greek and Macedonian were distantly related, but, in Classical times, mutually unintelligible languages. See Eugene N. Borza, *In the Shadow of Olympus: The Emergence of Macedon*, 2nd edition (Princeton, 1990), pp. 77–79. We have neither sufficient vocabulary nor grammar to determine conclusively whether Macedonian was a separate language or a Greek dialect, possibly related to Northwest or Doric Greek—the latter position an article of faith by modern Greek nationalists today. Inscriptions from the Kingdom of Macedon in the Archaic and Classical periods are in the Greek dialect spoken by the stone cutter rather than Macedonian (and the same is true from contemporary inscriptions in Thrace). Macedonian, along with other Balkan languages such as Illyrian, Paeonian, and Thracian, were spoken vernaculars not committed to writing. King Archelaus (413–399 BC) declared Attic Greek the language of the Macedonian court in a deliberate effort to Hellenize his kingdom. Greeks, however, regarded Macedonians as barbarians speaking an unintelligible language, even though the royal family since the reign of Alexander I (ca. 490–454 BC) was accorded the Hellenic status by the Olympic commission. See especially Plutarch *Alexander* 52; Penguin translation, Plutarch, *The Age of Alexander*, revised edition, translated by Ian Scott-Kilvert and Timothy E. Duff (New York, 2011), p. 276, when Alexander the Great shouts orders to his bodyguard in Macedonian so that the Greeks present cannot understand.

48   The archaeological break between Early Helladic III and Middle Helladic I, in ca. 1900 BC (and represented by destruction levels at sites on mainland Greece and followed by a new material culture with Minyan ware as the marker), is considered the date of the arrival of the first Greek speakers. See R. J. Hopper, *The Early Greeks* (New York, 1976),

pp. 16–25. For decipherment of Linear B as Greek, see John Chadwick, *The Decipherment of Linear B*, 2nd edition (Cambridge, 2014). Linear A and the earlier hieroglyphic syllabary from Crete are still not deciphered, but the language of these tablets was not Indo-European.

49   See Herodotus. VII. 73 and VIII. 138 (Penguin translation, pp. 397–398 and 495). Herodotus also notes that the Macedonians first settled near the Gardens of Midas in Mygdonia, where the Phrygians had dwelled before they migrated into Asia Minor. See Bartomeu Obrador-Cursach, "On the Place of Phrygian among the Indo-European Languages," *Journal of Language Relationship* 17 (2019), pp. 234–239, for links between Greek and Phrygian.

50   See Mallory, *Indo-Europeans*, pp. 76–84.

51   See Pablo Librado *et al.*, "The Origins and Spread of Domestic Horses from the Western Eurasian Steppes," *Nature* 598 (2021), pp. 634–640. For chariot at Sintashta and spread of chariot warfare, see P. J. Kuznetsov, "The Emergence of Bronze Age Chariots in Eastern Europe," *Antiquity* 80 (2006), pp. 638–645, and Stephen Lindner, "Chariots in the Eurasian Steppe: a Bayesian Approach to the Emergence of Horse-Drawn Transport in the Early Second Millennium B.C.," *Antiquity* 94 (2020), pp. 361–380.

52   See E. E. Kuzmina, *The Prehistory of the Silk Road*, edited by Victor H. Mair (Philadelphia, 2008), pp. 57–58 and 88–93.

53   See Kohl, *Making of Bronze Age Eurasia*, pp. 104-213.

54   Meluhha is used as the preferred name of this first civilization of India; it is also designated the Indus Valley Civilization or the Harappan civilization. The latter name is from the major site of Harappa first excavated by Sir John Hubert Marshall in 1921–1922. See Romila Thapar, *Early India from the Origins to A.D. 1300* (Berkeley, 2002), pp. 79–94. For the trade routes, see E. C. L. During Caspers, "Sumer, Coastal Arabia and the Indus Valley in Protoliterate and Early Dynastic Eras: Supporting Evidence for a Cultural Linkage," *Journal of the Economic and Social History of the Orient* 22 (1979), pp. 121–135, and Julian Reade, "The Indus-Mesopotamia Relationship Reconsidered," *Intercultural Relations between South and Southwest Asia: Studies in Commemoration of E. C. L. During Caspers (1934–1996)*, edited by E. Olijdam and R. H. Spoor (Oxford, 2008, BAR International Series 1826), pp. 12–18.

55   See Asko Parpola, *The Roots of Hinduism: The Early Aryans and Indus Civilization* (Cambridge, 2015), pp. 69–91.

56   See Richard L. Bulleit *et al.*, "Camel," *Encyclopedia Iranica* IV. 7 (New York, 1990), pp. 730–739. The root word may be derived from Proto-Indo-European *ues*, "to be wet," denoting the ejaculation of semen by camels. See Mallory, *Indo-Europeans*, pp. 35–56, for the close relationship of Avestan Iranian and Vedic Sanskrit.

57   See Thapar, *Early India*, pp. 104–117, and Parpola, *Roots of Hinduism*, pp. 92–106, for the controversy over the transmission and historical context of the *Vedas*.

58   See S. Dhammika, *The Edicts of King Asoka: An English Rendering* (Kandy Sri Lanka, 1993), The Wheel Publication No. 386/387. The translations are available online: https://web.archive.org/web/20140328144411/ http://www.cs.colostate.edu/~malaiya/ashoka.html.

59   See W. King and R. C. Thompson, *The Sculptures and Inscription of Darius the Great on the Rock of Behistûn in Persia: A New Collation of the Persian, Susian and Babylonian Texts* (London, 1907). For the Persian text, see George G. Cameron, "The Old Persian Text of the Bisitun Inscription," *Journal of Cuneiform Studies* 5 (1951), pp. 47–54.

60   See Stefano de Martino, "The Mittani State: The Formation of the Kingdom of Mittani," in *Constituent, Confederate and Conquered Space: The Emergence of the Mittani State*, edited by Eva Cancik-Kirschbaum, Nicole Brisch, and Jesper Eidem (Berlin, 2014), pp. 61–74.

61   See Paul Thieme, "The 'Aryan' Gods of the Mitanni Treaties," *Journal of the American Oriental Society* 80 (1960), pp. 301–317.

62   For text of the cuneiform tablet (now in the Pergamon Museum, Berlin), see Gerhard F. Probst, Joachim Marzahn, and Peter Raulwing, *Kikkuli–Text* (Lexington, KY, 2010). See online translation: http://imh.org/exhibits/past/legacy-of-the-horse/kikkuli-1345-bce/. The site is maintained by the International Museum of the Horse. See discussion by O. R. Gurney, *The Hittites* (Baltimore, 1953), pp. 124–125.

63   See Jane R. MacIntosh, *A Peaceful Realm: The Rise and Fall of the Indus Civilization* (Boulder, CO, 2002) and *The Ancient Indus Valley: New Perspectives* (Santa Barbara, 2008). Recommended website for Harappan civilization is: www.harappa.com.

64   The language is most likely descended from a proto-Dravidian language. For controversy over the language recorded on the glyphs, see Travatham Mahadevan, "Study of Recent Attempts to Decipher the Indus Script: Aryan or Dravidian or Neither?"(1995–2002), *Electronic Journal of Vedic Studies* 8 (2002), pp. 1–19. The definitive scholarly study on decipherment is Walter A. Fairservice Jr., *The Harappan Civilization: A Model for the Decipherment of the Indus Script* (Leiden, 1992). For the corpus of inscriptions, see Sayid Ghulam Shah and Asko Parpola, eds., *Corpus of Indus Seals and Inscriptions*, 2 vols. (Helsinki, 1992).

65   See Thapar, *Early India*, pp. 117–136, for the Aryan impact on the transformation of Indian culture in the Early Iron Age.

66   See Mallory and Mair, *Tarim Mummies*, pp. 185–187 and 329–330, and C. Keyser, C. Bouakaze, and E. Crubézy, *et al.*, "Ancient DNA Provides New Insights into the History of South Siberian Kurgan People," *Human Genetics* 126 (2009), pp. 395–410.

67   See R. E. Emmerick, "Iranian Settlement East of the Pamirs," in *The Cambridge History of Iran*, Volume III. 2: *The Seleucid, Parthian, and Sasanian Periods*, edited by Ehsan Yarshater (Cambridge, 1986), pp. 265–266, and Edwin G. Pulleyblank, "The Wu-sun and Sakas and the Yüeh-chih Migration," *Bulletin of the School of Oriental and African Studies* 33 (1970), pp. 154–160. For the Saka language and its importance for Buddhist litera-

ture at Khotan, see Carsten Colfe, "Development of Religious Thought," in *Cambridge History of Iran*, III. 2, pp. 849–851.

68 See Grousset, *The Empire of the Steppes*, pp. 50–53.

69 See Nicola di Cosmo, "The Northern Frontier in Pre-Imperial China," in *The Cambridge History of Ancient China from the Origins of the Civilization to 221 B.C.*, edited by Michael Loewe and Edward L. Shaughnessy (Cambridge, 1999), pp. 941–944.

70 See Herodotus IV. 11-13 (Penguin translation, pp. 220–221). Recent DNA analysis supports these migrations reported by Herodotus. See Mari Järve *et al.*, "Shifts in the Genetic Landscape of the Western Eurasian Steppe Associated with the Beginning and End of the Scythian Dominance," *Current Biology* 29 (2019), pp. 2430–2441, and Maja Krzewińska, *et al.*, "Ancient Genomes Suggest the Eastern Pontic-Caspian Steppe as the Source of Western Iron Age Nomads," *Science Advances* 4 (2018), pp. 1–13.

71 See Sarah C. Melville, *The Campaigns of Sargon II, King of Assyria, 721–705 B.C.* (Norman, 2016), pp. 126–128 and 207–220.

72 See H. W. R. Saggs, *The Might That Was Assyria* (London, 1984), pp. 96–87, and Melville, *Campaigns of Sargon II*, pp. 187–192.

73 Strabo, *Geographica* I. 3. 21, dated either to 696 (by Eusebius) or 676 (by Julius Africanus). See Selim Ferruh Adali, "Cimmerians and Scythians: The Impact of Nomadic Powers on the Assyrian Empire and the Ancient Near East," in *Eurasian Empires in Antiquity and the Early Middle Ages: Contact and Exchange between the Greco-Roman World, Inner Asia and China*, edited by Hyun Jin Kim, Frederick Juliaan Vervaet, and Selim Ferruh Adali (Cambridge, 2017), pp. 67–68.

74 See *ibid.*, pp. 73–75.

75 See Mallory, *Indo-Europeans*, pp. 48–56.

76 See Amelie Kurt, *The Persian Empire: A Corpus of Sources from the Achaemenid Period* (London/New York, 2007), pp. 31–33, with translations of the cuneiform sources.

77 See Georges Roux, *Ancient Iraq*, 3rd edition (New York, 1992), pp. 372–388.

78 See Herodotus I. 116-134 (Penguin translation, pp. 48–56), and Pierre Briant, *From Cyrus to Alexander: A History of the Persian Empire*, translated by Peter T. Daniels (Winona Lake, Indiana, 2002), pp. 13–30.

79 See *ibid.*, pp. 31–61 and 107–164.

2 Surviving on the Eurasian Steppes

1 See John of Plano Carpini, "History of the Mongols," in *Mission to Asia*, translated by Christopher Dawson (New York, 1966), p. 8.

2 Herodotus, *Histories*, IV. 46–47; translations from Penguin edition of Herodotus, *Histories*, revised edition, translated by Aubrey de Selincourt (New York, 1972), pp. 230–231.

3   See Erik Hildinger, *Warriors of the Steppe: A Military History of Central Asia, 500 B.C. to 1700 A.D.* (New York, 1977), pp. 7–8.

4   See *Ibn Fadlan and Land of Darkness*, pp. 14–16 (Penguin translation).

5   See William of Rubruck, "The Journey of William of Rubruck," in *Mission to Asia*, pp. 129–131.

6   See Robert N. Taaffe, "The Geographic Setting," in *The Cambridge History of Early Inner Asia*, edited by Denis Sinor (Cambridge, 1990), pp. 19–40.

7   See Michael H. Glantz, "Creeping Environmental Disasters: Central Asia's Aral Sea," in *The Aral Sea Environment*, edited by Andrey G. Kostianoy and Aleksey N. Kosarev (Leiden, 2010), pp. 305–315.

8   See Peter B. Golden, *Central Asia in World History* (Oxford, 2011), pp. 12–17.

9   See Denis Sinor, "The Establishment and Dissolution of the Türk Empire," in *The Cambridge History of Early Inner Asia*, edited by Denis Sinor (Cambridge, 1990), pp. 297–302.

10 For the campaign of Genghis Khan against Khwarazm, see Michael Prawdin, *The Mongol Empire: Its Rise and Legacy*, translated by Eden and Cedar Pau (New York, 1961), pp. 157–159. For Tamerlane's campaign against Tokhtamysh, Khan of the Golden Horde, see Justin Marozzi, *Tamerlane, Sword of Islam, Conqueror of the World* (New York, 2004), pp. 180–184.

11 See Jack Weathersfield, *Genghis Khan and the Making of the Modern World* (New York, 2002), pp. 13–14, and see also pp. xxxiii–xxxv for his invaluable observations based on five years' experience living among the Mongols.

12 Ammianus Marcellinus 31. 2. 1–12; Penguin translation, Ammianus Marcellinus, *The Later Roman Empire (A.D. 354-378)*, translated by Walter Hamilton (New York, 1986), pp. 411–412.

13 See William of Rubruck, "Journey," *Mission to Asia*, pp. 98–99.

14 See John of Plano Carpini, *Mission to Asia*, pp. 16–17. William of Rubruck, *ibid.*, pp. 95–101, likewise so reports the Mongol diet.

15 See Paul Ratchnevsky, *Genghis Khan: His Life and Legacy*, translated by Thomas N. Haining (Oxford, 1991), pp. 19–23.

16 See Herodotus, *Histories* IV. 17 and 54 (Penguin translation), pp. 223 and 233. See Thomas S. Noonan, "The Grain Trade of the Northern Black Sea in Antiquity," *American Journal of Philology* 94 (1973), pp. 231–242. The high king of the Royal Scythians exacted tribute from the agriculturalists and taxed the grain trade to pay for the luxury imports from the Greek world; see Boardman, *Greeks Overseas*, pp. 256-264.

17 See Ross and Thomsen, "Orkhon Inscriptions," *Bulletin of the School of Oriental Studies, University of London* 5 (1930), pp. 863–864.

18 See Golden, *Central Asia*, pp. 16–20.

19   See Craig Benjamin, *Empires of Ancient Eurasia: The First Silk Roads Era,*
      100 BCE–250 CE (Cambridge, 2018), pp. 91–175, and *contra* Valerie Han-
      sen, *Silk Road: A New History* (Oxford, 2012), pp. 235–242, who mini-
      mizes the economic significance of the international trade.

20   See Richard Stoneman, *Palmyra and Its Empire: Zenobia's Revolt against*
      Rome (Ann Arbor, 1994), pp. 31–50. For the range of goods taxed in tar-
      iff law, see John F. Matthews, "The Tax Law of Palmyra: Evidence for
      Economic History in a City of the Roman East," *Journal of Roman Stud-*
      ies 74 (1984), pp. 157–180.

21   The routes traversed by caravans from the Roman Empire were recorded
      by Isidore of Charax in the first century BC; see Wilfred H. Schoff, trans.,
      Parthian Stations by Isidore of Charax: The Greek Text, with a Translation and
      Commentary (Philadelphia, 1914). The emperor Augustus ordered a Latin
      translation.

22   For the role of Sogdian merchants, see Richard N. Frye, *The Heritage of*
      Central Asia from Antiquity to the Turkish Expansion (Princeton, 1998), pp.
      183–198. The range of exotic and luxury goods which Sogdian merchants
      carried to China is well-documented in the early Islamic era; see Edward
      H. Schafer, *The Golden Apples of Samarkand* (Berkeley, 1963), pp. 58–278.

23   See Thomas Thilo, "Chang'an: China's Gateway to the Silk Road," *Be-*
      tween Rome and China: History, Religions and Material Culture of the Silk
      Road, edited by Samuel N. C. Lieu and Gunner Mikkelsen (Turnhout,
      2016), pp. 91–100.

24   See Benjamin, *Empires of Ancient Eurasia,* pp. 183–192, for the crucial role
      of the Kushan Emperors in promoting these routes.

25   See *ibid.,* and pp. 204–237, for scale and importance of Roman com-
      merce in the Indian Ocean. For text and translation of the *Periplus Maris*
      Erythraei, see Lionel Casson, trans., *The Periplus Maris Erythraei: Text with*
      Introduction, Translation, and Commentary (Princeton, 1989).

26   See Michael McCormick, *Origins of the European Economy: Communication*
      and Commerce, A.D. 300–900 (Cambridge, 1), pp. 237–254. The slave trade
      of Western Eurasia fed the demand for labor in the early Islamic world. The
      trade in Turkish slaves met the demand for soldiers in the Abbasid Caliphate;
      see Hugh Kennedy, *The Armies of the Caliphs: Military and Society in the Early*
      Islamic State (London/New York, 2001), pp. 118–147.

27   See Richard Bulliet, *Cotton, Climate, and Camels in Early Islamic Iran: A*
      Moment in World History (New York, 2009), pp. 96–126.

28   Modu Chanyu employed scribes who used Chinese ideogram to keep
      records in Chinese and the language of the Xiongnu. Chinese chroni-
      clers and historians assume that later chanyu of the Xiongnu could rec-
      ognize ideograms. Buddhist missionaries translated religious texts into
      Iran, Tocharian, and Turkish languages by adapting the North Indian
      scripts Brahmi and Karosthi; see György Kara, "Aramaic Scripts for Al-
      taic Languages," *The World's Writing Systems,* edited by Peter T. Daniels
      and William Bright (Oxford, 1996), pp. 536–539. The Turkish runic
      alphabet was ultimately derived from the Aramaic alphabet and it was

widely used among Turks, Uyghurs, Bulgars, and Magyars between the seventh and tenth centuries. See Wolfgang Scharlipp, *An Introduction to the Old Turkish Runic Inscriptions* (Engelschoff, 2000).

29 See Anthony, *Horse, Wheel, and Language*, pp. 117–120 and 140–143.

30 See Weathersfield, *Genghis Khan*, pp. 37–41.

31 See Kahn, trans., *Secret History of the Mongols*, pp. 3–4.

32 Yelu Dashi (1087–1143) was the direct descendant of Abaoji, also known as the Emperor Taizu of the Liao dynasty (916–926), head of the Yelu clan of Khitans who founded the Liao Empire in northern China.

33 For the efficacy of animal sacrifice, see Walter Burkert, *Homo Necans: The Anthropology of Greek Sacrificial Ritual and Myth* (Berkeley, 1996), pp. 1–82.

34 See Anthony, *Horse, Wheel, and Language*, p. 128.

35 See M. L. West, *Indo-European Poetry and Myth* (Oxford, 2007), pp. 166–193, and Mallory, *Indo-Europeans*, pp. 130–134 and 140–142.

36 See Ehsan Yashater, "Iranian Common Beliefs and World View," *Cambridge History of Iran*, III. 1, pp. 347–353.

37 See Mallory, *Indo-Europeans*, pp. 131–133, for the prominent role of Indra in Vedic myth.

38 See *ibid.*, p. 135, for twin fraternal gods.

39 See Marozzi, *Tamerlane*, pp. 95–96 and 397–398.

40 See West, *Indo-European Poetry and Myth*, pp. 26–119, for the meters and rules of oral poetry.

41 Calvert Watkins, *How to Kill a Dragon: Aspects of Indo-European Poetics* (Oxford, 1995), pp. 397–304.

42 Hesiod, *Theogony*, ll. 839–852; Penguin translation, Hesiod, *Theogony and Works and Days*, translated by Dorothea Wender (New York, 1973), pp. 50–51. See also Watkins, *How to Kill a Dragon*, pp. 448–452.

43 The earliest telling of the combat is in *Rig-Veda* I. 32, and it is expanded in the later Mandala, *Riga-Veda* IV. 18. See Watkins, *How to Kill a Dragon*, pp. 464–470.

44 See H. A. Hoffner, *Hittite Myths* (Atlanta, 1990), pp. 11–14, for the translation of the myth which was reenacted at the annual Purulli festival held at Hattusas, the Hittite capital. See discussion by Trevor Bryce, *Life and Society in the Hittite World* (Oxford, 2002), pp. 215–219, and Watkins, *How to Kill a Dragon*, pp. 452–460.

45 Völuspá, ll. 54–55; see translation of Lee M. Hollander, *Poetic Edda* (Austin, 1962), p. 11. Snorri Sturluson retells the story in the *Prose Edda*, translated by Jesse L. Byock (New York, 2005), p. 53. See Calvert, *How to Slay a Dragon*, pp. 429–440.

46 For the techniques of recitation of oral poetry, see seminal works of Millman Parry, *The Making of Homeric Verse: The Collective Papers of Milliman*

Parry, edited by Adam Parry (Oxford, 1989), and Albert Lord, *The Singer of Tales*, 3rd edition (Cambridge, MA, 2019).

47 These were then the tributaries of the Indus, which have since shifted course to the east, and the Sarasvati has since disappeared altogether.

48 See Jules Cashford, trans., *The Homeric Hymns* (New York, 2001). See also Richard Janko, *Homer, Hesiod and the Hymns: Dichronic Development in Oral Poetry* (Cambridge, 1982), pp. 18–41.

49 See Jean-Paul Roux, *Die alttürkische Mythologie* (Klett-Cotta, 1997), p. 255.

50 See Ross and Thomsen, "Orkhon Inscriptions," *Bulletin of the School of Oriental Studies, University of London* 5 (1930), pp. 864.

51 See Ratchnevsky, *Genghis Khan*, pp. 153–155.

52 See John A. Boyle, "Turkish and Mongol Shamanism in the Middle Ages," *Folklore* 83 (1972), pp. 177–193, and Reuven Amitai-Preiss, "Sufis and Shamans: Some Remarks on the Islamization of the Mongols in the Ilkhanate," *Journal of the Economic and Social History of the Orient* 42 (1999), pp. 27–46.

53 See Gülten Yener, "The Creation and Procreation: The Turkish Epic in English Translation with an Introduction and Commentary," M.A. Thesis, Emporia State University, Kansas, 1965. The myth is based on the folklore collected by Mustafa Sepetcioglu in 1965. For English rendition of the myth in verse, see https://larryavisbrown.com/turkish-creation-myth/. The site is maintained by Professor Larry Avis Brown, Department of Theater, Lipscomb University.

54 See Richard Foltz, *Religions of the Silk Road: Premodern Patterns of Globalization*, 2nd edition (New York, 2010), pp. 37–58.

55 See Susan Whitfield, *Life along the Silk Road* (London, 1999), pp. 27–35.

56 The Mauryan emperor Ashoka (268–232 BC) embraced the faith, presided over the Third Buddhist Council, backed missionaries, and promulgated edicts promoting dharma throughout his empire. See Thapar, *Early India*, p. 222. The Indo-Greek King Menander (165–130 BC) was more likely a patron rather than a convert, but he was remembered as both just and an adherent of dharma by later Buddhist writers; see Tarn, *Greeks in Bactria and India*, pp. 265–268. The Kushan Emperor Kanishka (127–150) presided over the Fourth Buddhist Council, built and endowed stupas, and supported missionaries; see Benjamin, *Empires of Ancient Eurasia*, pp. 192–197.

57 For reforms of Kartir, see R. N. Frye, "The Political History of Iran under the Sasanians," *The Cambridge History of Iran*, Vol. 3. 1 (Cambridge, 1983), pp. 128–130. The inscriptions concerning the reforms were displayed at the royal complex at Naqsh-e Rajab, five miles north of Persepolis. Four colossal reliefs cut in the living rock celebrate the investitures of the Shahs Ardashir I and Shapur I, the victories of Shapur I over the Roman emperor Philip I, and the reforms of Kartir, promoted by Shah Hormizd I (272–273). For text and translation of the inscription, see David N. MacKenzie, "Kerdir's inscription," in *The Sasanian Rock Re-*

liefs at Naqsh-i Rustam. Naqsh-i Rustam 6, Iranische *Denkmäler.* Lief. 13. Reihe II: *Iranische Felsreliefs* I (Berlin, 1989), pp. 35–72.

58   See Garth Fowden, *Empire to Commonwealth: Consequences of Monotheism in Late Antiquity* (Princeton, 1994), pp. 61–79 and 138–152.

59   See Samuel N. C. Lieu, *Manichaeism in the Later Roman Empire and Medieval China: A Historical Survey* (Manchester, 1985), pp. 117–152. Our understanding of Manichaeism as world religion rather than a Christian heresy was profoundly changed by the discovery and publication of the Mani Codex from Cologne; see Albert Henrichs and Ludwig Koenen, "Ein griechischer Mani-Codex (P. Colon. inv. nr. 4780)," *Zeitschrift für Papyrologie und Epigraphik* 5 (1970), pp. 97–216. For English translation, see Iain Gardner and Samuel N. C. Lieu, *Manichaean Texts from the Roman Empire* (Cambridge, 2004), pp. 46–103.

60   See Larry Clark, "Manichaeism among the Uygurs: The Uygur Khan of the Bokug Cvlan," *New Light on Manichaeism*, edited by Jason D. BeDuhn (Leiden, 2009), pp. 61–72.

61   See Fowden, *Empire to Commonwealth*, pp. 76–79 and 121–124, and Foltz, *Religions of the Silk Road*, pp. 59–84.

62   Theophylactus Simocatta, *History* V. 10. For the translation, see Michael and Mary Whitby, trans., *The History of Theophylact Simocatta* (Oxford, 1986), pp. 146–147. In 588, Shah Khusrau II sent to Constantinople Turkish captives who had been tattooed with crosses on their foreheads.

63   See Alphonse Mingana, *The Early Spread of Christianity in Central Asia and the Far East: A New Document.* (Manchester, 1925), pp. 8–9.

64   See Kevin Alan Brook, *The Jews of Khazaria*, 3rd edition (New York, 2018), pp. 77–108.

65   See Golden, *Central Asia*, pp. 63–75.

66   See West, *Indo-European Poetry and Myth*, pp. 411–504, for the celebration of these deeds in verse.

67   See Anthony, *Horse, Wheel, and Language*, pp. 300–305.

68   H. W. E. Saggs, *Civilization before Greece and Rome* (New Haven, 1989), pp. 213–215.

69   See P. Librado *et al.*, "The Origins and Spread of Domestic Horses," *Nature* 598 (2021), pp. 634–640.

70   See Herodotus, *Histories*, IV. 22-23 (Penguin translation, p. 238).

71   Strabo, *Geographica* XIV. 2. See also C. Bennett Pascal, "October Horse," *Harvard Studies in Classical Philology* 85 (1981), pp. 261–29, for comparable Roman horse sacrifice.

72   See Mallory, *Indo-Europeans*, pp. 135–136, for the *ashvamedha*, which was promoted by the Gupta emperors.

73   See Robert Drews, *The End of the Bronze Age: Changes in Warfare and the Catastrophe ca. 1200 B.C.* (Princeton, 1995), pp. 104–147.

74   See Hildinger, *Warriors of the Steppes*, pp. 33–56.

75   See Ross and Thomsen, "Orkhon Inscriptions," *Bulletin of the School of Oriental Studies, University of London* 5 (1930), pp. 868–869.

76   See Michael Sullivan, *The Arts of China*, 6th edition, revised (Berkeley, 2018), p. 135. The reliefs of the horses were placed in the mausoleum of Taizong at Zhao, Shaanxi.

77   See Herodotus, *Histories* IV. 110–115 (Penguin translation), pp. 249–251.

78   See Morris Rossabi, *Kublai Khan, His Life and Times* (Berkeley, 1986), pp. 104–105.

3 Scythians and the Great King of Persia

1   Hdt IV. 132 (Penguin translation, p. 256).

2   Herodotus IV. 83–146 (Penguin translation, pp. 242–261). Herodotus is the main source of the expedition, dated to either 515 or 512 BC. See Pierre Briant, *From Cyrus to Alexander: A History of the Persian Empire*, translated by Peter T. Daniels (Winona Lake, 2002), pp. 141–146.

3   See Herodotus I. 205–216 (Penguin translation, pp. 81–85), and Briant, *From Cyrus to Alexander*, pp. 38–40 and 49–50.

4   For the size and logistics of the Achaemenid army, see F. Maurice, "The Size of the Army of Xerxes in the Invasion of Greece in 480 B.C.," *Journal of Hellenic Studies* 50 (1930), pp. 210–235. See Herodotus VII. 60, 64–66 (Penguin translation, pp. 395–397), for his description of Persian, Median, Bactrian, and Sogdian cavalry in the army of Xerxes. See Xenophon, *Anabasis*, III. 2; Penguin translation Xenophon, Persian Expedition, translated by Rex Warner (New York, 1872), pp. 151–153, for exhorting his fellow Greek mercenaries, armed as hoplites (heavy infantry), on how to oppose Persian horsemen.

5   See John L. Myers, *Herodotus, Father of History* (Chicago, 1958), pp. 168–172, for the sources of Herodotus on the Scythians.

6   Herodotus IV. 136 (Penguin translation, p. 258).

7   See Herodotus IV. 137–139 (Penguin translation, pp. 258–259).

8   See Herodotus V. 23–25 (Penguin translation, pp. 287–288).

9   See Herodotus V. 35–36 (Penguin translation, pp. 291–292). Aristagoras was already inclined to revolt because he had compromised himself in the eyes of King Darius by promoting the ill-fated Persian expedition against Naxos. For the role of Histiaeus in fomenting the Ionian Revolt (499–494 BC), see A. Blamire, "Herodotus and Histiaeus," *Classical Quarterly* 53 (1959), pp. 142–154, and G. A. H. Chapman, "Herodotus and Histiaeus' Role in the Ionian Revolt," *Historia* 21 (1972), pp. 546–568.

10   See Herodotus V. 37–126 and VI. 1–43, pp. 93–338, for the Ionian Revolt (499–494 BC), and A. R. Burn, *Persia and the Greeks: Defense of the West, 546–478 B.C.* (New York, 1962), pp. 193–220.

11   See Briant, *From Cyrus to Alexander*, pp. 357–471.

12   See *ibid.*, pp. 783–800, and Muhammad A. Dandamaev and Vladimir G. Lukonin, *The Culture and Social Institutions of Ancient Iran* (Cambridge, 1989), pp. 177–237.

13   See most recent analysis by G. A. Gnecchi-Ruscon *et al.*, "Ancient Genomic Time Transect from the Central Asian Steppe Unravels the History of the Scythians," *Science Advances* 7 (2021), pp. 1–14.

14   See Galen, *De Temperamentis*. 2, and Ammianus Marcellinus, *Histories* XXI. 2. 2, describing the Alans. See also remarks of Pliny the Elder, *Natural History* 6. 24.

15   Herodotus IV. 8 (Penguin translation, p. 219), crediting the Pontic Greeks for his information.

16   See Barry Cunliffe, *The Scythians: Nomad Warriors of the Steppes* (Oxford, 2019), pp. 265–289; Tamara Talbot Rice, *The Scythians*, 3rd edition (London, 1961), pp. 146–177; and Hermann Parzinger, "Burial Mounds of Scythian Elites in the Eurasian Steppe: New Discoveries," *Journal of British Archaeology* 5 (2017), 331–355.

17   Herodotus IV. 22–23 (Penguin translation, p. 238).

18   See Talbot Rice, *Scythians*, pp. 92–124.

19   See *ibid.*, pp. 96–97.

20   See *ibid.*, pp. 77–78 and 97–99.

21   See *ibid.*, pp. 154–161.

22   Herodotus IV. 110–117 (Penguin translation, pp. 249–251).

23   Plutarch, *Pyrrhus*, 16. King Pyrrhus was referring to the orderly legionary camp of the Romans.

24   See John Boardman, *The Greek Overseas: Their Early Colonies and Trade*, 4th edition (New York, 1999), pp. 232–264.

25   See Zopfia H. Archibald, "The Bosporan Kingdom," in *Cambridge Ancient History*, Volume IV (1994), pp. 476–511.

26   See David MacDonald, *An Introduction to the History and Coinage of the Kingdom of the Bosporus* (Lancaster, PA, 2005), pp. 13–38 and 69–122.

27   See Herodotus IV. 46. 76–77 (Penguin translation), pp. 239–240.

28   See Plutarch, *Solon* 5, for a meeting between the Athenian lawgiver and Ancharsis. See Diogenes Laertius, *Lives of the Philosophers* I. 41–42 and 101–105, who credits Anacharsis as a proponent of the Cynic philosophy; see J. F. Kindstrand, *Anacharsis: The Legend and the Apophthegmata* (Uppsala, 1981), pp. 85–95.

29   Herodotus IV. 78–80 (Penguin translation, pp. 240–241).

30   Atheas or Ateas is mentioned briefly in Classical sources, see notably Plutarch, *Moralia* 174; Justin, *Epitome* 9. 2; Lucian, *Macrobii* 10; and Orosius, *Against the Pagans* 3. 13; see CAH article on Scythians, and John Gardiner-Garden, "Ateas and Theopompus," *Journal of Hellenic Studies* 109 (1989), 29–40.

31   See Tamara Talbot Rice, "The Scytho-Sarmatian Tribes of South-Eastern Europe," in *The Roman Empire and Its Neighbors*, by Fergus Millar, 2nd edition (New York, 1981), pp. 270–275.

32   For the development of cataphracti, see A. D. H. Bivar, "Cavalry Equipment and Tactics on the Euphrates Frontier," *Dumbarton Oaks Papers* 26 (1972), pp. 271–291.

33   See Cicero, *Acad.* 3. 2. 1, who made the comparison to exalt the fame of his political ally Pompey the Great (Cn. Pompeius Magnus), who finally defeated Mithridates.

34   See Adrienne Mayor, *The Poison King: The Life and Legend of Mithradates, Rome's Deadliest Enemy* (Princeton, 2010), pp. 332–358.

35   Tacitus, *Germania* 3. 3; Penguin translation, Tacitus, *The Agricola and Germania*, translated by S. A. Handford (New York, 1973) p. 129.

36   See Talbot Rice, "Scytho-Samartian Tribes," *Roman Empire and Its Neighbors*, pp. 289–293.

37   See Pat Southern, *Domitian, Tragic Tyrant* (Bloomington, 1997), pp. 93 and 99–100, and Julian Bennett, *Trajan: Optimus Princeps*, 2nd edition (Bloomington, 2001), pp. 163–166, for the Roxolani and Jazyges allying with Dacians against Rome. For their alliance with the Germanic Quadi and Marcomanni in 167–180, see Anthony Birley, *Marcus Aurelius* (New Haven, 1989), pp. 208–209. The Roxolani had the singular distinction of annihilating the Legio XXI Rapax in 92 AD.

38   See Cassius Dio 72. 19 (LCL translation, Vol. 9, pp. 59–61), for treaty arrangements imposed on the Jazyges by Marcus Aurelius in 178–179. Marcus Aurelius had contemplated the incorporation of the Roxolani and Jazyges as a new province Sarmatia; see SHA, *Vita Marci* 24. 5 and 27. 10 (LCL translation, Vol. 1 t, pp. 191 and 201).

39   Josephus, *The Jewish War* VII. 230; Penguin translation, Josephus, *The Jewish War*, revised edition, translated by G. A. Williamson (New York, 1970), pp. 392–393.

40   For the most readily available translation of the text of Arrian's *Tactica*, see online translation at https://members.tripod.com/~S_van_Dorst/Ancient_Warfare/Rome/Sources/ektaxis.html.

For analysis of Arrian's tactical formation, see A. K. Goldsworthy, *The Roman Army at War, 100 B.C.–200 A.D.* (Oxford, 1996), pp. 136–138, and Everett Wheeler, "The Legion as Phalanx," *Chiron* 9 (1979), pp. 303–318.

4 Alexander the Great: Walling off Gog and Magog

1   Arrian, *Anabasis* IV. 4. 1–3; Arrian, *Campaigns of Alexander*, revised edition, translated by Aubrey de Selincourt (New York, 1971), pp. 204–205. See also A. B. Bosworth, *Conquest and Empire: The Reign of Alexander the Great* (1988), pp. 116–119.

2   For Greek conceptions of Central Asia and India in 329 BC, see M. Cary
        and E. H. Warmington, *The Ancient Explorers*, revised edition (Baltimore,
        1963), pp. 174–179.

3   Herodotus IV. 44 (Penguin translation, pp. 239–240).

4   For conquest of Upper Satrapies, see Bosworth, *Conquest and Empire*, pp.
        104–116. For the expansion of the Macedonian army by recruiting Greek
        mercenaries and Iranian cavalry, see *ibid.*, pp. 266–277, and see also H. W.
        Parke, *Greek Mercenary Soldiers from the Earliest Times to the Battle of Ipsus*
        (Oxford, 1933), pp. 186–199, and G. Griffith, "A Note on the Hipparchies
        of Alexander," *Journal of Hellenic Studies* 82 (1963), pp. 68–74.

5   See Frank L. Holt, *Alexander the Great and Bactria: The Formation of a Greek
        Frontier in Central Asia*, Mnemosyne Supplement 104 (Leiden, 1995), pp.
        61–70, and Bosworth, *Conquest and Empire*, pp. 245–250, for the fortified
        settlements along the northern frontier.

6   Arrian, *Anabasis*. IV. 3. 3–5.1 (Penguin translation, pp. 204–206); Cur-
        tius Rufus VII. 8–10; Penguin translation, Quintus Curtius Rufus, *The
        History of Alexander*, translated by John Yardley (New York, 1984), pp.
        167–173. See J. F. C. Fuller, *The Generalship of Alexander the Great* (New
        York, 1959), pp. 236–241.

7   Private communication from my colleague and dear friend Professor
        Eugene N. Borza, the leading expert of Macedon, who held many such
        polls during his career.

8   Arrian, *Anabasis* I. 3–4 (pp. 46–47, Penguin translation), and Diodorus
        Siculus XVI. 84–98 and XVII. 1–16; translation, Diodorus of Sicily, *The
        Library, Books 16–20*, translated by Robin Waterfield (Oxford, 2018), pp.
        76–94. See also Bosworth, *Conquest and Empire*, pp. 28–35, and Fuller,
        Generalship of Alexander, pp. 61–85 and 219–226.

9   See Goldsworthy, *Roman Army at War*, pp. 129–134, and A. B. Bosworth,
        "Arrian and the Alani," *Harvard Studies in Classical Philology* 81 (1977),
        pp. 247–255.

10   Joseph P. Yap, *The Western Regions: Xiongnu and Han: From the Shiji, Hanshu
        and Hou Hanshu* (Independent Publication, 2019), pp. 59–70.

11   See Ralph D. Sawyer, "Military Writings," in *A Military History of China*,
        edited by David Graff and Robin Higham (Lexington, KY, 2012), pp.
        97–114. The most important manual was *Wujing Zongyao*, compiled on or-
        ders of the Song emperor Renzong (1022–1063), with the earliest formula
        for black gunpowder and descriptions of incendiary arrows and bombs.

12   See G. T. Dennis, *Maurice's Strategikon: Handbook of Byzantine Military
        Strategy* (Pennsylvania, 1984), the first Byzantine manual discussing how
        to cope with nomadic foes. For later manuals, see G. T. Dennis, *Three
        Byzantine Military Treatises* (Washington, DC, 1986) and *The Tactica of
        Leo VI*, revised edition (Washington, DC, 2014), for text (translation
        and commentary of anonymous manuals of the late sixth and tenth cen-
        turies, with stress on stealth, ambush, and skirmishing by cavalry). See

discussion by Sir Charles Oman, *A History of the Art of War in the Middle Ages*, Volume 1 (London, 1925), pp. 200–217.

13 See Brent Nosworthy, *The Anatomy of Victory: Battle Tactics, 1689-1763* (New York, 1989), pp. 223–227.

14 See Holt, *Alexander and Bactria*, pp. 78–86, and W. W. Tarn, *The Greeks in Bactria and India*, 3rd edition, revised by Frank L. Holt (Chicago, 1986), pp. 5–32.

15 See M. Rostovtzeff, *The Social and Economic History of the Hellenistic World*, Volume II (Oxford, 1941), pp. 1238–1300, and Susan Sherwin-White and Amelie Kuhrt, *From Samarkand to Sardis: A New Approach to the Seleucid Empire* (Berkeley, 1993), pp. 10–113.

16 See excavation reports by Paul Bernard, "Alexandre et Aï Khanoum," *Journal des Savants* 2 (1982), 125–138, and *Fouilles d'Ai Khanoum I (Campagnes 1965, 1966, 1967, 1968).* Memoires de la Delegation Archeologique Francaise en Afghanistan 21 (Paris, 1973). For English summary of the finds, see https://www.worldhistory.org/article/165/ai-khanum-the-capital-of-eucratides/.

17 The French documentary is by P. Cabouat and A. Moreau, "Eurasia-L'Alexandrie oubliée," NHK-France 5-Point du Jour, 2004.

18 See Cary and Warmington, *Ancient Explorers*, pp. 163–167 and 173–189.

19 See Sherwin-White and Kuhrt, *From Samarkand to Sardis*, pp. 91–103. Megasthenes, envoy of Seleucus I (395–281 BC), resided at the court of King Chandragupta Maurya in Pataliputra (modern Patna), in ca. 290–280 BC. His account was incorporated by later authors, most notably by Arrian in his own *Indica*. See Richard Stoneman, *The Greek Experience of India from Alexander to the Indo-Greeks* (Princeton, 2019), pp. 129–238.

20 See Cary and Warmington, *Ancient Explorers*, pp. 222–232.

21 For circulation of Greco-Bactrian tetradrachmae as international trade coins, see Frank L. Holt, "The Euthydemid Coinage of Bactria: Further Hoard Evidence from Aï Khanoum," *Revue numismatique* 6, 23 (1981), pp. 7–44. The standard catalog remains Osmund Bopearachchi, *Monnaies gréco-bactriennes et indo-grecques: Catalogue raisonné* (Paris, 1991).

22 See Richard Stoneman, trans., *The Greek Alexander Romance* (New York, 1991), pp. 8–23.

23 See Richard Stoneman, *Alexander the Great: A Life in Legend* (London/New York, 2008), pp. 230–245, with detailed summary of growth of the legend among the many versions.

24 See *ibid.*, pp. 128–149, for the many different versions about Alexander's dealings with the Amazons. *The Greek Alexander Romance* III, 25–26 (Penguin translation, pp. 141–144) does report the visit of Queen Thalestris; Plutarch, *Alexander* 46 (Penguin translation, p. 330) and Diodorus Siculus XVII. 77 (Oxford translation, p. 143) first report the encounter. See Elizabeth Baynham, "Alexander and the Amazons," *Classical Quarterly* 21 (2001), pp. 115–126.

25   Arrian, *Anabasis* IV. 15 (Penguin translation, pp. 227–228).

26   See Justin, *Epitome*, II. 4; *Justin, Epitome of the Philippic Histories*, trans-
     lated by John S. Watson and revised by Giles Lauren (Sophron Editor,
     2017), pp. 30–32.

27   See John B. Friedman, *The Monstrous Races in Medieval Art and Thought*
     (Cambridge, MA, 1981), pp. 170–172.

28   *Alexander Romance*, III. 1–35 9 (Penguin translation, pp. 7–23 and 128–
     159). See George Cary, *The Medieval Alexander* (Cambridge, 1956), pp.
     71–163, and Andrew R. Anderson, *Alexander's Gate: Gog and Magog, and
     the Inclosed Nations* (Cambridge, MA, 1932), pp. 3–57.

29   See Stoneman, *Alexander the Great*, pp. 170–189, for the diverse tales of
     Alexander's dealing with the unclean nations.

30   Suetonius, *Nero* 19. 2 (Penguin trans., p. 222); Tacitus, *Hist*. I. 6. 2 (Pen-
     guin trans., p. 24); Cassius Dio 63. 8. 1 (LCL Vol. 8, p. 149), and Pliny
     the Elder, *Natural History* VI. 40 (LCL Vol. 2, p. 367).

31   See Barbara Levick, *Vespasian* (New Haven, 1999), pp. 168–169, and Barry
     W. Jones, *The Emperor Domitian* (London/New York, 1992), pp. 156–159.

32   Josephus, *Jewish War* VII. 244 (Penguin trans., pp. 392–293), who iden-
     tifies the Derbent Pass as the Gates of Alexander. See also Anderson,
     Alexander's Gate, pp. 58–86.

33   *Revelation* 19. 11-21. 8.

34   See Scott D. Westrem, "Against Gog and Magog," *Text and Territory:
     Geographical Imagination in the European Middle Ages*, edited by Sylvia To-
     masch, Sylvia and Gilles Sealy (Philadelphia, 1998), pp. 54–78, and An-
     derson, *Alexander's Gate*, pp. 87–90.

35   *Koran*, sura 18 (Al Kahf) and sura 21 (Al-Anbiya); see Emeri J. van Donzel
     and Andrea Barbara Schmidt, *Gog and Magog in Early Eastern Christian and
     Islamic Sources: Sallam's Quest for Alexander's Wall* (Leiden, 2010), pp. 50–54.

36   See Anderson, *Alexander's Gate*, pp. 91–105.

37   See van Donzel and Schmidt, *Gog and Magog*, pp. 90–93.

38   See Richard Stoneman, "Alexander the Great in Arabic Tradition," *The
     Ancient Novel and Beyond*, edited by Stelios Panayotakis, Maaike Zim-
     merman, and Wytse Keulen (Leiden, 2003), pp. 1–21.

39   See *Ibn Fadlan and the Land of Darkness: Arab Travellers in the Far North*,
     translated by Paul Lund and Carol Stone (New York, 2012), pp. 40–41.

40   *Ibid.*, p. 41.

41   See van Donzel and Schmidt, *Gog and Magog*, pp. 86–117.

5 Modu Chanyu and the Great Wall of China

1   See Derk Bodde, "The State and Empire of Ch'in," *The Cambridge History
     of China*, Vol. I, edited by Denis Twitchett and Michael Loewe (Cam-
     bridge, 1986), pp. 40–51.

2   See Jonathan Clements, *The First Emperor of China* (Stroud, 2006), pp. 113–138.

3   See Hiromi Kinoshita, "Qin Palaces and Architecture," *The First Emperor: China's Terracotta Army*, edited by Hiromi Kinoshita and Jane Portal (Cambridge, MA, 2007), pp. 83–92. See also Charles Sanft, "The Construction and Deconstruction of Epanggong: Notes from the Crossroads of History and Poetry," *Oriens Extremus* 47 (2003), pp. 160–176.

4   See Jessica Rawson, "The First Emperor's Tomb: The Afterlife Universe," in *The First Emperor*, pp. 114–151.

5   Lukas Nickel, "The Terracotta Army," *The First Emperor*, pp. 158–159.

6   See Pengliang Lu, "The Ingenuity of Qin and Han Craftsmanship," *Age of Empires: Art of the Qin and Han Dynasties*, edited by Zhixin Jason Sun (New York, 2017), pp. 30–50.

7   See Arthur Waldron, *The Great Wall of China: From History to Myth* (Cambridge, 1990), pp. 30–52.

8   See Nicola di Cosmo, *Ancient China and Its Enemies: The Rise of Nomadic Power in East Asian History* (Cambridge, 2002), pp. 127–138.

9   See Clements, *First Emperor*, pp. 103–109.

10   See John Man, *The Great Wall* (New York, 2008), pp. 29–36.

11   See *ibid.*, pp. 15–18, and Clements, *First Emperor*, p. 111.

12   The Emperor Qin Shi Huang inherited a long-established policy among the northern Chinese Kingdoms of building walls on distant frontiers to regulate the movement of nomads; see di Cosmo, *Ancient China and Enemies*, pp. 141–149.

13   See David Graf and Robin Higham, eds., *A Military History of China* (Lexington, KY, 2012), pp. 76–77.

14   See Edward Burman, *The Terracotta Warriors* (New York, 2018), pp. 105–131, and Yang Hong, "The Military Armaments of the Qin and Han," in *Age of Empires*, pp. 51–61.

15   See di Cosmo, *Ancient China and Enemies*, pp. 174–175. For the strategic importance of the Ordos triangle, see Waldron, *The Great Wall of China*, pp. 61–71.

16   See Bodde, "State and Empire of Ch'in," in *Cambridge History of China*, I, pp. 64–66.

17   See Thomas J. Barfield, *The Perilous Frontier: Nomadic Empires and China, 221 B.C. to A.D. 1757* (Oxford, 1989), pp. 32–34.

18   See Vu Ying-Shih, "The Hsiung-nu," in *The Cambridge History of Early Inner Asia*, edited by Denis Sinor (Cambridge, 1990), pp. 110–125.

19   See Joseph J. Yap, *The Western Regions, Xiongnu and Han from the Shiji, Hanshu and Hou Hanshu* (Independent Publisher, 2019), pp. 287–299.

20   See the perceptive comparison of the two historians by Thomas R. Martin, *Herodotus and Sima Qian: The First Great Historians of Greece and China* (Boston, 2010), pp. 1–28.

21   See di Cosmo, *Ancient China and Enemies*, pp. 175–178. The source is *Hanshu* 6. 6–7; see Yap, *Western Regions*, pp. 286–287.

22   Barfield, *Perilous Frontier*, p. 57. See Michael Loewe, "The Structure and Practice of Government," *Cambridge History of China*, I, pp. 470–475. In 140 AD, the Han Empire comprised eighty commanderies or tax districts, with populations between two hundred fifty thousand and two million per commandery. At an average of seven hundred fifty thousand residents per commandery, the Han Empire of the mid-second century AD was comparable in size and population to the Roman Empire, whose population is estimated at 65 million.

23   See Bodde, "The State and Empire of Ch'in," *Cambridge History of China*, I, pp. 71–84.

24   See Michael Loewe, "Structure and Practice of Government," *Cambridge History of China*, I, pp. 463–490. For the widespread acceptance of the emperor's Mandate of Heaven, see Marianne Bujard, "State and Local Cults in Han Religion," *Early Chinese Religion*, Volume II, edited by John Lanerwey and Marc Kalinowski (Leiden, 2009), pp. 777–812. For the significance of mastery of the Confucian canon, see Michael Nylan, "Classics without Canonization: Learning and Authority in Qin and Han," *ibid.*, pp. 721–776.

25   See di Cosmo, *Ancient China and Enemies*, pp. 35-36, and *Hanshu* 6. 13–16; see Yap, *Western Regions*, pp. 292–297.

26   See Yu Ying-shih, "Han Foreign Relations," *Cambridge History of China*, Vol. I, pp. 436–460, for Han expansion into Korea and the southern lands of the Yangtze.

27   See Yu Ying-shih, *Trade and Expansion in Han*, pp. 36–54.

28   See di Cosmo, *Ancient China and Enemies*, pp. 190–196.

29   See Barfield, *Perilous Frontier*, pp. 47–49, for the significance of distributing gifts to Xiongnu elite and vassal rulers.

30   See Yu Ying-shih, *Trade and Expansion*, pp. 92–132, for the economic benefits of frontier trade.

31   *Hanshu* 6. 17; see Yap, *Western Regions*, pp. 297–299. See also Yu Ying-shih, "The Hsiung-nu," *Cambridge History of Early Inner Asia*, p. 127, and di Cosmo, *Ancient China and Enemies*, pp. 188–190.

32   *Hanshu* 8-9 and 12; see Yap, *Western Regions*, pp. 287–289 and 292. See also Yu Ying-shih, "The Hsiung-nu," *Cambridge History of Early Inner Asia*, pp. 127–128.

33   See di Cosmo, *Ancient China and Enemies*, pp. 176–181.

34   *Hanshu* 6. 10; see Yap, *Western Regions*, pp. 288–289. See also di Cosmo, *Ancient China and Enemies*, pp. 181–183.

35   See *ibid.*, pp. 185–188.

36   *Shiji* 3; see Joseph P. Yap, *Wars with the Xiongnu: A Translation from Zizhi Tongjian* (Bloomington, 2009), pp. 109–111.

37   See Hyun Jin Kim, *The Huns, Rome and the Birth of Europe*, pp. 60–69, arguing that Attila and his Huns were the heirs to an imperial bureaucratic tradition of the Xiongnu.

38   See *ibid.*, pp. 127–131.

39   See David N. Keightley, "The Shang: China's First Historical Dynasty," *The Cambridge History of Ancient China from the Origins of Civilization to 221 B.C.*, edited by Michael Lowe and Edward L. Shaughnessy (Cambridge, 1999), pp. 236–246.

40   See Hyuan Jin Kim, *Huns, Rome and Birth of Europe*, pp. 21–26, for a perceptive comparison of the Xiongnu and Scythian confederations.

41   J. C. Greenfield, "Aramaic in the Achaemenid Empire," *The Cambridge History of Iran*, Volume II: *The Median and Achaemenid Periods*, edited by Ilya Gershevitch (Cambridge, 1985), pp. 698–713.

42   See Keith Hopkins, "Taxes and Trade in the Roman Empire (200 B.C.–400 A.D.)," *Journal of Roman Studies* 70 (1980), pp. 120–121; during the later Roman Empire or Dominate, the ratio increased perhaps to one senior official to every one hundred fifty thousand subjects. By Chinese standards, the Roman Empire was woefully under-governed. For Han administration, with comparison to the Roman imperial counterpart, see Dingxin Zhao, "The Han Bureaucracy: Its Origin, Structure and Development," *State Power in Rome and China*, edited by Walter Scheibel (Oxford, 2015), pp. 56–89. The fundamental study remains Hans Bielenstein, *The Bureaucracy of Han Times* (Cambridge, 1980).

43   See Barfield, *Perilous Frontier*, pp. 65–67.

44   *Hanshu* 6.29; see Yap, *Western Regions*, pp. 308–310.

6 The Xiongnu and Chinese Emperors at War

1   *Shiji* 1. 1–13; see Yap, *Western Regions*, pp. 1–15. See also Michael Loewe, "Zhang Qian," *A Biographical Dictionary of Qin, Former Han, and Xin Periods* (Leiden, 2000), pp. 687–689.

2   *Shiji* 1. 18; see Yap, *Western Regions*, pp. 20–21.

3   See Benjamin, *Empires of Ancient Eurasia*, p. 68, for significance of the report of Zhang Qian.

4   See Michael Loewe, "The Campaigns of the Han Wu-ti," in *Chinese Ways in Warfare*, edited by Frank Kierman and John Fairbanks (Cambridge, 1974), pp. 80–95.

5   See di Cosmo, *Ancient China and Enemies*, pp. 201–205, and Barfield, *Perilous Frontier*, pp. 53–54.

6   See di Cosmo, *Ancient China and Enemies*, pp. 232–236, and Michael Loewe, "The Western Han Army: Organization, Leadership, and Operation," in *Military Culture in Imperial China*, edited by Nicolas di Cosmo (Cambridge, MA, 2009), pp. 71–97.

7   See di Cosmo, *Ancient China and Enemies*, pp. 231–233.

8   See *ibid.*, pp. 229–232.

9   See Loewe, "Campaigns of Wu-ti," in *Chinese Ways in Warfare*, pp. 67–122.

10   Yap, *Wars with Xiongnu*, pp. 146–153.

11   See *ibid.*, pp. 154–176.

12   *Hanshu* 2. 1–6; see Yap, *Western Regions*, pp. 59–68. See also di Cosmo, *Ancient China and Enemies*, pp. 237–240.

13   *Hanshu* 2. 14 and 4. 1–9; see Yap, *Western Regions*, pp. 74–76 and 162–172. See also di Cosmo, *Ancient China and Enemies*, pp. 241–244.

14   See Yap, *Wars with Xiongnu*, pp. 186–194.

15   See Barfield, *Perilous Frontier*, pp. 56–57, for losses. See also Loewe, "Western Han Army," in *Chinese Ways of Warfare*, pp. 71–77 and 81–82, for the Han expeditionary armies.

16   *Shiji* 1. 15–17; see Yap, *Western Regions*, pp. 17–20. See also Yu Ying-shih, "Hsiung-nu," *Cambridge History of Early Inner Asia*, pp. 141–142.

17   See Yap, *Wars with Xiongnu*, pp. 205–220.

18   See *ibid.*, pp. 200–229, for the primary account from the *Shiji* on the War of the Heavenly Horses.

19   *Ibid.*, pp. 257–262; this was the third unsuccessful expedition of Li Guangi Li in 90 BC. He suffered defeats at the hands of the Xiongnu in 99 and 97 BC; see *ibid.*, pp. 235–240 and 243–244.

20   *Hanshu* 2. 16; see Yap, *Western Regions*, p. 78.

21   See Barfield, *Perilous Frontier*, pp. 267–270.

22   See Walter Scheibel, "State Revenue and Expenditure in the Han and Roman Empires," *State Power in Rome and China*, pp. 150–180.

23   See Yu Ying-shih, *Trade and Expansion*, pp. 65-88, for perceptions of the Xiongnu and treatment of captives.

24   See Yu Ying-shih, "Hsiung-nu," *Cambridge History of Early Inner Asia*, pp. 135–138, and Barfield, *Perilous Frontier*, pp. 60–63.

25   *Hanshu* 7. 1–11; see Yap, *Western Regions*, pp. 352–368, and Joseph P. Yap, *Wars with the Xiongnu: A Translation from Zhizi Tongjian* (Independent Publication, 2009), pp. 348–352 (account of *Shiji*). See Barfield, *Perilous Frontier*, pp. 60–63, and Yu Ying-shih, "Hsiung-nu," *Cambridge History of Early Inner Asia*, pp. 135–144.

26   See Hans Bielenstein, "Wang Mang, the Restoration of the Han Dynasty, and Later Han," *Cambridge History of China*, Vol. I, pp. 224–232.

27   See *ibid.*, pp. 232–240.

28   For the currency reforms of Wang Mang, see Robert Tye, *Wang Mang* (South Uist, 1993), and compare the currency reforms of Diocletian (284–30); see Kenneth W. Harl, *Coinage in the Roman Economy 300 B.C.*

to A.D. 300 (Berkeley, 1996), pp. 148–157. Both rulers instituted a new fiduciary currency to meet state expenditures.

29   *Hanshu* 7. 33–40; see Yap, *Western Regions*, pp. 382–394, and pp. 526–545. See also Barfield, *Perilous Frontier*, pp. 71–80.

30   *Houhan Shu* 8. 1–3; Yap, *Western Regions*, pp. 413–414.

31   Yap, *Wars with Xiongnu*, pp. 562–601; *Shiji* 17 deals exclusively with the demise of Wang Mang.

32   See Barfield, *Ancient China and Enemies*, pp. 71–78.

33   See Yu Ying-shih, "Hsiung-nu," *Cambridge History of Early Inner Asia*, pp. 143–149.

34   See Yu Ying-shih, "Han Foreign Relations," *Cambridge History of China*, I, pp. 400–405, for the diplomacy deployed by the Han emperors Ming (57–75) and Zhang (75–88) against the Xiongnu.

35   The later Han emperors discontinued conscription into the imperial army except in the frontier commanderies where barbarians and provincials of mixed origin were recruited. See Rafe de Crespigny, "The Military Culture of the Later Han," *Military Culture in Imperial China*, pp. 93–95.

36   See Barfield, *Perilous Frontier*, pp. 77–80.

37   *Hou Hanshu* 23–29; see Yap, *Western Regions*, pp. 517–526. See also Yu Ying-shih, "Han Foreign Relations," *Cambridge History of China*, I, pp. 404–405, and de Crespigny, "Military Culture of Later Han," pp. 97–103.

38   Laurie Chen, "Archaeologists Discover Story of China's Ancient Military Might Carved in Cliff Face," *South China Morning Post* (21 August 2017). The text of the inscription was reported in *Hou Hanshu* 10.32; see Yap, *Western Regions*, p. 94. For poetic inscriptions, see also David Knechtges, "From the Eastern Han to the Western Jin (A.D. 25–317)," in *The Cambridge History of Chinese Literature*, Vol. I, edited by Kang-i Sun Chang and Stephen Owen (Cambridge, 2010), p. 138.

39   *Hou Hanshu* 9. 32–45 and 49–50; see Yap, *Western Regions*, pp. 527–542 and 548–549. See also Yu Ying-shih, "Han Foreign Relations," *Cambridge History of China*, I, pp. 412–415.

40   *Hou Hanshu* 9, 30–31 and 46–49; see Yap, *Western Regions*, pp. 526–527 and 542–549.

41   See Benjamin, *Empires of Ancient Eurasia*, pp. 188–190.

42   See John E. Hill, *Through the Jade Gate, China to Rome: A Study of the Silk during the Later Han Dynasty 1st to 2nd Centuries CE* (Charleston, SC, 2009), Vol. I, pp. 21–31.

43   See *ibid.*, II, pp. 16–20.

44   Translation from *ibid.*, I, pp. 26–27.

45   See Julian Bennett, *Trajan, Optimus Princeps* (New Haven, 1997), pp. 184–185.

46   See Liu Xinru, "Looking towards the West: How the Chinese Viewed the Romans," in *Silk: Trade and Exchange along the Silk Roads between Rome*

and China in Antiquity, edited by Erit Hilderbrandt and Carole Gillis (Oxford, 2016), pp. 1–6.

47   See Yu Ying-shih, "Han Foreign Relations," *Cambridge History of China*, I, pp. 415–432.

48   See Benjamin, *Empires of Ancient Eurasia*, pp. 191–192.

49   See Barfield, *Perilous Frontier*, pp. 85–97.

50   See B. J. Mansvelt Beck, "The Fall of the Han," *Cambridge History of China*, I, pp. 341–376.

7 The Sons of Heaven and the Silk Road

1   See Sally Hovey Wriggins, *The Silk Road Journey with Xuanzang*, revised edition (Boulder, CO, 2004), pp. 45–48. The statues were carved during the rule of the Hephthalites. The smaller Eastern Buddha, depicting Gautama Buddha as Sakyamuni, stands nearly 125 feet (39 meters) high and was carved in ca. 570. The Western Buddha, depicting Gautama Buddha as Vairocana, was carved ca. 618 BC and stands nearly 197 feet (60 meters) high. The mural frescoes dated from the late sixth through eighth centuries.

2   See Benjamin Borse, *Xuanzang, China's Legendary Pilgrim and Translator* (Boulder, CO, 2021), pp. 201–202.

3   See Robert Ford Company, "Buddhism Enters China in Early Medieval China," *Old Society, New Belief: Religious Transformation of China and Rome, ca. 1st–6th Centuries*, edited by Mu-chou Poo, H. A. Drake, and Lisa Raphals (Oxford, 2017), pp. 13–34.

4   Wiggins, *Silk Road Journey*, pp. 19–45.

5   See *ibid.*, pp. 119–136.

6   See Mallory and Mair, *Tarim Mummies*, pp. 315–331. The Tocharians and Iranians of the Andronovo culture likely transmitted wheeled vehicles and skills in metallurgy to the Chinese of the Shang Dynasty (1554–1046 BC) and the nomadic way of life to the peoples on the Mongolian steppes. See di Cosmo, *Ancient China and Enemies*, pp. 15–59.

7   *Hanshu* 6. 17, and see Yap, *Western Regions*, pp. 297–299. See also A. K. Narain, "The Indo-Europeans in Inner Asia," *Cambridge History of Early Inner Asia*, pp. 155–156.

8   *Shiji* 1. 1–9; with notes by Yap, *Western Regions*, pp. 1–9. For the probable route of the migration west, see Narain, "Indo-Europeans," *Cambridge History of Early Inner Asia*, pp. 156–157. The Yuezhi reached their new homes first in the grasslands of the Ili valley, and then on the grasslands of north of the Oxus River in Bactria (Chinese Daxia).

9   See A. D. H. Bivar, "The History of Eastern Iran," *Cambridge History of Iran*, Vol. 3. 1: *The Seleucid, Parthian, and Sasanian Periods*, edited by Ehsan Yarshater (Cambridge, 1983), pp. 192–194, for migration of the Sacae.

10   See *ibid.*, pp. 194–198.

11   See Craig, *Empires of Ancient Eurasia*, pp. 181–183.

12   *Shiji* 1. 4–5, and see Yap, *Western Regions*, pp. 6-7. See also Narain, "Indo-Europeans," *Cambridge History of Early Inner Asia*, pp. 157–158.

13   See Narain, "Indo-Europeans," *Cambridge History of Early Inner Asia*, pp. 159–160, discussing the Chinese references in the *Hou Hanshu* 128. 9a. For the coins, see David Jongeward and Joe Cribb, *Kushan, Kushano-Sasanian, and Kidarite Coins: A Catalogue of Coins from the American Numismatic Society* (New York, 2015), pp. 23–27.

14   See *ibid.*, p. 90, nos. 37. The fractional silver coins depict Heraeus standing; see p. 90, nos. 38–44. The identification of Heraeus as Kujula Kadphises is incorrect. See below note 14.

15   See Razieh Taasob, "Heraios Coinage and Khalchayan, Attribution and Chronology: Revisited," *Anabasis: Studia Classica et Orientalia* 10 (2019), pp. 219–160, redating the coins to ca. 1–30 AD, and *contra* Joe Cribb, "The Heraeus Coins: Their Attribution to the Kushan King Kujula Kadphises, c. AD 30–80," *Essays in Honour of Robert Carson and Kenneth Jenkins*, edited by Martin Price, Andrew Burnett, and Roger Bland (London, 1993), pp. 116–140, who attributed the coins to the first Kushan emperor Kujula Kadphises. See now Robert C. Senior, *The Coinage of Hermaios and Its Imitations Struck by the Scythians: A Study* (Lancaster, PA, 2000).

16   See Craig, *Empires of Ancient Eurasia*, pp. 183–185.

17   See Jongeward and Cribb, *Kushan Coins*, pp. 44 and 80–81, nos. 248–251. Vima Taku is styled in Greek as the "Great Savior" (*soter megas*).

18   See Craig, *Empires of Ancient Eurasia*, pp. 190–193.

19   See Craig, *Empires of Ancient Eurasia.*, pp. 185–188, with full discussion of the sources.

20   See Jongeward and Cribb, *Kushan Coins*, pp. 65–69.

21   See B. N. Mukherjee, "The Great Kushana Testament," *Indian Museum Bulletin* 32 (1995), 1–105. See discussion by Nicholas Sims-Williams and Joe Cribb, "A New Bactrian Inscription of Kanishka the Great," *Silk Road Art and Archaeology* 4 (1995–1996), 76–142.

22   See David Jongeward and Joe Cribb, *Kushan Coins*, p. 70, nos. 370–373.

23   The headless statue, in the museum at Mathura, has been identified as that of Kanishka. See V. S. Agrawala, "Catalogue of the Mathura Museum," *The Journal of Uttar Pradesh Historical Society* 21 (1950), pp. 71–79.

24   The illumination is from Rabanus Maurus (Archbishop of Mainz), *De Laudibus Sancti Crucis*, ca. 840; now in the Bodleian Museum, Oxford.

25   See Jongeward and Cribb, *Kushan Coins*, p. 71, nos. 375–376.

26   See *ibid.*, p. 70, no. 370.

27   See *ibid.*, p. 105, nos. 752–754.

28   See Joe Cribb, "Kanishka's Buddha Image Coins Revisited," *Silk Road Art and Archaeology* 6 (2000), pp. 151–189.

29   See Matthew W. King, *In the Forest of the Blind: The Eurasian Journey of Faxian's Record of Buddhist Kingdom* (New York, 2022), pp. 159 and 175. The stupa was seen by Faxian, in ca. 399–414, Sung Yun (who gives the fullest description) in 518, and Xuanzang in 630.

30   See David B. Spooner, "Excavations at Shāh-ji-Dherī," *Archaeological Survey of India, Annual Report (1908-1909)*, p. 49.

31   John H. Marshall, "The Stūpa of Kanishka and Relics of the Buddha," *Journal of the Royal Asiatic Society* 41 *(*1909), pp. 1056–1061.

32   See Benjamin, *Empires of Ancient Eurasia*, pp. 192–193.

33   See Karl Potter, *Abhidharma Buddhism to 150 A.D.* (New Delhi, 1998), pp. 111–117.

34   See David Whitehouse, "Begram, the Periplus and Gandharan Art," *Journal of Roman Archaeology* 2 (1989), pp. 93–100, and S. Mehendale, "Begram: Along Ancient Central Asia and Indian Trade Routes," *Cahiers d'Asia centrale* 1 (1986), pp. 47–64.

35   See Osmund Bopearachchi, "Greeks, Scythians, and Parthians in Central Asia and India," in *Eurasian Empires in Antiquity and the Early Middle Ages: Contact and Exchange between the Graeco-Roman World, Inner Asia and China*, edited by Hyun Jin Kim, Frederik J. Vervaet, and Selim Ferruh Adali (Cambridge, 2017), pp. 264–268.

36   See Benjamin, *Ancient Empires of Eurasia*, pp. 193–197.

37   See John Marshall, *A Guide to Sanchi* (Calcutta, 1918), still a perceptive report of the sculpture and architecture, and Julia Shaw, *Buddhist Landscapes in Central India: Sanchi Hill and Archaeologies of Religious and Social Change, c. Third Century BC to Fifth Century AD* (London/New York, 2013), pp. 50–53.

38   See Wriggins, *Silk Road Journey*, pp. 97–118.

39   See Thapar, *Early India*, pp. 313–317, for the prosperity and patronage of Buddhist sanctuaries by wealthy members of the Vaishya caste.

40   See *ibid.*, pp. 288–289.

41   See Wriggins, *Silk Road Journey*, pp. 160–165, and Brose, *Xuanzang*, pp. 149–151.

42   See Foltz, *Religions of the Silk Road*, pp. 37–58.

43   See Cary and Warmington, *Ancient Explorers*, pp. 123–131.

44   See Lionel Casson, trans., *The Periplus Maris Erythraei* (Princeton, 1989), pp. 22–29, and Steven E. Sidebotham, *Roman Economic Policy in the Erythra Thalassa, 30 B.C.–217 A.D.* (Leiden, 1986), pp. 48–112. This trade did not result in a significant drain of gold and silver specie from the Roman world to India and China. See Kenneth W. Harl, *Coinage in the Roman Economy, 300 B.C. to A.D. 700* (Berkeley, 1987), pp. 297–300.

45   Strabo, 2. 5. 12. See Casson, *Periplus Maris Erythraei*, pp. 188–191, 201–206, and 210–223, for the ports of Barbaricum, Barygaza, and Muzaris.

46   See Benjamin, *Ancient Empires of Eurasia*, pp. 213–236, for the routes and ports frequented by Roman merchants. See Thapar, *Early India*, for the rise of prosperity in the Indian ports due to this trade.

47   See Narain, "Indo-Europeans," *Cambridge History of Early Inner Asia*, pp. 169–173, and Benjamin, *Ancient Empires of Eurasia*, pp. 243–249.

48   See Richard N. Frye, "The Political History of Iran under the Sasanians," *Cambridge History of Iran* II. 1, pp. 126–127.

49   See Thapar, *Early India*, pp. 282–288.

50   The destruction commenced on March 2, 2001, and took several weeks to complete. The mural frescos are forever lost. The meticulous efforts to reassemble the fragments will likely never be completed under the current Taliban regime. A number of replicas have been erected, most notably the eighty-foot statue in the gardens of the Thai temple at Sarnath in 2011, where Gautama Buddha first taught his rule of dharma.

8 The Parthians, Nomadic Foes of Imperial Rome

1   Plutarch, *Crassus* 19–33; Penguin translation, Plutarch, *Fall of the Roman Republic*, translated by Rex Warner (New York, 1972), pp. 134–155, and Dio 60. 16–20 (Loeb Classical Library, volume 3, pp. 435–447). See also A. K. Goldsworthy, (New Haven, 2010), pp. 304–320, and Neilson C. Debevoise, *A Political History of Parthia* (Chicago, 1938), pp. 70–95, for analysis of the campaign and battle.

2   See A. D. H. Bivar, "The Political History of Iran under the Arsacids," *Cambridge History of Iran*, III. 1, pp. 24–28.

3   *Ibid.*, pp. 27–31.

4   Edwyn R. Bevan, *The House of Seleucus: A History of the Hellenistic Near East under the Seleucid Dynasty* (London, 1902), pp. 233–235, and Debevoise, *Poliltical History of Parthia*, pp. 22–25.

5   See M. Rahim Shayean, *Arsacids and Sasanians: Political Ideology in Post-Hellenistic and Late Antique Persia* (Cambridge, 2011), pp. 39–45, for the significance of the title for the Arsacid kings.

6   See Bevan, *House of Seleucus*, pp. 242–244, and Debevoise, *A Political History of Parthia*, pp. 30–35.

7   *Ibid.*, pp. 244–246.

8   *Ibid.*, pp. 247–250.

9   Painting by Charles Antoine Coypel, 1749.

10   The play was performed in 1644 and was published three years later in 1647. Pierre Corneille, however, was anticipated by the little-known French poet and playwright who composed his own *Rodogune* at the court of Queen Christina of Sweden in 1642.

11   Justin, *Epitome* 42. 1–2; and see Bivar, "History of Eastern Iran," *Cambridge History of Iran*, III. 1, pp. 195–196.

12   See Wilhelm Eilers, "Iran and Mesopotamia," *Cambridge History of Iran* III. 1, pp. 481–493.

13   See Malcolm A. B. Colledge, *The Parthians* (London, 1967), pp. 77–88. Cuneiform text reveals the sophistication of the grain market in Babylonia. See Peter Temin, *The Roman Market Economy* (Princeton, 2017), pp. 66–70.

14   See Benjamin, *Ancient Eurasian Empire*, pp. 268–274.

15   Isidore of Charax, *Parthian Stations: An Account of the Overland Trade Route Between the Levant and India in the First Century B.C.; The Greek Text with a Translation and Commentary*, translated by Wilfred H. Schoff (Philadelphia, 1914).

16   See David Sellwood, *An Introduction to the Coinage of Parthia* (London, 1971), pp. 16–20, types 1–4.

17   See *ibid.*, pp. 57–72, types 23–27.

18   See *ibid.*, pp. 73–75, types 28–29.

19   See David Sellwood, "Parthian Coins," *Cambridge History of Iran*, III. 1, pp. 282–288.

20   See Matthew P. Canepa, *The Iranian Expanse: Transforming Royal Identity through Architecture, Landscape, and the Built Environment, 550 BCE–642 CE* (Berkeley, 2018), pp. 81–82.

21   *Hanshu* 62; see William Watson, "Iran and China," *Cambridge History of Iran*, p. 545. See critique of report by Wang Tao, "Parthia in China: A Re-examination of the Historical Records," *The Age of the Parthians*, edited by Vesta Sarkhosh Curtis and Sarah Stewart (London, 2007), pp. 93–95.

22   See Canepa, *The Iranian Expanse,* pp. 81–84.

23   See *ibid.*, pp. 324–332, and Colledge, *Parthians*, pp. 166–177.

24   See Matthew Canepa, *The Two Eyes of the Earth: Art and Ritual of Kingship between Rome and Sasanian Iran* (Berkeley, 2009), pp. 138–145.

25   See Plutarch, *Antony* 34–52; Penguin translation, Plutarch, *Rome in Crisis*, translated by Ian Scott-Kilvert and Christopher Pelling (New York, 2010), pp. 357–376, and Dio 49. 21. 1–31. 4 Loeb Classical Library, Vol. 5, pp. 389–407. Antony invaded on invitation of Median King Artavades I, who planned to revolt from Phraates IV; see Sherwin-White, *Roman Foreign Policy*, pp. 307–310, and Debevoise, *Poliltical History of Parthia*, pp. 121–142. Phraata, on the highway between Lake Umiah and Ecbatana (modern Hamadan) in Azerbaijan, is unlocated. It might have been near Takht-e Sueyman ("Fires of Suleiman"), later seat of a Zoroastrian fire altar complex.

26   See Dio 54. 7. 36–8. 3 (Loeb Classical Library, Vol. 6, pp. 301–303); Suetonius, *Augustus*, 21. 3; Penguin translation, Suetonius, *The Twelve Caesars*, translated by Robert Graves (New York, 1957), pp. 53–54; and Vellius Paterculus, *Roman History* 2. 100. 1 Loeb Classical Library, p. 257. See Sherwin-White, *Roman Foreign Policy*, pp. 322–341, and Bivar, "History of Iran under Arsacids," *Cambridge History of Iran*, III. 1, pp. 66–68.

27   See A. K. Goldsworthy, *The Roman Army at War, 100 B.C.–A.D. 200* (Oxford, 1996), pp. 183–191 and 228–235. For evolution of Roman logistics, see Jonathan P. Roth, *The Logistics of the Roman Army at War (264 BC.–A.D. 235)* (Leiden, 1990), pp. 279–320.

28   See Paul Zanker, *The Power of Images in the Age of Augustus*, translated by A. Shapiro (Ann Arbor, 1988), pp. 105–115. For depiction of the returned standards on coins, see C. H. V. Sutherland and R. A. G. Carson, *Roman Imperial Coinage*, second edition, Volume I (London, 1984), p. 62, no. 286–297 (aurei and denarii) and p. 83, nos. 508–510 (cistophori).

29   Josephus, *Antiquities of the Jews* 18. 40. 2–4. See also Debevoise, *Political History of Parthia*, pp. 147–150.

30   See Bivar, "Political History of Iran under Arsacids," *Cambridge History of Iran*, III. 1., pp. 67–68.

31   Sellwood, *Coinage of Parthia*, pp. 176–178, types 55–58.

32   Bivar, "Political History of Iran under Arsacids," *Cambridge History of Iran*, III. 1, pp. 67–68.

33   See David Magie, *Roman Rule in Asia Minor to the End of the Third Century after Christ* (Princeton, 1950), pp. 497–499 and 548–553, for the turbulent succession crises in Armenia.

34   See A. N. Sherwin-White, *Roman Foreign Policy in the East, 168 B.C.–A.D. 1* (Norman, 1986), pp. 194–195.

35   See Kenneth W. Harl, "Rome's Greatest Foes: Parthia and Sassanid Persia," *Great Strategic Rivalries from the Classical World to the Cold War*, edited by James Lacey (Oxford, 2016), pp. 112–113.

36   See *ibid.*, pp. 110–115.

37   See Tac., *Ann.* 13. 35. 3; Penguin translation, Tacitus, *The Annals of Imperial Rome*, translated by Michael Grant (New York, 1956), p. 300, contrasting the disciplinarian Corbulo to the depraved Nero. In 58, Corbulo commanded the legions III Gallica, IV Scythica, V Macedonica, and VI Ferrarta and a strong *vexillatio* of X Fretensis; see H. M. D. Parker, *The Roman Legions* (Cambridge, 1958), pp. 182–188.

38   Tac., *Ann.* 13. 6–9 and 34–41 (Penguin translation, pp. 287–288 and 299–305); and Dio 62. 19. 2–4 Loeb Classical Library, Vol. 8. pp. 119–127. For chronology of the campaign, see Magie, *Roman Rule*, p. 414, n. 46. For the Parthian perspective, see Bivar, "History of Iran under Arsacids," *Cambridge History of Iran*, III. 1, pp. 79–86, and Debevoise, *Political History of Parthia*, pp. 179–202.

39   Tac., *Ann.* 15. 24–26 (Penguin translation, pp. 355–359).

40   Suet., *Nero* 13 (Penguin translation, p. 214) and Dio 62. 28. 1–7 (Loeb Classical Library, Vol. 8, pp. 135–137).

41   See Parker, *Roman Legions*, pp. 106–115 and 145–160. The legions VI Ferrata, XII Fulminata, and XVI Flavia were stationed in Cappadocia; legions III Gallica, IV Scythica, were stationed in Syria; and X Fretensis

was stationed in Palestine after 70. See Magie, *Roman Rule in Asia Minor*, pp. 566–592. The kingdom of Commagene was annexed in 72, and the provinces of Galatia and Cappadocia were united under a propraetorian legate. For construction of highways, see Stephen Mitchell, *Anatolia: Land, Men, and Gods in Asia Minor* (Oxford, 1993), Vol. I, pp. 118–142.

42 See Bennett, *Trajan*, pp. 184–185.

43 See *ibid.*, pp. 190–198. For the movements of Trajan and chronology of his Parthian War, the reconstruction of Christopher C. Lightfoot, "Trajan's Parthian War and the Fourth Century Perspective," *Journal of Roman Studies* 80 (1990), pp. 114–120, is preferred over the one proposed by Bennett, *Trajan*, pp. 192–196. For the Parthian perspective, see Bivar, "History of Iran under Arsacids," *Cambridge History of Iran*, III. 1, pp. 86–92.

44 See Bennett, *Trajan*, p. 199.

45 See *ibid.*, pp. 200–202.

46 See E. M. Smallwood, *The Jews under Roman Rule* (Leiden, 1981), pp. 389–427.

47 SHA, *Vita Had.* 22; Penguin translation, *Lives of the Later Caesars*, translated by Anthony Birley (New York, 1976), pp. 80–81.

48 See Bennett, *Trajan*, p. 202. Trajan had crowned Parthamaspates as the philo-Roman Parthian king whose realm comprised Babylonia and the client kingdoms of Charax, Elymais, and Persis.

49 See, notably, Benjamin Isaac, *The Limits of Empire: The Roman Army in the East*, revised edition (Oxford, 1993), p. 26, and E. N. Luttwak, *Grand Strategy of the Roman Empire: From the First Century CE to the Third*, revised edition (Baltimore, 2016), pp. 73–74.

50 A. Birley, *Marcus Aurelius* (New York, 1987*)*, pp. 123–125, and Bivar, "History of Iran under Arsacids," *Cambridge History of Iran*, III. 1., pp. 93–94.

51 See Harl, "Rome's Greatest Foe," *Great Strategic Rivalries*, pp. 124–125.

52 See J. F. Gilliam, "The Plague under Marcus Aurelius," *American Journal of Philology* 82 (1961), pp. 225–251.

53 See Birley, *Marcus Aurelius*, pp. 184–189.

54 Harl, "Rome's Greatest Foe," *Great Strategic Rivalries*, pp. 124–125.

55 See Anthony Birley, *Septimius Severus: The African Emperor* (New Haven, 1988), pp. 108–120 and 130–135, and Bivar, "History of Iran under Arsacids," *Cambridge History of Iran*, III. 1., pp. 94–95.

56 Dio 79. 7–8 (Loeb Classical Library), Vol. 9, pp. 349–352, and see Pat Southern, *The Roman Empire from Severus to Constantine* (London/New York, 2001), pp. 53–54 and 169, n. 69.

57 See *ibid.*, pp. 54–55.

58 See Bivar, "History of Iran under Arsacids," *Cambridge History of Iran*, III. 1, pp. 95–97.

9 Heirs of the Xiongnu: The Northern Wei

1   These are now known as caves 16–20; see Joy Lidu Yi, *Yungang, Art, History, Archaeology, Liturgy* (London/New York, 2017), pp. 54–77.

2   See Scott Pearce, "Northern Wei," in *The Cambridge History of China*, Volume II: *Six Dynasties, 220–589*, edited by Albert E. Dien and Keith N. Knapp (Cambridge, 2019), pp. 168–172, for the reign of Wencheng.

3   See Scott Pearce, "A King of Two Bodies: The Northern Wei Emperor Wencheng and Representations of the Power of the Monarchy," *Frontiers of History in China* 7 (2012), pp. 90–105.

4   See Barfield, *Perilous Frontier*, pp. 118–119, for unification of the Xianbei under Tuoba Gui. The ethnic and linguistic identity of the Xianbei is still in dispute, but they were apparently vassals of the Xiongnu who formed their own loose confederacy after the collapse of the Xiongnu Confederation at the end of the first century AD.

5   See Zhang Xunliao, "Daoist Stelae of the Northern Dynasties," *Early Chinese Religion, Part Two: The Period of Division (220–589 AD)*, edited by John Lagerwey (Leiden, 2009), pp. 535–539. In 446, the emperor Taiwu, at the urging of the Taoist reformers Kou Qianzhi and Cui Hao, permitted the destruction of Buddhist monasteries. The other three state persecutions of Buddhism were ordered by the emperor Wu of the Northern Zhou Dynasty in 567; the emperor Wuzong of the Tang Dynasty in 845; and Shizong of the Later Zhou Dynasty in 955. For a perceptive comparison of the persecution of Buddhists by the Chinese emperors to the persecution of Christians by Roman emperors, see Hyun Jin Kim, "Justin Martyr and Tatian: Christian Reactions to Encounters with Greco-Roman Culture and Imperial Persecution," *Old Society, New Belief: Religious Transformation of China and Rome, ca. 1st–6th Centuries*, edited by Mu-chou Poo, H. A. Drake, and Lisa Raphalos (Oxford, 2017), pp. 78–79.

6   See Stephen R. Bokenkamp, "Daoism," *Cambridge History of China*, II, pp. 559–571, for the revelations and innovations of the Taoist Celestial Masters who reconciled Taoist beliefs with popular Chinese religion. From the late second century AD, Taoists denounced Buddhist monks as sorcerers.

7   See Robert Ford Company, "Buddhism Enters China in Early Medieval China," *Old Society, New Belief*, pp. 13–34.

8   See E. Zürcher, *The Buddhist Conquest of China* (Leiden, 1959), pp. 22–25. The reconstruction was permitted by Han emperor Ming (57–75).

9   See Mallory and Mair, *Tarim Mummies*, pp. 289–301.

10 See Flotz, *Religions on the Silk Road*, pp. 39–49.

11 See Jan Nattier, *A Guide to the Earliest Chinese Buddhist Translations: Texts from the Eastern Han and Three Kingdoms Period* (Tokyo, 2008), pp. 18–41 and 73–76.

12 For the translation of Faxian's account, see James Legge, *A Record of Buddhistic Kingdoms: Being an account by the Chinese Monk Fa-Hien of his travels in India and Ceylon (A.D. 399–414)* (Oxford, 1886); reprinted by Paragon Book (New York, 1965).

13 See Mark Edward Lewis, *China between Empires: The Northern and South-ern Dynasties* (Cambridge, MA, 2009), pp. 54–86.

14 See John Kieschnick, "Buddhist Monasteries," *Early Chinese Religion*, pp. 545–574.

15 See Gil Raz, "Buddhism Challenged, Adopted and in Disguise: Daoist and Buddhist Interaction in Medieval China," *Old Society, New Belief*, pp. 109–128.

16 See Edwards, *China between Empires*, pp. 28–53.

17 See Barfield, *Perilous Frontier*, pp. 85–101, for raids by nomads and the rise of border states after 220.

18 See di Cosmo, *Ancient China and Enemies*, pp. 286–290, and Barfield, *Perilous Frontier*, pp. 76–80.

19 See B. J. Mansvelt Beck, "The Fall of Han," *Cambridge History of China*, I, pp. 335–340.

20 See *ibid.*, pp. 355–357.

21 See Ian Rafe de Crespigny, "Wei" and "Wu," *Cambridge History of China*, I, pp. 35–49 and 50–65, respectively, and J. Michael Farmer, "Shu-Han," *ibid.*, pp. 67–78.

22 These were the Gallo-Roman Empire founded by Postumus (260–267), comprising the Western provinces, the central empire held by Gallienus (253–268) and centered on Italy, the Balkans and North Africa, and the eastern provinces under the control of the rulers of Palmyra Odenathus (263–267) and Zenobia (268–272). See Southern, *From Severus to Constantine*, pp. 81–101.

23 See Alaric Watson, *Aurelian and the Third Century* (London/New York, 1999), pp. 70–100, for reunification of the Roman Empire by Aurelian (270–275).

24 See Damien Chaussende, "Western Jin," *Cambridge History of China*, II, p. 93, and Barfield, *Perilous Frontier*, p. 93. This so-called disaster of Yongjia ended the power of the Western Jin emperors, and shifted the political axis of northern China to the Eastern Jin dynasty (317–420) with its capital at Jiankang (today Nanjing).

25 See Heather, *Fall of the Roman Empire*, pp. 227–232. Alaric, however, maintained strict discipline among his Visigoths. Churches were respected and violence against the residents was prohibited. Alaric conducted a massive blackmail rather than a sack.

26 See Valerie Hansen, *The Silk Road: A New History* (Oxford, 2012), pp. 117–118. This is Sogdian letter 5. A translation is available online by Nicholas Sims-Williams at the Silk Road website maintained by the University of Washington, Seattle: http://depts.washington.edu/silkroad/texts/sogdlet.html.

27 The rulers assumed the imperial names Yuan and Cheng, respectively. Sima Yan should not be confused with his namesake and predecessor who

ruled under the imperial name of Wu. See Charles Holcomb, "Eastern Jin," *Cambridge History of China*, II, pp. 96–98.

28 See Lewis, *China between Empires*, pp. 11–17 and 51–71.

29 See *ibid.*, pp. 54–85, and Barfield, *Perilous Frontier*, pp. 100–114.

30 See *ibid.*, pp. 104–114 and 172–177.

31 See *ibid.*, pp. 118–119, and Lewis, *China between Empires*, pp. 77–81.

32 Edwards, *China between Empires*, pp. 100–102 and 126–217. See Shing Muller, "Northern Material Culture," *Cambridge History of China*, II, pp. 384–4417, for the archaeological evidence that points to a distinct northern Chinese society.

33 See Edwards, *China between Empires*, pp. 127–128.

34 See Lan Dong, *Mulan's Legend and Legacy in China and the United States* (Philadelphia, 2010). To date, Hua Mulan has been celebrated in three theatrical dramas, fourteen films, six TV series, eight novels, three children's books, and six video games.

35 See Barfield, *Perilous Frontier*, pp. 118–119.

36 See Grousset, *The Empire of the Steppes*, pp. 60–61. Chinese chroniclers and historians also call these barbarians Juan-Juan. DNA analysis confirms the nomadic Avars (Abars) of Central Europe during the sixth and seventh centuries were East Asian ancestry, thereby confirming their claims as descendants of the Rouran. See V. Csáky, D. Gerber, I. Koncz *et al.* "Genetic Insights into the Social Organisation of the Avar Period Elite in the 7th century AD Carpathian Basin," *Scientific Reports* 10, 948 (2020), 1–14, and Walter Pohl, "Ethnicity and Empire in Western Eurasian Steppes," *Empires and Exchanges*, pp. 193–202.

37 See Barfield, *Perilous Frontier*, pp. 120–122.

38 See Nikolay N. Kradin, "From Tribal Confederation to Empire: The Evolution of the Rouran Society," *Acta Orientalia Academiae Scientiarum Hungaricae* 58 (2005), pp. 49–151.

39 See *ibid.*, pp. 152–169.

40 See Hyun Jin Kim, *The Huns, Rome and the Birth of Europe*, p. 40.

41 See Hyun Jin Kim, *Huns*, p. 46.

42 See Kradin, "From Tribal Confederation to Empire," *Acta Orientalia Academiae Scientiarum Hungaricae* 58 (2005), pp. 149–169.

43 See Nicola di Cosmo, "The Relations between China and the Steppe: From the Xiongnu to the Türk Empire," *Empires and Exchanges in Eurasian Late Antiquity: Rome, China, Iran, and the Steppe, ca. 250–750*, edited by Nicola di Cosmo and Michael Maas (Cambridge, 2018), pp. 47–49, for the early Northern Wei emperors as heirs to the military traditions and foreign policy of the Han emperor Wudi.

44 See Barfield, *Perilous Frontier*, pp. 122–123.

45 See *ibid.*, p. 123.

46   See David A. Graff, "The Art of War," *Cambridge History of China*, II, pp. 289–295.

47   See Scott Pearce, "The Northern Wei," *Cambridge History of China*, I, pp. 165–168.

48   Livy. 34. 9. 12; see Livy, *Rome and the Mediterranean*, translated by Henry Bettenson (New York, 1976), p. 152.

49   See Barfield, *Perilous Frontier*, pp. 124–127; Lewis, *China between Empires*, pp. 81–82; and Pearce, "Northern Wei," *Cambridge History of China*, II, pp. 169, for the Sinified policies of Xiaowen.

50   See *ibid.*, pp. 172–173. See also A. G. Wenley, *The Great Empress Dowager Wen Ming and the Northern Wei Necropolis at Fang Shan* (Washington, DC, 1947), pp. 1–10.

51   See Pearce, "Northern Wei," *Cambridge History of China*, II, pp. 173–175.

52   See *ibid.*, pp. 172–173.

53   See Barfield, *Perilous Frontier*, p. 127, and Pearce, "Northern Wei," *Cambridge History of China*, II, pp. 178–182.

54   See Andrew Eisenberg, "Collapse of a Eurasian Hybrid: The Case of the Northern Wei," *Empires and Exchanges*, pp. 375–377.

55   See *ibid.*, pp. 179–183, and Albert E. Dien, "Eastern Wei and Northern Qi," *Cambridge History of China*, II, pp. 103–107, and "Western Wei and Northern Zhou," in *ibid.*, pp. 210–224.

56   Barfield, *Perilous Frontier*, pp. 126–127.

57   See Denis Sinor, "The Establishment and Dissolution of the Türk Empire," *Cambridge History of Early Inner Asia*, pp. 297–301.

58   See Arthur F. Wright, "The Sui Dynasty" (581–617), *The Cambridge History of China*, Volume 3: *Sui and T'ang China, 589–906*, edited by Denis Twitchett (Cambridge, 1979), pp. 57–73.

59   Hyun Jin Kim, *The Huns, Rome and the Birth of Europe*, pp. 62–64.

60   See Richard Lim, "Trade and Exchanges along the Silk and Steppe Routes," *Empires and Exchanges*, p. 80, for the Rouran kaghans driving the Hephthalites west and southwest into Transoxiana.

10 The Hephthalites: Huns in Iran

1   Shah Peroz waged three campaigns against the Hephthalites, most likely in 474, 478, and 484. The date of the first campaign, and subsequent ransom of Peroza by Zeno, was likely either the late summer or fall of 474. On January 9, 475, the usurper Basilicus staged a revolt and Zeno fled Constantinople. Zeno crushed the revolt and retook Constantinople in August of the next year, 476. Zeon, an untutored Isaurian, earned the hatred of the ruling classes of the capital. He and his wife, Ariadne, had been crowned emperor and empress on January 29, 474, as guardians of their sickly son Leo II, age seven, who was the preferred successor of the

emperor Leo I, who had died on January 18, 474. Leo II, however, died in November. The two prime accounts by the historians Procopius and Joshua the Stylite are confused as to the dates and details of Peroz's campaigns against the Hephthalites. Procopius reports only two campaigns, whereas Joshua the Stylite briefly reports three. See Rezakhani, *ReOrienting the Sasanians*, pp. 127–128, and Ilkka Syväne, "The Three Hephthalite Wars of Peroz 474/5–484," *Historia I Świat* 10 (2010), pp. 95–116, for the chronology of Peroz's camapigns. See Bury, *History of the Later Roman Empire*, I, pp. 389–394, for events in Constantinople.

2   Theophylact Simocatta IV. 11. 2–3 (Whitby translation, pp. 117–118).

3   See Michael Whitby, *The Emperor Maurice Tiberius and His Historian: Theophylact Simocatta on the Persian and Balkan Wars* (Oxford, 1988), pp. 297–304. The emperor Maurice Tiberius provided Khusrau II with an army so that Shah recovered his throne.

4   See Bury, *History of the Later Roman Empire*, I, pp. 319–322 and 389–394.

5   See R. N. Frye, "The Political History of Iran under the Sasanians," *Cambridge History of Iran*, III. 1, p. 147, and Rezakhani, *ReOrienting Sasanians*, pp. 126–127.

6   See Hyun Jim Kim, *The Huns* (London/New York, 2018), pp. 45–47. Étienne de la Vaissière, "The Steppe World and the Rise of the Huns," in *The Cambridge Companion to the Age of Attila*, edited by Michael Maas (Cambridge, 2015), pp. 184–185.

7   Procopius, *Persian War* I. 3. 1–5. Loeb Classical Library translation of Procopius, *History of the Wars*, Vol. I, translated by H. B. Dewing (Cambridge MA, 1914), pp. 13–15.

8   See Klaus Vondrovec, *Coinage of the Iranian Huns and Their Successors from Bactria to Gandhara (4th to 8th Centuries CE)*, Vol. I (Vienna, 2014), pp. 307–405.

9   See Rezakhani, *ReOrienting Sasanians*, pp. 87–89, and A. D. B. Bivar, "The History of Eastern Iran," *Cambridge History of Iran*, III. 1, pp. 211–212.

10   Ammianus Marcellinus, *History* 16. 9. 1–4; for Loeb Classical Library translation, see Ammianus Marcellinus, translated by John C. Rolfe, Vol. I (Cambridge, MA, 1963), pp. 241–243. The Roman emperor Constantius II learned from his envoys sent to negotiate a truce that Shah Shapur had departed to deal with the Kidarites.

11   Ammianus Marcellinus, *History* 17. 5. 1 (LCL translation, Vol. I, p. 333).

12   Ammianus Marcellinus, *History* 18. 6. 22 (LCL translation, Vol. I, pp. 447–449).

13   Ammianus Marcellinus, *History*. 18. 7. 1–19. 9. 9 (LCL translation, Vol. 1, pp. 449–515), for the campaign of Shapur II and siege of Amida. See Kimberly Kagan, *The Eye of Command* (Ann Arbor, 2008), pp. 23–51, for the accuracy of Ammianus's account. On three occasions, in 2002, 2010, and 2011, I have examined the walls of Diyarbakır (ancient Amida) and thereby verified the details of Ammianus's account of the siege.

14   Ammianus Marcellinus, *History* 19. 1. 7–10 (LCL translation, pp. 473–479).

15   See Vondrovec, *Coinage of the Iranian Huns*, Vol. I, pp. 26–38 and 43–97, for a catalog of gold, silver, and copper coins.

16   See Hyun Jin Kim, *The Huns, Rome and the Birth of Europe*, pp. 36–37.

17   See Rezakhani, *ReOrienting the Sasanians*, p. 124.

18   Procopius, *Persian Wars*, I. 3. 3–6 (Loeb Classical Library translation, p. 15).

19   See E. A. Thompson, "The Foreign Policies of Theodosius II and Marcian," *Hermathena* 76 (1950), pp. 56–75.

20   See Prudence O. Harper and Pieter Meyers, *Silver Vessels of the Sasanian Period*, Volume I, *The Royal Imagery* (New York, 1981), pp. 40–88.

21   See Rezakhani, *ReOrienting the Sasanians*, pp. 127–128, and Syväne, "Three Hephthalite Wars," *Historia I Świat* 10 (2010), pp. 95–108.

22   See *ibid.*, pp. 109–113.

23   See Frye, "History of Iran under the Sasanians," *Cambridge History of Iran*, III. 1, p. 149, and Payne, "Reinvention of Iran," *Age of Attila*, p. 288.

24   See Patricia Crone, "Kavad's Heresy and the Mazdakite Revolt," *Iran* 29 (1991), pp. 21–42, and "Zoroastrian Communism," *Comparative Studies in Society and History* 36 (1994), pp. 447–462.

25   Parvaneh Pourshariati, *Decline and Fall of the Sasanian Empire: The Sasanian-Parthian Confederation and the Arab Conquest of Iran* (London/New York, 2008), p. 267, and Tourai Daryaee, *Sasanian Persia: The Rise and Fall of an Empire* (London/New York, 2009), p. 27.

26   See Procopius I. 6. 7–10 (LCL translation, Vol. 1, pp. 45–47), for Kavad's escape with the aid of his wife. See C. E. Bosworth, trans. and ed., *The History of al-Ṭabarī*, Volume V: *The Sāsānids, the Byzantines, the Lakhmids, and Yemen* (Albany, NY, 1999), p. 136, for escape with the aid of his sister.

27   Khodadad Rezakhani, *ReOrienting the Sasanians*, pp. 132–134.

28   Frye, "History of Iran under Sasanians," *Cambridge History of Iran*, III. 1, pp. 149–151.

29   See Daniel T. Potts, "Sasanian Iran and its Northeastern Frontier," *Empires and Exchanges in Eurasian Late Antiquity*, edited by Michael Mass and Nicola di Cosmo (Cambridge, 2018), pp. 296–297.

30   See Vondrovec, *Coinage of the Iranian Huns* I, pp. 397–403 and 419–426. The Hephthalites also countermarked many Sassanid dirhems received in tribute; see Robert Göbl, *Dokumente zur Geschichte der iranischen Hunnen in Dokumente zur Geschichte der iranischen Hunnen in Baktrien und Indien Volume II* (Munich, 1967), pp. 112–138 and for catalog of the countermarks.

31   See Potts, "Sasanian Iran and its Northeastern Frontier," *Empires and Exchanges*, pp. 297–299.

32   See Hyun Jin Kim, *The Huns, Rome and the Birth of Europe*, pp. 37–38.

For the contemporary history of the caravan cities of the Tarim basin, see R. E. Emmerich, "Iran Settlement East of the Pamirs," *Cambridge History of Iran*, III. 1, pp. 263–275.

33   See Canepa, *Two Eyes of the Earth*, p. 143.

34   See Eberhard W. Sauer, *Persia's Imperial Power in Late Antiquity: The Great Wall of Gorgan and Frontier Landscapes of Sasanian Iran* (Oxford, 2013).

35   See Thapasr, *Early India*, p. 286, and and Rezakhani, *ReOrienting the Sasanians*, pp. 99–102.

36   See Vondrovec, *Coinage of the Iranian Huns* I, pp. 220–222, with full discussion of the Chinese sources, and Rezakhani, *ReOrienting the Sasanians*, pp. 94–95.

37   See *ibid.*, pp. 99–102.

38   See Vondrovec, *Coinage of Iranian Huns*, pp. 23–50.

39   See Rezakhani, *ReOrienting the Sasanians*, pp. 104–109.

40   See *ibid.*, pp. 183–185 and 291–300, types 44–81.

41   For Xuanzang's complaint about Mihirakula's destruction of Buddhist monasteries and stupas, see translation by Li Rongxi, trans., *The Great Tang Dynasty Record of the Western Regions* (Berkeley, 1996), pp. 97–100.

42   See Vondrovec, *Coinage of the Iranian Huns*, Vol. I, pp. 86–214, for coinages of the later rulers of the Alchon Huns. For the high volume of coinage by the Alchon Huns, see Pankaj Tandon, "The Identity of Prakāśāditya," *Journal of the Royal Asiatic Society.* 25 (2015), pp. 667–668.

43   See Rezakhani, *ReOrienting the Sasanians*, pp. 111–113, and Thapar, *Early India*, p. 287.

44   See Rezakhani, *ReOrienting the Sasanians*, pp. 157–161.

45   See Vondrovec, *Coinage of the Iranian Huns*, Vol. I, pp. 447–459.

46   *Mahabharata* 2. 50, where the Hunas participate as allies in the Rajasuya sacrifice for the consecration of Yudhishthira.

47   See Roger C. Blockley, "The Division of Armenia between the Romans and the Persians at the End of the Fourth Century A.D.," *Historia* 36 (1987), pp. 222–234.

48   See R. W. Thomson, "Armenia in the Fifth and Sixth Century," *The Cambridge Ancient History, Volume XIV: Late Antiquity, Empire, and Successors, A.D. 425–600*, edited by Averil Cameron, Bryan Ward-Perkins, and Michael Whitby (Cambridge, 2000), pp. 662–677. Armenian resistance to enforced Zoroastrianism by the Persian Shahs climaxed in the revolt of Vardan Mamikonian, who fell at the Battle of Avarayr in 451. Vardan Mamikonian is still hailed as a martyr and one of the greatest national heroes of Armenia.

49   See Maenchen-Helfen, *World of the Huns*, pp. 51–58.

50   See C. D. Gordon, "Subsidies in Roman Imperial Defence," *Phoenix* 3 (1949), pp. 60–69, and critique by Roger C. Blockley, "Subsidies and

Diplomacy: Rome and Persia in Late Antiquity," *Phoenix* 39 (1985), pp. 62–74.

51   See Bivar, "History of Eastern Iran," *Cambridge History of Iran*, III. 1, pp. 214–216.

11 Huns, Allies and Foes of Rome

1   Ammianus Marcellinus XXX1. 3. 1–8 (Loeb Classical Library, Vol. 3, pp. 394–409). See Michael Kulikowski, *Rome's Gothic Wars from the Third Century to Alaric* (Cambridge, 2007), pp. 111–112. I accept the view that Ermanaric ruled over a confederation of Goths and Iranian-speaking tribes on the Pontic-Caspian steppes; see Herwig Wolfram, *History of the Goths*, translated by Thomas J. Dunlap (Berkeley, 1979), pp. 86–9, and contra the skepticism of Peter Heather, *Goths and Romans 332–489* (Oxford, 1991), pp. 86–89, who argues Ermanaric was only king of the Tervingi Goths.

2   See *ibid.*, p. 106. The surviving fortifications comprise a southern and northern section of 77 miles (125 kilometers) and 75 miles (120 kilometers), respectively. The project testifies to the engineering and strategic thinking which the Goths had learned from the Romans.

3   See Noel Lenski, *Failure of Empire Valens and Roman State in the Fourth Century A.D.* (Berkeley, 2002), pp. 320–325.

4   Jordanes, *Getica* 23. 129–130. See Jordanes, *The Origins of the Goths*, translated by Charles C. Mierow (Princeton, 1998), pp. 15–16. The translation is also available online at: https://people.ucalgary.ca/~vandersp/Courses/texts/jordgeti.html.

5   The story is celebrated in the *Hamðismál* and *Guðrúnarhvöt* in the *Poetic Edda*; see Hollander, *Poetic Edda*, pp. 311–321. The tale is retold by Snorri Sturluson, *Prose Edda* (Penguin translation, pp. 101–103), and in the *Volsunga Saga*. See Jesse L. Byock, trans., *The Saga of the Volsungs* (New York, 1990), pp. 106–108. Bragi Boddason also alluded to the story in the oldest skaldic poem, *Ragnarsdrápa*. The combat was depicted on the shield of Ragnar Lodbrok.

6   For the accuracy and historical method of Ammianus Marcellinus, see John Matthews, *The Roman Empire of Ammianus* (Baltimore, 1989), pp. 8–32.

7   Ammianus Marcellinus 31. 2. 1–12 (Penguin translation, p. 411).

8   See Maenchen-Helfen, *World of Huns*, pp. 291–255, for Hun way of war. For the accuracy of Ammianus Marcellinus, see John Matthews, *The Roman Empire of Ammianus* (Baltimore, 1989), pp. 17–32.

9   See Kulikowski, *Rome's Gothic Wars*, pp. 84–86.

10   For the Battle of Abrittus, see Zosimus, *New History* I. 23, and Zonares XX. 21. See Parker, *History of Roman World*, p. 161. The bodies of Trajan Decius and his son Herennius Etruscus were never recovered. The next emperor Trebonnianus Gallus (251–253) allowed the Goths to retire with their loot and captives, and subsequently paid a subsidy. See Aleksander Bursche, "The Battle of Abrittus, the Imperial Treasury and

Aurei in Barbaricum," *Numismatic Chronicle* 173 (2013), pp. 151–170, for Goths capturing the imperial treasury after the battle.

11 See Wolfram, *History of the Goths*, pp. 36–43.

12 See Ammianus Marcellinus, XXXI. 3, 4–5. 8 (LCL translation, Vol. 3, pp. 401–413), and see also Lenski, *Failure of Empire*, pp. 341–355.

13 See Ammianus Marcellinus XXXI. 12–14 (LCL translation, Vol. 3, pp. 463–489), and see Lenski, *Failure of Empire*, pp. 325–341 and 355–368, and Thomas S. Burns, "The Battle of Adrianople: A Reconsideration," *Historia* 22 (1973), pp. 336–345.

14 See Thomas S. Burns, *Barbarians within the Gates of Rome: A Study of Roman Policy and the Barbarians, ca. 375–425 A.D.* (Bloomington, 1994), pp. 69–79.

15 See Kim, *Huns*, pp. 66–74. Prior to the report of Ammianus Marcellinus, the Roman world had no knowledge of the Huns; see Thompson, *Huns*, pp. 19–25.

16 Maenchen-Helfen, *World of the Huns*, pp. 376–382 and 441–443.

17 See *ibid.*, pp. 297–357.

18 See *ibid.*, pp. 260–270.

19 See *ibid.*, pp. 51–52.

20 There is no direct evidence that the Huns of the fourth and fifth century AD inherited imperial institutions of the Xiongnu Confederacy of the second and first centuries BC. Therefore, do not accept the view that the Huns of Europe were the direct political heirs of the Xiongnu as argued by Hyun Jin Kim, *The Huns, Rome and the Birth of Europe*, pp. 17–42, and "The Political Organization of Steppe Empires and Their Contribution to Eurasian Interconnection: The Case of the Huns and Their Impact on the Frankish West," *Eurasian Empires in Antiquity and the Early Middle Ages: Contact and Exchange between the Greco-Roman World, Inner Asia and China*, edited by Hyun Jin Kim, Frederick J. Vervaet, and Selim Ferruh Adali (Cambridge, 2017), pp. 15–33. Attila employed Roman engineers, soldiers, and scribes; see Maenchen-Helfen, *World of Huns*, pp. 125–128. Attila's chief secretary (*notarius*) in 449–452 was Orestes, who kept records in Latin. Orestes later returned to Roman service and elevated his son Romulus Augustulus (475–476) as last Western Roman emperor.

21 See Maenchen-Helfen, *World of the Huns*, pp. 18–19.

22 See *ibid.*, pp. 26–50, and Thompson, *Huns*, pp. 29–35.

23 This is readily documented by the Huns adopting personal names of Germanic and Iranian origin; see *ibid.*, pp. 386–392.

24 See Thompson, *Huns*, pp. 35–36 and 63–65, and Maenchen-Helfen, *World of Huns*, pp. 59–73.

25 See Pat Southern and Karen R. Dixon, *The Late Roman Army* (New Haven, 1996), pp. 67–75, and J. H. W. G. Liebeschuetz, *Barbarians and*

Bishops: Army, Church, and State in the Age of Arcadius and Chrysostom (Oxford, 1991), pp. 7–88, for recruitment of *foederati,* "federates."

26 See Heather, *Fall of Roman Empire*, pp. 216–217.

27 See Liebeschuetz, *Barbarians and Bishops*, pp. 90–91 and 125–127.

28 See O'Flynn, *Generalissimos*, pp. 33–41.

29 See Heather, *Fall of the Roman Empire*, pp. 216–218.

30 See Bury, *History of the Later Roman Empire*, I, pp. 110–115, and Heather, *Fall of the Roman Empire*, pp. 211–213.

31 See Bury, *History of the Later Roman Empire*, I, pp. 115–121.

32 See *ibid.*, I, pp. 132–135, and Liebeschuetz, *Barbarians and Bishops*, pp. 111–125.

33 See Maenchen-Helfen, *World of Huns*, p. 59.

34 See Heather, *Fall of the Roman Empire*, pp. 225–226.

35 See Bury, *History of the Later Roman Empire*, I, pp. 160–166.

36 See Heather, *Fall of Roman Empire*, pp. 194–196, noting that Radagaisus's people likely migrated to escape the Huns. See also Jeroen W. P. Wijnendaele, "Stilicho, Radagaisus, and the So-Called Battle of Faesulae (406 CE)," *Journal of Late Antiquity* 9 (2016), 267–284.

37 See Guy Halsall, *Barbarian Migrations and the Roman West, 376–568* (Cambridge, 2007), pp. 210–212, and Heather, *Fall of the Roman Empire*, pp. 209–211.

38 See Halsall, *Barbarian Migrations*, pp. 220–224, for Roman civil wars compromising imperial defense. For the withdrawal of Roman forces from Britain, see Sheppard Frere, *Britannia: A History of Roman Britain* (London, 1974), pp. 407–410.

39 O'Flynn, *Generalissimos*, pp. 56–59, and Halsall, *Barbarian Migrations*, pp. 212–214.

40 See Bury, *History of the Later Roman Empire*, I, pp. 174–185, and Heather, *Fall of the Roman Empire*, pp. 227–232. For the disbelief and shock among Romans at the sack of Rome, see Samuel Dill, *Roman Society in the Last Century of the Western Empire*, second edition (New York, 1958), pp. 303–321.

41 See Wolfram, *History of the Goths*, pp. 161–167, for the settlement of Visigoths in Aquitania.

42 See Liebeschuetz, *Barbarians and Bishops*, pp. 127–128.

43 See Norman H. Baynes, "The Decline of the Roman Empire in Western Europe: Some Modern Explanations," *Journal of Roman Studies* 33 (194), pp. 29–35, for perceptive comparison of the resources and leadership of the Western and Eastern Roman Empires.

44 See Kenneth G. Holum, *Theodosian Empresses: Women and Imperial Dominion in Late Antiquity* (Berkeley, 1982), pp. 48–78 and 79–111, for the empresses Aelia Eudocia and Aelia Pulcheria, respectively.

45 See Doug Lee, "Theodosius and His Generals," *Theodosius II: Rethinking the Roman Empire in Late Antiquity*, edited by Christopher Kelly (Cambridge, 2013), pp. 90–108. After the fall of Ganias, the emperor and his civil officials kept the generals in check so that none could aspire to the position of their counterparts in the Western Roman Empire.

46 See R. C. Blockley, *East Roman Foreign Policy: Formation and Conduct from Diocletian to Anastasius* (London, 1992), pp. 45–58, for cordial relations between Rome and Persia during the reigns of Arcadius and Theodosius II. For the threat of the Hephthalites, see Potts, "Sasanian Iran and Its Northeastern Frontier," in *Empires and Exchanges*, pp. 287–301.

47 See J. B. Bury, *History of the Later Roman Empire*, I, pp. 112–114.

48 See Alexander van Millingen, *Byzantine Constantinople: The Walls of the City and Adjoining Historical Sites* (London, 1899), pp. 40–94.

49 See Stephen Trumbull, *The Walls of Constantinople, A.D. 324–1453* (Oxford, 2004), pp. 110–19, for building and matériel of the Theodosian Wall with excellent illustrations.

50 See van Millingen, *Byzantine Constantinople*, pp. 55–58.

51 See *ibid.*, pp. 40–51.

52 See *ibid.*, pp. 53–55.

53 See *ibid.*, pp. 51–53.

54 Hendrik W. Dey, *The Aurelian Wall and the Refashioning of Imperial Rome, A.D. 271–855* (Cambridge, 2011), pp. 1–48 and 110–122.

55 See J. B. Bury, *History of the Later Roman Empire*, Vol. II (New York, 1925), pp. 180–195 and 238–252, for the Gothic sieges of Rome in 537–539, 546 and 549. For the damage to Rome from the sieges during the Gothic War, see Dey, *Aurelian's Wall*, pp. 48–62.

56 See Donald Queller, *The Fourth Crusade: The Conquest of Constantinople*, revised edition, pp. 172–192.

57 See Stephen Runciman, *The Fall of Constantinople 1453* (Cambridge, 1965), pp. 133–144.

58 See Gordon, *Age of Attila*, pp. 59–60, and Maenchen-Helfen, *World of the Huns*, pp. 73–74, for the mission of Olympiodorus to the Hun court.

59 See *ibid.*, pp. 74–75.

60 See Thompson, *Huns*, pp. 227–230, and Maenchen-Helfen, *World of Huns*, pp. 81–82.

61 See *ibid.*, pp. 82–83.

62 *Ibid.*, pp. 89–90, and Bury, *History of the Later Roman Empire*, I, p. 271.

63 See *ibid.*, pp. 358–375. For DNA analysis, see Endre Neparáczki, Zoltán Maróti *et al.*, "Y-chromosome Haplogroups from Hun, Avar and Conquering Hungarian Period Nomadic People of the Carpathian Basin," *Scientific Reports* 9 (2019), published online at https://doi.org/10.1038/s41598-019-53105-5, and Zoltán Maróti *et al.*, "Whole Genome Analysis Sheds

Light on the Genetic Origin of Huns, Avars and Conquering Hungarians," *BioRXiv* (2020), published online: https://www.biorxiv.org/content/
10.1101/2022.01.19.476915v1.full.

64   See Gordon, *Age of Attila*, pp. 84–85.

65   See Burns, *Romans and Barbarians*, pp. 356–360.

66   See Gordon, *Age of Attila*, pp. 85–90.

12 Attila, the Scourge of God

1   See Gordon, *Age of Attila*, pp. 69–101, for the translation of the mission
    of Priscus. See also Bury, *History of the Later Roman Empire*, I, pp. 279–
    289 (also providing a translation of Priscus's account), and Kelly, *End of
    Empire*, pp. 153–173.

2   See Gordon, *Age of Attila*, pp. 74–75.

3   See *ibid.*, pp. 78–81. Attila had many encampments, and Priscus reports
    that he was received at an encampment that might have been the Theiss
    River; see Thompson, *Huns*, pp. 276–277. It is surmised that the prin-
    cipal settlement was near Aquincum, which might have functioned as
    a capital for the Huns. Aetius likely ceded Aquincum and the province
    of Valeria, in return for military assistance either from Ruglia in 425 or
    from Attila in 437; see Bury, *History of the Later Roman Empire*, I, p. 272
    (favoring the former date) and Maenchen-Helfen, *World of Huns*, pp.
    87–89 (favoring the latter date).

4   See Gordon, *Age of Attila*, pp. 94–96, and Kelly, *End of Empire*, pp. 174–
    188, for the banquet and the reception of the Western envoys.

5   See Gordon, *Age of Attila*, p. 61. Priscus's description is preserved by Jor-
    danes, *Getica*, 34. 182.

6   Gordon, *Age of Attila*, p. 95.

7   See Thompson, *Huns*, pp. 69–70, and Kelly, *End of Empire*, pp. 93–97.

8   See Bury, *History of the Later Roman Empire*, I, p. 275.

9   See Thompson, *Huns*, p. 97, and Kelly, *End of Empire*, pp. 104–105.

10 See Bury, *History of the Later Roman Empire*, I, pp. 273–274, and Maenchen-
    Helfen, *World of Huns*, pp. 110 and 116–117.

11 Thompson, *Huns*, pp. 81–82, and Kelly, *End of Empire*, pp. 186–188.

12 See Kelly, *End of Empire*, pp. 183–184 and 267–269. Attila almost cer-
    tainly wanted to transmit the lordship of the empire to his favored son,
    Emac, but the plan risked civil war among the brothers.

13 See O'Flynn, *Generalissimos*, pp. 88–103, and Thompson, *Huns*, pp. 36–39.

14 See Kim, *Huns, Rome and the Birth of Europe*, pp. 3–60, supporting the
    older opinions by Thompson, *Huns*, pp. 177–185, and Maenchen-Helfen,
    World of the Huns, pp. 94–129, and *contra* revisionist opinion, diminish-
    ing the significance of the Huns, see Peter Heather, "The Huns and the
    End of the Roman Empire in Western Europe," *English Historical Re-*

view 110 (1995), pp. 4–41, and Lindner, "Nomadism," *Past and Present* 92 (1981), pp. 1–19.

15   See Kim, *Huns, Rome and the Birth of Europe*, pp. 127–130, and see also Penny MacGeorge, *Late Roman Warlords* (Oxford, 2002), pp. 276–282.

16   See Bury, *History of the Later Roman Empire*, I, pp. 274–278.

17   See Thompson, *Huns*, p. 136. See Thompson, "Foreign Policies," *Hermathena* 76 (1950), pp. 62–65. Theodosius II saw as his priority the recapture of Carthage and the rich African provinces rather than the northern frontier along the lower Danube.

18   See Thompson, *Huns*, pp. 89–98.

19   See Thompson, "Foreign Policies," *Hermathena* 76 (1950), pp. 60–66, and Ferrill, *Fall of the Roman Empire*, pp. 137–138, for Aspar's two campaigns against the Vandals in 432–434 and 442.

20   See Thompson, *Huns*, pp. 99–100, and Maenchen-Helfen, *World of Huns*, pp. 119–123.

21   See Alan Cameron, *Circus Factions: Blues and Greens at Rome and Byzantium* (Oxford, 1976), pp. 100–104.

22   See Thompson, *Huns*, pp. 101–102.

23   See Harl, *Coinage in the Roman Economy*, p. 310. The sum of 18,500 pounds of gold was equivalent to 1,334,600 gold solidi. The solidus (4.74 grs.) was struck 72 to the Roman Pound.

24   See *ibid.*, pp. 311–312, for payoff of Philip I to Shah Shapur in 244 and Justinian's Eternal Peace with Shah Khusru I in 532. These were 10,000 and 11,000 Roman pounds of gold, respectively but each was a single payment rather than annual tribute.

25   See Holum, *Theodosian Empresses*, pp. 207–208.

26   See *ibid.*, pp. 209–211, for marriage of Marcian and Aelia Pulcheria. See Thompson, "Foreign Policies," *Hermathena* 76 (1950), pp. 69–70, suggesting that Marcian too put the defeats of the Vandals as a top priority and so contemplated a new expedition against the Vandals. Marcian, however, preferred diplomacy to war, and during his seven-year reign amassed a reserve of 100,000 pounds of gold. See Warren Treadgold, *Byzantium and Its Army, 284–1081*, pp. 193–195 and 202–203.

27   O'Flynn, *Generalissimos*, pp. 77–78. For Aetius's stay among the Huns, see Thompson, *Huns*, pp. 38 and 60.

28   See Bury, *History of the Later Roman Empire*, I, pp. 221–225.

29   See O'Flynn, *Generalissimos*, pp. 75–76. See Stewart I. Oost, *Galla Placidia Augusta*, pp. 189–190, for the hostility of the empress Galla Placidia to Aetius. See *ibid.*, pp. 226–234, for intrigues against Aetius and her promotion of Count Boniface, governor of Africa, as a rival to Aetius.

30   See Thompson, *Huns*, p. 40.

31   Procopius, *Vandal Wars* I. 3. 14–15 (LCL translation), volume 2, p. 27, praising both Aetius and Boniface. See Edward Gibbon, *The Decline*

and Fall of the Roman Empire, annotated by J. B. Bury (The Modern Library, New York) II, p. 170, for his laudatory assessment of Aetius: "His prudence, rather than his virtue, engaged him to leave the grandson of Theodosius in the possession of the purple; Valentinian was permitted to enjoy the peace and luxury of Italy, while the patrician appeared in the glorious light of a hero and patriot, who supported near twenty years the ruins of the Western Empire." Undoubtedly, the empress Galla Placidia would challenge Gibbon's judgment.

32 O'Flynn, *Generalissimos*, pp. 88–95, and see J. R. Moss, "The Effects of the Policies of Aetius on Western Europe," *Historia* 22 (1973), pp. 711–731.

33 See Stewart Oost, *Galla Placidia Augusta*, pp. 200–211 and 230–235. For Aetius's schemes to link himself by marriage into the imperial family, see O'Flynn, *Generalissimos*, pp. 95–100.

34 See Thompson, *Huns*, pp. 72–74.

35 For the evolution of the legend, see Turville-Petre, *Heroic Age of Scandinavia*, pp. 27–37, and de Vries, *Heroic Song and Heroic Legend*, pp. 44–49.

36 See Bury, *History of the Later Roman Empire*, I, pp. 288–291, and Kelly, *End of Empire*, pp. 224–230.

37 These would be the "Five Baits" employed by the Chinese emperor, including the marriage of the Xiongnu chanyu to a Chinese princess and recognition of the chanyu as an equal ruler. See Yu Ying-shih, *Trade and Expansion in Han*, pp. 36–54. Attila likely had similar expectations from a marriage proposal.

38 See Bury, *History of the Later Roman Empire*, I, pp. 291–293; Thompson, *Huns*, pp. 143–151; and Kelly, *End of Empire*, pp. 231–245.

39 See *ibid.*, pp. 152–153, for Aetius's alliance with Theoderic.

40 See Arther Ferrill, *The Fall of the Roman Empire: The Military Explanation* (London, 1986), pp. 145–151, and Ulf Tackholm, "Aetius and the Battle on the Catalaunian Fields," *Opuscula Romana* 7.15: (1969), pp. 259–276, for reconstruction of the battle.

41 See Maenchen-Helfen, *World of Huns*, p. 268.

42 See Kelly, *End of Empire*, pp. 248–249, for the ferocity of the fighting.

43 See O'Flynn, *Generalissimos*, pp. 97–98, for Aetius's long-term aims of renewing the alliance with Attila. See Kelly, *End of Empire*, pp. 249–251, for withdrawal of the Hun army.

44 Bury, *History of the Later Roman Empire*, I, pp. 294–296.

45 See Kelly, *End of Empire*, pp. 262–264, Thompson, *Huns*, pp. 160–163, and Bury, *History of Later Roman Empire*, I, pp. 295–296.

46 See Thompson, *Huns*, pp. 163–166, and Kelly, *End of Empire*, p. 263.

47 See Thompson, *Huns*, pp. 167–174.

48 Se Kelly, *End of Empire*, pp. 267–268, and Maenchen-Helfen, *World of Huns*, pp. 144–149.

49   See Heather, *Goths and Romans*, pp. 242–244. The emperor Marcian permitted the Ostrogoths to settle in Pannonia.

50   See Thompson, *Huns*, pp. 175–176.

51   Bury, *History of the Later Roman Empire*, I, pp. 298–299, and O'Flynn, *Generalissimos*, pp. 101–103.

52   Bury, *History of the Later Roman Empire*, I, pp. 299–301, and Heather, *Fall of the Roman Empire*, pp. 375–379.

53   Gibbon, *The Decline and Fall of the Roman Empire*, II, p. 319.

54   The exception was Majorian (457–461), the last effective emperor of the Roman West. See MacGeorge, *Late Roman Warlords*, pp. 201–214, and Stewart I. Oost, "Aëtius and Majorian," *Classical Philology* 59 (1964), pp. 23–29.

55   See O'Flynn, *Generalissimos*, pp. 104–128, and Penny MacGeorge, *Late Roman Warlords* (Oxford, 2002), pp. 165–293.

56   See O'Flynn, *Generalissimos*, pp. 129–148, and MacGeorge, *Late Roman Warlords*, pp. 270–280. The constitutional position of Odoacer and significance of the deposition of Romulus Augustulus are still subject to debate. See A. H. M. Jones, "The Constitutional Position of Odovacar and Theoderic," *Journal of Roman Studies* 52 (1962), pp. 126–130; Michael McCormick, "Odoacer, Emperor Zeno, and the Rugian Victory Legation," *Byzantion* 47 (1977), pp. 212–222; and Brian Croke, "A.D. 476: The Manufacture of a Turning Point," *Chiron* 13 (1983), 81–119.

57   Jordanes, *Getica* 35, citing as his source Priscus of Pantium. See in Gordon, *Age of Attila*, pp. 93–94, for the translation of Priscus's report. See also Kelly, *End of Empire*, pp. 102–104 and Maenchen-Helfen, *World of Huns*, pp. 278–280, who stresses the sacred sword as the manifestation of divine kingship.

58   See Peter Heather, "Christianity and the Vandals in the Reign of Geiseric," *Bulletin of the Institute of Classical Studies*. 50 (2007), pp. 137–147. See Victor of Vita, *History of the Vandal Persecutions*, translated by John Moorhead (Liverpool, 1992), who records the confessors who defied the Arian Vandal kings.

59   See Gordon, *Age of Attila*, pp. 94–96.

60   See *Saga of Volsungs* (Penguin translation), pp. 96–105.

61   See *Nibelungenlied*, translated by A. T. Hatto (New York, 1965), pp. 242–290.

62   See John C. G. Röhl, *Kaiser Wilhelm II, 1859–1941: A Concise Life*, translated by Sheila de Bellaigue (Cambridge, 2014), pp. 68–69.

63   See Laurence V. Moyer, *Victory Must Be Ours: Germany in the Great War 1914–1918* (New York, 1995), pp. 95–97.

64   See Jon Solomon, *The Ancient World in Cinema* (New Haven, 2001), pp. 115–120.

65   See *ibid.*, pp. 96–98.

66   See Thompson, *Huns*, pp. 226–231, for a judicious assessment of Attila's achievement.

67   See Kim, *Huns, Rome and the Birth of Europe*, pp. 69–88.

68   See Peter Brown, "Eastern and Western Christendom in Late Antiquity: A Parting of the Ways," *Orthodox Churches and the West*, edited by Derek Baker (Oxford 1976), pp. 1–24; reprinted in Peter Brown, *Society and the Holy in Late Antiquity* (Berkeley, 1982), pp. 166–195.

13 The Heirs of Attila and the New Rome

1   See H. Turtledove, *The Chronicle of Theophanes Anni Mundi 6095–6305 (A.D. 602–813)* (Philadelphia, 1982), pp. 22–23, and Geoffrey Dodgeon and Samuel N. C. Lieu, trans., *The Roman Eastern Frontier and the Persian Wars Part II. A.D. 363–630* (London/New York, 2002), pp. 205–207, for the account of Theophanes. See also Walter E. Kaegi, *Heraclius, Emperor of Byzantium* (Cambridge, 2003), pp. 132–141 and 146–147, and Walter Pohl, *The Avars: A Steppe Empire in Central Europe, 567–522* (Ithaca, NY, 2015), pp. 274–275 and 290–292.

2   See Averil Cameron, "The Theotokos in Sixth Century Constantinople: A City Finds Its Symbol," *Journal of Theological Studies* 29 (1978), pp. 79–108, for the veneration of Mary as the protectress of the city.

3   See Pohl, *Avars*, pp. 90–93, and James Howard-Johnston, *The Last Great War of Antiquity* (Oxford, 2021), pp. 207–213, for the Avars' inability to assault the Long Walls of Constantinople in 626.

4   See *Chronicle of Theophanes*, pp. 23–30, and Kaegi, *Heraclius*, pp. 100–191, for Heraclius's campaigns against Sassanid Persia.

5   See *ibid.*, pp. 177–180. The Sassanid aristocracy deposed Shah Khusrau II in 628, and elevated to the throne Khusrau's son Kavad II, who concluded the peace with Heraclius. In 629, Heraclius assumed the Greek title basileus, "king," which had previously been used as the title for the Persian Shah. As a result of the peace in 636, the Shah of Persia was no longer deserving of the title.

6   See Sinor, "The Establishment and Dissolution of the Türk Empire," *Cambridge History of Early Inner Asia*, pp. 297–301, for the overthrow of the Rouran Kaghanate by the Gök Turks.

7   See Pohl, *Avars*, pp. 11–38, for the migration of the Avars to the Pontic-Caspian Steppes in 554–557, covering over 3,000 mile (5,000 kilometers).

8   See Constantine Porphyrogenitus, *De Administrando Imperio*, revised edition, translated by G. Moravcsik, and R. J. H. Jenkins (Washington, DC, 2002), pp. 49–50. Since the sixth century, the task of the Byzantine governor in Cherson was to placate the leading nomadic confederation on the Pontic-Caspian steppes.

9   See Alexander Sarantis, *Justinian's Balkan Wars: Campaigning, Diplomacy and Development of Illyricum, Thrace, and the Northern World A.D. 527–65*

(Prenton, 2016), pp. 333–336. The Avar envoys arrived in Constantinople either in 557 or 558.

10 See Peter Heather, *Rome Resurgent: War and Empire in the Age of Justinian* (Oxford, 2018), pp. 303–332, for the losses in the Roman West in the generation after Justinian's death. For the high costs of Justinian's wars, Harl, *Coinage in the Roman Economy*, pp. 195–199, and Michael F. Hendy, *Studies in the Byzantine Monetary Economy c. 300–1450* (Cambridge, 1985), pp. 164–173.

11 See Heather, *Rome Resurgent*, pp. 285–286 and 316. See Pohl, *Avars*, pp. 36–37, for the refusal of Justin II to grant land or a subsidy to the Avars out of fears of reprisals by the Ishtemi, Kaghan of the Gök. In 572, under the fifty-year treaty negotiated by Justinian with Khusrau I in 562, Roman payments of 30,000 solidi were to be paid annually. Justin, regarding such payments as tribute, refused payment and so provoked the Persian War of 572–590. See Theophylact Simocatta III. 9. 3. 11. See Michael Whitby, *The Emperor Maurice and His Historian: Theophylact Simocatta on Persian and Balkan Warfare* (Oxford, 1988), pp. 250–254.

12 See J. A. S. Evans, *The Age of Justinian: The Circumstances of Imperial Power* (London/New York, 1996), pp. 267–268, and Pohl, *Avars*, pp. 36–37 and 78–83. The empress Sophia arranged for the adoption and elevation of the general Tiberius II Constantine as Caesar in 574. The madness of Justin II is reported by John of Ephesus, *Ecclesiastical History* III. 1-6, see online translation https://www.tertullian.org/fathers/ephesus_3_book3.htm. Translation from William Cureton, trans., *The Third Part of the Ecclesiastical History of John, Bishop of Ephesus* (Piscataway, NJ), 2012.

13 Theophylact Simocatta I. 3. 25; see Michael and Mary Whitby, trans., *The History of Theophylact Simocatta: An English Translation with Introduction and Notes* (Oxford, 1985), p. 24. See also Pohl, *Avars*, p. 89.

14 See Paul the Deacon, *History of the Lombards*, translated by William D. Foulke (Philadelphia, 1974), III. 22, p. 43, who omits the contribution of the Avars. See Pohl, *Avars*, pp. 62–68. For the migration of the Lombards into Italy in 567, see Neil Christie, *The Lombards: The Ancient Langobards* (Oxford, 1999), pp. 63–91. Since the Battle of Nedao (454), the Gepidae had posed a threat to Byzantine provinces in the Balkans. See Alexander Sarantis, "War and Diplomacy in Pannonia and the Northwest Balkans during the Reign of Justinian: The Gepid Threat and Imperial Responses," *Dumbarton Oaks Papers* 63 (2009), pp. 15–40.

15 See Pohl, *Avars*, pp. 62–68, for Avars taking possession of Pannonia in 567. For the DNA analysis demonstrating the Avars' descent from nomads of the eastern Eurasian steppes, see Maróti *et al.*, "Whole Genome Analysis Sheds Light on the Genetic Origin of Huns, Avars and Conquering Hungarians," *BioRXiv* (2020), published online: https://www.biorxiv.org/content/10.1101/2022.01.19.476915v1.full.

16 See Samuel Szádeczky-Kardoss, "The Avars," in *Cambridge History of Early Inner Asia*, pp. 225–228.

17   For the migration of Slavs into the Balkans, see Florin Curta, *Southeastern Europe in the Middle Ages, 500–1250* (Cambridge, 2008), pp. 58–100.

18   See Menander the Guardsman, *History*, fragment 23. 3; see R. C. Blockley, trans., *The History of Menander the Guardsman* (Liverpool, 1985), p. 240. See also Whitby, *Emperor Maurice*, p. 88, preferring 581 for the date of the surrender, and Pohl, *Avars*, pp. 83–89, for the Avar siege and capture of Sirmium in 582.

19   See Florin Curta, "Avar *Blitzkrieg*, Slavic and Bulgar Raiders, and Roman Speical Ops: Mobile Warriors in the Sixth Century Balkans," *Central Eurasia in the Middle Ages: Studies in Honour of Peter B. Golden*, edited by Osman Karatay and István Zimonyi (Wiesbaden, 2016) pp. 69–90.

20   The unknown author of the *Strategikon* composes his treatise to counter the cavalry tactics of the Avars. See comments by Dennis, trans., Maurice's *Strategikon*, pp. 11–14.

21   See John V. A. Fine Jr., *The Early Medieval Balkans: A Critical Survey from the Sixth to the Late Twelfth Century* (Ann Arbor), pp. 25–40. The Greek speakers of Thrace and Moesia fled to the Greek cities on the Aegean and Euxine shores. Latin speakers of Pannonia and Dalmatia settled in the Dalmatian coastal cities.

22   See Peter Brown, "A Dark Age Crisis: Aspects of the Iconoclastic Controversy," *English Historical Review* 88 (1971), pp. 21–22, for the efficacy of appeals of intercession to Saint Demetrius.

23   Theophylact Simocatta IV. 11. 2-3 (Whitby translation, pp. 117–118). See also Whitby, *Emperor Maurice*, pp. 292–304.

24   See *ibid.*, pp. 156–165, and Pohl, *Avars*, pp. 163–194.

25   See *Chronicle of Theophanes*, pp. 1–2 (Turtledove translation) and Theophylact Simocatta VIII. 10. 4–5 (Whitby translation, pp. 225–227). See also Walter E. Kaegi, *Byzantine Military Unrest, 471–843: An Interpretation* (Amsterdam, 1981), pp. 110–119, for grievances of soldiers and breakdown of discipline. For the hostile sources on Phocas, see David M. Olster, *The Politics of Usurpation in the Seventh Century: Rhetoric and Revolution in Byzantium* (Amsterdam, 1993), pp. 1–22 and 165–186.

26   Theophylact Simocatta IV. 11. 2–3 (Whitby translation, pp. 117–118), and see Whitby, *Emperor Maurice*, pp. 292–304.

27   See Kaegi, *Heraclius*, pp. 37–54.

28   See *Chronicle of Theophanes*, pp. 23–30. See also Kaegi, *Heraclius*, pp. 100–191, and Howard-Johnston, *Last Great War*, pp. 214–320, for Heraclius's campaigns against Sassanid Persia. To pay for the war, Heraclius borrowed gold and silver plates from the Orthodox church to strike gold solidi and silver hexagrams in great numbers, and he debased the copper coinage; see Harl, *Coinage in Roman Economy*, pp. 199–203. Heraclius is often credited with major reforms in civil administration, and reorganization of the army based on themes. These reforms, however, were likely the work of his heirs, Constans II (641–668) and Constantine IV (668–585).

See J. F. Haldon, *Byzantium in the Seventh Century: The Transformation of a Culture* (Cambridge, 1990), pp. 202–215.

29 See Pohl, *Avars*, pp. 305–311 and 376–396.

30 For the Revolt of Samo and establishment of the Slavic Kingdom of Great Moravia, see Pohl, *Avars*, pp. 305–318 and 392–395, and Francis Dvornik, *The Making of Central and Eastern Europe* (London, 1949), pp. 11–19 and pp. 288–291.

31 See Pohl, *Avars*, pp. 372–387.

32 See Fine, *Early Medieval Balkans*, pp. 66–69, and Pohl, *Avars*, pp. 326–335, for the migration of the Bulgars into Moesia. For the nomadic origins of the Bulgars, who spoke a distinct Western Turkish dialect, see Peter B. Golden, "The Peoples of the South Russian Steppes," *Cambridge History of Early Inner Asia*, pp. 260–262, and Warwick Ball, *The Eurasian Steppe: People, Movement, Ideas* (Edinburgh, 2021), pp. 233–239.

33 *Chronicle of Theophanes,* pp. 170–173 (Turtledove translation). See also Warren Treadgold, *The Byzantine Revival, 780–842* (Stanford, 1988), pp. 68–73, and Dennis P. Hupchick, *The Bulgarian-Byzantine Wars for Early Medieval Balkan Hegemony: Silver-Lined Skulls and Blinded Armies* (Cham, Switzerland, 2017), pp. 83–87.

34 See *ibid.*, pp. 89–114.

35 See *ibid.*, pp. 123–127. The treaty was negotiated in 814, ratified in 816, and renewed in 836. For frontier of the kaghanate, see J. B. Bury, "The Bulgarian Treaty of A.D. 814, and the Great Fence of Thrace," *English Historical Review* 25 (1910), pp. 276–287.

36 See Treadgold, *Byzantine Revival*, pp. 283–285. For description and explanation of the mechanics of the throne room, see Gerard Brett, "The Automata in the Byzantine Throne Room of Solomon," *Speculum* 29 (1954), pp. 477–478, and Allegra Iafrate, *The Wandering Throne of Solomon: Objects and Tales of Kingship in the Medieval Mediterranean* (Leiden, 2015), pp. 55–105.

37 See Dimitri Oblensky, *The Byzantine Commonwealth: Eastern Europe, 500–1453* (Crestwood, N.Y., 1971), pp. 117–121, and, for the Patriarchate of Great Preslav, pp. 160–172.

38 See Hupchick, *Bulgarian-Byzantine Wars*, pp. 149–220. During the second war (913–924), Symeon pressured the regents Patriarch Nicholas Mysticus (913–915) and Zoe Carbospina (915–920) to grant a marriage of his daughter to the young emperor Constantine VII Porphyrogenitus. In 920, the admiral Romanus Lecapenus seized power in Constantinople, married his daughter Helena Lecapena to Constantine VII, and thwarted Symeon's imperial ambitions by refusing battle and bribing Slavic princes to revolt. See Stephen Runciman, *The Emperor Romanus Lecapenus and His Reign: A Study in Tenth Century Byzantium* (Cambridge, 1929), pp. 81–101.

39 See *ibid.*, pp. 155–167, and Shaun Tougher, *The Reign of Leo VI (886–912): Politics and People* (Leiden, 1997), pp. 177–185, for the Byzantine-Bulgarian

War of 894–896. The war was ignited over the Byzantine withdrawal of Bulgarian trading rights.

40   See Peter B. Golden, "The Peoples of the Russian Forest Belt," *Cambridge History of Early Inner Asia*, pp. 242–247, for the origins of the Magyars. See Tougher, *Reign of Leo VI*, pp. 176–177, and C. A. Macarthy, *The Magyars in the Ninth Century* (Cambridge, 1930), pp. 177–179, for the Byzantine diplomatic agreement calling for a Magyar invasion of Bulgaria.

41   See Hupchick, *Bulgarian-Byzantine Wars*, pp. 160–162. Tsar Symeon courted the Pechenegs into an alliance to attack the Magyars in 895. For the migration of the Magyars and settlement on the Hungarian grasslands in the winter of 895–896, see Macarthy, *Magyars in Ninth Century*, pp. 179–188, and Z. I. Kosztolnyik, *Hungary under the Early Árpáds, 890s to 1063* (New York, 2002), pp. 83–112.

42   See Charles R. Bowlus, *The Battle of Lechfeld and its Aftermath, August 955: The End of the Age of Migrations in the Latin West* (London, 2016), pp. 97–130.

43   See Pál Engel and Andrew Ayton, ed., *The Realm of St Stephen: History of Medieval Hungary, 895–1526*, translated by Tamás Pálosfalvi (London/ New York, 2006), pp. 26–29, and Kosztolnyik, *Hungary under Early Árpáds*, pp. 113–136. King Stephen received a royal coronation, compliments of the Holy Roman Emperor Otto III and Pope Sylvester III.

44   See Hupchick, *Bulgarian-Byzantine Wars*, pp. 247–320, and Mark Whittow, *The Making of Byzantium, 600–1025* (Berkeley, 1996), pp. 374–390. The emperor John Tzimisces annexed the eastern realm of Bulgaria, along with its capital Preslav in 971, after he defeated the Rus invasion of Prince Sviatoslav of Kiev. Basil II waged a ruthless, methodical conquest of Western Bulgaria in 990–1018.

45   See Peter F. Sugar, *Southeastern Europe under Ottoman Rule, 1354–1804* (Seattle, 1977), pp. 224–234, for the significant demographic and ethnic changes.

46   Menander the Guardsman, *History*, fragment 4 (Whitby translation, p. 53); see also Pohl, *Avars*, pp. 50–53.

47   See *ibid.*, fragment 19 (Whitby translation), pp. 171–173.

48   See Kaegi, *Heraclius*, pp. 143–145, for the alliance of Heraclius and the Western Turks.

49   See Kevin A. Brook, *The Jews of Khazaria*, third edition (Lanham, MD, 2018), pp. 1–19 and pp. 125–138.

50   For the Arab sieges of Constantinople in 674–677 and 717–718, see respectively, *Chronicle of Theophanes*, pp. 52–54 and 82–91 (Turtledove translation). See also Romily Jenkins, *Byzantium: The Imperial Centuries, 610–1071* (New York, 1966), pp. 42–44 and 60–65. See Whittow, *Making of Byzantium*, pp. 25–37, for the daunting logistical and geographic barriers faced by Arab armies in waging war in Anatolia or against Constantinople.

51   See Brook, *Jews of Khazaria*, pp. 199–205.

52   See Golden, "Peoples of the Russian Steppes," *Cambridge History of Early Inner Asia*, p. 264. In 737, the future Umayyad caliph Marwan II (744–750) defeated and compelled the Khazar Kaghan to embrace Islam.

53   See *Chronicle of Theophanes*, pp. 66–67 (Turtledove translation), for the overthrow and exile of Justinian II in 695, and pp. 70–72 for the Khazar alliance and the return of Justinian II in 705. See also *Constance Head, Justinian II of Byzantium* (Madison, 1972), pp. 99–107.

54   See *ibid.*, pp. 142–150.

55   Brook, *Jews of Khazaria*, pp. 45–48.

56   See *The Chronicle of Theophanes*, pp. 101–102 (Turtledove translation). See also Lynda Garland, *Byzantine Empresses: Women and Power in Byzantium, 527–1204* (London/New York, 1999), pp. 73–74, and Brook, *Jews of Khazaria*, pp. 123–124. The marriage was arranged in 732 when envoys of Leo III concluded an alliance with the Khazar Kaghan Bihar against the Abbasid Caliphate. The Greek rendition of the princess's name in Turkish. Tzitzak is derived from same root word as çiçek in modern Turkish.

57   The contest is recorded in the life of Saint Philaretus; see M. H. Lourmy and M. Leroy, "La vie de Saint Philarète," *Byzantion* 9 (1934), pp. 135–143. See Garland, *Byzantine Empresses*, pp. 8–81, and Treadgold, *Byzantine Revival*, pp. 90–91, for the first detailed report of the bridal competition in 788, when the empress Irene arranged for the fixed contest so that her choice, Mary of Amnia, married her son Constantine VI. It is surmised that a similar contest might have been held when Irene was selected as the wife of Leo IV, the Khazar (775–780).

58   See Brook, *Jews of Khazaria*, pp. 67–76.

59   See *ibid.*, pp. 37–40 and 71–73.

60   See Gun Westholm, "Gotland and the Surrounding World," *The Spilling Hoard: Gotland's Role in the Viking Age World Trade*, edited by Gun Westholm (Visby, 2009), pp. 139–143 and fig. 21.

61   Similar political considerations might have influenced Uyghur Bögü Qaghan (759–789) to embrace Manichaeism rather than Buddhism, which was widespread in northern China and a recognized religion under the Tang emperors. See Vladimir Perukhin, "The Choice of Faith in the Turkic Empires: The Uighurs and the Khazars," *Central Eurasia in the Middle Ages*, pp. 285–292.

62   See Brook, *Jews of Khazaria*, pp. 77–108, for the conversion of Khazars to Judaism.

63   See D. M. Behar *et al.* (October 2003), "Multiple Origins of Ashkenazi Levites: Y Chromosome Evidence for Both Near Eastern and European Ancestries," *American Journal of Human Genetics* 73 (2003), pp. 768–779. Ashkenazi Jews share both Middle Eastern and European ancestries, but not Central Asia. See also Danielle Venton, "Highlight: Out of Khazaria—Evidence for Jewish Genome Lacking," *Genome Biology and Evolution* 5 (2013), pp. 75–76.

64   See Whittow, *Making of Byzantium*, pp. 248–252.

65   See Gwyn Jones, *A History of the Vikings* (Oxford, 1968), pp. 241–258. For the range of trade goods the Rus brought back to Gotland and Sweden, see Count Eric Oxenstierna, *The Norsemen*, translated by Catherine Hutter (Greenwich, CT, 1965), pp. 122–144.

66   See Golden, "Peoples of South Russian Steppes," *Cambridge History of Early Inner Asia*, pp. 270–275, for the Pecheneg confederacy.

67   Constantine Porphyrogenitus, *De Administrando Imperio*, pp. 48–50 (Moravcsik and Jenkins translation).

68   See Jones, *History of Vikings*, pp. 245–245, and Simon Franklin and Jonathan Shepard, *The Emergence of Rus, 750–1200* (London, 1996), pp. 27–49.

69   See Androshchuk, "Rural Vikings and Viking Helgo," *Archaeology, Artefacts and Human Contacts in Northern Europe: Cultural Interactions between East and West*, edited by Ulf Fransson and Ingmar Jansson (Stockholm, 2007), pp. 153–163. The statuette is now on display in the Swedish History Museum in Stockholm.

70   See *Ibn Fadlan and Land of Darkness*, pp. 89–95 (Penguin translation).

71   See *ibid.*, pp. 54–55.

72   Translation from A. M. Talbot and D. E. Sullivan, *The History of Leo the Deacon* (Washington, DC, 2005), pp. 199–200.

73   See Samuel H. Cross and Olgerd P. Sherbowitz-Wetzor, trans., *The Russian Primary Chronicle: Laurentian Text* (Cambridge, MA, 1973), pp. 5–61. See Jones, *History of Vikings*, pp. 245–247, for possible identification of Rurik with Erik, a brother of Harald Klak (827–852), the duplicitous Viking vassal of Louis the Pious who was granted Frisia.

74   Cross and Sherbowitz-Wetzor, *Russian Primary Chronicle*, p. 60. See A. A. Vasiliev, *The First Russian Attack Constantinople in 860* (Cambridge, MA, 1946), for detailed study of the sources.

75   Constantine Porphyrogenitus, *De Administrando Imperio*, pp. 57–65 (Moravcsik and Jenkins translation).

76   Prince Oleg of Kiev (ON Helgi) launched an attack in 907; see Cross and Sherbowitz-Wetzor, *Russian Primary Chronicle*, p. 64. The attack is not recorded in Byzantine sources, but there is reason to doubt the report's veracity. See Romily Jenkins, "The Supposed Russian Attack on Constantinople in 907: Evidence of the Pseudo-Symeon," *Speculum* 24 (1949), pp. 405–406. Prince Igor (ON Ingvar) launched two attacks in 943 and 944, and secured a favorable commercial treaty; see Franklin and Shepard, *Emergence of Rus*, pp. 112–138.

77   See Adrienne Mayor, *Greek Fire, Poison Arrows, and Scorpion Bombs: Biological and Chemical Warfare in the Ancient World* (Woodstock, NY, 2003), pp. 215–216. The philosopher Callinicus of Heliopolis (today Baalbek, Lebanon) discovered the formula, and carried it to Constantinople. The emperor Constantine IV equipped siphon-bearing warships (*siphonophoroi*) that could deliver the incendiary against the Arab ships during the

first Arabic siege of the city in 674–677. See *Chronicle of Theophanes*, p. 53 (Turtledove translation).

78   See Cross and Sherbowitz-Wetzor, *Russian Primary Chronicle*, pp. 214–216. The Chronicle dates the conversion to 957, but she may have been baptized or accepted the status of a catacheum during an earlier visit in ca. 955. See Omeljan Pritsak, "When and Where Was Olga Baptized?" *Harvard Ukrainian Studies* 9 (1985), pp. 5–24.

79   See Franklin and Shepard, *Emergence of Rus*, pp. 144–145. For political and institutional decline of the Khazar confederacy, see, *Jews of Khazaria*, pp. 133–142.

80   Alice-Mary Talbot and Denis F. Sullivan, trans., *The History of Leo the Deacon: Byzantine Military Expansion in the Tenth Century* (Washington, DC, 2003), v. 2–3 (pp. 129–133) and VIII. I–IX. 12 (pp. 187–199), Cross and Sherbowitz-Wetzor, *Russian Primary Chronicle*, pp. 86–90. See also Whittow, *Making of Byzantium*, pp. 260–262, and Franklin and Shepard, *Emergence of Rus*, pp. 139–151.

81   Leo the Deacon, *History* IX. 11–12, pp. 199–201.

82   See Michael McCormick, *Eternal Victory, Triumphal Rulership in Late Antiquity, Byzantium, and the Early Medieval West* (Cambridge, 1986), pp. 170–175.

83   See Golden, "Peoples of South Russian Steppes," *The Cambridge History of Inner Asia*, pp. 277–279.

84   For the revolt of the eastern army under Bardas Phocas (986–989), see Michael Psellus, *Fourteen Byzantine Rulers*, translated by E. R. A. Sewter (New York, 1966), pp. 40–43, and John Skylitzes, *A Synopsis of Byzantine History, 811–1057*, translated by John Wortley (Cambridge, 2010), pp. 318–321. See also Whittlow, *Making of Byzantium*, pp. 362–374, and Anthony Kaldellis, *Streams of God, Rivers of Blood: The Rise and Fall of Byzantium, 955 A.D. to the First Crusade* (Oxford, 2017), pp. 94–102. For the Varangian Guard, see Sigfús Blöndel, *The Varangians of Byzantium*, translated by Benedikt S. Benedikz (Cambridge, 1978), pp. 32–53.

85   See Oblensky, *Byzantine Commonwealth*, pp. 254–260.

86   See Cross and Sherbowitz-Wetzor, *Russian Primary Chronicle*, pp. 91–111.

87   See Franklin and Shepard, *Emergence of the Rus*, pp. 209–244 and 323–364.

88   See *ibid.*, pp. 252–256, 271–273, and 327–329, and Golden, "Peoples of the South Russian Steppes," *Cambridge History of Early Inner Asia*, pp. 280–284.

89   Anna Komnene, *The Alexiad*, second edition, translated by E. R. Sewter (New York, 2003), pp. 219–234. See also Michael Angold, "Belle époque or crisis (1025–1118)?" *The Cambridge History of the Byzantine Empire, c. 599–1492*, edited by Jonathan Shepard (Cambridge, 2008), pp. 611–612, and Golden, "Peoples of the South Russian Steppes," *Cambridge History of Early Inner Asia*, p. 275.

90   See Franklin and Shepard, *Emergence of Rus*, pp. 294–295 and 365–367.

91   See Serge A. Zenkovsky, trans., *Medieval Russia's Epics, Chronicles and*

Tales, revised edition (New York, 1974), pp. 167–192, for a translation of the epic of Prince Igor.

92   See Oblensky, *Byzantine Commonwealth*, pp. 266–308.

14 Turkish Kaghans and Tang Emperors

1   See Ross and Thomsen, "The Orkhon Inscriptions" *Bulletin of the School of Oriental Studies, University of London* 5 (1930), pp. 861–871. For the purpose of the propaganda of the inscription and the monument, see Sören Stark, "Aspects of Elite Representation among the Sixth and Seventh Century Türks," *Empires and Exchanges*, pp. 333–334.

2   See Denis Sinor, "The Establishment and Dissolution of the Türk Empire," *Cambridge History of Early Inner Asia*, pp. 287–291, and Peter B. Golden, *An Introduction to the History of the Turkic Peoples* (Wiesbaden, 1992), pp. 115–124.

3   See Sinor, "Türk Empire," *Cambridge History of Early Inner Asia*, pp. 291–297, and Barfield, *Perilous Frontier*, pp. 131–133.

4   See Nikolai M. Ziniakov, "Ferrous Metallurgy and Blacksmith Production of the Altay Turks in the Sixth to Tenth Centuries A.D.," *Arctic Anthropology* 25 (1988), pp. 48–100.

5   See Barfield, *Perilous Frontier*, pp. 132–133.

6   See *ibid.*, p. 132, and Jonathan K. Skaff, *Sui-Tang China and Its Turko-Mongol Neighbors: Culture, Power, and Connections, 580–800* (Oxford, 2017), pp. 205–207.

7   See Barfield, *Perilous Frontier*, pp. 133–135.

8   See Pohl, *Avars*, pp. 33–37, for the migration of Avars west.

9   See Sinor, "Türk Empire," *Cambridge History of Early Inner Asia*, pp. 298–299.

10   Menander, *History*, fragment 10, pp. 111–125 (Blockley translation). See Pohl, *Avars*, pp. 51–52.

11   Ross and Thomsen, "The Orkhon Inscriptions," *Bulletin of the School of Oriental Studies* 5 (1930), p. 864.

12   See Saim Sakaoğlu, "From Tale to Fact: On the Concept of Sovereignty in Altaic Communities," in *Altaica Berolinensia: The Concept of Sovereignty in the Altaic World*, edited by Barbara Kellner-Heinkele (Berlin, 1993), pp. 209–213, and Golden, *History of Turkic Peoples*, pp. 149–150.

13   See Sinor, "Türk Empire," *The Cambridge History of Inner Asia*, pp. 288–289, Bumin promoting the tribal legend of descent from the wolf.

14   See Ross and Vilhelm Thomsen, "The Orkhon Inscriptions," *Bulletin of the School of Oriental Studies, University of London* 5 (1930), p. 865, for the Turks fighting like wolves.

15   See Golden, *History of Turkic Peoples*, pp. 15–26.

16   The only Lir language still spoken is Chuvash, descended from the lan-

guage of the Volga Bulgars. Since the nineteenth century, most of the Chuvash people have converted to Orthodox Christianity and employ the Cyrillic alphabet.

17   Béla Kempf, "Old Turkic Runiform Inscriptions in Mongolia: An Overview," *Turkic Languages* 8 (2004), pp. 43–52, and Golden, *History of Turkic Peoples*, pp. 140–151.

18   See Vilhelm Thomsen, *Inscriptions de l'Orkhon Déchiffrées* (Helsinki, 1896), and see Golden, *History of Turkic Peoples*, pp. 151–152.

19   See Hildinger, *Warriors of Steppe*, pp. 18–20 and 78–79.

20   See Lynn White Jr., *Medieval Technology and Social Change* (Oxford, 1966), pp. 14–28, who has argued for a date of the ninth century for the introduction and widespread use of metal stirrups. The date is too late. The author of the *Strategikon* notes the use of metal stirrups by Byzantine cavalry of the later sixth century. See Kelly DeVries, *Medieval Military Technology* (Petersborough, 1992), pp. 95–122.

21   See Hans J. van de Ven, *Warfare in Chinese History* (Leiden, 2000), pp. 6–7. The manual is entitled *Questions and Replies between Emperor Taizong of Tang and Li Weigong*. For the tactics and treatise of Li Jin, see David Graff, *Medieval Chinese Warfare, 300–900*, pp. 192–196.

22   See Hugh Kennedy, *Armies of the Caliphs: Military and Society in the Early Islamic State* (London/New York, 2001), pp. 134–141, for recruitment of Oghuz and Kipchak Turks into Islamic armies from the ninth century on.

23   Translation from S. C. Levi and R. Sela, *Islamic Central Asia: An Anthology of Historical Sources* (Bloomington, 2010), p. 56.

24   See Barfield, *Perilous Frontier*, pp. 136–137, and Michael R. Drompp, "Infrastructures of Legitimacy in Inner Asia: The Early Türk Empires," *Empires and Exchanges*, pp. 308–316.

25   See A. C. Peterson, "Court and Province in Mid- and Late Tang," *Cambridge History of China*, III, pp. 238–551, for analysis of the wealth and population of the Tang Empire in the eighth century.

26   See Ross and Thomsen, "Orkhon Inscriptions," *Bulletin of the School of Oriental Studies* 5 (1930), pp. 867–868.

27   See Barfield, *Perilous Frontier*, pp. 147–148, and Golden, *History of Turkic Peoples*, pp. 137–138, for the roles of Kül Tegin and his senior commander, Tonuykuk.

28   See Arthur F. Wright, "The Sui Dynasty (581–617)," *Cambridge History of China*, III, pp. 57–72.

29   Golden, *History of Turkic Peoples*, pp. 136–138, and Barfield, *Perilous Frontier*, pp. 131–134.

30   See Pourshariati, *Decline and Fall of the Sasanian Empire*, pp. 126–127, and Rezakhani, *ReOrienting the Sasanians*, p. 217. Tardu Kaghan likely had backed Bagha Kaghan in an effort to break Sassanid power; see Golden, *History of Turkic Peoples*, pp. 132–133.

31   See Pourshariati, *Decline and Fall of the Sasanian Empire*, pp. 129–134. Shah Khusrau II, with the detachment provided by Maurice Tiberius and his rallied followers, defeated Bahram Chobin at the Battle of Blarathon (near modern Ganzak in northwestern Iran) in August 591.

32   See Barfield, *Perilous Frontier*, p. 138, and *Golden, History of Turkic Peoples*, pp. 132–135.

33   See Howard J. Wechsler, "The Founding of the Tang Dynasty: Kao-tsu (reign 618–26)," *Cambridge History of China*, III, pp. 153–167. The emperor Gaozu took over the Sui military and administration forged by the first Sui emperor Wen (581–604). See Graff, *Chinese Medieval Warfare*, pp. 160–176, for the decisive role of Prince Li Shimin (the future emperor Taizong) in defeating rivals for the imperial throne.

34   For Tang armies, see *ibid.*, pp. 183–204. For the Tang adoption of tactics of their nomadic foes, see Jonathan K. Skaff, "Tang Military Culture and Its Inner Asia Influences," *Military Culture in Imperial China*, pp. 185–191.

35   See Man, *Great Wall*, pp. 88–89, for Tang repairs to the Great Wall. For imperial promotion of prosperity and improvements to the Grand Canal, see Charles Benn, *China's Golden Age: Everyday Life in Tang Dynasty* (Oxford, 2002), pp. 19–70 and 177–194.

36   See Wechsler, "Kao-tsu," *Cambridge History of China*, III, pp. 181–182.

37   Barfield, *Perilous Frontier*, pp. 139–140.

38   See Nicola di Cosmo, "The Relations between China and the Steppe: From Xiongnu to the Türk Empire," *Empires and Exchanges*, pp. 51–53.

39   See Wechsler, "Kao-tsu," *Cambridge History of China*, III, p. 181, and Graff, *Medieval Chinese Warfare*, pp. 185–186.

40   See Wechsler, "Kao-tsu," *Cambridge History of China*, III, pp. 182–187, and Barfield, *Perilous Frontier*, pp. 140–142, for the rivalry between Li Shimin (the future emperor Taizong) and his older brother Li Jiancheng.

41   See Howard J. Wechsler, "T'ai-tsung (reign 626–49)," *Cambridge History of China*, III, pp. 188–193.

42   See Skaff, *Sui-Tang China*, pp. 93–99.

43   See *ibid.*, pp. 100–101.

44   See Ross and Vilhelm Thomsen, "The Orkhon Inscriptions," *Bulletin of the School of Oriental Studies, University of London* 5 (1930), p. 865.

45   See Thomas S. Burns, *Barbarians within the Gates of Rome: A Study of Roman Military Policy and the Barbarians, ca. 375–425 A.D.* (Bloomington, 1993), pp. 73–111.

46   See Barfield, *Perilous Frontier*, pp. 140–141, and Skaff, *Sui-Tang China*, pp. 53–60. The emperor Taizong was exceptionally open to considering the recommendations of his mandarin ministers; see Wechsler, "T'ai-stung," *Cambridge History of China*, III, pp. 193–200.

47   Skaff, *Sui-Tang China*, pp. 56–58, and Wechsler, "T'ai-stung," *Cambridge History of China*, III, pp. 193–194 and 197–198.

48   See Skaff, *Sui-Tang China*, pp. 62–94, and Barfield, *Perilous Frontier*, p. 142.

49   See Wechsler, "T'ai-tsung," *Cambridge History of China*, III, pp. 224–232.

50   See Wechsler, "T'ai-tsung," *Cambridge History of China*, III, p. 223, and Skaff, *Sui-Tang China*, pp. 55–58.

51   See Jonathan K. Skaff, "Tang China's Horse Power: The Borderland Breeding Ranch System," *Eurasian Empires in Antiquity and the Early Middle Ages: Contact and Exchange between the Graeco-Roman World, Inner Asia, and China*, edited by Hyun Jim Kim, Frederick J. Vervaet, and Selim Ferruh Adali (Cambridge, 2017), pp. 34–59.

52   See Wechsler, "T'ai-tsung," *Cambridge History of China*, III, p. 223, and Skaff, *Sui-Tang China*, pp. 55–58.

53   See Denis Twitchett and Howard J. Wechsler, "Kao-tsung (reign 649–91) and the Empress Wu: The Inheritor and the Usurper," *Cambridge History of China*, III, pp. 279–281.

54   Graff, *Warfare in Medieval China*, pp. 205–226, for the costs of Tang military success.

55   See Twitchett and Wechsler, "Kao-tsung," *Cambridge History of China*, III, pp. 244–250, and Jonathan Clemens, *Wu: The Chinese Empress Who Schemed, Seduced and Murdered Her Way to Become a Living God* (Albert Ridge Books, 2014), pp. 34–46.

56   See *ibid.*, pp. 34–46, 55–86, and Twitchett and Wechsler, "Kao-tsung," *Cambridge History of China*, III, pp. 251–273.

57   See *ibid.*, pp. 282–285.

58   See *ibid.*, pp. 279–281, and Barfield, *Perilous Frontier*, pp. 146–147.

59   See E. Denison Ross and Vilhelm Thomsen, "The Tonyukuk Inscription: Being a Translation of Professor Vilhelm Thomsen's Final Danish Rendering," *Bulletin of the School of Oriental Studies, University of London* 6 (1930), pp. 37–43. See also Barfield, *Perilous Frontier*, pp. 148–149, and Golden, *History of Turkic Peoples*, pp. 137–138.

60   For the monumental stelai and tumuli, see Edward Tryjarski, "On the Archaeological Traces of Old Turks in Mongolia," *East and West* 21 (1971), pp. 121–135.

61   See Denis Twitchett, "Hsüan-tsung (reign 712–757)," *Cambridge History of China*, III, pp. 379–382.

62   See *ibid.*, pp. 430–435. The defeats were humiliating given the efforts to reform the army earlier in the reign; see *ibid.*, pp. 415–418.

63   See Michael T. Daley, "Court Politics in Late T'ang Times," *Cambridge History of China*, III, pp. 561–563.

64   See *ibid.*, pp. 563–564.

65   See Graff, *Medieval Chinese Warfare*, pp. 227–251, for long-term consequences.

66   See Colin MacKerras, "The Uighurs," *Cambridge History of Early Inner Asia*, pp. 317–318.

67   See Barfield, *Perilous Frontier*, pp. 153–155.

68   See Twitchett, "Court Politics," *Cambridge History of China*, III, pp. 166–169. Uyghur cavalry proved vital in the recapture of the capital Chang'an from An Lushan, but the Emperor Suzong and Bögü Kaghan quarreled throughout the campaign in 756.

69   See Skaff, *Sui-Tang Ching*, pp. 209–218. Bayanchur Kaghan (749–759) married Princess Xiaogu; Bogu Kaghan (759–780) married Princess Congbui; Tun Baga Tarkhan (780–789) married Princess Xian'an; Baoyi Kaghan (808–821) married Princess Yong'an; and Chongde Kaghan (821–824) married Princess Taihe, who was welcomed back to the Tang court in 843.

70   See MacKerras, "Uighurs," *Cambridge History of Early Inner Asia*, p. 328, for a description of the city by the Arab visitor Tamim ibn-Bahr in 821, and pp. 335–341, for the prosperity stimulated by supplying the capital.

71   See Rong Xinjiang, "Sogdian Merchants and Sogdian Culture on the Silk Road," *Empires and Exchanges*, pp. 84–95.

72   See Clark, "Manichaeism among the Uygurs," *New Light on Manichaeism*, pp. 61–72, and MacKerras, "Uighurs," *Cambridge History of Early Inner Asia*, pp. 329–335.

73   See Lieu, *Manichaeism*, pp. 117–152, for career and doctrines of Mani.

74   For the translation of the Mani Codex, see Gardner and Lieu, *Manichaean Text*, pp. 46–103.

75   See Foltz, *Religions of Silk Road*, pp. 71–77. See Scott F. Johnson, "The Languages of Christianity on the Silk Road and the Transmission of Mediterranean Culture into Central Asia," *Empires and Exchanges*, pp. 220–234, for Aramaic employed by Christian missionaries.

76   See Daley, "Court Politics," *Cambridge History of China*, III, pp. 666–669. In 843, the emperor Wuzong targeted Manichaeism, because over one hundred thousand armed Uyghur refugees had crossed into Northern China after the collapse of the Kaghanate.

77   See Fowden, *Empire to Commonwealth*, pp. 76–79 and 121–124.

78   See Barfield, *Perilous Frontier*, pp. 155–157.

79   See Robert M. Somers, "The End of the T'ang," *Cambridge History of China*, III, pp. 773–781.

15 Turks and the Caliphate

1   John Haldon, *The Byzantine Wars* (Stroud, Glouchestershire, 2001), pp. 82–86 and, for analysis of the sources, pp. 212–213. See also Treadgold, *Byzantine Revival*, pp. 300–301. The battle is sometimes called after Azen, the location near Dazimon where the battle was fought.

2   See Walter E. Kaegi, "The Contribution of Archery to the Turkish Con-

quest of Anatolia," *Speculum* 39 (1964), pp. 99–102; reprinted in *Army, Society and Religion in Byzantium* (London, 1982), chapter XIX.

3   See Treadgold, *Byzantine Revival*, pp. 302–305, and pp. 444–445, note pp. 413–414, for the chronology of the siege and capture of Amorium, and the Abbasid retreat.

4   The embassy is reported in the *Annales Bertiniani*; see L. Nelson, trans., *The Annals of St-Bertin* (Manchester, 1991), p. 44. See also Treadgold, *Byzantine Revival*, pp. 309–310. The Byzantine envoys were accompanied by Rus, who had arrived in Constantinople from lands north of the Black Sea and could not return home. These Rus, who were Swedes, represented themselves as agents of a Swedish Kaghan, presumably dwelling on the banks of the middle Volga River. They could not return home through the northern routes because of hostile Turkomen tribes on the south Russian steppes, most likely Magyars or Pechenegs. Louis the Pious and his court were astonished to learn that these Rus were Swedes, and so Northmen or Vikings whose kin were raiding the Frankish Empire.

5   See Kennedy, *Armies of the Caliphs*, pp. 104–106.

6   See Barfield, *Perilous Frontier*, pp. 148–150, and Golden, *History of Turkic Peoples*, pp. 138–140.

7   See *ibid.*, pp. 233–236, for Khazar Kaghans uniting sundry Turkic- and Altaic-speaking tribes on the western steppes.

8   See Kaegi, *Heraclius*, pp. 141–149, and Howard-Johnston, *Last Great War*, pp. 295–304. It is also possible that Ziebel might have been a subordinate commander of the Kaghan.

9   See Golden, *History of Turkic Peoples*, pp. 97–105, for the Sabirs and Onoğurs, likely Turkic-speaking tribes designated Huns by Byzantine authors, who occupied the Pontic-Caspian steppes after the collapse of the empire of Attila in 454.

10   See Peter B. Golden, "The Karakhanids and Early Islam," *Cambridge History of Early Inner Asia*, pp. 348–352, and *History of the Turkic Peoples*, pp. 196–199.

11   For the cultural and political world of Transoxiana in 650, see Johan Elverskog, *Buddhism and Islam on the Silk Road* (Philadelphia, 2010), pp. 9–55, and E. V. Zeimal, "The Political History of Transoxiana," *Cambridge History of Iran*, I, pp. 263–278.

12   See Helmut Hoffman, "Early and Medieval Tibet," *Cambridge History of Early Inner Asia*, pp. 382–385, for the conquests of the cities of the Tarim Basin by the Tibetan emperor Khri-srong-Ide-btsan (755–797).

13   See Skaff, *Sui-Tang China*, pp. 182–184 and 280–282.

14   See Fred M. Donner, *The Early Islamic Conquests* (Princeton, 1991), pp. 82–220, and Hugh Kennedy, *The Great Arab Conquests: How the Spread of Islam Changed the World We Live In* (New York, 2007), pp. 66–199.

15   See P. Crone and G. M. Hinds, *God's Caliph: Religious Authority in the First Centuries of Islam* (Cambridge, 1980), pp. 4–43 and 80–96, and Hugh

Kennedy, *The Prophet and the Age of the Caliphates: The Islamic Near East from the Sixth to the Eleventh Century*, 3rd Edition (London/New York, 2015), pp. 69–75.

16   See J. J. Saunders, *A History of Medieval Islam* (London, 1965), pp. 59–76; Kennedy, *Prophet and Caliphates*, pp. 75–81; and M. A. Shaban, *Islamic History: A New Interpretation*, Volume I: *A.D. 600–750 (A.H. 132)* (Cambridge, 1971), pp. 60–78, for the civil war and victory of Muawiya in 661.

17   For the Arab sieges of Constantinople in 674–677 and 717–718, see respectively, *Chronicle of Theophanes*, pp. 52–54 and 82–91 (Turtledove translation). See also Kennedy, *Great Arab Conquests*, pp. 328–334, and Hoyland, *In God's Path*, pp. 105–110 and 172–178.

18   See Kennedy, *Great Arab Conquests*, pp. 225–254.

19   For imitative Sassanid silver dirhems, see Heinz Gaube, *Arabo-sasanidische Numismatik* (Braunschweig, 1973).

20   See Kennedy, *Armies of Caliphs*, pp. 104–105, and M. A. Shaban, *The Abbasid Revolution* (Cambridge, 1970), pp. 24–26, for recruitment of Iranians of Khurasan into the heavy cavalry and infantry.

21   See Kennedy, *Great Arabic Conquests*, pp. 255–276, and H. A. R. Gibb, *The Arabic Conquests in Central Asia* (New York, 1923), pp. 29–58, for the campaigns of Qutayba ibn Muslim.

22   See *ibid.*, pp. 276–289, and Khalid Yahya Blankinship, *The End of the Jihad State: The Reign of Hisham ibn 'Abd al-Malik and the Collapse of the Umayyads* (Albany, NY, 1994), pp. 109–110 and 125–129.

23   See Shaban, *Abbasid Revolution*, pp. 138–168, and Saunders, *History of Medieval Islam*, pp. 96–105, and Blankinship, *The End of the Jihad State*, pp. 206–222.

24   See Paul M. Cobb, *White Banners: Contention in 'Abbasid Syria, 750–880* (Albany, NY, 2001), pp. 43–47. Eighty Umayyad princes were invited to the banquet held at abu-Futrus, near Jaffa, on June 22, 750.

25   Roger Collins, *Early Medieval Spain: Unity in Diversity, 400–1000* (New York, 1983), pp. 169–174.

26   See Kennedy, *Prophet and Caliphates*, pp. 123–132, and Hugh Kennedy, *When Baghdad Ruled the Muslim World: The Rise and Fall of Islam's Greatest Dynasty* (New York, 2004), pp. 12–15.

27   See Eliyahu Ashtor, *A Social and Economic History of the Near East in the Middle Ages* (Berkeley, 1978), pp. 86–124 and 132–146, for population growth and expansion of cities stimulating trade and prosperity.

28   See Kennedy, *When Baghdad Ruled the Muslim World*, pp. 112–159.

29   See Bernard Lewis, "The Isma'ilites and the Assassins," *A History of the Crusades*, Volume I, edited by Kenneth M. Setton and Marshall W. Baldwin (Madison, 1959), pp. 99–104.

30   See A. R. Gibb, "The Isma'ilites and the Assassins," in *History of Crusades*,

I, pp. 99–156, and Fahhad Daftary, *A Short History of the Ismalis: Tradition of a Muslim Community* (Edinburgh, 1998), pp. 45–106.

31 See Skaff, *Sui-Tang China*, pp. 180–184 and 280–284, for the emperor Xuanzong's policy in the Western Regions.

32 See Robert G. Hoyland, *In God's Path: The Arab Conquests and the Creation of an Islamic Empire*, pp. 185–186.

33 See *ibid.*, pp. 186–187. The campaign was beyond the limits of Tang logistics; see David Graff, "The Reach of the Military: Tang," *Journal of Chinese History* 1 (2017), pp. 243–268.

34 See Kennedy, *Great Arab Conquests*, pp. 293–295, and H. A. R. Gibb, *The Arab Conquests in Central Asia* (New York, 1923), pp. 97–98.

35 Hyunbee Park, *Mapping the Chinese and Islamic Worlds: Cross-Cultural Exchange in Pre-Modern Asia* (Cambridge, 2012), pp. 25–27. The first paper mill in Baghdad was in 794–795, a generation after the Battle of Talas, and no source records the transfer of the technology of paper-making to the Islamic world by the Chinese captured at the battle.

36 See Golden, *History of the Turkic Peoples*, pp. 189–210.

37 See Ashtor, *Social and Economic History*, pp. 71–91.

38 See Ashtor, *Social and Economic History*, pp. 36–70, and Andrew M. Watson, *Agricultural Innovation in the Early Islamic World* (Cambridge, 1983), pp. 1–76.

39 See Michael McCormick, *The Origins of the European Economy: Communications and Commerce, A.D. 300–900* (Cambridge, 2001), pp. 237–264. See also Peter Spufford, *Money and Its Use in Medieval Europe* (Cambridge, 1989), pp. 66–71, for movement of silver specie vital for the slave trade in Central and Eastern Europe providing labor for the Islamic world.

40 See Ashtor, *Social and Economic History*, pp. 115–121, and Ghada Hashem Talhami, "The Zanj Rebellion Reconsidered," *The International Journal of African Historical Studies.* 10 (1977), pp. 443–461. It was the greatest African slave rebellion until the successful revolt and foundation of the state of Haiti by François-Dominique Toussaint Louverture in 1789–1798.

41 See Kennedy, *Armies of the Caliphs*, pp. 120–122, and Daniel Pipes, *Slave Soldiers and Islam: The Genesis of a Military System* (New Haven, 1981), pp. 35–45.

42 See Kennedy, *Prophet and Caliphates*, pp. 156–169.

43 Lewis, "Isma'ilites and the Assassins," *History of the Crusades*, I, pp. 104, and Daftary, *History of the Ismalis*, p. 88. He was Muhammad ibn al-Hasan al-Mahdī, descendant of Ali and Fatima through their younger son Husain, recognized as the third iman and killed at the Battle of Karbala in 680.

44 See Kennedy, *Armies of the Caliphs*, pp. 120–124, and *Prophets and Caliphates*, pp. 156–169.

45 See Kennedy, *When Baghdad Ruled the Muslim Word*, pp. 261–296. Samarra was the Abbasid capital in 836–892. The Turkish bodyguard (*haras*)

dominated the court in the decade of 861–870, during the so-called
anarchy of Samarra; see *ibid.*, pp. 169–172. The four caliphs were al-
Mutawakkil (847–861), who was murdered during his dinner; al-Must'in
(862–866), who was forced to abdicate, tortured and died in prison; al-
Mu'tazz (866–869), who was deposed and murdered in prison; and al-
Muhtadi (869–870), who was murdered. A fifth al-Muntasir (861-862)
either died of illness or from poisoning on orders of his Turkish officers.

46   See Saunders, *History of Medieval Islam*, pp. 106–124.

47   See Frye, "Samanids," *Cambridge History of Iran*, IV, p. 143.

48   See Peter Golden, *Central Asia in World History* (Oxford, 2011), pp. 64–68.

49   See Foltz, *Religions of Silk Road*, pp. 91–93, and Golden, *Central Asia*,
     pp. 69–71.

50   For an introduction to Islam, see Alfred Guillaume, *Islam* (Baltimore,
     1954). Still fundamental for the career and tenets of the Prophet Mu-
     hammad is W. Montgomery Watt, *Muhammad, Prophet and Statesman*
     (Oxford, 1975).

51   The evening of June 18, 2010, at the village of Menzil. I was accompa-
     nied by my friend and alumnus Stephanos Roulakis, who had discovered
     the order's presence and the mosque.

52   See Foltz, *Religions of Silk Road*, pp. 92–93 and 127–128.

53   See J. A. Boyle, "Turkish and Mongol Shamanism in the Middle Ages,"
     Folklore 83 (1972), pp. 184–193.

54   See Michael Khodarkovsky, *Russia's Steppe Frontier: The Making of a Colo-
     nial Empire, 1500–1800* (Bloomington, 2002), pp. 175–176 and 195–196.

55   See Peter M. Golden, "The Peoples of the Russian Forest Belt," *Cam-
     bridge History of Early Inner Asia*, pp. 237 and 239, and *History of Turkic
     Peoples*, pp. 212–213. In 965, the Bulgar Kaghan sent envoys to exhort
     Prince Vladimir of Kiev to embrace Islam.

56   See Michael Crichton, *Eaters of the Dead: The Manuscript of Ibn Fadlan, Re-
     lating to His Experience with the Northmen in A.D. 922* (New York, 1976).

57   See Golden, *History of Turkic Peoples*, p. 213. The Oghuz Turks had gained
     familiarity with Islam after long dealings with Muslim merchants of the
     Samanid Emirate.

58   See Golden, "Karakhanids," *Cambridge History of Early Inner Asia*, p. 357.

59   See Frye, "Samanids," *Cambridge History of Iran*, IV, p. 137.

60   See Edgar Knobloch, *Beyond the Oxus: Archaeology, Art and Architecture
     of Central Asia* (Totowa, NJ, 1972), pp. 27–28, and Melanie Michaili-
     dis, "Dynastic Politics and the Samanid Mausoleum," *Ars Orientalis* 44
     (2014), pp. 20–39.

61   See C. E. Bosworth, "The Development of Persian Culture under the
     Early Ghaznavids," *Iran* 6 (1968), pp. 33–44, for the creation of the high
     culture of Eastern Islam in the ninth through eleventh centuries.

62   See Oleg Grabar, "The Visual Arts," *Cambridge History of Iran*, IV, pp.

329–363, and G. Lazard, "The Rise of the New Persian Language," *ibid.*, pp. 595–632.

63   Sir Richard Burton so commented in his "Terminal Essay" after completing *The Book of the Thousand and One Arabian Nights* in 1888.

64   See Abolgasem Ferdowsi, *Shahnameh: The Persian Book of Kings*, translated by Dick Davis (New York, 1997), pp. xiii–xx.

65   See A. C. S. Peacock, *The Great Seljuk Empire* (Edinburgh, 2015), pp. 181–183. For a translation of his compendium, see Maḥmud ibn al-Husain al-Kashgari, *Compendium of the Turkic Dialects (Diwan lugat at-turk)*, 2 volumes, translated by Robert Dankoff and James Kelly (Cambridge, MA, 1984). The map is housed in the National Library, Topkapi Palace, Istanbul.

16 The Seljuk Turks and Their Sultanate

1   See Haldon, *Byzantine Wars*, pp. 168–181, for the course of battle, and pp. 216–117, for the sources. For the best analysis of the battle and the sources, see J.-C. Cheynet, "Manzikert: un désastre militaire?" *Byzantion* 59 (1980), pp. 410–438. Michael Attaleiates, John Skylitzes (or his continuator), and Michael Psellus are the prime Byzantine sources. See Michael Attaleiates, *The History*, translated by Anthony Kaldellis and Dimitris Krallis (Washington, DC, 2012), 20. 9–29, pp. 270–302; Eric McGeer, trans., *Byzantium in the Time of Troubles: The Continuation of the Chronicle of John Skylitzes (1057–1079)* (Leiden, 2020), V. 1–18, pp. 111–129; and Michael Psellus, *Fourteen Byzantine Rulers*, translated by E. R. A. Sewter (New York, 1966), pp. 354–355. Michael Psellus, hostile to Romanus Digenes, offers little other than snide remarks about the emperor's mistakes and cruelty to the Empress Eudocia.

2   My comments are based on my visits of Malazgirt and a survey of the battlefield in 2010 and 2011, with thanks to the observations by my friends Stephanos Roulakis and Jason Sanchez, who accompanied me on the first and second visit, respectively.

3   See Golden, *History of the Turkic Peoples*, pp. 205–211, for the migration of Oghuz Turks.

4   See Bulliet, *Cotton, Climate, Camels*, pp. 102–114.

5   See McCormick, *Origins of European Economy*, pp. 237–264. For the slave trade in the early Islamic world, see F. Ragib, "Les marchés aux esclaves en terre d'Islam," *Merrati e mercanti nel'alto medioevo*, *Settimane* 40 (Spoleto, 1993), pp. 721–764.

6   See *Ibn Fadlan and Land of Darkness*, pp. 45–46.

7   *Ibid.*, pp. 8–9.

8   *Ibid.*, pp. 9–10.

9   *Ibid.*, pp. 14–15.

10   *Ibid.*, p. 13.

11   *Ibid.*, pp. 12–13.

12 *Ibid.*, p. 18.

13 *Ibid.*, pp. 14 and 20.

14 See Golden, "Karakhanids," *Cambridge History of Early Inner Asia*, pp. 361–362.

15 See Golden, *History of Turkic Peoples*, pp. 209–210, and Claude Cahen, "The Turkish Invasion: The Selchükids," *History of the Crusades*, I, pp. 139–140.

16 See Peacock, *Great Seljuk Empire*, pp. 25–27 and 246–247.

17 See R. N. Frye, "The Samanids," *The Cambridge History of Iran*, Volume IV: *From the Arab Invasion to the Saljuqs*, edited by R. N. Frye (Cambridge 1975), p. 160.

18 See *ibid.*, pp. 159–160.

19 See Golden, "Karakhanids," *Cambridge History of Early Inner Asia*, pp. 363–365.

20 See Golden, *History of Turkic Peoples*, pp. 214–216.

21 See C. E. Bosworth, "The Political and Dynastic History of the Iranian World," *The Cambridge History of Iran*, Volume V: *The Saljuq and Mongol Periods*, edited by J. A. Boyle (Cambridge, 1968), pp. 18–19.

22 See C. E. Bosworth, *The Ghaznavids: Their Empire in Afghanistan and Eastern Iran, 994–1040* (Edinburgh, 1983), pp. 48–56.

23 See *ibid.*, pp. 129–144.

24 See *ibid.*, pp. 39–44.

25 See Bosworth, "Political History," *Cambridge History of Iran* V, pp. 6–7. This Samanid emir Alp Tigin is not to be confused with the Bughra Khan Alip Tigin of the Karakhanid dynasty.

26 See Bosworth, *Ghaznavids*, pp. 78–79 and 227, and Keay, *India*, pp. 205–212, for Mahmud's campaigns into India.

27 A. C. S. Peacock, *The Great Seljuk Empire* (Edinburgh, 2015), pp. 33–35, and Bosworth, *Ghaznavids*, pp. 219–226.

28 Bosworth, "Political History," *Cambridge History of Iran* V, p. 19.

29 See *ibid.*, pp. 19–20.

30 See Peacock, *Great Seljuk Empire*, pp. 39–43, and Bosworth, "Political History," *Cambridge History of Iran* V, pp. 21–23.

31 See Peacock, *Great Seljuk Empire*, pp. 135–136.

32 See Peacock, *Great Seljuk Empire*, pp. 37–38, and C. E. Bosworth, *The Later Ghaznavids: Splendour and Decay: The Dynasty in Afghanistan and Northern India. 1040–1186* (Edinburgh, 1977), p. 128, and "Early Ghaznavids," *Cambridge History of Iran* IV, p. 195.

33 See Bosworth, *Later Ghaznavids*, pp. 9–33.

34 See Bosworth, "Political History," *Cambridge History of Iran* V, pp. 23–24.

35 See Claude Cahen, *Pre-Ottoman Turkey: A General Survey of the Mate-*

rial and Spiritual Culture and History, c. 1071–1330, translated by J. Jones-Williams (London, 1968), pp. 66–71, for the first Turkish raids into Anatolia directed against the Armenian cities of Ani and Kars.

36 See Herbert Busse, "Iran under the Buyids," *The Cambridge History of Iran*, Volume IV: *From the Arab Invasion to the Saljuqs*, edited by R. N. Frye (Cambridge 1975), pp. 262–289.

37 See Peacock, *Great Seljuk Empire*, pp. 48–50, and Bosworth, "Political History," *Cambridge History of Iran* V, pp. 42–53.

38 See Peacock, *Great Seljuk Empire*, pp. 52–54, and Bosworth, "Political History," *Cambridge History of Iran* V, pp. 65–66. Securing Khurasan and the northeastern frontier of the Jaxartes River were the priorities of Alp Aralan rather than waging war against the Byzantine Empire.

39 See Michael Brett, *The Fatimid Empire* (Edinburgh, 2017), pp. 13–20, and Stanley Lane-Poole, *A History of Egypt under the Saracens* (New York, 1969), pp. 92–116.

40 See Lewis, "Ismal'ilites and Assassins," *History of Crusades* I, pp. 104–106, and Saunders, *History of Medieval Islam*, pp. 131–132.

41 See Brett, *Fatimid Empire*, pp. 13–37, and Lane-Poole, *History of Egypt*, pp. 117–120.

42 See Brett, *Fatimid Empire*, pp. 60–83.

43 See *ibid.*, pp. 171–176 and 269–273.

44 See Peacock, *Great Seljuk Empire*, pp. 50–51; Brett, *Fatimid Empire*, pp. 193–197; and A. R. Gibb, "The Caliphate and Arab States," *History of Crusades* I, pp. 89–92.

45 See Peacock, *Great Seljuk Empire*, pp. 53–54.

46 See Yaacov Lev, "The Fatimids and Byzantium, 10th–12th Centuries," *Graeco-Arabica* 6 (1995), pp. 203–205. Although al-Hakim, who descended into madness in his later years, destroyed the Church of the Holy Sepulcher in 1009, the church was repaired by Byzantine artists under his successor al-Zahir (1021–1036). For the madness of the Caliph and his persecution of Christians, see Stanley-Poole, *History of Egypt*, pp. 125–136. The treaty enabled ever more pilgrims from Western Europe to travel to Jerusalem and Bethlehem in the eleventh century; see Steven Runciman, "The Pilgrimages to Palestine before 1095," *History of Crusades* I, pp. 74–78.

47 See Peter Charanis, "The Byzantine Empire in the Eleventh Century," *History of Crusades* I, p. 219.

48 Michael Psellus, *Fourteen Byzantine Rulers*, pp. 53–380 (Penguin translation), is the prime source for the political failure of the heirs of Basil II (956–1025). For the decline of the professionalism of the Byzantine army, see Warren Treadgold, *Byzantium and Its Army, 284–1081* (Stanford, 1992), pp. 39–42. For the debasement of the gold currency initiated by Constantine IX Monomachus (1042–1055), see Michael F. Hendy, *Studies in the Byzantine Monetary Economy c. 300–1450* (Cambridge, 1986),

pp. 506–512. The gold nomisma (4.54 grs) was debased from 90.5% to 10.5% fine in 1042–1092.

49 See Peacock, *Great Seljuk Empire*, p. 55.

50 See *ibid.*, pp. 58–59.

51 See Cahen, *Pre-Ottoman Turkey*, pp. 72–83.

52 See *ibid.*, pp. 91–96, and Alexander D. Beilhammer, *Byzantium and the Emergence of Muslim-Turkish Anatolia, ca. 1040–1130* (London/New York, 2017), pp. 202–204 and 268–285.

53 See Cahen, *Pre-Ottoman Turkey*, pp. 78–83, and Beilhammer, *Emergence of Muslim-Turkish Anatolia*, pp. 171–179 and 204–231.

54 See Cahen, *Pre-Ottoman Turkey*, pp. 61–64. The Caliph Harun ar-Raschid established a military settlement with a mosque at Tyana (today Kemerhisar) on the Anatolian plateau in 806. Most of the Arab colonists abandoned the city after the first winter. See Treadgold, *Byzantine Revival*, p. 145.

55 See Speros Vryonis Jr., *The Decline of Medieval Hellenism in Asia Minor and the Process of Islamization from the Eleventh through Fifteenth Century* (Berkeley, 1971), pp. 1–68, for the state of Byzantine Asia Minor in 1071. For the geography of Asia Minor, see Hendy, *Studies in the Byzantine Monetary Economy*, pp. 21–68.

56 See Steven Runciman, *A History of the Crusades*, Volume I (Cambridge, 1952), pp. 175–194, for the First Crusade march across Asia Minor from Nicaea to Antioch. In the march of four months (July–October 1097), it is estimated that 4,500 cavalry and 30,000 infantry set out from Nicaea, suggesting a total of 100,000 crusaders and noncombatant pilgrims. Between one-third and one-half of those who began the march did not reach Antioch.

57 See Anna Komnene, *Alexiad*, pp. 87–88, and Paul Magdalino, *The Empire of Manuel Komnenos, 1143–1180* (Cambridge, 1993), pp. 180–227.

58 See Vyronis, *Decline of Middle Hellenism*, pp. 85–120.

59 See Vryonis, *Decline of Medieval Hellenism*, pp. 223–224 and 351–402, and Cahen, *Pre-Ottoman Turkey*, pp. 110–142.

60 See Vyronis, *Decline of Medieval Hellenism*, pp. 452–461. These Christians of Karaman, classified as Greeks in 1923, were deported to Greece, a homeland their ancestors never knew. These Christians were descendants of the Luvian and Hattian populations of the Bronze Age who had adopted Greek in the Hellenistic Age and converted to Christianity in the fourth through sixth centuries.

61 See Tamara Talbot Rice, *The Seljuks in Asia Minor* (New York, 1961), pp. 115–186, and J. M. Rogers, "Çifte Minare Medrese at Erzurum and Gök Medrese at Sivas," *Anatolian Studies* 15 (1965), pp. 63–85. The medresses far more than the mosques transformed the urban landscape. Over 3,500 memorial türbler and tekkler to pious Muslims erected between 1100 and 1350 Islamized the sacred space of the countryside.

62   See Vryonis, *Decline of Medieval Hellenism*, pp. 288–350, for the decline of Christian institutions in Asia Minor.

63   See Cahen, *Pre-Ottoman Turkey*, pp. 192–193, 214–215, and 351–358. See also Afzal Iqbal, *The Life and Work of Jalal-ud-Din Rumi* (Kuala Lumpur, 2014).

64   See A. J. Arberrry, trans., *Mystical Poems of Rumi* (Chicago, 1968).

65   The Museum of the Mevlana (Mevlana Müzesi) houses numerous votive offerings of the pious since his death in 1273, and it is still the most frequently visited site by tourists and Muslim pilgrims.

66   For DNA of the Turkish population today, see Can Alkan *et al.*, "Whole Genome Sequencing of Turkish Genomes Reveals Functional Private Alleles and Impact of Genetic Interactions with Europe, Asia and Africa," *Geonomics* 15 (2014), pp. 1–12; available online: https://bmcgenomics. biomedcentral.com/articles/10.1186/1471-2164-15-963. My wife, Sema, a native of Siverek in southeastern Turkey, had her DNA tested by Ancestry. com soon after our marriage in 2014. We learned that her descent was nearly 75% Armenian, 19% Mediterranean (consistent with Greek and Italian ancestry), and 6% Middle Eastern. I surmise her ancestors were Armenian, Byzantine Greek, and Syrian Christians, all of whom learned Turkish and converted to Islam between the thirteenth and sixteenth centuries. There was no ancestry from Central Asia. Successive regimes in Ankara have been reluctant to permit widespread DNA testing because the results shatter the nationalist Turkish myth of a common origin from Central Asia.

67   See John Keay, *India: A History* (New York, 2001), pp. 241–327. All Muslim regimes from the first sultans of Delhi to the Mughal emperors faced the same constraints.

68   See A. A. Vasiliev, *History of Byzantine Empire*, Volume I (Madison, 1952), p. 356.

69   Michael Psellus, *Fourteen Byzantine Rulers*, pp. 282–283 (Penguin translation), and Michael Attaleiates, *History* 21. 8, pp. 316–319.

70   See Anna Komnene, *Alexiad*, pp. 50–78 (Penguin translation). See also Vasiliev, *History of Byzantine Empire*, II, pp. 380–389, and Anthony Kaldellis, *Streams of Gold, Rivers of God: The Rise and Fall of Byzantium 985 A.D. to First Crusade* (Oxford, 2017), pp. 261–270.

71   Runciman, *A History of the Crusades*, I, p. 71.

72   See Barbara Hill, "Actions Speak Louder Than Words: Anna Komnene's Attempted Usurpation," *Anna Komnene and Her Times*, edited by Thalia Gouma-Peterson (New York, 2000), pp. 45–62.

73   See Anna Komnene, *Alexiad*, pp. 127–236 and 508–519, and see also Vasiliev, *History of Byzantine Empire*, II, pp. 380–389. There is need of a modern biography of Alexius I. The fundamental work is still Ferdinand Chalandon, *Essai sur le règne d'Alexis Ier Comnène 1081–1118* (Paris, 1900), reprinted by Hachette Livre & Bibliothèque nationale, 2018. For

the Norman invasion, see Graham Loud, *The Age of Robert Guiscard: Southern Italy and the Norman Conquest* (Singapore, 2000), pp. 209–222.

74   See Hendy, *Studies in Byzantine Monetary Economy*, pp. 513–519.

75   See Jonathan Harris, *Byzantium and the Crusades*, second edition (London, 2014), pp. 59–76, and Peter Charanis, "Byzantium, the West and the Origin of the First Crusade," *Byzantion* 19 (1949), pp. 24–36. The purported letter Alexius, in Latin, to Count Robert of Flanders with a request for mercenaries was likely composed in 1106–1108, as a means to justify the crusade of Bohemond against Constantinople. The author might have used a Latin translation of a genuine letter of Alexius for the composition of the middle sections of the letter; see J. Joranson, "The Problem of the Spurious Letter of the Emperor Alexius to the Count of Flanders," *American Historical Review* 55 (1950), pp. 812–815.

76   Anna Komnene, *The Alexiad*, revised edition, translated by E. R Sewter (New York, 2009), pp. 377–37, and see pp. 122–123 for her comments on the irresistible charge of European knights. For her prejudices toward Western Europeans, whom she calls Celts, see Peter Frankopan, "Perception and Projection of Prejudice: Anna Comnena, the Alexiad, and the First Crusade," in *Gendering the Crusades*, edited by Susan Edgington and Sarah Lambert (New York, 2002), pp. 59–76.

77   Five versions of the speech of Pope Urban II have come down to us; see Edward Peters, trans., *The First Crusade: The Chronicle of Fulcher of Chartres and Other Source Materials* (Philadelphia, 1971), pp. 1–16. See also Frederic Duncalf, "The Councils of Piacenza and Clermont," *History of Crusades*, I, pp. 220–252.

17 The Legend of Prester John and the Gurkhans of Cathay

1   Otto, Bishop of Freising, *The Two Cities: A Chronicle of Universal History to the Year 1146 A.D.*, translated by Charles C. Mirrow (New York, 1928), VII. 33, pp. 443–444. Latin text with English translation is also in Keagan Brewer, *Prester John: The Legend and its Sources* (Farnham, Surrey, 2015), pp. 42–45.

2   See Runciman, *History of Crusades*, II, pp. 225–246, for the capture of Edessa by Imad al-Din Zengi atabeg of Mosul.

3   See Robert Silverberg, *The Realm of Prester John* (Athens, Ohio, 1972), pp. 3–39, and I. de Rachewiltz, *Papal Envoys to the Great Khans* (Stanford, 1971), pp. 29–40, for the origins and development of the legend of Prester John.

4   See Jonathan Phillips, *The Second Crusade: Extending the Frontiers of Christendom* (New Haven, 2007), pp. 37–60. Saint Bernard, Abbot of Clairvaux, assumed the leading role in inspiring many to assume the cross.

5   See Runciman, *History of Crusades*, II, pp. 278–290, and Phillips, *Second Crusade*, pp. 207–227.

6   See Geoffrey Barraclough, *The Origins of Modern Germany*, second edition (New York, 1947), pp. 163–164.

7   See Ralph V. Turner, *Eleanor of Aquitaine, Queen of France, Queen of England* (New Haven, 2009), pp. 70–122, and W. L. Warren, *Henry II* (Berkeley), pp. 42–45.

8   See Brewer, *Prester John*, pp. 67–91, for Latin text and English translation of the purported letter of Prester John. The letter has survived in a number of versions with later interpolations.

9   See Silverberg, *Realm of Prester John*, pp. 40–73, and Brewer, *Prester John*, pp. 13–17.

10   See *ibid.*, pp. 92–96, for letter of Pope Alexander II to John, King of the Indians.

11   See Runciman, *History of Crusades*, II, pp. 436–474.

12   See Michal Biran, *The Empire of the Qara Khitai in Eurasian History between China and the Islamic World* (Cambridge, 2005), pp. 41–47; Peacock, *Great Seljuk Empire*, pp. 104–105; and Charles E. Nowell, "The Historical Prester John," *Speculum* 38 (1953), pp. 441–443.

13   See *ibid.*, pp. 105–118.

14   See Biran, *Qara Khitai*, pp. 107–113.

15   See Peacock, *Great Seljuk Empire*, pp. 105–106.

16   See Herbert Franke, "The Forest Peoples of Manchuria: Khitans and Jurchens," *Cambridge History of Early Inner Asia*, pp. 400–403.

17   See Barfield, *Perilous Frontier*, pp. 164–165, and Denis Twitchett and Klaus-Peter Tietze, "The Liao," *The Cambridge History of China*, Volume VI: *Alien Regimes and Border States, 907–1368*, edited by Herbert Franke and Denis Twitchett (Cambridge, 1994), pp. 42–53.

18   See Barfield, *Perilous Frontier*, pp. 168–169.

19   Twitchett and Tietze, "The Liao," *Cambridge History of China*, VI, pp. 60 aetiological 62.

20   See Franke, "The Forest Peoples," *Cambridge History of Early Inner Asia*, pp. 403–407, for aetiological myths of the Khitans.

21   See F. W. Mote, *Imperial China, 900–1800* (Cambridge, MA, 1999), p. 31. The legend about the birth of Abaoji is comparable to that of Temujin, the future Genghis Khan.

22   See Barfield, *Perilous Frontier*, pp. 167–168. Chinese advisers encouraged the imperial pretensions of Abaoji.

23   See Robert M. Somers, "The End of the T'ang," *Cambridge History of China*, III, p. 781.

24   See *ibid.*, pp. 781–782, and Gungwu Wang, *The Structure of Power in North China during the Five Dynasties* (Stanford, 1967), pp. 191–121.

25   Somers, "End of T'ang," *Cambridge History of China*, III, p. 784.

26   See Wang, *The Structure of Power*, pp. 125–126.

27   See Twitchett and Tietze, "Liao," *Cambridge History of China*, VI, pp. 60–67.

28   The offer was hardly attractive, because Abaoji and his successor repeatedly campaigned on the Mongolian steppes to assert their hegemony over Turkic and Mongolian tribes; see Mote, *Imperial China*, pp. 56–68. Furthermore, the Khitans had occupied the Orkhon valley since the late ninth century; see Barfield, *Perilous Frontier*, p. 165. Many Uyghurs, who had settled in northern China after the fall of their kaghanate, served as bureaucrats and merchants to the Khitan emperor; see Mote, *Imperial China*, pp. 35–36.

29   See Biran, *Qara Khitai*, pp. 2–7. The Khitans were accorded an official chronicle, *History of Liao (Liao Shi)*, which survives in an early fourteenth century version, which is based on sources dating from the tenth century; see Biran, *Qara Khitai*, pp. 13–15.

30   See Barfield, *Perilous Frontier*, p. 175, for population estimates.

31   See *ibid.*, pp. 173–174, and Mote, *Imperial China*, pp. 39–40. Abaoji instituted the fiction that his Chinese subjects were a separate tribe within the Khitan Confederacy, even though they governed by mandarin officials employing Chinese law. See *ibid.*, pp. 40–41, for resentment of the Khitan tribal leaders over Abaoji's authoritarian administration and preference for Chinese ways and officials.

32   See Franke, "Forest Peoples," *Cambridge History of Early Inner Asia*, pp. 407–408.

33   See Mote, *Imperial China*, p. 41.

34   See *ibid.*, pp. 43–44 and 81–86. See Twitchett and Tietze, "Liao," *Cambridge History of China*, VI, pp. 63–64, for Abaoji ordering the construction of Buddhist, Daoist, and Confucian temples in his Chinese-style capital, Shangjing. See also Herbert Franke, "The Chin Dynasty," *Cambridge History of China*, VI, pp. 312–314, stressing that the Jurchen emperors of the Jin Dynasty were following the Khitan traditions of patronizing Buddhism.

35   See Twitchett and Tietze, "Liao," *Cambridge History of China*, VI, pp. 60, and Mote, *Imperial China*, p. 49.

36   See *ibid.*, pp. 49–51 and 54–56.

37   See Twitchett and Tietze, "Liao," *Cambridge History of China*, VI, pp. 68–69.

38   See *ibid.*, pp. 69–75. The entrance of Yelü Deguang into Kaifeng was the high point of his reign.

39   See *ibid.*, pp. 76–80, and Mote, *Imperial China*, pp. 62–68.

40   See Ruth Dunnel, "The Hsi Hsia," *Cambridge History of China*, VI, pp. 154–158, and Mote, *Imperial China*, pp. 168–171.

41   Dunnel, "Hsi Hsia," *Cambridge History of China*, VI, pp. 158–164, and Mote, *Imperial China*, pp. 171–179.

42   See Dunnel, "Hsi Hsia," *Cambridge History of China*, VI, pp. 176–179, and Mote, *Imperial China*, pp. 179–182.

43   See *ibid.*, pp. 351–354, for the population estimates of the Song Empire. For the revenues of the Song Empire, see Mote, *Imperial China*, pp. 359–364, and Peter J. Golan, "The Sung Fiscal Administration," in *The Cambridge History of China*, Volume V, Part 2: *Sung China, 960–1279*, edited by John W. Chaffee and Denis Twitchett (Cambridge, 2015), pp. 139–213.

44   See Mote, *Imperial China*, pp. 289–298.

45   See Dieter Kuhn, *The Age of Confucian Rule: The Song Transformation of China* (Cambridge, MA, 2009), pp. 99–137, and Mote, *Imperial China*, pp. 253–351, for the Neo-Confucian examination system and domination of the Confucian mandarins.

46   See Charles Hartman, "Sung Government and Politics," *Cambridge History of China*, V.2, pp. 32–80.

47   See Kuhn, *Confucian Rule*, pp. 29–48, and Mote, *Imperial China*, pp. 98–112, for the rituals and ideology of the Song court.

48   For technological innovations and economic growth, see Dieter Kuhn, *The Age of Confucian Rule: The Song Transformation of China* (Cambridge, MA, 2009), pp. 213–232, and Joseph P. McDermott, "Economic Change in China, 960–1279," in *The Cambridge History of China*, Volume V. 2, pp. 321–409. William McNeill, *Pursuit of Power: Technology, Armed Force, and Society since A.D. 1000*, second edition (Chicago, 1984), pp. 25–62, concludes that the Song Empire was on the brink of an industrial revolution in the late tenth century.

49   See Wang Tseng-Yü, "A History of the Sung Military," *Cambridge History of China*, V. 2, pp. 214–249. The lack of cavalry hindered Song offensive operations, while innovations in artillery, firebombs, fortifications, and the navy were aimed to negate the advantage in cavalry enjoyed by the Khitans and Jurchens; see Graff, *Military History of China*, pp. 220–223.

50   Barfield, *Perilous Frontier*, p. 174, Mote, *Imperial China*, pp. 70–71, and Twitchett and Tieze, "Liao," *Cambridge History of China*, VI, pp. 104–110. The treaty has been dated to either 1004 or 1005.

51   See Franke, "Forest Peoples of Manchuria," *Cambridge History of Early Inner Asia*, pp. 411–419, and Herbert Franke, "The Chin Dynasty," *Cambridge History of China*, VI, pp. 216–220.

52   See Herbert Franke, "Chinese Texts on the Jurchen: A Translation of the Jurchen Monograph," *San ch'ao pei meng hui pien, Zentralasiastische Studien* 9 (1979), pp. 153–154.

53   See Mote, *Imperial China*, pp. 194–199.

54   See Franke, "Chin Dynasty," *Cambridge History of China*, VI, pp. 223–224.

55   See Twitchett and Tietze, "Liao," *Cambridge History of China*, VI, pp. 149–153, and Mote, *Imperial China*, pp. 199–206.

56   See *ibid.*, pp. 206–211.

57   See *ibid.*, pp. 307–308, for the terms of the treaty of Shaoxing in 1141.

58   For the Song navy, see Angela Schottenhammer, "China's Emergence as a Maritime Power," *Cambridge History of China*, V. 2, pp. 454–460. Song engineers excelled in fortifying cities and Song generals were expert in defending fortified cities. See Herbert Franke, "Siege and Defense of Towns in Medieval China," *Chinese Ways in Warfare*, pp. 151–201.

59   See Barfield, *Perilous Frontier*, pp. 180–181, and Mote, *Imperial China*, pp. 229–236, for the Jin emperors centralizing government and adopting Chinese ideology and diplomacy.

60   See Barfield, *Perilous Frontier*, pp. 182–184.

61   See Biran, *Qara Khitai*, pp. 19–22.

62   See *ibid.*, pp. 22–26.

63   See *ibid.*, pp. 26–28.

64   See *ibid.*, pp. 28–30.

65   See *ibid.*, pp. 35–37, for the march west, and pp. 33–35, for Khitans who had fled west before 1130.

66   See *ibid.*, p. 38.

67   See *ibid.*, pp. 38–40

68   For analysis of ruins, see online publication of H. Yamaguchi, K. Kiyama, N. Shimizu, and Altangerel, "Archaeological Research of the Khitai Dynasty's Balgash City Ruins, Cultural Heritage on the Steppes, Using GIS," *Proceedings of the 22nd CIPA Symposium, October 11-15, 2009, Kyoto, Japan* (Kyoto, 2009).

69   See Biran, *Qara Khitai*, p. 41.

70   See Peacock, *Great Seljuk Empire*, pp. 101–103, and Bosworth, "Political History," *Cambridge History of Iran*, V, pp. 140–144.

71   See Biran, *Qara Khitai*, pp. 41–45.

72   See *ibid.*, pp. 180–191.

73   See *ibid.*, pp. 48–59.

74   See *ibid.*, pp. 171–191.

75   See *ibid.*, pp. 196–201.

76   See *ibid.*, pp. 102–128 and 146–160, for the Karakhitan Chinese-style bureaucracy and nomadic military.

77   See *ibid.*, pp. 191–194.

78   See Brewer, *Prester John*, pp. 98–100, for Latin text and English translation of the letter of Jacques de Vitry, Bishop of Acre, written in March 1221.

79   See James M. Powell, *Anatomy of a Crusade, 1213–1221* (Philadelphia, 1986), pp. 175–194.

18 From Temujin to Genghis Khan

1   See Kahn, trans., *Secret History of the Mongols*, pp. 114–125. See also Ratchnevsky, *Genghis Khan*, pp. 89–96; Weatherford, *Genghis Khan*, pp. 65–66; and Michael Prawdin, *The Mongol Empire: Its Rise and Legacy*, revised edition, translated by Eden and Cedar Paul (New York, 1961), pp. 85–90.

2   See Ratchnevsky, *Genghis Khan*, pp. 90–91, who proposes the title is best translated as "oceanic ruler," and so in keeping with the traditional rendering of the title as "universal lord."

3   Peter B. Golden, "Inner Asia in c. 1200," *The Cambridge History of Inner Asia: The Chinggisid Age*, edited by Nicola di Cosmo, Allen J. Frank, and Peter B. Golden (Cambridge, 2009), pp. 9–25, and David Morgan, *The Mongols* (Oxford, 1986), pp. 32–54.

4   See Bosworth, *History of Turkic Peoples*, pp. 26–27, and consult Juha Janhunen, *Mongolian* (Amsterdam, 2012), for origins of Mongol language and its divergence from the Turkic languages.

5   See Ratchnevsky, *Genghis Khan*, p. 95. Genghis Khan ordered the keeping of records in Mongolian written in the Uyghur script from 1206 on. In ca. 1269, Kublai Khan ordered a new alphabet known as the square script (Phags-pa), which was devised by the Tibetan monk Drogön Chogyal Phagpa. See Mote, *Imperial China*, p. 484.

6   See Morgan, *Mongols*, pp. 87–89, on the size of Mongol armies. Muslim chroniclers claim Genghis Khan invaded Khwarazm with an army of 800,000. The number, while exaggerated, included the engineers, infantry, and cavalry of allied and subject populations. Based on a national levy of 129,000 horsemen at the death of Genghis Khan, the population of eastern steppes is often reckoned between 750,000 and 1 million. The current population of the Republic of Mongolia is nearly 3.4 million.

7   See Morgan, *Mongols*, pp. 50–54, and Golden, "Inner Asia," *The Cambridge History of Inner Asia*, pp. 18–25, for the distribution of tribes in Mongolia in 1162.

8   See Barfield, *Perilous Frontier*, pp. 192–185, and Mote, *Imperial China*, pp. 236–243, for the diplomacy of Jin emperors.

9   Ratchnevsky, *Genghis Khan*, pp. 8–14.

10   Weatherford, *Genghis Khan*, pp. 12–13.

11   See Kuhn, *Secret History*, p. 13. See also Weatherford, *Genghis Khan*, pp. 13–15.

12   See Ratchnevsky, *Genghis Khan*, pp. 16–20, and Weatherford, *Genghis Khan*, pp. 19–25, for the family hierarchy.

13   See Ratchnevsky, *Genghis Khan*, pp. 21–22, for the betrothal of Börte to Temujin.

14   See Kuhn, *Secret History*, pp. 15–16, and Ratchnevsky, *Genghis Khan*, pp. 22–23.

15   See *ibid.*, pp. 23–24, and Weatherford, *Genghis Khan*, pp. 19–23, for Hoelum's role in preserving the family.

16   See Kuhn, *Secret History*, p. 18. See also Ratchnevsky, *Genghis Khan*, pp. 23–24, and Weatherford, *Genghis Khan*, pp. 23–27, for Temujin's murder of Begter.

17   See Kuhn, *Secret History*, p. 19. See also Ratchnevsky, *Genghis Khan*, p. 24, and Weatherford, *Genghis Khan*, p. 25, for the curse of Hoelum.

18   Ratchnevsky, *Genghis Khan*, pp. 25–28.

19   See Kahn, trans., *Secret History of Mongols*, pp. 50–51.

20   See Ratchnevsky, *Genghis Khan*, p. 31, and Weatherford, *Genghis Khan*, pp. 28–29.

21   See Ratchnevsky, *Genghis Khan*, pp. 31–33, and Prawdin, *Mongol Empire*, pp. 40–41.

22   See Ratchnevsky, *Genghis Khan*, pp. 19–20, and Weatherford, *Genghis Khan*, pp. 63–64.

23   See Morgan, *Mongols*, pp. 9–23, for judicious evaluation of the *Secret History*, Chinese chronicles, and the accounts of the Persian historians Ata-Malik Juvayni and Rashid al-Din.

24   See Ratchnevsky, *Genghis Khan*, pp. 34–35, for the abduction of Börte.

25   See *ibid.*, pp. 36–37, and Weatherford, *Genghis Khan*, pp. 31–37.

26   See *ibid.*, p. 36.

27   See Ratchnevsky, *Genghis Khan*, pp. 37–41.

28   See *ibid.*, pp. 50–51, and Biran, *Qara Khitai*, pp. 64–65.

29   See Ratchnevsky, *Genghis Khan*, pp. 51–52.

30   See *ibid.*, pp. 53–61, and Prawdin, *Mongol Empire*, pp. 54–63.

31   See Ratchnevsky, *Genghis Khan*, pp. 66–67.

32   See *ibid.*, pp. 32 and 53.

33   See *ibid.*, pp. 67–71, and Prawdin, *Mongol Empire*, pp. 68–70.

34   See Ratchnevsky, *Genghis Khan*, pp. 71–73, and Prawdin, *Mongol Empire*, pp. 70–72.

35   See Ratchnevsky, *Genghis Khan*, pp. 73–83, and Prawdin, *Mongol Empire*, pp. 71–74.

36   See Ratchnevsky, *Genghis Khan*, pp. 79–80, and Prawdin, *Mongol Empire*, p. 75.

37   See Ratchnevsky, *Genghis Khan*, pp. 90–87, and Prawdin, *Mongol Empire*, pp. 77–81.

38   Biran, *Qara Khitai*, pp. 76–77.

39   See Ratchnevsky, *Genghis Khan*, pp. 87–88, and Weatherford, *Genghis Khan*, pp. 62–64.

40   See Kuhn, *Secret History*, pp. 87–88, and Weatherford, *Genghis Khan*, p. 64, for the final words of Jamuka.

41   See Richard A. Gabriel, *Genghis Khan's Greatest General: Subotai the Valiant* (Westport, CT, 2005), pp. 15–16.

42   See Ratchnevsky, *Genghis Khan*, pp. 145–149.

43   See Mote, *Imperial China*, pp. 378–389, for the ritualized diplomacy of the Song, Jin, and Xi Xia court that hindered perception of emerging Mongol threat.

44   See Ratchnevsky, *Genghis Khan*, pp. 149–150, and Prawdin, *Mongol Empire*, pp. 129–130.

45   See Ratchnevsky, *Genghis Khan*, pp. 164–165, and Weatherford, *Genghis Khan*, pp. 36–38.

46   See Ratchnevsky, *Genghis Khan*, p. 106.

47   See *ibid.*, p. 146, figure 18, and pp. 145–147. The painting is now in the National Museum, Tapei.

48   See *ibid.*, pp. 152–169.

49   See *ibid.*, pp. 197–198, and Morgan, *Mongols*, pp. 40–44.

50   See Ratchnevsky, *Genghis Khan*, pp. 96–101, and Prawdin, *Mongol Empire*, pp. 97–101.

51   See Ratchnevsky, *Genghis Khan*, pp. 134–136, and Prawdin, *Mongol Empire*, pp. 200–209.

52   See Ratchnevsky, *Genghis Khan*, p. 197. Nestorian Christianity was favored at the Mongol court because it was the faith of the Keraits and his favorite daughter-in-law, Sorghaghtani Beki, wife of his son Tolui.

53   See Theophylactus Simocatta, *History* V. 10, pp. 146–147 (Whitby translation).

54   See Ratchnevsky, *Genghis Khan*, p. 197, who stresses Genghis Khan showed little interest in the doctrine of Buddhism in contrast to his grandson Kublai Khan.

55   See *ibid.*, pp. 136–140, and Peter Jackson, *The Mongols and the Islamic World from Conquest to Conversion* (New Haven, 2017), pp. 92–93, for the administrative arrangements for the Islamic lands when Genghis Khan gained familiarity with Islam.

56   See Prawdin, *Mongol Empire*, pp. 180–181. Genghis Khan shared the views of the Karakhitan rulers toward Islam; see Birat, *Qara Khitai*, pp. 180–191. See also Jackson, *The Mongols and Islamic World*, pp. 89–92, noting the Muslims found Genghis Khan tolerable after the overthrow of Muhammad Shah.

57   See Ratchnevsky, *Genghis Khan*, pp. 187–196, and Morgan, *Mongols*, pp. 84–95.

58   Ratchnevsky, *Genghis Khan*, pp. 149–150.

59   Stephen Pow and Jingjing Liao, "Subutai: Sorting Fact from Fiction Surrounding the Mongol Empire's Greatest General (With Translations of Subutai's Two Biographies in the Yuan Shi)," *Journal of Chinese Military History* 7 (2018), pp. 43-52.

60   Gabriel, *Subotai the Valiant*, pp. 21–22, and Stephen Pow, "The Last Campaign and Death of Jebe Noyan," *Journal of the Royal Asiatic Society* 27 (2016), pp. 32–34. For Jelme administering to the wound of Temujin, see Ratchnevsky, *Genghis Khan*, p. 63.

61   See Kahn, trans., *Secret History*, p. 111. See also Prawdin, *Mongol Empire*, pp. 79–80.

62   See Gabriel, *Subotai the Valiant*, pp. 1–24 and 137–142.

63   See Condoleezza Rice, "The Making of Soviet Strategy," *Makers of Modern Strategy from Machiavelli to the Nuclear Age*, edited by Peter Paret (Princeton, 1986), pp. 648–676, for the decisive role of Nikolayevich Tukhachevsky in creating the Soviet strategic doctrine of deep battle.

64   The NKVD, Naródnyy komissariát vnútrennikh del, translated as People's Commissariat for Internal Affairs, was the secret police of Josef Stalin and the predecessor of the later Soviet KGB (Komitet gosudarstvennoy bezopasnosti), or the Committee for State Security in 1954–1991.

65   See Simon Sebag Montefiore, *Stalin: The Court of the Red Tsar* (New York, 2005), pp. 222–226. The trial was a sham, complete with forged documents. The reputation of Nikolayevich Tukhachevsky was only rehabilitated in 1957.

66   See Weatherford, *Genghis Khan*, pp. 295–296. Subetai retired to his encampment on the Tuul River near modern Ulaanbaatar and died in 1248 at the age of seventy-two.

67   See Morgan, *Mongols*, pp. 88–90, and Timothy May, *The Mongol Art of War: Chinggis Khan and the Mongol Military System* (Yardley, PA, 2007), for organization of army.

68   See Morgan, *Mongols*, pp. 90–91, and May, *Mongol Art of War*, pp. 58–85.

69   See Morgan, *Mongols*, p. 90, and Ratchnevsky, *Genghis Khan*, pp. 92–94, for the officers drawn from bodyguard (*keshig*).

70   See Peter Jackson, *The Mongols and the Islamic World from Conquest to Conversion* (New Haven, 2017), pp. 154–173, for the best analysis of the Mongol use of terror and assessment of the numbers of people massacred reported in the sources.

71   See Ratchnevsky, *Genghis Khan*, p. 117.

72   See Jackson, *The Mongols and the Islamic World*, pp. 169–173.

73   Ratchnevsky, *Genghis Khan*, p. 164.

74   See Barfield, *Perilous Frontier*, pp. 183–184, for the Jin emperors pursuing a traditional policy of *divide et impera* ("divide and conquer") on the

steppes. See also Prawdin, *Mongol Empire*, pp. 82–83, for the reception of the news of coronation of Genghis Khan in 1206. See Ratchnevsky, *Genghis Khan*, pp. 105–106, who stresses Genghis Khan saw the Jin emperors as personal foes.

19 Genghis Khan, the World Conqueror

1   See Kahn, *Secret History*, pp. 114–135, recording the words of Genghis Khan in bestowing rewards and pronouncing laws. See also Prawdin, *Mongol Empire*, pp. 166–168 and Weatherford, *Genghis Khan*, pp. 3–9.

2   Prawdin, *Mongol Empire*, pp. 165–166.

3   See Ratchnevsky, *Genghis Khan*, pp. 131–132, and Weatherford, *Genghis Khan*, pp. 3–9.

4   See Ratchnevsky, *Genghis Khan*, p. 131, for conscription of males into hashar service in future sieges. See Prawdin, *Mongol Empire*, pp. 170–173, for the assault of Samarkand.

5   See Frye, "Samanids," *Cambridge History of Iran*, IV, pp. 142–143, for literary culture of the city and its renowned library. See Grabar, "Visual Arts," *ibid.*, pp. 331–343, for Samanid architecture.

6   See J. Spencer Trimingham, *The Sufi Orders in Islam* (Oxford, 1998), pp. 63–65.

7   See G. Michell, *Architecture of the Islamic World* (London, 1995), pp. 258–259. Mohammad Arslan Khan had constructed the minaret in 1127.

8   See Prawdin, *Mongol Empire*, pp. 174–178.

9   See Weatherford, *Genghis Khan*, pp. 142–145.

10 See Bowsorth, *History of Turkic Peoples*, pp. 225–228, and Jackson, *Mongols and Islamic World*, pp. 46–70.

11 See Ratchnevsky, *Genghis Khan*, pp. 101–105, and Prawdin, *Mongol Empire*, pp. 103–107.

12 See Ratchnevsky, *Genghis Khan*, pp. 96–101, and Prawdin, *Mongol Empire*, pp. 97–101.

13 See Ratchnevsky, *Genghis Khan*, pp. 92–94.

14 See May, *Mongol Way of War*, pp. 36–38.

15 See Ratchnevsky, *Genghis Khan*, pp. 90–92 and 95–96.

16 See Agnes Birtalan, "Ritual of Sworn Brotherhood (Mong, anda bol-, Oir, and Ax düü bol-) in Mongol Historic and Epic Tradition," *Chronica. Annual of the Institute of History, University Szeged.* 7–8. (2007–2008), pp. 44–56.

17 See May, *Mongol Way of War*, pp. 32–36.

18 See *ibid.*, pp. 57–60 and 89–90.

19 See Mote, *Imperial China*, p. 427, and Barfield, *Perilous Frontier*, pp. 194–195.

20   See Weatherford, *Genghis Khan*, pp. 67–77.

21   See Prawdin, *Mongol Empire*, pp. 105–107 and 113–115.

22   See Dunnel, "Hsi Hsia," *Cambridge History of China*, VI, p. 207.

23   See Ratchnevsky, *Genghis Khan*, p. 104, and Prawdin, *Mongol Empire*, pp. 107–108.

24   See "Hsi Hsia," *Cambridge History of China*, VI, pp. 208–209.

25   See *ibid.*, p. 208, Barfield, *Perilous Frontier*, p. 199, and Mote, *Imperial China*, p. 255.

26   See Ratchnevsky, *Genghis Khan*, pp. 108–109, and Weatherford, *Genghis Khan*, pp. 81–84.

27   See Ratchnevsky, *Genghis Khan*, pp. 109–110, and Prawdin, *Mongol Empire*, pp. 117–122.

28   See Mote, *Imperial China*, pp. 283–288.

29   See Ratchnevsky, *Genghis Khan*, pp. 107–108, and Mote, *Imperial China*, pp. 242–243, for the decline in the professionalism and training of the Jin army.

30   See Mote, *Imperial China*, pp. 236–243, and Barfield, *Perilous Frontier*, pp. 181–182, for disaffection of the Han Chinese, Uyhgur, and Khitan subjects of the Jin emperor.

31   See Prawdin, *Mongol Empire*, p. 119, and Man, *Great Wall*, p. 165. See *ibid.*, pp. 166–169, for the Mongols easily overrunning the Great Wall and Jin defenses.

32   Weatherford, *Genghis Khan*, p. 90.

33   See Ratchnevsky, *Genghis Khan*, p. 110. When Genghis Khan refused to negotiate, the Jin envoy Ming'an promptly defected and entered the service of Genghis Khan.

34   See Ratchnevsky, *Genghis Khan*, p. 110, for the wounding of Genghis Khan.

35   Ratchnevsky, *Genghis Khan*, p. 110–111.

36   Ratchnevsky, *Genghis Khan*, p. 112, and Franke, "Chin Dynasty," *Cambridge History of China*, V, pp. 252–254.

37   Ratchnevsky, *Genghis Khan*, p. 114.

38   See Ratchnevsky, *Genghis Khan*, pp. 114–115, and Weatherford, *Genghis Khan*, pp. 96–97.

39   See Prawdin, *Mongol Empire*, pp. 138–139.

40   Prawdin, *Mongol Empire*, pp. 139–140, and Weatherford, *Genghis Khan*, pp. 97–100.

41   See *ibid.*, pp. 101–107.

42   See Prawdin, *Mongol Empire*, pp. 130–135.

43   See Ratchnevsky, *Genghis Khan*, pp. 115–116.

44   See *ibid.*, pp. 116–117.

45   See *ibid.*, p. 117.

46   See Biran, *Qara Khitai*, pp. 60–74.

47   See Ratchnevsky, *Genghis Khan*, p. 86, and Weatherford, *Genghis Khan*, p. 62.

48   See Biran, *Qara Khitai*, pp. 76–77.

49   See *ibid.*, pp. 77–78.

50   Se *ibid.*, pp. 78–79.

51   See *ibid.*, pp. 80–84.

52   See *ibid.*, pp. 82 and 194–196.

53   See Ratchnevsky, *Genghis Khan*, pp. 118–119, Weatherford, *Genghis Khan*, pp. 103–104, and Prawdin, *Mongol Empire*, pp. 145–146.

54   See Ratchnevsky, *Genghis Khan*, p. 119.

55   See *ibid.*, pp. 120–121, and Weatherford, *Genghis Khan*, pp. 105–106.

56   See Ratchnevsky, *Genghis Khan*, pp. 119–120, and Prawdin, *Mongol Empire*, pp. 143–149.

57   See Ratchnevsky, *Genghis Khan*, pp. 122–123, and Prawdin, *Mongol Empire*, pp. 155–156.

58   See *ibid.*, pp. 164–166.

59   See Jackson, *Mongols and Islamic World*, pp. 51–54. Muhammad Shah's perception of the Mongols was based on Islamic views of the Turkish nomads.

60   See Kennedy, *Armies of Caliphs*, pp. 168–182. The slave soldiers of Muhammad Shah were comparable to those of the Abbasid Caliph and Samanid emirs.

61   See James M. Powell, *Anatomy of a Crusade, 1213-1221* (Philadelphia, 1986), pp. 157–173, and Runciman, *History of Crusades*, III, pp. 156–162, for the advance of the Fifth Crusade in 1219. See Jackson, *Mongols and Islamic World*, pp. 43–45 and 73, for Muslim perceptions of the Crusader threat. Hence, Muhammad Shah spent most of his reign conquering Iran and Iraq so that he could obtain the fatwa of the Abbasid Caliph to champion jihad against the Crusaders; see Prawdin, *Mongol Empire*, pp. 154–156.

62   See Joinville and Villehardouin, *Chronicles of the Crusades*, translated by M. R. B Shaw (New York, 1963), pp. 245. Jean de Joinville, who fell captive during the Seventh Crusade, was spared because of his kinship to Frederick II, whom the Muslims respected as a great sovereign.

63   See Powell, *Anatomy of Crusade*, pp. 175–194, and Runciman, *History of Crusades*, III, pp. 165–170. Pope Gregory IX, frustrated by the emperor's repeated delays, excommunicated Frederick II in 1228; see *ibid.*, pp. 178–179.

64   See Prawdin, *Mongol Empire*, pp. 157–159, and May, *Mongol Way of War*, pp. 54–57.

65 See Prawdin, *Mongol Empire*, pp. 164–166, and Jackson, *Mongols and Islamic World*, pp. 77–78.

66 See Prawdin, *Mongol Empire*, pp. 166 and 171–172, and Jackson, *Mongols and Islamic World*, p. 78.

67 See *ibid.*, p. 78, and John Man, *Genghis Khan: Life, Death, and Resurrection* (New York, 2007), p. 163, but the incident may be apocryphal.

68 See Prawdin, *Mongol Empire*, pp. 165 and 170.

69 See Jackson, *Mongols and Islamic World*, pp. 76–77 and 89–92, and Weatherford, *Genghis Khan*, pp. 113–117, for the terms offered cities that surrendered and punishment for those cities that resisted.

70 See Ratchnevsky, *Genghis Khan*, pp. 132–133, and Prawdin, *Mongol Empire*, pp. 170–171.

71 See Ratchnevsky, *Genghis Khan*, p. 135, and Jackson, *Mongols and Islamic World*, p. 78.

72 See John Fennell, *The Crisis of Medieval Russia, 1200-1304* (London, 1983), pp. 64–68.

73 See Prawdin, *Mongol Empire*, pp. 173–176, and J. A. Boyle, "The Political and Dynastic History of the Il-Khans," *Cambridge History of Iran*, V, pp. 312–314.

74 See Prawdin, *Mongol Empire*, p. 176, and Jackson, *Mongols and Islamic World*, p. 80.

75 See Prawdin, *Mongol Empire*, pp. 176–177, and Jackson, *Mongols and Islamic World*, p. 80. For the atrocities committed in the sack of Nishapur, see Weatherford, *Genghis Khan*, pp. 117–118, and Boyle, "Political History," *Cambridge History of Iran*, V, p. 314.

76 See Ratchnevsky, *Genghis Khan*, pp. 163–165, Prawdin, *Mongol Empire*, pp. 193–194, and Weatherford, *Genghis Khan*, pp. 117–119.

77 See Ratchnevsky, *Genghis Khan*, pp. 133–134, Jackson, *Mongols and Islamic World*, p. 80, and Prawdin, *Mongol Empire*, pp. 185–186.

78 See Ratchnevsky, *Genghis Khan*, p. 134, Boyle, "Political History," *Cambridge History of Iran*, V, pp. 318–319, and Prawdin, *Mongol Empire*, pp. 194–197.

79 See Boyle, "Political History," *Cambridge History of Iran*, V, pp. 319–320, Jackson, *Mongols and the Islamic World*, p. 80, and Prawdin, *Mongol Empire*, pp. 197–199.

80 Prawdin, *Mongol Empire*, pp. 179–181.

81 See Ratchnevsky, *Genghis Khan*, pp. 140–141, and Mote, *Imperial China*, pp. 255–256.

82 See Jackson, *Mongols and Islamic World*, pp. 153–181, and Thomas T. Allsen, *Culture and Conquest in Mongol Eurasia* (Cambridge, 2001), pp. 41–50.

83 See Saunders, *History of Medieval Islam*, pp. 170–176, and see also Jackson,

Mongols and Islamic World, pp. 22–40, for the Islamic historical traditions concerning the Mongols.

84   See Golden, *History of Turkic Peoples*, pp. 307–308.

85   See Claude Cahen, "Mongols and the Near East," *History of Crusades*, II, pp. 729–730.

86   See Cahen, *Pre-Ottoman Turkey*, pp. 192–193, 214–215, and 351–358. Jalāl al-Dīn Rūmī (1207–1273) was born in Balkh, and his family fled to Nishapur in 1218–1219, then to Baghdad, and finally to Karaman in Asia Minor by 1225. In 1228, the Seljuk Sultan Ala ad-Dīn Kayqubad (1220–1237) invited Baha ud-Dīn Walad to settle in Konya.

87   See Golden, *History of the Turkic Peoples*, pp. 357–358.

88   See Silverberg, *Realm of Prester John*, pp. 71–73, and Brewer, *Prester John*, pp. 98–100.

89   See Prawdin, *Mongol Empire*, pp. 189–190, and Gabriel, *Subotai the Valient*, pp. 90–96.

90   See Kuhn, *Secret History*, pp. 154–156. See also Weatherford, *Genghis Khan*, pp. 120–123, Prawdin, *Mongol Empire*, pp. 225–227, and Jackson, *Mongols and Islamic World*, pp. 97–100.

91   See Weatherford, *Genghis Khan*, p. 123.

92   See Weatherford, *Genghis Khan*, pp. 124–125, Jackson, *Mongols and Islamic World*, pp. 78 and 89, and Boyle, "Political History," *Cambridge History of Iran*, V, p. 317.

93   See Weatherford, *Genghis Khan*, pp. 124–125. See also Jackson, *Mongols and Islamic World*, p. 104, Genghis Khan conferring the city on Jochi.

94   See Kuhn, *Secret History*, pp. 158–159. See also Weatherford, *Genghis Khan*, pp. 124–125, and Boyle, "Political History," *Cambridge History of Iran*, V, p. 319.

95   See Beatrice Forbes Manz, "Temür and the Early Timurids to c. 1450," *Cambridge History of Inner Asia*, pp. 185–186.

96   See Ratchnevsky, *Genghis Khan*, pp. 136–137, and Prawdin, *Mongol Empire*, pp. 218–220.

97   See Morgan, *Mongols*, pp. 112–114, and Jackson, *Mongols and the Islamic World*, pp. 96–100.

20 Batu and the Devil's Horsemen

1   See Gabriel, *Subotai the Valiant*, pp. 98–99. See Prawdin, *Mongol Empire*, p. 217, and Weatherford, *Genghis Khan*, pp. 139–140.

2   See Gabriel, *Subotai the Valiant*, pp. 99–101. See also John Fennell, *The Crisis of Medieval Russia, 1200-1304* (London, 1983), p. 66.

3   See Mote, *Imperial China*, pp. 434–436; Gabriel, *Subotai the Valiant*, pp. 101–102; and Weatherford, *Genghis Khan*, pp. 140–142.

4   See Charles Halperin, *Russia and the Golden Horde: The Mongol Impact on Medieval Russian History* (Bloomington, 1987), pp. 64–74 and 126–130, and Fennell, *Crisis of Medieval Russia*, pp. 162–168, for the Russian view of Tartar yoke.

5   From *Chronicle of Novgorod*; translation by Serge A. Zenkovsky, *Medieval Russia's Epics, Chronicles and Tales*, revised edition (New York, 1974), p. 196.

6   See Prawdin, *Mongol Empire*, pp. 211–220, and Weatherford, *Genghis Khan*, pp. 139–143.

7   See Prawdin, *Mongol Empire*, pp. 211–214.

8   See Weatherford, *Genghis Khan*, pp. 142–145. See Jackson, *The Mongols and the West* (London, 2005), pp. 45–47, noting that the campaign was waged to advance an ideology of world conquest.

9   See Morgan, *Mongols*, pp. 108–111, and Jackson, *Mongols and Islamic World*, pp. 95–97, for the diversity of the empire and the challenge confronting Ögedei.

10   See Mote, *Imperial China*, pp. 436–439, for Ögedei's apprecation of Chinese civilization. See also Michael C. Bose, "Uyghur Technologists of Writing and Literacy in Mongol China," *T'oung Pao*, Ser. 2, 91 (2005), pp. 396–435, for the prevalence of literacy among the heirs of Genghis Khan in the second and third generations and members of the aristocracy.

11   See David Morgan, "Who Ran the Mongol Empire?" *Journal of the Royal Asiatic Society* 2 (1982), p. 135. See Weatherford, *Genghis Khan*, p. 90, for the career of Yelü Chucai.

12   See Morgan, "Who Ran the Mongol Empire?" *Journal of the Royal Asiatic Society* 2 (1982), pp. 124–136. See also Prawdin, *Mongol Empire*, pp. 238–240, and Golden, "Rise of Chinggisids," *The Cambridge History of Inner Asia*, pp. 33–36.

13   See Prawdin, *Mongol Empire*, p. 240, and Michael Rossabi, *Khubilai Khan: His Life and Times* (Berkeley, 1988), pp. 123–124. The Mongols adopted the paper currency (*jiaochao*) issued by the Jin Emperors. For the origins and development of paper currency, see John Pickering, "The History of Paper Money in China," *Journal of the American Oriental Society* 1. 2 (1844), pp. 136–142.

14   See Weatherford, *Genghis Khan*, pp. 132–133.

15   See *ibid.*, pp. 133–136, and Mote, *Imperial China*, p. 435, for the construction of Karakorum. For excavations by the German team of archaeologists, see Helmut R. Roth, ed., *Qara Qorum-City (Mongolia). 1: Preliminary Report of the Excavations* (Bonn, 2002). The excavation team maintains a website: https://dbpedia.org/page/Karakorum.

16   Prawdin, *Mongol Empire*, pp. 240–244.

17   See Weatherford, *Genghis Khan*, pp. 136–139.

18   See J. J. Saunders, *The History of the Mongol Conquests* (Philadelphia, 1971), pp. 75–76, and Mote, *Imperial China*, p. 248. The Song emperor Lizong

rejected overtures from the Jin emperor Aizong to make common cause against the Mongols.

19 See Saunders, *History of Mongol Conquests*, pp. 75–76, and Wang Tseng-Yü, "A History of the Sung Military," *Cambridge History of China*, V. 2, pp. 247–248.

20 See Weatherford, *Genghis Khan*, pp. 150–152, and Prawdin, *Mongol Empire*, pp. 250–251.

21 See Ross and Thomsen, "The Orkhon Inscriptions," *Bulletin of the School of Oriental Studies, University of London* 5 (1930), pp. 864–865.

22 See Peter Jackson, *The Mongols and the West* (Harlow, 2005), pp. 45–49, Weatherford, *Genghis Khan*, pp. 142–145, and Fennell, *Crisis of Medieval Russia*, p. 77.

23 See Prawdin, *Mongol Empire*, pp. 240–244, and Saunders, *History of Mongol Conquests*, pp. 76–77.

24 See Prawdin, *Mongol Empire*, pp. 249–251, and Denis Sinor, "The Mongols in the West," *Journal of Asian History* 33 (1999), pp. 6–7.

25 See Carpini, "History of Mongols," *Mission to Asia*, p. 57.

26 See Saunders, *History of Mongol Conquests*, pp. 81–82.

27 See Saunders, *History of Mongol Conquests*, p. 81.

28 See Saunders, *History of Mongol Conquests*, p. 82, and Sinor, "Mongols in West," *Journal of Asian History* 33 (1999), pp. 9–10.

29 See Jackson, *Mongols and West*, pp. 47–49.

30 See Fennell, *Crisis of Medieval Russia*, pp. 75–76, for the disunity among the princes of Russia.

31 See May, *Mongol Art of War*, pp. 78–80.

32 L. R. Partington, *A History of Greek Fire and Gunpowder* (Baltimore, 1999), pp. 176–177, 242–246, and 262–265. Batu's Chinese engineers employed fire arrows (nicknamed "flying dragons"), ignited by black powder and hurled by torsion artillery. The Southern Song army had devised this siege technology in the twelfth century.

33 See Fennell, *Crisis of Medieval Russia*, pp. 78–79, and Saunders, *History of Mongol Conquests*, pp. 82–83.

34 See Fennell, *Crisis of Medieval Russia*, p. 79.

35 See Robert Michell and Nevill Forbes, trans., *The Chronicle of Novgorod, 1016–1471* (London, 1914), pp. 31–32, and Prawdin, *Mongol Empire*, p. 250.

36 See Michell and Forbes, *Chronicle of Novgorod*, pp. 33–34. See also Fennell, *Crisis of Medieval Russia*, pp. 79–80, and Runciman, *History of the Crusades*, III, p. 251.

37 See Janet Martin, *Medieval Russia 980–1584* (Cambridge, 1995), pp. 138–

139. The prime source for the battle is Robert Michell and Nevill Forbes, eds., *The Chronicle of Novgorod* (London, 1914), p. 83.

38   See Jackson, *Mongols*, pp. 68–75, for Mongols overrunning Russia and Eastern Europe in 1238–1241. For suffering and demographic impact, see Charles J. Halperin, *Russia and the Golden Horde: The Mongol Impact on Medieval Russian History* (Bloomington, 1985), pp. 75–86.

39   See Saunders, *History of Mongol Conquests*, p. 101.

40   See *ibid.*, pp. 84–85, and Sinor, "Mongols in West," *Journal of Asian History* 33 (1999), pp. 11.

41   See George Perfecky, *The Hypatian Codex* (Munich, 1973), pp. 43–49. The Hypatian Codex, dating from 1425, preserves excerpts of three older chronicles reporting events of the twelfth through fourteenth centuries. It reports only two thousand of the fifty thousand residents of Kiev survived the massacre.

42   See Jackson, *Mongols and West*, pp. 51–63.

43   See Peter Jackson, "Medieval Christendom's Encounter with the Alien," *Historical Research* 74 (2001), pp. 353–354, for Pseudo-Methodius's classification of nomadic barbarians as Ishmaelites and offsprings of Gog and Magog. See Benjamin Garstad, ed. and trans., *Apocalypse of Pseudo-Methodius. An Alexandrian World Chronicle* (Cambridge, MA, 2012), pp. 15–52, for the vilification of the Ishmaelites.

44   Matthew Paris, *Chronica Maiora*, anno 1240; see translation by John Allen, *Matthew Paris's English History from 1235 to 1273* (London, 1852), pp. 253–257. Translation available online at https://archive.org/details/matthewparissen01rishgoog/page/256/mode/2up. See also Silverberg, *Realm of Prester John*, pp. 74–76, and Weatherford, *Genghis Khan*, pp. 148–149.

45   See Halperin, *Russia and Golden Horde*, pp. 87–103.

46   See *ibid.*, pp. 77–86 and 90–103.

47   See Isabel de Madariaga, *Ivan the Terrible, First Tsar of Russia* (New Haven, 2005), pp. 86–89, and Robert L. Frost, *The Northern Wars, 1558–1721* (Harlow, Essex, 2000), pp. 16–22, for the military innovations of Ivan IV, the Terrible.

48   See de Madariaga, *Ivan the Terrible*, pp. 92–106, and Michael Khodarkovsky, *Russia's Steppe Frontier: Making of a Colonial Empire, 1500–1800* (Bloomington, 2002), pp. 100–125.

49   See W. Bruce Lincoln, *The Conquest of a Continent: Siberia and the Russians* (Ithaca, NY, 1994), pp. 33–72, and Khodarkovsky, *Russia's Steppe*, pp. 126–184.

50   See Saunders, *History of Mongol Conquest*, p. 84, and Weatherford, *Genghis Khan*, pp. 150–152.

51   See Saunders, *History of Mongol Conquests*, p. 85, and Sinor, "The Mongols in the West," *Journal of Asian History* 33 (1999), pp. 11–13.

52 See Jackson, *Mongols and West*, p. 63, and Saunders, *History of the Mongol Conquests*, p. 85. For the Medieval sources, see Radosław Liwoch, "The Mongols in Poland in the 13th century. Traces of the Invasions," *Archaeology of Conflicts*, edited by Pavel Drnovský and Petr Hejhal (Červený Kostelec, 2020), pp. 55–67.

53 See Saunders, *History of the Mongol Conquests*, p. 85, and Gabriel, *Subotai the Valiant*, p. 112.

54 See Saunders, *History of Mongol Conquests*, p. 85.

55 See Gabriel, *Subotai the Valiant*, pp. 112–121; Jackson, *Mongols and West*, pp. 63–64; and Prawdin, *Mongol Empire*, pp. 257–259.

56 Prawdin, *Mongol Empire*, p. 259.

57 See Saunders, *History of the Mongol Conquests*, pp. 85–86; Z. J. Kosztolnyik, *Hungary in the Thirteenth Century* (New York, 1996), pp. 152–153; and Prawdin, *Mongol Empire*, pp. 260–261.

58 See Prawdin, *Mongol Empire*, pp. 261–262.

59 Sinor, "The Mongols in the West," *Journal of Asian History* 33 (1999), p. 14.

60 See Prawdin, *Mongol Empire*, pp. 263–264, and Gabriel, *Subotai the Valiant*, pp. 122–123.

61 See Saunders, *History of Mongol Conquests*, p. 86; Kosztolnyik, *Hungary*, pp. 156–157; and Gabriel, *Subotai the Valiant*, p. 123.

62 See *ibid.*, pp. 124–125, and Kosztolnyik, *Hungary*, pp. 158–159.

63 See Prawdin, *Mongol Empire*, pp. 264–265, and Weatherford, *Genghis Khan*, pp. 154–155. See Curta, *Southeastern Europe*, pp. 312–413, noting that the devastation was comparable to the later Black Death. The Italian prelate Roger of Torre Maggiore, who witnessed the invasion, wrote *Carmen Miserabile super Destructione Regni Hungariae per Tartaro* (*Song of Lamentation of the Destruction of the Kingdom of Hungary*).

64 See Thomas of Spalato, *Historia* 161, and see also Gabriel, *Subotai the Valiant*, p. 124. Hungarian losses are reported at fifty thousand to seventy thousand out of a force of eighty thousand.

65 See Curta, *Southeastern Europe*, pp. 410–112; Weatherford, *Genghis Khan*, pp. 155–156; and Prawdin, *Mongol Empire*, p. 265.

66 See Kosztolnyik, *Hungary*, p. 169, and Prawdin, *Mongol Empire*, p. 267.

67 See Saunders, *History of the Mongol Conquests*, p. 233, note 48, and Kosztolnyik, *Hungary*, pp. 151–168. For Mongol use of disinformation, see Jackson, *Mongols and West*, pp. 47–49.

68 See Saunders, *History of the Mongol Conquests*, pp. 87–88, and Sinor, "The Mongols in the West," *Journal of Asian History* 33 (1999), pp. 19–20, stressing losses in battles and logistics as the prime reasons for the withdrawal.

69 See Saunders, *History of the Mongol Conquests*, pp. 86–87.

70 See Weatherford, *Genghis Khan*, pp. 158–159, and Jack Weatherford, *The

Secret History of the Mongol Queens: How the Daughters of Genghis Khan Rescued his Empire (New York, 2010), pp. 95–96. But see Jackson, *Mongols and Islamic World*, pp. 106–107, for a more judicious assessment of the role of Mongol princesses during succession crises.

71   See Weatherford, *Mongol Queens*, pp. 96–100.

72   See Jackson, *Mongols and Islamic World*, pp. 100–106, stressing how succession crises limited Mongol expansion.

73   See Carpini, "History of Mongols," *Mission to Asia*, pp. 32–38 and 43–59.

74   See DeVries, *Medieval Military Technology*, pp. 213–250, and Philippe Contamine, *War in the Middle Ages*, translated by Michael Jones (Oxford, 1984), pp. 101–115.

75   See W. L. Warren, *King John* (Berkeley, 1961), pp. 57–59 and 96–99, for his castle building and loss of Normandy in 1202–1204.

76   See Runciman, *History of Crusades*, III, pp. 175–176, who has penned the best description of Frederick II.

77   See Contamine, *War in the Middle Ages*, pp. 65–100, for the arms, organization, and tactics of Western armies in the thirteenth century.

78   See David Abulafia, *Frederick II: A Medieval Emperor* (Oxford, 1988), pp. 355 and 359–360.

79   Kosztolnyik, *Hungary*, pp. 170–171.

80   See David Abulafia, *Frederick II: A Medieval Emperor* (Oxford, 1988), p. 25. See also Jackson, *Mongols and West*, p. 68, for rumors that Frederick considered recruiting Mongols as allies against the Papacy.

81   See Abulafia, *Frederick II*, p. 267.

82   Thomas Curtis van Cleve, *The Emperor Frederick II of Hohenstaufen, Immutator Mundi* (Oxford, 1972), pp. 392–409, and Abulafia, *Frederick II*, pp. 290–307.

83   See van Cleve, *Frederick II*, pp. 405–407, and Abulafia, *Frederick II*, pp. 303–305.

84   See Abulafia, *Frederick II*, p. 359, and van Cleve, *Frederick II*, pp. 434–435.

85   See Abulafia, *Frederick II*, pp. 359–360.

86   See *ibid.*, p. 355.

87   See Abulafia, *Frederick II*, p. 359, and van Cleve, *Frederick II*, pp. 434–435.

88   See Abulafia, *Frederick II*, pp. 380–389. For the destruction of the Hohenstaufen monarchy, see Norman Housley, *The Italian Crusades: The Papal-Angevin Alliance and the Crusade against the Christian Lay Powers, 1254–1343* (Oxford, 1982), pp. 15–34.

89   See Abulafia, *Frederick II*, p. 366–373.

90   See de Rachewiltz, *Papal Envoys*, pp. 84 and 110–112.

21 The Mongol Sack of Baghdad

1   See Prawdin, *Mongol Empire*, pp. 308–309, and Jackson, *Mongols and Islamic World*, p. 130.

2   See Saunders, *History of Mongol Conquests*, p. 110.

3   See *ibid.*, pp. 109–110. Hulagu and his older brother, the Great Khan Möngke, had agreed that the expedition's aim was to destroy any Muslim spiritual authority that might oppose Mongol rule.

4   Marco Polo, *The Description of the World*, translated by Sharon Kinoshita (Indianapolis, 2016), chapter 25, pp. 20–21. The story was circulated among Christian writers soon after the capture of the city. See Saunders, *History of the Mongol Conquests*, p. 231, note 76, and J. A. Boyle, "The Death of the Last Abbasid Caliph," *Journal of Semitic Studies* 6 (1961), pp. 145–161.

5   See Saunders, *History of Mongol Conquests*, p. 231, note 75.

6   See Weatherford, *Genghis Khan*, pp. 181 and 183–184.

7   See Prawdin, *Mongol Empire*, pp. 359–360, and Saunders, *History of Mongol Conquests*, pp. 111–112.

8   See Runciman, *History of the Crusades*, I, pp. 285–288.

9   See Jackson, *Mongols and Islamic World*, pp. 348–349.

10 See *ibid.*, pp. 353–380.

11 See Prawdin, *Mongol Empire*, pp. 303–304, and Jackson, *Mongols and Islam*, pp. 125–126.

12 See Jackson, *Mongols and Islamic World*, pp. 97–98.

13 See Jack Weatherford, *The Secret History of the Mongol Queens: How the Daughters of Genghis Khan Rescured his Empire* (New York, 2010), pp. 93–94.

14 See Mote, *Imperial China*, p. 446, and Weatherford, *Genghis Khan*, p. 143.

15 See Weatherford, *Mongol Queens*, pp. 95–99.

16 See Jackson, *Mongols and West*, pp. 100–101, and Weatherford, *Genghis Khan*, p. 165.

17 See Weatherford, *Genghis Khan*, pp. 167–168.

18 Weatherford, *Mongol Queens*, pp. 95 and 99–100, for the clash between Güyük and Töregene. Güyük resented the influence of his mother's protégée counselor Fatima, a Shi'ite Persian or Tajik.

19 See Prawdin, *Mongol Empire*, pp. 292–293, for Ögedei preferring Shiremum over Güyük.

20 See William of Rubruck, "Journey," *Mission to Asia*, chapter 30, pp. 175–181.

21 See Weatherford, *Mongol Queens*, p. 101.

22   See Jackson, *Mongols and West*, p. 103.

23   See Mote, *Imperial China*, p. 447, and Weatherford, *Genghis Khan*, pp. 165–166.

24   See Weatherford, *Mongol Queens*, pp. 101–105, who fails to account for the crucial role of Batu in assisting Sorgkaghtani Beki to assume the regency.

25   See Weatherford, *Genghis Khan*, pp. 165–167.

26   See *ibid.*, pp. 167–170, and *Mongol Queens*, pp. 108–110.

27   See *ibid.*, pp. 106–108.

28   See Jackson, *Mongols and Islamic World*, pp. 122–123.

29   See William of Rubruck, "Journey," *Mission to Asia*, chapter 30, pp. 175–176. See also Weatherford, *Genghis Khan*, pp. 199–200.

30   See Prawdin, *Mongol Empire*, pp. 303–304, and Weatherford, *Genghis Khan*, pp. 131–135.

31   See Jackson, *Mongols and Islamic World,* pp. 107–113.

32   See Runciman, *History of Crusades*, III, pp. 249–250.

33   See Saunders, *History of Mongol Conquests*, p. 78, and Jackson, *Mongols and Islamic World*, pp. 81–83.

34   See Saunders, *History of Mongol Conquests*, p. 61, and Runciman, *History of Crusades*, III, p. 250.

35   See Saunders, *History of Mongol Conquests*, pp. 78–79; Jackson, *Mongols and Islamic World*, pp. 82–83; and Runciman, *History of Crusades*, III, p. 250.

36   See Claude Cahen, "The Turks in Iran and Anatolia before the Mongol Invasions," *History of Crusades*, II, pp. 672–674.

37   See Runciman, *History of Crusades*, III, pp. 224–226.

38   See Cahen, *Pre-Ottoman Europe*, pp. 135–136.

39   See *ibid.*, pp. 136–137, and Talbot Rice, *Seljuks*, pp. 74–75.

40   See Claude, *Pre-Ottoman Turkey*, pp. 269–314.

41   See Saunders, *History of Mongol Conquests*, pp. 79–80. King Hethum of Cilician Armenia (1226–1270) sent envoys to Karakorum in hopes of convincing the Mongol court, then dominated by Töregene, to back his alliance with the princes of Outremer to recapture Jerusalem.

42   See Jackson, *Mongols and Islamic West*, p. 121.

43   See *ibid.*, pp. 133–142, for the advantages of Hulagu's army over its opponents.

44   See Saunders, *History of Mongol Conquests*, pp. 108–109, and Weatherford, *Genghis Khan*, pp. 177–178.

45   See A. C. Boyle, "Dynastic and Political History of the Il-Khans," *Cambridge History of Iran*, V, pp. 340–341. The army pitched camp in the grasslands immediately east of the city.

46 See Marshall G. S. Hodgson, *The Secret Order of the Assassins: The Struggle of the Early Nizari Ismailis Against the Islamic World* (Philadelphia, 2008), pp. 41–78 and 115–120, and Bernard Lewis, *The Assassins: A Radical Sect in Islam* (New York, 2008), pp. 64–89.

47 See Hodgson, *Assassins*, pp. 260–263, and Lewis, *Assassins*, pp. 93–94.

48 See Hodgson, *Assassins*, pp. 82–83, 110–114, and 133–138. See also Lewis, *Assassins*, pp. 10–12, and "Isma'lites and Assassins," *History of Crusades*, I, pp. 108–11.

49 See Bernard, *Assassins*, pp. 95–96. See also Hodgson, *Assassins*, pp. 22–28, for the hostile Sunni writers about the sect who approved of the order's destruction.

50 See Bernard, *Assassins*, pp. 94–95.

51 See Jackson, *Mongols and Islamic World*, pp. 128–129, and Saunders, *History of Mongol Conquests*, p. 110.

52 See Jackson, *Mongols and Islamic World*, pp. 129–130; Prawdin, *Mongol Empire*, pp. 308–309; and Saunders, *History of Mongol Conquest*, p. 110.

53 See Weatherford, *Genghis Khan*, pp. 182–183.

54 See Prawdin, *Mongol Empire*, pp. 308–309, and Jackson, *Mongols and Islamic World*, p. 130.

55 See Jackson, *Mongols and Islamic World*, p. 130.

56 See Saunders, *History of Mongol Conquests*, pp. 112–113.

57 See *ibid.*, p. 130, and Reuven Amitai-Preiss, *Mongols and Mamluks: The Mamluk-Ilkhanid War, 1260–1281* (Cambridge, 1995), pp. 26–27.

58 See Jackson, *Mongols and Islamic World*, p. 130, and H. A. R. Gibb, "The Ayyubids," *History of Crusades*, p. 714.

59 See Jackson, *Mongols and Islamic World*, p. 130.

60 See Weatherford, *Genghis Khan*, pp. 184–185, and Runciman, *History of Crusades*, III, pp. 307–308.

61 David O. Morgan, "Mongols in Syria," *Crusade and Settlement*, edited by P. W. Edbury (Cardiff, 1985), pp. 231–235, and Amitai-Preiss, *Mongols and Mamluks*, pp. 28–29.

62 See Louise B. Robbert, "Venice and the Crusades," *History of Crusades*, V, pp. 408–445, and William H. McNeill, *Venice, The Hinge of Europe, 1081–1797* (Chicago, 1974), pp. 52–57. Venetian vessels supplied the Ayyubid and Mamluk regimes in Cairo with metals, timber, grain, and slaves for the Mamluk army.

63 See Runciman, *History of Crusades*, III, pp. 308 and 311–312.

64 See Rossabi, *Khubilai Khan*, pp. 47–62; Prawdin, *Mongol Empire*, pp. 317–218; and Weatherford, *Genghis Khan*, pp. 187–190.

65 See Amitai-Preiss, *Mongols and Mamluks*, pp. 27–28, and Jackson, *Mongols and Islamic World*, pp. 131–132.

66   See Amitai-Preiss, *Mongols and Mamluks*, p. 36, and Jackson, *Mongols and Islamic World*, p. 132.

67   See P. M. Holt, *The Age of Crusades: The Near East from the Eleventh Century to 1517* (Harlow, Essex), pp. 86–89.

68   See Mustafa M. Ziada, "The Mamluk Sultans to 1293," *History of Crusades*, II, pp. 737–740.

69   See Runciman, *History of Crusades*, III, pp. 261–265, and Joseph R. Strayer, "The Crusades of Louis IX," *History of Crusades*, II, pp. 494–498.

70   See Runciman, *History of Crusades*, III, pp. 265–290, and Joseph R. Strayer, "The Crusades of Louis IX," *History of Crusades*, II, pp. 498–503.

71   See William C. Jordan, *Louis IX and the Challenge of the Crusade: A Study in Rulership* (Princeton, 1979), pp. 65–104, for the revenues of the French monarchy and its ability to pay for the Seventh Crusade and the ransom.

72   See Amitai-Preiss, *Mongols and Mamluks*, pp. 37–39, and Runciman, *History of Crusades*, III, pp. 311–312.

73   See Jackson, *Mongols and Islamic World*, pp. 132–133.

74   Amitai-Preiss, *Mongols and Mamluks*, pp. 39–45.

75   See Runciman, *History of Crusades*, III, pp. 324–329 and 387–425.

76   Amitai-Preiss, *Mongols and Mamluks*, pp. 46–48.

77   See *ibid.*, pp. 56–63, and Ziada, "Mamluks," *History of Crusades*, II, pp. 746–747.

22 Kublai Khan and the Unification of China

1   Polo, *Description of World*, chapter 75, pp. 64–67.

2   See Polo, *Description of World*, chapters 76 and 83, pp. 67 and 72, on greatness of Kublai Khan. See also Mote, *Imperial China*, pp. 444–445, and Laurence Bergreen, *Marco Polo from Venice to Xanadu* (New York, 2007), pp. 154–166.

3   See Polo, *Description of World*, chapter 96, pp. 86–88.

4   See Rossabi, *Khubilai Khan*, pp. 123–124, and Mote, *Imperial China*, pp. 449–451.

5   See David Morgan, "Who Ran the Mongol Empire?" *Journal of the Royal Asiatic Society* 2 (1982), p. 135, and Weatherford, *Genghis Khan*, p. 90.

6   See Rossabi, *Khubilai Khan*, pp. 28–30, and Mote, *Imperial China*, pp. 448–450.

7   See Rossabi, *Khubilai Khan*, pp. 70–75.

8   See Rossabi, *Khubilai Khan*, pp. 22–23, and Prawdin, *Mongol Empire*, pp. 303–304.

9   See Rossabi, *Khubilai Khan*, pp. 14–16 and 28–31, and Mote, *Imperial China*, pp. 450–451.

10 See Kuhn, *Age of Confucian Rule*, pp. 99–119, for the Neo-Confucian values of kingship. Chinese accounts invariably attribute the achievements of Kublai Khan to his Confucian advisers, but this is a conceit and Kublai Khan decided based on his own knowledge and judgment; see Rossabi, *Khubilai Khan*, pp. 14–16.

11 See Bin Yang, *Between Wind and Clouds: The Making of Yunnan (Second Century BCE to Twentieth Century CE)* (New York, 2009), pp. 265–276.

12 Yang, *Between Wind and Clouds*, pp. 81–92.

13 Rossabi, *Khubilai Khan*, pp. 24–25, and Prawdin, *Mongol Empire*, pp. 308–315. The *noyan* Bayan was indispensable in organizing the shipments of supplies and military equipment by river transportation.

14 See Rossabi, *Khubilai Khan*, pp. 24–25, and Mote, *Imperial China*, p. 452.

15 See Rossabi, *Khubilai Khan*, pp. 25–27; Mote, *Imperial China*, p. 452; and Yang, *Between Wind and Clouds*, pp. 277–281.

16 See Rossabi, *Khubilai Khan*, pp. 27–28.

17 See Prawdin, *Mongol Empire*, pp. 315–316, and Rossabi, *Khubilai Khan*, pp. 43–45, and "Reign of Khubilai Khan," *Cambridge History of China*, VI, p. 421.

18 See Rossabi, *Khubilai Khan*, pp. 45–46, and Weatherford, *Genghis Khan*, p. 188.

19 See Rossabi, *Khubilai Khan*, pp. 47–49, and Mote, *Imperial China*, p. 455.

20 See Rossabi, *Khubilai Khan*, p. 50, and Prawdin, *Mongol Empire*, p. 316.

21 See Rossabi, *Khubilai Khan*, pp. 47–48 and 50–51, and "Reign of Khubilai Khan," *Cambridge History of China*, VI, pp. 421–422.

22 See Rossabi, *Khubilai Khan*, pp. 55–56; "Reign of Khubilai Khan," *Cambridge History of China*, VI, pp. 423–424; and Prawdin, *Mongol Empire*, p. 318.

23 See Rossabi, *Khubilai Khan*, pp. 50–51, and Weatherford, *Genghis Khan*, pp. 189–190.

24 See Boyle, "Political History of Il-Khans," *Cambridge History of Iran*, V, pp. 353–354.

25 See Rossabi, *Khubilai Khan*, pp. 57–59, and Prawdin, *Mongol Empire*, pp. 319–320.

26 See Rossabi, *Khubilai Khan*, pp. 59–61, and "Reign of Khubilai Khan," *Cambridge History of China*, VI, p. 424.

27 See Rossabi, *Khubilai Khan*, pp. 61–62, and Weatherford, *Genghis Khan*, p. 190.

28 See Boyle, "Political History of Il-Khans," *Cambridge History of Iran*, V, pp. 354–355. Hulagu died on February 8, 1261.

29 See Rossabi, *Khubilai Khan*, pp. 59–61, and Prawdin, *Mongol Empire*, p. 321.

30 See Mote, *Imperial China*, pp. 136–144, and Charles Hartman, "Sung Government and Politics," *Cambridge History of China*, V. 2, pp. 80–138.

31 See Weatherford, *Genghis Khan*, p. 208.

32 See Richard L. Davis, *Wind Against the Mountain: The Crisis of Politics and Culture in Thirteenth-Century China* (Cambridge, MA, 1996), pp. 29–30, but in fairness to the emperor, Duzong was born with paralysis in his limbs due to the efforts of his mother, Princess Huang Dingxi, to abort the pregnancy.

33 See Mote, *Imperial China*, pp. 318–320.

34 See Tseng-Yü, "Sung Military," *Cambridge History of China*, V. 2, pp. 233–238. For fortifications and artillery of Song army, see Franke, "Siege and Defense of Towns," *Chinese Ways in Warfare*, pp. 152–179.

35 See Mote, *Imperial China*, p. 319. Given the state of the Song army and expectations of the mandarin elite, Jia Sidao pursued the only policy acceptable to the court.

36 See Rossabi, *Khubilai Khan*, pp. 77 and 104–105.

37 See Morris Rossabi, "The Reign of Khubilai Khan," *Cambridge History of China*, VI, p. 433, and *Khubilai Khan*, p. 86. Kublai's nephew and Ilkhan Abaqa Khan (1262–1282) sent the unit of Arab and Persian engineers commanded by the veteran officers Ismma'il and Ala ad-Din.

38 See Rossabi, *Khubilai Khan*, pp. 83–84, and Mote, *Imperial China*, p. 461–462.

39 See Rossabi, *Khubilai Khan*, p. 25, and Prawdin, *Mongol Empire*, p. 322, for Bayan as commander.

40 See Tseng-Yü, "Sung Military," *Cambridge History of China*, V. 2, pp. 248–249, for indispensable expertise of Liu Cheng in siege warfare.

41 See Rossabi, *Khubilai Khan*, pp. 81–83, and Rossabi, "The Reign of Khubilai Khan, *Cambridge History of China*, VI, p. 433.

42 Rossabi, *Khubilai Khan*, pp. 84–85.

43 Rossabi, *Khubilai Khan*, pp. 85–87, and "Reign of Khubilai Khan," *Cambridge History of China*, VI, p. 432–433.

44 See *ibid.*, p. 433, and Mote, *Imperial China*, p. 319.

45 See Rossabi, *Khubilai Khan*, pp. 87–90, and "Reign of Khubilai Khan," *Cambridge History of China*, VI, pp. 434–435.

46 See Mote, *Imperial China*, pp. 320 and 463.

47 Rossabi, *Khubilai Khan*, p. 88, and "Reign of Khubilai Khan," *Cambridge History of China*, VI, p. 434.

48 See Rossabi, *Khubilai Khan*, pp. 90–91, and Tseng-Yü, "History of Sung Military," *Cambridge History of China*, V. 2, pp. 248–249.

49 Rossabi, *Khubilai Khan*, pp. 92–93, and "Reign of Khubilai Khan," *Cambridge History of China*, VI, pp. 435–436.

50   See William E. Henthorn, *Korea: The Mongol Invasions* (Leiden, 1963), pp. 208–210. See also Randall J. Sasaki, *The Origins of the Lost Fleet of the Mongol Empire* (College Station, Texas, 2015), pp. 57–141, for the limitations of the naval technology.

51   See Richard W. Unger, *The Ship in the Medieval Economy, 600-1600* (London, 1980), pp. 119–200, who argues that Christian Europe enjoyed the advantage of two separate traditions of naval technology, one based in the Mediterranean and the other based in the North and Baltic Seas. The frequent exchanges of technology between the two regions led to the launching of oceangoing vessels in the fifteenth century.

52   See Henthorn, *Korea*, pp. 150–172, and Weatherford, *Genghis Khan*, pp. 210–211.

53   Weatherford, *Genghis Khan*, p. 209, and Ishii Susumu, "The Decline of the Kamakura Bakufu," translated by Jeffrey Mass and Hitomi Tonomura, *Medieval Japan*, Volume III, edited by Kozo Yamamura (Cambridge, 1990), pp. 131–135.

54   See Kozo Yamamura, "The Growth of Commerce in Medieval Japan," *Cambridge History of Japan*, III, pp. 344–376.

55   See Rossabi, *Khubilai Khan*, pp. 100–102, and Susumu, "Decline of Kamakura Bakufu," *Cambridge History of Japan*, III, pp. 136–138.

56   Rossabi, *Khubilai Khan*, p. 102, and Susumu, "Decline of Kamakura Bakufu," *Cambridge History of Japan*, III, pp. 138–140.

57   Rossabi, *Khubilai Khan*, p. 103, and Susumu, "Decline of Kamakura Bakufu," *Cambridge History of Japan*, III, p. 140.

58   See Rossabi, *Khubilai Khan*, pp. 208–209, Weatherford, *Genghis Khan*, pp. 211–212, and Susumu, "Decline of Kamakura Bakufu," *Cambridge History of Japan*, III, pp. 145–146.

59   See *ibid.*, pp. 143–144.

60   See Rossabi, *Khubilai Khan*, pp. 209–212, and Susumu, "Decline of Kamakura Bakufu," *Cambridge History of Japan*, III, pp. 146–147.

61   See Rossabi, *Khubilai Khan*, p. 212, and Susumu, "Decline of Kamakura Bakufu," *Cambridge History of Japan*, III, pp. 147–148.

62   See Rossabi, *Khubilai Khan*, p. 212.

63   See *ibid.*, pp. 67–70, for Chabai's role as counselor to Kublai Khan, and pp. 224–226, for the death of Chabai plunging Kublai Khan into grief and loneliness.

64   See *ibid.*, pp. 206 and 227.

65   See *ibid.*, p. 225.

66   See *ibid.*, pp. 226–227.

67   Rossabi, *Khubilai Khan*, pp. 213–114. The conditions are well-known to me given my own experiences traveling in Thailand and Cambodia in 1999.

68   See Marco Polo, *Description of World*, chapter 122, pp. 110–112.

69   See Rossabi, *Khubilai Khan*, pp. 214–215, and Weatherford, *Genghis Khan*, p. 212.

70   See Rossabi, "Reign of Khubilai Khan," *Cambridge History of China*, VI, pp. 484–487.

71   See Rossabi, *Khubilai Khan*, pp. 217–218, and Weatherford, *Genghis Khan*, p. 213.

72   See Rossabi, *Khubilai Khan*, p. 219.

73   See *ibid.*, p. 220, and Weatherford, *Genghis Khan*, p. 213.

74   See Rossabi, *Khubilai Khan*, p. 220.

75   See Weatherford, *Genghis Khan*, pp. 213–214, for an assessment of the limits of Mongol and Chinese naval power in comparison to Western states.

76   See István Vásáry, "The Jochid Realm: The Western Steppe and Eastern Europe," *The Cambridge History of Inner Asia: The Chinggisid Age*, edited by Nicola di Cosmo, Allen J. Frank, and Peter Golden (Cambridge, 2009), pp. 76–77.

77   See Rossabi, *Genghis Khan*, p. 115, and Boyle, "Political History of Il-Khans," *Cambridge History of Iran*, V, pp. 355–356.

78   See Allen, *Culture and Conquest*, pp. 144–188.

79   Rossabi, "Reign of Khubilai Khan," *Cambridge History of China*, VI, pp. 442–445.

80   See Weatherford, *Mongol Queens*, pp. 121–124.

81   See Rossabi, *Khubilai Khan*, pp. 127–129 and 172–176.

82   Rossabi, *Khubilai Khan*, pp. 229–231.

83   See Rossabi, *Khubilai Khan*, pp. 28–30, and Mote, *Imperial China*, pp. 452 and 457–458.

84   See Mote, *Imperial China*, pp. 459–460.

85   Rossabi, *Khubilai Khan*, pp. 137–138, and "Reign of Khubilai Khan," *Cambridge History of China*, VI, pp. 457–458.

86   See Rossabi, *Khubilai Khan*, p. 226.

87   Rossabi, *Khubilai Khan*, pp. 226 and 228.

88   See Rossabi, *Khubilai Khan*, pp. 31–35, and Weatherford, *Genghis Khan*, pp. 197–198.

89   Polo, *Description of World*, chapter 75, pp. 64–67.

90   Rossabi, "Reign of Khubilai Khan," *Cambridge History of China*, VI, pp. 454–457, and Weatherford, *Genghis Khan*, pp. 198–200.

91   See *ibid.*, p. 199.

92   Polo, *Description of World*, pp. 84–85 and 73–76.

93   See Rossabi, *Khubilai Khan*, pp. 188–190, and "Reign of Khubilai Khan," *Cambridge History of China*, VI, pp. 448 and 476–478.

94   Rossabi, *Khubilai Khan*, pp. 134–135.

95   See Ratchnevsky, *Genghis Khan*, pp. 145–147. The paintings are now in the National Museum, Taipei.

96   See Rossabi, *Khubilai Khan*, pp. 161–172.

97   See *ibid.*, pp. 131–137, and Mote, *Imperial China*, pp. 450–452.

98   See Rossabi, *Khubilai Khan*, pp. 179–183, and "Reign of Khubilai Khan," *Cambridge History of China*, VI, pp. 473–478.

99   Rossabi, *Khubilai Khan*, pp. 131–137, and "Reign of Khubilai Khan," *Cambridge History of China*, VI, pp. 459–460.

100   See Rossabi, *Khubilai Khan*, pp. 183–184.

101   See *ibid.*, pp. 189–199, and "Reign of Khubilai Khan," *Cambridge History of China*, VI, pp. 478–482 and 496–499.

102   See Rossabi, *Khubilai Khan*, pp. 116–127, and Mote, *Imperial China*, pp. 503–507.

103   See Polo, *Description of World*, chapters 86–90, pp. 77–81.

104   See Rossabi, *Khubilai Khan*, pp. 141–143.

105   See *ibid.*, p. 141.

106   See *ibid.*, p. 228.

107   See *ibid.*, p. 141.

108   See *ibid.*, pp. 155–156, and Mote, *Imperial China*, p. 484. The script was far better adapted for the Mongolian language than the Uyghur script.

109   Rossabi, *Khubilai Khan*, pp. 156–159.

110   See John Dardess, "Shun-ti and the End of Yüan Rule in China," *Cambridge History of China*, VI, pp. 572–580, and Prawdin, *Mongol Empire*, pp. 380–389.

111   See Dardess, "Shun-ti," *Cambridge History of China*, VI, pp. 580–584, and Mote, *Imperial China*, pp. 541–563.

112   See Man, *Great Wall*, pp. 244–273.

23 Papal Envoys, Missionaries, and Marco Polo

1   See Laurence Bergreen, *Marco Polo from Venice to Xanadu* (New York, 2008), pp. 324–332, and Stephen G. Haw, *Marco Polo's China: A Venetian in the Realm of Khubilai Khan* (London/New York, 2006), pp. 41–42 and 176–178. There is no reason to believe that the work is a fabrication by Rustichello.

2   Polo, *Description of World*, chapter 75, pp. 64–67.

3   See Bergreen, *Marco Polo*, pp. 13–25. Although the Polos traveled on the golden passport of Kublai Khan as envoys from the Papacy, they were motivated by the business opportunities shared by the great Venetian families of merchant princes.

4   See Haw, *Marco Polo's China*, pp. 52–67. Critics have stressed that Marco Polo reports neither the Great Wall nor Chinese ideograms, but the Great Wall had fallen in disrepair under Mongol rule and was more a military highway rather than the masonry barrier of the Ming Dynasty; see Man, *Great Wall*, pp. 114–117. Marco Polo was one of many foreign officials employed by Kublai Khan who neither knew nor needed Chinese; see Rossabi, *Khubilai Khan*, pp. 127–219 and 179–200.

5   See *ibid.*, pp. 147–148, noting Marco Polo very likely exaggerated his importance within the bureaucratic hierarchy of Kublai Khan.

6   See Carpini, "History of Mongols," *Mission to Asia*, pp 63–68. Giovanni da Pian del Caprine was awed by the number of envoys and vassal rulers across Eurasia who paid court to the Great Khan Güyük.

7   Friar Benedict penned a summary report of the mission without details about the Mongol court and life. See "The Narrative of Brother Benedict the Pole," *Mission to Asia*, pp. 79–84.

8   See Carpini, "History of Mongols," *Mission to Asia*, pp. 32–38 and 43–59.

9   See de Rachewiltz, *Papal Envoys*, p. 89.

10   See Rubruck, "Journey," *Mission to Asia*, pp. 156–175.

11   See de Rachewiltz, *Papal Envoys*, p. 141.

12   See Bergreen, *Marco Polo*, pp. 315–316.

13   Polo, *Description of World*, pp. 1–2.

14   See Bergreen, *Marco Polo*, pp. 330–335 and 347–349.

15   See de Rachewiltz, *Papal Envoys*, pp. 84–88.

16   See Jackson, *Mongols and West*, pp. 87 and 91–92, and de Rachewiltz, *Papal Envoys*, pp. 86–87.

17   See Jackson, *Mongols and West*, pp. 60–61, and de Rachewiltz, *Papal Envoys*, pp. 41–42.

18   See *ibid.*, pp. 84–86.

19   See Mark G. Pegg, *The Corruption of Angels: The Great Inquisition of 1245–1246* (Princeton, 2001), pp. 48–50.

20   See Powell, *Anatomy of Crusade*, pp. 158–160.

21   See de Rachewiltz, *Papal Envoys*, pp. 89–90.

22   See *ibid.*, pp. 90–91.

23   See Carpini, "History of Mongols," *Mission to Asia*, pp. 3–4.

24   See *ibid.*, pp. 50–51, and de Rachewiltz, *Papal Envoys*, pp. 90–92.

25   See Carpini, "History of Mongols," *Mission to Asia*, pp. 51–52, and see also de Rachewiltz, *Papal Envoys*, p. 93.

26   See Carpini, "History of Mongols," *Mission to Asia*, p. 53.

27   See *ibid.*, pp. 53–54.

28   See *ibid.*, p. 54.

29   See *ibid.*, pp. 54–55.

30   See *ibid.*, pp. 56–57.

31   See *ibid.*, p. 57. Father Benedict agreed in Carpine's judgment of Batu; see Benedick, "Report," *Mission to Asia*, p. 80.

32   See Carpini, "History of Mongols," *Mission to Asia*, p. 57.

33   See *ibid.*, p. 57. Father Giovanni received from Batu a golden pass, but he was not quite sure of the meaning of the metal object.

34   See *ibid.*, pp. 58–61.

35   See de Rachewiltz, *Papal Envoys*, p. 96.

36   See Carpini, "History of Mongols," *Mission to Asia*, pp. 63–67. Father Benedict was equally impressed by the coronation; see Benedick, "Report," *Mission to Asia*, pp. 82–84.

37   See Carpini, "History of Mongols," *Mission to Asia*, pp. 6–14.

38   See *ibid.*, pp. 14–18.

39   See *ibid.*, pp. 43–50.

40   See "Two Papal Bulls of Pope Innocent IV Addressed to the Emperor of the Tartars," *Mission to Asia*, pp. 73–78.

41   See "Guyuk Khan's Letter to Pope Innocent IV (1246)," in *Mission to Asia*, pp. 85–88. See also de Rachewiltz, *Papal Envoys*, pp. 102–106.

42   See Carpini, "History of Mongols," *Mission to Asia*, p. 69–71.

43   See *ibid.*, pp. 71–72.

44   See de Rachewiltz, *Papal Envoys*, pp. 109–110.

45   See *ibid.*, p. 111.

46   See *ibid.*, p. 112. No reports have survived about the outcome of these missions, and so the missions were most likely unsuccessful.

47   See *ibid.*, p. 115.

48   See *ibid.*, pp. 115–117.

49   See Prawdin, *Mongol Empire*, pp. 283–285.

50   See de Rachewiltz, *Papal Envoys*, p. 117.

51   See *ibid.*, pp. 117–118.

52   See Runciman, *History of Crusades*, III, p. 260, and de Rachewiltz, *Papal Envoys*, p. 120.

53   See *ibid.*, pp. 120–122.

54   See Weatherford, *Mongol Queens*, p. 102, and de Rachewiltz, *Papal Envoys*, p. 123.

55   See Runciman, *History of Crusades*, III, p. 260, and de Rachewiltz, *Papal Envoys*, pp. 123–124.

56   See *ibid.*, p. 125.

57   See *ibid.*, pp. 126–127.

58   See Bernard Hamilton, "The Latin Empire and Western Contacts with Asia," *Contact and Conflict in Frankish Greece and the Aegean, 1204–1453: Crusade, Religion and Trade between Latins, Greeks and Turks*, edited by Nikolaos G. Chrissis and Mike Carr (Farnham, Surrey, 2016), p. 50.

59   See William of Rubruck, "Journey," *Mission to Asia*, pp. 89–91, and de Rachewiltz, *Papal Envoys*, p. 127.

60   See William of Rubruck, "Journey," *Mission to Asia*, p. 92.

61   See *ibid.*, p. 113.

62   See *ibid.*, p. 108.

63   See *ibid.*, pp. 111–112 and 123–124, and Runciman, *History of Crusades*, III, p. 297.

64   See *ibid.*, pp. 133–114, and de Rachewiltz, *Papal Envoys*, p. 126.

65   See *ibid.*, pp. 128 and 131–133.

66   See William of Rubruck, "Journey," *Mission to Asia*, pp. 119–120.

67   See *ibid.*, p. 114.

68   See *ibid.*, pp. 125–128.

69   See *ibid.*, p. 127.

70   See *ibid.* p. 99.

71   See *ibid.*, pp. 131–149.

72   See *ibid.*, pp. 130–131.

73   See *ibid.*, pp. 149–151.

74   See *ibid.*, pp. 154–155.

75   See *ibid.*, pp. 157–158.

76   See *ibid.*, pp. 147–197.

77   See *ibid.*, pp. 138–141 and 191–194.

78   See *ibid*, pp. 187–194, and de Rachewiltz, *Papal Envoys*, p. 138.

79   See William of Rubruck, "Journey," *Mission to Asia*, pp. 194–197.

80   See *ibid.*, pp. 206–209 and 213–218.

81   See *ibid.*, p. 219.

82   See de Rachewiltz, *Papal Envoys*, pp. 138–143.

83   See *ibid.*, pp. 160–167.

84   See *ibid.*, pp. 201–204.

85   See Liu, *Silk Road*, pp. 109–126; Jackson, *Mongols and Islamic World*, pp. 210–241; and Allen, *Culture and Conquest*, pp. 115–188. For Kublai Khan's promotion of trade and prosperity, see Rossabi, *Khubilai Khan*, pp. 119–127, and Weatherford, *Genghis Khan*, pp. 220–227. For the economic revival of Iran and Transoxiana from the reign of Ilkhan Abaqa (1265–1282)

on, see I. P. Petrusneysky, "The Socio-Economic Condition of Iran under the Il-Khans," *Cambridge History of Iran*, V, pp. 499–514.

86   See Polo, *Description of World*, p. 2, and Bergreen, *Marco Polo*, pp. 25–26.

87   See Robbert, "Venice and Crusades," *History of Crusades*, V, pp. 408–445, and Donald M. Nicol, *Byzantium and Venice: A Study in Diplomatic and Cultural Relations* (Cambridge, 1988), pp. 148–165, for the expansion of Venetian trade and naval power in the thirteenth century.

88   See Polo, *Description of World*, pp. 2–3, and Bergreen, *Marco Polo*, pp. 27–28.

89   Polo, *Description of World*, p. 4. See also Bergreen, *Marco Polo*, pp. 28–30, and Prawdin, *Mongol Empire*, pp. 333–334.

90   Polo, *Description of World*, pp. 5–8, and Bergreen, *Marco Polo*, pp. 31–33.

91   See *ibid.*, pp. 33–35, and Prawdin, *Mongol Empire*, pp. 334–335.

92   See Bergreen, *Marco Polo*, pp. 35–37. It is remarkable that none of the surviving sources report the reunion of Marco Polo with his father in Venice.

93   See Polo, *Description of World*, pp. 8–9. See also Bergreen, *Marco Polo*, pp. 39–41, and Prawdin, *Mongol Empire*, pp. 335–336.

94   Bergreen, *Marco Polo*, pp. 135–136.

95   See Haw, *Marco Polo's China*, pp. 60–63.

96   Polo, *Description of World*, chapter 62, p. 50. Campçio has been identified as Ganzhou; see Haw, *Marco Polo's China*, p. 90.

97   Benjamin of Tudela (1130–1172), the Jewish traveler from Spain, wrote in Arabic a detailed account of his journey in the Middle East. See Benjamin of Tudela, *The Itinerary of Benjamin of Tudela: Travels in the Middle Ages*, translated by Marcus Nathan Adler (Malibu, CA, 1993). Ibn Battuta (1304–1369) composed the most detailed of Arabic travelogue from Morocco to Central Asia and India. See Ibn Battuta, *The Travels of Ibn Battuta*, translated by Timothy Mackintosh-Smith (Toronto, 2003).

98   See Polo, *Description of World*, chapters 41–43, pp. 33–36, and chapter 52, pp. 61–62, for descriptions of the Assassins and Samarkand, respectively.

99   See Polo, *Description of World*, chapter 54, p. 42. See also Bergreen, *Marco Polo*, pp. 77–79.

100   See Polo, *Description of World*, chapter 46, pp. 37–38.

101   See *ibid.*, chapters 58–59, pp. 45–46. See also Bergreen, *Marco Polo*, pp. 83–85, 195–197, and 278–283.

102   See Polo, *Description of World*, chapters 65–69, pp. 52–59.

103   See *ibid.*, chapter 68, pp. 54–55. See also Silverberg, *Realm of Prester John*, pp. 119–132.

104   Bergreen, *Marco Polo*, p. 117.

105   Polo, *Description of World*, chapters 76–82, pp. 67–72, 92–93, and 103–104.

106   See *ibid.*, chapter 79, pp. 69-70.

107   See Bergreen, *Marco Polo*, pp. 131–133.

108   See *ibid.*, pp. 141–166.

109   See Polo, *Description of World*, chapters 140–157, pp. 123–143. See also Haw, *Marco Polo's China*, pp. 82–123.

110   See Polo, *Description of World*, chapter 130, p. 116 (lion hunts), chapters 140–157, pp. 123–143 (cities of China), and chapter 158, pp. 143–144 (ship building).

111   See Bergreen, *Marco Polo*, pp. 300–303.

112   See *ibid.*, pp. 303–304.

113   See *ibid.*, pp. 305–308.

114   See *ibid.*, pp. 315–316.

115   See C. W. R. D. Moseley, trans., "Introduction," *The Travels of Sir John Mandeville* (New York, 1983), pp. 9–18.

116   See *The Travels of Sir John Mandeville*, pp. 103–190.

117   See Bergreen, *Marco Polo*, pp. 348–350.

118   See *ibid.*, p. 354. Christopher Columbus also read the fabulous account of Sir John Mandeville.

24 Tamerlane, Prince of Destruction

1   Tamerlane is the English rendition of the Persian Timur-e lang, Timur the Lame. His birth name is Timur or Temur, Turkish for "iron." I have used Tamerlane throughout as this form of his name is most readily recognized.

2   See Marozzi, *Tamerlane*, pp. 31–32, and Mikhail Gerasimov, *The Face Finder* (Philadelphia, 1971), pp. 129–157.

3   See Beatrice F. Manz, "Tamerlane's Career and Its Uses," *Journal of World History* 13 (2002), pp. 1–25.

4   For the legend of the curse, which Gerasimov denied, see Oksanam, "Facial Reconstruction, Nazis, and Siberia: The story of Mikhail Gerasimov," *Atlas Obscura*, January 25, 2011; online publication: https://www.atlasobscura.com/articles/facial-reconstruction-nazis-and-siberia-the-story-of-mikhail-gerasimov.

5   R. Pinder-Wilson, "Timurid Architecture," *The Cambridge History of Iran*, Volume VI: *The Timurid and Safavid Periods*, edited by Peter Jackson and Laurence Lockhart (Cambridge, 1986), pp. 737–738.

6   See *ibid.*, pp. 737–744, and Marozzi, *Tamerlane*, pp. 207–230.

7   See Beatrice F. Manz, *The Rise and Rule of Tamerlane* (Cambridge, 1989), pp. 107–127.

8   See H. R. Roemer, "Tīmūr in Iran," *The Cambridge History of Iran*, Volume VI: *The Timurid and Safavid Periods*, edited by Peter Jackson and Laurence Lockhart (Cambridge, 1986), pp. 83–97.

9   See Marozzi, *Tamerlane*, pp. 211–212, and Ruy González de Clavijo, *Embassy to Tamerlane*, 1403–1406, translated by Guy Le Strange (Roan, Kilberran, 2009), pp. xvi–xvii.

10 See de Clavijo, *Embassy to Tamerlane*, pp. 245–266.

11 See de Clavijo, *Embassy to Tamerlane*, pp. 181–182. See also Marozzi, *Tamerlane*, pp. 378–379.

12 Edgar Allan Poe published his poem "Tamerlane" in 1827 in a collection entitled *Tamerlane and Other Poems*. Text is available online at https://poets.org/poem/tamerlane.

13 See Park Honan, *Christopher Marlowe: Poet and Spy* (Oxford, 2005), pp. 323–325, and Leslie Hotson, *The Death of Christopher Marlowe* (London, 1925), pp. 39–40 and 65–66. Scholarly and numerous popular books have speculated on a conspiracy to assassinate Marlowe; see Charles Nicholl, *The Reckoning: The Murder of Christopher Marlowe*, revised edition (New York, 2002).

14 See review by Dominic Cavendish (25 August 2018), "Tamburlaine, RSC: A Very Modern Reading of Marlowe's Violent Play," *The Daily Telegraph*, September 16, 2018.

15 See Charles Stewart, *The Mulfuzat Timury, or, Autobiographical Memoirs of the Moghul Emperor Timur* (Cambridge, 2013).

16 See Marozzi, *Tamerlane*, pp. 101–106.

17 See *ibid.*, *Tamerlane*, pp. 46–47, and Ilker Evrim Binbas, "The Histories of Sharaf al-Din 'Ali Yazdi: A Formal Analysis," *Acta Orientalia* 65 (2012), pp. 391–417.

18 See Marozzi, *Tamerlane*, pp. 84–85, and Ilker Evrim Binbas, *Sharaf Al-Dīn 'Alī Yazdī (ca. 770s–858/ca. 1370s–1454), Prophecy, Politics, and Historiography in Late Medieval Islamic History* (Chicago, 2009), pp. 1-19.

19 Marozzi, *Tamerlane*, pp. 77–78.

20 See *ibid.*, pp. 8–9 and 85–86. See Ahmad ibn Arabshah, *Tamerlane: The Life of the Great Amir*, translated by Robert McChesney (New York, 2017).

21 See Mazorri, *Tamerlane*, pp. 7–9, and Roemer, "Tīmūr," *Cambridge History of Iran*, VI, pp. 43–44.

22 See Marozzi, *Tamerlane*, pp. 32–39.

23 See *ibid.*, pp. 7–8, and Manz, *Tamerlane*, p. 60.

24 See Boyle, "Political History of Il-Khans," *Cambridge History of Iran*, V, pp. 413–417, for the fragmenting of the Ilkhanate after the death of Abu Sa'id (1305–1335).

25 See I. P. Petrushevsky, "The Socio-Economic Conditions of Iran under the Il-Khans," *Cambridge History of Iran*, V, pp. 494–514, for the revival of commerce and prosperity from the late thirteenth century on.

26 See Marozzi, *Tamerlane*, pp. 22–24, and Roemer, "Tīmūr," in *The Cambridge History of Iran*, VI, p. 43.

27   Marozzi, *Tamerlane*, pp. 24–25, and Roemer, "Tīmūr," *Cambridge History of Iran*, VI, pp. 43–45.

28   See *ibid.*, pp. 29–30.

29   See *ibid.*, pp. 29–30, and Roemer, "Tīmūr,"*Cambridge History of Iran*, VI, p. 45.

30   See Marozzi, *Tamerlane*, p. 30, and Roemer, "Tīmūr," *Cambridge History of Iran*, VI, pp. 44–45.

31   See Marozzi, *Tamerlane,* pp. 27–29.

32   Roemer, "Tīmūr in Iran," *Cambridge History of Iran*, VI, p. 41.

33   See Marozzi, *Tamerlane*, p. 31. Ababshah and the fictional memoirs of Timur report the unlikely tale that Tamerlane was wounded by a shepherd who fended off Tamerlane in an ambush to steal sheep.

34   See de Clavijo, *Embassy to Tamerlane*, pp. 181–182. See also Marozzi, *Tamerlane*, pp. 378–379. The historian Ibn Khaldun gives a similar description after his meeting with Tamerlane outside of Damascus in 1401; see *ibid.*, p. 306.

35   See *ibid.*, p. 40; Manz, *Tamerlane*, pp. 58–60; and Grousset, *The Empire of the Steppes*, pp. 412–414.

36   Marozzi, *Tamerlane*, pp. 40–43, and Manz, *Tamerlane*, pp. 56–57.

37   See Marozzi, *Tamerlane*, pp. 45–46, and Manz, *Tamerlane*, p. 57.

38   See Marozzi, *Tamerlane*, pp. 43–44, 64–66, and 273–274. See remarks of de Clavijo, *Embassy to Tamerlane*, pp. 225–230, about the wives and offspring of Tamerlane.

39   See Manz, *Tamerlane*, pp. 58–64, and Grousset, *The Empire of the Steppes*, pp. 442–426.

40   See *ibid.*, pp. 409–412.

41   See Marozzi, *Tamerlane*, pp. 348–349. See also Dardess, "Shun-ti," *Cambridge History of China*, VI, pp. 580–584, and Mote, *Imperial China*, pp. 541–563. In 1370, Tamerlane acknowledged a distant overlordship of the Ming Emperor Hongwu (1368–1398), who had, in effect, succeeded to the throne of Kublai Khan.

42   Marozzi, *Tamerlane*, pp. 96–96 and 396–397.

43   See Manz, *Tamerlane,* pp. 66–89, and Marozzi, *Tamerlane*, pp. 99–102.

44   See *ibid.*, pp. 294–295 and 327. These elephants also played an important ceremonial role at the court of Samarkand; see de Clavijo, *Embassy to Tamerlane*, pp. 230–233.

45   See Manz, *Tamerlane*, pp. 90–106.

46   See Marozzi, *Tamerlane*, pp. 114–117.

47   See *ibid.*, pp. 118–125, offering insightful comment based on his direct experience and visit of the city.

48   See *ibid.*, pp. 116–117.

49   See *ibid.*, pp. 125–126.

50   See *ibid.*, pp. 64–67 and 97–99, and Roemer, "Tīmūr," *Cambridge History of Iran*, VI, pp. 51–57.

51   See Marozzi, *Tamerlane*, pp. 131–154, and Roemer, "Tīmūr," *Cambridge History of Iran*, VI, pp. 57–64.

52   See Marozzi, *Tamerlane*, p. 131.

53   See *ibid.*, pp. 132–138.

54   See *ibid.*, pp. 91 and 132

55   See *ibid.*, pp. 137–138. Ilkhan Öljaitü (1305–1316) founded the city as his capital. See Boyle, "Political History of Il-Khans," *Cambridge History of Iran*, V, pp. 399–406. See de Calvijo, *Embassy to Tamerlane*, pp. 132–133, for the city as a hub of the silk and spice markets a century later.

56   See Marozzi, *Tamerlane*, p. 137.

57   See Marozzi, *Tamerlane*, pp. 142–143, and Roemer, "Tīmūr," *Cambridge History of Iran*, VI, pp. 58–59.

58   See Marozzi, *Tamerlane*, p. 143.

59   See Vásáry, "Jochid Realm," *The Cambridge History of Inner Asia*, pp. 79–82, for the civil wars in the Jochid realm, and the early career of Tokhtamysh.

60   See Marozzi, *Tamerlane*, pp. 76–77, and Vásáry, "Jochid Realm," *The Cambridge History of Inner Asia*, pp. 82–83.

61   See Marozzi, *Tamerlane*, pp. 159–161, and Vásáry, "Jochid Realm," *The Cambridge History of Inner Asia*, pp. 82–83.

62   See Marozzi, *Tamerlane*, pp. 139–140.

63   Robert O. Crummey, *The Formation of Moscovy, 1304–1613* (London/New York, 1987), pp. 49–54, and Halperin, *Russia and Golden Horde*, pp. 56–57. Tokhtamysh avenged the defeat that Grand Duke Dimitry Ivanovitch inflicted on the forces of the Golden Horde under the commander Mamai at the Battle of Kulikovo on September 8, 1380. The Grand Duke had won the first victory of the Russians over the Mongols.

64   See Marozzi, *Tamerlane*, pp. 143–148. Tamerlane only waged jihad against the Christians of Georgia, whereas all his other foes and victims were overwhelmingly Muslims.

65   See Marozzi, *Tamerlane*, pp. 146–147, and Roemer, "Tīmūr," *Cambridge History of Iran*, VI, p. 59.

66   See Marozzi, *Tamerlane*, pp. 150–154.

67   See *ibid.*, pp. 162–165, and Manz, *Tamerlane*, pp. 71–72.

68   See Marozzi, *Tamerlane*, pp. 177–188.

69   See *ibid.*, pp. 188–191.

70   See *ibid.*, p. 192.

71   See *ibid.*, pp. 192–193.

72   See *ibid.*, pp. 193–196.

73   See *ibid.*, pp. 197–198, and Vásáry, "Jochid Realm," *The Cambridge History of Inner Asia*, p. 84. The new khan Temur Qutlugh (1397–1399) was the grandson of Urus Khan (1369–1377) and an implacable enemy of Tokhatmish.

74   See Marozzi, *Tamerlane*, pp. 207–230. The beauty of the city's architecture awed de Calvijo, *Embassy to Tamerlane*, pp. 188–205.

75   See de Madariaga, *Ivan the Terrible*, pp. 92–106, and Khodarkovsky, *Russia's Steppe Frontier*, pp. 100–125.

76   See Keay, *India*, pp. 263–278.

77   See Marozzi, *Tamerlane*, pp. 237–240.

78   See Keay, *India*, pp. 247–249.

79   See *ibid.*, p. 256.

80   See *ibid.*, p. 24.

81   See *ibid.*, pp. 241–245, and Roemer, "Tīmūr," *Cambridge History of Iran*, VI, pp. 69–70.

82   See Marozzi, *Tamerlane*, pp. 239 and 263.

83   See *ibid.*, pp. 264–269.

84   See *ibid.*, pp. 269–274. The Hindu population was either massacred or enslaved thereby giving Tamerlane the pretext of waging jihad. See Keay, *India*, p. 278.

85   See Marozzi, *Tamerlane*, pp. 275–284.

86   See *ibid.*, pp. 284–286.

87   See Roemer, "Tīmūr," *Cambridge History of Iran*, VI, pp. 64–65.

88   See Marozzi, *Tamerlane*, pp. 277–279.

89   See *ibid.*, pp. 280–282.

90   See *ibid.*, pp. 282–283.

91   See Roemer, "Tīmūr," *Cambridge History of Iran*, VI, pp. 65–66.

92   Marozzi, *Tamerlane*, pp. 314–316, and Roemer, "Tīmūr," *Cambridge History of Iran*, VI, pp. 66–67.

93   Marozzi, *Tamerlane*, pp. 287–288, and Roemer, "Tīmūr," *Cambridge History of Iran*, VI, p. 77.

94   See Marozzi, *Tamerlane*, pp. 292–294, and Roemer, "Tīmūr," *Cambridge History of Iran*, VI, pp. 76–77.

95   See Marozzi, *Tamerlane*, pp. 294–297.

96   See *ibid.*, pp. 297–300.

97   See *ibid.*, pp. 301–306, and Manz, *Tamerlane*, p. 17.

98   See Marozzi, *Tamerlane*, pp. 307–312.

99   See *ibid.*, pp. 308–310.

100 See Runciman, *History of Crusades*, III, pp. 458–461, and Aziz S. Ativa, "The Crusade in the Fourteenth Century," *History of Crusades*, III, pp. 23–26.

101 Howard Crane, "Art and Architecture. 1300–1453," *Cambridge History of Turkey*, Volume I: *Byzantium to Turkey, 1071–1453*, edited by Kate Fleet (Cambridge, 2009), pp. 288–292.

102 Runciman, *Fall of Constantinople*, pp. 40–41, and Nevra Necipoğlu, *Byzantium between the Ottomans and the Latins: Politics and Society in the Late Empire* (Cambridge, 2009), pp. 149–183.

103 See Marozzi, *Tamerlane*, pp. 327–331.

104 See *ibid.*, pp. 331–333, and Roemer, "Tīmūr," *Cambridge History of Iran*, VI, pp. 77–78.

105 See *ibid.*, pp. 334–337.

106 See *ibid.*, pp. 338–341.

107 See *ibid.*, pp. 333–334.

108 See Halil Inalcik, *The Ottoman Empire: The Classical Age 1300–1600* (London, 1973), pp. 17–19.

109 See *ibid.*, pp. 19–27, and Rudi P. Lindner, "The Incorporation of the Balkans into the Ottoman Empire," *Cambridge History of Turkey*, I, pp. 134–137.

110 See *ibid.*, pp. 352–353.

111 See *ibid.*, pp. 354–356, and de Clavijo, *Embassy to Tamerlane*, p. 192.

112 See Marozzi, *Tamerlane*, pp. 394–400, and Roemer, "Tīmūr," *Cambridge History of Iran*, V, pp. 80–82.

113 See Marozzi, *Tamerlane*, pp. 400–404, and Roemer, "Tīmūr," *Cambridge History of Iran*, VI, p. 83.

114 See *ibid.*, pp. 405–413, and H. R. Romer, "The Successors of Tīmūr," *Cambridge History of Iran*, VI, pp. 98–101.

115 See Livy, History XXII. 51; see Penguin translation, and Livy, *The War with Hannibal*, translated by Aubrey de Selincourt (New York, 1965), p. 151. Maharbal replied to Hannibal's refusal to march on Rome after his victory at Cannae in 216 BC: "Assuredly, Maharbal replied, no one has been blessed with all the gods' gifts. You know, Hannibal, how to win a fight; you do not know how to use your victory."

Index